Lecture Notes in Computer Science　　15469

Founding Editors

Gerhard Goos
Juris Hartmanis

AF147640

The series Lecture Notes in Computer Science (LNCS), including its subseries Lecture Notes in Artificial Intelligence (LNAI) and Lecture Notes in Bioinformatics (LNBI), has established itself as a medium for the publication of new developments in computer science and information technology research, teaching, and education.

LNCS enjoys close cooperation with the computer science R & D community, the series counts many renowned academics among its volume editors and paper authors, and collaborates with prestigious societies. Its mission is to serve this international community by providing an invaluable service, mainly focused on the publication of conference and workshop proceedings and postproceedings. LNCS commenced publication in 1973.

Timothy Bourke · Liqian Chen ·
Amir Goharshady
Editors

Dependable Software Engineering

Theories, Tools, and Applications

10th International Symposium, SETTA 2024
Hong Kong, China, November 26–28, 2024
Proceedings

 Springer

Editors
Timothy Bourke 🆔
Inria
Paris, France

Liqian Chen 🆔
National University of Defense Technology
Changsha, China

Amir Goharshady 🆔
Hong Kong University of Science
and Technology
Hong Kong, China

ISSN 0302-9743 ISSN 1611-3349 (electronic)
Lecture Notes in Computer Science
ISBN 978-981-96-0601-6 ISBN 978-981-96-0602-3 (eBook)
https://doi.org/10.1007/978-981-96-0602-3

Preface

This volume presents the proceedings of the 10th International Symposium on Dependable Software Engineering: Theories, Tools and Applications (SETTA 2024), which was held in Hong Kong SAR, China, on November 26–28, 2024. SETTA is a leading Chinese conference on formal methods. In 2024, it was held outside of mainland China for the first time and hosted by the City University of Hong Kong. The purpose of the SETTA symposium series is to bring international researchers together to exchange research results and ideas on bridging the gap between formal methods and software engineering. Topics of interest to SETTA include, but are not limited to:

- Requirements specification and analysis
- Formalisms for modeling, design and implementation
- Model checking, theorem proving and decision procedures
- Scalable approaches to formal system analysis
- Formal approaches to simulation, run-time verification and testing
- Integration of formal methods into software engineering practice
- Contract-based engineering of components, systems and systems of systems
- Formal and engineering aspects of software evolution and maintenance
- Parallel and multicore programming
- Embedded, real-time, hybrid, probabilistic and cyber-physical systems
- Mixed-critical applications and systems
- Formal aspects of service-oriented and cloud computing
- Safety, reliability, robustness and fault-tolerance
- Dependability of smart software and systems
- Empirical analysis techniques and their integration with formal methods
- Applications and industrial experience reports
- Software tools to assist the construction or analysis of software systems

This edition of SETTA received 47 complete submissions for single-blind peer review. Each submission was rigorously reviewed by three to five members of the program committee and external reviewers. This was followed by an online discussion among the reviewers, overseen by the PC chairs. In the end, consensus was reached to accept 21 high-quality papers with novel contributions for presentation at SETTA 2024 and inclusion in the present proceedings.

SETTA 2024 was also honored to feature invited talks and contributions by the following internationally recognized keynote speakers:

- Jean-François Raskin, Université Libre de Bruxelles
- Wang Yi, Uppsala University
- Shengchao Qin, Huawei

In this edition of SETTA, a best paper award was established. This award was sponsored by Springer and, based on the votes cast by the PC members, went to the following contribution:

– *An Assertion-Based Logic for Local Reasoning about Probabilistic Programs* by Huiling Wu, Anran Cui and Yuxin Deng

Additionally, the following PC members were selected for the Distinguished Reviewer Award, also based on votes cast by other PC members:

– Guillaume Dupont, Institute of Research in Informatics of Toulouse
– Thomas Sewell, University of New South Wales
– Guannan Wei, Purdue University
– Đorđe Žikelić, Singapore Management University

We are very thankful to the organizing committee at the City University of Hong Kong for their superb hosting of this edition of SETTA, and to the program committee members and external reviewers for their much-appreciated voluntary contribution in the form of detailed and high-quality reviews, which enabled us to choose the best submissions for presentation at SETTA. Finally, SETTA would not exist without the excellent research contributions of its authors. We are thus grateful to them for choosing SETTA as the venue for publication of their results. We hope that you enjoy reading their work.

November 2024

Timothy Bourke
Liqian Chen
Amir Goharshady

Organization

General Chairs

Ahmed Bouajjani   Université Paris Cité, France
Nan Guan   City University of Hong Kong, China

Technical Program Committee Chairs

Timothy Bourke   Inria, France
Liqian Chen   National University of Defense Technology, China
Amir Goharshady   Hong Kong University of Science and Technology, China

Local Chairs'

Heqing Huang   City University of Hong Kong, China
Yu Pei   Hong Kong Polytechnic University, China

Web Chair

Ruoxiang Li   City University of Hong Kong, China

Program Committee

S. Akshay   IIT Bombay, India
Thomas Bourgeat   EPFL, Switzerland
Lei Bu   Nanjing University, China
Supratik Chakraborty   IIT Bombay, India
Mingshuai Chen   Zhejiang University, China
Yuxin Deng   East China Normal University, China
Wei Dong   National University of Defense Technology, China
Guillaume Dupont   IRIT, France

Yufeng Zhang	Hunan University, China
Min Zhou	Tsinghua University, China
Yu Zhou	Nanjing University of Aeronautics and Astronautics, China
Đorđe Žikelić	Singapore Management University, Singapore

External Reviewers

Martin Berger	University of Sussex, UK
Jintao Chen	Zhejiang University, China
Yifan Dong	Aarhus University, Denmark
Nils Husung	Saarland University, Germany
Michael Kirsten	Karlsruhe Institute of Technology, Germany
Romain Pascual	Karlsruhe Institute of Technology, Germany
Yutao Sun	Zhejiang University, China
Hünkar Can Tunç	Aarhus University, Denmark
Siyuan Zhu	Peking University, China
Dominic Zimmer	Saarland University, Germany

Advisory Board

Jifeng He	East China Normal University, China
Cliff Jones	Newcastle University, UK
Deepak Kapur	University of New Mexico, USA
Wei Li	Beihang University, China
Chaochen Zhou	Institute of Software, CAS, China

Steering Committee

Zhenhua Duan	Xidian University, China
Martin Fränzle	University of Oldenburg, Germany
Kim Larsen	Aalborg University, Denmark
Xuandong Li	Nanjing University, China
Zhiming Liu	Southwest University, China
Sriram Rajamani	Microsoft Research, India
Ji Wang	National University of Defense Technology, China
Kwangkeun Yi	Seoul National University, South Korea
Naijun Zhan (Chair)	Institute of Software, CAS, China

Abstracts of Invited Talks

MIMOS: A New Paradigm and Tools for Embedded Systems Design and Updates

Wang Yi

Department of Information Technology, Uppsala University, Sweden
yi@it.uu.se

MIMOS is a tool environment for the design, simulation, verification, scheduling, and code generation of embedded real-time systems on heterogeneous multi-core platforms. MIMOS primarily targets safety-critical applications, where correct functional and timing behaviors are essential. The MIMOS tools provide a seamless approach to safe system development, ensuring that specified functionalities and timing behaviors specified and verified during the design phase are faithfully realized in the final implementation. This allows for customizable embedded real-time systems, enabling modifications to the design model without touching the executables in the final implementation.

Unlike existing tools such as Simulink and SCADE, which are all rooted in the synchronous design paradigms, MIMOS employs an asynchronous yet deterministic semantics model. This model is designed to not only guarantee (1) **determinism** but also facilitate (2) **composability** throughout all design stages, from system modeling to final implementation. This allows for dynamic updates for systems in operation. Furthermore, the asynchronous semantics of MIMOS enables pipelined parallel computation for (3) **optimal performance** with respects to both end-to-end latency and system throughput.

Essentially, a MIMOS model consists of a network of independent components that communicate through two types of channels: FIFO queues and registers. The FIFO queues are designed to support both non-blocking reads where no data is also considered an input, and non-blocking write operations. In contrast, a register is a single-capacity storage location that allows non-blocking read and write operations, overwriting its previous value with any new incoming data. Unlike FIFO queues, the contents of a register remain unchanged after a read operation. More precisely, a MIMOS model is a timed Kahn Process Network (KPN), where each node represents a periodic real-time task computing a mathematical function at a given rate. At the beginning of each period, the task reads its inputs; if the required inputs are available, it must compute the function before the period ends (ensured through schedulability analysis) and deliver the output by the end of the period or at a predetermined time point, such as the worst-case response time. If no inputs are available on the input channels when the period starts, essentially no computation is required. Thanks to the periodic timing behavior of reading, computation, and writing at each node, we can demonstrate that the non-blocking reading of inputs from both registers and FIFO channels is equivalent to a function over timed streams. Consequently, the MIMOS model operates under deterministic timed semantics. Further details for the MIMOS model and tools can be found in [1–3].

References

1. Yi, W.: Towards customizable CPS: composability, efficiency and predictability. In: Duan, Z., Ong, L. (eds.) Formal Methods and Software Engineering. ICFEM 2017. Lecture Notes in Computer Science, vol. 10610, pp. 3–15. Springer, Cham (2017). https://doi.org/10.1007/978-3-319-68690-5_1
2. Yi, W.: Design and dynamic update of real-time systems. In: 2019 IEEE Real-Time Systems Symposium (RTSS), pp. 1–3. IEEE (2019)
3. Yi, W., Mohaqeqi, M., Graf, S.: MIMOS: A deterministic model for the design and update of real-time systems. In: ter Beek, M.H., Sirjani, M. (eds.) Coordination Models and Languages. COORDINATION 2022. IFIP Advances in Information and Communication Technology, vol. 13271, pp. 17–34. Springer, Cham (2022). https://doi.org/10.1007/978-3-031-08143-9_2

Synthesis from LTL with Reward Optimization in Sampled Oblivious Environments

Jean-François Raskin[1] and Yun Chen Tsai[2,3]

[1] Université libre de Bruxelles, Brussels, Belgium
[2] National Institute of Informatics, Tokyo, Japan
[3] The Graduate University for Advanced Studies (SOKENDAI), Hayama, Japan

Abstract. This paper addresses the synthesis of reactive systems that enforce hard constraints while optimizing for quality-based soft constraints. We build on recent advancements in combining reactive synthesis with example-based guidance to handle both types of constraints in stochastic, oblivious environments accessible only through sampling. Our approach constructs examples that satisfy LTL-based hard constraints while maximizing expected rewards—representing the soft constraints—on samples drawn from the environment. We formally define this synthesis problem, prove it to be NP-complete, and propose an SMT-based solution, demonstrating its effectiveness with a case study.

This work was supported by Fondation ULB, and the fund Thelam from the Fondation Roi Baudouin. Author Y.C. Tsai was previously funded by HKUST and the Lee Hysan Foundation, and is currently supported by the ERATO HASUO Metamathematics for Systems Design Project (No. JPMJER1603) and the ASPIRE grant No. JPMJAP2301, JST on this project.

Contents

Invited Talks

Synthesis from LTL with Reward Optimization in Sampled Oblivious Environments

Jean-François Raskin[1(✉)] and Yun Chen Tsai[2,3]

[1] Université libre de Bruxelles, Brussels, Belgium
jraskin@ulb.ac.be
[2] National Institute of Informatics, Tokyo, Japan
[3] The Graduate University for Advanced Studies (SOKENDAI), Hayama, Japan

Abstract. This paper addresses the synthesis of reactive systems that enforce hard constraints while optimizing for quality-based soft constraints. We build on recent advancements in combining reactive synthesis with example-based guidance to handle both types of constraints in stochastic, oblivious environments accessible only through sampling. Our approach constructs examples that satisfy LTL-based hard constraints while maximizing expected rewards—representing the soft constraints—on samples drawn from the environment. We formally define this synthesis problem, prove it to be NP-complete, and propose an SMT-based solution, demonstrating its effectiveness with a case study.

1 Introduction

When designing reactive systems, we are often required to enforce *hard* constraints, such as those related to safety-critical features. In addition, we need to address more flexible, *softer* constraints, such as quality of service. While formal methods typically provide powerful tools for handling hard constraints, there are fewer solutions available for addressing soft constraints. In this paper, we build on recent work [BFR23] that demonstrates how to combine reactive synthesis, based on game theory and automata theory, with learning from examples. We extend this approach to propose a new tool for addressing *both* hard and soft constraints. We concentrate in this paper on the case of reactive synthesis with an unknown oblivious[1] and stochastic environment that is only accessible by sampling.

---

[1] An environment whose behavior is unaffected by the behavior of the reactive system.

This work was supported by Foundation ULB, and the fund Thelam from the Fondation Roi Baudouin. Author Y.C. Tsai was previously funded by HKUST and the Lee Hysan Foundation, and is currently supported by the ERATO HASUO Metamathematics for Systems Design Project (No. JPMJER1603) and the ASPIRE grant No. JPMJAP2301, JST on this project.

T. Bourke et al. (Eds.): SETTA 2024, LNCS 15469, pp. 3–21, 2025.
https://doi.org/10.1007/978-981-96-0602-3_1

In [BFR23], the following setting is studied. A linear temporal logic (LTL) formula, with atomic propositions partitioned into *inputs* controlled by an environment (Env) and *outputs* controlled by a system (Sys), defines the *core specifications* for a reactive system to be designed, where correctness must hold regardless of the environment's behavior. Alongside these core specifications, examples of desired system behaviors on sequences of environment inputs help guide the synthesis algorithm toward preferred solutions. This combination is advantageous because, while core correctness properties are easily expressible in LTL, specific implementation details, which may be challenging to capture in LTL, can be effectively illustrated through examples or scenarios. The algorithm proposed in [BFR23] addresses this synthesis problem by attempting to generalize the behaviors given in the examples, using automata learning techniques, while ensuring that these generalizations lead to a solution that enforce the core specification of the system.

In this paper, we consider another practically relevant design scenario. Here, we aim to synthesize a reactive system embedded in an oblivious environment, which needs to enforce a LTL formula (as above) which formalizes hard constraints for the system that needs to be enforced no matter what the environment does. However, instead of receiving a set of examples that demonstrate how to make "good" or "optimal" decisions on a set of prefixes of input sequences, we assume that we only receive a statistically representative set of samples of input sequences from the oblivious environment. Along with the samples, we are also given a reward machine $\mathcal{R}$, which maps prefixes of input/output sequences to rewards. The reward machine is used to formalize the *soft* constraints: the reactive system to be developed should aim to maximize the expected long-run average reward during its interaction with the environment while enforcing the hard constraints with certainty.

The goal of our procedure is to extend input samples from the environment into full prefixes of executions (alternating sequences of inputs and outputs) that serve as complete *examples* for the procedure in [BFR23]. The output choices used to complete these samples must meet two conditions: (1) the resulting set of examples must be extendable into a Mealy machine (a solution) that enforces the hard constraints specified by the LTL formula, so our completion of the input sequences must not compromise the realizability of the LTL specification; and (2) the expected mean reward across the samples is maximized. Once these examples are completed, we can apply the techniques from [BFR23], which combine learning from examples and synthesis as recalled above, to generalize the decisions made on the samples and produce a full solution that enforces the LTL specification. Since these examples are completed with an emphasis on maximizing the expected reward, we anticipate that their generalization will lead to strong overall performance.

Our technical contributions are as follows. First, we formally define the problem described above. Second, we demonstrate that determining the optimal decisions for the set of input sequences obtained by sampling the environment is computationally hard, even when the actions required to satisfy the hard constraints defined by the LTL specification are known. Specifically, we establish that this problem is NP-complete. Third, we propose an SMT-based approach to solve the optimization problem. Finally, we illustrate our method with a case study.

Related Works. The LTL synthesis problem was first introduced in [PR89]. Since then, several works have contributed to the development of efficient algorithms to solve this problem, e.g. [KV05, SF07, FJR11, LMS20]. Although the worst-case complexity is known to be high (2ExpTime-complete), tools for solving the LTL realizability problem have been implemented; see, for example, the tools described in the following papers: [FFT18, BBF+12, FFT18, LMS20, CP23].

The algorithm presented in this paper builds on the new synthesis methods for LTL and example-based guidance introduced recently in [BFR23]. Our paper demonstrates how to leverage these methods to synthesize a robust and efficient reactive system that interacts with an unknown, oblivious stochastic environment for which no model is available and only sampling is possible.

When a model of the stochastic environment is known, methods based on Markov Decision Processes (MDPs) can be applied to synthesize optimal reactive systems (see, e.g., [BK08]). These methods have been implemented in tools such as Storm [HJK+22] and Prism [KNP09].

MDP-based methods have been extended to handle multiple objectives, as in [CRR14, RRS17, QK21]; however, they do not account for constraints that must not be violated (hard constraints.) Additionally, the MDP model has been adapted to accommodate both properties that must be enforced with certainty (such as hard constraints) and those that cannot be guaranteed but for which we aim to maximize the probability of satisfaction (see, for example, [BFRR14]). However, these approaches differ from those presented here, as they assume the existence of a model for the stochastic environment, whereas we assume access only to samples and not to a full model.

Structure of the Paper. In Sect. 2, we introduce the necessary preliminaries for formally defining our setting and the problem we aim to solve. In Sect. 3, we present a formal problem definition along with a high-level overview of our algorithm. Our approach focuses on finding the optimal decisions for samples obtained from the stochastic environment, ensuring that these decisions also maintain the realizability of the hard constraints. In Sect. 4, we analyze the computational complexity of identifying these optimal decisions and propose a practical algorithm using SMT solvers. In Sect. 5, we demonstrate our approach with a case study.

2 Preliminaries

2.1 LTL and the Realizability Problem

We briefly review the syntax and semantics of LTL. For further details, interested readers may refer to, e.g., [BK08]. Given a set of atomic proposition AP, a LTL formula over AP adheres to the following syntax:

$$\varphi := p \in \mathsf{AP} \mid \neg\varphi \mid \varphi_1 \vee \varphi_2 \mid X\varphi \mid \varphi_1 U\varphi_2$$

Where X is the next operator and U is the until operator, we also define the globally operator $G(\varphi) := \neg(\mathbf{True}\ U\ \neg\varphi)$.

A LTL formula is evaluated over the positions on an infinite trace $\pi := \pi_1\pi_2\pi_3... \in (2^{\mathsf{AP}})^\omega$, i.e. an infinite sequences of valuations, which defines for every index $i \in \mathbb{N}$, the set atomic propositions $\pi_i \subseteq \mathsf{AP}$ that hold in that index. The truth value of a formula φ along a trace π at index i is defined as follows:

- for $p \in \mathsf{AP}$, $\pi, i \models p \iff p \in \pi_i$
- $\pi, i \models X\varphi \iff \pi, i+1 \models \varphi$
- $\pi, i \models \varphi_1 U\varphi_2 \iff \exists j \geq i \cdot (\pi, j \models \varphi_2 \wedge \forall k \cdot i \leq k < j : \pi, k \models \varphi_1)$

A trace π *satisfies* a LTL formula φ, denoted as $\pi \models \varphi$, if $\pi, 1 \models \varphi$, i.e. if π satisfies φ in its first position. Finally, we denote the set of traces that satisfies a formula φ as follows: $\llbracket\varphi\rrbracket := \{\pi : \mathbb{N} \mapsto 2^{\mathsf{AP}} | \pi \models \varphi\}$.

In the sequel, we partition the set of atomic propositions AP into $\mathsf{AP}_I \uplus \mathsf{AP}_O$, called *inputs* and *outputs* respectively. Given AP_I, we note Σ_I the set of valuations for the atomic propositions in AP_I, i.e. $\Sigma_I = 2^{\mathsf{AP}_I}$, and $\Sigma_O = 2^{\mathsf{AP}_O}$, and we interprete a pair $(\sigma_I, \sigma_0) \in \Sigma_I \times \Sigma_O$ as a valuation for the entire set of atomic propositions AP.

Realizability Game. Let ψ be an LTL formula over the set of atomic propositions $\mathsf{AP} = \mathsf{AP}_I \uplus \mathsf{AP}_O$. The realizability game with objective ψ is played by two players: Env, who controls the atomic propositions in AP_I (i.e. the inputs), and Sys, who controls the atomic propositions in AP_O (i.e. the outputs). The game proceeds for infinitely many rounds, and the interaction between the two players produces an infinite sequence π of valuations over the atomic propositions AP. The valuations in this sequence are built over successive rounds. In each round $j \in \mathbb{N}$, Env first chooses $\sigma_I \in \Sigma_I$, i.e., a valuation for the atomic propositions in AP_I, and then Sys responds by choosing $\sigma_O \in \Sigma_O$, a valuation for the atomic propositions in AP_O. The pair (σ_I, σ_O), which is a valuation for the entire set of atomic propositions in AP, is appended to the sequence of valuations constructed in previous rounds. After infinitely many rounds, we thus obtain an infinite trace π on which the truth value of the formula ψ can be evaluated. Sys wins the interaction if $\pi \models \psi$; otherwise, Env wins. This game is therefore a zero-sum game.

The way Sys plays in the game above can be formalized by the notion of a *strategy*, which is a function $\lambda_O : \Sigma_I^+ \rightarrow \Sigma_O$ that prescribes the choice $\lambda_O(h) \in \Sigma_O$ after a history of inputs $h = \sigma_{I,1}\sigma_{I,2}...\sigma_{I,n} \in \Sigma_I^+$, i.e., after a sequence of moves by player Env. Given an infinite sequence of valuations $\sigma_{I,1}\sigma_{I,2}...\sigma_{I,n}... \in \Sigma_I^\omega$ for the input variables in AP_I, if Sys plays according to λ_O, the outcome of the interaction is the following infinite sequence of valuations:

$$\pi = (\sigma_{I,1}, \lambda_O(\sigma_{I,1})), (\sigma_{I,2}, \lambda_O(\sigma_{I,1}, \sigma_{I,2}))...(\sigma_{I,n}, \lambda_O(\sigma_{I,1}\sigma_{I,2}...\sigma_{I,n}))...$$

We note this outcome $\lambda_O(\sigma_{I,1}\sigma_{I,2}\ldots\sigma_{I,n}\ldots)$. In the sequel, we will say that given a prefix $(\sigma_{I,1}, \sigma_{O,1})(\sigma_{I,2}, \sigma_{O,2})\ldots(\sigma_{I,n}, \sigma_{O,n}) \in (\Sigma_I \times \Sigma_O)^*$ is compatible with strategy λ_O if for all positions i, $1 \le i \le n$, $\sigma_{O,i} = \lambda_O(\sigma_{I,1}\sigma_{I,2}\ldots\sigma_{I,i})$.

We are now in position to recall the formal definition of the LTL realizabilty problem [PR89]. The *realizability* problem for a formula ψ over $\mathsf{AP} = \mathsf{AP}_I \uplus \mathsf{AP}_O$ asks if there exists a strategy $\lambda_O : \Sigma_I^+ \to \Sigma_O$ for Sys such that for all $\sigma_{I,1}\sigma_{I,2}\ldots\sigma_{I,n}\cdots \in (\Sigma_O)^\omega$,

$$\lambda_O(\sigma_{I,1}\sigma_{I,2}\ldots\sigma_{I,n}\ldots) \models \psi$$

(or equivalently if $\lambda_O(\sigma_{I,1}\sigma_{I,2}\ldots\sigma_{I,n}\ldots) \in [\![\psi]\!]$). In other words, the realizability problem asks whether there exists a strategy for Sys such that all possible interactions with Env result in an infinite trace that satisfies the specification. This problem is decidable as stated in the following theorem.

Theorem 1. *The realizability problem for LTL is* 2ExpTime-C.

Like LTL, automata over infinite words define languages of infinite traces, or words, over a finite alphabet. From the definition of the realizability problem, it follows that we can replace the LTL formula with an ω-regular language defined by an automaton over infinite words and evaluate the realizability of that language. Consequently, several automata-based solutions have been developed to decide the LTL realizability problem [PR89]. Here, we recall one approach based on *universal coBüchi automata*, variants of this approach were first introduced in [KV05,SF07,FJR09].

Automata-Based Approach to Realizablility. Let $\Sigma = \Sigma_I \times \Sigma_O$, a *universal coBüchi automaton* over Σ is a 5-tuple $\mathcal{A} = (Q, Q_{\mathsf{init}}, \Delta, F)$ where: Q is a finite set of states, $Q_{\mathsf{init}} \in 2^Q \setminus \emptyset$ is the non-empty set of initial states, $\Delta : Q \times \Sigma \to 2^Q \setminus \emptyset$ is the *universal* transition relation, and $F \subseteq Q$ is the set of Büchi states. A *run* of $\mathcal{A}$ over an infinite word $w = \sigma_1\sigma_2\cdots\sigma_n\cdots \in \Sigma^\omega$ is an infinite sequence $r = q_1 q_2 \ldots q_n \ldots$ such that $q_1 \in Q_{\mathsf{init}}$, and for all indices $i \ge 1$, we have that $q_{i+1} \in \Delta(q_i, \sigma_i)$. According to the coBüchi acceptance condition, a run is *accepting* if the number of visits to F along the run is *finite*, i.e. $\exists i \in \mathbb{N} \cdot \forall j \ge i : r(i) \notin F$. A word w is *accepted* by $\mathcal{A}$ if *all* its run on w are accepting. In what follows, we also rely on a *stronger* acceptance condition, which is called the K-coBüchi condition, with $K \in \mathbb{N}_0$, which imposes that a run $r = q_1 q_2 \ldots q_n \ldots$ visits F at most K times (instead of finitely many times) to be accepting, i.e. $|\{i \mid q_i \in F\}| \le K$. We denote by $L(\mathcal{A})$ the language defined by $\mathcal{A}$ under the coBüchi acceptance condition, and by $L(\mathcal{A}, K)$ the language defined by $\mathcal{A}$ with the K-coBüchi condition. Clearly, we have $L(\mathcal{A}, K) \subseteq L(\mathcal{A})$ for all $K \in \mathbb{N}_0$, as the acceptance condition is strengthened. For all LTL formulas ψ over AP, we can construct a universal coBüchi automaton $\mathcal{A}_\psi$ such that $L(\mathcal{A}_\psi) = [\![\psi]\!]$. Thus, we can reduce the realizability of an LTL formula ψ to the realizability of the language defined by the automaton $\mathcal{A}_\psi$. Furthermore, the following theorem extends this by linking the realizability of an LTL formula to the realizability of the associated K-coBüchi automata.

Theorem 2. *Let ψ be a LTL formula and $\mathcal{A}_\psi$ be a universal coBüchi automaton such that $L(\mathcal{A}_\psi) = [\![\psi]\!]$. Then for all $K \in \mathbb{N}_0$, if λ_O realizes $L(\mathcal{A}_\psi, K)$ then λ_O realizes ψ. Furthermore, if ψ is realizable then there exists $K \in \mathbb{N}_0$, such that $L(\mathcal{A}_\psi, K)$ is realizable.*

The advantage of the K-coBüchi approach lies in the fact that the automaton $(\mathcal{A}_\psi, K)$ defines a *safety language*. A word that does not belong to the language will have a finite prefix, and a partial run on this prefix that will exceed K visits to F. As a consequence, the determinization of K-coBüchi automata $\mathcal{A}$ relies on the following generalization of the subset construction: in addition to tracking the set of states that can be reached by a prefix of a run while reading an infinite word, the construction also counts the maximal number of times that a run prefix reaches states in the set F. Remember that a run can visit at most K times such states to be accepting. The states of the deterministic automaton are called *counting functions* (that generalize subsets of states). These are formally defined for a coBüchi automaton $\mathcal{A} = (Q, Q_{\text{init}}, \Sigma, \Delta, F)$ and $K \in \mathbb{N}_0$ as the set, denoted $\mathsf{CF}(\mathcal{A}, K)$, of functions $f : Q \to \{-1, 0, 1, \ldots, K, K+1\}$. If $f(q) = -1$ for some state q, it indicates that q is inactive (i.e., no run of $\mathcal{A}$ reaches q on the current prefix). If $f(q) = x$, where $0 \leq x \leq K$, it means that q is active, and the run leading to q with maximal number of visits to F, has done x visits to F. On the other hand, if $f(q) = K + 1$, this indicates that a run on the current prefix has reached q and visited F more than K times, implying that the word being read will be rejected. The initial counting function f_{init} maps all initial states in $Q_{\text{init}} \cap F$ to 1, all other initial states to 0, and all other states to -1 (which means that the state is not active). The deterministic automaton obtained by this determinization procedure is denoted by $\mathcal{D}(\mathcal{A}, K) = (Q^{\mathcal{D}}, q_{\text{init}}^{\mathcal{D}}, \Sigma, \Delta^{\mathcal{D}}, Q_{\text{reject}}^{\mathcal{D}})$, where $Q^{\mathcal{D}} = CF(\mathcal{A}, K)$, $q_{\text{init}}^{\mathcal{D}} = f_{\text{init}}$, the transition function $\Delta^{\mathcal{D}}$ follows the intuition developed above, and $Q_{\text{reject}}^{\mathcal{D}}$ are all the counting functions that maps a state q to $K + 1$.

As the automaton $\mathcal{D}(\mathcal{A}, K)$ defines a safety language, its realizability problem is a *safety game*. During the realizability game, if by reading the prefixes of the word which is built by the interaction, the automaton never reaches $Q_{\text{reject}}^{\mathcal{D}}$, Sys wins, otherwise Env wins. Solving this safety games, can be done with classical algorithms based on backward induction, as shown e.g. in [FJR11]. In the context of safety games, there exists a well-defined notion of the *most general winning strategy*, which can be characterized using the subset of counting functions $\mathsf{Win} \subseteq \mathsf{CF}(\mathcal{A}, K)$. This subset consists of the counting functions that are winning for Sys in the associated safety game—specifically, all counting functions reached by prefixes of words from which Sys has a winning strategy. Furthermore, if $f \in \mathsf{Win}$, then for all f' such that, for all $q \in Q$, $f'(q) \leq f(q)$, then $f' \in \mathsf{Win}$, that is the set of winning counting functions is *downward closed*. This is a direct consequence of the fact that the language of suffixes accepted from f' includes the set of prefixes accepted from f. Another interesting consequence of this fact is that we can equivalently represent Win by considering its maximal elements (as their downward closure is equal to Win.) We write this set of maximal elements as $\lceil \mathsf{Win} \rceil$. Details on how to compute symbolically the winning counting function can be found in [FJR11]. As shown in that paper, the set of winning counting functions enjoys the following important properties.

Theorem 3. *Let ψ be a LTL formula over $\mathsf{AP}_I \uplus \mathsf{AP}_O$, $\mathcal{A}_\psi$ be the coBüchi automaton over the alphabet $\Sigma = \Sigma_I \times \Sigma_O$ such that $L(\mathcal{A}_\psi) = \llbracket \psi \rrbracket$, $K \in \mathbb{N}_0$, and Win be the set of winning counting functions of the determinization of $(\mathcal{A}_\psi, K)$, then if $h \in (\Sigma_I \times \Sigma_0)^*$ is such that by reading h in $\mathcal{D}(\mathcal{A}_\psi, K)$, the run on h stays wining Win, then we know that there exists a strategy λ_O for Sys that realizes ψ and is compatible with h.*

2.2   Pre-mealy, Mealy and Reward Machines

Strategies for the Sys that uses finite memory can be encoded with Mealy machines. It is known that whenever a LTL specification is realizable, then it is realizable with a finite memory strategy and so with a Mealy machine.

A *pre-Mealy machine* $\mathcal{M}$ over Σ_I and Σ_O is defined as a 4-tuple $\langle M, m_0, \delta, \mathcal{O} \rangle$, where M is a finite set of states, sometimes called *memory states*, $m_0 \in M$ is the *initial state*, and $\delta : M \times \Sigma_I \mapsto M$, $\mathcal{O} : M \times \Sigma_I \mapsto \Sigma_O$ are partial functions called, respectively, the *transition* function and the *output* function. A *Mealy machine* is a pre-Mealy machine with δ and $\mathcal{O}$ being complete, i.e. $\mathrm{dom}(\delta) = \mathrm{dom}(\mathcal{O}) = M \times \Sigma_I$.

Let $\sigma_{I,1} \sigma_{I,2} \ldots \sigma_{I,n} \in \Sigma_I^*$, the extended transition function δ^* of $\mathcal{M}$ is defined inductively as follows:

- if $n = 1$, $\delta^*(m, \sigma_{I,1}) = \delta(m, \sigma_{I,1})$
- if $n > 1$, $\delta^*(m, \sigma_{I,1}\sigma_{I,2} \ldots \sigma_{I,n}) = \delta^*(\delta(m, \sigma_{I,1}), \sigma_{I,2} \ldots \sigma_{i,n})$.

We also define the finite language defined by a Mealy machine $\mathcal{M}$, noted $L^*(\mathcal{M})$, and the infinite language, noted $L^\omega(\mathcal{M})$, as follows:

- $L^*(\mathcal{M}) = \{\sigma_{I,1}\sigma_{O,1} \ldots \sigma_{I,n}\sigma_{O,n} \in (\Sigma_I \times \Sigma_O)^* \mid \forall j \cdot 1 \leq j \leq n : \sigma_{O,j} = \mathcal{O}(\delta^*(m_0, \sigma_{I,1} \ldots \sigma_{I,j-1}), \sigma_{I,j})\}$
- $L^\omega(\mathcal{M}) = \{\sigma_{I,1}\sigma_{O,1} \ldots \sigma_{I,n}\sigma_{O,n} \cdots \in (\Sigma_I \times \Sigma_O)^\omega \mid \forall j \in \mathbb{N} : \sigma_{O,j} = \mathcal{O}(\delta^*(m_0, \sigma_{I,1} \ldots \sigma_{I,j-1}), \sigma_{I,j})\}$

A *reward machine* is a Mealy machine with input alphabet $\Sigma_I \times \Sigma_O$ that maps finite sequences from this alphabet to integer rewards. The output alphabet of the reward machine is defined by a pair of integers $r_{\min} < r_{\max}$, such that the output alphabet is the set $\mathbb{Z} \cap [r_{\min}, r_{\max}]$. We denote a reward machine by $\mathcal{R} = \langle S^{\mathcal{R}}, s_{\mathsf{init}}, \delta, r \rangle$, where $S^{\mathcal{R}}$ is a finite set of states, s_{init} is the initial state, $\delta : S^{\mathcal{R}} \times (\Sigma_I \times \Sigma_O)) \to S^{\mathcal{R}}$ is the transition function, and $r : S^{\mathcal{R}} \to \mathbb{Z} \cap [r_{\min}, r_{\max}]$ is the reward function. For any finite word $\sigma_{I,1}\sigma_{O,1} \ldots \sigma_{I,n}\sigma_{O,n} \in (\Sigma_I \times \Sigma_O)^*$, we define

$$\mathcal{R}\left(\sigma_{I,1}\sigma_{O,1} \ldots \sigma_{I,n}\sigma_{O,n}\right) := \sum_{j=1}^{n} r\left(\delta^*(s_{\mathsf{init}}, \sigma_{I,1}\sigma_{O,1} \ldots \sigma_{I,j}\sigma_{O,j})\right) \qquad (1)$$

to be the sum of rewards gained over the finite word $\sigma_{I,1}\sigma_{O,1} \ldots \sigma_{I,n}\sigma_{O,n}$.

2.3   Sample Trees

We assume that our environment, which is stochastic and oblivious, is modelled as a sequence of random variables $\{I_i\}_{i \in \mathbb{N}}$ that can be sampled. Samples are provided via a function $\mathcal{E} : \mathbb{N} \mapsto \Sigma_I^*$ which, for every $L \in \mathbb{N}$, returns a sequence $\mathcal{E}(L)$ of inputs of length L from the environment: $\sigma_{I,1}\sigma_{I,2}\ldots\sigma_{I,L} \in \Sigma_I^L$, so $\mathcal{E}(L)$ is itself a random variable that can be sampled multiple times. A sample obtained by sampling $\mathcal{E}(L)$ multiple times can be seen as a multiset[2] $S : \Sigma_I^L \to \mathbb{N}_0$ of finite sequences of input symbols of length L.

Let S be a sample obtained by drawing n observations from $\mathcal{E}(L)$. We organize this sample, which consists of n input sequences of length L, into a sample tree, defined as follows. Let $\mathsf{Pref}(S)$ denote the set of all prefixes of sequences that appear (possibly multiple times) in S. The sample tree of S, denoted $T_S = (V, v_\epsilon, E, p)$, is a tree with vertices $V = \mathsf{Pref}(S)$, representing the prefixes of input sequences found in S. We denote the root of this tree by v_ε (the vertex associated with the empty word ϵ).

The set of edges, $E \subseteq V \times V$, contains an edge $(v, v') \in E$ if there exists $\sigma_I \in \Sigma_I$ such that $v' = v \cdot \sigma_I$, i.e. if v' extends v with one additional input. We refer to maximal prefixes $v \in V$ as *leaves*, and a *branch* is defined as a path from the root to a leaf, or equivalently as a sequence of inputs of length L. We denote by $\mathcal{B}(T_S)$ the set of branches in T_S. Additionally, we define a function $p : E \to [0, 1]$ that assigns a probability to each edge, reflecting the relative frequency of prefixes in the sample S, formally defined as follows:

$$p(v, v') = \frac{\text{number of sequences in } S \text{ with prefix } v}{\text{number of sequences in } S \text{ with prefix } v'}$$

Clearly, for all $v \in V \setminus \mathcal{B}(T_S)$, i.e. for all vertices that are not leaves, we have $\sum_{v' \in V \mid (v,v') \in E \setminus \mathcal{B}(T_S)} p(v, v') = 1$. Consequently, T_S forms a *finite Markov chain* with sink vertices, which correspond to the leaves of the tree.

2.4   Partial Strategy and Expected Reward

Let $T_S = (V, v_\epsilon, E, p)$ be a sample tree for S that contains n input sequences of length L drawn from $\mathcal{E}(L)$. A *partial Σ_O-strategy* over T_S is a function $\sigma : V \setminus \{v_\varepsilon\} \to \Sigma_O$. Intuitively, a partial strategy associates an output with each vertex of the sample tree, and thus with each prefix of inputs in $\mathsf{Pref}(S)$. Clearly, a partial strategy can be encoded as a pre-Mealy machine.

As each branch $b = v_\varepsilon v_1 v_2 \ldots v_L$ in T_S corresponds to a sequence of inputs $\sigma_{I,1}\sigma_{I,2}\ldots\sigma_{I,L}$ in $\mathsf{Pref}(S)$. We denote by $p(b)$ the probability of the branch b in T_S, calculated as $\prod_{i=1}^{L-1} p(v_i, v_{i+1})$.

Additionally, let $\lambda_O(b)$ represent the sequence $\sigma_{I,1}\sigma_{O,1}\sigma_{I,2}\sigma_{O,2}\ldots\sigma_{I,L}\sigma_{O,L} \in (\Sigma_I \times \Sigma_O)^L$ where $\sigma_{O,i} = \lambda_O(v_i)$ and $v_i = \sigma_{I,1}\sigma_{I,2}\ldots\sigma_{I,i}$, for all i, $1 \leq i <$

---

[2] This is a multiset and not a set as identical sequences may appear multiple times when sampling $\mathcal{E}(L)$.

L. Thus, $\lambda_O(b)$ is the outcome of the strategy λ_O on the sequences of inputs associated to the branch b.

Finally, let $\mathcal{R}(\lambda_O(b))$ denote the total sum of rewards obtained along branch b when following strategy λ_O, as defined in Eq. 1. We can now define the expected $\mathcal{R}$-reward of the partial strategy λ_O over T_S as follows:

$$\mathbb{E}_{\lambda_O}(\mathcal{R}, T_S) := \sum_{b \in \mathcal{B}(T_S)} p(b) \cdot \mathcal{R}(\lambda_O(b)) \tag{2}$$

3   The Problem and Its Algorithm

We present the general problem we aim to solve, along with a high-level overview of the algorithm we use to address it. The problem is defined as follows:

Problem 1. Given a realizable LTL formula ψ over the set of atomic propositions $\mathsf{AP} = \mathsf{AP}_I \uplus \mathsf{AP}_O$, a sample tree T_S of input sequences sampled from the oblivious stochastic environment, and a reward machine $\mathcal{R}$, compute a strategy λ_O that satisfies the following: (i) realizes ψ, and (ii) maximizes the expected total reward over the sample tree T_S.

To obtain a solution to this problem, we proceed as follows:

– First, we compute the optimal outputs for each vertex in the sample tree to maximize the expected reward. This selection of optimal outputs defines a partial strategy that must also preserve the realizability of the LTL specification ψ, ensuring that the partial strategy can be extended into a complete strategy for Sys that satisfies ψ. We denote by $\mathsf{Ex} \subseteq (\Sigma_I \times \Sigma_O)^*$ the set of complete examples resulting from defining the partial strategy on S. Formally, $\mathsf{Ex} = \bigcup_{b \in \mathcal{B}(T_S)} \lambda_O(b)$.
– Second, we apply the algorithm LearnSynth, as defined in [BFR23], to the set of examples Ex (obtained in the first phase) and the specification ψ to derive a complete strategy that realizes ψ and generalizes Ex.

Let us make two important remarks here. First, as noted, we assume that ψ is realizable; otherwise, there would be no solution to satisfy the hard constraints defined by ψ, and thus no solution to the overall problem we aim to solve. Additionally, we assume access to the universal coBüchi automaton $\mathcal{A}_\psi$, along with the maximal elements of a non-empty set of winning states $\lceil \mathsf{Win} \rceil$ for a given $K \in \mathbb{N}$. This additional input is a byproduct of testing the realizability of ψ using a reactive synthesis tool such as ACACIA [BBF+12, CP23], and hence incurs no additional cost in our context.

This setup allows us to apply Theorem 3 to verify that the partial strategy defined on the sample tree can be extended into a complete strategy that realizes ψ. Specifically, a partial strategy is compatible with the set $\lceil \mathsf{Win} \rceil$ if the following condition holds: for all branches $b \in \mathcal{B}(T_S)$, when reading $\lambda_O(b)$ with the universal K-coBüchi automaton $\mathcal{A}_\psi$ associated with ψ, the corresponding counting functions remain within the downward closure of $\lceil\mathsf{Win}\rceil$, see Lemma 2 in [BFR23].

Second, the purpose of using LearnSynth to derive a complete strategy that realizes ψ is to generalize the examples in Ex. These examples demonstrate optimal decisions on input traces from the sample set among strategies that realize ψ. Since these examples represent optimal responses to inputs in the sample, applying LearnSynth generalizes these decisions to produce a complete strategy—represented as a Mealy machine—which we expect to perform well in the unknown, oblivious environment.

To apply the above algorithm and use SynthLearn, we must provide a method to optimally label a sample tree with the outputs of a partial strategy while ensuring the realizability of ψ. The worst-case complexity of this problem is analyzed in the following section, where we also present a practical solution to solve it.

4   Computing the Partial Strategy

In this section, we address the problem of computing a partial strategy for a sample tree T_S that meets two key requirements: (1) the partial strategy can be extended into a full strategy that realizes ψ, meaning it maintains the realizability of ψ; and (2) it maximizes the expected reward on T_S while satisfying the first requirement. The formal statement of this problem is given below:

Problem 2. Given a realizable LTL formula ψ over the set of atomic propositions $\mathsf{AP} = \mathsf{AP}_I \uplus \mathsf{AP}_O$, a sample tree T_S of input sequences sampled from the oblivious stochastic environment, and a reward machine $\mathcal{R}$, a universal KcoBüchi automaton $\mathcal{A}_\psi$ for the formula ψ, and a non-empty set of winning counting functions $\lceil\mathsf{Win}\rceil$ for $L(\mathcal{A}_\psi, K)$, compute a strategy λ_O that satisfies the following: (i) it maintains the realizability of ψ, and (ii) maximizes the expected total reward (defined by $\mathcal{R}$) over the sample tree T_S.

4.1   Hardness

We start by showing unless $\mathsf{PTime} = \mathsf{NP}$, there is no polynomial time algorithm to solve problem 2. Indeed, we prove in the next theorem that the decision version of this problem, which asks for the existence of a solution with an expected reward larger than or equal to a threshold $C \in \mathbb{Z}$ is NP-complete.

Theorem 4. *The decision version of problem 2 is* NP-complete.

Proof: The NP-membership follows from the following arguments. Given a partial strategy λ_O, which has polynomial size relative to the sample tree and can therefore be guessed in polynomial time, we can verify two properties in deterministic polynomial time. First, to ensure that λ_O preserves the realizability of ψ, we compute the counting functions reached by reading $\lambda_O(b)$ with $\mathcal{A}$ for all $b \in \mathcal{B}(T_S)$ and confirm that each of these counting functions falls within the downward closure of $\lceil \mathsf{Win} \rceil$. Second, we verify that the expected reward achieved by λ_O on the Markov chain T_S is at least C. This is accomplished by running the reward machine $\mathcal{R}$ on $\lambda_O(b)$ for each branch $b \in \mathcal{B}(T_S)$ to obtain its reward and then computing the weighted sum of these rewards based on the probability $p(b)$ of each branch b.

To establish NP-hardness, we present a reduction from the graph independent set problem, which is defined as follows.

Problem 3 (Graph Independent Set Problem). Given a undirected graph $G = (U, H)$, where U is a finite set of vertices and H is a set of edges (pairs of adjacent vertices), and a parameter $\kappa \in \mathbb{N}$, determine if there exists a subset of vertices $I \subseteq U$ with cardinality at least κ, i.e., $|I| \geq \kappa$, such that for all $u, v \in I$, $\{u, v\} \notin H$.

Given a graph $G = (U, H)$ and a parameter κ, we now show how to reduce this instance to an instance of our decision problem. We start by fixing the input and output alphabet, we choose $\Sigma_I := U = \{u_1 u_2 ... u_n\}$ and $\Sigma_O := \{0, 1\}$. We consider as the sample the unique sample sequence $u_1 u_2 \ldots u_n$. Intuitively, a strategy $\lambda_O : V \backslash \{v_\varepsilon\} \mapsto \Sigma_O$ will assign 1 after the history up to u_j if the vertex u_j is selected to be in the independent set I, and 0 otherwise. We must then verify two properties. First, that I is indeed an independent set in G. Second, that we have selected at least κ vertices in I. The first property will be coded in the universal KcoBüchi automaton, while the second will be enforced by the reward machine.

To ensure that the set of vertices selected by λ_O forms an independent set, we encode the independence property using a KcoBüchi automaton (with $K = 0$) over the alphabet $\Sigma_I \times \Sigma_O$. Additionally, we demonstrate that the winning counting functions Win for this universal KcoBüchi automaton have a compact representation.

First, we define the automaton. For each edge $\{u_i, u_j\} \in H$ with $i < j$, the universal 0-coBüchi automaton has an initial state q_{ij} where control remains (with appropriate self-loops) until the letter $(u_i, 1)$ is read, indicating that vertex u_i has been selected for the independent set. Upon reading this letter, the automaton transitions to a state where it waits for the letter $(u_j, 1)$ (with additional self-loops). If this second letter is read, signifying that vertex u_j has also been selected, the automaton moves to a state in F, where it remains indefinitely, thus violating the 0-coBüchi condition. Clearly, if such a state in F is reached, it means that the strategy λ_O has selected two vertices connected by an edge in set I, which makes the choice invalid. This setup forces the universal automaton to reject any continuation of $\lambda_O(u_1 u_2 \ldots u_n)$, preventing us from completing the partial strategy λ_O into a strategy that realizes the language defined by the universal automaton.

Conversely, if the local strategy λ_O selects vertices that form an independent set, no run reaches a state in F upon completing the sample, allowing λ_O to be trivially extended into a strategy that realizes the language defined by the K universal automaton, as no accepting state is ever reached.

From this description of the universal automaton, it follows that all counting functions where no active state in F are winning, as Sys can always emit 0 (indicating it is not selecting any more vertices). There is a unique maximal counting function that represents this set of winning functions: all states q not in F are mapped to 0, while the states in F are mapped to -1 (indicating they are inactive).

We still need to encode the requirement that λ_O must select at least κ vertices to form an independent set with the appropriate size. This can be accomplished by defining a reward machine $\mathcal{R}$ that rewards λ_O with reward 1 each time it emits the letter 1, indicating a vertex selection, and it does not reward when the letter 0 is emitted. By setting a reward threshold $C = \kappa$, we ensure that λ_O selects at least κ vertices.

With these constructions, it is straightforward to see that every positive instance of the independent set problem translates to a positive instance of Problem 2, and every negative instance of the independent set problem translates to a negative instance of Problem 2.   □

Therefore, we cannot expect to solve Problem 2 with a polynomial-time algorithm unless PTime = NP. Let us note that this result is somewhat surprising, as it can be shown that verifying the existence of a local strategy that meets condition (1) can be done efficiently (since we have access to the universal automaton $\mathcal{A}_\psi$ and the set $\lceil \mathsf{Win} \rceil$). Similarly, computing an optimal local strategy that maximizes the expected reward on T_S can also be done in polynomial time (by treating T_S as a Markov Decision Process (MDP)). Thus, it is the combination of these two constraints that makes the problem NP-complete.

4.2 SMT Based Solution

Now that we have established that Problem 2 is NP-complete, we show how to solve it using a SMT solver.

We begin by providing some intuition. To encode the decision version of Problem 2, we need to track the execution of two machines along the branches of T_S, which are annotated by the choices made by the partial strategy λ_O: the universal automaton, to monitor the counting functions reached, and the reward machine, to compute the reward. Since the partial strategy is not yet fixed—discovering it is the purpose of the SMT-based procedure—we maintain two sets of variables: one to represent the output choices at each vertex of the sample tree and another to track the counting functions. The constraints should then specify rules for assigning values to these variables so that the transitions of both machines are correctly simulated, ensuring the realizability of the hard constraints.

Formally, given a universal K-coBüchi automaton $\mathcal{A}$ with access to the antichain of realizable counting functions $\lceil \mathsf{Win} \rceil$, a sample tree T_S, and a reward machine $\mathcal{R}$, we define two sets of variables. The first set consists of boolean variables used to determine the strategy to be applied at each vertex v:

$$\{x_{v,s,o} \mid \forall v \in V, S \in S^{\mathcal{R}}, o \in \Sigma_O\}$$

The second set consists of integer variables used to track the counting function after executing the action determined by the previous set of variables:

$$\{y_{v,q} \mid \forall v \in V, q \in Q\}$$

We then encode the initial conditions, transitions, and realizability constraints and pass these to an SMT solver to obtain a partial strategy λ_O that solves the decision version of Problem 2 with respect to a given parameter C. The encoding techniques used are mostly standard, so we omit them here for brevity; interested readers may refer to [RT24] for a full construction. To achieve optimality, we note that the reward machine has a finite set of edges, thus bounding the maximum and minimum rewards. This bounded range allows for a straightforward binary search over the interval to find the optimal partial strategy. Further details are provided in [RT24].

5   Case Study: Weather Monitoring System

In this section, we illustrate how our formal framework and synthesis algorithm apply to a system that must meet *both* hard and soft constraints while interacting with a unknown, oblivious stochastic environment.

The design scenario is as follows: the objective is to automatically synthesize a weather monitoring system capable of issuing *warnings* and *alarms* to alert road administration teams of freezing hazards, enabling timely deployment of salt trucks and other preventive measures when road conditions become unsafe. In this scenario, Env controls the evolution of temperature, while the Sys manages the warning and alarm signals. Clearly, the Env is *oblivious* to the behavior of Sys, as it is independent of the system's decisions; that is, temperature evolution is unaffected by the issuance of alarms or warnings.

Similar to real-world conditions, the monitoring system is developed without a fully defined probabilistic model of temperature evolution. Instead, the system relies on previous observations of temperature patterns, leveraging statistical trends to optimize warning issuance based on historical data. This historical data will be played by our sample tree.

According to our framework, the specifications governing the system's operation are divided into two categories: *hard constraints* related to *alarms* and *soft constraints* related to *warnings*.

Informal Description. We begin with a description of the hard constraints. An *alarm* is triggered whenever the temperature reaches or falls below $0\,°C$. Once active, the alarm remains on until the temperature rises above $0\,°C$ for at least two consecutive time steps, after which it automatically deactivates. While an alarm is active, all warnings are disabled to prevent redundancy. Below, we show how to formalize these hard constraints in LTL.

Now, let us turn to the *soft constraints* related to warnings. A *warning* is triggered when the temperature is nearing $0°$ but has not yet reached it. A warning is considered valid *in insight* if the temperature subsequently reaches

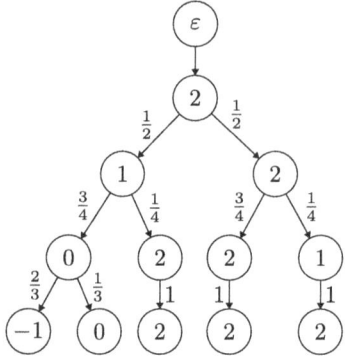

Fig. 1. An example of sample tree.

$0°$; otherwise, it is deemed a false alarm if the temperature rises again without reaching the critical threshold. To assess system performance, a cost function evaluates the accuracy of warnings, penalizing false alarms (negative rewards) while incurring no penalty for legitimate warnings.

While it is straightforward to design a system that meets the hard constraints for alarms *alone*, achieving both the hard constraints *and* optimal adherence to the soft constraints for warnings is more complex. Consider the following multiset of samples (eight sequences of four inputs each) drawn from the environment:

$$S(2; 1; 0; -1) = 2, S(2; 1; 0; 0) = 1, S(2; 1; 2; 2) = 1, S(2; 2; 2; 2) = 3, S(2; 2; 1; 2) = 1$$

which correspond to the sample tree depicted in Fig. 1. In the node labeled 1 on the left branch, there is a higher likelihood that the temperature will reach $0°C$, so the system may issue a warning. However, there is also a chance that the temperature will subsequently rise to 2, rendering the warning unnecessary and suboptimal. Conversely, if the strategy chooses not to issue a warning at node 1, it violates the intended warning protocol, as the temperature reaches 0 in some samples.

This simple example demonstrates that a flawless warning system cannot be designed due to the probabilistic nature of the environment. Instead, the system should issue warnings when conditions indicate a high probability of need. Here, the prefix 2; 1 suggests a decrease in temperature, with a corresponding probability indicating a higher likelihood of reaching 0 compared to branches with the prefix 2; 2. If this pattern is confirmed by a larger number of samples, it can be used to issue warnings more effectively. Indeed, such a pattern naturally suggests that a warning should be issued for prefix 2; 1 but not for prefix 2; 2. This example illustrates that gathering statistical information from the environment through sampling is valuable and highlights the importance of distinguishing between hard and soft constraints.

Formalization. We now turn to a formal description of the two types of constraints. The hard constraints are expressed using LTL, while the soft constraints are defined by a reward machine (where negative rewards are interpreted as costs). This reward machine assigns negative rewards for false warnings detected in hindsight (i.e., when the temperature does not drop to 0 after a warning) and imposes no penalty for accurate warnings. This balanced approach enables the system to optimize its responses while managing the inherent uncertainties in temperature evolution.

To formalize the scenario above, we begin by establishing notation and encoding conventions. First, we assume that the temperature is sampled frequently enough so that the temperature difference between any two consecutive inputs is at most 1. We focus only on the interval $[-1, 2]$, with any value outside this interval abstracted as -1 or 2, respectively. Furthermore, all values are rounded to the nearest integer to allow encoding as discrete inputs. Let $\{M_1, M_2\}$ be the set of input atomic propositions AP_I; we assign temperatures to their binary encoding as follows:

1. $t = 2 \iff \,!M_1 \,\&\, !M_2$
2. $t = 1 \iff M_1 \,\&\, !M_2$
3. $t = 0 \iff \,!M_1 \,\&\, M_2$
4. $t = -1 \iff M_1 \,\&\, M_2$

Let $\mathsf{AP}_O = \{\mathsf{Warn}, \mathsf{Alarm}\}$ be the set of output atomic propositions, where the assignment of each atomic proposition corresponds to an action taken by the system. The case where both Warn and Alarm are active simultaneously is ruled out by encoding this restriction as part of the hard constraint φ_{hard}.

The hard constraints are encoded as the conjunction of the following LTL formulas, each with its corresponding natural language interpretation:

1. Alarm must be issued when the temperature is below or equal to 0:

$$G(M_2 \to \mathsf{Alarm})$$

2. Alarm can only be released when the temperature is above zero for two consecutive steps:

$$G((!M_1 \,\&\, M_2) \,\&\, X(!M_2)) \to X(\mathsf{Alarm})$$

$$G(!M_2 \,\&\, X(!M_2)) \to X(!\mathsf{Alarm})$$

3. Warning and Alarm should not be issued at the same time:

$$G(!\mathsf{Alarm} \,|\, !\mathsf{Warn})$$

For the soft constraint on warnings, we construct the reward machine depicted in Fig. 2, where s_0 is the initial state, corresponding to no signal being issued; s_1 and s_2 correspond to states reached when a warning has been issued and the temperature is equal to 1 and 2, respectively; and s_3 corresponds to the state when an alarm has been issued. Intuitively, the following three types of behavior incur a reward of -1:

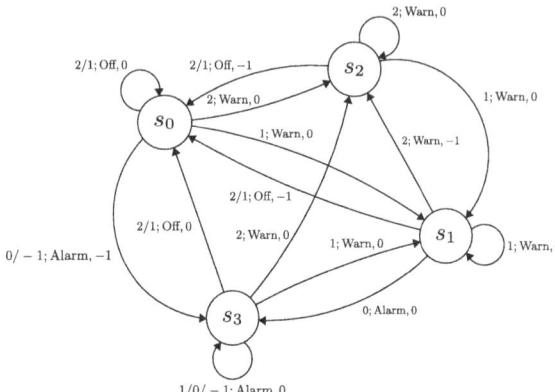

Fig. 2. The reward machine is designed to penalize false warning signals in hindsight.

1. Alarm is directly issued without warning ahead, which corresponds to the edge from s_0 to s_3.
2. Warn is taken off without being reached to zero, which corresponds to the edge from s_1 and s_2 to s_0.
3. The temperature increase while the Warn is being issued, which corresponds to the arrow from s_1 to s_0.

For readability, the edge labels are shown as temperature values and issued signals rather than their binary encodings. Some input-output pairs are omitted here, as they correspond to actions that would violate the hard constraint φ_{hard}. Our synthesis method will always avoid these edges and can therefore be safely omitted.

Prototypal Implementation. To demonstrate the practicality of our framework, we developed a prototype in Python. We used ACACIA-BONSAI [CP23] to translate the hard constraints expressed in LTL into universal coBüchi automata and employed its antichain solver to compute $\lceil \mathsf{Win} \rceil$. For constructing and solving the SMT instances, we utilized the PYSMT library [LAK+14] with Z3 [dMB08] as the underlying solver. This setup allowed us to compute the optimal partial strategy on the sample tree, generating complete examples for a given set of samples. Finally, we applied the SynthLearn algorithm [BFR23] to obtain a Mealy machine that realizes the hard constraints and generalizes the examples computed on the sample tree.

To enable the sampling of a representative environment, we modeled the environment as the finite Markov chain shown in Fig. 3[3]. This model allowed us to draw representative samples. We used the parameters $n = 100$ and $L = 6$ for sampling. Our implementation successfully built a partial strategy on the sample tree constructed from these 100 samples, achieving an optimal value of

---

[3] The model was used exclusively for sampling in alignment with our framework, given that Env is accessible only through sampling.

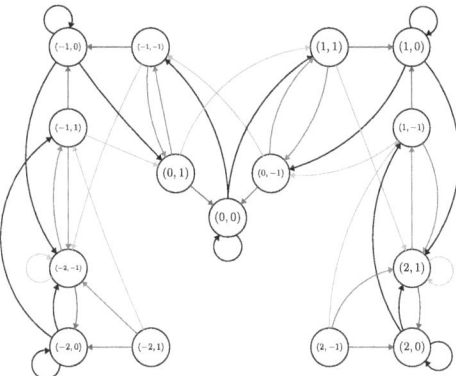

Fig. 3. The Markov Chain was used to model the environment, providing samples both during synthesis and for validation purposes, i.e. for model-checking the Mealy machine produced by our algorithm.

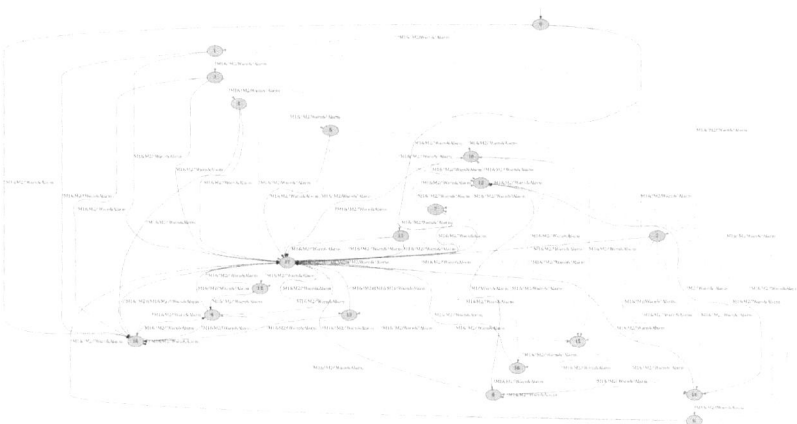

Fig. 4. The completed Mealy machine, obtained using SynthLearn on φ_{hard} and examples from Ex that were constructed by computing an optimal local strategy based on the samples.

$C = -0.25$ while maintaining the realizability of φ_{hard}. When this partial function is applied to the 100 samples, it generates 100 complete examples, which are then passed to the SynthLearn algorithm along with φ_{hard}. This produces a complete Mealy machine that realizes φ_{hard} and generalizes the examples, resulting in a Mealy machine with 20 states, as depicted in Fig. 4.

To evaluate the quality of the solution produced by SynthLearn, we model-checked this machine within the environment shown in Fig. 3 and the reward machine in Fig. 2 using STORM to compute the expected mean-payoff of the solution in the long run. The result was a long-run average reward of -0.0707, which is reasonably close to the sample tree's average reward of $\frac{-0.25}{6} = -0.0417$. This indicates that the SynthLearn algorithm has effectively generalized the optimal local decisions computed from the samples to synthesize a complete strategy that enforces φ_{hard} with certainty while achieving strong performance in the environment. This outcome is particularly notable since we did not use the full model of the environment during synthesis, relying instead solely on samples drawn from it.

6   Conclusion

In this paper, we presented a framework for the automatic synthesis of reactive systems that must enforce *both* hard and soft constraints in an unknown, oblivious stochastic environment that can only be sampled. Our approach relies on an LTL specification to formalize the hard constraints, while a reward machine assigns rewards to finite sequences of inputs and outputs to capture the soft constraints.

Given a set of sampled input sequences from the environment, we demonstrated how to compute a partial strategy that is optimal with respect to the reward machine while preserving the realizability of the hard constraints. We established that computing this optimal strategy is computationally hard (the associated decision problem was shown NP-complete), and provided an SMT-based solution to tackle this problem.

Once this partial strategy is applied to the sample, it produces complete examples, which can then be generalized using the SynthLearn algorithm [BFR23]. This results in a complete strategy that not only enforces the hard constraints with certainty but also generalizes the behaviors illustrated by the examples.

We implemented a prototype tool to validate our framework and applied it to a simple yet insightful case study, showcasing its practical applicability and effectiveness.

References

[BBF+12] Bohy, A., Bruyère, V., Filiot, E., Jin, N., Raskin, J.-F.: Acacia+, a tool for LTL synthesis. In: Madhusudan, P., Seshia, S.A. (eds.) CAV 2012. LNCS, vol. 7358, pp. 652–657. Springer, Heidelberg (2012). https://doi.org/10.1007/978-3-642-31424-7_45

[BFR23] Balachander, M., Filiot, E., Raskin, J.F.: LTL reactive synthesis with a few hints. In: Sankaranarayanan, S., Sharygina, N. (eds.) TACAS 2023. LNCS, vol. 13994, pp. 309–328. Springer, Cham (2023). https://doi.org/10.1007/978-3-031-30820-8_20

[BFRR14] Bruyère, V., Filiot, E., Randour, M., Raskin, J.-F.: Meet your expectations with guarantees: beyond worst-case synthesis in quantitative games. In: Mayr, E.W., Portier, N. (eds.) STACS 2014. LIPIcs, vol. 25, pp. 199–213. Schloss Dagstuhl - Leibniz-Zentrum für Informatik (2014)

[BK08] Baier, C., Katoen, J.-P.: Principles of Model Checking. MIT Press, Cambridge (2008)

[CP23]   Cadilhac, M., Pérez, G.A.: Acacia-Bonsai: a modern implementation of downset-based LTL realizability. In: Sankaranarayanan, S., Sharygina, N. (eds.) TACAS 2023. LNCS, vol. 13994, pp. 192–207. Springer, Cham (2023). https://doi.org/10.1007/978-3-031-30820-8_14

[CRR14] Chatterjee, K., Randour, M., Raskin, J.-F.: Strategy synthesis for multi-dimensional quantitative objectives. Acta Inform. **51**(3–4), 129–163 (2014)

[dMB08] de Moura, L., Bjørner, N.: Z3: an efficient SMT solver. In: Ramakrishnan, C.R., Rehof, J. (eds.) TACAS 2008. LNCS, vol. 4963, pp. 337–340. Springer, Heidelberg (2008). https://doi.org/10.1007/978-3-540-78800-3_24

[FFT18] Faymonville, P., Finkbeiner, B., Tentrup, L.: BoSy: an experimentation framework for bounded synthesis. CoRR, abs/1803.09566 (2018)

[FJR09] Filiot, E., Jin, N., Raskin, J.-F.: An antichain algorithm for LTL realizability. In: Bouajjani, A., Maler, O. (eds.) CAV 2009. LNCS, vol. 5643, pp. 263–277. Springer, Heidelberg (2009). https://doi.org/10.1007/978-3-642-02658-4_22

[FJR11] Filiot, E., Jin, N., Raskin, J.-F.: Antichains and compositional algorithms for LTL synthesis. Formal Methods Syst. Des. **39**(3), 261–296 (2011)

[HJK+22] Hensel, C., Junges, S., Katoen, J.-P., Quatmann, T., Volk, M.: The probabilistic model checker storm. Int. J. Softw. Tools Technol. Transf. **24**(4), 589–610 (2022)

[KNP09] Kwiatkowska, M.Z., Norman, G., Parker, D.: PRISM: probabilistic model checking for performance and reliability analysis. SIGMETRICS Perform. Evaluation Rev. **36**(4), 40–45 (2009)

[KV05]   Kupferman, O., Vardi, M.Y.: Safraless decision procedures. In: FOCS 2005, pp. 531–542. IEEE Computer Society (2005)

[LAK+14] Li, Y., Albarghouthi, A., Kincaid, Z., Gurfinkel, A., Chechik, M.: Symbolic optimization with SMT solvers. In: POPL, pp. 607–618. ACM (2014)

[LMS20] Luttenberger, M., Meyer, P.J., Sickert, S.: Practical synthesis of reactive systems from LTL specifications via parity games. Acta Inform. **57**(1–2), 3–36 (2020)

[PR89]   Pnueli, A., Rosner, R.: On the synthesis of a reactive module. In: POPL 1989, pp. 179–190. ACM Press (1989)

[QK21]   Quatmann, T., Katoen, J.-P.: Multi-objective optimization of long-run average and total rewards. In: TACAS 2021. LNCS, vol. 12651, pp. 230–249. Springer, Cham (2021). https://doi.org/10.1007/978-3-030-72016-2_13

[RRS17] Randour, M., Raskin, J.-F., Sankur, O.: Percentile queries in multi-dimensional Markov decision processes. Formal Methods Syst. Des. **50**(2–3), 207–248 (2017)

[RT24]   Raskin, J.-F., Tsai, Y.C.: Synthesis from LTL with reward optimization in sampled oblivious environments. CoRR, ArXiv (2024)

[SF07]   Schewe, S., Finkbeiner, B.: Bounded synthesis. In: Namjoshi, K.S., Yoneda, T., Higashino, T., Okamura, Y. (eds.) ATVA 2007. LNCS, vol. 4762, pp. 474–488. Springer, Heidelberg (2007). https://doi.org/10.1007/978-3-540-75596-8_33

Regular Papers

An Assertion-Based Logic for Local Reasoning about Probabilistic Programs

Huiling Wu, Anran Cui, and Yuxin Deng[⊠]

Shanghai Key Laboratory of Trustworthy Computing,
East China Normal University, Shanghai, China
{51255902019,arcui}@stu.ecnu.edu.cn, yxdeng@sei.ecnu.edu.cn

Abstract. We introduce an assertion-based logic specifically designed for local reasoning about probabilistic programs featuring unbounded loops. Distribution formulas and their extensions facilitate the representation of invariants for unbounded loops in probabilistic programs. The assertions connected by separating conjunction exhibit probabilistic independence, which more intuitively displays the mutually independent properties of variables and ensures that the logic supports local reasoning. We prove the soundness of our logic and showcase its effectiveness through the formal verification of a wide range of examples including probabilistic inference in Bayesian networks and security analysis of cryptographic schemes.

Keywords: Probabilistic programs · Separation logic · Local reasoning

1 Introduction

Probabilistic programs are ubiquitous across various domains, including reliability analysis of networks [21,46] and cyberphysical systems [30,37], verification of randomized algorithms [40], security of cryptographic algorithms [8], privacy protocols [10], and machine learning, particularly Bayesian network analysis [23]. With the development of these fields, there is a growing recognition of the importance of formally verifying probabilistic programs to ensure their correctness. This is particularly crucial due to the challenges posed by the probabilistic nature of their execution, necessitating rigorous verification methods to mitigate potential risks and ensure reliable performance.

H. Wu and A. Cui contributed equally to this work.

Deng was supported by the National Key R&D Program of China under Grant No. 2023YFA1009403, the National Natural Science Foundation of China under Grants Nos. 62472175 and 62072176, Shanghai Trusted Industry Internet Software Collaborative Innovation Center, and the "Digital Silk Road" Shanghai International Joint Lab of Trustworthy Intelligent Software under Grant No. 22510750100.

T. Bourke et al. (Eds.): SETTA 2024, LNCS 15469, pp. 25–45, 2025.
https://doi.org/10.1007/978-981-96-0602-3_2

$$x := 0;$$
$$\textbf{while } x < 5 \textbf{ do}$$
$$n :=_\$ \{\tfrac{1}{2} \cdot 0 + \tfrac{1}{2} \cdot 1\};$$
$$\textbf{if } (n = 1) \textbf{ then}$$
$$x := x + 1;$$
$$\textbf{else}$$
$$\textbf{skip};$$
$$\textbf{fi}$$
$$\textbf{od}$$

Fig. 1. The program $Prog_1$

Since Kozen's seminal work [35] established the semantics of probabilistic programs, different techniques have emerged to verify the correctness of programs. Early methods rely on mathematical models derived from probabilistic semantics, utilizing structures like Markov chains, Markov decision processes [3,29], probabilistic input-output automata [45,50], and probabilistic transition systems [26,28]. However, the complexities of some probabilistic programs often make precise model construction difficult, hindering traditional verification methods. As an alternative, a systematic approach for formally verifying probabilistic programs without computing their semantics has received much attention. Techniques such as probabilistic process algebra [2], stochastic processes [19], and model checking [16] have been proposed.

The most mature approach in this area, which bypasses the need for computing semantics, is the expectation-based technique [36,39]. These works primarily utilize the weakest pre-expectation calculus or the weakest precondition calculus, triggering a series of research in this direction [25,31–34,41]. Another popular family of approaches is the assertion-based techniques, first proposed by Ramshaw [42]. These techniques enable concurrent verification of properties involving multiple probabilities and offer more intuitive specifications for loop reasoning.

Challenge. In the realm of probabilistic programs, assertion-based techniques require assessing whether an assertion is satisfied. Very often, the Boolean condition in the guard of a loop may not deterministically evaluate to true or false after an iteration; instead, it forms a Boolean distribution. This kind of loops, termed *unbounded loops* in this paper, lack a guarantee of termination within any fixed number of iterations and may potentially diverge with certain probability. The infinitary nature of unbounded loops complicates reasoning tasks, posing a significant challenge in the design of while rules and invariants for probabilistic programs. Many prior works in assertion-based systems lack adequate rules to support the inference for unbounded loops [9,13,38]. A few works attempt to address this issue but impose constraints on invariants [43] or introduce conditions that are challenging to verify [5,27].

Let us consider a simple probabilistic program, called $Prog_1$, as given in Fig. 1. Intuitively, the property $x = 5$ holds upon the termination of the program.

However, after each iteration of the loop, there remains a non-zero probability that the Boolean condition $x < 5$ holds. Establishing a suitable invariant for this program is crucial for verifying that the postcondition is $x = 5$.

We take advantage of distribution formulas [18] to specify properties of distribution states. An invariant for $Prog_1$ can be expressed as $x < 5 \oplus x = 5$, which intuitively means that both properties $x < 5$ and $x = 5$ are satisfied probabilistically, though the precise probabilities are not explicitly stated.

As discussed in [18], distribution formulas serve as a useful tool for constructing invariants of while loops, thus avoiding the infinite sequences of assertions discussed in [5].

Contribution. We present an assertion-based logic for local reasoning about probabilistic programs featuring unbounded loops. Our contributions are summarized as follows:

– We propose a new separation logic for probabilistic programs with discrete distributions, which uses distribution formulas to specify probabilistic behavior. These formulas play a crucial role in establishing an invariant condition in the proof rule for unbounded loops, effectively preventing the occurrence of infinite assertion sequences.
– The separating conjunction in our work can represent probabilistic independence, as inherited from [9], and is combined with a frame rule to facilitate local reasoning. We then prove the soundness of the separation logic; a key ingredient of the proof is the property that the denotation of every assertion is a closed set.
– We demonstrate the effectiveness of our logic by establishing the correctness of various probabilistic programs featuring unbounded loops. The case studies encompass examples for Bayesian networks and cryptographic schemes, highlighting the versatility and applicability of our approach.

Organization. The rest of the paper is structured as follows. In Sect. 2, we recall some basic notations about probability distributions. Section 3 gives the syntax and denotational semantics of a probabilistic language. Section 4 defines an assertion language and provides its semantics. In Sect. 5, we present a proof system for local reasoning about probabilistic programs. In Sect. 6, we verify the correctness of $Prog_1$ and a program for encoding a Bayesion Network. We discuss related work and compare with ours in Sect. 7. Finally, we conclude and discuss possible future work in Sect. 8.

2 Preliminaries

Let S be a countable set. A (discrete) *sub-distribution* on S is a function $\mu : S \to [0,1]$ with $\|\mu\| \triangleq \sum_{s \in S} \mu(s) \leq 1$. If $\|\mu\| = 1$, then μ is a *distribution*. We denote the set of all sub-distributions on S as **SDist**$[S]$. For any set $S' \subseteq S$, we write $\mu(S')$ for $\sum_{s \in S'} \mu(s)$. The support of a sub-distribution μ is defined

(**Aexp**)	a	::=	$r \mid x, y, \ldots \mid f_m(a, \ldots, a)$
(**Bexp**)	b	::=	**true** $\mid$ **false** $\mid P_m(a, \ldots, a) \mid b \wedge b \mid \neg b$
(**Com**)	c	::=	**skip** $\mid$ **abort** $\mid x := a \mid x :=_{\$} d_A \mid c; \, c$
			$\mid$ **if** b **then** c **else** c **fi** $\mid$ **while** b **do** c **od**

Fig. 2. Syntax of PIMP

as $\lceil \mu \rceil \triangleq \{ s \in S \mid \mu(s) > 0 \}$. If $\mu(s) = 0$ for all $s \in S$, then μ is an empty sub-distribution, denoted by ϵ_S.

Let $\mu_1, \mu_2 \in \mathbf{SDist}[S]$ such that $\|\mu_1\| + \|\mu_2\| \leq 1$. The sum of $\mu_1 + \mu_2$ is also a sub-distribution in $\mathbf{SDist}[S]$, defined by letting $(\mu_1 + \mu_2)(s) \triangleq \mu_1(s) + \mu_2(s)$, for all $s \in S$. Let $\mu \in \mathbf{SDist}[S]$ and $p \in [0, 1]$. Then $p \cdot \mu$ is also a sub-distribution in $\mathbf{SDist}[S]$, defined by letting $(p \cdot \mu)(s) \triangleq p \cdot \mu(s)$, for all $s \in S$. Let $S' \subseteq S$ and $\mu \in \mathbf{SDist}[S]$. The restriction $\mu_{S'}$ of μ to S' is also a sub-distribution, defined by

$$\mu_{S'}(s) \triangleq \begin{cases} \mu(s), & \text{if } s \in S' \\ 0, & \text{otherwise.} \end{cases}$$

Let S_1 and S_2 be two countable sets, $\mu_1 \in \mathbf{SDist}[S_1]$, and $\mu_2 \in \mathbf{SDist}[S_2]$. The *joint sub-distribution* $\mu_1 \otimes \mu_2 \in \mathbf{SDist}[S_1 \times S_2]$ is defined by letting

$$\mu_1 \otimes \mu_2(s_1, s_2) \triangleq \mu_1(s_1) \cdot \mu_2(s_2),$$

for any $s_1 \in S_1$ and $s_2 \in S_2$. Let S_1 and S_2 be two countable sets and $\mu \in \mathbf{SDist}[S_1 \times S_2]$. The two projection operators $\pi_{S_1}(\cdot)$ and $\pi_{S_2}(\cdot)$ yield two sub-distributions in the sets $\mathbf{SDist}[S_1]$ and $\mathbf{SDist}[S_2]$, called the *first* and *second marginals* respectively, defined by

$$\pi_{S_1}(\mu)(s_1) \triangleq \sum_{s_2 \in S_2} \mu(s_1, s_2) \qquad \pi_{S_2}(\mu)(s_2) \triangleq \sum_{s_1 \in S_1} \mu(s_1, s_2).$$

The events in S_1 and S_2 are mutually independent if any $\mu \in \mathbf{SDist}[S_1 \times S_2]$ can be factored as $\pi_{S_1}(\mu) \otimes \pi_{S_2}(\mu)$.

3 A Probabilistic Imperative Language

In this section, we introduce the syntax and denotational semantics of a probabilistic language, known as PIMP, obtained by extending the imperative language in [49] with random assignments.

3.1 Syntax

The syntax of PIMP is given in Fig. 2. Let $\mathbb{Q}$ be the set of rational numbers, and **Var** be the set of variables. Arithmetic operators (e.g., $+$, $-$, $*$, etc.) are denoted by f_m, and Boolean predicates (e.g., $=$, $\leq$, $\geq$, etc.) are denoted by P_m, where m is the arity of f or P. The set **Aexp** of arithmetic expressions includes constant rational numbers $r \in \mathbb{Q}$, variables x, y, ... in **Var**, as well as other arithmetic expressions constructed by arithmetic operators f_m. Similarly, the set **Bexp** of Boolean expressions encompasses Boolean constants **true** and **false**, and other Boolean expressions created by Boolean predicates P_m and Boolean connectives such as $\wedge$ and $\neg$. We collectively refer to arithmetic expressions a and Boolean expressions b as expressions, denoted by e. Here we use d_A to represent a distribution on the finite set A consisting of arithmetic expressions. The set **Com** includes **skip** (no-op command), **abort** (halt command), the classical assignment, the random assignment, the sequential statement, the conditional statement and the **while**-loop statement.

3.2   Partial States and Distribution States

Recall that a classical state is a mapping from **Var** to $\mathbb{Q}$. We introduce a notion of partial state in order to facilitate local reasoning.

Definition 1. *Let X be any subset of **Var**. A classical partial state on X is a function $\sigma : X \to \mathbb{Q}$, where $\sigma(x)$ represents the value of the classical variable x.*

We abbreviate a classical (partial) state as a state hereafter. We denote the set of all states on X by Σ_X and the domain of any state $\sigma \in \Sigma_X$ by $\mathrm{dom}(\sigma) \triangleq X$. Note that the set $\Sigma_\emptyset$ has only one element $\mathbf{0} : \emptyset \to \mathbb{Q}$. We denote the set of all states by Σ. Suppose $X \subseteq Y \subseteq$ **Var**. For any $\sigma \in \Sigma_Y$, we use the notation σ_X to denote the state obtained by restricting the state σ to the domain Σ_X, such that $\sigma_X(x) = \sigma(x)$. The updated state denoted by $\sigma[a/x]$ is defined as

$$\sigma[a/x](y) \triangleq \begin{cases} a & \text{if } y = x \\ \sigma(y) & \text{otherwise.} \end{cases}$$

Let the set of (sub)-distribution states on X be **SDist**$[\Sigma_X]$. For any $\mu \in$ **SDist**$[\Sigma_X]$, its domain $\mathrm{dom}(\mu) \triangleq X$. For simplicity, we abbreviate (sub)-distribution states as distribution states hereafter. We denote the set of all distribution states by

$$\Delta = \{\mu \in \mathbf{SDist}[\Sigma_X] \mid X \subseteq \mathbf{Var}\}.$$

The updated distribution state $\mu[a/x]$ is defined by letting

$$(\mu[a/x])(\sigma) \triangleq \sum_{\sigma' \in \lceil \mu \rceil} \{\mu(\sigma') \mid \sigma'[a/x] = \sigma\}.$$

Definition 2. *Let X and Y be two sets of disjoint variables, $\mu_1 \in \mathbf{SDist}[\Sigma_X]$ and $\mu_2 \in \mathbf{SDist}[\Sigma_Y]$. We write $\mu_1 \otimes \mu_2$ for a new distribution state in the set $\mathbf{SDist}[\Sigma_{X \cup Y}]$, which satisfies $(\mu_1 \otimes \mu_2)(\sigma) = \mu_1(\sigma_X) \cdot \mu_2(\sigma_Y)$, for any $\sigma \in \Sigma_{X \cup Y}$.*

$$\llbracket n \rrbracket_\sigma \qquad\qquad = n$$

$$\llbracket x \rrbracket_\sigma \qquad\qquad = \sigma(x)$$

$$\llbracket f_m(a,...,a) \rrbracket_\sigma \quad = f_m(\llbracket a \rrbracket_\sigma,...,\llbracket a \rrbracket_\sigma)$$

$$\llbracket \mathbf{true} \rrbracket_\sigma \qquad\quad = \mathbf{true}$$

$$\llbracket \mathbf{false} \rrbracket_\sigma \qquad\quad = \mathbf{false}$$

$$\llbracket P_m(a,...,a) \rrbracket_\sigma \quad = P_m(\llbracket a \rrbracket_\sigma,...,\llbracket a \rrbracket_\sigma)$$

$$\llbracket b_1 \wedge b_2 \rrbracket_\sigma \qquad = \llbracket b_1 \rrbracket_\sigma \wedge \llbracket b_2 \rrbracket_\sigma$$

$$\llbracket \neg b \rrbracket_\sigma \qquad\qquad = \neg(\llbracket b \rrbracket_\sigma)$$

$$\llbracket a \rrbracket_\mu \qquad\qquad = d_{\{\llbracket a \rrbracket_\sigma | \sigma \in \lceil \mu \rceil\}}, \text{ where } d(\llbracket a \rrbracket_\sigma) = \sum_{\sigma' \in \lceil \mu \rceil, \llbracket a \rrbracket_{\sigma'} = \llbracket a \rrbracket_\sigma} \mu(\sigma')$$

$$\llbracket b \rrbracket_\mu \qquad\qquad = d_{\{\llbracket b \rrbracket_\sigma | \sigma \in \lceil \mu \rceil\}}, \text{ where } d(\llbracket b \rrbracket_\sigma) = \sum_{\sigma' \in \lceil \mu \rceil, \llbracket b \rrbracket_{\sigma'} = \llbracket b \rrbracket_\sigma} \mu(\sigma')$$

Fig. 3. Evaluation for expressions

Suppose $X \subseteq Y \subseteq \mathbf{Var}$. We project a distribution state $\mu \in \mathbf{SDist}[\Sigma_Y]$ to a distribution state $\pi_X(\mu) \in \mathbf{SDist}[\Sigma_X]$ via the projection operator π in the following way:

$$\pi_X(\mu)(\sigma) \triangleq \sum_{\sigma' \in \lceil \mu \rceil} \{\mu(\sigma') \mid \sigma'_X = \sigma\}.$$

If any distribution μ in $\mathbf{SDist}[\Sigma_{X_1 \cup X_2}]$ can be factored as $\pi_{X_1}(\mu) \otimes \pi_{X_2}(\mu)$, we say the variables in X_1 and X_2 are mutually independent, denoted by $X_1 \perp X_2$.

3.3   Denotational Semantics

We interpret expressions in both partial states and distribution states. For any expression e, we use $\mathbf{V}(e)$ to denote the set of variables occurring in e. The denotation of an arithmetic expression a is a mapping of type $\Sigma_X \to \mathbb{Q}$, and that of a Boolean expression b is a mapping of type $\Sigma_{X'} \to \{\mathbf{true}, \mathbf{false}\}$, where $\mathbf{V}(a) \subseteq X$ and $\mathbf{V}(b) \subseteq X'$. Given a distribution state μ, the evaluation of expressions under μ is defined inductively in Fig. 3 and most of them are self-explanatory. Note that for an expression e and distribution state μ, the notation $\llbracket e \rrbracket_\mu$ stands for a distribution over the values $\llbracket e \rrbracket_\sigma$ for all $\sigma \in \lceil \mu \rceil$.

$$\llbracket \textbf{skip} \rrbracket \mu = \quad \mu$$

$$\llbracket \textbf{abort} \rrbracket \mu = \quad \varepsilon$$

$$\llbracket x := a \rrbracket \mu = \quad \sum_{\sigma \in \lceil \mu \rceil} \mu(\sigma) \cdot \sigma[\llbracket a \rrbracket_\sigma / x]$$

$$\llbracket x :=_\$ d_A \rrbracket \mu = \quad \sum_{a \in A} d(a) \cdot \llbracket x := a \rrbracket \mu$$

$$\llbracket c_0 ; c_1 \rrbracket \mu = \quad \llbracket c_1 \rrbracket_{\llbracket c_0 \rrbracket \mu}$$

$$\llbracket \textbf{if } b \textbf{ then } c_0 \textbf{ else } c_1 \textbf{ fi} \rrbracket \mu = \quad \llbracket c_0 \rrbracket_{(b?\mu)} + \llbracket c_1 \rrbracket_{(\neg b?\mu)}$$

$$\llbracket \textbf{while } b \textbf{ do } c \textbf{ od} \rrbracket \mu = \quad \lim_{n \to \infty} \llbracket (\textbf{if } b \textbf{ then } c \textbf{ fi})^n ; \textbf{if } b \textbf{ then abort fi} \rrbracket \mu$$

Fig. 4. Denotational semantics for commands

(Deterministic formulas) $P ::= \textbf{true} \mid \textbf{false} \mid P_m(a, ..., a) \mid P \wedge P \mid \neg P \mid \exists x. P(x)$

(Probabilistic formulas) $\phi ::= P \mid \oplus_{i \in I} p_i \phi_i \mid \oplus_{i \in I} \phi_i \mid \phi \odot \phi \mid \phi \wedge \phi \mid \phi \vee \phi$

Fig. 5. Syntax of assertions

The denotation of a command c is a mapping of type $\textbf{SDist}[\Sigma_{\textbf{Var}}] \to$ $\textbf{SDist}[\Sigma_{\textbf{Var}}]$, presented in Fig. 4. Here $b?$ is a function from Δ to Δ, which satisfies

$$b?\mu(\sigma) = \begin{cases} \mu(\sigma), & \textbf{iff} \quad \llbracket b \rrbracket_\sigma = \textbf{true} \\ 0, & \textbf{iff} \quad \llbracket b \rrbracket_\sigma = \textbf{false}. \end{cases}$$

The **skip** command does not change any states and **abort** maps any input distribution state to the empty distribution state ϵ. The classical assignment statement changes the value of variable x in every state of the input distribution and the random assignment statement may assign any expression $a \in A$ to variable x with probability $d(a)$, where A is a finite set.

As usual, the denotation of $c_0 ; c_1$ is the composition of these commands. For the conditional statement, we need to divide the distribution state μ into two parts $b?\mu$ and $\neg b?\mu$, then combine the semantics c_0 and c_1 in the two parts, respectively. Following the work of Barthe et al. [5], we define the semantics of a loop (**while** b **do** c **od**) as the limit of its lower approximations, where the n-th lower approximation of $\llbracket \textbf{while } b \textbf{ do } c \textbf{ od} \rrbracket_\mu$ is $\llbracket (\textbf{if } b \textbf{ then } c \textbf{ fi})^n ; \textbf{if } b \textbf{ then abort fi} \rrbracket_\mu$. The statement (**if** b **then** c **fi**) is a shorthand for (**if** b **then** c **else skip fi**) and $c^{n+1} = c; c^n$ with $c^0 \equiv \textbf{skip}$. By [5, Definition 7], the sequence $(\llbracket (\textbf{if } b \textbf{ then } c \textbf{ fi})^n ; \textbf{if } b \textbf{ then abort fi} \rrbracket_\mu)_{n \in \mathbb{N}}$ is convergent; its limit exists because the sequence is strictly increasing and bounded.

4 Assertions

Assertions in our logic contain two categories of formulas: deterministic and probabilistic ones. The latter are characterized by distribution formulas, which draw inspiration from the work of [18] to describe the properties of distributions.

$$\begin{aligned}
[\![\textbf{true}]\!] \quad &= \Sigma \\
[\![\textbf{false}]\!] \quad &= \emptyset \\
[\![P_m(a_1,...,a_n)]\!] \quad &= \{\sigma \in \Sigma_X \mid P_m([\![a_1]\!]_\sigma,...,[\![a_n]\!]_\sigma) = \textbf{true} \\
&\quad \text{and} \bigcup_{i=1,...,n} \mathbf{V}(a_i) = X\} \\
[\![P_1 \wedge P_2]\!] \quad &= [\![P_1]\!] \cap [\![P_2]\!] \\
[\![\neg P]\!] \quad &= \Sigma \setminus [\![P]\!] \\
[\![\exists x.P(x)]\!] \quad &= \{\sigma \mid \exists r \in \mathbb{Q}, \sigma \in [\![P[r/x]]\!]\}
\end{aligned}$$

Fig. 6. Semantics of deterministic formulas

4.1 Syntax of Assertions

In Fig. 5, we give the syntax of assertions. Deterministic formulas can be Boolean constants, built from arithmetic expressions by Boolean predicates, or formed by other deterministic formulas using connectives $\wedge$, $\neg$ and $\exists$. Probabilistic formulas include deterministic formulas, distribution formulas, and other probabilistic formulas built by some connectives such as $\odot$, $\wedge$ and $\vee$. Recall distribution formulas in the form $\oplus_{i \in I} p_i \phi_i$ from [18], which consist of various formulas ϕ_i composed by the connective $\oplus$, with each formula weighted by p_i. These weights satisfy the condition $\sum_{i \in I} p_i = 1$ and the index set I is finite. The formula $\oplus_{i \in I} \phi_i$ is a relaxed form of $\oplus_{i \in I} p_i \phi_i$ as the individual probabilities p_i are not important. The connective $\odot$ describes the properties of two independent sets of variables. Other connectives are standard.

4.2 Semantics of Assertions

We first formally describe the combining operation on distribution states following the Kripke resource semantics, where the set of possible worlds forms a partial, pre-order commutative monoid $\mathcal{M} = (M, \circ, \mathbf{I}, \sqsubseteq)$.

Definition 3 ([20])**.** *A (partial) Kripke resource monoid consists of a set M of possible worlds, a partial binary combining operation $\circ : M \times M \to M$, an element $\mathbf{I} \in M$, and a pre-order $\sqsubseteq$ on M, such that the monoid operation*

- *has identity $\mathbf{I}$: for all $x \in M$, we have $\mathbf{I} \circ x = x \circ \mathbf{I} = x$;*
- *is associative: $x \circ (y \circ z) = (x \circ y) \circ z$, where both sides are either defined and equal, or both undefined; and*
- *is compatible with pre-order: if $x \sqsubseteq y$ and $x' \sqsubseteq y'$ and if both $x \circ x'$ and $y \circ y'$ are defined, then $x \circ x' \sqsubseteq y \circ y'$.*

Proposition 1. *Let Δ be the set of all distribution states and $\mathbf{I}$ be the element in $\textbf{SDist}[\Sigma_\emptyset]$ such that $\mathbf{I}(0) = 1$. The partial binary combining operation $\circ$ is defined as:*

$$\mu \circ \mu' \triangleq \begin{cases} \mu \otimes \mu' & \text{if } \mathrm{dom}(\mu) \cap \mathrm{dom}(\mu') = \emptyset \\ \text{undefined} & \text{otherwise.} \end{cases}$$

$$[\![P]\!] \qquad =\{\mu \mid \mu \models P\}$$

$$[\![\oplus_{i\in I}p_i \cdot \phi_i]\!] \quad =\{\mu \mid \exists\mu_1 \cdots \exists\mu_m. \ [(\bigwedge_{i\in I}(\mu_i \models \phi_i) \wedge (\|\mu_i\| = \|\mu\|))$$

$$\wedge \mu = \sum_{i\in I}p_i \cdot \mu_i]\}, \text{ for } I = \{1,\ldots,m\}$$

$$[\![\oplus_{i\in I}\phi_i]\!] \quad =\{\mu \mid \exists p_1 \cdots p_m. \sum_{i\in I}p_i = 1 \wedge \mu \models \oplus_{i\in I}p_i \cdot \phi_i\}$$

$$[\![\phi_1 \odot \phi_2]\!] \quad =\{\mu \mid \exists\mu_1,\mu_2. \ (\mu_1 \circ \mu_2 \sqsubseteq \mu) \wedge \mu_1 \in [\![\phi_1]\!] \wedge \mu_2 \in [\![\phi_2]\!]\}$$

$$[\![\phi_1 \wedge \phi_2]\!] \quad =[\![\phi_1]\!] \cap [\![\phi_2]\!]$$

$$[\![\phi_1 \vee \phi_2]\!] \quad =[\![\phi_1]\!] \cup [\![\phi_2]\!]$$

Fig. 7. Semantics of probabilistic formulas

The pre-order $\sqsubseteq$ is defined as

$$\mu \sqsubseteq \mu' \quad \textbf{iff} \quad \mathrm{dom}(\mu) \subseteq \mathrm{dom}(\mu') \text{ and } \pi_{\mathrm{dom}(\mu)}(\mu') = \mu.$$

Then $(\Delta, \circ, \mathbf{I}, \sqsubseteq)$ is a Kripke resource monoid.

The semantics of a deterministic formula P on partial states is denoted by $[\![P]\!]$, as shown in Fig. 6. For a deterministic formula P and a partial state σ, we say $\sigma \models P$ if and only if $\sigma \in [\![P]\!]$. For a deterministic formula P and a distribution state μ, we say

$$\mu \models P \quad \textbf{iff} \quad \forall\sigma \in \lceil\mu\rceil, \ \sigma \models P.$$

The semantics of a probabilistic formula ϕ, denoted by $[\![\phi]\!]$, is given in Fig. 7. The denotation of $\oplus_{i\in I}p_i \cdot \phi_i$ is the set including all the distribution states that are linear combinations of some μ_i with weight p_i, and each μ_i is in the denotation of ϕ_i. The denotation of $\oplus_{i\in I}\phi_i$ comprises all the distribution states that are in the denotation of $\oplus_{i\in I}p_i \cdot \phi_i$ for some arbitrary weights p_i such that their sum is 1. The denotation for the formula $\phi_1 \odot \phi_2$ contains all the up-closures of distribution states that dominate the combination of two distributions μ_1 and μ_2 with disjoint domains such that μ_1 and μ_2 are in the denotations of ϕ_1 and ϕ_2, respectively. Finally, other types of formulas are self-explanatory. The satisfaction relation between distribution state μ and probabilistic formula ϕ is defined as: $\mu \models \phi$ if and only if $\mu \in [\![\phi]\!]$.

We then propose the following important property to prove the soundness of our logic. The proof is proceeded by induction on the structure of ϕ.

Proposition 2. *For any probabilistic formula ϕ, its denotation $[\![\phi]\!]$ is a closed set.*

5 Proof System

In this section, we present a proof system which consists of some rules to reason about the correctness of PIMP programs. As usual, we use Hoare triples of the form $\{\phi_1\}\; c\; \{\phi_2\}$, where c is a program fragment and ϕ_1, ϕ_2 are two assertions.

The rules are given in Fig. 8. Some of them are adapted from [18] and we just give explanations for several new rules. The [RAssn] rule is used for the random assignment, which is different from rule [DAssn] used for the deterministic assignment. If the formula $\phi_a[a/x]$ holds at the current state for any a in a finite set A, the post-condition $\oplus_{a \in A} d(a) \cdot \phi_a$ holds after executing the random assignment. The [While] rule is derived from [18], where ϕ_0 and ϕ_1 in the invariant ϕ are the assertions presented in Fig. 5. Note that the invariant ϕ represents a special form of distribution formulas with arbitrary probability coefficients. This indicates that we allow the probability coefficients of the distributions to differ after each loop, as long as the support sets remain the same. This weaker property enables us to handle a broader class of unbounded while loops.

The [OFrame] rule in our work is similar to the [QFrame] rule in the work of [18], with the distinction lying in the side condition. Let $\mathbf{V}(c)$ be the set of all variables occurring in program c and $\mathbf{MV}(c)$ the set of all variables modified by program c. Besides, given a formula ϕ, we denote the set of all free variables in ϕ by $\mathbf{FV}(\phi)$. The condition $\mathbf{FV}(\phi_3) \cap \mathbf{V}(c)$ stipulates that both the modified and read variables in c are restricted from appearing as free in assertion ϕ_3, while rule [QFrame] in [18] allows read variables in the side condition. This distinction from rule [QFrame] is required for handling the unique semantics of the $\odot$ connective in the current work. Here the assertion $\phi_1 \odot \phi_2$ denotes the independence relation between the variables in $\mathbf{FV}(\phi_1)$ and $\mathbf{FV}(\phi_2)$ for any assertions ϕ_1, ϕ_2. Consequently, even if the free variables in ϕ_3 are not modified by the program c, being read by c may still result in the non-independence between $\mathbf{FV}(\phi_2)$ and $\mathbf{FV}(\phi_3)$ after the execution of c. This point is illustrated further in Example 1.

Example 1. Let $\phi_1 = \mathbf{true}$, $\phi_2 = (x = 0) \oplus (x = 1)$, $\phi_3 = \frac{1}{2}(y = 0) \oplus \frac{1}{2}(y = 1)$ and let c be the program in Fig. 9. We encounter a situation where $\{\phi_1\}\; c\; \{\phi_2\}$ holds, and additionally, $\mathbf{FV}(\phi_3) \cap \mathbf{MV}(c) = \emptyset$. Despite these conditions, the Hoare triple

$$\{\phi_1 \odot \phi_3\}\; c\; \{\phi_2 \odot \phi_3\}$$

is still invalid. This is because the variables x and y are clearly not independent. Actually, we get the Hoare triple $\{\phi_1 \odot \phi_3\}\; c\; \{\frac{1}{2}(x = 0 \wedge y = 0) \oplus \frac{1}{2}(x = 1 \wedge y = 1)\}$ in Fig. 9, where the post-condition is not equal to $\phi_2 \odot \phi_3$.

The [Frame] rule adheres to the conventions of classical Hoare logic. Since the assertion $\phi_1 \wedge \phi_2$ does not have any particular constraints between the variables in the assertions ϕ_1 and ϕ_2, the side condition of the free variables in ϕ_3 remains unmodified by the program c, which is enough. Rule [Exists] is inspired by the work of [17].

Figure 10 displays several rules for auxiliary reasoning. Some already appear in [18], we only explain the rules that are new in our work. The [OdotD] rule aids in distributing $\odot$ into the connective $\oplus$. The connective operator $\oplus$ is commutative and associative according to rules [OplusC] and [OplusA].

$$\frac{}{\{\phi\}\ \mathbf{skip}\ \{\phi\}}[\text{Skip}] \qquad \frac{}{\{\phi\}\ \mathbf{abort}\ \{\mathbf{false}\}}[\text{Abort}]$$

$$\frac{}{\{\phi[a/x]\}\ x := a\ \{\phi\}}[\text{DAssn}] \qquad \frac{}{\{\bigwedge_{a\in A}\phi_a[a/x]\}\ x :=_\$ d_A\ \{\oplus_{a\in A}d(a)\cdot\phi_a\}}[\text{RAssn}]$$

$$\frac{\{\phi_0\}\ c_0\ \{\phi_1\}\quad \{\phi_1\}\ c_1\ \{\phi_2\}}{\{\phi_0\}\ c_0;c_1\{\phi_2\}}[\text{Seq}]$$

$$\frac{\{\phi_1\wedge b\}\ c_1\ \{\phi_1'\}\quad \{\phi_2\wedge\neg b\}\ c_2\ \{\phi_2'\}}{\{p(\phi_1\wedge b)\oplus(1-p)(\phi_2\wedge\neg b)\}\ \mathbf{if}\ b\ \mathbf{then}\ c_1\ \mathbf{else}\ c_2\ \mathbf{fi}\ \{p\phi_1'\oplus(1-p)\phi_2'\}}[\text{Cond}]$$

$$\frac{\phi=(\phi_0\wedge b)\oplus(\phi_1\wedge\neg b)\quad \{\phi_0\wedge b\}\ c\ \{\phi\}}{\{\phi\}\ \mathbf{while}\ b\ \mathbf{do}\ c\ \mathbf{od}\ \{\phi_1\wedge\neg b\}}[\text{While}]$$

$$\frac{\phi_0\Rightarrow\phi_1\quad \{\phi_1\}\ c\ \{\phi_2\}\quad \phi_2\Rightarrow\phi_3}{\{\phi_0\}\ c\ \{\phi_3\}}[\text{Conseq}]$$

$$\frac{\{\phi_1\}\ c\ \{\phi_1'\}\quad \{\phi_2\}\ c\ \{\phi_2'\}}{\{\phi_1\wedge\phi_2\}\ c\ \{\phi_1'\wedge\phi_2'\}}[\text{Conj}] \qquad \frac{\{\phi_1\}\ c\ \{\phi_1'\}\quad \{\phi_2\}\ c\ \{\phi_2'\}}{\{\phi_1\vee\phi_2\}\ c\ \{\phi_1'\vee\phi_2'\}}[\text{Disj}]$$

$$\frac{\{\phi_1\}\ c\ \{\phi_2\}\quad \mathbf{FV}(\phi_3)\cap\mathbf{V}(c)=\emptyset}{\{\phi_1\odot\phi_3\}\ c\ \{\phi_2\odot\phi_3\}}[\text{OFrame}] \qquad \frac{\{\phi_1\}\ c\ \{\phi_2\}\quad \mathbf{FV}(\phi_3)\cap\mathbf{MV}(c)=\emptyset}{\{\phi_1\wedge\phi_3\}\ c\ \{\phi_2\wedge\phi_3\}}[\text{Frame}]$$

$$\frac{\forall i\in I.\ \{\phi_i\}\ c\ \{\phi_i'\}\quad \Sigma_{i\in I}\,p_i=1}{\{\oplus_{i\in I}p_i\cdot\phi_i\}\ c\ \{\oplus_{i\in I}p_i\cdot\phi_i'\}}[\text{Sum}] \qquad \frac{\forall r.\ r\in\mathbb{Q}\ \wedge\ \{P(r)\}\ c\ \{\phi'\}}{\{\exists x.\ P(x)\}\ c\ \{\phi'\}}[\text{Exists}]$$

Fig. 8. Inferences rules for PIMP programs

$$\{\mathbf{true}\odot\tfrac{1}{2}(y=0)\oplus\tfrac{1}{2}(y=1)\}$$

$$\{\tfrac{1}{2}(y=0)\oplus\tfrac{1}{2}(y=1)\} \qquad\qquad [\text{OdotE}]$$

if $(y=0)$ **then**

$\qquad x := 0;$

else

$\qquad x := 1;$

fi

$$\{\tfrac{1}{2}(x=0\wedge y=0)\oplus\tfrac{1}{2}(x=1\wedge y=1)\} \quad [\text{Cond}]$$

Fig. 9. Example 1

We write $\vdash\{\phi_1\}\ c\ \{\phi_2\}$ if the Hoare triple $\{\phi_1\}\ c\ \{\phi_2\}$ can be derived from the rules of our proof system. Semantically, the Hoare triple is valid, written as $\models\{\phi_1\}\ c\ \{\phi_2\}$, if for any distribution state μ, $\mu\models\phi_1$ implies $[\![c]\!]_\mu\models\phi_2$.

Theorem 1 (Soundness). *For any assertions ϕ_1, ϕ_2 and any program c, we have that $\vdash\{\phi_1\}\ c\ \{\phi_2\}$ implies $\models\{\phi_1\}\ c\ \{\phi_2\}$.*

Proof. We prove by induction that all the rules in the proof system are sound. Here we only consider rule [While], which is the most difficult case.

Suppose $\phi=(\phi_0\wedge b)\oplus(\phi_1\wedge\neg b)$ and $\models\{\phi_0\wedge b\}\ c\ \{\phi\}$. We aim to prove that $\models\{\phi\}\ \mathbf{while}\ b\ \mathbf{do}\ c\ \mathbf{od}\ \{\phi_1\wedge\neg b\}$.

$$\frac{}{\phi \vdash \mathbf{true}} \, [\text{PT}] \qquad \frac{}{\phi \odot \mathbf{true} \dashv\vdash \phi} \, [\text{OdotE}]$$

$$\frac{}{(\oplus_{i \in I} p_i \phi_i) \odot (\oplus_{j \in J} q_j \phi_j) \vdash \oplus_{i \in I, j \in J} p_i q_j (\phi_i \odot \phi_j)} \, [\text{OdotD}]$$

$$\frac{}{\phi_1 \odot \phi_2 \dashv\vdash \phi_2 \odot \phi_1} \, [\text{OdotC}] \qquad \frac{}{\phi_1 \odot (\phi_2 \odot \phi_3) \dashv\vdash (\phi_1 \odot \phi_2) \odot \phi_3} \, [\text{OdotA}]$$

$$\frac{}{\phi_1 \odot \phi_2 \vdash \phi_1 \wedge \phi_2} \, [\text{OdotO}] \qquad \frac{}{\phi_1 \odot (\phi_2 \wedge \phi_3) \vdash (\phi_1 \odot \phi_2) \wedge (\phi_1 \odot \phi_3)} \, [\text{OdotOC}]$$

$$\frac{}{\phi_1 \oplus \phi_2 \dashv\vdash \phi_2 \oplus \phi_1} \, [\text{OplusC}] \qquad \frac{}{\phi_1 \oplus (\phi_2 \oplus \phi_3) \dashv\vdash (\phi_1 \oplus \phi_2) \oplus \phi_3} \, [\text{OplusA}]$$

$$\frac{}{p_0 \cdot P \oplus p_1 \cdot P \oplus p_2 \cdot P' \dashv\vdash (p_0 + p_1) \cdot P \oplus p_2 \cdot P'} \, [\text{OMerg}]$$

$$\frac{}{\oplus_{i \in I} p_i \cdot \phi_i \vdash \oplus_{i \in I} \phi_i} \, [\text{Oplus}] \qquad \frac{\forall i \in I, \; \phi_i \vdash \phi_i'}{\oplus_{i \in I} p_i \cdot \phi_i \vdash \oplus_{i \in I} p_i \cdot \phi_i'} \, [\text{OCon}]$$

Fig. 10. Rules for entailment reasoning

For any $n \geq 0$, we write $\mathbf{while}^n$ for the n-th iteration of the while loop, i.e.

$$(\mathbf{if} \; b \; \mathbf{then} \; c \; \mathbf{fi})^n; \mathbf{if} \; b \; \mathbf{then} \; \mathbf{abort} \; \mathbf{fi}.$$

We claim that if $\mu \models \phi$ then $[\![\mathbf{while}^n]\!]_\mu \models \phi_1 \wedge \neg b$ for any $n \geq 0$. This can be proved by induction on n. Note that if $\mu \models \phi$ then there exist some p, μ_0 and μ_1 such that $\mu = p\mu_0 + (1 - p)\mu_1$ with $\mu_0 \models \phi_0 \wedge b$ and $\mu_1 \models \phi_1 \wedge \neg b$.

– $n = 0$. In this case we have that

$$\begin{aligned}
[\![\mathbf{while}^0]\!]_\mu &= [\![\mathbf{if} \; b \; \mathbf{then} \; \mathbf{abort} \; \mathbf{fi}]\!]_\mu \\
&= p[\![\mathbf{if} \; b \; \mathbf{then} \; \mathbf{abort} \; \mathbf{fi}]\!]_{\mu_0} + (1 - p)[\![\mathbf{if} \; b \; \mathbf{then} \; \mathbf{abort} \; \mathbf{fi}]\!]_{\mu_1} \\
&= p\varepsilon + (1 - p)\mu_1 \\
&= (1 - p)\mu_1.
\end{aligned}$$

Since $\mu_1 \models \phi_1 \wedge \neg b$, it implies that $(1 - p)\mu_1 \models \phi_1 \wedge \neg b$.

– $n = k + 1$. We infer that

$$\begin{aligned}
[\![\mathbf{while}^{k+1}]\!]_\mu &= [\![\mathbf{if} \; b \; \mathbf{then} \; c \; \mathbf{fi}; \; \mathbf{while}^k]\!]_\mu \\
&= p[\![\mathbf{if} \; b \; \mathbf{then} \; c \; \mathbf{fi}; \; \mathbf{while}^k]\!]_{\mu_0} + (1 - p)[\![\mathbf{if} \; b \; \mathbf{then} \; c \; \mathbf{fi}; \; \mathbf{while}^k]\!]_{\mu_1} \\
&= p[\![\mathbf{while}^k]\!]_{[\![c]\!]_{\mu_0}} + (1 - p)[\![\mathbf{while}^k]\!]_{\mu_1} \\
&= p[\![\mathbf{while}^k]\!]_{[\![c]\!]_{\mu_0}} + (1 - p)\mu_1.
\end{aligned}$$

Note that $[\![c]\!]_{\mu_0} \models \phi$. Therefore, it follows from the induction hypothesis that

$$[\![\mathbf{while}^k]\!]_{[\![c]\!]_{\mu_0}} \models \phi_1 \wedge \neg b.$$

As in the last case, we have $(1 - p)\mu_1 \models \phi_1 \wedge \neg b$. Then we immediately have that $[\![\mathbf{while}^{k+1}]\!]_\mu \models \phi_1 \wedge \neg b$.

Thus we have completed the proof of the claim. Finally, by Proposition 2, we know that the denotation $[\![\phi_1 \wedge \neg b]\!]$ for $\phi_1 \wedge \neg b$ is a closed set. This implies that if a sequence $\{\nu_n\}$ of distributions is in the set $[\![\phi_1 \wedge \neg b]\!]$ and the sequence has a limit $\lim_{n \to \infty} \nu_n$, then the limit is still in $[\![\phi_1 \wedge \neg b]\!]$. So we can obtain $[\![\mathbf{while}]\!]_\mu = \lim_{n \to \infty} [\![\mathbf{while}^n]\!]_\mu \models \phi_1 \wedge \neg b$. $\qquad \square$

6 Case Studies

6.1 A Simple Program

Recall the program $Prog_1$ given in the introduction, which has an unbounded loop. The correctness of this program can be specified by the following Hoare triple:

$$\{\mathbf{true}\} \; Prog_1 \; \{x = 5\}.$$

We outline the correctness proof in Fig. 11. Although this example is straightforward, it effectively illustrates the advantages of our logic when reasoning about loops involving an unknown number of iterations.

6.2 Bayesian Network

First of all, we use the symbol $\mathbb{P}_\mu(P)$ to represent the probability of deterministic formula P being satisfied by μ, and $\mathbb{P}_\mu(P|Q)$ to represent the conditional probability of formula P given Q. That is,

$$\mathbb{P}_\mu(P) \triangleq \frac{1}{\|\mu\|} \sum_{\sigma \in \lceil \mu \rceil} \{\mu(\sigma) \mid \sigma \models P\},$$

$$\mathbb{P}_\mu(P|Q) \triangleq \frac{\mathbb{P}_\mu(P \wedge Q)}{\mathbb{P}_\mu(Q)}.$$

Lemma 1. *Let μ be a distribution state, if $\mu \models \oplus_{i \in I} p_i \cdot P_i$ for some p_i and P_i, then $\mathbb{P}_\mu(P_i) \geq p_i$.*

For reasoning about Bayesian networks at the source code level, Batz et al. translated the Bayesian network, along with observations, into the *Bayesian Network Language* (BNL) in [11]. Then they derived dedicated proof rules to determine exact expected outcomes and runtimes of such loops based on the weakest pre-expectation calculus. We borrow the *Bayesian Network* (BN) depicted in Fig. 12 from [11]. The network consists of four binary random variables, including exam difficulty (D), student preparation (P), achieved grade (G), and resulting mood (M), with inherent dependencies shown in Fig. 12. Each node x_v has a conditional probability table, with rows for the random variable values and columns for the corresponding probabilities of x_v.

$\{\mathbf{true}\}$

$\{0 = 0\}$ [Conseq]

$x := 0;$

$\{x = 0\}$ [DAssn]

$\{x < 5 \oplus x = 5\}$ [Conseq]

while $x < 5$ **do**

    $\{x < 5\}$ [Conseq]

    $\{x < 5 \odot \mathbf{true}\}$ [OdotE]

    $\Longrightarrow \{0 = 0 \land 1 = 1\}$ [Conseq]

    $n :=_\$ \{\frac{1}{2} \cdot 0 + \frac{1}{2} \cdot 1\};$

    $\Longleftarrow \{\frac{1}{2} \cdot (n = 0) \oplus \frac{1}{2} \cdot (n = 1)\}$ [RAssn]

    $\{(x < 5) \odot (\frac{1}{2} \cdot n = 0 \oplus \frac{1}{2} \cdot n = 1)\}$ [OFrame]

    $\{\frac{1}{2}((x < 5) \odot n = 0) \oplus \frac{1}{2}((x < 5) \odot n = 1)\}$ [OdotD]

    $\{\frac{1}{2}((x < 5) \land n = 0) \oplus \frac{1}{2}((x < 5) \land n = 1)\}$ [OdotO OCon]

    if $(n = 1)$ **then**

        $\{(x < 5) \land n = 1\}$ [Conseq]

        $\{(x + 1 < 5) \oplus (x + 1 = 5)\}$ [Conseq]

        $x := x + 1;$

        $\{(x < 5 \oplus x = 5)\}$ [DAssn]

    else

        $\{(x < 5) \land n = 0\}$ [Conseq]

        $\{x < 5\}$ [Conseq]

        skip;

        $\{x < 5\}$ [Skip]

    fi

    $\{\frac{1}{2}(x < 5 \oplus x = 5) \oplus \frac{1}{2}(x < 5)\}$ [Cond]

    $\{(x < 5 \oplus x = 5) \oplus (x < 5)\}$ [Conseq Oplus]

    $\{(x < 5) \oplus (x = 5)\}$ [OplusC OplusA OMerg]

od

$\{x = 5\}$ [While]

Fig. 11. Proof outline for program $Prop_1$

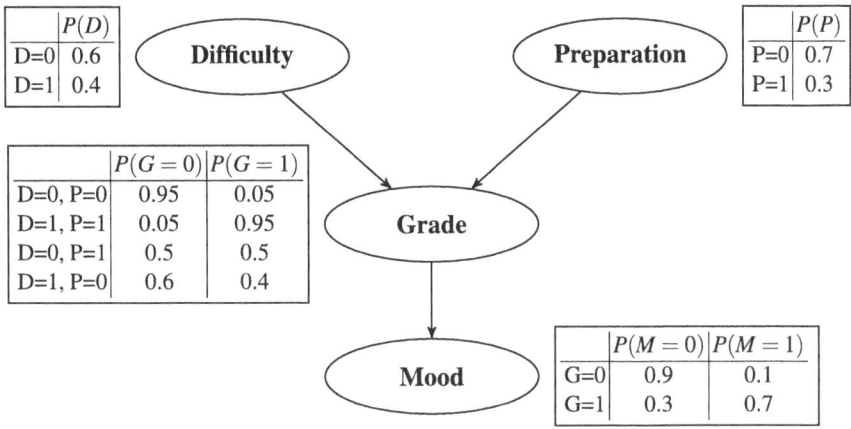

Fig. 12. A Bayesian network

We make some minor adjustments to the syntax of BNL fragment to align it with our language, and the entire program is named BN, as shown in Fig. 13. We can still use this BN to compute the probability of a student having a bad mood $(x_M = 0)$, after receiving a bad grade $(x_G = 0)$ for an easy exam $(x_D = 0)$, given that he was well-prepared $(x_P = 1)$.

In [11] the conditional probability given an observation on $P = 1$ is computed as:

$$\mathbb{P}(D = 0, G = 0, M = 0 | P = 1) = \frac{\mathbb{P}(D = 0, G = 0, M = 1, P = 1)}{\mathbb{P}(P = 1)}.$$

However, according to our semantics, this property can be expressed by

$$\{\textbf{true}\} \; BN \; \{x_P = 1 \wedge F_1\},$$

where F_1 is

$(\frac{0.0054}{0.3}(x_G = 0 \wedge x_D = 1 \wedge x_M = 0) \oplus \frac{0.0006}{0.3}(x_G = 0 \wedge x_D = 1 \wedge x_M = 1)$
$\oplus \frac{0.0342}{0.3}(x_G = 1 \wedge x_D = 1 \wedge x_M = 0) \oplus \frac{0.0798}{0.3}(x_G = 1 \wedge x_D = 1 \wedge x_M = 1)$
$\oplus \frac{0.081}{0.3}(x_G = 0 \wedge x_D = 0 \wedge x_M = 0) \oplus \frac{0.009}{0.3}(x_G = 0 \wedge x_D = 0 \wedge x_M = 1)$
$\oplus \frac{0.027}{0.3}(x_G = 1 \wedge x_D = 0 \wedge x_M = 0) \oplus \frac{0.063}{0.3}(x_G = 1 \wedge x_D = 0 \wedge x_M = 1)).$

Then by Lemma 1, we get $\mathbb{P}_\mu(x_D = 0, x_G = 0, x_M = 0) \geq \frac{0.081}{0.3}$ when $x_P = 1$.

With our program logic, we can reason about the correctness of other interesting examples such as encodings of cryptographic schemes including one-time pad, private information retrieval, and oblivious transfer. They are omitted due to lack of space.

$x_P := 0;$
while $x_P \neq 1$ **do**
    $x_D :=_\$ \{0.6 \cdot 0 + 0.4 \cdot 1\};$
    $x_P :=_\$ \{0.7 \cdot 0 + 0.3 \cdot 1\};$
    if $(x_D = 0 \wedge x_P = 0)$
       $x_G :=_\$ \{0.95 \cdot 0 + 0.05 \cdot 1\};$
    else if $(x_D = 1 \wedge x_P = 1)$
       $x_G :=_\$ \{0.05 \cdot 0 + 0.95 \cdot 1\};$
    else if $(x_D = 0 \wedge x_P = 1)$
       $x_G :=_\$ \{0.5 \cdot 0 + 0.5 \cdot 1\};$
    else if $(x_D = 1 \wedge x_P = 0)$
       $x_G :=_\$ \{0.6 \cdot 0 + 0.5 \cdot 1\};$
    fi
    if $(x_G = 0)$
       $x_M :=_\$ \{0.9 \cdot 0 + 0.1 \cdot 1\};$
    else if $(x_G = 1)$
       $x_M :=_\$ \{0.3 \cdot 0 + 0.7 \cdot 1\};$
    fi
od

Fig. 13. Probabilistic program BN

7 Related Work

In addition to the approaches mentioned above, there are many other well-established methods for the verification of probabilistic programs, such as martingale-based methods [14,15,48] or symbolic integration-based methods [12, 22,44]. Here, we mainly focus on probabilistic assertions within probabilistic programs.

7.1 Comparison of Assertion-Based Work

In this sub-section, we compare our work with the most relevant assertion-based approaches in the literature, specifically focusing on Ellora [5], PSL [9], and Lilac [38].

    Barthe et al. introduce ELLORA, a novel assertion logic that integrates probabilistic independence and other distribution law properties into first-order logic. This extension enables assertions to directly describe the probabilities of events and offers comparable expressive power to expectation-based approaches. However, Barthe et al. also recognize ELLORA's limitations in handling conditional control flow in independence logic. To address this issue, they later introduce PSL, a refined logic that draws from separation logic and treats independence in a structural manner. The separating conjunction in PSL models probabilistic independence by combining distributions over disjoint domains of random variables, with the restriction that random variables cannot appear on both sides of the conjunction. Moreover, the frame rule imposes extra side conditions to capture the program's data-flow properties, which can make the application of the frame rule cumbersome. In contrast, the [OFrame] rule in our work simplifies these conditions to a simpler constraint that is easier to verify while still sufficient for the verification of relevant examples. Li et al. introduce Lilac, a modal separation logic that innovatively reinterprets the separating conjunction by combining probability spaces, analogous to the disjoint union of heap fragments in ordinary separation logic. This work models probabilistic systems using standard objects from probability theory, where the measurability of a random variable mirrors ownership in heap logic. Furthermore, they expand the application scope of probabilistic separation logic by incorporating conditional independence.

7.2 pRHL

Another method for reasoning about the properties of probabilistic programs involves establishing logical relations to recast reasoning problems as program equivalence problems. The equivalence is characterized using a step-indexed biorthogonal logical relation constructed over an operational semantics.

One prominent work in this trend is the relational Hoare logic pRHL proposed by Barthe et al. [7]. The logic compares a pair of commands from a given pre-relation to a given post-relation of sub-distributions over states in the language of pWHILE programs. It is widely used for verifying cryptographic protocols, such as private information retrieval and multi-party computation. While pRHL is very useful for verifying the equivalence between two commands, we can also analyze program equivalence using our Hoare logic. Our definition of program equivalence is more targeted at state transitions caused by variables modified by program fragments. Furthermore, logical relations are less well-suited for proving intricate post-conditions such as the convergence of distributions and the specific probability value of the occurrence of an event. Another restriction of pRHL is that the coupled programs must execute synchronously. This is a very strict requirement, though in [24] they propose a way to relax the requirement by introducing the presampling steps and storing the results on a tape.

7.3 Conditional Independence

Li et al. [38] propose a logic that supports conditioning and continuous random variables, integrating a substructural approach to independence. They add a new modality to handle conditional independence, which is based on disintegration theory. The verification process involves expressing probabilistic programs in a monadic style, similar to Haskell's style of pure functional language.

Several prior systems have explored the concept of conditional independence. For example, Batz et al. [11] employ the weakest precondition style to analyze both expected outcomes and expected runtimes of a syntactic fragment of pGCL, which is called the Bayesian Network Language (BNL). Simultaneously, Barthe et al. [6] investigate a relational type system named PrivInfer, designed for Bayesian inference within a functional programming language. In another direction, Bao et al. extend the standard logic of bunched implications, which underlies separation logic, to handle conditional independence through the introduction of doubly-bunched implications [4]. On the foundational side, Ackerman et al. [1] delve into computability issues for (conditional) independence, motivated in part by exchangeable sequences closely related to independence. Language-based investigations of exchangeable sequences are explored by Staton et al. [47].

8   Conclusion and Future Work

Our work builds upon the previous work [18]. Initially, we developed a method for the local reasoning of quantum programs. However, recognizing the broader applicability of our methodology, we now adapt it to the probabilistic setting. Proposition 2 is newly added, which is not explicitly stated in [18], but is crucial to prove the soundness of the [While] rule. Besides, since we are no longer dealing with quantum states, the semantics of assertions involving separation conjunction is changed to represent probabilistic independence, which also necessitated a change in the side condition of the [OFrame] rule. Moreover, we now allow conjunction and disjunction of distribution formulas, which is not the case in [18] because the syntax of assertions given there is more restricted. In summary, we have introduced a probabilistic separation logic tailored for handling unbounded loops, with distribution formulas serving as useful invariants. Our interpretation of separating conjunction aligns with the concept of probabilistic independence, enhancing the versatility of our logic. We have proved the soundness of the logic and its effectiveness is illustrated through the formal verification of several intricate examples from probabilistic inference of Bayesian network to cryptographic schemes.

As to the future work, we plan to analyze more randomized algorithms and cryptographic protocols, addressing specific challenges in these domains through the proposed logic. Additionally, further theoretical development and embedding the logic into a proof assistant are also being considered.

References

1. Ackerman, N.L., Avigad, J., Freer, C.E., Roy, D.M., Rute, J.M.: On the computability of graphons. arXiv preprint arXiv:1801.10387 (2018)
2. Andova, S.: Probabilistic process algebra. Ph.D. thesis, Mathematics and Computer Science (2002). https://doi.org/10.6100/IR561343
3. Baier, C., Kwiatkowska, M., Norman, G.: Computing probability lower and upper bounds for LTL formulae over sequential and concurrent Markov chains. Technical report, University of Birmingham (1998)
4. Bao, J., Docherty, S., Hsu, J., Silva, A.: A bunched logic for conditional independence. In: Proceedings of the 36th Annual ACM/IEEE Symposium on Logic in Computer Science (LICS 2021), pp. 1–14. IEEE (2021)
5. Barthe, G., Espitau, T., Gaboardi, M., Grégoire, B., Hsu, J., Strub, P.-Y.: An assertion-based program logic for probabilistic programs. In: Ahmed, A. (ed.) ESOP 2018. LNCS, vol. 10801, pp. 117–144. Springer, Cham (2018). https://doi.org/10.1007/978-3-319-89884-1_5

6. Barthe, G., et al.: Differentially private Bayesian programming. In: Proceedings of the 2016 ACM SIGSAC Conference on Computer and Communications Security, pp. 68–79 (2016)
7. Barthe, G., Grégoire, B., Zanella Béguelin, S.: Formal certification of code-based cryptographic proofs. In: Proceedings of the 36th Annual ACM SIGPLAN-SIGACT Symposium on Principles of Programming Languages, pp. 90–101 (2009)
8. Barthe, G., Grégoire, B., Zanella Béguelin, S.: Probabilistic relational Hoare logics for computer-aided security proofs. In: Gibbons, J., Nogueira, P. (eds.) MPC 2012. LNCS, vol. 7342, pp. 1–6. Springer, Heidelberg (2012). https://doi.org/10.1007/978-3-642-31113-0_1
9. Barthe, G., Hsu, J., Liao, K.: A probabilistic separation logic. Proc. ACM Program. Lang. **4**(POPL), 1–30 (2019)
10. Barthe, G., Köpf, B., Olmedo, F., Zanella Beguelin, S.: Probabilistic relational reasoning for differential privacy. In: Proceedings of the 39th annual ACM SIGPLAN-SIGACT Symposium on Principles of Programming Languages, pp. 97–110 (2012)
11. Batz, K., Kaminski, B.L., Katoen, J.-P., Matheja, C.: How long, O Bayesian network, will I sample thee? In: Ahmed, A. (ed.) ESOP 2018. LNCS, vol. 10801, pp. 186–213. Springer, Cham (2018). https://doi.org/10.1007/978-3-319-89884-1_7
12. Beutner, R., Ong, C.H.L., Zaiser, F.: Guaranteed bounds for posterior inference in universal probabilistic programming. In: Proceedings of the 43rd ACM SIGPLAN International Conference on Programming Language Design and Implementation, pp. 536–551 (2022)
13. Chadha, R., Cruz-Filipe, L., Mateus, P., Sernadas, A.: Reasoning about probabilistic sequential programs. Theoret. Comput. Sci. **379**(1–2), 142–165 (2007)
14. Chakarov, A., Sankaranarayanan, S.: Probabilistic program analysis with martingales. In: Sharygina, N., Veith, H. (eds.) CAV 2013. LNCS, vol. 8044, pp. 511–526. Springer, Heidelberg (2013). https://doi.org/10.1007/978-3-642-39799-8_34
15. Chatterjee, K., Novotný, P., Žikelić, Đ.: Stochastic invariants for probabilistic termination. In: Proceedings of the 44th ACM SIGPLAN Symposium on Principles of Programming Languages, pp. 145–160 (2017)
16. De Alfaro, L.: Formal verification of probabilistic systems. Stanford university (1998)
17. Den Hartog, J., de Vink, E.P.: Verifying probabilistic programs using a Hoare like logic. Int. J. Found. Comput. Sci. **13**(03), 315–340 (2002)
18. Deng, Y., Wu, H., Xu, M.: Local reasoning about probabilistic behaviour for classical-quantum programs. In: Dimitrova, R., Lahav, O., Wolff, S. (eds.) VMCAI 2024. LNCS, vol. 14500, pp. 163–184. Springer, Cham (2024). https://doi.org/10.1007/978-3-031-50521-8_8
19. D'Argenio, P.R., Katoen, J.P., Brinksma, E.: General purpose discrete event simulation using. In: Proceedings of 6th International Workshop on Process Algebras and Performance Modeling, PAPM, vol. 98, pp. 85–102 (1998)
20. Galmiche, D., Mery, D., Pym, D.: The semantics of BI and resource tableaux. Math. Struct. Comput. Sci. **15**(6), 1033–1088 (2005)
21. Gehr, T., Misailovic, S., Tsankov, P., Vanbever, L., Wiesmann, P., Vechev, M.: Bayonet: probabilistic inference for networks. ACM SIGPLAN Not. **53**(4), 586–602 (2018)
22. Gehr, T., Misailovic, S., Vechev, M.: PSI: exact symbolic inference for probabilistic programs. In: Chaudhuri, S., Farzan, A. (eds.) CAV 2016, Part I. LNCS, vol. 9779, pp. 62–83. Springer, Cham (2016). https://doi.org/10.1007/978-3-319-41528-4_4
23. Ghahramani, Z.: Probabilistic machine learning and artificial intelligence. Nature **521**(7553), 452–459 (2015)

24. Gregersen, S.O., Aguirre, A., Haselwarter, P., Tassarotti, J., Birkedal, L.: Asynchronous probabilistic couplings in higher-order separation logic. Proc. ACM Program. Lang. **8**(POPL) (2024)

25. Gretz, F., Katoen, J.P., McIver, A.: Operational versus weakest pre-expectation semantics for the probabilistic guarded command language. Perform. Eval. **73**, 110–132 (2014)

26. Hartog, D.J.J.: Comparative semantics for a process language with probabilistic choice and non-determinism. Vrije Universitt (1998)

27. den Hartog, J.I.: Probabilistic extensions of semantical models. Ph.D. thesis, Vrije Universiteit Amsterdam (2002)

28. den Hartog, J.I., de Vink, E.P.: Mixing up nondeterminism and probability: a preliminary report. Electron. Notes Theor. Comput. Sci. **22**, 88–110 (1999)

29. Hermanns, H.: Interactive Markov chains. In: Hermanns, H. (ed.) Interactive Markov Chains. Lecture Notes in Computer Science, vol. 2428, pp. 57–88. Springer, Heidelberg (2002). https://doi.org/10.1007/3-540-45804-2_4

30. Holtzen, S., Junges, S., Vazquez-Chanlatte, M., Millstein, T., Seshia, S.A., Van den Broeck, G.: Model checking finite-horizon Markov chains with probabilistic inference. In: Silva, A., Leino, K.R.M. (eds.) CAV 2021. LNCS, vol. 12760, pp. 577–601. Springer, Cham (2021). https://doi.org/10.1007/978-3-030-81688-9_27

31. Hurd, J.: Formal verification of probabilistic algorithms. Technical report, University of Cambridge, Computer Laboratory (2003)

32. Kaminski, B.L.: Advanced weakest precondition calculi for probabilistic programs. Ph.D. thesis, RWTH Aachen University (2019)

33. Kaminski, B.L., Katoen, J.-P., Matheja, C.: Inferring covariances for probabilistic programs. In: Agha, G., Van Houdt, B. (eds.) QEST 2016. LNCS, vol. 9826, pp. 191–206. Springer, Cham (2016). https://doi.org/10.1007/978-3-319-43425-4_14

34. Kaminski, B.L., Katoen, J.P., Matheja, C., Olmedo, F.: Weakest precondition reasoning for expected runtimes of randomized algorithms. J. ACM (JACM) **65**(5), 1–68 (2018)

35. Kozen, D.: Semantics of probabilistic programs. In: 20th Annual Symposium on Foundations of Computer Science (SFCS 1979), pp. 101–114. IEEE (1979)

36. Kozen, D.: A probabilistic PDL. In: Proceedings of the Fifteenth Annual ACM Symposium on Theory of Computing, pp. 291–297 (1983)

37. Lee, E.A., Seshia, S.A.: Introduction to Embedded Systems: A Cyber-Physical Systems Approach. MIT Press, Cambridge (2016)

38. Li, J.M., Ahmed, A., Holtzen, S.: Lilac: a modal separation logic for conditional probability. Proc. ACM Program. Lang. **7**(PLDI), 148–171 (2023)

39. McIver, A., Morgan, C.: Abstraction, Refinement and Proof for Probabilistic Systems. Springer, Heidelberg (2005). https://doi.org/10.1007/b138392

40. Motwani, R., Raghavan, P.: Randomized Algorithms. Cambridge University Press, Cambridge (1995)

41. Ngo, V.C., Carbonneaux, Q., Hoffmann, J.: Bounded expectations: resource analysis for probabilistic programs. ACM SIGPLAN Not. **53**(4), 496–512 (2018)

42. Ramshaw, L.H.: Formalizing the analysis of algorithms. Ph.D. thesis, Stanford University (1979)

43. Rand, R., Zdancewic, S.: VPHL: a verified partial-correctness logic for probabilistic programs. Electron. Notes Theor. Comput. Sci. **319**, 351–367 (2015)

44. Sankaranarayanan, S., Chakarov, A., Gulwani, S.: Static analysis for probabilistic programs: inferring whole program properties from finitely many paths. In: Proceedings of the 34th ACM SIGPLAN Conference on Programming Language Design and Implementation, pp. 447–458 (2013)

45. Segala, R.: Modeling and verification of randomized distributed real-time systems. Ph.D. thesis, MIT (1996)
46. Smolka, S., et al.: Scalable verification of probabilistic networks. In: Proceedings of the 40th ACM SIGPLAN Conference on Programming Language Design and Implementation, pp. 190–203 (2019)
47. Staton, S., Stein, D., Yang, H., Ackerman, N.L., Freer, C.E., Roy, D.M.: The Beta-Bernoulli process and algebraic effects. In: Proceedings of the 45th International Colloquium on Automata, Languages, and Programming (ICALP 2018). LIPIcs, vol. 107, pp. 141:1–141:15. Schloss Dagstuhl - Leibniz-Zentrum für Informatik (2018)
48. Wang, P., Fu, H., Goharshady, A.K., Chatterjee, K., Qin, X., Shi, W.: Cost analysis of nondeterministic probabilistic programs. In: Proceedings of the 40th ACM SIGPLAN Conference on Programming Language Design and Implementation, pp. 204–220 (2019)
49. Winskel, G.: The Formal Semantics of Programming Languages - An Introduction. The MIT Press, Cambridge (1993)
50. Wu, S.H., Smolka, S.A., Stark, E.W.: Composition and behaviors of probabilistic I/O automata. Theoret. Comput. Sci. **176**(1–2), 1–38 (1997)

Extending Symbolic Heap to Support Shared Ownership

Jiyang Wu and Qinxiang Cao[✉]

Shanghai Jiao Tong University, Shanghai, China
wujiyang@sjtu.edu.cn, caoqinxiang@gmail.com

Abstract. The symbolic heap is widely used in verification of pointer-manipulating programs because it supports forward symbolic execution. While it can describe disjoint data structures easily, it is not suitable to describe overlapping data structures. Based on the observations that overlapping structures are often immutable in practical programs, we propose read-only assertions and extended separation logic to solve the problem. Our logic simplifies the specifications and verifications of overlapping structures. We formalize our logic, its soundness proof, and program verification examples in Coq.

Keywords: separation logic · program verification · interactive theorem proving

1 Introduction

Separation logic [15] has been widely used in program verification. Many authors prefer to use symbolic heaps:

$$(\phi_1 \wedge \phi_2 \wedge \cdots \wedge \phi_n) \wedge (\psi_1 * \psi_2 * \cdots * \psi_m)$$

where ϕ_i are non-spatial predicates, ψ_j are spatial predicates, and $*$ is the separating conjunction operator[1]. For example, the canonical assertion of Verified Software Toolchain (VST) [5] has the form

$$\mathrm{PROP}(\phi_1; \phi_2; \cdots)\mathrm{LOCAL}(\rho_1; \rho_2; \cdots)\mathrm{SEP}(\psi_1; \psi_2; \cdots)$$

where ϕ_i are independent of the stack and heaps, ρ_i are only dependent of the stack, and ψ_i are predicates over heaps. A state s and a heap h satisfy the assertion if and only if $\phi_1 \wedge \phi_2 \wedge \cdots \wedge \psi_1(s) \wedge \psi_2(s) \wedge \cdots$ holds and h satisfies $\psi_1 * \psi_2 * \cdots$. Also, Iris proof mode [10] contains three proof contexts: the pure Coq context, the persistent context and the spatial context. Both examples can be considered special cases of the symbolic heap.

---

[1] The separating conjunction $P * Q$ describes a heap composed of two disjoint parts, one satisfying P and another satisfying Q.

T. Bourke et al. (Eds.): SETTA 2024, LNCS 15469, pp. 46–63, 2025.
https://doi.org/10.1007/978-981-96-0602-3_3

One important reason for using symbolic heaps is to support forward symbolic execution. Updates of the concrete heap can be represented as in-place updates of a spatial predicate in the symbolic heap, and reading from the concrete heap corresponds to looking up the spatial predicates:

$$\{\phi \wedge (e_1 \mapsto e_0 * \psi)\}\ [e_1] := e_2\ \{\phi \wedge (e_1 \mapsto e_2 * \psi)\}$$
$$\{\phi \wedge (e \mapsto e_0 * \psi)\}\ x := [e]\ \{\exists x'.(x = e_0[x'/x] \wedge \phi[x'/x]) \wedge (e \mapsto e_0 * \psi)[x'/x]\}$$

Although the use of symbolic heap has achieved great success in verification, we found that it is not suitable to describe overlapping data structures, where several structures share some of their memory. Such circumstances are common in real-world programming. For example, we may have multiple iterators of a linked list. Since iterators can be used to access the contents of the list, each of them should be given read permission of the list, leading to logical sharing of the list contents (Fig. 1a). As another example, one argument of a string comparison function can be a substring of another argument, in which case the arguments are overlapping. Also, memory sharing is unavoidable if we use persistent data structures [14]. When updating a persistent structure, instead of destroying the existing structure, we create a new version of it and keep the original one unchanged. Nodes unaffected by the update are shared between two versions.

In order to write specifications for such structures in the symbolic heap, we have to divide the heap into several disjoint parts. We note that the shared memory are often read-only in practice, so reasoning about the flexible and intricate sharing of memory is often unnecessary. Intuitively, we wish to reason about the read-only data structures as if we were reasoning about purely functional data structures.

In this paper, we present a way to define representation predicates for overlapping data structures, and propose an extension of separation logic to enable local reasoning of immutable shared memory. The rest of the paper is structured as follows. Section 2 describes a motivating example. Section 3 gives an overview

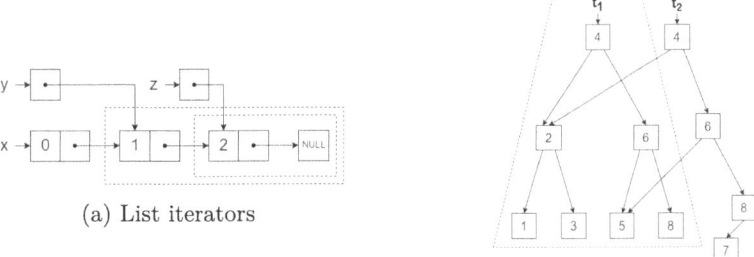

(a) List iterators

(b) Persistent binary search tree insertion

Fig. 1. Examples

$$V ::= x, y, z, \cdots \qquad \qquad \text{(variable name)}$$

$$E ::= n \mid V \mid E + E \mid E - E \mid E * E \mid \cdots \qquad \text{(expression)}$$

$$C ::= \textbf{skip} \mid V := E \mid C_1; C_2 \mid \textbf{if } E \textbf{ then } C_1 \textbf{ else } C_2 \mid$$

$$\qquad \textbf{while } E \textbf{ do } C \textbf{ end} \qquad \qquad \text{(command)}$$

$$K ::= \textbf{KStop} \mid C \cdot k \qquad \qquad \text{(continuation)}$$

Fig. 2. Syntax of the object language

$$\frac{}{(\textbf{skip}, k, \sigma) \to (\bot, k, \sigma)} \qquad \frac{}{(\bot, c \cdot k, \sigma) \to (c, k, \sigma)}$$

$$\frac{}{(x := e, k, \sigma) \to (\bot, k, \sigma[\llbracket e \rrbracket(\sigma)/x])} \qquad \frac{}{(c_1; c_2, k, \sigma) \to (c_1, c_2 \cdot k, \sigma)}$$

$$\frac{\llbracket e \rrbracket(\sigma) \neq 0}{(\textbf{if } e \textbf{ then } c_1 \textbf{ else } c_2, k, \sigma) \to (c_1, k, \sigma)} \qquad \frac{\llbracket e \rrbracket(\sigma) = 0}{(\textbf{if } e \textbf{ then } c_1 \textbf{ else } c_2, k, \sigma) \to (c_2, k, \sigma)}$$

$$\frac{\llbracket e \rrbracket(\sigma) \neq 0}{(\textbf{while } e \textbf{ do } c \textbf{ end}, k, \sigma) \to (c, \textbf{while } e \textbf{ do } c \textbf{ end} \cdot k, \sigma)}$$

$$\frac{\llbracket e \rrbracket(\sigma) = 0}{(\textbf{while } e \textbf{ do } c \textbf{ end}, k, \sigma) \to (\bot, k, \sigma)}$$

Fig. 3. Small-step semantics of the object language

of our extended separation logic. Section 4 and Sect. 5 discuss more details about assertion entailment rules and Hoare logic proof rules. We discuss related works in Sect. 6. We conclude in Sect. 7.

2   A Motivating Example

The motivating example is an interpreter for the while language (Fig. 2), which contains sequential compositions, if-commands and while-commands. In this paper, we will call this while language the *object* language in order to distinguish it from the *source* language, which is used to implement the interpreter.

The program presented in Fig. 4 is a naive implementation of the small step semantics for the object language (Fig. 3). To make the memory structure explicit, the program is written in C. The implementation of the interpreter in the source language is similar. A program state σ is a function from variable names to integers, which is represented by a hash table in the interpreter. For simplicity, we assume that the expressions are side effect free, and thus their semantics are defined using denotational semantics. The denotation of an expression e is typed $\llbracket e \rrbracket$: state $\to \mathbb{Z}$. It is worth noting that the semantics in Fig. 3 is not the standard one. It is based on continuations, which is similar to the semantics of Clight, the source language of CompCert [13]. In this semantics, $(c, k, \sigma) \to (c', k', \sigma')$ means that one step in the evaluation of focused command c and continuation k in state σ yields focused command c' and continuation k' in state σ'. In order to match the null pointers in the implementation, we use $\bot$ to represent that there is no focused command. A residual program is a pair of

```
1    struct com {
2      enum com_type t;
3      union {
4        struct { void *none; } SKIP;
5        struct { struct com *left; struct com *right; } SEQ;
6        struct { struct exp *cond; struct com *body; } WHILE;
7        ... } d; }
8    struct cont_list { struct com *c; struct cont_list *link; }
9    struct res_prog { struct com *foc; struct cont_list *ctx; }
10
11   int eval(struct hash_table *t, struct exp *e);
12   void step(struct hash_table *t, struct res_prog *r) {
13     struct cmd *c; struct cont_list *k, *k2;
14     struct exp *e; int b;
15     c = r->foc; k = r->ctx;
16     if (c == NULL) {
17       r->foc = k->c; r->ctx = k->link; free(k);
18     } else {
19       if (c->t == T_SKIP) { r->foc = NULL; }
20       else if (c->t == T_SEQ) {
21         k2 = malloc(sizeof(struct cont_list));
22         k2->c = c->d.SEQ.right; k2->link = k;
23         r->foc = c->d.SEQ.left; r->ctx = k2; }
24       else if ... else {   // c->t == T_WHILE
25         e = c->d.WHILE.cond; b = eval(t, e);
26         if (b) {
27           k2 = malloc(sizeof(struct cont_list));
28           k2->c = c; k2->link = k;
29           r->foc = c->d.WHILE.body; r->ctx = k2; }
30         else { r->foc = 0; } } } }
```

Fig. 4. Simple interpreter

a focused command and a continuation, which are represented as a pointer to a command and a linked list of commands.

The interpreter is composed of two functions. The `eval` function returns the value of the input expression in the given state. Its implementation is simple and omitted. The `step` function takes as input a residual program and a hash table mapping variable names to values, and write the result of execution in-place. For illustration, the memory layout while executing command **while** $a < b$ **do** $a = 2 * a$ **end**; $c = a - b$ is shown in Fig. 5. We want to prove the functional correctness of the `step` function.

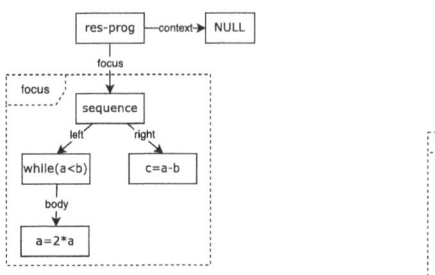

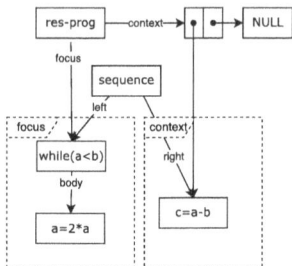

(a) focus:
while a < b **do** a = 2 ∗ a **end**; c = a − b
cont: (none)

(b) focus: **while** a < b **do** a = 2 ∗ a **end**
cont: c = a − b

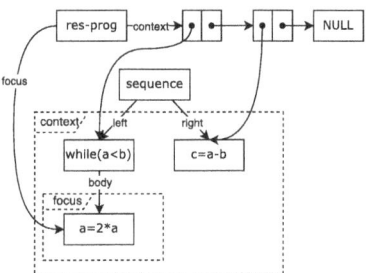

(c) focus: a = 2 ∗ a, cont #1: **while** a < b **do** a = 2 ∗ a **end**, cont #2: c = a − b

Fig. 5. Memory layout of **while** a < b **do** a = 2 ∗ a **end**; c = a − b

Suppose we have defined the representation predicates for hash tables, expressions and commands, which are named *table_rep*, *exp_rep* and *com_rep*, respectively. The eval function satisfies the specification

$$\{table\_rep(t, \sigma) * exp\_rep(e, E)\}$$
$$\texttt{eval}(t, e)$$
$$\{res = [\![E]\!](\sigma) \wedge table\_rep(t, \sigma) * exp\_rep(e, E)\}$$

where *res* represents the return value.

For the step function, we need to define a representation predicate for the continuation, and we call it *cont_rep*. Since the continuation has a typical linked list structure, we may try to define the following predicate:

$$cont\_rep(p, K) := (p = 0 \wedge K = \textbf{KStop} \wedge \text{emp}) \vee$$
$$(\exists q_1, q_2, C, K'.K = C \cdot K' \wedge p \mapsto q_1, q_2 * com\_rep(q_1, C) * cont\_rep(q_2, K'))$$

Then we can define the representation predicate for residual programs and the specification for the `step` function.

$$resprog\_rep(r, C, K) := \exists q_1, q_2.r \mapsto q_1, q_2 * com\_rep(q_1, C) * cont\_rep(q_2, K)$$

$$\{(C \neq \bot \vee K \neq \mathbf{KStop}) \wedge table\_rep(t, \sigma) * resprog\_rep(r, C, K)\}$$

$$\mathtt{step}(t, r)$$

$$\{\exists C', K', \sigma'.(C, K, \sigma) \rightarrow (C', K', \sigma') \wedge table\_rep(t, \sigma') * resprog\_rep(r, C', K')\}$$

The condition $C \neq \bot \vee K \neq \mathbf{KStop}$ ensures that the execution is not terminated.

This specification, although looking quite reasonable, is unprovable. Consider the case for the while command. When the loop condition evaluates to true, the whole while command is pushed into the continuation, and the loop body becomes the new focused command, as shown in Fig. 5c. It is impossible to prove the postcondition, because we connect the focused command and the continuation using the separating conjunction in the postcondition, while the focused command is actually included in the first command in the continuation. The unexpected sharing of memory brings great difficulty to the verification.

3   Main Idea

3.1   Read-Only Assertions

As introduced above, the most critical problem is to represent shared memory. To describe a heap with multiple temporary read-only and possibly overlapping regions, we introduce a new separation logic assertion:

$$P[R_1; R_2; \cdots ; R_n]$$

It is defined as $(P \wedge (R_1 * \mathrm{True}) \wedge (R_2 * \mathrm{True}) \wedge \cdots \wedge (R_n * \mathrm{True}))$. It means that the heap satisfies P, and there are subheaps satisfying $R_1, R_2, \cdots , R_n$. We write $[R_1; R_2; \cdots ; R_n]$ for $\mathrm{True}[R_1; R_2; \cdots ; R_n]$.

We can define the representation predicates for continuations and residual programs using the read-only assertions.

$$cont\_rep(p, \vec{p_k}) := (p = 0 \wedge \vec{p_k} = [\,] \wedge \mathrm{emp}) \vee$$

$$(\exists q_1, q_2, \vec{p'_k}.\vec{p_k} = q_1; \vec{p'_k} \wedge p \mapsto q_1, q_2 * cont\_rep(q_2, \vec{p'_k}))$$

$$resprog\_rep(r, p_0, C_0, C, K) := \exists q_1, q_2, \vec{p_k}, \vec{C_k}.$$

$$K = C_{k1} \cdot ... \cdot C_{kn} \cdot \mathbf{KStop} \wedge r \mapsto q_1, q_2 * cont\_rep(q_2, \vec{p_k}) *$$

$$com\_rep(p_0, C_0)[com\_rep(q_1, C); com\_rep(p_{k1}, C_{k1}); \cdots ; com\_rep(p_{kn}, C_{kn})]$$

The new *cont_rep* only describes the mutable part of the continuation, where $\vec{p_k}$ represents a list of pointers to commands in the continuation. The *resprog_rep* takes two extra parameters p_0 and C_0. Here, C_0 represents the complete program, and p_0 is a pointer to it. The focused command and the commands in the continuation are parts of C_0, so the read-only assertion is used to describe the sharing of memory.

Now we can define a correct specification for the step function.

$$\{(C \neq \bot \vee K \neq \textbf{KStop}) \wedge table\_rep(t, \sigma) * resprog\_rep(r, c_0, C_0, C, K)\}$$
$$\texttt{step}(t, r)$$
$$\left\{ \begin{array}{l} \exists C', K', \sigma'.(C, K, \sigma) \rightarrow (C', K', \sigma') \wedge \\ \qquad table\_rep(t, \sigma') * resprog\_rep(r, c_0, C_0, C', K') \end{array} \right\}$$

Remark. Fractional permission [3] is widely used to reason about shared data structures in concurrent programs, and it may be used to verify this example. However, this verification strategy involves complex arithmetic accounting about permissions, and our read-only assertions are easier to use.

Another solution is to use overlapping conjunctions [9]. This method can be used to define good specifications, but overlapping conjunctions interacts badly with the FRAME rule. For example, it is unclear how to find a frame F such that $P \uplus Q = P * F$, so it is hard to apply the FRAME rule.

Vindum and Birkedal [16] define a persistent points-to predicate $l \mapsto^\square v$, which denotes that l always points to v. The predicate is duplicatable, so it can simplify reasoning about overlapping data structures. A disadvantage of the persistent points-to predicate is the permanent loss of reclamation permission. While their language uses a garbage collector to automatically reclaim memory blocks, our C-like language requires manual memory management, and using the persistent points-to predicate leads to memory leaks.

Krishna et al. [11] use flows to encode structural properties and data invariants of data structures. They introduce flow interfaces to express the constraints a heap relies upon and guarantees the heap provides. Their approach can be used to reason about overlapping data structures, and the data structures are not necessarily immutable. Many intricate data structures, such as the Harris list, can be verified using flow interfaces. However, their method requires great proof efforts. We need to define a flow domain and a good condition for the heap. It is also difficult to prove entailments about assertion with flow interfaces.

3.2   New Hoare Triple

With read-only assertions, it becomes difficult to use the original FRAME rule:

$$\frac{\{P\} \; c \; \{Q\} \quad modify(c) \cap fv(R) = \emptyset}{\{P * R\} \; c \; \{Q * R\}}$$

Here, $fv(R)$ is the set of free variables in R, and $modify(c)$ is the set of variables assigned to within c.

When verifying the call to `eval` in Fig. 4 line 25, we know that the program state satisfies the following assertion:

$$table\_rep(t, \sigma) * com\_rep(c_0, C_0)[exp\_rep(e, E); \vec{P}] * \mathbb{Q}$$

where $\vec{P}$ and $\mathbb{Q}$ are irrelevant to the function call. Using the traditional FRAME rule, we need to turn this assertion into the following form:

$$\underline{table\_rep(t, \sigma) * exp\_rep(e, E)} * \text{R}$$

where these underlined parts are called function's precondition. However, it is difficult to get a separate $exp\_rep(e, E)$ from read-only assertions. A common solution to the problem is to use the separating implication, and try to prove that $H = exp\_rep(e, E) * (exp\_rep(e, E) \mathbin{-\!*} H)$, where H represents the assertion $com\_rep(c_0, C_0)[exp\_rep(e, E); \vec{P}]$. This is very difficult, because $\vec{P}$ may have pointers into $exp\_rep(e, E)$. The difficulty is also demonstrated by Hobor and Villard [9].

We find that splitting the memory into disjoint parts is unnecessary if part of the memory is read-only. Our solution to the problem is to extend the Hoare triple, enabling it to describe read-only subheaps. New pre/postconditions have the following form:

$$P\langle R_1; R_2; \cdots; R_n \rangle$$

where P and R_i are separation logic assertions. Informally, a heap satisfies the assertion if it can be divided into two disjoint parts, one of them satisfying P, and the other having several subheaps satisfying $R_1, \cdots, R_n$ respectively. The conditions can also be existentially quantified, written as $\exists x. P\langle \vec{R} \rangle$.

The definition of a Hoare triple $\{\mathbb{Q}\}\ c\ \{\mathbb{Q}'\}$, where $\mathbb{Q}$ and $\mathbb{Q}'$ are the new pre-/postconditions, is standard, except that the heap is divided into mutable part and immutable part, and we require that the immutable part is not modified when executing c. To improve readability, we sometimes use $\{P\}\langle \vec{R} \rangle\ c\ \{P'\}\langle \vec{R}' \rangle$ to represent a Hoare triple with precondition $P\langle \vec{R} \rangle$ and postcondition $P'\langle \vec{R}' \rangle$. Read-only parts of such extended Hoare triples can connect with read-only assertions introduced in Sect. 3.1. If command c satisfies $\{P\}\langle R_1; R_2 \rangle\ c\ \{P'\}\langle R_1'; R_2' \rangle$, then we have the triple $\{P * Q[R_1; R_2]\}\ c\ \{P' * Q[R_1'; R_2']\}$ and also the triple $\{P * Q_1[R_1] * Q_2[R_2]\}\ c\ \{P' * Q_1[R_1'] * Q_2[R_2']\}$ for arbitrary Q, Q_1 and Q_2.

With the new Hoare triple, We can rewrite the specification for `eval`.

$$\{emp\}\ \langle table\_rep(t, \sigma); exp\_rep(e, E) \rangle$$
$$\texttt{eval}(t, e)$$
$$\{res = [\![E]\!](\sigma) \wedge emp\}\ \langle \text{True}; \text{True} \rangle$$

This new specification above claims that the `eval` function can read from the hash table and the expression, but it is not allowed to modify them, which is more precise than the original specification.

We provide two more examples to demonstrate how to write concise specifications with the new Hoare triple. We consider only memory safety for simplicity.

The first example is a string comparison function. When comparing a string with itself or its substring, the two arguments are overlapping, so we can't use the separating conjunctions, but should use the read-only assertions instead.

$$\{\text{emp}\} \langle string\_rep(p); string\_rep(q)\rangle \texttt{strcmp}(p,q)\{\text{emp}\} \langle \text{True}; \text{True}\rangle$$

The second example is a function retrieving the next item from a list iterator. The list is not modified by the function, so it is specified in the read-only part of the triple. The $list\_rep(q')$ in the postcondition is wrapped inside the read-only assertion, since it only occupies part of the heap denoted by $list\_rep(q)$.

$$\{q \neq 0 \wedge p \mapsto q\} \langle list\_rep(q)\rangle \texttt{next\_item}(p)(\exists q'.\{p \mapsto q'\} \langle [list\_rep(q')]\rangle)$$

Remark. Hance et al. [8] present a framework for reasoning about temporary sharing. They introduce a novel guard relationship $G \rightarrowtail P$, which means that the proposition G can be used as a shared P. Nontrivial guard relations can be deduced by defining a proper storage protocols. In their guard relation, G is typically a ghost state, while in our read-only assertions $P[\vec{R}]$, P is an ordinary separation logic assertion. They use $[X]\{P\}e\{Q\}$, which is a shorthand for $\forall G.\{P * G * (G \rightarrowtail X)\}e\{Q * G\}$, to mean that execution of e requires the shared resource X. There is only one read-only proposition in their triple, and they use ghost states to avoid information loss. In contrast, we prefer to have read-only assertions in both precondition and postcondition and describe the read-only memory directly. For instance, in the $\texttt{next\_item}$ example, the postcondition asserts that the shared memory contains a linked list with head q'.

4   Read-Only Assertions

The read-only assertion $P[R_1; \cdots; R_n]$, introduced in the previous section, is defined as $(P \wedge (R_1 * \text{True}) \wedge \cdots \wedge (R_n * \text{True}))$. The shared predicates $\vec{R}$ can be freely duplicated, split, merged and discarded:

$$P[R_1; R_2; \cdots; R_n] \vdash P[R_1; R_1; R_2; \cdots; R_n] \qquad \text{(RO-DUP)}$$
$$P[R_1; R_2; \cdots; R_n] \vdash P[R_2; \cdots; R_n] \qquad \text{(RO-DROP)}$$
$$P[R_{11} * R_{12}; R_2; \cdots; R_n] \vdash P[R_{11}; R_{12}; R_2; \cdots; R_n] \qquad \text{(RO-SPLIT)}$$
$$P[\exists x.R_1(x); R_2; \cdots; R_n] \vdash \exists x.P[R_1(x); R_2; \cdots; R_n] \qquad \text{(RO-EXISTS)}$$

We can finish most of the proof of the motivating example using ordinary Hoare rules and these useful properties. Figure 6 shows the proof sketch for the while case of the interpreter, where $com\_reps(\vec{c_k}, \vec{C_k})$ is a shorthand for the list $com\_rep(c_{k1}, C_{k1}); \cdots; com\_rep(c_{kn}, C_{kn})$. Most of the verification is straightforward. The most interesting part is the first entailment, which makes use of several important properties of read-only assertions. Knowing that there is a while command rooted at c, we need to derive that there are subheaps satisfying $exp\_rep(e, E)$, $com\_rep(c', C')$ and also $com\_rep(c, C)$. The $exp\_rep(e, E)$ is required by the function call to `eval`. When the while condition evaluates to true, Commands C' and C will become the new focused command and part of the new continuation. Since the other two predicates are part of $com\_rep(c, C)$, the entailment requires subtle reasoning of shared memory. We first make a copy of the while command using RO-DUP. For the first copy, we repeatedly apply the RO-SPLIT rule, and then discard the useless $c \mapsto$ T_WHILE, e, c' by RO-DROP. For the second one, we simply fold the definition of com_rep, and get $com\_rep(c, C)$. Verification of the function call to `eval`, which involves the new FRAME rule, is left to the next section.

$$// \left\{ \begin{array}{c} K = C_{k1} \cdot \ldots \cdot C_{kn} \cdot \mathsf{KStop} \wedge \mathit{table\_rep}(t, \sigma) * r \mapsto c, k * \mathit{cont\_rep}(k, \vec{c_k}) * \\ \mathit{com\_rep}(c_0, C_0)[c \mapsto \mathrm{T\_WHILE}, e, c' * \mathit{exp\_rep}(e, E) * \mathit{com\_rep}(c', C'); \\ \mathit{com\_reps}(\vec{c_k}, \vec{C_k})] \end{array} \right\}$$

$//$ (by RO-Dup, RO-Split and RO-Drop)

$$// \left\{ \begin{array}{c} K = C_{k1} \cdot \ldots \cdot C_{kn} \cdot \mathsf{KStop} \wedge \mathit{table\_rep}(t, \sigma) * r \mapsto c, k * \mathit{cont\_rep}(k, \vec{c_k}) * \\ \mathit{com\_rep}(c_0, C_0)[\mathit{exp\_rep}(e, E); \mathit{com\_rep}(c', C'); \mathit{com\_rep}(c, C); \\ \mathit{com\_reps}(\vec{c_k}, \vec{C_k})] \end{array} \right\}$$

```
b = eval(t, e);
```

$$// \left\{ \begin{array}{c} K = C_{k1} \cdot \ldots \cdot C_{kn} \cdot \mathsf{KStop} \wedge b = [\![E]\!](\sigma) \wedge \\ \mathit{table\_rep}(t, \sigma) * r \mapsto c, k * \mathit{cont\_rep}(k, \vec{c_k}) * \\ \mathit{com\_rep}(c_0, C_0)[\mathit{com\_rep}(c', C'); \mathit{com\_rep}(c, C); \mathit{com\_reps}(\vec{c_k}, \vec{C_k})] \end{array} \right\}$$

```
if (b) {
    k2 = malloc(sizeof(struct cont_list));
    k2->c = c; k2->link = k;
    r->foc = c->d.WHILE.body; r->ctx = k2;
```

$$// \left\{ \begin{array}{c} [\![E]\!](\sigma) = \mathrm{true} \wedge \mathit{table\_rep}(t, \sigma) * r \mapsto c', k2 * k2 \mapsto c, k * \mathit{cont\_rep}(k, \vec{c_k}) * \\ \mathit{com\_rep}(c_0, C_0)[\mathit{com\_rep}(c', C'); \mathit{com\_rep}(c, C); \mathit{com\_reps}(\vec{c_k}, \vec{C_k})] \end{array} \right\}$$

$//$ (folding resprog_rep)

$$// \left\{ \begin{array}{c} [\![E]\!](\sigma) = \mathrm{true} \wedge \mathit{table\_rep}(t) * \mathit{resprog\_rep}(r, c_0, C_0, C', C \cdot K) * \\ \mathit{com\_rep}(c_0, C_0)[\mathit{com\_rep}(c', C'); \mathit{com\_rep}(c, C); \mathit{com\_reps}(\vec{c_k}, \vec{C_k})] \end{array} \right\}$$

```
} else { r->foc = 0; }
```

Fig. 6. Proof sketch of the interpreter

5 Extended Separation Logic

5.1 Simple Shorthand Definitions

When there is only one read-only region, the triple $\{P\}\langle R\rangle\ c\ \{P'\}\langle R'\rangle$ can be defined as a shorthand for $\forall X.\{P * X[R]\}\ c\ \{P' * X[R']\}$. The definition works well, but it is difficult to extend to more read-only regions. As we discuss below, two possible definitions for the triple $\{P\}\langle R_1; R_2\rangle\ c\ \{P'\}\langle R'_1; R'_2\rangle$ suffer from some shortcomings.

One definition is $\forall X_1 X_2.\{P * X_1[R_1] * X_2[R_2]\}\ c\ \{P' * X_1[R'_1] * X_2[R'_2]\}$. As X_1 and X_2 must be disjoint, this definition does not support aliasing assertions. Therefore, if R_1 and R_2 may represent the same heap region, we need to prove another triple: $\{P\}\langle[R_1; R_2]\rangle\ c\ \{P'\}\langle[R'_1; R'_2]\rangle$. We have to prove two similar triples for the same statement, which requires more efforts.

Another definition is $\forall X.\{P * X[R_1; R_2]\}\ c\ \{P' * X[R'_1; R'_2]\}$. This definition allows aliasing assertions, but it is too weak. Suppose that we want to execute the command c from a heap satisfying $P * P_1[R_1] * P_2[R_2]$, and we expect that after execution the heap satisfies $P' * P_1[R_1; R'_1] * P_2[R_2; R'_2]$. However, with this definition of extended triple, we can only instantiate X with $P_1[R_1] * P_2[R_2]$ and prove the much weaker postcondition $P' * (P_1[R_1] * P_2[R_2])[R'_1; R'_2]$.

5.2 Extended Pre/Postcondition

As proposed in Sect. 3, the syntax of pre/postconditions $\mathbb{Q}$ of our extended Hoare triples is defined as

$$\mathbb{Q} ::= P\langle R_1; R_2; \cdots; R_n\rangle \mid \exists x.\mathbb{Q}$$

We use $h, \vec{h_r} \vDash \mathbb{Q}$ to denote that the mutable heap h and read-only heaps $\vec{h_r}$ satisfy $\mathbb{Q}$. The satisfaction relation is defined by structural induction:

- $h, [h_{r1}, \cdots, h_{rn}] \vDash P\langle R_1; \cdots; R_n\rangle \iff h \vDash P \wedge h_{r1} \vDash R_1 \wedge \cdots \wedge h_{rn} \vDash R_n$
- $h, \vec{h_r} \vDash \exists x.\mathbb{Q} \iff h, \vec{h_r} \vDash \mathbb{Q}[v/x]$ for some v

The assertion P corresponds to the mutable heap, while $R_1, R_2, \cdots, R_n$ are used to describe immutable heaps. The assertion R_i usually has the form $[R_{i1}; \cdots; R_{in}]$, in order to describe possibly-overlapping internal structure. The extended pre/postconditions enable us to write more precise specifications by specifying the mutability of different parts of the heap.

Some useful properties of the pre/postconditions are given below. The E-MONO rule reduces entailments between two conditions to entailments between their components, while the E-EXISTS rule shows existential quantifiers can be extracted from inner read-only regions.

$$\frac{P \vdash P' \quad R_1 \vdash R'_1 \quad \cdots \quad R_n \vdash R'_n}{P\langle R_1; R_2; \cdots; R_n\rangle \vdash P'\langle R'_1; R'_2; \cdots; R'_n\rangle} \text{ E-MONO}$$

$$\frac{}{P\langle \exists x.R_1(x); R_2; \cdots; R_n\rangle = \exists x.P\langle R_1(x); R_2; \cdots; R_n\rangle} \text{ E-EXISTS}$$

5.3   Extended Hoare Triple

A Hoare triple $\{\mathbb{Q}\}\ c\ \{\mathbb{Q}'\}$ is valid if and only if starting from a state where the heap can be divided into two disjoint parts, the exclusively owned part h and the read-only part h_r, and h_r contains several possibly overlapping immutable regions $\vec{r}$, if h and $\vec{r}$ satisfy the precondition $\mathbb{Q}$, then the execution of c either loops infinitely or terminates safely. When it terminates, the updated exclusively owned heap h' and the unmodified $\vec{r}$ satisfies the postcondition $\mathbb{Q}'$.

In this definition, there are several points worth highlighting.

1. We require the mutable heap h and immutable heap h_r to be disjoint, so mutations of h do not influence h_r.
2. It is trivial to prove that when c terminates, the read-only part of $\mathbb{Q}$ remains true. Thus, we do not need to mention the original overlapping regions $\vec{r}$ in the postcondition, which simplifies the specifications.
3. Although h_r is unchanged, we can gain more knowledge about it as we read from it. It is important to pass the extra information to the caller. It is best exemplified by the specification for next_item in Sect. 3, which asserts that the new value q' stored in p after the function call is still a valid list pointer. Without that information, the caller could not make use of the new iterator.
4. Different elements of $\vec{r}$ can be either disjoint or overlapping. For example, the specification for strcmp in Sect. 3 can be used when p and q represent disjoint strings. It can also be used when $p = q$ or even p points to the middle of the string pointed by q. With traditional separation logic, we may need to provide several specifications for different use cases (Fig. 7).

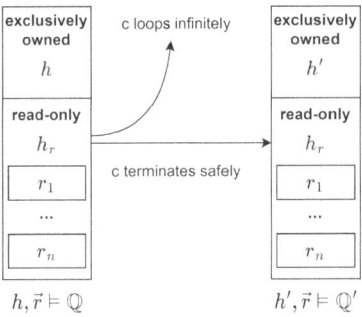

Fig. 7. Definition of extended Hoare triple

5.4   Load and Store Rules

Most rules in traditional separation logic have simple counterparts in the extended separation logic, which are omitted for simplicity. Among the non-standard rules are the load and store rules, which are related to the heap:

$$\frac{P \vdash e \mapsto e_0 * \text{True}}{\Delta \vdash \{P\} \langle \vec{R} \rangle \; x := [e] \; (\exists x'. \{x = e_0[x'/x] \wedge P[x'/x]\} \langle \vec{R}[x'/x] \rangle)} \; \text{LOAD}$$

$$\frac{R_1 \vdash e \mapsto e_0 * \text{True}}{\Delta \vdash \{P\} \langle \vec{R} \rangle \; x := [e] \; (\exists x'. \{x = e_0[x'/x] \wedge P[x'/x]\} \langle \vec{R}[x'/x] \rangle)} \; \text{R-LOAD}$$

$$\frac{}{\Delta \vdash \{e_1 \mapsto e_0 * P\} \langle \vec{R} \rangle \; [e_1] := e_2 \; \{e_1 \mapsto e_2 * P\} \langle \vec{R} \rangle} \; \text{STORE}$$

We write $\Delta \vdash \{Q\} \; c \; \{Q'\}$ to represent that the triple is provable under assumption Δ, which is a set of function specifications. The LOAD rule allows us to read from the mutable heap. The R-LOAD rule allows us to read from the read-only regions. We can modify the mutable heap using the STORE rule, but we can't mutate the read-only heap, so there is not an R-STORE rule.

5.5 Function Call and Frame Rule

The following CALL rule and FRAME rule are useful to handle function calls.

$$\frac{\{P\} \langle \vec{R} \rangle \; f \; (\exists x. \{P'\} \langle \vec{R'} \rangle) \in \Delta}{\Delta \vdash \{P\} \langle \vec{R} \rangle \; \text{call} \; f \; (\exists x. \{P'\} \langle \vec{R'} \rangle)} \; \text{CALL}$$

$$\frac{\Delta \vdash \{P\} \langle \vec{R} \rangle \; c \; (\exists x. \{P'\} \langle \vec{R'} \rangle) \quad modify(c) \cap (fv(F) \cup fv(\vec{R_F})) = \emptyset}{\Delta \vdash \{P * F\} \langle \vec{R}; \vec{R_F} \rangle \; c \; (\exists x. \{P' * F\} \langle \vec{R'}; \vec{R_F} \rangle)} \; \text{FRAME}$$

To call a function, we simply look up the function specification from the assumption Δ. The new FRAME rule is a simple extension of the ordinary FRAME rule, allowing us to frame out read-only assertions as well as mutable assertions.

5.6 Manipulation of Read-Only Regions

The rules described in previous sections only interact with existing read-only regions. To use them, we need rules to create and manipulate read-only regions:

$$\frac{\begin{array}{c} \Delta \vdash \{P\} \langle \vec{R_1}; \vec{R} \rangle \; c \; (\exists x. \{P'\} \langle \vec{R_1'}; \vec{R'} \rangle) \\ modify(c) \cap (fv(P_0) \cup fv(\vec{R_2})) = \emptyset \end{array}}{\Delta \vdash \left\{ P_0[\vec{R_1}; \vec{R_2}] * P \right\} \langle \vec{R} \rangle \; c \; (\exists x. \left\{ P_0[\vec{R_1'}; \vec{R_2}] * P' \right\} \langle \vec{R'} \rangle)} \; \text{R-INTRO}$$

$$\frac{\Delta \vdash \{P\} \langle R_1; R_2; \vec{R} \rangle \; c \; (\exists x. \{P'\} \langle R_1'; R_2'; \vec{R'} \rangle)}{\Delta \vdash \{P\} \langle R_1 \wedge R_2; \vec{R} \rangle \; c \; (\exists x. \{P'\} \langle R_1' \wedge R_2'; \vec{R'} \rangle)} \; \text{R-SPLIT-}\wedge$$

$$\frac{\Delta \vdash \{P\} \langle R_1; R_2; \vec{R} \rangle \; c \; (\exists x. \{P'\} \langle R_1'; R_2'; \vec{R'} \rangle)}{\Delta \vdash \{P\} \langle R_1 * R_2; \vec{R} \rangle \; c \; (\exists x. \{P'\} \langle R_1' * R_2'; \vec{R'} \rangle)} \; \text{R-SPLIT-}*$$

$$\frac{s \text{ is a permutation function} \quad \Delta \vdash \{P\} \langle s(\vec{R}) \rangle \; c \; (\exists x. \{P'\} \langle s(\vec{R'}) \rangle)}{\Delta \vdash \{P\} \langle \vec{R} \rangle \; c \; (\exists x. \{P'\} \langle \vec{R'} \rangle)} \; \text{R-PERM}$$

The R-INTRO rule marks some part of the mutable heap temporary immutable by moving some assertions into read-only regions. The R-SPLIT-∧ and R-SPLIT-∗ rule allow us to split one read-only assertion in two different ways, either duplicating the whole immutable subheap or split it into two disjoint parts. The R-PERM rule is handy when dealing with multiple read-only regions.

With these reasoning rules, we can finish the verification of the call to `eval` in the motivating example. The proof sketch is shown in Fig. 8. Using the FRAME rule and the R-INTRO rule, we frame out irrelevant assertions, and move the $exp\_rep(e, E)$ to the read-only part of the triple. Note that $table\_rep(t, \sigma) = table\_rep(t, \sigma)[table\_rep(t, \sigma)]$, so we can move $table\_rep(t, \sigma)$ to the read-only part by applying another R-INTRO rule. Now the triple correctly matches the specification for `eval`, and can be proved by the CALL rule.

$$
// \left\{ \begin{array}{c} K = C_{k1} \cdot ... \cdot C_{kn} \cdot \text{KStop} \wedge \textbf{\textit{table\_rep}}(t, \sigma) * r \mapsto c, k * \text{cont\_rep}(k, \vec{c_k}) * \\ com\_rep(c_0, C_0)[\textbf{\textit{exp\_rep}}(e, E); com\_rep(c', C'); \\ com\_rep(c, C); com\_reps(\vec{c_k}, \vec{C_k})] \end{array} \right\}
$$

```
//  local reasoning begins
    //{ table_rep(t, σ)} ⟨exp_rep(e, E)⟩
    //{emp} ⟨table_rep(t, σ); exp_rep(e, E)⟩
        b = eval(t, e);
    //{b = ⟦E⟧(σ) ∧ emp} ⟨True; True⟩
    //{b = ⟦E⟧(σ) ∧ table_rep(t, σ)} ⟨True⟩
//  local reasoning ends
```

$$
// \left\{ \begin{array}{c} K = C_{k1} \cdot ... \cdot C_{kn} \cdot \text{KStop} \wedge b = \llbracket E \rrbracket(\sigma) \wedge \\ \textbf{\textit{table\_rep}}(t, \sigma) * r \mapsto c, k * cont\_rep(k, \vec{c_k}) * \\ com\_rep(c_0, C_0)[com\_rep(c', C'); com\_rep(c, C); com\_reps(\vec{c_k}, \vec{C_k})] \end{array} \right\}
$$

Fig. 8. Verification of function call

5.7   Soundness

We prove that the rules are sound for partial correctness with respect to the language's denotational semantics [18]. Given the denotation for callee functions χ, the denotation for command c, written as $\llbracket c \rrbracket(\chi)$, consists of two parts: the terminate part $\llbracket c \rrbracket(\chi).(\text{nrm}) \subseteq \text{Mem} \times \text{Mem}$, and the error part $\llbracket c \rrbracket(\chi).(\text{err}) \subseteq \text{Mem}^2$. Formally, $(h_1, h_2) \in \llbracket c \rrbracket(\chi).(\text{nrm})$ means that the execution of c from state h_1 terminates safely in h_2, while $h \in \llbracket c \rrbracket(\chi).(\text{err})$ means that a runtime

---

[2]   In order to keep the presentation of the soundness proof simple, we omit variable environments.

error occurs if c is executed from state h. For function definitions D and a function name f, the denotation of the function is written as $[\![D]\!](f)$.

We write $\alpha : \{\mathbb{Q}\}\{\mathbb{Q}'\}$, where α is a command denotation, to represent that $\mathbb{Q}$ and $\mathbb{Q}'$ are valid pre/postcondition for the denotation α. It is defined as

$$\forall h_1, h_{11}, h_{12}, \vec{h_r}.h_1 = h_{11} \oplus h_{12} \wedge (\forall h \in \vec{h_r}.h \leq h_{12}) \wedge h_{11}, \vec{h_r} \vDash \mathbb{Q} \Rightarrow$$

$$h_1 \notin \alpha.(\mathrm{err}) \wedge (\forall h_2, (h_1, h_2) \in \alpha.(\mathrm{nrm}) \Rightarrow \exists h_{21}.h_2 = h_{21} \oplus h_{12} \wedge h_{21}, \vec{h_r} \vDash \mathbb{Q}')$$

where $\oplus$ represents disjoint union, and $h_1 \leq h_2$ is defined as $\exists h_3.h_1 \oplus h_3 = h_2$. We define $\beta : \{\mathbb{Q}\}\{\mathbb{Q}'\}$ for function denotation β similarly. Theorem 1 states the soundness of the logic.

Theorem 1 (Soundness). *For function definitions D and specifications Δ, if every function specification is provable*

$$\forall \{\mathbb{Q}_f\} \ f \ \{\mathbb{Q}'_f\} \in \Delta.\exists c.(f, c) \in D \wedge \Delta \vdash \{\mathbb{Q}_f\} \ c \ \{\mathbb{Q}'_f\}$$

then the specifications are all valid

$$\forall \{\mathbb{Q}_f\} \ f \ \{\mathbb{Q}'_f\} \in \Delta.[\![D]\!](f) : \{\mathbb{Q}_f\}\{\mathbb{Q}'_f\}$$

Since the rules involve the assumption Δ, it is helpful to define the validity of a triple with assumption [1]. We use $\Delta \vDash \{\mathbb{Q}\} \ c \ \{\mathbb{Q}'\}$ to represent that the triple is valid given assumption Δ, which is defined as:

$$\forall \chi.(\forall \{\mathbb{Q}_f\} \ f \ \{\mathbb{Q}'_f\} \in \Delta.\chi(f) : \{\mathbb{Q}_f\}\{\mathbb{Q}'_f\}) \Rightarrow [\![c]\!](\chi) : \{\mathbb{Q}\}\{\mathbb{Q}'\}$$

The soundness theorem follows immediately from the following lemmas.

Lemma 1. *If $\Delta \vdash \{\mathbb{Q}\} \ c \ \{\mathbb{Q}'\}$ then $\Delta \vDash \{\mathbb{Q}\} \ c \ \{\mathbb{Q}'\}$.*

Lemma 2. *If*

$$\forall \{\mathbb{Q}_f\} \ f \ \{\mathbb{Q}'_f\} \in \Delta.\exists c.(f, c) \in D \wedge \Delta \vDash \{\mathbb{Q}_f\} \ c \ \{\mathbb{Q}'_f\}$$

then

$$\forall \{\mathbb{Q}_f\} \ f \ \{\mathbb{Q}'_f\} \in \Delta.[\![D]\!](f) : \{\mathbb{Q}_f\}\{\mathbb{Q}'_f\}$$

Lemma 1 states that every provable triple is valid, provided that the assumption Δ is valid. It can be proved by simple structural induction on c. Since $[\![D]\!]$ is defined as the least fixpoint, Lemma 2 can be proved by Scott's fixpoint induction [18], i.e., by showing the property holds of every approximate to $[\![D]\!]$.

6   Related Works

Bornat et al. [2] proposed to use the construction $(A * \text{True}) \wedge B$ to describe inclusion sharing, which is similar to our read-only assertions. They showed how this idiom can be used to provide good postcondition for functions creating internal structures of the input structures, and proposed to use $A * ((B * \text{True}) \wedge C) * ((D * \text{True}) \wedge E) \vdash (B * D * \text{True}) \wedge (A * C * E)$ to combine such assertions. They did not show that this idiom is also useful for function precondition, and how it interacts with the FRAME rule.

Charguéraud and Pottier [6] presented a general mechanism for temporarily converting any assertion to a read-only form. They introduced a read-only modality, written $\text{RO}(H)$ where H is a traditional separation assertion, to represent that the heap covered by H is read-only. The modality has many good properties. For example, $\text{RO}(H_1 * H_2) \vdash \text{RO}(H_1) * \text{RO}(H_2)$ and $\text{RO}(H) = \text{RO}(H) * \text{RO}(H)$. The read-only modality is introduced by the following read-only frame rule:

$$\frac{\{H * \text{RO}(H')\} \ t \ \{Q\} \quad \text{normal } H'}{\{H * H'\} \ t \ \{Q * H'\}}$$

where normal H' means that RO does not occur in H'. A shortcoming of their method is that their read-only permissions can only occur in the precondition because of the side condition of the read-only frame rule, so they can only be passed down from caller to callee and never from callee to caller. Thus, it cannot be used to define a simple specification for iterators. By contrast, a concise specification for iterators can be defined using our extended separation logic.

Fractional permissions [3] can be used to reason about shared data structures. A rational number π in the range $(0, 1]$ is associated with each heap location. A share π with value 1 represents exclusive ownership, while $0 < \pi < 1$ only allows read access. The permissions can be split or combined using the rule $x \overset{\pi_1}{\mapsto} e * x \overset{\pi_2}{\mapsto} e = x \overset{\pi_1 + \pi_2}{\mapsto} e$. Fractional permission is suitable for fork-join programs, since it enables symmetrical splitting and unbounded division. To regain write permission for the resources, one need to prove that all shares have been collected, which requires arithmetic accounting.

Fractional permissions interact badly with inductive predicates. For predicate A, we write A^π to denote that every memory cell of the heap covered by A has π permission. The entailment $A^\pi * B^\pi \vDash (A * B)^\pi$ is false, because A and B may be aliased. Another difficulty is that the entailment $A^{\pi_1} * A^{\pi_2} \vDash A^{\pi_1 + \pi_2}$ is also false, so it is difficult to combine shares. Le and Hobor [12] solved the problem by using tree shares [7] and side conditions requiring the predicates to be precise or uniform. Brotherston et al. [4] provided another solution by using two separating conjunction, the strong one $*$ and the weak one $\circledast$.

The overlapping conjunction $P \uplus Q$, which is defined as $h \vDash P \uplus Q \iff \exists h_1, h_2, h_3.(h_1 \oplus h_2 \oplus h_3 = h) \wedge (h_1 \oplus h_2 \vDash P) \wedge (h_2 \oplus h_3 \vDash Q)$, means that P and Q may overlap in the heap. Hobor and Villard [9] demonstrated that it is suitable to describe overlapping data structures such as graphs. Instead of using FRAME rule, they propose to use the following RAMIFY rule:

$$\frac{\{P\}\ c\ \{Q\} \quad R \vdash P * (Q \twoheadrightarrow R')}{\{R\}\ c\ \{R'\}}$$

where the separating implication is defined as $h \vDash P \twoheadrightarrow Q \iff \forall h'.h' \vDash P \Rightarrow h \oplus h' \vDash Q$. Wang et al. [17] developed a LOCALIZE rule, an upgrade of RAMIFY rule, to enable modular reasoning about graph-manipulating programs.

7   Conclusion

We proposed an extension of separation logic to reason about read-only overlapping data structures. We use the read-only assertions to define representation predicates for overlapping structures, and enable local reasoning by extending the pre/postconditions of the Hoare triple. The proposed method can be used to define concise specifications for many functions and simplify the verification, which is demonstrated on the interpreter example. We formalized our logic in Coq and build a lightweight symbolic execution library. We plan to try applying our extended separation logic to concurrent program verification in the future.

Acknowledgements. This material is based upon work supported by NSF China 92370201.

References

1. Apt, K.R., de Boer, F.S., Olderog, E.: Verification of Sequential and Concurrent Programs. Texts in Computer Science. Springer, Heidelberg (2009). https://doi.org/10.1007/978-1-84882-745-5

2. Bornat, R., Calcagno, C., O'Hearn, P.: Local reasoning, separation and aliasing. In: Proceeddings of the Workshop on Semantics, Program Analysis, and Computing Environments (2004)

3. Boyland, J.: Checking interference with fractional permissions. In: Cousot, R. (ed.) SAS 2003. LNCS, vol. 2694, pp. 55–72. Springer, Heidelberg (2003). https://doi.org/10.1007/3-540-44898-5_4

4. Brotherston, J., Costa, D., Hobor, A., Wickerson, J.: Reasoning over permissions regions in concurrent separation logic. In: Lahiri, S.K., Wang, C. (eds.) CAV 2020. LNCS, vol. 12225, pp. 203–224. Springer, Cham (2020). https://doi.org/10.1007/978-3-030-53291-8_13

5. Cao, Q., Beringer, L., Gruetter, S., Dodds, J., Appel, A.W.: VST-Floyd: a separation logic tool to verify correctness of C programs. J. Autom. Reason. **61**(1–4), 367–422 (2018)

6. Charguéraud, A., Pottier, F.: Temporary Read-Only Permissions for Separation Logic. In: Yang, H. (ed.) ESOP 2017. LNCS, vol. 10201, pp. 260–286. Springer, Heidelberg (2017). https://doi.org/10.1007/978-3-662-54434-1_10

7. Dockins, R., Hobor, A., Appel, A.W.: A fresh look at separation algebras and share accounting. In: Hu, Z. (ed.) APLAS 2009. LNCS, vol. 5904, pp. 161–177. Springer, Heidelberg (2009). https://doi.org/10.1007/978-3-642-10672-9_13

8. Hance, T., Howell, J., Padon, O., Parno, B.: Leaf: modularity for temporary sharing in separation logic. Proc. ACM Program. Lang. **7**(OOPSLA2), 31–58 (2023)

9. Hobor, A., Villard, J.: The ramifications of sharing in data structures. In: Giacobazzi, R., Cousot, R. (eds.) The 40th Annual ACM SIGPLAN-SIGACT Symposium on Principles of Programming Languages, POPL 2013, Rome, Italy, 23–25 January 2013, pp. 523–536. ACM (2013)

10. Krebbers, R., Timany, A., Birkedal, L.: Interactive proofs in higher-order concurrent separation logic. In: Castagna, G., Gordon, A.D. (eds.) Proceedings of the 44th ACM SIGPLAN Symposium on Principles of Programming Languages, POPL 2017, Paris, France, 18–20 January 2017, pp. 205–217. ACM (2017)

11. Krishna, S., Shasha, D.E., Wies, T.: Go with the flow: compositional abstractions for concurrent data structures. Proc. ACM Program. Lang. **2**(POPL), 37:1–37:31 (2018)

12. Le, X.-B., Hobor, A.: Logical reasoning for disjoint permissions. In: Ahmed, A. (ed.) ESOP 2018. LNCS, vol. 10801, pp. 385–414. Springer, Cham (2018). https://doi.org/10.1007/978-3-319-89884-1_14

13. Leroy, X.: Formal certification of a compiler back-end or: programming a compiler with a proof assistant. In: Morrisett, J.G., Jones, S.L.P. (eds.) Proceedings of the 33rd ACM SIGPLAN-SIGACT Symposium on Principles of Programming Languages, POPL 2006, Charleston, South Carolina, USA, 11–13 January 2006, pp. 42–54. ACM (2006)

14. Okasaki, C.: Purely Functional Data Structures. Cambridge University Press, Cambridge (1999)

15. Reynolds, J.C.: Separation logic: a logic for shared mutable data structures. In: Proceedings of the 17th IEEE Symposium on Logic in Computer Science (LICS 2002), 22–25 July 2002, Copenhagen, Denmark, pp. 55–74. IEEE Computer Society (2002)

16. Vindum, S.F., Birkedal, L.: Contextual refinement of the Michael-Scott queue (proof pearl). In: Hritcu, C., Popescu, A. (eds.) CPP 2021: 10th ACM SIGPLAN International Conference on Certified Programs and Proofs, Virtual Event, Denmark, 17–19 January 2021, pp. 76–90. ACM (2021)

17. Wang, S., Cao, Q., Mohan, A., Hobor, A.: Certifying graph-manipulating C programs via localizations within data structures. Proc. ACM Program. Lang. **3**(OOPSLA), 171:1–171:30 (2019)

18. Winskel, G.: The Formal Semantics of Programming Languages - An Introduction. Foundation of Computing Series. MIT Press (1993)

Constraint Based Invariant Generation with Modular Operations

Yuchen Li(ID), Hongfei Fu(✉)(ID), Haowen Long(ID), and Guoqiang Li(ID)

Shanghai Jiao Tong University, Shanghai, China
{unicronli,jt002845,longhaowen,li.g}@sjtu.edu.cn

Abstract. Invariant generation is a fundamental problem in program verification that targets the automated generation of invariants that capture the set of reachable program states. Modular operations that calculate the remainder of an integer variable against a divisor are common in programs, and therefore the generation of invariants with modular information is indispensible for proving the correctness of such programs. In this paper, we propose a novel approach for generating affine invariants with modular information via constraint solving. Our approach first transforms affine programs with modular operations into affine transition systems, and then applies existing approaches in Farkas' Lemma to solve the invariants. Experimental results over a suite of benchmarks that involve complex modular operations show that our approach is time efficient and can generate tight or even accurate linear invariants with modular information.

1 Introduction

An invariant at a program location is an assertion that is always satisfied when the program executes to that location. Invariants provide an over-approximation for the set of reachable program states, and hence can be used for the analysis of safety [9–11], reachability [13–16] and time complexity [12] in program verification. Invariant generation aims at the automated generation of invariants, and thus is fundamental to verify the correctness of programs. As its importance in program verification, various approaches have been proposed to address the invariant generation problem, such as abstract interpretation [26–28], constraint solving [18–20], recurrence analysis [23–25], machine learning [32–35], etc.

In programming languages, modular operation is fundamental to calculate the remainder (e.g. $x\%2$) of an integer variable against a positive integer (e.g. 2). Remainder computation widely exists in various kinds of programs. Hence, the invariant generation with modular information plays a crucial role in verifying the correctness of programs with remainder computation. In the literature, this problem is addressed by several approaches, including recurrence analysis [31], path dependency automata [29,30], etc. In this work, we consider to leverage constraint solving methods to address this problem.

T. Bourke et al. (Eds.): SETTA 2024, LNCS 15469, pp. 64–84, 2025.
https://doi.org/10.1007/978-981-96-0602-3_4

Most constraint solving methods (such as [18–20]) generates polynomial invariants without modular information. A disadvantage of these approaches is that they cannot handle modular operations since they cannot be described by polynomial constraints. In this work, we extend the constraint solving methods which are based on Farkas' Lemma [6–8,17,36] to modular operations. Farkas' Lemma [5] is a fundamental theorem in the theory of linear inequalities, and we show how one can adapt existing constraint solving methods in Farkas' Lemma to handle modular operations.

Our Contribution. In detail, we make the following contributions:

– We propose a general method of generating linear invariants in affine programs with modular operations. To achieve this, we first introduce our paradigm and main technique in a simple example. Then, we classify the modular operation in transition systems into three basic types: multiple modular information in branch conditions, update function of modular related variables referring to other variables and modular operation in update functions, and provide the corresponding detailed method following our paradigm to solve them. Further, we show how to integrate them together and thus our method is applicable to linear transition systems with any types of the modular operation by transforming the given transition system into equivalent pure linear transition system and generating linear invariants by the well-developed methods respect to linear transition systems off the shelf.
– We classify the types of such systems and establish the benchmarks of general systems with linear and modular expressions.
– We implement our method by integrating it into the implementation of Sting [3] and carry out soundness experiments on the benchmarks.

Our experiments show the effectiveness and time efficiency of our method and our method outperforms the state-of-the-art tool CPAchecker [1] in all of the examples in our benchmarks, which means our method is a good complement of current tools.

2   Preliminaries

2.1   Transition Systems and Invariants

We first present some formal definitions and concepts. A *linear constraint* over a real-valued variable set $X = \{x_1, \ldots, x_n\}$ is of the form $a_1 x_1 + \cdots + a_n x_n + b \bowtie 0$, where $a_1, \cdots, a_n, b$ are known real-valued coefficients, and $\bowtie \in \{\leq, =\}$, corresponding to linear inequality and linear equality respectively. A *linear assertion* over X is a conjunction of linear constraints over X. A *propositional linear predicate* over X is a propositional formula with atomic proposition in the form of linear constraints. A propositional formula is recognized as disjunctive (resp. conjunctive) normal form when it is a finite disjunction of linear assertions (resp. a finite conjunction of finite disjunctions of linear assertions), respectively.

Given this basic concepts, we can define *linear transition systems* and *linear invariants*.

Definition 1 (Linear Transition System). *A linear transition system (LinTS) with modular operation can be symbolically represented as $P = \langle X, X', L, l_0, \theta, \mathcal{T} \rangle$ consists of:*

- *$X = \{x_1, \ldots, x_n\}$ and the corresponding primed version $X' = \{x'_1, \ldots, x'_n\}$ represent the finite set of current-state variables and next-state variables accordingly.*
- *L is a finite set of locations and $l_0 \in L$ is the initial location.*
- *θ is the propositional linear predicate over the initial states of variables X and standalone variables $e \% n$ where e is a linear expression over the initial states of variables X and n is a positive integer.*
- *$\mathcal{T}$ is a finite set of transitions and each transition $\tau \in \mathcal{T}$ is a triplet $\langle l, l', \rho_\tau \rangle$ where $l, l' \in L$ is the current-state location and the next-state location, and ρ_τ is the guard condition of the transition in the form of the propositional formula over $X \cup X'$ and standalone variables $e \% n$ where e is a linear expression over $X \cup X'$ and n is a positive integer.*

The definition of LinTS is an extension of linear transition systems in [6,8]. The extension is that θ and ρ_τ include modular operations that calculate the remainder.

The control-flow graph (CFG) of a linear transition system P is a directed graph whose vertices are the locations of P and whose edges are the transitions pointed from current-state location to next-state location. Apart from this basic structure, we define valuation functions, configurations and satisfaction relation to describe the semantics of a linear transition system.

A *valuation function* $\sigma : X \to \mathbb{R}$ is an assignment function over a finite set of variables X to real numbers set $\mathbb{R}$. For a given linear transition system, a *configuration* is a pair (l, σ) where l denotes the location and σ is the valuation function which specifies the variable values at this location. Without loss of generality, we assume an implicit linear order among variables in X and formalize every valuation function σ as a real vector so that its i-th coordinate $\sigma[i]$ is the real value for the i-th variable in the linear order. We introduce three kinds of *satisfaction relation* $\models$ in this work. The first one is $\sigma \models \phi$, where ϕ denotes an assertion over variable set X and σ denotes a valuation function over variable set X. This relation means that σ satisfies ϕ, i.e., ϕ is true when assigning the variables in X using the valuation function σ. The second one is $\sigma, \sigma' \models \phi$, where ϕ denotes an assertion over variable set $X \cup X'$ and σ, σ' denote a valuation function over X, X' respectively. This relation means that σ, σ' satisfy ϕ, i.e., ϕ is true when assigning the variable in X using the valuation function σ and assigning the variable in X' using the valuation function σ'. The third one is $\phi \models \psi$, where ϕ and ψ denote an assertion over variable set X. This relation means that ϕ satisfies ψ, i.e., for every valuation function σ over X, we have that $\sigma \models \phi$ implies $\sigma \models \psi$.

Next we introduce the semantics of linear transition systems, which is formally specified by the notion of paths through its CFG. A path π of the linear transition system P is symbolically represented as a finite sequence of configurations $(l_0, \sigma_0), \ldots, (l_k, \sigma_k)$ with the requirement that

- **(Initialization)** For the start of the path, we have $l_0 = l^*$ and $\sigma_0 \models \theta$
- **(Consecution)** For every two consecutive configurations $(l, \sigma), (l', \sigma')$ in the path, there exists a transistion $\tau = \langle l, l', \rho_\tau \rangle$ such that $\sigma, \sigma' \models \rho_\tau$

We define that a configuration (l, σ) is *reachable* if there exists a path $\pi = (l_0, \sigma_0), \ldots, (l, \sigma)$. Intuitively, every path π in the linear transition system P starts with some legitimate initial configuration i.e., at the initial location l_0 with an initial valuation function σ_0 such that $\sigma_0 \models \theta$ and proceeds by repeatedly applying the transitions to the current-state configuration. Thus, every path π corresponding to a possible execution of the underlying linear transition system.

Definition 2 (Invariants). *An invariant of a linear transition system P at a location l is a logical formula ϕ over X that for every reachable configuration (l, σ), we have $\sigma \models \phi$.*

Intuitively, an invariant ϕ at a location l provides an over-approximate of the set of reachable configurations at l. As the standard method for proving a given invariant is to find an *inductive* invariant that strengthens it, invariant automatically generation methods are normally methods for generating inductive invariant. We present inductive invariants in the form of inductive assertion maps in this work. An *assertion map* (AM) over a linear transition system is a function η which maps every location l of the linear transition system to an assertion $\eta(l)$ over the real-valued variable set X. We say an AM η is inductive if it follows:

- **(Initialization)** $\theta \models \eta(l_0)$
- **(Consecution)** For every transition $\tau = \langle l, l', \rho \rangle$, $\eta(l) \wedge \rho \models \eta(l')$ where $\eta(l)$ is the assertion over X and $\eta(l')$ is the assertion over X'.

It has been established that all the assertions in an inductive AM are invariant. In this work, we focus on the automated synthesis of inductive AM and invariants in disjunctive form.

2.2   Farkas' Lemma and Invariant Generation

Farkas' Lemma [5] is a classical theorem in the theory of linear algebra and provides a sound and complete method for reasoning about systems of real linear inequalities. Many works [6–8,17] have applied the theorem to constraint solving methods for linear invariant generation and implement the integer-valued variable version.

Theorem 1 (Farkas' Lemma). *Consider a linear assertion ϕ over a real-valued variable set $X = \{x_1, \ldots, x_n\}$ as shown in Fig. 1a. When ϕ is satisfiable, it entails a linear inequality ψ as shown in Fig. 1b (i.e.,$\phi \models \psi$) if and only if there exist non-negative real numbers $\lambda_0, \ldots, \lambda_m$ such that it follows the tabular form*

$$\phi : \quad \begin{matrix} a_{11} \cdot x_1 + \cdots + a_{1n} \cdot x_n + b_1 \geq 0 \\ \vdots \qquad \vdots \quad \vdots \\ a_{m1} \cdot x_1 + \cdots + a_{mn} \cdot x_n + b_m \geq 0 \end{matrix}$$

(a) ϕ in Farkas' Lemma

$\psi : c_1 \cdot x_1 + \cdots + c_n \cdot x_n + d \geq 0$

(b) ψ in Farkas' Lemma

$$\begin{array}{c|c} \lambda_0 & \hspace{3cm} 1 \geq 0 \\ \lambda_1 & a_{11} \cdot x_1 + \cdots + a_{1n} \cdot x_n + b_1 \bowtie_1 0 \\ \vdots & \vdots \qquad \vdots \quad \vdots \\ \lambda_m & a_{m1} \cdot x_1 + \cdots + a_{mn} \cdot x_n + b_m \bowtie_m 0 \\ \hline & c_1 \cdot x_1 + \cdots + c_n \cdot x_n + d \geq 0 \leftarrow \psi \\ & -1 \geq 0 \leftarrow false \end{array} \Big\} \phi$$

(c) The Tabular Form for Farkas' Lemma

Fig. 1. The ϕ, ψ and Tabular Form for Farkas' Lemma [6,7]

in Fig. 1c, i.e. $c_j = \sum_{i=1}^{m} \lambda_i \cdot a_{ij}$ for all integer $j \in [1, n]$ and $d = \lambda_0 + \sum_{i=1}^{m} \lambda_i \cdot b_i$. Moreover, ϕ is unsatisfiable if and only if the false inequality $-1 \leq 0$ can be derived from the tabular form.

Existing approaches [6–8,17] apply Farkas' Lemma to linear invariant generation follow the template-based paradigm:

- Represent the inductive linear AM to be solved by a linear template η with unknown coefficients over the input LinTS with variable set $X = \{x_1, \ldots, x_n\}$ at each location l, i.e. $\eta(l) = c_{l1} \cdot x_1 + \cdots + c_{ln} \cdot x_n + d \geq 0$.
- Obtain constraints drawing from the initialization condition $\theta \models \eta(l_0)$ and consecution conditions that for every transition $\tau = \langle l, l', \rho \rangle$, $\eta(l) \wedge \rho \models \eta(l')$.
- Apply Farkas' Lemma to simplify the constraints from initialization and consecution collected in the previous step according to Fig. 1c. The technical details are shown in Fig. 2a. Note that in Fig. 2b, there introduces a fresh non-negative multiplier variable μ to the template $\eta(l)$, and thus the constraint no longer remains linearity.
- Simplify the constraints by choosing appropriate μ values and solve the simplified constraints concretely, and thus obtain the value of the unknown coefficient in the template η.

3 Linear Invariant Generation with Modular Operation

We propose a paradigm of converting modular operation in linear transition systems into equivalent linear expressions through location-splitting techniques. We illustrate our paradigm in the context of transition systems with linear operation and modular operation. With the aid of this method, we can extend the existing constraint solving methods which are based on Farkas' Lemma to modular operation, and thus our work is a good supplement to the current invariant generation methods. Our paradigm can be applied to arbitrary types of modular operation in programs, for example, in the branch conditions, in the update functions, etc. Moreover, the numbers and the structures of the modular operations are not limited, which means there may be multiple modular operations in one program and the modular operation may also be against multiple integers.

$$
\begin{array}{r|l}
\lambda_0 & \qquad\qquad\qquad 1 \geq 0 \\
\lambda_1 & a_{11}x_1+\cdots+\ a_{1n}x_n+\ b_1 \bowtie_1 0 \\
\vdots & \ \ \vdots \qquad\quad \vdots \qquad\ \vdots \\
\lambda_m & a_{m1}x_1+\cdots+a_{mn}x_n+b_m\bowtie_m 0 \\
\hline
& c_{l^*,1}x_1+\cdots+c_{l^*,n}x_n+d_{l^*} \geq 0 \leftarrow \eta(l^*) \\
& \qquad\qquad\qquad\qquad -1 \geq 0 \leftarrow false
\end{array} \Bigg\} \theta
$$

(a) Initialization Tabular

$$
\begin{array}{r|l}
\mu & c_{l,1}x_1+\cdots+\ c_{l,n}x_n \qquad\qquad\qquad\quad +\ d_l \geq 0 \leftarrow \eta(l) \\
\lambda_0 & \qquad\qquad\qquad\qquad\qquad\qquad\qquad 1 \geq 0 \\
\lambda_1 & a_{11}x_1+\cdots+\ a_{1n}x_n+\ a'_{11}x'_1+\cdots+\ a'_{1n}x'_n+\ b_1 \bowtie_1 0 \\
\vdots & \ \ \vdots \qquad\quad \vdots \qquad\ \vdots \qquad\ \vdots \qquad\ \vdots \\
\lambda_m & a_{m1}x_1+\cdots+a_{mn}x_n+a'_{m1}x'_1+\cdots+a'_{mn}x'_n+b_m\bowtie_m 0 \\
\hline
& \qquad\qquad c_{l',1}x'_1+\cdots+c_{l',n}x'_n+d_{l'} \geq 0 \leftarrow \eta(l')' \\
& \qquad\qquad\qquad\qquad\qquad\qquad -1 \geq 0 \leftarrow false
\end{array} \Bigg\} \rho
$$

(b) Consecution Tabular

Fig. 2. Tabular for Initialization and Consecution [6,7]

We first give an overview of our paradigm in Sect. 3.1 through a simple running example. Then, we classify three basic modular operations: Modular Information in Branch Condition in Sect. 3.2, Update Function of modular related variable referring to other variables in Sect. 3.3 and Modular Operation in Update Function in Sect. 3.4. We briefly introduce how to generalize our paradigm in these different basic components in each section respectively. It is worth noting that a general modular transition system may contain any combination of these three components, and these components may have an influence on the calculation of each other. Thus in Sect. 3.5, we mainly introduce the general methods of handling any combination of these three components, i.e. a general transition system with modular and linear operation based on the methods from the previous subsections in detail. We also provide a complex running example for better understanding.

3.1 Overview of Our Paradigm

The nature of our paradigm is to carry modular remainder information in the location through location-splitting techniques and can be summarized as the following three steps.

Step A1. In the first step, for each original location l which is related to the modular operation, split it to $l_0, l_1, \ldots, l_{m-1}$, where m is the number of all possible kinds of remainder results and the subscript of the newly-created locations represent the remainder results.

Step A2. In the second step, for the original transition $\tau = \langle l, l', \rho_\tau \rangle$ that is related to modular operation, i.e. l and l' is the location which are split in Step A1, transform it to the form $\tau = \langle l_i, l'_j, \rho_{\tau ij} \rangle$, where l_i is split from l and l'_j is split from l_j. Adjust the original ρ_τ to $\rho_{\tau ij}$ according to the modular remainder results i and j.

Step A3. There is no change to original X, X' and θ. For l_0, if it is split in Step A1, change it to the corresponding location $l_0 = l_{0j}$ according to the initial modular information and remains no change if l_0 is not split. Also, revise L and $\mathcal{T}$ accordingly by the transformation in Step A1 and Step A2. Build the equivalent LinTS $P = \langle X, X', L, l_0, \theta, \mathcal{T} \rangle$.

```
int x = 0;
int y = 0;
while (x <= 100) {
    if (y%2 == 0) {
        x = x + 2;
        y = y + 1;
    }
    else {
        x = x + 1;
        y = y + 1;
    }
}
```

(a) A Loop with Modular Information

$$X = \{x, y\}, \; L = \{l_0, l_e\},$$
$$\mathcal{T} = \{\tau_1, \tau_2, \tau_3, \tau_4\},$$
$$\theta : x = 0 \wedge y = 0,$$
$$\tau_1 : \langle l_0, l_0, \rho_1 \rangle, \; \tau_2 : \langle l_0, l_0, \rho_2 \rangle,$$
$$\tau_3 : \langle l_0, l_e, \rho_3 \rangle, \; \tau_4 : \langle l_0, l_e, \rho_4 \rangle,$$

$$\rho_1 : \begin{bmatrix} x < 99 \\ y\%2 = 0 \\ x' = x + 2 \\ y' = y + 1 \end{bmatrix}, \rho_2 : \begin{bmatrix} x < 100 \\ y\%2 = 1 \\ x' = x + 1 \\ y' = y + 1 \end{bmatrix}$$

$$\rho_3 : \begin{bmatrix} x = 100 \\ y\%2 = 1 \\ x' = x + 1 \\ y' = y + 1 \end{bmatrix}, \rho_4 : \begin{bmatrix} 99 \le x \le 100 \\ y\%2 = 0 \\ x' = x + 2 \\ y' = y + 1 \end{bmatrix}$$

(b) The Corresponding Linear Transition System P

Fig. 3. A while loop with modular information and its corresponding linear transition system

To exhibit our idea, we first show a simple program in Fig. 3a and the corresponding linear transition system in Fig. 3b. Then, we present the process of transforming this transition system to an equivalent pure LinTS with our paradigm. The details are shown in Example 1 and Example 2.

Example 1. Consider a while loop with modular operation in Fig. 3a with integer-valued variables x, y. Before the loop, the values of the variables x, y are both initialized to 0. In each loop iteration, if y is odd, the execution passes through the if-branch and the value of x is incremented by one, and if y is even, the execution passes through the else-branch and then the value of x is incremented by two. In both cases, the value of y is incremented by one.   □

In Fig. 3b, we present a linear transition system of the program in Fig. 3a. The details are listed below.

- We have the set of integer variables $X = \{x, y\}$ and the initialization condition θ corresponds to the initialization of the variables before the while loop in Fig. 3a.
- We have two locations. The location l_0 represents the start of the execution in the loop body and l_e is the termination location after the whole execution of the while loop. The initial location is l_0.
- We have four transitions $\tau_1, \ldots, \tau_4$. The transition τ_1 specifies that current loop iteration passes through the **if**-branch, for which the guard condition ρ is the conjunction of $x < 100$ (which specifies the condition for the values of variables at the start of the current loop iteration derived from the loop guard and the similar condition derived for the values at the start of the next loop iteration) and $y\%2 = 0$ (which specifies the condition for the pass into the **if**-branch). The transition τ_2 can be derived by similar logic to the transition τ_1. τ_3 and τ_4 specifies two possible transition that from the loop iteration to the exit of the loop, which means that x satisfied the loop guard $x \leq 100$, while x' not and the execution will jump out of the loop and reach the exit location l_e.

$X = \{x, y\}$, $L = \{l_{00}, l_{01}, l_e\}$, $\mathcal{T} = \{\tau_1, \tau_2, \tau_3, \tau_4\}$, $\theta : x = 0 \wedge y = 0$,
$\tau_1 : \langle l_{00}, l_{01}, \rho_1 \rangle$, $\tau_2 : \langle l_{01}, l_{00}, \rho_2 \rangle$, $\tau_3 : \langle l_{01}, l_e, \rho_3 \rangle$, $\tau_4 : \langle l_{00}, l_e, \rho_4 \rangle$,

$$\rho_1 : \begin{bmatrix} x < 99 \\ x' = x+2 \\ y' = y+1 \end{bmatrix}, \rho_2 : \begin{bmatrix} x < 100 \\ x' = x+1 \\ y' = y+1 \end{bmatrix} \rho_3 : \begin{bmatrix} x = 100 \\ x' = x+1 \\ y' = y+1 \end{bmatrix}, \rho_4 : \begin{bmatrix} 99 \leq x \leq 100 \\ x' = x+2 \\ y' = y+1 \end{bmatrix}$$

Fig. 4. Equivalent Transformed LinTS to Fig. 3b

Example 2. Consider the linear transition system in Fig. 3b, follow the paradigm and we can transform it to the equivalent pure LinTS in Fig. 4. The specific process is as follows. First split the location l_0 to l_{00} and l_{01}, which represent the value of y in the current state is an even integer and an odd integer respectively (**Step A1**). Then, transform the original transition $\tau = \langle l, l', \rho \rangle$ that refers to the l_0. All the transition refer to the l_0 and the current location can be directly confirmed by the guard condition in each transition. For example, the current-state of τ_1 is l_{00} while the current-state of τ_2 is l_{01}. For τ_3 and τ_4, the next-state location is l_e and they do not need extra analysis since l_e is not split. For τ_1 and τ_2, the next-state location needs to be inferred through the update of variable y. For τ_1, $y' = y+1$ and the original remainder result $y \bmod 2 == 0$, we can deduce

$$y' \bmod 2 = (y \bmod 2 + 1 \bmod 2) \bmod 2 = 1,$$

and thus the next-state location of τ_1 is l_{01}. Similarly, the next-state location of τ_2 is l_{00}. Finally revise the guard condition for each transition τ and we can get the equivalent transition relations $\tau_1, \ldots, \tau_4$ (**Step A2**). Revise L and $\mathcal{T}$ according to Step A1 and Step A2, and we can get the equivalent transformed LinTS in Fig. 4 (**Step A3**).

3.2 Multiple Modular Information in Branch Condition

In this section, we introduce our method in the aspect of handling multiple modular information in the branch condition. There are two kinds of structure of branch conditions: parallel structure and nested structure in Fig. 5a and Fig. 6a respectively.

```
int y = 0;
for (int i = 0; i < 1000; i++){
    if (y%3 == 0){
        y = y + 3;
    }
    if (y%6 != 0){
        y = y - 1;
    }
    if (y%3 != 2){
        y = y + 2;
    }
}
```

(a) Parallel Structure

```
int y = 0;
for (int i = 0; i < 1000; i++){
    if (y%6 == 0){
        y = y + 2;
    }
    elif (y%3 == 0){
        y = y + 5;
    }
    else{
        y = y + 1;
    }
}
```

(b) Parallel Exclusive Structure

Fig. 5. A parallel loop with modular information and its equivalent transformed parallel exclusive structure

For both these two structure, we propose a universal solution to them. We notice that we can transform the nested structure to the parallel exclusive version by stretching the inner nested condition out and compounding it with the outer branch condition. For example, we can transform the nested structure in Fig. 6a to Fig. 6b. Further, we can combine the parallel conditions and corresponding update function to let every branch be mutually exclusive, and thus reduce the location and the step of the execution path. For example, we can transform the parallel structure in Fig. 5a to the parallel mutually exclusive structure Fig. 5b. Then, we propose the method of handling multiple modular information in the parallel mutually exclusive structure. There are two cases: (1) For each variable there is modular information against only one positive integer and modular information may refer to multiple variables. (2) For each variable, there may be modular information that against multiple positive integers, such as Fig. 5b. For the first case, each modular information is individual as it refers to different variables, and thus we can solve it by the following procedure

– Split the locations to $l_{r_1,r_2,...}$, where $r_1, r_2, \cdots$ are the remainder results for each piece of modular information I_i against positive integer m_i, and r_i ranges from 0 to $m_i - 1$. As a result, the number of split locations for each modular information branch is $\prod_{i=1}^{k} m_i$, where k is the total amount of the modular information.

- For each transition $\tau = \langle l, l', \rho \rangle$ whose location l is related to modular information branches, we establish a new series of $\tau' = \langle l_{r_1,r_2,\cdots}, l'_{r'_1,r'_2,\cdots}, \rho' \rangle$ where
ρ' is the update function in the execution path that the current remainder
result $r_1, r_2, \cdots$ corresponds to. Then, we can calculate $r'_1, r'_2, \cdots$ similar to
the example in the Sect. 3.1.
- Build the equivalent LinTS $P = \langle X, X', L, l_0, \theta, \mathcal{T} \rangle$.

For the second case, it is more complicated as multiple modular information
for one variable may not be independent. We can also solve this problem in the
manner of the first type that splits each original location l using the subscript r_i
and r_j to represent the remainder result of this variable against positive integer
m_i and m_j. However, when the greatest common divisor of m_i and m_j is not
equal to one, there exist redundant locations. We propose that for the variable
that has multiple modular information, we can use the least common multiple
of all the modular positive integer related to this variable as the overall modular constant integer and use the corresponding remainder result as part of the
subscript to carry all the modular information related to this variable. Then, we
can reuse the methods for type 1 to handle this complicated type.

```
int a = b = 0;
for (int i = 0; i < 1000; i++){
    if (a%5 != 0){
        a = a + 2;                     int a = b = 0;
        if (b%3 != 0){                 for (int i = 0; i < 1000; i++){
            b = b + 2;                     if (a%5 != 0 && b%3 != 0){
        }                                      a = a + 2;
        else{                                  b = b + 2;
            b = b + 1;                     elif (a%5 != 0 && b%3 == 0){
        }                                      a = a + 2;
    }                                          b = b + 1;
    else{                                  }
        a = a + 1;                         elif (a%5 == 0 && b%3 != 0){
        if (b%3 != 0){                         a = a + 1;
            b = b + 2;                         b = b + 2;
        }                                  }
        else{                              else{
            b = b + 1;                         a = a + 1;
        }                                      b = b + 1;
    }                                      }
}                                      }
```

(a) Nested Structure   (b) Transformed Parallel Structure

Fig. 6. A nested loop with modular information and its corresponding parallel mutually
exclusive structure

3.3 Update Related to Other Variables

We define a variable x_m is modular related if its modular remainder is used in at least one branch condition. In this subsection, we mainly focus on the update function of the modular-related variables that are related to other variables. That is to say, the transition relation of the modular-related variable x_m will refer to multiple variables and some constants, i.e. in the form $x'_m = a_1x_1 + a_2x_2 + \cdots + a_nx_n + c$. In this case, we not only need to concern about x_m as in Sect. 3.2, but also keep track of the modular remainder of $x_1, x_2, \ldots$. An example is shown in Fig. 7a. For this case, our method can be presented as the following high-level description:

```
int y = 0;
for (int i = 1; i < 1000; i++){
    if (y%2 == 0){
        y = y + i + 1;
    }
    else{
        y = y + i + 3;
    }
}
```

(a) Update related to other variable(s)

```
int y = 0;
for (int i = 0; i < 1000; i++){
    y = y + (i%3) + (i%5) + 1;
}
```

(b) Modular Operation: Type 2

```
int y = b = 0;
for (int i = 0; i < 1000; i++){
    y = y + (b + i)%3 + 1;
    b = (y + i)%3 + 1;
}
```

(c) Modular Operation: Type 3

Fig. 7. Examples of Modular Expressions

- Find all the variables related to the modular information, i.e. we need to find the modular-related variable set whose each element will influence the value of x_m as well as the modular remainder x_m mod m. We can find these variables in a Breadth First Search(BFS) manner. First, we find the variables that directly influence the value of x_m by scanning all the update equations of $x'_m = a_{m1}x_1 + a_{m2}x_2 + \cdots + a_{mn}x_n + c$ and add all the variables whose coefficients are not equal to 0 in these equations to the modular-related set. Then, for all the newly-added element x_i in the modular-related set, find the variables that indirectly influence the value of x_m by scanning all the update equations of $x'_i = a_{i1}x_1 + a_{i2}x_2 + \cdots + a_{in}x_n + c$, and add all the variables whose coefficients are not equal to 0 in these equations to the modular-related set. Repeat this procedure to find all the indirect modular-related variables and terminate when there is no newly added element to the modular-related variables.

– Split the number of locations that are related to the modular information to $\prod_{i=1}^{n} m \mathbb{I}\{x_i$ is in the modular-related set$\}$, where $\mathbb{I}\{x_i$ is in the modular-related set $\}$ is an indicator function and equals to 0 when x_i is not in the modular-related set and equals to 1 when x_i is in the modular-related set, i.e. we need to split the number of locations to m^k different locations $l_j r_1 r_2 \cdots$ where $k \leq n$ is the size of the modular-related set, j is the current location index in the original system and $r_1, r_2, \cdots$ is the modular remainder of the variables in the modular-related set. For each variable, there are m possible results $0 \rightarrow m - 1$, and thus the total state of the current location is m^k and every location $l_j r_1 r_2 \cdots$ corresponds to a particular remainder result list of current variable value.

– Analyze the transition $\tau = \langle l, l', \rho \rangle$. For every possible current state location $l_{r_1, r_2, \cdots}$, calculate and obtain the remainder results of the next-state variable through the analysis of the following equation

$$x'_m \bmod m = (a_1 x_1 \bmod m + \cdots + a_n x_n \bmod m + c) \bmod m$$

we can directly obtain the remainder result of x_m and all the variable in the modular-related set by substituting $x_i \bmod m$ with the remainder results $r_1, r_2, \cdots$, and thus we can transform the original transition τ to a series of $\tau' = \langle l_{r_1, r_2, \cdots}, l'_{r'_1, r'_2, \cdots}, \rho \rangle$, where $r'_1, r'_2, \cdots$ are the remainder results of x_m and all the variable in the modular-related set.

– Build the equivalent LinTS $P = \langle X, X', L, l_0, \theta, \mathcal{T} \rangle$.

3.4 Modular Operation in Update Function

For the update of variables in the transition function, there are three types:

– **Type 1.** The modular operations only apply to constant
– **Type 2.** The modular operations apply to one or multiple variables, and are against one or multiple positive integers
– **Type 3.** The modular operations apply to compound expressions

For the first type, we can directly substitute this constant modular operation with its constant result, and thus we remove the modular operation. For the second type, for example, in Fig. 7b, we can solve it similar to the way in Sect. 3.3 that maintain the modular reminders of each modular related and indirect modular related variables by label-splitting technique. The method can be summarized as follows and the details can refer to Sect. 3.3.

– For each modular constant integer, establish the modular-related set and add all the variables related to it in a BFS manner.
– Split current state location l to $l_{r_1, r_2, \cdots}$ where $r_1, r_2, \cdots$ are the remainder results of the variables in the modular-related set for each corresponding modular constant integer in sequence, and thus different location subscripts indicates different corresponding remainder result of the variables in all the modular-related set.

– Establish a series of new transitions $\tau = \langle l_{r_1,r_2,...}, l'_{r'_1,r'_2,...}, \rho' \rangle$ from the original transition $\tau = \langle l, l', \rho \rangle$. Substitute the modular expression in ρ according to the subscript of current state location $l_{r_1,r_2,...}$ and thus obtain ρ in linear form. Analyze the corresponding next state subscript $r'_1, r'_2, \cdots$ through the transition function and the subscript $r_1, r_2, \cdots$ of the current state location.
– Build the equivalent LinTS $P = \langle X, X', L, l_0, \theta, \mathcal{T} \rangle$.

For the third type, as in the example in Fig. 7c, we can transform the compound operation in the following equation: $(a_1 x_1 + \cdots + a_n x_n) \bmod m = (a_1 x_1 \bmod m + \cdots + a_n x_n \bmod m) \bmod m$. Then we can first use the method of type 2 to eliminate the inner modular operation with constant and then we can use the method of type 1 to eliminate the outer modular operation.

3.5   General Modular Transition System

Having the basis of the above method for every individual components, we now introduce the method of combining all these cases together and can be applied to general modular transition system.

– First, if there is multiple modular information, transform it into a parallel mutually exclusive structure. If there exist modular operations applying to constant, calculate and substitute it with constant.
– Establish the modular-related set for each modular constant integer. First, add the directly related variable to these sets, namely the variables in modular expression in the system, including first the assignment statement and then the judgment statement. Then, add all the indirectly related variables to these sets by searching the assignment statement of the newly added element of these sets in the transition relation in a BFS manner.
– Split the locations to $l_{r_1,r_2,...}$, where $r_1, r_2, \cdots$ are the remainder results for each variable in at least one modular related set, and r_i ranges from 0 to $m_i - 1$, where m_i equals to the modular constant integer if the variable is only in one modular related set and m_i equals to least common multiple of all the modular constant integer of the modular set this variable in. As a result, the number of split locations for each modular information branch is $\prod_{i=1}^{k} m_i$, where k is the total amount of the variable that has relation to modular information.
– For each transition $\tau = \langle l, l', \rho \rangle$ whose current state location l is related to modular information, we establish a new series of $\tau' = \langle l_{r_1,r_2,...}, l'_{r'_1,r'_2,...}, \rho' \rangle$ where ρ' is the update function in the execution streams where the current remainder result $r_1, r_2, \cdots$ corresponds to. If there are modular operations in ρ', we utilize the subscript $r_1, r_2, \cdots$ which carries all the modular information to substitute the modular expression in the ρ' correspondingly. Finally, we utilize the subscript $r_1, r_2, \cdots$ to calculate the corresponding next state remainder result $r'_1, r'_2, \cdots$.
– Build the equivalent LinTS $P = \langle X, X', L, l_0, \theta, \mathcal{T} \rangle$.

14   Y. Li et al.

```
int i = y = b = 0;
while (i <= 1000){
    if (y%2 == 0){
        y = y + b + i%4 + 1;
        b = b + i%3 + 1;
        i = i + 1
    }
    else{
        y = y + b + i%3 + 1;
        b = b + i%4 + 1;
        i = i + 1
    }
}
```

$X = \{i, y, b\}$, $L = \{l_0, l_e\}$,
$\mathcal{T} = \{\tau_1, \tau_2, \tau_3, \tau_4\}$,
$\theta : y = 0 \wedge b = 0 \wedge i = 0$,
$\tau_1 : \langle l_0, l_0, \rho_1 \rangle$, $\tau_2 : \langle l_0, l_0, \rho_2 \rangle$,
$\tau_3 : \langle l_0, l_e, \rho_3 \rangle$, $\tau_4 : \langle l_0, l_e, \rho_4 \rangle$,

$$\rho_1 : \begin{bmatrix} i < 1000 \\ y\%2 == 0 \\ y' = y + b + i\%4 + 1 \\ b' = b + i\%3 + 1 \\ i' = i + 1 \end{bmatrix}, \rho_2 : \begin{bmatrix} i < 1000 \\ y\%2 == 1 \\ y' = y + b + i\%3 + 1 \\ b' = b + i\%4 + 1 \\ i' = i + 1 \end{bmatrix}$$

$$\rho_3 : \begin{bmatrix} i == 1000 \\ y\%2 == 1 \\ y' = y + b + i\%3 + 1 \\ b' = b + i\%4 + 1 \\ i' = i + 1 \end{bmatrix}, \rho_4 : \begin{bmatrix} i == 1000 \\ y\%2 = 0 \\ y' = y + b + i\%4 + 1 \\ b' = b + i\%3 + 1 \\ i' = i + 1 \end{bmatrix}$$

(a) An Example of General Modular System

(b) The Corresponding Linear Transition System P

Fig. 8. Running example of our method

Then, we can utilize this equivalent pure LinTS P and linear invariant generation methods off the shelf and obtain linear invariants. We denote ϕ_j as the invariant at location l_j. To calculate the invariant ϕ at location l in the original LinTS, we need to merge invariant ϕ_j of each location l_j which is split from location l, i.e. $\phi = \phi_0 \vee \phi_1 \vee \cdots \vee \phi_{m-1}$.

In Fig. 8, we present a program and its corresponding linear transition system as a running example of our methods. The procedures of our methods are listed below. Following our methods, we first check the structure of the program and find it already in the parallel exclusive version and build the corresponding LinTS in Fig. 8b. First consider the modular operation in update function and we establish modular 3 and modular 4 set and add i to it. Then, we consider the modular information and establish a modular 2 set. We first add the directly related value y to it and then add b to it. It is worth noting that since we have already added i to the modular 4 and 3 set, the value $i \bmod 4$ and the value $i \bmod 3$ is constant through the information the location will carry, and thus we no longer need to add i to the modular 2 set.

Then, split the location l_0 to l_{r_1, r_2, r_3, r_4}, where r_1 represents the results of $i \bmod 3$, r_2 represents the results of $i \bmod 4$ and r_3 represents the results of $y \bmod 2$ and r_4 represents the results of $b \bmod 2$.

After that, we can modify the original transition related to l_0 correspondingly. For our example, all the current-state locations of the original transition are l_0, and thus we need to transform all of the transition. We first replace the current-state location with l_{r_1, r_2, r_3, r_4}, and we can directly get the modular information of $y \bmod 2$ through r_3. As a result, $l_{r_1, r_2, 0, r_4}$ applies to τ_1, τ_4 and $l_{r_1, r_2, 1, r_4}$ applies to τ_2 and τ_3, and we no longer need to contain this guard condition in our transformed transition. For all the transitions, we can first replace the modular operation $i \bmod 3$ and $i \bmod 4$ in the update function with r_1 and r_2, then the update function is transformed to the equivalent linear version. For τ_1 and τ_2, we also need to infer the next-state location, i.e. r'_1, r'_2, r'_3 and r'_4. For r'_1 and r'_2, we infer through

$$i' \bmod c = (i+1) \bmod c = (i \bmod c + 1) \bmod c = (r+1) \bmod c$$

Thus, we replace r with r_1 and r_2 and c with 3 and 4 to get r'_1 and r'_2 respectively. For r'_3, we infer through

$$b' \bmod 2 = (b + i \bmod c + 1) = (b \bmod 2 + r + 1) \bmod 2$$

Thus, we replace r with r_1 and r_2 to get r'_4 for τ_1 and τ_2 respectively. For r'_4, we infer through

$$y' \bmod 2 = (y + b + i \bmod c + 1) \bmod 2 = (r_4 + r_3 + r + 1) \bmod 2$$

Thus, we replace r with r_1 and r_2 to get r'_4 for τ_2 and τ_1 respectively. In this way, we transform all the original transitions to an equivalent linear version. We can also deduce from the first current state location l_{0000} to find all the reachable states to eliminate the redundant location. In this way, we build equivalent LinTS.

4   Experimental Results

4.1   Implementation

We implement our linear invariant generator of generalized modular transition system in C++ referring to the implementation of StInG [3] according to our method in Sect. 3.5. We first transform the input program into LinTS manually. Then, we keep the modular information by splitting the location and revise the transition correspondingly, and thus transform the original generalized modular transition system to equivalent pure LinTS. After that, we follow the StInG [3] and uses PPL 1.2 [2] for polyhedra manipulation (e.g., projection, generation computation, etc.). This method generates invariants by applying invariant-generation with Farkas' Lemma in a constraint solving manner. All the experiments are conducted on an Intel Core i7 (2.00 GHz) machine with 64 GB memory, running Ubuntu 18.04.

4.2   Benchmarks

Current benchmarks lack comprehensive examples of modular programs and thus we establish general benchmarks of programs with modular and linear operations based on extending the modular program examples in Competition on Software Verification [4]. To best test the capabilities of each method, we illustrate ten detailed types of programs with modular and linear information and operation. The description and examples of these ten types are shown in Table 1.

Table 1. Description and Examples of Benchmarks

Type	Description
I	Modular information related to one variable but is against multiple positive integers
II	Modular information related to multiple variables
III	Transition relation of the modular related variable includes other variable(s)
IV	Modular operation applies to individual variable(s)
V	Modular operation applies to compound expression
VI	The combination of the above five types

For Type I, we illustrate three sub-types: (1)these positive integers which modular information against are relatively prime (2) these positive integers which modular information against are in a multiple relationship and (3) other types. For Type IV, we also illustrate three sub-types: (1) Modular operations refer to only one variable and is against one constant modular integer (2) Modular operations refer to one variable and are against multiple positive integers (3) Modular operation refers to multiple variables. We establish examples for all these types and sub-types. Some examples are shown in this paper, and we will publish all the benchmarks.

4.3 Evaluation

We evaluate our methods on the established benchmarks and compare our results with the state-of-the-art verification tool CPAchecker [1]. We use the latest version (2.3.1) of CPAchecker and follow the default configuration.

Table 2. Evaluation Results Under Benchmarks

Example	Our method	Time(s)	#loc	CPAchecker
Example 1	$3 * y \leq 4 * i + 5 \wedge 3 * y \geq 4 * i$	20.56	15	UNKNOWN
Example 2	$y \leq 2 * i \wedge y \geq 2 * i - 1$	<0.01	3	UNKNOWN
Example 3	$y \leq 4 * i \wedge y \geq 4 * i - 2$	<0.01	3	UNKNOWN
Example 4	$3 * a \leq 5 * i \wedge 3 * a \geq 5 * i - 2 \wedge$ $9 * a \leq 10 * b + 5 \wedge 9 * a \geq 10 * b - 6$	0.04	6	UNKNOWN
Example 5	$2 * y \geq 3 * i + 1 \wedge 2 * y \leq 9 * i$	<0.01	4	UNKNOWN
Example 6	$3 * y \leq 10 * i \wedge 3 * y \geq 10 * i - 7$	<0.01	3	UNKNOWN
Example 7	$y \leq 3 * i \wedge y \geq 3 * i - 4$	20.9	15	UNKNOWN
Example 8	$y \leq 2 * i \wedge y \geq 2 * i - 2 \wedge$ $3 * y - 4 * b \leq 0 \wedge 3 * y - 4 * b \geq -8$	0.02	5	UNKNOWN
Example 9	$y \leq 2 * i \wedge y \geq 2 * i - 1 \wedge y == b$	0.04	6	UNKNOWN
Example 10	$6 * b \leq 13 * i \wedge 6 * b \geq 13 * i - 11$	2.64	12	UNKNOWN

We show the content of our evaluation results under the benchmarks in Table 2, where each horizontal block corresponds to one type in Table 1 in sequence. In the table, "Our method" represents the column of the result obtained by our method, "Time" represents the runtime for linear invariant generation of our methods in seconds, "#loc" represents the number of the split locations in the equivalent linear transition system and "CPAchecker" represents the verification verdict of the CPAchecker corresponds to the original system with our generated invariant as the assertion. There are three different verification verdicts CPAchecker may report: "TRUE" or "FALSE" if it can proves the assertion(s) respect to the program is correct or wrong; "UNKNOWN" if it cannot decide the verification task. From Table 2, it can be found that our methods generate meaningful invariants for all of the benchmarks and the runtime has a positive relation to the complexity of the modular information and the operation. This is intuitive as when the modular information or the modular operation gets richer, the number of locations we need to split to represent the modular information gets larger and so does the transition, and then the equivalent linear transition system gets more complex. In addition, we find that the CPAchecker can not obtain the verification results under the default configuration, i.e. with the time limit of 900 s and then output "UNKNOWN". Further, we find the CPAchecker can output "TRUE" when the loop size is small, while the variance of the loop size has nearly no influence on the runtime of our method to generate the invariants, which means our methods find the inherent loop information while CPAchecker is just forcefully unfolding the loop and conduct the calculation.

5   Related Work

There are many representative patterns of invariant generation methods. In this paper, our method can be classified as a constraint solving method.

Constraint Solving. Constraint Solving methods follow the pattern that first initializes an objective invariant template with unknown variables and then calculates the unknown variables from the constraints stretched from the inductive invariant conditions. Various invariant templates have been adopted include polynomial invariants [18–20] and linear invariants [7,21,22]. In this paper, we generate linear invariants automatically over transition systems with modular information while current constraint solving methods mainly focus on the linear transition systems and lack the ability to handle modular information.

Abstract Interpretation. Abstract Interpretation is also a mainstream method for invariant generation [26–28]. The framework of such methods can be summarized as setting up the abstract domain for the objective invariants and calculating the fixed point in this domain. The precision of the invariants these methods generate is not guaranteed for most cases [7] while our methods follow the constraint solving pattern and thus guarantee the precision.

Recurrence Analysis. Recurrence Analysis transforms the invariant generation problem into finding the closed form solution of the corresponding recurrence relation [23–25]. However, the existence of closed form solution is not guaranteed in some cases.

Other Methods. There are other methods for invariant generation such as machine learning [32–35], inference [37–42], etc. However, these methods can provide no theoretical guarantee on the accuracy of the generated invariants and some methods also require large sets of data, which is also costly.

6   Conclusion and Future Work

In this paper, we conduct solid research on the transition systems with modular operations and achieve good results, which can extend current invariant generation methods based on Farkas' Lemma. We propose effective methods to generate linear invariants over transition systems with linear and modular operations. We implement our methods and build the formal benchmarks for such linear transition system. The experimental results demonstrate that our approach outperforms the state of the art verification tool CPAchecker in both the efficiency and the effectiveness. We propose a general way to deal with modular expression and this will lead us to many other various transition systems with modular operation and the cases that when some variable plays the role of modular integer.

Acknowledgments. We thank anonymous reviewers for constructive comments. This work is partially supported by the National Natural Science Foundation of China (NSFC) under Grant No. 61872232 and No. 62172271.

References

1. Beyer, D., Keremoglu, M.E.: CPACHECKER: a tool for configurable software verification. In: Gopalakrishnan, G., Qadeer, S. (eds.) CAV 2011. LNCS, vol. 6806, pp. 184–190. Springer, Heidelberg (2011). https://doi.org/10.1007/978-3-642-22110-1_16

2. Bagnara, R., Ricci, E., Zaffanella, E., Hill, P.M.: Possibly not closed convex polyhedra and the parma polyhedra library. In: Hermenegildo, M.V., Puebla, G. (eds.) SAS 2002. LNCS, vol. 2477, pp. 213–229. Springer, Heidelberg (2002). https://doi.org/10.1007/3-540-45789-5_17

3. StInG. StInG: Stanford Invariant Generator (2006). http://theory.stanford.edu/~srirams/Software/sting.html

4. SV-COMP 2022. Software Verification Competition. https://sv-comp.sosy-lab.org

5. Farkas, J.: A Fourier-féle mechanikai elv alkalmazásai (Hungarian). Math. Természettudományi Értesitö **12**(1894), 457–472 (1894)

6. Colón, M.A., Sankaranarayanan, S., Sipma, H.B.: Linear invariant generation using non-linear constraint solving. In: Hunt, W.A., Somenzi, F. (eds.) CAV 2003. LNCS, vol. 2725, pp. 420–432. Springer, Heidelberg (2003). https://doi.org/10.1007/978-3-540-45069-6_39

7. Sankaranarayanan, S., Sipma, H.B., Manna, Z.: Constraint-based linear-relations analysis. In: Giacobazzi, R. (ed.) SAS 2004. LNCS, vol. 3148, pp. 53–68. Springer, Heidelberg (2004). https://doi.org/10.1007/978-3-540-27864-1_7

8. Liu, H., Fu, H., Yu, Z., Song, J., Li, G.: Scalable linear invariant generation with Farkas' Lemma. Proc. ACM Program. Lang. **6**(OOPSLA2) (2022). https://doi.org/10.1145/3563295

9. Manna, Z., Pnueli, A.: Temporal Verification of Reactive Systems - Safety. Springer, New York (1995). https://doi.org/10.1007/978-1-4612-4222-2

10. Padon, O., McMillan, K.L., Panda, A., Sagiv, M., Shoham, S.: Ivy: safety verification by interactive generalization. In: PLDI, pp. 614–630. ACM (2016). https://doi.org/10.1145/2908080.2908118

11. Albarghouthi, A., Li, Y., Gurfinkel, A., Chechik, M.: UFO: a framework for abstraction- and interpolation-based software verification. In: Madhusudan, P., Seshia, S.A. (eds.) CAV 2012. LNCS, vol. 7358, pp. 672–678. Springer, Heidelberg (2012). https://doi.org/10.1007/978-3-642-31424-7_48

12. Chatterjee, K., Fu, H., Goharshady, A.K.: Non-polynomial worst-case analysis of recursive programs. ACM Trans. Program. Lang. Syst. **41**(4), 20:1–20:52 (2019). https://doi.org/10.1145/3339984

13. Colón, M.A., Sipma, H.B.: Synthesis of linear ranking functions. In: Margaria, T., Yi, W. (eds.) TACAS 2001. LNCS, vol. 2031, pp. 67–81. Springer, Heidelberg (2001). https://doi.org/10.1007/3-540-45319-9_6

14. Bradley, A.R., Manna, Z., Sipma, H.B.: Linear ranking with reachability. In: Etessami, K., Rajamani, S.K. (eds.) CAV 2005. LNCS, vol. 3576, pp. 491–504. Springer, Heidelberg (2005). https://doi.org/10.1007/11513988_48

15. Alias, C., Darte, A., Feautrier, P., Gonnord, L.: Multi-dimensional rankings, program termination, and complexity bounds of flowchart programs. In: Cousot, R., Martel, M. (eds.) SAS 2010. LNCS, vol. 6337, pp. 117–133. Springer, Heidelberg (2010). https://doi.org/10.1007/978-3-642-15769-1_8

16. Podelski, A., Rybalchenko, A.: A complete method for the synthesis of linear ranking functions. In: Steffen, B., Levi, G. (eds.) VMCAI 2004. LNCS, vol. 2937, pp. 239–251. Springer, Heidelberg (2004). https://doi.org/10.1007/978-3-540-24622-0_20

17. Ji, Y., Fu, H., Fang, B., Chen, H.: Affine loop invariant generation via matrix algebra. In: Shoham, S., Vizel, Y. (eds.) CAV 2022. LNCS, vol. 13371, pp. 257–281. Springer, Cham (2022). https://doi.org/10.1007/978-3-031-13185-1_13

18. Kapur, D.: Automatically generating loop invariants using quantifier elimination. In: Deduction and applications. In: Deduction and Applications (Dagstuhl Seminar Proceedings, vol. 05431). Internationales Begegnungs- und Forschungszentrum für Informatik (IBFI), Schloss Dagstuhl, Germany (2005). http://drops.dagstuhl.de/opus/volltexte/2006/511

19. Yang, L., Zhou, C., Zhan, N., Xia, B.: Recent advances in program verification through computer algebra. Frontiers Comput. Sci. China **4**(1), 1–16 (2010). https://doi.org/10.1007/s11704-009-0074-7

20. Chatterjee, K., Fu, H., Goharshady, A.K., Goharshady, E.K.: Polynomial invariant generation for non-deterministic recursive programs. In: PLDI, pp. 672–687. ACM (2020). https://doi.org/10.1145/3385412.3385969

21. de Oliveira, S., Bensalem, S., Prevosto, V.: Synthesizing invariants by solving solvable loops. In: D'Souza, D., Narayan Kumar, K. (eds.) ATVA 2017. LNCS, vol. 10482, pp. 327–343. Springer, Cham (2017). https://doi.org/10.1007/978-3-319-68167-2_22

22. Gupta, A., Rybalchenko, A.: InvGen: an efficient invariant generator. In: Bouajjani, A., Maler, O. (eds.) CAV 2009. LNCS, vol. 5643, pp. 634–640. Springer, Heidelberg (2009). https://doi.org/10.1007/978-3-642-02658-4_48

23. Farzan, A., Kincaid, Z.: Compositional recurrence analysis. In: FMCAD, pp. 57–64. IEEE (2015)

24. Kincaid, Z., Cyphert, J., Breck, J., Reps, T.W.: Non-linear reasoning for invariant synthesis. Proc. ACM Program. Lang. **2**(POPL), pp. 54:1–54:3 (2018). https://doi.org/10.1145/3158142

25. Wang, C., Lin, F.: Solving conditional linear recurrences for program verification: the periodic case. In: OOPSLA. ACM (2023)

26. Cousot, P., Halbwachs, N.: Automatic discovery of linear restraints among variables of a program. In: POPL, pp. 84–96. ACM Press (1978). https://doi.org/10.1145/512760.512770

27. Bagnara, R., Hill, P.M., Ricci, E., Zaffanella, E.: Precise widening operators for convex polyhedra. In: Cousot, R. (ed.) SAS 2003. LNCS, vol. 2694, pp. 337–354. Springer, Heidelberg (2003). https://doi.org/10.1007/3-540-44898-5_19

28. Singh, G., Püschel, M., Vechev, M.: Fast polyhedra abstract domain. In: Proceedings of the 44th ACM SIGPLAN Symposium on Principles of Programming Languages (POPL 2017), pp. 46–59. Association for Computing Machinery, New York (2017). https://doi.org/10.1145/3009837.3009885

29. Xie, X., Chen, B., Liu, Y., Le, W., Li, X.: Proteus: computing disjunctive loop summary via path dependency analysis. In: Proceedings of the 2016 24th ACM SIGSOFT International Symposium on Foundations of Software Engineering (FSE 2016), pp. 61–72. Association for Computing Machinery, New York (2016). https://doi.org/10.1145/2950290.2950340

30. Lin, Y., et al.: Inferring loop invariants for multi-path loops. In: 2021 International Symposium on Theoretical Aspects of Software Engineering (TASE), Shanghai, China, pp. 63–70 (2021). https://doi.org/10.1109/TASE52547.2021.00030

31. Wang, C., Lin, F.: Solving conditional linear recurrences for program verification: the periodic case. Proc. ACM Program. Lang. **7**(OOPSLA1), 28 p. (2023). https://doi.org/10.1145/3586028. Article 76

32. Garg, P., Neider, D., Madhusudan, P., Roth, D.: Learning invariants using decision trees and implication counterexamples. In: POPL, pp. 499–512. ACM (2016). https://doi.org/10.1145/2837614.2837664

33. He, J., Singh, G., Püschel, M., Vechev, M.T.: Learning fast and precise numerical analysis. In: PLDI, pp. 1112–1127. ACM (2020). https://doi.org/10.1145/3385412.3386016

34. Ryan, G., Wong, J., Yao, J., Gu, R., Jana, S.: CLN2INV: learning loop invariants with continuous logic networks. In: 8th International Conference on Learning Representations, ICLR 2020, Addis Ababa, Ethiopia, 26–30 April 2020. OpenReview.net (2020). https://openreview.net/forum?id=HJlfuTEtvB

35. Yao, J., Ryan, G., Wong, J., Jana, S., Gu, R.: Learning nonlinear loop invariants with gated continuous logic networks. In PLDI, pp. 106–120. ACM (2020). https://doi.org/10.1145/3385412.3385986

36. Liu, H., Li, G.: Empirically scalable invariant generation leveraging divide-and-conquer with pruning. In: Chin, W.N., Xu, Z. (eds.) TASE 2024. LNCS, vol. 14777, pp. 324–342. Springer, Cham (2024). https://doi.org/10.1007/978-3-031-64626-3_19

37. Gulwani, S., Srivastava, S., Venkatesan, R.: Constraint-based invariant inference over predicate abstraction. In: Jones, N.D., Müller-Olm, M. (eds.) VMCAI 2009.

LNCS, vol. 5403, pp. 120–135. Springer, Heidelberg (2008). https://doi.org/10.1007/978-3-540-93900-9_13

38. Sharma, R., Aiken, A.: From invariant checking to invariant inference using randomized search. Form Methods Syst. Des. **48**, 235–256 (2016). https://doi.org/10.1007/s10703-016-0248-5

39. McMillan, K.L.: Quantified invariant generation using an interpolating saturation prover. In: Ramakrishnan, C.R., Rehof, J. (eds.) TACAS 2008. LNCS, vol. 4963, pp. 413–427. Springer, Heidelberg (2008). https://doi.org/10.1007/978-3-540-78800-3_31

40. Garg, P., Löding, C., Madhusudan, P., Neider, D.: ICE: a robust framework for learning invariants. In: Biere, A., Bloem, R. (eds.) CAV 2014. LNCS, vol. 8559, pp. 69–87. Springer, Cham (2014). https://doi.org/10.1007/978-3-319-08867-9_5

41. Gan, T., Xia, B., Xue, B., Zhan, N., Dai, L.: Nonlinear Craig interpolant generation. In: Lahiri, S.K., Wang, C. (eds.) CAV 2020. LNCS, vol. 12224, pp. 415–438. Springer, Cham (2020). https://doi.org/10.1007/978-3-030-53288-8_20

42. Dillig, I., Dillig, T., Li, B., McMillan, K.: Inductive invariant generation via abductive inference. In: Proceedings of the 2013 ACM SIGPLAN International Conference on Object Oriented Programming Systems Languages & Applications (OOPSLA 2013), pp. 443–456. Association for Computing Machinery, New York (2013). https://doi.org/10.1145/2509136.2509511

Data-Dependent WAR Analysis for Efficient Task-Based Intermittent Computing

Juxin Niu[1] , Yunlong Yu[2], Wei Zhang[2], and Nan Guan[1(✉)]

[1] City University of Hong Kong, Kowloon, Hong Kong SAR
`juxinniu2-c@my.cityu.edu.hk, nanguan@cityu.edu.hk`
[2] Shandong University, Jinan, China
`202317004@mail.sdu.edu.cn, sduzhangwei@sdu.edu.cn`

Abstract. Energy harvesting systems provide power solutions for Internet-of-Things (IoT) devices, liberating them from battery life constraints. However, unstable power supplies can cause frequent power failures. This leads to the non-progress problem, where the system loses its state and, upon power restoration, is unable to resume unfinished programs, forcing it to start from the beginning. To tackle this issue, task-based Intermittent Computing (ImC) has been proposed. This approach breaks the program into multiple tasks and uses non-volatile memory (NVM) to store the results of completed tasks. When power is restored, the system can resume from the last unfinished task, avoiding the need to restart the entire program. However, a specific type of data, known as write-after-read (WAR) data, can introduce consistency errors during execution. Current approaches prevent these errors by backing up WAR data before task execution, but identifying such data precisely remains a challenge. Runtime detection methods can accurately find WAR data but introduce significant performance overhead. Meanwhile, static analysis techniques tend to be overly conservative, resulting in excessive and unnecessary backups. In this paper, we first examine the limitations of existing methods, then propose a hybrid WAR analysis method. This approach combines static analysis and leverages information during runtime to more accurately identify WAR data, with nearly no increase in run-time overhead. Experimental results indicate that compared to existing methods, our approach can significantly reduce system backup overhead and achieve up to a $9.20\times$ performance improvement.

Keywords: Intermittent Computing · WAR Data · Data Consistency · Static Analysis

1 Introduction

The rapid advancement of tiny IoT devices foresees their numbers surpassing tens of billions in the near future [1]. This growth presents a unique challenge:

T. Bourke et al. (Eds.): SETTA 2024, LNCS 15469, pp. 85–101, 2025.
https://doi.org/10.1007/978-981-96-0602-3_5

how to power such a vast array of devices. Traditional batteries require periodic charging or replacement, posing restrictions on device placement, contributing to environmental pollution, and escalating maintenance costs. Energy harvesting, which draws power from the surrounding environment using various sources such as RFID and solar energy, is a promising alternative [13,21]. However, unpredictable and insufficient harvested energy can lead to frequent system power failures [10], causing a non-progress issue: when a power failure occurs during system operation, the system state, including data stored in registers and RAM, is lost. Even if power is restored, these data cannot be recovered to their pre-failure state. As a result, the system is forced to restart execution from the beginning.

To address this issue, *task-based intermittent computing (ImC)* has been proposed [5,15,17,22]. In this approach, the system breaks down the program into multiple tasks that are interconnected through control flows. The system leverages non-volatile memory (NVM, such as FRAM [8] or Flash) to store certain critical data, referred to as *global* data, ensuring it remains intact at power failures. Once a task is completed, it writes its execution results to the global data. As a result, upon system restart, previously completed tasks do not need to be re-executed. However, if a power failure occurs and interrupts a task that is currently executing, re-executing it might lead to data inconsistency issues. Specifically, if the task involves a write-after-read (WAR) operation on certain global data, and the interruption happens after the write operation has completed, re-execution would result in the read operation accessing the already modified data [16]. To prevent this issue, it is essential to back up all global data involved in WAR operations before executing the task to ensure that the data can be restored to its correct state for re-execution [15]. In the following, we refer to data involved WAR operations as *WAR data*.

Accurately identifying WAR data is crucial yet challenging, particularly when dealing with *data-dependent memory access*, where "data-dependent" refers to memory accesses determined dynamically at runtime based on the values of the data, rather than being statically declared. Examples include array indexing and pointer dereferencing [11]. Currently, there are two primary approaches for managing data-dependent memory access: static analysis-based methods and runtime methods. Static analysis-based methods [15,23] utilize data-flow analysis and adopt a conservative strategy to ensure safety. These methods assume that any data-dependent access could potentially access all possible data. Consequently, the entire range of data must be backed up before task execution, resulting in significant unnecessary backup overhead. Runtime methods [17] actively monitor each data read and write operation as the program runs, recording the addresses of accessed data. If a WAR operation on the same address is detected, the relevant data is backed up. While this approach minimizes backup overhead, it incurs considerable runtime overhead for access-intensive program.

We observed that existing static analysis techniques still rely on coarse-grained methods, resulting in a considerable disparity between the obtained results and the desired precision. Besides, due to the decoupling of static analysis and run-time backing-up in current approaches, the results of static analysis cannot be effectively leveraged to achieve more accurate data management. To tackle these challenges, we first identify two main limitations in existing methods when handling data-dependent access: *over-range* and *false-positive*, and then propose a *data-dependent WAR analysis method*. The hybrid approach builds on existing static analysis methods, introducing a finer-grained static analysis specifically for data-dependent memory access. The results of the static analysis are applied at runtime, allowing for more precise data backups without the need to track every read and write operation. Our experimental results demonstrate performance improvements of up to 9.20×.

The rest of this paper is organized as follows: Sect. 2 provides background knowledge and related work on task-based intermittent computing. Section 3 first identifies and discusses the two primary limitations of existing methods, then explains the motivation behind our proposed method, with an illustration using motivating example. Section 4 offers a formal description of our methodology. Section 5 includes a discussion on the proposed method and its limitations. Finally, Sect. 6 presents the evaluation results.

2 Background and Related Work

2.1 Task-Based ImC and Data Inconsistency Issue

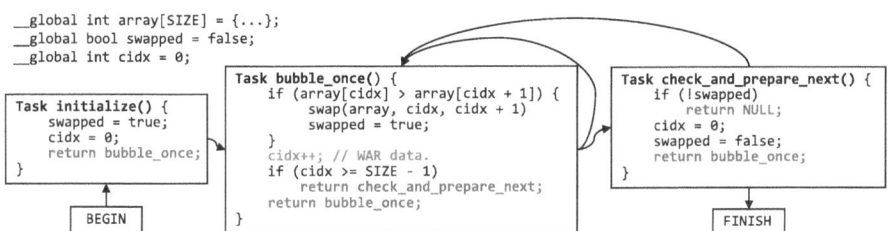

Fig. 1. An illustration of task-based intermittent computing method.

The energy harvesting system draws power from environmental sources like solar, tidal, and wind energy [13,21]. However, the inherent unpredictability of these environmental conditions often leads to power failures, making it difficult to provide a continuous power supply long enough to ensure the complete execution of a program. Consequently, the system operates *intermittently*, functioning normally when sufficient energy is available and entering a sleep mode during power shortages. However, when the execution is interrupted by power failures, data stored in registers and RAM is lost, therefore the system state is erased. Thus, upon power restoration, the system must restart from the beginning, resulting in the issue of *non-progress*.

Task-based intermittent computing offers a solution for ensuring forward progress. In this approach, the program is divided into multiple segments statically, with each segment referred to as a *task*. These tasks are connected through control flows, forming a task graph. As shown in Fig. 1 with the example of the bubble-sort algorithm, the task check_and_prepare_next manages the array scan, while each round of comparison and swapping is handled by the task bubble_once. The control flow between these two tasks forms the loop of the algorithm. Since each task is designed to be small enough, the system can ensure that each task completes within a single cycle of power supply. To prevent state loss, certain data is declared as *global data*. This global data is stored in non-volatile memory (NVM), ensuring its value are not lost after power failures. After a task is executed, its results are written into the global data. As illustrated in the bubble_once task in Fig. 1, the swapping of two elements is directly written into the variable array. As a result, these already completed tasks do not need to be re-executed after power failures. Therefore, with each power supply cycle, the system can guarantee some forward progress until the entire program is successfully completed.

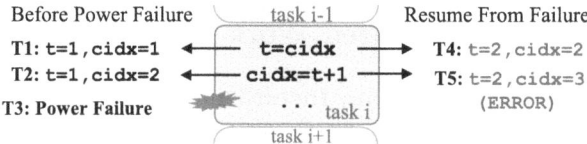

Fig. 2. An illustration of the WAR problem.

However, Task-based methods encounter **data inconsistency issues** when write-after-read (WAR) operations are performed on global data. As illustrated by the task bubble_once in Fig. 1, we highlight that the variable cidx falls into a WAR dependency. We will use this example to explain the inconsistency in more detail. The self-increment operation shown in the code can be viewed as two steps, as illustrated in Fig. 2: first, reading the value of cidx, and then assigning its updated value. Consider a situation where, before the task is executed, the value of cidx is set to 1. At time T1, both cidx and t are 1. As execution progresses, cidx is incremented to 2 at T2. If a power failure occurs at T3 and the program subsequently resumes execution, it reads the value of cidx as 2 at T4. At T5, the value of cidx is assigned to 3, which is incorrect and may lead to an erroneous system output. This inconsistency arises because cidx is first read and then written, indicating it is subject to a WAR dependency. Here, we refer to data that falls into write-after-read dependencies as WAR data. To ensure consistent execution, the system should detect the WAR data for each task and back it up before execution. This way, if a task is interrupted during execution, the system can restore the WAR data to its previous state using the backup before re-executing the task.

2.2   Related Work on Task-Based ImC

Starting with Mementos [18], existing work began incorporating checkpointing to back up system states, ensuring forward progress in execution. Task-based methods [5,7,9,14,15,20] simplifies the design and implementation of intermittent computing systems by dividing the program into atomic sub-tasks and only placing checkpoints between tasks. Modern chips, such as TI's MSP430 development board [19], come equipped with advanced NVMs like FRAM [8]. These NVMs offer RAM-like speed, durability, and low energy consumption. As a result, data can be directly stored and accessed in these memories, enabling persistence with almost no additional overhead [16]. DINO [16] firstly highlighted the consistency issue in this case when performing WAR operations in NVM, and pointed out that the system must back up all WAR data at each checkpoint. In energy-sensitive ImC environments, the amount of backup data directly affects execution efficiency [22]. Therefore, the challenge lies in minimizing the amount of backup data while ensuring that no WAR data is missed.

Methods for identifying WAR data can be classified into static analysis-based and runtime methods. For static analysis-based methods, LATICS [15] applies reachability analysis on the control flow graph to identify all potential WAR dependencies in the tasks. InK [20] implements a dual-buffer mechanism and utilizes pointers to achieve efficient atomic commits. Chain [5] introduces the concept of channels, allowing programmers to explicitly define how WAR data is transferred between tasks. The system automatically ensures atomicity for these data transfers. However, since static analysis-based methods require all WAR data to be identified at compile time, they must back up the entire possible data range for data-dependent accesses. Runtime methods check for WAR dependencies during execution and only back up the precise data when a dependency is detected. For instance, Alpaca [17] uses a version array for each array data, tracking read and write operations at each position to identify WAR dependencies and perform precise backups. However, for memory-intensive tasks, this approach can result in significant runtime overhead. Based on the discussions, a straightforward idea is to combine static analysis-based methods with runtime methods to propose a hybrid approach. To the best of our knowledge, no existing work has yet explored the potential of such an approach.

3   Challenges and Motivation

In this section, we first demonstrate the difficulties that current static analysis-based methods. Building on these observations, the insights that inspire our proposed method are then presented.

Figure 3 presents three tasks as our motivating examples. Each task incorporates indexed array accesses aimed at three different arrays, namely A, B, and C. Considering that for all three arrays, a write access is found subsequent to a read access, current methods classify them as WAR data. We use the notation L2 to signify the loop in TASK2, and L31 and L32 to denote different levels of the nested loop in TASK3.

```
1    __global int sel, hp, p, A[1024];
2    void TASK1() {
3        if (sel == 0)          hp = p;
4        else if (sel == 1)     hp = 2 * p + 1;
5        else if (sel == 2)     hp = 2 * p + 2;
6        else                   hp = 0;
7        A[hp] += 2;
8    }
9
10   __global int beg, B[1000];
11   void TASK2() {
12       for (int i = beg; i <= beg + 100; ++i) // L2
13           B[i]++;
14   }
15
16   __global int rw, cl, C[50][50];
17   void TASK3() {
18       for (int i = 1; i <= rw; ++i) // L31
19           for (int j = 1; j <= cl; ++j) // L32
20               C[i][j] = C[i - 1][j] + C[i][j - 1];
21   }
```

Fig. 3. The motivating example.

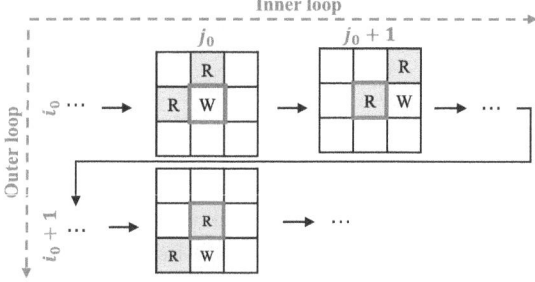

Fig. 4. An illustration of the false-positive issue.

Static analysis-based methods lack the ability to accurately determine which data should be backed up in the presence of data-dependent memory accesses. This uncertainty arises because the static analysis-based method requires that all checkpoints be determined at compile time, but the specific data accessed depends on variables that can only be known during run-time. For instance, consider TASK1 from Fig. 3. Here, the location of the accessed element is based on the value of the index hp, which could potentially have four different values. However, these values are dependent on the run-time values of p and sel, which are inaccessible statically. Array accesses in TASK2 and TASK3 have similar situations. Due to this data dependency, even though it is clear that only a tiny portion of the data may be accessed, the system still has to back up the entire three arrays for safety reasons, leading to considerable energy wastage. We further demonstrate that pessimism primarily manifests in two ways: issues of *over-range* and *false-positive*:

– The **over-range issue** directly arises when the system cannot precisely determine the range of accessed data. As a result, it conservatively assumes that all elements could potentially be accessed to ensure that the actual WAR data is always included. In our motivating example, TASK1 and TASK2 are representative of this issue.

– The **false-positive issue** arises when the system incorrectly identifies data as WAR data. We illustrate this issue with TASK3. Consider a single element in array C. It has one write and two read accesses that occur in different loop iterations, as shown in the line 20 of Fig. 4. Each 3×3 grid in the figure symbolizes the elements of array C accessed in one iteration. We focus on the access pattern of the center element (outlined in red). The directional arrows demonstrate the iterative process. From the figure, the write access always **before** the read access, indicating that the data is not WAR data.

However, there are already static analysis methods that can capture the aforementioned information during the static phase. Therefore, a straightforward idea is whether it is possible to combine static analysis with runtime backup, applying the results of static analysis to runtime backup, in order to further improve the precision of backup without increasing runtime overhead. We find that when a program runs to a certain checkpoint, all the global variables involved in the task are known. Thus, in this paper, we deploy a parameterized WAR analysis method, representing all WAR data using global variables as parameters, and calculate the locations of these WAR data at run-time and then perform accurate backups. Taking TASK2 as an example, at the checkpoint, we can directly obtain the value of the variable beg, thus accurately determining the boundaries of the array access from B[beg] to B[beg+100]. This insight leads us to propose a **data-dependent WAR analysis**, a *hybrid* approach that leverages both static analysis methods and system run-time information. With almost negligible runtime overhead, it accurately locates the range of data-dependent WAR data.

4 Methodology

In this section, we provide details of our proposed data-dependent WAR analysis. Our method is outlined as follows, consisting of two main components: *static analysis* and *runtime dynamic backup*. During the static analysis phase, we first identify data-dependent memory accesses within the program and attempt to represent these access locations as parameterized expressions. Next, in the WAR analysis, these expressions and the values of their parameters are combined to form constraints. By evaluating whether these constraints can be satisfied, we can determine if WAR dependencies will occur at runtime. At runtime, information about the access expressions that constitute WAR dependencies is passed to the tasks. Before a task begins execution, it will dynamically calculate the values of these expressions in real-time and back up the relevant data based on the results.

The structure of the remaining content is as follows: In Sect. 4.1, we present some assumptions of our method and the notation used. Sections 4.2 through Sect. 4.4 detail the static analysis part of our method, and Sect. 4.5 covers the runtime dynamic backup component.

4.1   Assumption and Notation

Our method is performed on the control flow graph (CFG) of a task $\mathcal{T}$, denoted as $\mathcal{G} = (\mathcal{B}, \mathcal{E})$, where $\mathcal{B} = \{bb_i\}$ is the set of basic blocks composed by a set of statements, and $\mathcal{E} = \{e_i\}$ is the set of edges that represent the control flow between blocks. The CFG has a unique *entry* node, bb_{entry}, from which all control flows that lead to the task start their execution. A *path* from bb_s to bb_t is defined as an ordered sequence of blocks $\{bb_s, \cdots, bb_t\}$ where an edge exists between each pair of adjacent blocks.

The illustration of our method uses the C code example shown in Fig. 3, where all data is declared as variables. Therefore, in the following context, the terms "variable" and "data" are interchangeable. Moreover, data-dependent memory accesses appear in the form of array indexing. In the following discussion, we will explain how this method is also applicable to other forms of data-dependent memory access. We use $\mathcal{V} = \{v_i\}$ to represent all non-array variables in the task. These variables can be either global or local. Before a task starts executing, all global variables have initial values that can be obtained. We use v_i^{ini} to denote the initial value of a global variable v_i. For local variables, their initial value is represented as NAA, indicating an unknown value.

Loops are in the task. In the following discussions, we focus solely on *natural loops* [12], which have a single-entry node known as the *header* and a *back-edge* targeting back to the header. Note that all `for`, `while`, and `do-while` loops are natural loops. For a natural loop, whenever the back-edge returns to the header, it signifies the end of one iteration of the loop. A loop counter of a natural loop is used to indicate the sequence number of the current iteration, and is treated as a special global variable. The value of the loop counter is set to NAA when outside the loop. Upon first entering the loop, it is initialized to 0 and increments by 1 with each iteration. In our motivating example, we use lc_2, lc_{31}, and lc_{32} to denote the loop counters of loops L2, L31, and L32, respectively.

4.2   Representing Data-Dependent Memory Access

The locations of WAR data need to be determined prior to task execution for backup. However, only the values of global variables can be accessed at task boundaries, and these global variables may undergo multiple changes during execution. Therefore, in this section, we first obtain an expression to represent each access location using the *initial value* of global variables.

The main idea of the proposed approach is to use a *symbolic execution* algorithm to generate a set of expressions for each access, representing the potential memory locations that might be accessed during runtime. To begin, we consider a scenario where no loops are present in the task and illustrate the symbolic execution process. In the next section, we will address cases where loops are present in the program.

Given a memory access in block bb_t, we start by using a depth-first search (DFS) algorithm to identify all the paths from the entry block bb_{entry} to bb_t. For each path, we utilize a symbolic execution-like approach to maintain a mapping for every global variable, ensuring that its value depends solely on the initial value of the global variables. Otherwise, its value cannot be captured during the backup process. Before scanning any statements, we initialize this mapping as follows:

$$m(v_i) = \begin{cases} v_i^{ini} & \text{if } v_i \text{ is a global variable;} \\ \text{NAA} & \text{if } v_i \text{ is a local variable.} \end{cases} \tag{1}$$

Here, NAA represents an unknown and arbitrary value, while the superscript "ini" denotes the initial value of the variable. While scanning the path, if a statement s assigns a value to v_i, we update the mapping using the following transfer function:

$$m'(v_i) = \text{Transfer}\,(v_i, s) =$$
$$\begin{cases} c_0 + \sum_{k=1}^{|\mathcal{V}|} c_k m(v_k) & \text{if } v_i \text{ is assigned by } s \text{ to } c_0 + \sum_{k=1}^{|\mathcal{V}|} c_k v_k, \\ & \text{where for each } k \in [1, |\mathcal{V}|]\,, \text{ either} \\ & c_k = 0 \text{ or } m(v_k) \neq \text{ NAA}; \\ \text{NAA} & \text{otherwise.} \end{cases} \tag{2}$$

For example, consider two global variables, v_1 and v_2. Suppose the next assignment statement is $v_1 = 3 + 2v_2$, and the current mapping for v_2 is $m(v_2) = 2v_2^{ini} + 2$. To apply the transfer function, we compute $m'(v_1) = 3 + 2 \cdot m(v_2)$. Substituting $m(v_2) = 2v_2^{ini} + 2$ into the equation, we get $m'(v_1) = 3 + 2 \cdot (2v_2^{ini} + 2) = 4v_2^{ini} + 7$.

After performing scanning for all paths, we aggregate the results as a set of expressions to finalize the interpretation process. Note that we only focus on *affine expressions* [12] in the form of $c_0 + \sum_i (c_i v_i^{ini})$, where $\{c_i\}$ are constants. The transfer function in (2) guarantees this affine nature due to the closure property of linear expressions, except for NAA-labeled mappings.

Figure 5 provides the CFG for `TASK1` and a table detailing the outcomes of the symbolic execution process. As observed, there exist four distinct paths from the entry block ① to the access within block ⑧. Each of these paths assigns a unique expression to the variable `hp`, thus generating four possible values that converge at block ⑧ given as follows.

$$\{0, 2 \times p^{ini} + 1, 2 \times p^{ini} + 2, p^{ini}\} \tag{3}$$

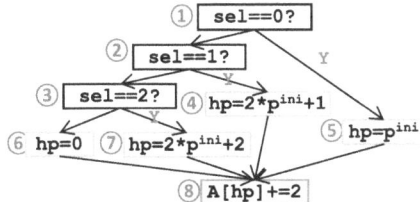

Path	Interpretation
①②③⑥⑧	0
①②③⑦⑧	2*p^ini+2
①②④⑧	2*p^ini+1
①⑤⑧	p^ini

Fig. 5. The CFG of `TASK1` and an illustration of symbolic execution process.

4.3 Handling In-Loop Memory Access

Symbolic execution faces the *path explosion problem* [3] when loops are in the task. To tackle this, our approach introduces an initial *region-based analysis* [2] step. Based on the definition in [12], every natural loop is a *region*, which is a subset of nodes dominated by a single leader node and enclosed by a back edge leading to the leader. By reducing all loops in the task to a single node and hiding the back edges within the reduced nodes, the DFS algorithm can always search out all paths within a finite time. To interpret locations of accesses in loops, variables in loops need to be represented as expressions. We classify each variable within loops based on their assignment patterns throughout loop iterations into the following three categories:

– **Invariant variables** remain constant throughout a loop's execution, and their values are established prior to the loop.
– **Induction variables** change by a fixed value each iteration, and the values are essentially linear expressions with respect to loop counters and invariant variables. In specific, an induction variable v can be formally represented as follows:

$$m(v_i)(t) = E_{\mathrm{ini}}(v_i) + lc \times d \qquad (4)$$

Here, $E_{\mathrm{ini}}(v_i)$ denotes the value before entering the loop, d is the constant change in v_i, and lc is the loop counter. Notably, an induction variable assumes distinct values in different loop iterations, leading to the (4) also dependent on the loop counter. In Fig. 3, variables i in TASK2, i and j in TASK3 are induction variables, with representations as follows:

$$\begin{aligned} \text{TASK2:} \quad & m(\texttt{i})(lc_2) = lc_2 \\ \text{TASK3:} \quad & m(\texttt{i})(lc_{31}) = 1 + lc_{31} \quad m(\texttt{j})(lc_{32}) = 1 + lc_{32} \end{aligned} \qquad (5)$$

– **Unknown Variables** are the variables that do not fit into the above two categories. Their values are unknown or not applicable, also denoted as NAA.

Based on the expressions for variables, we further derive the access addresses for memory accesses. In the motivating example, within TASK2, the index expression for accessing array B is:

$$\texttt{B[i]} : m(i)(lc_2) = lc_2 \qquad (6)$$

In TASK3, accessing array C involves three accesses with expressions:

$$\begin{aligned} \texttt{C[i][j]} &: 50 \times m(\texttt{i})(lc_{31}) + m(\texttt{j})(lc_{32}) = 50 \times lc_{31} + lc_{32} + 51 \\ \texttt{C[i-1][j]} &: 50 \times (m(\texttt{i})(lc_{31}) - 1) + m(\texttt{j})(lc_{32}) = 50 \times lc_{31} + lc_{32} + 1 \\ \texttt{C[i][j-1]} &: 50 \times m(\texttt{i})(lc_{31}) + (m(\texttt{j})(lc_{32}) - 1) = 50 \times lc_{31} + lc_{32} + 50 \end{aligned} \qquad (7)$$

An observation is that memory access in loops often corresponds to accessing a contiguous memory space due to the updating of induction variables through iterations [4]. Thus, we also represent the ranges of loop counters. Taking TASK2 in Fig. 3 as an example. The range of the loop counter lc_2 for loop L2 is $0 \leq lc_2 \leq$ 100. This means that only 100 elements of the array B are modified. It's worth noting that the representation of the loop counter's range aligns with the *loop-counter analysis* problem, which can be tackled using a symbolic execution-like approach [6].

4.4 Identifying WAR Data

In this section, we show the process of WAR analysis utilizing the expressions obtained in the preceding section. A pair of Read and Write accesses results in a WAR dependency only when it satisfies the following conditions [15]:

1. Both accesses potentially target the same data location;
2. The write access occurs after the read access.

The process of verifying the establishment of the first condition, after interpreting accessed locations as expressions, translates to a problem of solvability. Specifically, consider a given pair of read-write memory accesses, represented as (ρ_r, ρ_w). We use $\mathcal{I}(\rho_r)$ and $\mathcal{I}(\rho_w)$ to denote the expression sets for the read and write accesses, respectively. The set of write access expressions that may potentially participate in a WAR is denoted as $\mathcal{I}^*$, where for each expression $\eta_i^* \in \mathcal{I}^*$, there exists a corresponding expression $\eta_j^r \in \mathcal{I}(\rho_r)$ such that the following equation is solvable:

$$\eta_i^* - \eta_j^r = 0 \tag{8}$$

The second condition necessitates a check on the sequence of accesses to the same data location. Outside of loops, this can be determined by examining the CFG for reachability [15]. However, loops bring ambiguity and complexity, as they represent a code segment that could be executed multiple times consecutively, potentially involving different data locations in each execution. An important observation is that, for natural loops, loop counters serve as unique identifiers, allowing for a clear understanding of the execution order for each iteration. To address this issue, we incorporate additional *monotonicity constraints*. These represent the restrictions that must be met when the write access comes after the read one. Given a pair of read-write memory accesses (ρ_r, ρ_w), these operations occur within a loop controlled by a counter t. The specific counter values at the instances of reading and writing are denoted as t^r and t^w, respectively. The second condition is satisfied when the following constraint is met:

$$t^w - t^r \geq 0 \tag{9}$$

For a more detailed introduction, consider the loops in TASK3 as an example. Given (7), as shown in Fig. 3, during each loop iteration, there are two read accesses with the following expressions:

$$\{50 \times t_{31}^r + t_{32}^r + 1, 50 \times t_{31}^r + t_{32}^r + 50\} \tag{10}$$

Additionally, there's one write access with the expression:

$$\{50 \times t_{31}^w + t_{32}^w + 51\} \tag{11}$$

According to (8), WAR dependencies occur if either of the following equations is satisfied:

$$\begin{cases} t_{31}^w = t_{31}^r - 1 \\ t_{32}^w = t_{32}^r \end{cases} \quad \begin{cases} t_{31}^w = t_{31}^r \\ t_{32}^w = t_{32}^r - 1 \end{cases} \tag{12}$$

However, according to (9), a constraint is given to ensure that the write access follows the read access:

$$t_{31}^w \geq t_{31}^r, t_{32}^w \geq t_{32}^r \tag{13}$$

This directly contradicts with (12). Therefore, we can assert that for accesses to array C in TASK3, there is no WAR dependency.

4.5   Inserting Checkpoints and Backups

Once an expression-level WAR dependency is obtained, we backup the WAR data at run-time. Different backup strategies are applied based on various data access patterns. In the case of array accesses outside of loops, multiple expressions might determine memory access at runtime. Therefore, all possible access addresses are provided to the task. Before the task's execution, the values of these expressions can be computed, and the corresponding data is backed up. For example, in TASK1, once the initial value of p is obtained, we calculate the values of the expressions in (3) and back up the four corresponding elements. For array accesses within loops, these typically involve a contiguous memory space. The boundaries of this space can be determined by analyzing the range of the loop counter. Therefore, we calculate the specific boundary values at runtime and back up the entire range. In TASK2, the range of the array B being accessed can be identified by the left boundary at beg^{ini}, with the subsequent 100 contiguous elements included. For other types of WAR dependencies, such as those marked as NAA, we continue to use existing methods based on static analysis for processing.

5   Discussion

5.1   Extending to Other Forms of Data-Dependent Accesses

In our method, each memory access is represented by the expression $c_0 + c_i \times m(v_i)$, where c_0 is a statically known constant, and v_i is a scalar variable in C. This expression captures the index used for array accesses in C, but it can naturally extend to other forms of memory access. For instance, in the case of pointer dereferencing, this expression corresponds to the actual memory address being accessed. Similarly, for memory access instructions in binary code, it represents the address computed based on the values stored in registers. The unifying concept across these various forms of data-dependent memory accesses is the notion of an *offset*. In all cases, the access starts from a statically known base address c_0, and the specific location accessed depends on the value of v_i, which determines the offset relative to c_0. This generalization allows our method to extend beyond array accesses, capturing the behavior of any memory access where the accessed location depends on runtime variables.

5.2   Safety and Effectiveness

In this paper, we propose a static analysis method for more accurately detecting WAR dependencies in memory accesses involving data dependencies. The method is built upon existing static analysis techniques, ensuring the safety of the analysis results, which means that no WAR dependency will go undetected. Specifically, our analysis method represents array accesses in the form of the expression $c_0 + c_i \cdot m(v_i)$. This representation ensures that when these expressions are affine, WAR dependencies can be accurately detected. However, if the variable's value cannot be expressed as an affine expression through analysis, it is labeled as NAA, meaning that the array access may take arbitrary values at runtime. In such cases, the analysis degrades to the coarsest form of WAR dependency detection, assuming that the array access may potentially touch any location, and if a WAR dependency exists, all possible locations are backed up.

While this method guarantees the safety of the analysis results, it introduces some conservativeness. In certain scenarios, our method may back up more data than is actually required. The conservatism primarily stems from our restriction to affine expressions, as existing algorithms (e.g., polyhedral methods [2]) can effectively handle dependencies involving such accesses. However, for more general cases involving non-linear operations, the complexity of dependency analysis and runtime overhead would significantly increase. Therefore, our method does not handle non-affine accesses. That said, we emphasize that if suitable algorithms or techniques emerge in the future, our method can be naturally extended to handle non-affine array accesses.

Therefore, our approach can be viewed as a trade-off between static analysis complexity, runtime overhead, and data backup accuracy. While it cannot achieve absolute accuracy in all scenarios, our method demonstrates sufficient effectiveness in practice. As shown in the upcoming experimental evaluation, our method incurs minimal runtime overhead in common benchmark tests in the ImC field, while achieving high accuracy.

6   Evaluation

In this section, we evaluate the effectiveness of our proposed method. Our system is implemented on an existing task-based system, InK [20], and is deployed on the TI's MSP430FR5994 Launchpad [19] with a 256KB FRAM NVM. We compare our method with two state-of-the-art methods: the run-time method, Alpaca [17], and the static analysis-based method, Latics [15]. To assess the performance of our system, we select benchmark programs from [15,17,22], including Cuckoo

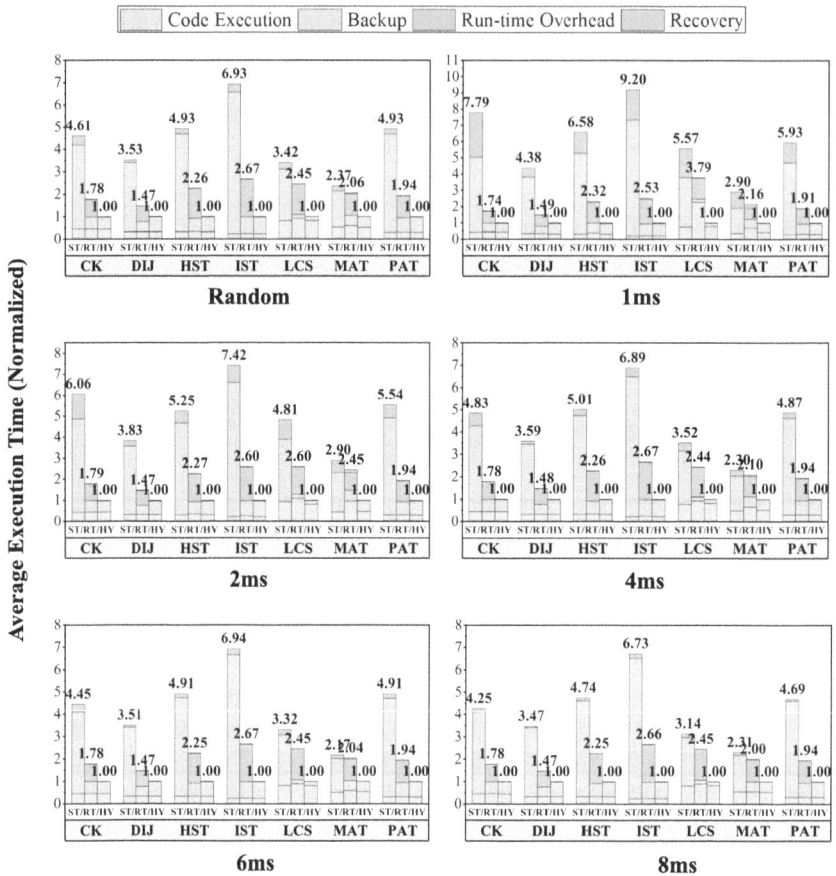

Fig. 6. Time comparison and breakdown under various power traces.

Filter (CK), Dijkstra's Shortest Path (DIJ), Heap Sort (HST), Insertion Sort (IST), Longest Common Substring (LCS), Matrix Multiplication (MAT), and the Patricia Tree (PAT). Our experimental setup is driven by a programmable power supply. This allows us to generate a variety of power traces, thus enabling us to assess our methodology under multiple power conditions. To benchmark the systems under different power supply conditions, we first execute tests with *periodic power traces*. In these tests, power failures happen periodically during system operation based on a predefined period, referred to as the *power cycle*. For our experiments, we chose to work with five distinct power cycles, varying from 1 ms to 8 ms. These settings are consistent with what was used in Latics [15]. Besides, we also performed tests on *random power traces* to mimic real-world scenarios. In these traces, the interval between two successive power failures is randomly selected from the range [1ms, 8 ms]. For each benchmark profiling, we run for 50 times and report the average time.

Table 1. Backup Size For All Tasks Under Various Power Traces (in MBytes)

		CK	DIJ	HST	IST	LCS	MAT	PAT
Random	Static	45.5	113.2	63.1	505.4	2251	56.9	13.5
	Runtime	1.5	4.5	1.8	14.6	3.9	4.1	0.4
	Hybrid	1.6	8.5	2.3	14.7	4.0	4.5	0.5
1 ms	Static	78.7	131.0	79.3	635.7	386.2	96.5	16.8
	Runtime	1.6	4.7	2.0	15.8	4.7	6.8	0.5
	Hybrid	1.6	8.9	2.4	15.9	4.9	6.9	0.5
2 ms	Static	55.9	119.1	68.1	545.0	289.8	72.8	14.8
	Runtime	1.5	4.6	1.8	15.0	4.1	5.2	0.4
	Hybrid	1.6	8.6	2.3	15.5	4.8	6.2	0.5
4 ms	Static	47.3	113.9	63.7	508.6	237.7	58.3	13.5
	Runtime	1.5	4.5	1.8	14.6	4.0	4.2	0.4
	Hybrid	1.6	8.5	2.3	14.8	4.1	4.3	0.5
6 ms	Static	44.5	112.3	62.4	498.5	218.4	54.7	13.3
	Runtime	1.5	4.5	1.8	14.5	3.9	4.0	0.4
	Hybrid	1.6	8.5	2.3	14.6	3.9	4.8	0.5
8 ms	Static	42.1	111.5	61.5	492.7	211.9	53.5	13.0
	runtime	1.5	4.4	1.8	14.4	3.9	3.9	0.4
	Hybrid	1.6	8.5	2.3	14.4	3.9	3.9	0.5

Figure 6 presents a comparison of the average execution times of three systems under different power traces. In the figure, ST, RT, and HY correspond to the static analysis-based method (Latics), the run-time method (Alpaca), and our proposed hybrid method, respectively. It can be observed that our method consistently outperforms the other methods for all traces and benchmarks, achieving a maximum performance improvement of 9.20 times.

We further divide the task execution time into four components: the *code execution* time of the program itself, the time required for *backup*, the *run-time overhead*, and the time for system state *recovery*. These times are depicted in the breakdown shown in Fig. 6. Additionally, in Table 1, we provide the sizes of backup data required for each benchmark when executed under different power traces and methods. While **static analysis-based methods** do not incur runtime overhead, they suffer from extreme backup overhead due to their overly pessimistic WAR analysis results, as evidenced in Table 1. Our method significantly reduces the unnecessary backup. On the other hand, **run-time method** always has the most negligible backup overhead. For some benchmarks, our method may still produce pessimistic WAR data analysis results (for example, the DIJ and HST), resulting in a backup overhead that is higher than that of run-time methods. Despite this, run-time methods carry a non-negligible run-time overhead due to the need for access monitoring. Thus, while our method may not always minimize backup overhead, it still achieves a lower total execution time than run-time methods.

7   Conclusion

In this paper, we propose an effective method for analyzing WAR data in intermittent computing systems. Our research reveals that existing methods encounter significant challenges when dealing with data-dependent memory accesses. These methods either introduce substantial run-time overhead or provide overly pessimistic analysis results, resulting in unnecessary backup costs. To address these issues, we propose a hybrid WAR analysis approach that combines static analysis techniques with the task run-time information to accurately identify WAR data with minimal impact on run-time performance. We implement our approach on TI's MSP series launchpad and conducted comparative evaluations against two state-of-the-art methods, namely Alpaca and Latics. The experimental results demonstrate that our approach yields a maximum performance improvement of up to $9.20\times$.

Acknowledgments. This work is supported by National Natural Science Foundation of China (Grant No. 62302270), Shandong Provincial Natural Science Foundation (Grant No. ZR20220F003).

References

1. IoT-analytics.   https://iot-analytics.com/state-of-the-iot-update-q1-q2-2018-number-of-iot-devices-now-7b/. Accessed September 2020
2. Alfred, V.A., Monica, S.L., Jeffrey, D.U.: Compilers Principles, Techniques & Tools. Pearson Education (2007)
3. Baldoni, R., Coppa, E., D'Elia, D.C., Demetrescu, C., Finocchi, I.: A survey of symbolic execution techniques. ACM Comput. Surv. **51**(3) (2018)
4. Bryant, R.E., David Richard, O., David Richard, O.: Computer Systems: A Programmer's Perspective, vol. 2. Prentice Hall, Upper Saddle River (2003)
5. Colin, A., Lucia, B.: Chain: tasks and channels for reliable intermittent programs. In: Proceedings of the 2016 ACM SIGPLAN International Conference on Object-Oriented Programming, Systems, Languages, and Applications, pp. 514–530 (2016)
6. De Michiel, M., Bonenfant, A., Cassé, H., Sainrat, P.: Static loop bound analysis of C programs based on flow analysis and abstract interpretation. In: 2008 14th IEEE International Conference on Embedded and Real-Time Computing Systems and Applications, pp. 161–166. IEEE (2008)
7. Dunkels, A., Gronvall, B., Voigt, T.: Contiki-a lightweight and flexible operating system for tiny networked sensors. In: 29th Annual IEEE International Conference on Local Computer Networks, pp. 455–462. IEEE (2004)
8. Goh, W., Dannenberg, A., He, J.: MSP430 FRAM technology-how to and best practices. Technical report, Texas Instruments (2014)
9. Hester, J., Storer, K., Sorber, J.: Timely execution on intermittently powered batteryless sensors. In: Proceedings of the 15th ACM Conference on Embedded Network Sensor Systems, pp. 1–13 (2017)

10. Hoseinghorban, A., Bahrami, M.R., Ejlali, A., Abam, M.A.: CHANCE: capacitor charging management scheme in energy harvesting systems. IEEE Trans. Comput.-Aided Design Integr. Circuits Syst. (2020)
11. Huynh, B.K., Ju, L., Roychoudhury, A.: Scope-aware data cache analysis for WCET estimation. In: 2011 17th IEEE RTAS, pp. 203–212. IEEE (2011)
12. Lam, M., Sethi, R., Ullman, J.D., Aho, A.: Compilers: Principles, Techniques, and Tools. Pearson Education (2006)
13. Lee, Y., et al.: A modular 1mm 3 die-stacked sensing platform with optical communication and multi-modal energy harvesting. In: 2012 IEEE International Solid-State Circuits Conference, pp. 402–404. IEEE (2012)
14. Levis, P., et al.: TinyOS: an operating system for sensor networks. Ambient intell. 115–148 (2005)
15. Liu, S., Zhang, W., Lv, M., Chen, Q., Guan, N.: LATICS: a low-overhead adaptive task-based intermittent computing system. IEEE Trans. Comput. Aided Des. Integr. Circuits Syst. 39(11), 3711–3723 (2020)
16. Lucia, B., Ransford, B.: A simpler, safer programming and execution model for intermittent systems. In: PLDI (2015)
17. Maeng, K., Colin, A., Lucia, B.: Alpaca: intermittent execution without checkpoints. Proc. ACM Program. Lang. 1(OOPSLA), 1–30 (2017)
18. Ransford, B., Sorber, J., Fu, K.: Mementos: system support for long-running computation on RFID-scale devices. In: Proceedings of the Sixteenth International Conference on Architectural Support for Programming Languages and Operating Systems, pp. 159–170 (2011)
19. Texas Instruments: MSP430FR58xx, MSP430FR59xx, and MSP430FR6xx Family User's Guide (Rev. P) (2020)
20. Yildirim, K.S., Majid, A.Y., Patoukas, D., Schaper, K., Pawelczak, P., Hester, J.D.: InK: reactive kernel for tiny batteryless sensors. In: Proceedings of the 16th ACM Conference on Embedded Networked Sensor Systems, SenSys, pp. 41–53 (2018)
21. Zhang, H., Gummeson, J., Ransford, B., Fu, K.: Moo: a batteryless computational RFID and sensing platform. University of Massachusetts Computer Science Technical Report UM-CS-2011-020 (2011)
22. Zhang, W., Liu, S., Lv, M., Chen, Q., Guan, N.: Intermittent computing with efficient state backup by asynchronous DMA. In: Design, Automation & Test in Europe Conference & Exhibition (DATE). IEEE (2021)
23. Zhang, W., et al.: Adaptive task-based intermittent computing system with parallel state backup. IEEE Trans. Comput.-Aided Design Integr. Circuits Syst. (2022)

Can Language Models Pretend Solvers?
Logic Code Simulation with LLMs

Minyu Chen[1], Guoqiang Li[1(✉)], Ling-I Wu[1], Ruibang Liu[1],
Yuxin Su[1], Xi Chang[2], and Jianxin Xue[2]

[1] Shanghai Jiao Tong University, Shanghai 200240, China
{minkow,li.g,edithwuly,628628,sshirley}@sjtu.edu.cn
[2] Shanghai Polytechnic University, Shanghai 201209, China
{changxi,jxxue}@sspu.edu.cn

Abstract. Logical solvers are typically employed for the static analysis
and formal verification of functional code that is not amenable to verification through execution. Concurrently, some research efforts aim to
convert natural language into logic code to bolster reasoning capabilities
with the aid of logical solvers. However, the transformation process from
code or natural language to a logical framework is costly. To address this
challenge, several studies have explored the use of large language models
(LLMs) to facilitate this transformation. Nevertheless, LLMs may introduce misalignment and formatting errors that are unacceptable for logical solvers. Considering the strong logical reasoning capabilities of LLMs
and their relative insensitivity to alignment and formatting errors, we
propose utilizing LLMs to emulate logical solvers for logic code simulation. In light of the characteristic fixed outputs of logical solvers, we introduce a novel LLM-based code simulation technique called Dual Chains of
Logic (DCoL). Additionally, we have compiled three new datasets specifically for the Logic Code Simulation task and conducted comprehensive
evaluations. These assessments demonstrate state-of-the-art performance
when compared to other LLM prompt strategies, achieving a notable
7.06% improvement in accuracy with GPT-4 Turbo.

Keywords: Large Language Models · Logic Solvers · Code
Simulation · Code Understanding · Evaluation

1 Introduction

Logic serves as the foundation for the majority of formal methodologies in software engineering. By translating specifications, constraints, and test cases into
logical frameworks like First Order Logic (FOL) or Satisfiability Modulo Theories (SMT), logic solvers can precisely judge arguments in problems or check
the satisfiability of problems. Thus, state-of-the-art solvers including Z3 [8] and
CVC5 [1] are applied in wide aspects of software engineering, including software verification [7], software testing [31], program synthesis [15], and program

T. Bourke et al. (Eds.): SETTA 2024, LNCS 15469, pp. 102–121, 2025.
https://doi.org/10.1007/978-981-96-0602-3_6

analysis [11]. However, logic remains a complex subject within human cognition, presenting several challenges to the deployment of logic solvers in software engineering. One key obstacle is the gap between natural language (NL) and the solver language (SL) of logical problems, impeding not only the programming process but also the comprehension of code segments within existing software systems. Besides, despite advancements, solvers encounter difficulties in effectively and precisely resolving logical problems, including those that are straightforward for humans. Furthermore, the integration of logic in software engineering often involves various extensions like arrays, integers, reals, strings, and bit-vectors. This diversity has led to the development of specialized solvers [5,11] tailored to different logical scopes.

Recent advances in transformer-based large language models (LLMs) such as GPT [4] and LLaMA [35] have showcased their ability to perform logic reasoning akin to humans [19,25]. By incentivizing LLMs to translate natural language into solver languages with in-context learning (ICL) [4] or model fine-tuning [10], LLMs can successfully solve simple propositional logic questions in NL form [28,34]. When faced with intricate logic-based queries in forms such as FOL [14] and SAT [47], LLMs exhibit challenges in direct problem-solving and show low successful execution rates of code generation. LLMs also fail to conduct relational reasoning [20]. Nonetheless, it is crucial to recognize the valuable bridge LLMs establish between natural language and solver language, along with the code intelligence LLMs bring to various aspects of software engineering, such as code generation [22,44,45], documentation [23,41], code understanding [36], and others [9,13,32,33,42]. On the other hand, a novel line of research, code simulation, is raised to discover the ability of LLMs to simulate the execution of code and algorithms. Preliminary research reports that the LLMs struggle to execute long and complex procedures [18].

This research focuses on previously overlooked areas that have been left unexplored by prior studies. While previous works have predominantly focused on directly solving logic problems presented in natural language (NL) form or employing external logical solvers, Large Language Models (LLMs) have primarily served as NL reasoners or NL-to-SL translators in those endeavors. LLMs have been extensively utilized for logic reasoning in NL; however, the most frequently encountered logic problems in software engineering are found in solvers. Solvers check the logic formulas inherently implicit within code, which are manifested through the code's execution. These logic code in solvers serve as fundamental components that guide the analysis process and influence the identification of defects, verification of correctness properties, and generation of test cases. Although the logic problems derived from code differ in format from those in NL, LLMs have demonstrated sufficient capability to resolve logic problems in solvers, such as code understanding and logic problem solving. Thus, we propose an intriguing research question: Can language models simulate logic codes?

To explore this question, we introduce our framework, *Dual Chains of Logic (DCoL)*, the first framework specifically designed for LLM-based logic solvers. Given the characteristics of logic solvers, with outputs typically fixed as `True`

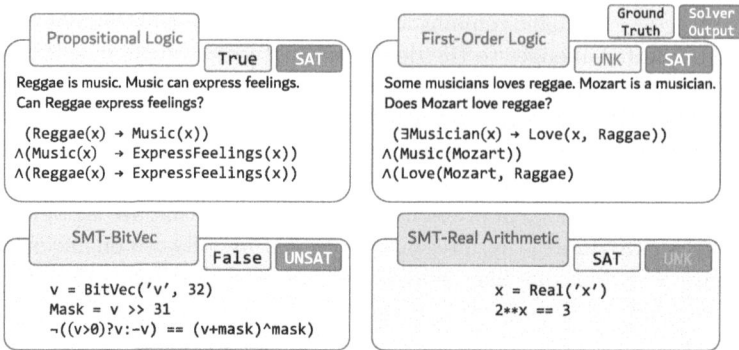

Fig. 1. Samples of logical problem to be studied in our research. The **light** gray boxes display the ground truth of the given problems, while the results given by the SMT solver are presented in the **dark** grey boxes. 'UNK' denotes unknown.

(SAT), `False` (UNSAT), or `Unknown` (UNK), DCoL directly processes code as input and guides LLMs to adopt a dual-path reasoning approach, enabling them to accurately infer the code's outcome. This framework helps LLMs effectively navigate reasoning challenges, such as handling multiple assignment problems, and reduces confusion during logical problem-solving. Through experiments, we demonstrate LLMs' competence in predicting the outcomes of codes involving logical reasoning. Additionally, we investigate the effectiveness of various prompting techniques in enhancing LLMs' performance in simulating code. Furthermore, we discuss the potential benefits that LLMs can bring to the current state of logic solvers, such as tolerance for slips in logic codes.

We highlight our contributions as follows:

– We are the **first** to propose a novel task, Logic Code Simulation, which assesses the ability of Large Language Models (LLMs) to directly reason the output of logical framework code based on their logical reasoning capabilities, unaffected by non-standard formats.
– We introduce a novel LLM-based code simulation technique, Dual Chains of Logic (DCoL), which leverages the fixed outputs characteristic of logic solvers. This technique incorporates the concept of backward chaining [16] by assuming an initial output and then guiding the LLM to determine whether contradictions exist, thereby achieving more reliable results.
– We have compiled three new datasets specifically for the Logic Code Simulation task: Z3Tutorial, Z3Test, and SMTSIM. Furthermore, we conducted comprehensive evaluations on various LLMs, demonstrating that DCoL achieves a notable 7.06% improvement in accuracy with GPT-4-Turbo.

2   Background and Related Work

Large Language Model. Large Language Models (LLMs) are generative models based on the pre-trained Transformer architecture. Most LLMs utilize a generative model architecture, where given a sentence of n tokens, the model is trained to maximize the likelihood of the ground-truth token t_i at the current time step t based on its preceding sequence $t_{i-1}, ..., t_1$. The training of LLMs typically follows three main processes: unsupervised training on large amounts of unlabeled text data without explicit human annotations, supervised fine-tuning on labeled data relevant to specific tasks or domains, and reinforcement learning on feedback from human annotators or evaluators. Leveraging extensive multimodal data and employing pre-training and fine-tuning techniques, LLMs have demonstrated state-of-the-art performance across various downstream tasks, such as machine translation, numerical reasoning, and code clone detection, with minimal examples (few-shot) or task-specific prompt instructions (zero-shot).

Logical Solver. We begin by identifying logical problems to be addressed in this work. Generally speaking, the hardest logical problem underlies the framework of satisfiability modulo theories (SMT). SMT is a variation of the SAT problem for first-order logic (FOL), with the interpretation of symbols constrained by specific theories, such as real arithmetic and bit vectors. Our study encompasses several subsets of SMT problems, including propositional logic, SMT problems themselves, and a segment of first-order logic within the solving ability of SMT, along with external theories defining constraints. Thus, we focus on SMT-based languages and solvers, to universally encode and solve those logical problems.

We elaborate on several samples to be solved in Fig. 1. In the realm of propositional logic, we incorporate variables like x to enhance conceptual clarity. The proposed hypothesis, *Reggae(x) → ExpressFeelings(x)*, can be derived with deductive reasoning. We transform the judgment process into a satisfiability dilemma by treating the assumption as a constraint. FOL supports quantifiers $\forall$ and $\exists$ on the basis of propositional logic, introducing uncertainty into problems. In this case, the assumption remains indeterminate. We check both the affirmation and negation hypotheses with SMT solvers, to align with the True/False/Uncertain output form. The uncertain cases are equivalent to UNSAT for both affirmation and negation hypotheses. Concerning SMT-based problems, theories also contribute to their complexity. In the SMT-BitVec case, the target is to ascertain whether the Left-Hand-Side (LHS) equals the Right-Hand-Side (RHS) for a bit-operation-oriented issue. The `True`/`False` corresponds to SAT/UNSAT. Conversely, the SMT-Real-Arthmetic is drawn from the Z3py manual. The Z3 solver produces an unknown result as x is involved in the exponentiation of 2^x, rendering this problem non-polynomial. In contrast, individuals can readily find a solution as $x = \log_2 3$.

Code Simulation with LLMs. Code simulation is a relatively new topic of interest. It is defined as predicting the concrete outputs of codes aligning with the execution results. Recent studies on Turing Completeness of transformers and LLMs [12,26,29,39] have suggested that LLMs are capable of interpreting instructions from code, showing potential to simulate the execution of code and algorithms as analog models. The previous works encourage LLMs to simulate a variety of tasks, such as keyboard and mouse actions on computers [17] and optimizers [42]. While transformer-based models are trained to predict the execution traces of codes [21] and UNSAT cores [30], a recent attempt at simulating code with LLMs has been proposed [18]. Their results indicate that LLMs can execute instructions sequentially.

When dealing with long programs and complex procedures, various strategies, such as memorization, can be employed. Our proposed logic code simulation framework focuses on simulating specialized codes for logical solvers rather than general-purpose code. The potential outcome space is constrained to either SAT or UNSAT, which makes accurate predictions more attainable, as logical codes can be more clearly expressed and understood in natural language.

3   DCoL: Dual Chains of Logic

In this section, we present a new prompt technique, *Dual Chains of Logic* (DCoL), aiming to improve the accuracy, reasoning process, and robustness of the logic code simulation task.

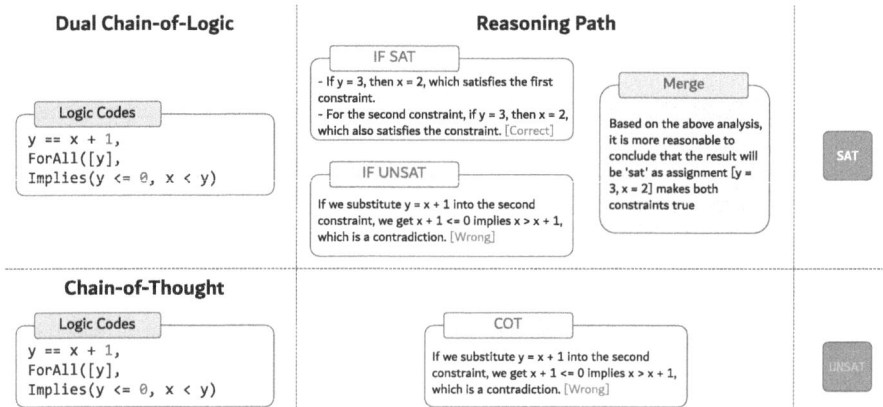

Fig. 2. Overview of the DCoL method: DCoL offers two hypotheses, SAT (satisfiable) and UNSAT (unsatisfiable), for logic code simulation. The LLMs verify these hypotheses individually before combining them to reach the final decision, while the COT method only outputs one possible reasoning path.

Since the concept of reasoning paths is crucial, they lead to more precise outcomes. Nevertheless, when dealing with general questions like mathematical computations and text generation, the answer search space is practically infinite, posing challenges in constructing reasoning paths. In contrast, logic problems that can be converted into solvers typically result in *dual* possible outcomes: SAT or UNSAT. The reasoning paths of humans for determining whether a set of constraints is SAT or UNSAT are diverse:

(1) If the result is SAT, we should find a legal assignment of variables to verify it. Consider the case presented in Fig. 3. Assuming that the given codes produce the output SAT, an arrangement of variables that fulfills all constraints

serves as compelling evidence. One possible assignment is $x = 2, y = 3$, which satisfies the first constraint $y \equiv x + 1$. In regard to the second constraint, $\forall y \, [(y \leq 0) \implies (x < y)]$, y is a **independent variable**[1], unrelated to the y defined in $y \equiv x + 1$. Therefore, only $x = 3$ is relevant in this context, and this assignment meets the second constraint.

(2) If the result is UNSAT, we should find a set of minimal constraints where conflicts always exist, which is also known as UNSAT core. Replacing $x > y$ with $x < y$ in the second constraint transforms the problem into an UNSAT one. The UNSAT core solely consists of the second constraint because, regardless of the value assigned to x, there exists a value for y that is non-positive and less than the given x value, meaning the second constraint cannot always be satisfied.

CoT Prompt	DCoL Prompt
Suppose you are one of the greatest mathematicians, logician, and programmer. Given the following code in Z3 solver, you are asked to determine the output of the code with #sat or #unsat. Let's think step by step. Code: [[CODE]]	Given the following code in Z3 solver, you are asked to determine the output of the code with #sat or #unsat. Follow instructions below: 1. List and understand variables and constraints added to the solver. 2. Based on the constraints, if I say the result is 'sat', is it correct? Can you find satisfied assignments for variables? Let's think step by step. 3. Based on the constraints, if I say the result is 'unsat', is it correct? Can you find conflict constraints? Let's think step by step. 4. Which is more correct and reasonable based on the above aspects? Answer your preferred hypothesis with #sat or #unsat. Let's think step by step. Code: [[CODE]]

Fig. 3. Prompting template of the DCoL method. Prompts can be modified slightly according to specific tasks.

However, LLMs cannot fully grasp the dual implicit reasoning chains for logic problems during one execution time. Among the dual paths, at least one leads to an accurate solution. Thus, by guiding LLMs to reason via both SAT/UNSAT paths, LLMs can produce different reasoning paths for contrary goals, and generate promising answers with explanations.

To this end, we propose a novel prompt method, Dual Chains of Logic (DCoL). Figure 2 illustrates our proposed DCoL approach. DCoL encourages LLMs to discard incorrect wrong prediction UNSAT after integrating dual paths

---

[1] Independent variable y can be replaced with any symbol, such as $\forall z \, [(z \leq 0) \implies (x < z)]$.

of thinking, while COT only generates a wrong reasoning path, leading to the prediction error. As illustrated in the template of DCoL from Fig. 3, the DCoL prompt begins by asking the user to analyze a given logic code, such as a SAT problem or Z3 solver code, to determine whether the result is #sat (satisfiable) or #unsat (unsatisfiable). It guides the user through a structured reasoning process: first, they are instructed to list and understand the variables and constraints added to the solver. Next, the prompt asks the user to verify if the result is #sat by checking if there are valid assignments for the variables. Then, the user is asked to consider if the result is #unsat and find any conflicting constraints. Finally, the user must decide which outcome—#sat or #unsat—is more reasonable based on their analysis and explain their conclusion. The logic code to be analyzed is represented by the placeholder "Code: [[CODE]]" at the bottom of the prompt, where the actual code would be inserted for evaluation.

DCoL, in contrast to COT, steers clear of falling into the erroneous reasoning trap illustrated in Fig. 2. Since y functions as an independent variable, it is inaccurate to interchangeably use $y = x + 1$ in the second constraint, given the realm that y in both constraints does not hold the same significance. This error, albeit subtle, often goes unnoticed even by humans lacking specialized knowledge. However, DCoL consistently provides a precise reasoning approach for obtaining accurate outcomes by thinking on the dual side of logic problems.

4   Experimental Results

In this section, we present the effectiveness and robustness of LLM-based logic solvers. We will provide a comprehensive analysis of the errors observed in unsuccessful results. Finally, we will discuss the performance of GPT-family-based logic solvers on challenging problems.

4.1   Involved LLMs

The objective of this study is to assess LLMs' reliability and limitations in simulating various forms of logic codes compared to conventional logical solvers like Z3. To accomplish this, we employ both open-source LLMs such as the LLaMA family [27,35], and close-source but strong LLMs such as the GPT family as our base models. We present details of these models as follows:

GPT-3.5 Turbo: GPT-3.5 Turbo, also known as ChatGPT, is a decoder-only network based on the Transformer architecture, comprising 175 billion parameters. It has undergone pretraining on 45 terabytes of text data gathered from diverse sources like books, articles, and websites. Moreover, GPT-3.5 Turbo is optimized for invoking its capability with Reinforcement Learning from Human Feedback (RLHF) technique. The GPT-3.5 Turbo-0125 supports a context window of 16,385 tokens.

GPT-4 Turbo. GPT-4 Turbo is an advancement of GPT-4, offering increased capabilities with an updated knowledge cutoff extended to April 2023. It also features a 128k context window in a single prompt.

LLaMA-2. LLaMA-2, an open-source foundational model introduced by Meta, has been trained on 2 trillion tokens and is designed to accommodate a context length of 4096 by default. LLaMA-2 models have been refined with the input of more than 1 million human annotations, specifically tailored for chat purposes. This study focuses on the evaluation of the 13B-Chat model.

Code LLaMA. Code LLaMA is a refined version of LLaMA-2 to support various code-related activities like coding, testing, explaining, and finishing code segments. We also deploy CodeLLaMA-13B-Instruct for our evaluation.

4.2 Datasets

To delve deeper into simulating real-life logical codes, we propose 3 new datasets from various sources. (1) We gathered 31 code examples from the Programming Z3 tutorial [3], culminating in a new dataset named *Z3Tutorial*. (2) Additionally, the Z3 official repository, Z3test², offers a range of test samples for the Z3 solver, from which we extracted 85 Python cases to form the *Z3Test* dataset. These cases were then categorized into three question types: logic-only, arithmetic, and type-inference. We discard the type-inference questions such as *is_add(x+y)* in our primary experimental setting, but will be introduced as a challenge for logic code simulation. (3) we included several codes in SMT-LIB format from the SMT-COMP 2023 [2]. These instances are predominantly derived from industrial software or established logical problem collections. We have chosen various external theories to enhance the intricacy of the problems, including real arithmetic (both linear and non-linear), bit vectors, uninterpreted functions, and strings. Our *SMTSim* dataset consists of 102 samples in total. For further insights, we present a comprehensive overview of our curated dataset in Table 1. Note that the complexity of a logic problem is determined by both the quantity of constraints and the difficulty of logic expressions. The number of lines is only a partial factor of the overall complexity. All those code snippets are ensured to only produce the result of SAT or UNSAT.

4.3 Prompting Baselines

The baseline Prompting methods considered in this work are listed below:

- Standard Prompting (SD) [4]. SD directly asks LLMs to predict the execution results of logic codes. The LLMs will return only SAT/UNSAT, sometimes with short explanations.
- Chain-of-Thought (COT) [40]. COT encourages LLMs to generate a systematic solution by explaining each step before presenting the final answer. The LLMs will return a reasoning path tackling the issue raised.
- Plan-and-Solve Prompting (PS) [37]. PS instructs LLMs to devise a detailed plan for addressing issues and solve plan targets sequentially.

---

² https://github.com/Z3Prover/z3test.

Table 1. Dataset information provided. Format means the input format of questions. Z3Py is based on Python, while SMTLIB is the standard language of SMT solvers. Mean LOC represents the average Lines of Code (LoC) of examples.

Dataset	Formulation	Format	# of Samples	Mean LoC
ProntoQA	PL	NL	500	-
Z3Tutorial	SMT	Z3Py	31	9.90
Z3Test	SMT	Z3Py	85	8.37
SMTSIM	SMT	SMTLIB	104	14.36

– Chain of Simulation (CoSm) [18]. The CoSm method enhances the conventional Chain of Thought prompting technique by circumventing the drawbacks associated with memorization in code simulation tasks. It aims to track the program trace and forces LLMs to simulate each instruction sequentially.

Additionally, Self-Consistency (SC) [38] utilizes a majority voting mechanism across different reasoning paths to enhance prediction robustness. The key insight behind this method is ensuring consistency in the reasoning process. Since SC operates as a parallel prompting method, it can be combined with other prompting approaches, including ours. Therefore, we evaluate it as a standalone plugin.

Note that our proposed task is a novel one focusing on codes as initial input. Thus, methods for processing natural language problems [25, 43, 46], are no longer compatible with our framework. Furthermore, these approaches are limited in their ability to address a specific portion of the task we have outlined, such as SAT [46] and SMT-Int (SMT questions with integer computing theory) [25, 43]. As a result, we do not include them as baselines in our study.

A notable observation is that the typical few-shot prompt, which is also known as in-context learning is ineffective in our experimental setting, which is also reported in similar tasks such as code simulation [18] and discussed in several works [24]. Few-shot prompt learning may not work on a task whose input-label correspondence is not already captured in the LLMs. In our logic code simulation task, elementary operations in different subtasks such as different function calls and various theories can be challenging for in-context learning. Besides, considering the intricate nature of logic problems, the templates heavily exceed the LLMs' context limit. Thus, we focus on the zero-shot prompting scheme in this research.

Table 2. Performance of LLMs with different prompt techniques. The **bolded** numbers denote the best performance in this dataset, while results in grey boxes represent the best result among all the prompt methods. All experiments are conducted three times.

Method		Z3Tutorial			Z3Test		
		Accuracy	Unknown	Exe. Acc.	Accuracy	Unknown	Exe. Acc.
Z3		100.0	-	100.0	98.80	1.20	100.0
GPT-3.5 Turbo	SD	67.74	-	67.74	70.59	-	70.59
	PS	67.74	-	67.74	72.54	3.52	75.19
	CoSm	63.44	-	63.44	71.76	-	71.76
	COT	68.82	-	68.82	74.11	0.39	74.40
	DCoL	70.97		70.97	74.90	-	74.90
GPT-4 Turbo	SD	84.95	-	84.95	76.47	3.53	79.27
	PS	**86.02**	-	86.02	82.35	-	82.35
	CoSm	81.72	-	81.72	80.39	2.35	82.32
	COT	**86.02**	-	86.02	81.18	2.35	83.13
	DCoL	**86.02**	-	86.02	**83.53**	1.76	84.52
LLaMA 2-13B	SD	38.70	19.35	48.00	40.00	8.23	43.03
	PS	54.83	9.67	60.71	42.35	8.23	46.15
	CoSm	61.29	9.67	67.85	34.11	2.35	34.93
	COT	53.22	8.06	57.89	50.00	5.88	52.79
	DCoL	64.51	6.45	68.96	54.11	1.17	54.76
Code LLaMA 13B	SD	58.06	3.22	60.00	57.64	5.88	61.25
	PS	51.61	12.90	59.25	55.29	10.58	61.84
	CoSm	70.96	-	70.96	61.17	9.41	67.53
	COT	56.45	17.74	68.62	58.23	3.52	60.36
	DCoL	70.96	6.45	75.86	62.35	-	62.35

4.4   Effectiveness

We employ four LLMs, GPT-3.5-Turbo, GPT-4-Turbo, LLaMA-2-13B, and CodeLLaMA-13B, with different prompting methods, to explore their capability of them on simulating logic codes. The results are provided in Table 2. Two datasets based on Z3Py are utilized for a comprehensive analysis.

We utilize two additional metrics, namely "unknown rate" and "execution accuracy" to further investigate the effectiveness of logic code simulation.

Unknown rate indicates the percentage of instances such as 'If a solution exists, the output will be SAT; otherwise UNSAT', where LLMs struggle to provide a definitive answer. An unknown output can be caused by errors in the program, such as 'The code should output ERROR rather than SAT or UNSAT'.

Execution accuracy refers to the precision among instances that LLMs confirm to be SAT/UNSAT. This measure aids in assessing the reliability of the outputs generated by LLMs. This metric can be computed as $EA = \frac{Acc}{1-UNK}$.

A model can have low accuracy while obtaining a high execution accuracy. If we apply a random guessing procedure on those unknown examples, the accuracy will be acceptable. Note that all methods obtain execution accuracy greater than 50%, which means LLMs can perform at least stronger than random guessing.

The main observations are summarized below:

GPT Can Pretend Logic Solvers. As shown in Table 2, GPT shows its capability to simulate logic codes even with the standard prompting method (SD). In the Z3Tutorial dataset analysis, it is evident that employing standard prompts can yield an accuracy exceeding 80% when utilizing GPT-4 Turbo, known for its high resilience among LLM options. Even when employing SD prompts with GPT-3.5, an accuracy of 67.74% can be attained. As for the Z3Test dataset, GPT-3.5 achieves over 70% accuracy, while GPT-4 successfully solved 80% logic problems in this dataset. This phenomenon comes from the combination of code understanding and logical reasoning for GPT models. Moreover, among all LLMs tested, the Dual Chains of Logic (DCoL) consistently enhances performance in logic code simulation across all datasets, with gains of up to 7.06% on GPT-4.

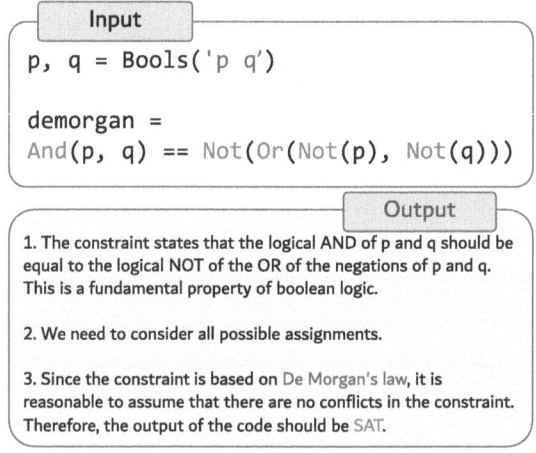

Fig. 4. An example of De Morgan's Law

Think on Logic Rather than Think on Code. A representative method performing 'Think on Code' is Chain of Simulation (CoSm), which forces LLMs to simulate the program instruction by instruction. However, this method is only suitable for simulating problems with sequential execution paths. Logic reasoning is a more complex issue as the execution chain of logic codes is hidden under external solver libraries such as the Conflict Driven Clause Learning algorithm applied in Z3 solver. To solve logic problems, LLMs should pay more attention to logical reasoning to derive the correct execution path. Nevertheless, the execution of code should not be ignored in our task. A typical error case involves adding constraints to a solver that are never actually verified, where LLMs should disregard these constraints.

LLMs Exceed Some Theoretical Limitations of Solvers. A motivated example of this strength is showcased in Fig. 1. Constraints like $2^x == 3$ go beyond the representation capability of SMT theories. Although it remains such a simple question for humans, typical solvers like Z3 output UNKNOWN in this case.

LLMs Leverage Explainable Knowledge for Reasoning. We provide an interesting example in Fig. 4 targeting checking the satisfiability of De Morgan's Law. Despite enumerating all assignments for proving, LLMs build the connection from logic codes to De Morgan's Law and make the correct prediction with this external knowledge. We suggest that leveraging formulas and theorems is a good manual for complex problem-solving, and LLMs show their capability of utilizing knowledge for more explainable reasoning.

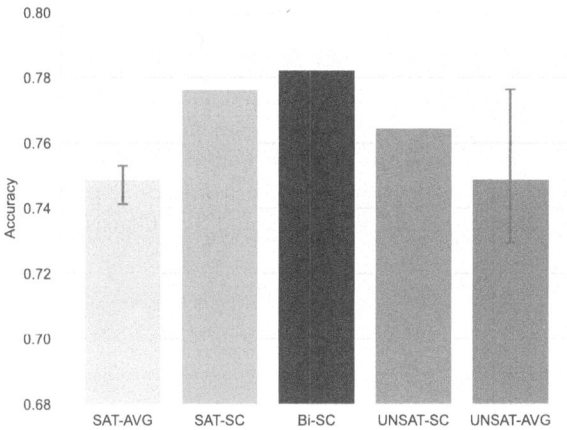

Fig. 5. Prompting template of the DCoL method. Prompts can be modified slightly according to specific tasks.

DCoL Prompt is Effective. Our proposed prompt method, Dual Chains of Logic (DCoL), offers a structured approach to LLM reasoning by encouraging two separate lines of problem-solving, and the results in Table 2 effectively support its efficacy. Across different datasets, particularly with the Z3Tutorial and Z3Test, we see that DCoL consistently outperforms other methods or shows competitive results, especially in the execution accuracy (Exe. Acc.) and accuracy rates, where it often achieves the best or near-best performance (highlighted in grey). For instance, GPT-4 Turbo achieves 86.02% accuracy using DCoL in the Z3Tutorial dataset, matching other top-performing methods while outperforming others in execution accuracy on the Z3Test dataset with 83.53%. This consistent performance boost suggests that the dual-reasoning structure introduced by DCoL is highly compatible with the evolving capabilities of LLMs. It facilitates multi-way reasoning, allowing the model to explore multiple solution paths, which can reduce the "unknown" output rate, indicating fewer situations where the model fails to provide meaningful answers. While the GPT models may occasionally follow a single reasoning pathway, as seen in experiments, the results show that DCoL still effectively improves overall model accuracy and reduces failure cases, confirming its utility in logic code simulation and problem-solving.

Bi-directional Self-consistency Improves Performance. A recent study suggests that the sequence in which premises are given to LLMs significantly impacts their performance in natural language reasoning tasks [6]. The Dual Chains of Logic prompt we introduced will present SAT and UNSAT questions to LLMs in a successive manner. By swapping the order of SAT/UNSAT reasoning path in DCoL, LLMs can show different tending for the final prediction. Inspired by the idea of self-consistency, To explore this further, a validation experiment was designed based on the concept of self-consistency. The experiment involved sending 3 SAT-first and 3 UNSAT-first DCoL prompts to Z3Test via GPT-3.5-Turbo separately, followed by aggregating the responses using a majority voting approach. The experimental results are depicted in Fig. 5, showing that the bi-directional Self-Consistency (Bi-SC) mechanism resulted in a 3.34% improvement to the average performance by bridging the gap between execution orders.

Based on the experimental results, we believe that LLMs, particularly the GPT family, **serve as highly effective simulators**, especially when utilizing our proposed DCoL prompt and Bi-directional Self-Consistency mechanism.

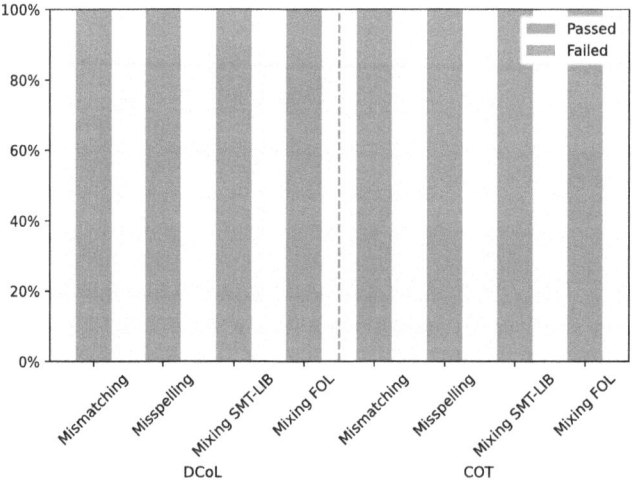

Fig. 6. Performance drop against code-level modifications

4.5   Robustness

We have already demonstrated the capability of Large Language Models (LLMs) in code simulation, indicating that LLMs can comprehend our intentions based on the provided code. Since LLMs can predict the outcome of code without actually executing it, they are more tolerant of syntax errors compared to logic solvers. To assess the robustness of code simulation in LLMs, we conducted an experiment involving four distinct syntax error patterns:

– Mismatched Parentheses: there is an inconsistency in the placement of parentheses, such as an unequal number of opening and closing parentheses or improper nesting, such as $(a + b$ or $func(a, b))$.
– Misspelled Variable or Function Names: incorrect spelling or naming of variables or functions within the code, such as $x1$ and xl.
– Mixing Z3 Library Grammar: elements specific to the SMT-LIB, such as $(declare - fun \langle symbol \rangle \langle sort \rangle^*)$, are incorrectly integrated into the code syntax.
– Mixing First-Order Logic Grammar: elements of first-order logic grammar, such as quantifiers $\forall$ and $\exists$, are incorrectly incorporated into the code syntax.

For each syntax error pattern, we randomly selected 10 cases from the Z3 Test dataset to introduce errors. Subsequently, we applied both COT and our proposed method (DCoT) on the poisoned Z3 Test dataset. As illustrated in Fig. 6, the code simulation of LLMs with COT was significantly misled by the introduced syntax errors, leading to a decrease in accuracy of approximately 40%. In contrast, syntax errors had minimal influence on the effectiveness of our method, which demonstrates **LLMs are robust simulators**.

Table 3. ProntoQA Comparison

Method	Accuracy
Direct Solving	
SD	51.20
COT	72.00
COT + CodeGen	76.80
Translation + Solver	
Logic-LM	61.00
Translation + Simulation	
Code Only	50.20
NL + Code	75.80

LLM Can Simulate Generated Logic Codes. This section is motivated by the limitations of Logic-LM [25], which tackles logic inference in natural language through a translation-solver approach. While Logic-LM achieves almost 100%

success in generating symbolic codes for the ProntoQA dataset, its accuracy sharply drops to 61% when interacting with symbolic solvers. This decline is largely due to **LLMs generating unreliable or implicit codes**, where hidden knowledge inferred by the LLM is not explicitly present in the generated code. For instance, an LLM might generate a code segment that assumes a certain variable should be non-negative based on common sense reasoning, even though this constraint is not included in the code itself. Consequently, a traditional symbolic solver, unaware of this implicit assumption, may infer an incorrect answer. To mitigate this issue, we propose ensuring consistency between code generation and the solver's understanding by simulating logic on generated outputs. As shown in Table 3, we conducted a comparative study based on Logic-LM's shortcomings. The $COT + CodeGen$ approach treats code generation as an auxiliary in-context task, while $NL + Code$ provides the original language input along with previously generated code. Our results indicate that even with low-quality code, direct simulation performs comparably to standard prompting for natural language tasks, with $NL + Code$ achieving an accuracy of 75.80%, which is comparable to $COT + CodeGen$ and outperforms the Logic-LM baseline that relies on external solvers.

4.6   Error Analysis

We analyzed results from the Z3Test dataset using three prompting methods: CoSm, COT, and DCoL, aiming to identify error types across different reasoning paths. The errors were categorized into six types:

Inference Error: Mistakes in logical deduction, such as misjudging $a \wedge b$ as false when both a and b are `True`, or conflicting conclusions like first inferring $a > 10$ and then $a < 10$.

Misunderstanding Satisfiability (SAT) Error: Occurs when an LLM correctly identifies a solution set for a satisfiable (SAT) problem but wrongly classifies it as unsatisfiable (UNSAT), due to misinterpreting the problem as having multiple solutions.

Partial UNSAT Error: Arises when the ground truth is satisfiable, but the LLM finds conflicting assignments while ignoring valid ones, wrongly classifying the problem as UNSAT. For example, $x = 1, y = 0$ is satisfiable, but the LLM may mistakenly label $x = 1, y = 2$ as an UNSAT core.

Bit-vector Arithmetic Error: Involves errors in handling bitwise operations on bit vectors, like incorrectly interpreting a left shift operation as an overflow.

Real Arithmetic Error: Includes computational mistakes with real numbers, such as confusion over the equality of positive and negative zeros in floating-point numbers.

Commonsense Error: Basic mathematical or logical mistakes, such as equating 1 with 2 or failing to recognize common library functions, indicating gaps in the LLM's understanding.

Our analysis (in Fig. 7) shows that DCoL improves LLMs' understanding of satisfiability problems, reducing misinterpretations and incorrect judgments.

In arithmetic tasks, DCoL enhances performance by guiding the LLM through initial steps.

While not the focus of our study, certain industry examples are noteworthy. For instance, the `is_add()` function in Z3Py, which checks if an expression is an addition, can lead to confusion; `is_add(1 + 2)` may return false as Z3Py treats $1 + 2$ as a constant, potentially confusing LLMs and users unfamiliar with this behavior.

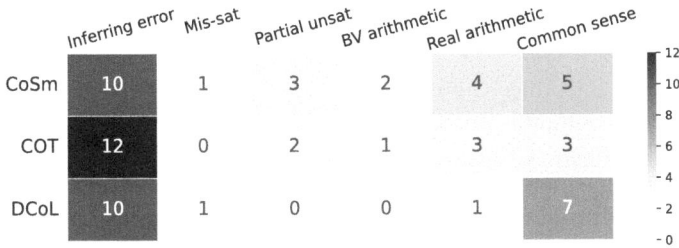

Fig. 7. Error analysis among different methods

Additionally, in the *SMTSim* dataset from SMT-COMP 2023, some SMT files generated by complex backend libraries contain numerous variables and formulas. Due to LLM token limits, we filtered out larger examples, yet many of these filtered cases remain unsolved by solvers like Z3, suggesting potential areas for future research.

4.7 Hard Problems

SMTSim dataset contains complicated logic code, with more lines of codes, variables, and theories. We regard it as a challenge for logic code simulation. We report the performance of GPT families in Table 4.

Table 4. SMTSim Results

Method		ACC.	UNK.	Exe. Acc
Z3 Solver		97.06	2.94	100.0
GPT-3.5 Turbo	COT	5.88	85.29	33.33
	CoSm	14.71	78.43	68.20
	DCoL	**54.9**	6.86	58.94
GPT-4 Turbo	COT	51.96	19.61	65.92
	CoSm	50.98	23.53	66.67
	DCoL	**58.82**	5.82	62.45

We observe that COT and CoSm suffer from UNKNOWN prediction, while our proposed DCoL achieves over 50% accuracy even with GPT-3.5-Turbo. However, the relatively low execution accuracy reveals that LLMs struggle to solve such complex datasets. This issue may stem from the abundance of variables and constraints present. In the SMTSim dataset, numerous instances occur infrequently but are deeply intertwined. Due to their limitations in handling extensive contexts, LLMs struggle to address complex logical compositions effectively.

5   Conclusion

In this work, we introduce the novel concept of logic code simulation to evaluate the ability to comprehend, analyze, and simulate logic problems encoded in programs. We propose DCoL, a novel prompt fashion designed to enhance reasoning performance on code-based logic problems. Furthermore, we release three datasets collected from the solver community and perform an extensible assessment to evaluate the capability of logic code simulation for various LLMs. In the conclusion, the authors mention a potential avenue for future work involving the application of the DCoL technique to convert natural language into logical code. Apriori, it is not immediately clear how this can be achieved, but exploring this direction could provide valuable insights.

One possible approach involves leveraging the dual reasoning paths central to DCoL, where the first path focuses on interpreting natural language inputs and extracting the logical structure or constraints embedded in the text. The second path could then focus on translating this understanding into executable logical code, ensuring consistency between the extracted logic and the generated code. This dual-path system could help bridge the gap between natural language reasoning and formal logic, addressing the ambiguity that often arises when translating nuanced human language into strict logical frameworks. Additionally, integrating techniques such as knowledge retrieval and structured prompting could allow LLMs to retrieve relevant logical patterns from a knowledge base while maintaining flexibility in the translation process.

This integration would represent a significant step forward in developing LLM-based solvers capable of handling not only traditional logic problems but also more complex, real-world scenarios where logical rules are derived from natural language descriptions. By enhancing DCoL in this way, future research could establish a new paradigm in logic-based problem-solving, where natural language inputs are seamlessly converted into formal logic programs. Furthermore, we plan to broaden DCoL's application beyond traditional solvers like SAT or UNSAT, ensuring its effectiveness across diverse logic code scenarios and complex logic programs, paving the way for more efficient LLM-driven logic solvers.

Acknowledgement. This work is supported by the National Natural Science Foundation of China Grant No. 61872232.

References

1. Barbosa, H., et al.: cvc5: a versatile and industrial-strength SMT solver. In: Fisman, D., Rosu, G. (eds.) TACAS 2022. LNCS, vol. 13243, pp. 415–442. Springer, Cham (2022). https://doi.org/10.1007/978-3-030-99524-9_24

2. Beyer, D.: Competition on software verification and witness validation: SV-COMP 2023. In: Sankaranarayanan, S., Sharygina, N. (eds.) TACAS 2023. LNCS, vol. 13994, pp. 495–522. Springer, Cham (2023). https://doi.org/10.1007/978-3-031-30820-8_29

3. Bjørner, N., de Moura, L., Nachmanson, L., Wintersteiger, C.M.: Programming Z3. In: Bowen, J.P., Liu, Z., Zhang, Z. (eds.) SETSS 2018. LNCS, vol. 11430, pp. 148–201. Springer, Cham (2019). https://doi.org/10.1007/978-3-030-17601-3_4

4. Brown, T., et al.: Language models are few-shot learners. In: Advances in Neural Information Processing Systems, vol. 33, pp. 1877–1901 (2020)

5. Cai, S., Li, B., Zhang, X.: Local search for SMT on linear integer arithmetic. In: Shoham, S., Vizel, Y. (eds.) CAV 2022. LNCS, vol. 13372, pp. 227–248. Springer, Cham (2022). https://doi.org/10.1007/978-3-031-13188-2_12

6. Chen, X., Chi, R.A., Wang, X., Zhou, D.: Premise order matters in reasoning with large language models. arXiv preprint arXiv:2402.08939 (2024)

7. Cordeiro, L., Fischer, B.: Verifying multi-threaded software using SMT-based context-bounded model checking. In: Proceedings of the 33rd International Conference on Software Engineering, pp. 331–340 (2011)

8. de Moura, L., Bjørner, N.: Z3: an efficient SMT solver. In: Ramakrishnan, C.R., Rehof, J. (eds.) TACAS 2008. LNCS, vol. 4963, pp. 337–340. Springer, Heidelberg (2008). https://doi.org/10.1007/978-3-540-78800-3_24

9. Deng, Y., Xia, C.S., Yang, C., Zhang, S.D., Yang, S., Zhang, L.: Large language models are edge-case generators: crafting unusual programs for fuzzing deep learning libraries. In: Proceedings of the 46th IEEE/ACM International Conference on Software Engineering, pp. 1–13 (2024)

10. Feng, J., et al.: Language models can be logical solvers. arXiv preprint arXiv:2311.06158 (2023)

11. Gadelha, M.R., Steffinlongo, E., Cordeiro, L.C., Fischer, B., Nicole, D.: SMT-based refutation of spurious bug reports in the clang static analyzer. In: 2019 IEEE/ACM 41st International Conference on Software Engineering: Companion Proceedings (ICSE-Companion), pp. 11–14. IEEE (2019)

12. Giannou, A., Rajput, S., Sohn, J., Lee, K., Lee, J.D., Papailiopoulos, D.: Looped transformers as programmable computers. In: International Conference on Machine Learning, pp. 11398–11442. PMLR (2023)

13. Gupta, P., et al.: Grace: language models meet code edits. In: Proceedings of the 31st ACM Joint European Software Engineering Conference and Symposium on the Foundations of Software Engineering, pp. 1483–1495 (2023)

14. Han, S., et al.: Folio: natural language reasoning with first-order logic. arXiv preprint arXiv:2209.00840 (2022)

15. Kang, E., Lafortune, S., Tripakis, S.: Automated synthesis of secure platform mappings. In: Dillig, I., Tasiran, S. (eds.) CAV 2019. LNCS, vol. 11561, pp. 219–237. Springer, Cham (2019). https://doi.org/10.1007/978-3-030-25540-4_12

16. Kazemi, M., Kim, N., Bhatia, D., Xu, X., Ramachandran, D.: Lambada: backward chaining for automated reasoning in natural language. arXiv preprint arXiv:2212.13894 (2022)

17. Kim, G., Baldi, P., McAleer, S.: Language models can solve computer tasks. In: Advances in Neural Information Processing Systems, vol. 36 (2024)
18. La Malfa, E., et al.: Code simulation challenges for large language models. arXiv preprint arXiv:2401.09074 (2024)
19. Lee, J., Hwang, W.: Symba: symbolic backward chaining for multi-step natural language reasoning. arXiv preprint arXiv:2402.12806 (2024)
20. Li, Z., et al.: LLMs for relational reasoning: How far are we? arXiv preprint arXiv:2401.09042 (2024)
21. Liu, C., et al.: Code execution with pre-trained language models. In: Findings of the Association for Computational Linguistics: ACL 2023, pp. 4984–4999 (2023)
22. Liu, M., Yang, T., Lou, Y., Du, X., Wang, Y., Peng, X.: Codegen4libs: a two-stage approach for library-oriented code generation. In: 2023 38th IEEE/ACM International Conference on Automated Software Engineering (ASE), pp. 434–445. IEEE (2023)
23. Ma, L., et al.: Knowlog: knowledge enhanced pre-trained language model for log understanding. In: Proceedings of the 46th IEEE/ACM International Conference on Software Engineering, pp. 1–13 (2024)
24. Min, S., et al.: Rethinking the role of demonstrations: What makes in-context learning work? In: Goldberg, Y., Kozareva, Z., Zhang, Y. (eds.) Proceedings of the 2022 Conference on Empirical Methods in Natural Language Processing, pp. 11048–11064. Association for Computational Linguistics, Abu Dhabi, United Arab Emirates (2022). https://doi.org/10.18653/v1/2022.emnlp-main.759. https://aclanthology.org/2022.emnlp-main.759
25. Pan, L., Albalak, A., Wang, X., Wang, W.: Logic-LM: empowering large language models with symbolic solvers for faithful logical reasoning. In: Findings of the Association for Computational Linguistics: EMNLP 2023, pp. 3806–3824 (2023)
26. Pérez, J., Barceló, P., Marinkovic, J.: Attention is turing-complete. J. Mach. Learn. Res. **22**(75), 1–35 (2021)
27. Roziere, B., et al.: Code llama: open foundation models for code. arXiv preprint arXiv:2308.12950 (2023)
28. Saparov, A., He, H.: Language models are greedy reasoners: a systematic formal analysis of chain-of-thought. In: The Eleventh International Conference on Learning Representations (2023). https://openreview.net/forum?id=qFVVBzXxR2V
29. Schuurmans, D.: Memory augmented large language models are computationally universal. arXiv preprint arXiv:2301.04589 (2023)
30. Shi, Z., et al.: Satformer: transformer-based unsat core learning. In: 2023 IEEE/ACM International Conference on Computer Aided Design (ICCAD), pp. 1–4. IEEE (2023)
31. Soltana, G., Sabetzadeh, M., Briand, L.C.: Practical constraint solving for generating system test data. ACM Trans. Softw. Eng. Methodol. (TOSEM) **29**(2), 1–48 (2020)
32. Sun, M., Yang, Y., Wang, Y., Wen, M., Jia, H., Zhou, Y.: SMT solver validation empowered by large pre-trained language models. In: 2023 38th IEEE/ACM International Conference on Automated Software Engineering (ASE), pp. 1288–1300. IEEE (2023)
33. Sun, Y., et al.: GPTScan: detecting logic vulnerabilities in smart contracts by combining GPT with program analysis. In: Proceedings of the IEEE/ACM ICSE (2024)
34. Tafjord, O., Dalvi, B., Clark, P.: Proofwriter: generating implications, proofs, and abductive statements over natural language. In: Findings of the Association for Computational Linguistics: ACL-IJCNLP 2021, pp. 3621–3634 (2021)

35. Touvron, H., S., et al.: Llama 2: open foundation and fine-tuned chat models. arXiv preprint arXiv:2307.09288 (2023)

36. Wang, C., Lou, Y., Liu, J., Peng, X.: Generating variable explanations via zero-shot prompt learning. In: 2023 38th IEEE/ACM International Conference on Automated Software Engineering (ASE), pp. 748–760. IEEE (2023)

37. Wang, L., et al.: Plan-and-solve prompting: Improving zero-shot chain-of-thought reasoning by large language models. In: Proceedings of the 61st Annual Meeting of the Association for Computational Linguistics (Volume 1: Long Papers), pp. 2609–2634 (2023)

38. Wang, X., et al.: Self-consistency improves chain of thought reasoning in language models. In: The Eleventh International Conference on Learning Representations (2022)

39. Wei, C., Chen, Y., Ma, T.: Statistically meaningful approximation: a case study on approximating turing machines with transformers. In: Advances in Neural Information Processing Systems, vol. 35, pp. 12071–12083 (2022)

40. Wei, J., et al.: Chain-of-thought prompting elicits reasoning in large language models. In: Advances in Neural Information Processing Systems, vol. 35, pp. 24824–24837 (2022)

41. Xu, J., et al.: Unilog: automatic logging via LLM and in-context learning. In: Proceedings of the 46th IEEE/ACM International Conference on Software Engineering, pp. 1–12 (2024)

42. Yang, A.Z., Le Goues, C., Martins, R., Hellendoorn, V.: Large language models for test-free fault localization. In: Proceedings of the 46th IEEE/ACM International Conference on Software Engineering, pp. 1–12 (2024)

43. Ye, X., Chen, Q., Dillig, I., Durrett, G.: SatLM: satisfiability-aided language models using declarative prompting. In: Advances in Neural Information Processing Systems, vol. 36 (2024)

44. Yu, H., et al.: Codereval: a benchmark of pragmatic code generation with generative pre-trained models. In: Proceedings of the 46th IEEE/ACM International Conference on Software Engineering, pp. 1–12 (2024)

45. Zhang, S., Gu, X., Chen, Y., Shen, B.: Infere: step-by-step regex generation via chain of inference. In: 2023 38th IEEE/ACM International Conference on Automated Software Engineering (ASE), pp. 1505–1515. IEEE (2023)

46. Zhang, Y., Zhen, H.L., Pei, Z., Lian, Y., Yin, L., Yuan, M., Yu, B.: Sola: solver-layer adaption of LLM for better logic reasoning. arXiv preprint arXiv:2402.11903 (2024)

47. Zhong, W., et al.: Analytical reasoning of text. In: Findings of the Association for Computational Linguistics: NAACL 2022, pp. 2306–2319 (2022)

Enhancing Multi-modal Regular Expression Synthesis via Large Language Models and Semantic Manipulations of Sub-expressions

Zipan Tang[1], Yixuan Yan[2,3], Rongchen Li[2,3], Hanze Dong[1],
Haiming Chen[2(✉)], and Hongyu Gao[1]

[1] Beijing University of Technology, Beijing, China
{tangzipan1999,1805739139}@emails.bjut.edu.cn, hygao@bjut.edu.cn
[2] Key Laboratory of System Software (Chinese Academy of Sciences)
and State Key Laboratory of Computer Science, Institute of Software,
Chinese Academy of Sciences, Beijing, China
{yanyx,lirc,chm}@ios.ac.cn
[3] University of Chinese Academy of Sciences, Beijing, China

Abstract. Real-world regular expressions (regexes) are widely used in practice. Since regexes are difficult to comprehend and write, automatically synthesizing regexes has been an important research problem. However, current techniques face challenges like weak capability in generalization and severely limited support of extended features of regexes. In this paper, we address these challenges via Large Language Models (LLMs) together with semantic manipulations of sub-expressions, and propose PowerSyn, a framework for regex synthesis based on both natural language descriptions and examples and supports extended features. Specifically, we design the prompt suitable for synthesizing regexes with LLMs and present novel algorithms to manipulate sub-expressions, which consider the matching relation, and are guided by examples. The evaluation results demonstrate the significant efficacy of our approach.

Keywords: regex synthesis · regex repair · programming by natural language descriptions · programming by examples · semantics · large language models

1 Introduction

Real-world regular expressions (regexes) are a potent tool extensively employed in software engineering, programming languages, network security, natural language processing (NLP), and other fields [3,4,6,7,17,18,20,23]. However, regexes pose challenges for comprehension and writing, and are prone to errors, even for the experts [4,13,16,17,22]. Therefore, developing techniques for automatic regex synthesis is essential. Many researchers have investigated various methods for solving this problem, which can be categorized into three main approaches: synthesizing regexes from natural language (NL) descriptions [10,14,18] [27,28], synthesizing regexes from examples [3,8,9], or synthesizing regexes from both resources [5,12,19,25,26]. Despite these efforts, the current techniques have the following problems.

Regex synthesis techniques based on NL descriptions suffer from ambiguity and impreciseness of human language [18,28,29]. Furthermore, existing techniques based on traditional machine learning models can only produce regexes that resemble the training data and have relatively low accuracy on benchmark datasets, due to the limitations of traditional models, such as having fewer parameters and using limited and lower-quality data for training.

On the other hand, example-based regex synthesis approaches rely on user-supplied high-quality examples. However, obtaining high-quality examples that fully capture the user's intent is challenging, making it difficult to apply purely example-based approaches effectively.

Since examples and NL descriptions provide complementary information, multi-modal approaches have the potential to leverage the advantages of both and are therefore promising. In fact, this practice is common. For instance, when users inquire about regex synthesis problems on Stack Overflow[1], they frequently refer to NL descriptions as a primary source and provide examples to clarify ambiguities in NL. However, effectively exploiting both of these resources remains a challenge. For example, the problem faced by NL descriptions-based techniques still exists for current multi-modal techniques based on traditional machine learning models: they heavily rely on training sets, resulting in their *limited generalization capabilities*, i.e. to synthesize accurate regexes for data excluded from the dataset.

Additionally, while regexes include many extended features commonly used in practice [15], current regex synthesis techniques have *severely limited support for these features*, significantly impacting their usability. In other words, it is necessary to synthesize regexes with extended features for real-world applications. For instance, in a question posed on Stack Overflow[2], the accepted answer is a regex with extended features: $\char"5E(?!.^*ins[a-z.]^*\backslash s).^*\backslash bpremium\backslash b.^*$[3]. Current regex synthesis methods fail to provide the correct solution when extended features such as *negative lookahead* $(?!r)$ and *word-boundary* $\backslash b$ are used, as these are not supported by existing techniques. Furthermore, certain studies have omitted operators such as *intersection* and *complement* which are pervasive in benchmark datasets [26].

Recent advances in large language models (LLMs) have demonstrated promising results in NL comprehension. The proficiency of LLMs is attributed

---

[1] https://stackoverflow.com/.

[2] We refine the user's question as: My task is to select all transactions that contain the word premium, but do not contain the word include lowercase letters and "." and start with "ins".

[3] https://stackoverflow.com/questions/73415312/regex-lookaround-does-not-work-with-quantifiers-in-sas.

to the extensive training on vast corpora. Therefore, leveraging LLMs provides a promising way to address the problem of weak capability in generalization faced by traditional machine learning models. However, it still faces challenges like ambiguity and impreciseness inherent in NL descriptions, lacking domain-specific semantic knowledge, and so on.

To address these challenges, we propose PowerSyn, a framework for regex synthesis based on both NL descriptions and examples. The key features of our approach include: **Supporting extended features**. As stated above, the synthesis of regexes with extended features is necessary for real-world applications. To tackle this problem, we leverage the capability of LLMs to synthesize from NL descriptions the syntax of regexes with extended features and propose a novel semantic framework to address the semantic errors that LLMs encounter when handling extended features. In this article, we have added support for the extended features of *lookarounds* and *anchors*. Additionally, we also provide support for Unicode-related extended features to enhance the usability of our framework. **Repairing regexes based on semantics.** There are still some errors in the regexes returned by LLMs due to the ambiguity and impreciseness inherent in the NL description. We have adopted an examples-guided and semantics-based approach to fix the errors. The core of this method is dividing regexes into sub-expressions and using the matching result with examples of the regex engine as the oracle for combining sub-expressions.

We evaluate our framework by comparison against the state-of-the-art tools for multi-modal regex synthesis, both on publicly available datasets and on a new dataset collected by us. The results illustrate the significant efficacy of our approach.

Our main contributions are summarized as follows:

- We design new prompts suited for the synthesizing task, and evaluate the consistent rate (see Sect. 6.1) of different LLMs (both open- and closed-sourced) in synthesizing regexes. We then utilize the models and prompt with the highest consistent rate for our work.
- We introduce a novel method for combining sub-expressions to repair regexes based on examples. The algorithm takes into account the semantics of sub-expressions for accurate combination and considers the extended features during combination.
- The evaluation results demonstrate that PowerSyn has significant advantages over other tools—it achieves the highest rate of consistent regexes compared to other tools.

2   Preliminary

Extended Regular Expressions. Let Σ be a finite alphabet of symbols. The set of extended regexes $\mathsf{ExReg}(\Sigma)$ is defined by the following abstract grammar:
$r, r' ::= a \mid \varepsilon \mid [C] \mid r + r' \mid r \mathbin{\&} r' \mid r \cdot r' \mid r\{m, n\} \mid \sim r \mid (?\text{=}r) \mid (?\text{<=}r) \mid (?!r)$
$\mid (?\text{<!}\ r) \mid \char`\^ \mid \$ \mid \backslash A \mid \backslash z \mid \backslash Z \mid \backslash b \mid \backslash B$, where $a \in \Sigma$, $C \subseteq \Sigma$ and C is not empty, $m \in \mathbb{N}$, $n \in \mathbb{N} \cup \{\infty\}$, and $m \leq n$. The empty word is represented by

ε, and the character classes are indicated by $[C]$. The *union, intersection, concatenation, quantifier* and *complement* operators are denoted by $+$, $\&$, $\cdot$, $\{m,n\}$ and $\sim$ respectively, with the priority increases from left to right. *Lookarounds* include: *positive lookahead* (?=r), *positive lookbehind* (?<=r), *negative lookahead* (?! r), *negative lookbehind* (?<! r). *Anchors* include: *start of line* ^, *end of line* $, *start of string* \A, *end of a string but for the line terminator (if any)* \Z, *end of string* \z, *word-boundary* \b, *non-word-boundary* \B. The line terminators include $\backslash n, \backslash r, \backslash u0085, \backslash u2028, \backslash u2029, \backslash r \backslash n$. Besides, $r\{i\}$, $r^?$, r^*, r^+ are abbreviations of $r\{i,i\}$, $r\{0,1\}$, $r\{0,\infty\}$, $r\{1,\infty\}$ respectively and $r \cdot r'$ is typically abbreviated as rr'. We have included *Unicode* in the alphabet Σ and support Unicode processing in subsequent sections.

Formal Semantics of Extended Regexes. Let s be a string and $s \in \Sigma^*$. A location of s is represented as an interval $[i,j]$, where i, j are called positions satisfying $0 \leq i \leq j \leq |s|$ where $|s|$ is the length of s. Then, we

String		!	a	b	a	b	;	
	↑	↑	↑	↑	↑	↑	↑	
Positions	0	1	2	3	4	5	6	

Fig. 1. String and positions

define the tuple $\langle s, [i,j] \rangle$ representing a (sub-)string of s from position i to j. Specially, $\langle s, [i,i] \rangle$ represents position i in s. Figure 1 illustrates a string along with its corresponding positions. The first row displays the string $s =$ "!abab;" with $|s| = 6$. The second row is the positions in the string, numbered from 0 to 6. For example, the sub-string "abab" within s appears between position 1 and 5 will be represented as $\langle s, [1,5] \rangle$. Moreover, we can utilize $\langle s, [5,5] \rangle$ to denote the position 5 that is between "b" and ";".

Let $r \in \mathsf{ExReg}(\Sigma)$ be a regex. We employ a satisfaction relation $\vDash: \Sigma^* \times \mathbb{N} \times \mathbb{N} \times \mathsf{ExReg}(\Sigma)$, which relates the tuple $\langle s, [i,j] \rangle$ with the regex r. We write $\langle s, [i,j] \rangle \vDash r$ to denote r can match s at the location $[i,j]$. For example, we have a regex "\w$^+$", it can match "abab" in $s =$ "!abab;", and we describe the matching relation by $\langle !abab;, [1,5] \rangle \vDash \backslash \mathtt{w}^+$. Then, we define the relation $\vDash$ by induction as shown in Fig. 2 where $\Longleftrightarrow$ is used to define the semantics of regexes. In addition, we define function $\mathrm{MATCH}: \Sigma^* \times \mathbb{N} \times \mathbb{N} \times \mathsf{ExReg}(\Sigma) \to \mathsf{Bool}$ as follows: $\mathrm{MATCH}(\langle s, [i,j] \rangle, r) = \mathbf{T}$ (true) if $\langle s, [i,j] \rangle \vDash r$, or $\mathbf{F}$ (false) otherwise.

3   Overview

This section presents an overview of PowerSyn as shown in Fig. 3, using the NL description and both the positive and negative examples given in Table 1.

Our method starts by synthesizing regexes from NL descriptions and a user-defined number of examples (i.e. a portion of the total examples) as input (i.e., *Result 1* in Fig. 3), and the detailed process is described in Sect. 4. After that, if any one of the synthesized regexes is consistent with the given examples, then PowerSyn outputs it. Otherwise, we propose SynReco, a novel examples-based and semantics-guided repair algorithm, to fix errors caused by ambiguity and imprecision in NL descriptions. For ease of understanding, the ambiguity and imprecision in Table 1 have been highlighted by the underlines. The key

Table 1. The NL Description and Examples Given By the User

Natural Language Description	Positive Examples	Negative Examples
Match strings start with upcase letters more than 3 times, which includes *UTF*. Then, strings have a character in [#_;]. Last, include the word *jack* in the strings.	UTFO#jack abc XYZUTF;jack EUTF#jack. UTFUTF#jack EUTF; jack! UTFB_you jack	UTF#jack utff_jack# 5H#jacka 123_jack UTFB#jackcc utf

$(1)\langle s,[i,j]\rangle \vDash \varepsilon \iff i = j \qquad (2)\langle s,[i,j]\rangle \vDash a \iff j = i+1 \wedge \langle s,[i,j]\rangle = a$

$(3)\langle s,[i,j]\rangle \vDash [C] \iff j = i+1 \wedge (\vee_{a\in C}\langle s,[i,j]\rangle \vDash a)$

$(4)\langle s,[i,j]\rangle \vDash r_1 + r_2 \iff \langle s,[i,j]\rangle \vDash r_1 \vee \langle s,[i,j]\rangle \vDash r_2$

$(5)\langle s,[i,j]\rangle \vDash r_1 \& r_2 \iff \langle s,[i,j]\rangle \vDash r_1 \wedge \langle s,[i,j]\rangle \vDash r_2$

$(6)\langle s,[i,j]\rangle \vDash r_1 \cdot r_2 \iff \langle s,[i,k]\rangle \vDash r_1 \wedge \langle s,[k,j]\rangle \vDash r_2, \exists k \in [i,j]$

$(7)\langle s,[i,j]\rangle \vDash r\{m,n\} \iff \vee_{m\leq k\leq n}\langle s,[i,j]\rangle \vDash \underbrace{rr...r}_{k} \qquad (8)\langle s,[i,j]\rangle \vDash \sim r \iff \langle s,[i,j]\rangle \nvDash r$

$(9)\langle s,[i,j]\rangle \vDash (?=r) \iff i = j \wedge \langle s,[i,k]\rangle \vDash r, \exists k \in [j,|s|] \qquad (13)\langle s,[i,j]\rangle \vDash \,\hat{}\, \iff i = j = 0$

$(10)\langle s,[i,j]\rangle \vDash (?!r) \iff i = j \wedge \langle s,[i,k]\rangle \nvDash r, \forall k \in [j,|s|] \qquad (14)\langle s,[i,j]\rangle \vDash \$ \iff i = j = |s|$

$(11)\langle s,[i,j]\rangle \vDash (?<=r) \iff i = j \wedge \langle s,[k,j]\rangle \vDash r, \exists k \in [0,i] \qquad (15)\langle s,[i,j]\rangle \vDash \backslash A \iff i = j = 0$

$(12)\langle s,[i,j]\rangle \vDash (?<!r) \iff i = j \wedge \langle s,[k,j]\rangle \nvDash r, \forall k \in [0,i] \qquad (16)\langle s,[i,j]\rangle \vDash \backslash z \iff i = j = |s|$

$(17)\langle s,[i,j]\rangle \vDash \backslash Z \iff \begin{cases} i = j = |s|-1 & \text{if } \langle s,[j-1,j]\rangle \vDash [\backslash n\backslash r\backslash u0085\backslash u2028\backslash u2029] \\ i = j = |s|-2 & \text{if } \langle s,[j-2,j]\rangle \vDash \backslash r\backslash n \\ i = j = |s| & \text{otherwise} \end{cases}$

$(18)\langle s,[i,j]\rangle \vDash \backslash b \iff i = j \wedge (i = 0 \vee j = |s| \vee (\text{MATCH}(\langle s,[i-1,i]\rangle, \backslash w) \neq$
$\qquad\qquad\qquad\qquad \text{MATCH}(\langle s,[i,i+1]\rangle, \backslash w) \wedge 1 \leq i = j \leq |s|-1))$

$(19)\langle s,[i,j]\rangle \vDash \backslash B \iff i = j \wedge (\text{MATCH}(\langle s,[i-1,i]\rangle, \backslash w) =$
$\qquad\qquad\qquad\qquad \text{MATCH}(\langle s,[i,i+1]\rangle, \backslash w) \wedge 1 \leq i = j \leq |s|-1)$

Fig. 2. Formal Semantics of Regexes with Extend Futures.

intermediate results of SynReco are shown as *Result 2–3* in Fig. 3 and details of the algorithm are introduced in Sect. 5. When SynReco successfully finds regexes that are consistent with positive and negative examples, it returns the one among them that is closest to the LLMs' completions; otherwise, it returns false. The specific explanation for each *Result* will be described in the section corresponding to the method. By utilizing examples to assist LLMs in synthesizing regexes and repairing possible errors in the synthesized completions, our method effectively addresses the ambiguity and inaccuracies from NL descriptions.

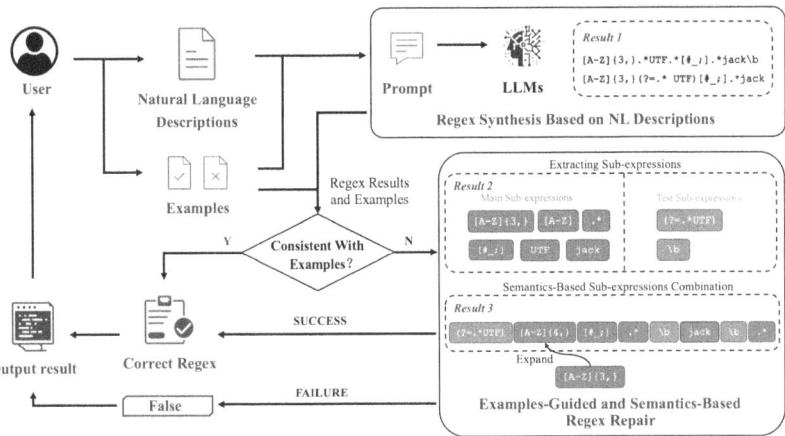

Fig. 3. The Framework of PowerSyn

4   Regex Synthesis Based on Natural Language Descriptions

In this section, we design two prompts for synthesizing regexes. We further process the completions returned by the LLMs and then extract the regexes from the processed completions.

Prompts Design. To align the completions of LLMs with our expectations, we design prompts for synthesizing regexes, as shown in Fig. 4 **Prompt** (lines 1–11). The prompt consists of two parts: a *System message* and a *User message*. The *System message* (lines 3–6 in Fig. 4) explains that the task of the LLMs is to synthesize regexes based on the user's questions and to place limits on the completions to facilitate the extraction of regexes from the completions. By providing a concise description of the task, LLMs gain clarity on the objectives and requirements of the task, allowing them to provide more relevant completions and prevent the generation of irrelevant information. The *User message* (lines 8–11 in Fig. 4) contains information of the user's questions for the concrete synthesizing task. Specifically, we designed two types of prompts: the *Simple* prompt, which depends on the NL descriptions (i.e. questions) (excluding the contents in the red box in Fig. 4), and the *Standard* prompt, which further includes example-related contents. We conducted experiments to compare the consistent rate of regexes synthesized by different LLMs and the designed prompts in Sect. 6.2, the results shown in Table 2 indicate that prompts with examples perform better than those without. The synthesis completions shown in Sect. 4 and the results from Syn-Reco presented in Sect. 5 are all based on standard prompts.

Completions Returned Directly by LLMs and Further Processing. Lines 13 to 14 of Fig. 4 we show one completion directly returned by *GPT-4o*. Since the randomness of regexes synthesized by LLMs, we will produce multiple

```
(01) I. Prompt
(02) System message:
(03) You are a software engineer. Your task is to synthesize the regular expression based on
(04) the following NL description. The regular expression must satisfy given Match exam-
(05) ples and Non-match examples. In addition, do not generate any additional information.
(06) You need return the answer within 3 back-ticks.
(07) User message:
(08) NL: Match strings start with uppercase letters more than 3 times, which includes UTF.
(09) Then, strings have a character in [#_;]. Last, include the word jack in the strings.
(10) Match examples: 1)"UTFO#jack abc" 2)"XYZUTF;jack" 3)"EUTF#jack."
(11) Non-match examples: 1)"UTF#jack" 2)"123_jack"

(12) II. Completion
(13) Below is a regular expression that matches the given description:
(14) ``` [A-Z]{3,}(?=.'UTF)[#_;].'jack ```
```

Fig. 4. Prompt and Completion for Synthesizing Regexes with LLMs

completions for each synthesis task to increase the likelihood of synthesizing the correct regex. Then, we extract content between "'from the completions as regex because, in the prompt, we require the regex to be enclosed within three back-ticks. This method effectively avoids interference from additional information in the completions. However, based on the observation of the completions, we found that they may synthesize regexes with syntax errors or anomalies (such as being excessively long). In such cases, we will let LLMs synthesize a new regex until it is normal and syntax correct. Referring back to the example in the Sect. 3, after processing the completion synthesized by LLMs, we remove the back-ticks and the content outside them (like line 13 in Fig. 4) to obtain the regexes. For demonstrating purpose, we only show two instances of the synthesized regexes as an example in Fig. 3, depicted in *Result 1*.

5   Examples-Guided and Semantics-Based Regex Repair

After conducting manual inspections and performing membership tests using the regex engines for the synthesized regexes, we find it is common that the regexes in all completions cannot accept all positive examples and reject all negative examples for one task. However, we notice that in this case the regexes often include sub-expressions that are aligned with the ground truth but are organized in the wrong order. It

---

Algorithm 1: SynReco

Input: Incorrect regexes $\mathcal{R}_I$, Positive examples $\mathcal{P}$, Negative examples $\mathcal{N}$
Output: Correct regex r
1 $\mathcal{R}_{\mathsf{sub}}:=\text{EXTRACT}(\mathcal{R}_I)$
2 $\mathcal{M}:=\text{INITIALIZE}(\mathcal{R}_{\mathsf{sub}}, \mathcal{P}, \mathcal{N})$
3 $\mathcal{R}_C:=\text{SEARCH}(\mathcal{M}, \mathcal{P}, \mathcal{N})$
4 $r:=\text{RANK}(\mathcal{R}_C, \mathcal{R}_I)$
5 **return** r

---

is not hard to grasp that this situation arises because of the inherent ambiguity of NL. Thus, we propose SynReco to derive a new and correct regex by manipulating sub-expressions, which are given below.

Algorithm 1 takes all incorrect regexes $\mathcal{R}_I$[4], all positive examples $\mathcal{P}$, and all negative examples $\mathcal{N}$ for one synthesis task as input, and returns a correct regex r. First, it extracts all sub-expressions from $\mathcal{R}_I$, and the results are stored in $\mathcal{R}_{\mathsf{sub}}$ (line 1). After extracting sub-expressions, it needs to combine sub-expressions into a regex. However, combining sub-expressions arbitrarily can lead to a combinatorial explosion. Therefore, we propose a heuristic strategy based on the semantics of sub-expressions. Through the INITIALIZE function, we obtained the matching results of sub-expressions in $\mathcal{P}$ and $\mathcal{N}$, denoted as $\mathcal{M}$ (line 2). The EXTRACT and INITIALIZE functions are described in Sect. 5.1. Then, we utilize the SEARCH function to search for correct regexes $\mathcal{R}_C$ that are consistent with examples based on $\mathcal{M}$ (line 3). We described the SEARCH function in Sect. 5.2. Finally, we use the RANK function to sort $\mathcal{R}_C$ and select the optimal regex r from the repaired regexes based on the regexes returned by LLMs (line 4), as detailed in Sect. 5.3.

5.1 Extracting and Initializing Sub-expressions

Extracting Sub-expressions. The EXTRACT function takes incorrect regexes $\mathcal{R}_I$ generated by LLMs as inputs and returns a set of sub-expressions. First, it constructed syntax trees for each regexes, based on the grammar (in Sect. 2). Then, it extracts the nodes of the syntax trees as a sub-expression, except for the root node. For instance, back to Sect. 3, we extract the sub-expressions from *Result 1* in Fig. 3. We demonstrate the key sub-expressions from the extraction results in *Result 2*, such as: "`[A-Z]{3,}`", "`UTF`", "`[#_;]`", "`.*`", "`jack`", "`(?=.*UTF)`", "`\b`".

Initializing Sub-expressions. We utilize Algorithm 2 to describe the implementation of the INITIALIZE function. Since some sub-expressions only match a specific position (such as lookaround or anchor), while others match a (sub-)string, we categorize the sub-expressions into the following two types and obtain their matching results on positive and negative examples respectively. (i) *Main Sub-Expressions*: Those sub-expressions have the potential to con-

---

Algorithm 2: Initialize

Input: Sub-expressions $\mathcal{R}_{\mathsf{sub}}$, Positive examples $\mathcal{P}$, Negative examples $\mathcal{N}$

Output: Matching results $\mathcal{M}$

1 $\mathcal{M}:=\emptyset$
2 **foreach** $e \in \mathcal{R}_{sub}$ **do**
3 $\quad T_\mathcal{P}:=\text{FINDALLMATCH}(e,\mathcal{P})$
4 $\quad T_\mathcal{N}:=\text{FINDALLMATCH}(e,\mathcal{N})$
5 $\quad \mathcal{M}:=\mathcal{M} \cup \{\langle e,T_\mathcal{P},T_\mathcal{N}\rangle\}$
6 **end**
7 $\mathcal{M}:=\text{MERGE}(\mathcal{M})$
8 **return** $\mathcal{M}$

---

[4] Which are the synthesized regexes returned from LLMs.

sume at least 1 character or more during a match, such as, "[A-Z]{3,}", "[#_;]" and ".*". (ii) *Test Sub-Expressions*: Those sub-expressions can not consume any characters during a match, but they constrain the other parts in a regex, such as, "(?=.*UTF)", "\b". In Fig. 3, we use red and blue respectively to represent these two types of sub-expressions.

textuiObtaining Matching Results. In INITIALIZE function, the set of matching results, i.e. $\mathcal{M}$, is initially an empty set (line 1). Then, the function iterates over each sub-expression e in the subset $\mathcal{R}_{sub}$. For each e, it utilizes the FINDALL-MATCH function to obtain matching results of e within $\mathcal{P}$ and $\mathcal{N}$, resulting in sets $T_{\mathcal{P},e}$ and $T_{\mathcal{N},e}$ respectively (lines 3–4). $T_{\mathcal{P},e}$ includes the matching results of e within each element of the set $\mathcal{P}$ and $T_{\mathcal{N},e}$ includes the matching results of e within each element of the set $\mathcal{N}$. These sets, along with the element e, are then grouped as a triple $\langle e, T_{\mathcal{P},e}, T_{\mathcal{N},e} \rangle$ and added to the set $\mathcal{M}$ (line 5). We define the FINDALLMATCH function to find all matching results of a given expression e within each element of examples S (represents $\mathcal{P}$ or $\mathcal{N}$). Let E_m be the set of *Main Sub-Expressions* and E_t be the set of *Test Sub-Expressions*. If $e \in E_m$, the set of matching results is defined as: $T = \{\langle s, [i, j] \rangle \mid s \in S, \ 0 \leq i \leq j \leq |s| \wedge \text{MATCH}(\langle s, [i, j] \rangle, e)\}$. If $e \in E_t$, the set of matching results is defined as: $T = \{\langle s, [i, i] \rangle \mid s \in S, \ 0 \leq i \leq |s| \wedge \text{MATCH}(\langle s, [i, j] \rangle, e)\}$. The formal semantics in Fig. 2 show that, despite the differing semantics of the two types of matching results, they can be unified within the same modeling framework. This allows our repair process to easily handle regexes with extended features.

textuiMerging Matching Results. At line 7, we employ the MERGE function to merge the matching results. The MERGE function is implemented by examining triples such as $\langle e_1, T_{\mathcal{P},e_1}, T_{\mathcal{N},e_1} \rangle$, $\langle e_2, T_{\mathcal{P},e_2}, T_{\mathcal{N},e_2} \rangle$, $\cdots$ within the set $\mathcal{M}$. If the function finds that $T_{\mathcal{P},e_1} = T_{\mathcal{P},e_2} = \cdots$ and $T_{\mathcal{N},e_2} = T_{\mathcal{N},e_2} = \cdots$, it merges these triples into a single consolidated output, expressed as $\langle [e_1, e_2, \cdots], T_{\mathcal{P},e_1}, T_{\mathcal{N},e_1} \rangle$. This function allows for the effective reduction of redundancy and the simplification of the search space.

5.2 Semantics-Based Sub-expressions Combination

In this section, we detail the SEARCH function through Algorithm 3. The purpose of this algorithm is to search for the correct regexes that are consistent with positive and negative examples. This is done by novel semantic-guided manipulation techniques of sub-expressions. Details are introduced below.

The algorithm takes the matching results $\mathcal{M}$, positive examples $\mathcal{P}$, and negative examples $\mathcal{N}$ as input, and outputs a set of correct regexes $\mathcal{R}_C$. Let r be a regex used to record temporary results of sub-expression combinations. First, the algorithm initializes the set of correct regexes $\mathcal{R}_C$ as the empty set, r as ε, $T_{\mathcal{P},r}$ as $\langle s, [0,0] \rangle$ where $s \in \mathcal{P}$ (lines 1–3) and stack S with initial state $\langle r, T_{\mathcal{P},r}, 0 \rangle$ (line 4). While stack S is not empty, the algorithm utilizes the POP function to get the top element $\langle r, T_{\mathcal{P},r}, i \rangle$ of the stack repeatedly (lines 5–6), where i denotes the number of attempts to combine sub-expressions in r. If i exceeds the threshold StepNum, the algorithm will exit the loop; otherwise, it attempts to combine new sub-expressions (lines 7–9). The threshold StepNum is the upper bound on the number of times the sub-expression has been combined and can be adjusted by the user.

Algorithm 3: Search

Input: Matching results $\mathcal{M}$, Positive examples $\mathcal{P}$, Negative examples $\mathcal{N}$

Output: Correct regexes $\mathcal{R}_C$

1   $\mathcal{R}_C := \emptyset$
2   $r := \varepsilon$
3   $T_{\mathcal{P},r} := \{ \langle s, [0,0] \rangle \mid s \in \mathcal{P} \}$
4   $S = [\langle r, T_{\mathcal{P},r}, 0 \rangle]$
5   **while** $S \neq \emptyset$ **do**
6     $\langle r, T_{\mathcal{P},r}, i \rangle = \text{POP}(S)$
7   **if** $i > $ StepNum **then**
8 | *break*
9   **end**
10    $\mathcal{M}' := \text{GETCANDIDATE}(\mathcal{M}, T_{\mathcal{P},r}, r)$
11   **if** $\text{FINDEXPAND}(r) < $ ExpNum **then**
12 | $\mathcal{M}' := \mathcal{M}' \cup \text{EXPAND}(\mathcal{M}')$
13   **end**
14    $\mathcal{M}_v := \text{VERIFY}(\mathcal{M}', \mathcal{P}, T_{\mathcal{P},r}, r)$
15   **foreach** $m \in \text{SORT}(\mathcal{M}')$ **do**
16     $\langle r', T'_{\mathcal{P},r} \rangle := \text{UPDATE}(m, r, T_{\mathcal{P},r})$
17   **if** $\text{SOLUTION}(r', \mathcal{P}, \mathcal{N})$ **then**
18 | $\mathcal{R}_C := \mathcal{R}_C \cup r'$
19   **end**
20     $\text{PUSH}(S, \langle r', T'_{\mathcal{P},r}, i+1 \rangle)$
21   **end**
22 **end**
23 **return** $\mathcal{R}_C$

Getting Candidates. The algorithm utilizes the GETCANDIDATE function to select candidates from $\mathcal{M}$ based on r and $T_{\mathcal{P},r}$ (line 10). During the selection process, we utilized the semantics of concatenation. Let $m = \langle m_e, T_{\mathcal{P},m_e}, T_{\mathcal{N},m_e} \rangle$ be one element in set $\mathcal{M}$. The set of candidates $\mathcal{M}'$ obtained from $\mathcal{M}$ using the GETCANDIDATE function is defined as follows: $\mathcal{M}' = \{m \mid m \in \mathcal{M}, \exists \langle s, [i,j] \rangle \in T_{\mathcal{P},r}, \langle s, [i',j'] \rangle \in T_{\mathcal{P},m_e} . \langle s, [i,j'] \rangle \vDash r \cdot m_e \}$, where $\langle s, [i,j] \rangle \vDash r$ and $\langle s, [i',j'] \rangle \vDash m_e$. The set $\mathcal{M}'$ include m when the new expression $r \cdot m_e$ can match at least one positive example $s \in \mathcal{P}$ at the location $[i,j']$. Thus, $\mathcal{M}'$ retains some promising candidates, which can be corrected using the EXPAND function. Next, the algorithm uses the FINDEXPAND function to determine the number of expanded sub-expressions present in the regex r (line 11). If this number is less than the threshold ExpNum, the algorithm will use the EXPAND function to expand the set of candidates $\mathcal{M}'$ (line 12). The threshold ExpNum is the upper bound on the number of extended sub-expressions present in the regex and can be adjusted by the user. A detailed explanation of the EXPAND function is given shortly. If some of the elements in $\mathcal{M}'$ fails to meet the concatenation semantics condition for any positive example $s \in \mathcal{P}$, these m do not need to try combining. The algorithm uses the VERIFY function to remove such m candidates and retain valid ones (line 14). The VERIFY function implements this feature according to the following definition: $\mathcal{M}_v = \{m | m \in \mathcal{M}', \forall s \in \mathcal{P} \exists \langle s, [i,j] \rangle \in T_{\mathcal{P},r}, \langle s, [i',j'] \rangle \in T_{\mathcal{P},m_e} \cdot \langle s, [i,j'] \rangle \vDash r \cdot m_e\}$.

Expanding Candidates. Based on our observation that although some sub-expressions are not directly suitable for the final regex, modifying or combining them (using + or &) may obtain new sub-expressions needed for the final regex, we design a series of rules listed below to generate a set of new sub-expressions and use the INITIALIZE function to initial this set, then add initializing results to candidate $\mathcal{M}'$. In the example from Sect. 3, we utilized the EXPAND function to extend the sub-expression "[A-Z]{3,}" to "[A-Z]{4,}" as shown in Fig. 3. This step corrects the error caused by the ambiguity in the NL description from Table 1 regarding "more than 3 times", and after modifying the quantifier of this sub-expression, the new sub-expression can effectively distinguish between positive and negative examples.

- *Adding existing quantifier*: This rule generates new expressions by adding quantifiers to quantifier-free sub-expressions in E_m, using quantifiers extracted from sub-expressions that already contain them.
- *Adding optional quantifier*: This rule generates new expressions by adding *optional quantifiers* ($^?$) to sub-expressions that belong to E_m.
- *Modifying quantifier*: This rule generates new expressions by modifying the quantifier in sub-expressions, where the minimum and maximum values are set based on the positive and negative examples.
- *Uniting and Intersecting sub-expressions*: This rule generates new expressions by combining sub-expressions by operators *union* (+) and *intersection* (&).

Sorting Candidates. The algorithm utilizes the SORT function to construct the candidate set $\mathcal{M}_v$ into a priority queue (line 15). We use $T'_{\mathcal{P},m_e}$ to denote all $\langle s, [i',j'] \rangle \in T_{\mathcal{P},m_e}$ satisfy $\langle s, [i,j'] \rangle \vDash r \cdot m_e$ in the definition of $\mathcal{M}_v$. The priority of the m is defined by the ratio $k_m = \frac{\sum_{s \in \mathcal{P}} max\{j-i : \langle s,[i,j] \rangle \in T'_{\mathcal{P},m_e}\}}{|T'_{\mathcal{P},m_e}|}$. The k_m is the average of the maximum matching lengths for each element s within the set $\mathcal{P}$, serving as our empirical assessment of the generalization capability of sub-expressions under the current search branch. This function, which sorts the candidates, utilizes the intuition that sub-expressions with moderate generalization ability (i.e., with a higher k_m value) are more likely to be selected. In this way, the final regex is more likely to reject negative examples. In this algorithm, due to the last-in-first-out (LIFO) nature of the stack, it arranges the priority queue in reverse order, ensuring that sub-expressions with higher priority are searched first.

Combining Candidates. At line 15, the algorithm iterates through m in the order of the results returned by the SORT function. Next, the algorithm updates r and $T_{\mathcal{P},r}$ based on the matching result m through the UPDATE function. The new regex r' is $r \cdot m_e$, and the $T'_{\mathcal{P},r}$ is the set of matching results $\langle s, [i,j] \rangle$ that satisfy $\langle s, [i,j] \rangle \vDash r \cdot m_e$ for each $s \in \mathcal{P}$ (line 16). Through the SOLUTION function, the algorithm determines whether r' is consistent with positive and negative examples (line 17). The function is implemented based on the following definition: $\text{SOLUTION}(r', \mathcal{P}, \mathcal{N}) = \forall p \in \mathcal{P}.\langle p, [0, |p|] \rangle \vDash r' \wedge \forall n \in \mathcal{N}.\langle n, [0, |n|] \rangle \nvDash r'$. If SOLUTION returns **T**, the algorithm uses the set $\mathcal{R}_C$ to record this regex r' (line 18). Then, the algorithm utilizes the PUSH function to push the current state $\langle r', T'_{\mathcal{P},r}, i+1 \rangle$ onto the stack S, allowing the algorithm to continue attempting to combine new sub-expressions in this state (line 20). Finally, after exiting the loop, the SEARCH function returns $\mathcal{R}$ (line 23).

Reflecting on Fig. 3, we combine the main sub-expressions ("`[#_;]`", "`.*`", "`jack`"), the test sub-expressions ("`(?=.*UTF)`", "`\b`"), and the expanded sub -expressions ("`[A-Z]{4,}`") into some regexes like r_1 = "`(?=.*UTF)[A-Z]{4,}[#_;].*\bjack\b.*`", as illustrated in *Result 3*. This combination step repairs two errors in the NL description from Table 1: "which include *UTF*" and "the word *jack*". In detail, based on the semantics with sub-expressions, (i) we place "`(?=.* UTF)`" before "`[A-Z]{4,}`" by adjusting the order of sub-expressions in the original regexes; (ii) we add "`\b`" on both sides of "`jack`" to ensure it meets the requirements of being a word. The final regex successfully accepts $\mathcal{P}$ and rejects $\mathcal{N}$.

5.3 Ranking Regexes

Note that the search algorithm introduced in Sect. 5.2 may return multiple regexes (i.e. $\mathcal{R}_C$) while we need to return one from them. So we propose a method for ranking $\mathcal{R}_C$ leveraging the signal of string similarity of $\mathcal{R}_C$ to $\mathcal{R}_I$, which is based on the observation that the set of regexes $\mathcal{R}_I$ is considered by LLMs to be aligned with the NL descriptions—thus although they are inconsistent with the positive or negative examples, they are very helpful for ranking.

Let $r_c \in \mathcal{R}_C$ be a repaired regex and $r_i \in \mathcal{R}_I$ be an incorrect regex. We use $\text{LEVD}(r_c, r_i)$ to represent the *Levenshtein Distance* between r_c and r_i, which effectively evaluates the similarity between two regexes. The Levenshtein Distance measures the similarity by counting the minimum number of edits (insertions, deletions, or substitutions) needed to transform one string into the other. And we define a function $f(r_c, \mathcal{R}_I)$ to calculate the average distance of r_c to $\mathcal{R}_I$ as: $f(r_c, \mathcal{R}_I) = \frac{\sum_{r_i \in \mathcal{R}_I} \text{LEVD}(r_c, r_i)}{|\mathcal{R}_I|}$, where $|\mathcal{R}_I|$ refers to the number of regexes in $\mathcal{R}_I$. The RANK function sorts each r_c based on the function $f(r_c, \mathcal{R}_I)$ and returns the regex with the smallest f value.

Return to the example from Sect. 3, besides the regex r_1 we have shown in *Result 3*, SEARCH function also has other repaired results, such as r_2 = "`(?=.*UTF)[A-Z] {3,}[A-Z][#_;].*\bjack\b.*`". Due to space limitations, we omit the others here. We separately calculated their f-values compared to the regexes returned by LLMs and found that $f(r_1, \mathcal{R}_I) < f(r_2, \mathcal{R}_I)$. Therefore, the result r_1 is selected as the final output.

6   Evaluation

We implemented our synthesis framework PowerSyn in Python, set thresholds StepNum to 10^3 and ExpNum to 2 in the experiments, and conducted experiments on a machine with an AMD EPYC 7763 3.50GHz CPU, NVIDIA A100 GPU and 512 GB of RAM, running Ubuntu 22.04 operating system. Our empirical investigation aims to address the following research questions:

RQ1. How well can LLMs synthesize regexes with our prompts?
RQ2. Does PowerSyn improve the effectiveness of regex synthesis?
RQ3. How effective are the different variants of PowerSyn?

We assess the impact of six LLMs with two different prompting strategies to validate RQ1. To address RQ2, we compare PowerSyn with existing regex-synthesis tools by evaluating our algorithm on both publicly available datasets and a dataset with extended features. We evaluate the effectiveness of each variant of PowerSyn to verify RQ3.

6.1   Experiment Setup

Datasets. We utilize two publicly available regex synthesis benchmarks, StructuredRegex [24] and Re(gEx|DoS)Eval [21]. StructuredRegex contains 996 pairs of NL descriptions and regexes, and contains 6 positive examples and 6 negative examples for each regex. Re(gEx|DoS)Eval contains 762 pairs of NL descriptions and regexes, and contains 13 positive examples and 12 negative examples for each regex. At the same time, we collected a dataset of 189 regexes with extended features from Stack Overflow [1] and Regex101[5], which is named Extended. We use GPT-4o to standardize user-supplied NL descriptions. To fulfill the criteria of having at least 6 positive examples and 6 negative examples, the insufficient examples were built by Xeger[6].

Baselines. In order to evaluate the effectiveness of PowerSyn, we perform a comparative analysis of PowerSyn, against three state-of-the-art multi-modal algorithms (Sketch [26], TransRegex [12] and Opsynth [25]). Some of the tools have made their source code publicly available, allowing us to reproduce their results, such as Sketch and Opsynth. However, for tools that do not provide source code or data, we rely on the information given in their papers. For those that both do not provide source code and do not have information in their papers, it is impossible to include them.

---

[5] https://regex101.com/.
[6] https://github.com/crdoconnor/xeger.

Models. Based on the rankings of LLMs maintained by a highly regarded Chatbot Arena[7] website, we have initially selected six popular models for synthesizing regexes. In the closed-source models, we selected *GPT-4o*, *GPT-3.5-turbo* developed by OpenAI[8] and *Claude-3.5-Sonnet* by Anthropic[9]. In the open-source models, we chose *Llama3.1-70B*, *Llama3.1-8B* developed by Meta[10], *Qwen2-72B* by Alibaba Cloud[11]. We set the models' temperature at 0.6 and configured models to return ten completions. In LLMs, the temperature regulates the randomness of text generation. For closed-source models, we use the models by invoking the API. For open-source models, we use llama-cpp-python[12] for local deployment. Additionally, considering both hardware resource constraints and the necessity for maintaining high model performance, this paper employs 4-bit quantization (Q4) for optimizing models with approximately 70 billion (70B) parameters and employs 8-bit quantization (Q8) for optimizing models with approximately 8 billion (8B) parameters.

Assessment. Many regexes synthesized by LLMs based on NL descriptions are inconsistent with positive and negative examples. Therefore, we have adopted the evaluation criteria, also known as the *consistent rate*, which is defined as: Consistent rate $= \frac{1}{|D|} \sum_{i=1}^{|D|} \text{SOLUTION'}(r_i, \mathcal{P}_i, \mathcal{N}_i)$, where $|D|$ refers to the size of the dataset D, and r_i denotes the synthesized regex, $\mathcal{P}_i$ and $\mathcal{N}_i$ denote the set of positive and negative examples of r_i respectively. The function SOLUTION'$(r_i, \mathcal{P}_i, \mathcal{N}_i)$ is defined in the same way as the function SOLUTION in Sect. 5.2 but it returns 1 for success and 0 otherwise, which evaluates the validation of regex r_i using the match function, by checking if the regex accepts all positive examples (i.e. $\mathcal{P}_i$) and rejects all negative examples (i.e. $\mathcal{N}_i$).

6.2 Effectiveness of LLMs and Prompts

In this evaluation, we utilized six selected LLMs, two types of prompts, and three benchmark datasets to evaluate the LLMs' ability to synthesize regexes to answer RQ1. As mentioned in Sect. 4, the Simple prompt instructs the LLMs to generate regex based on NL descriptions only, while the Standard prompt supplements the instructions with examples. In particular, three positive examples and two negative examples are used in the Standard prompt of this evaluation. Since the completions returned by the LLMs may contain various problems such as syntax errors (see Sect. 4), so before calculating the consistent rate, we process the completions returned by the LLMs as mentioned in Sect. 4.

Table 2 presents the consistent rate of six LLMs across three datasets, evaluated under two different types of prompts. It can be seen that closed-source

---

[7] https://chat.lmsys.org/.

[8] https://platform.openai.com/docs/overview.

[9] https://www.anthropic.com/api.

[10] https://ai.meta.com/blog/meta-llama-3-1/.

[11] https://qwenlm.github.io/blog/qwen2/.

[12] https://github.com/abetlen/llama-cpp-python.

Table 2. Performance Comparison of Different LLMs on Three Benchmark Datasets

		Closed-source LLMs			Open-source LLMs		
		GPT-4o	GPT-3.5-turbo	Claude-3.5-Sonnet	Llama3.1-70B	Llama3.1-8B	Qwen2-72B
Simple	StructureRegex	65.86%	49.29%	53.72%	63.35%	39.75%	44.97%
	Re(gEx|DoS)Eval	46.32%	38.97%	38.71%	40.68%	28.22%	29.92%
	Extended	57.67%	53.96%	49.20%	56.61%	48.14%	44.44%
	Average	57.32%	45.70%	47.41%	53.93%	36.05%	39.03%
Standard	StructureRegex	73.69%	57.53%	68.21%	67.46%	48.59%	49.89%
	Re(gEx|DoS)Eval	60.90%	45.53%	56.82%	48.95%	37.14%	40.81%
	Extended	65.60%	58.20%	61.37%	63.49%	56.61%	50.79%
	Average	**67.69%**	52.29%	63.09%	60.04%	44.89%	46.42%

* The values in the table represent consistent rate.

models generally have a higher consistent rate compared to open-source models. Among all the combinations, GPT-4o using Standard prompts yields the highest consistent rate at 67.69%. It is also noticeable that the consistent rate of synthesized regexes with the Standard prompt is, on average, 9.26% higher than with the Simple prompt. This demonstrates that prompts with provided examples help in synthesizing regexes.

Within the open-source models, Llama3.1-70B outperforms both GPT-3.5-turbo Turbo and Claude-3.5-Sonnet under the Simple prompt conditions, and under the Standard prompt conditions, it also surpasses GPT-3.5-turbo and is close to Claude-3.5-Sonnet. This shows that some open-source models also perform commendably in synthesizing regexes. Therefore, in the upcoming experiments, we will utilize the best model for each dataset, i.e. the one with the highest consistent rate.

6.3 Effectiveness and Efficiency of PowerSyn

To answer RQ2, we conduct a comparison between baselines and PowerSyn, as shown in Table 3, where each dataset has two columns indicating the consistent rate (*cons.*) and the average running time (*avg.*) respectively. Because PowerSyn can be integrated with various LLMs, its data is

Table 3. The Consistent Rate and the Average Running Time of the Results of Each Synthesis Algorithm on Three Datasets

	StructuredRegex		Re(gEx|DoS)Eval		Extended	
	cons.	*avg.*	*cons.*	*avg.*	*cons.*	*avg.*
Sketch	69.1%	22.43 s	0.15%	0.70 s	✗	✗
TransRegex	75.6%	13.93 s	-	-	✗	✗
Opsynth	80.4%	14.51 s	30.8%	238.29 s	✗	✗
PowerSyn	**86.4%**	2.32 s	**71.2%**	6.21 s	**77.8%**	2.81 s

derived from the results of using LLM which demonstrates the highest consistency rate. The "-" indicates that information about this dataset is not provided in their original paper, and further since its source code is not publicly available, we are unable to manually evaluate the tool's performance on this dataset. And the ✗ indicates that the tool does not support the extended features of that dataset.

The experimental results show that PowerSyn outperforms state-of-the-art tools. In the StructuredRegex dataset, PowerSyn achieves the highest consistent rate of 86.4%, followed by Opsynth with about 80.4%, which is 6% lower than PowerSyn. Similarly, on the Re(gEx|DoS)Eval dataset, PowerSyn achieves a consistent rate of 71.2%, which is 40.4% higher than Opsynth's 30.8%. In the Extended dataset, PowerSyn achieves a consistent rate of 77.8% and other tools fail to support the synthesis of regexes with extended features.

In terms of efficiency, on the StructuredRegex dataset, the most efficient tool apart from PowerSyn is TransRegex, with an average runtime of 13.93 s, whereas PowerSyn only requires 2.32 s, yielding a 6x speedup over TransRegex. Moreover, PowerSyn is up to 10x faster than the slowest tool, Sketch. In the Re(gEx|DoS)Eval dataset, our approach achieved an average runtime of 6.21 s, slightly slower than Sketch's 0.70 s. However, PowerSyn improves a hardly usable consistency rate at 0.15% to a substantial 71.2%. Notably, Opsynth took an unexpectedly long time of over 200 s, which may reflect its inefficiency in handling more complex examples. Noticeably, PowerSyn maintains a low average runtime of 2.81 s on the Extended dataset.

6.4 Evaluation of SynReco

To better explore the effect of Syn-Reco, we conducted experiments on the three variants of PowerSyn on the datasets mentioned in Sect. 6.1. Results are detailed in Fig. 5, where LLM refers to the use of standard prompts without employing Syn-Reco, LLM+SynReco⁻ refers to the use of SynReco on synthetic completions without applying the SORT and EXPAND functions to enhance the tool, LLM+SynReco represents the use of our complete synthesis framework.

The results indicate that Syn-Reco improves outcomes across different data and models, with an average repair rate of 13.4%. Notably, it performs the best on completions

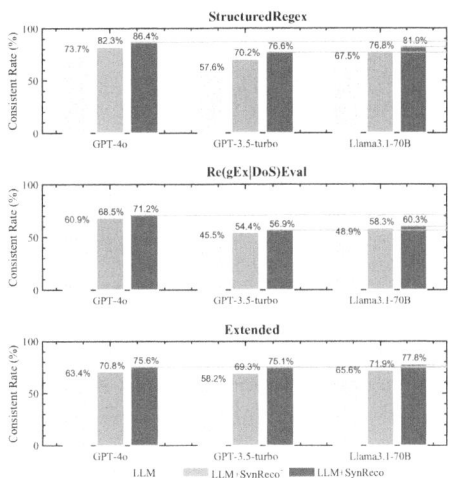

Fig. 5. The Consistent Rate of the Results of Different Variants

synthesized by the GPT-3.5-turbo model on the StructuredRegex dataset, improving a consistent rate of 19%. In comparing LLM+SynReco⁻ with LLM+SynReco, we also found that the SORT and EXPAND functions within SynReco affect the repair results, with an improvement of approximately 4%. Through the experiment, we have confirmed the remarkable impact each step of SynReco has on improving its effectiveness.

Additionally, we have observed that for some synthesis results with a relatively low consistent rate, the corrected consistent surpasses that of the synthesis results with an initially high consistent rate. For instance, on the StructuredRegex dataset, the GPT-3.5-turbo model achieved a repaired consistent rate of 76.6%, while the GPT-4o model reached a repaired consistent rate of 73.7%. Even on the Extended dataset, the repaired consistent rate of the GPT-3.5-turbo model was 75.13%, nearly the same as the repaired consistent rate of the other two models. In practice, GPT-4o requires significantly more computational resources than GPT-3.5-turbo. This indicates that by using SynReco, computational resource consumption can be reduced while achieving the same level of consistent rate.

7   Related Work

Regex Synthesis by NL: Several NLP techniques [10,14,18,28,29] have been developed for regex synthesis. SemRegex [28] and SoftRegex [18] proposed machine learning models to translate NL descriptions to regexes. Zhong et al. [29] applied the latest methods to synthesise regular expressions using real datasets. The existing techniques based on traditional models heavily rely on training sets, resulting in their weak capability in generalization. Recently, Zhang et al. [27] proposed a new method called InfeRE, which decomposes the generation of regexes into a chain of step-by-step. Siddiq et al. [21] evaluated the ability of some LLMs to synthesize regexes using their dataset. However, NL is characterized by ambiguity and impreciseness, which hampers the ability of tools based on traditional models and LLMs to accurately synthesize regexes.

Regex Synthesis by Example: There has been some works on regex synthesis based on examples, which are applied in different domains. Angluin [1] devised an algorithm that can derive finite-state machines and regexes in polynomial time from positive and negative examples. AlphaRegex [11] also synthesizes simple regexes from introductory automata assignments, using a search-based synthesis algorithm that leverages ideas from over-fitting and under-fitting to effectively prune a large portion of search space. Bartoli et al. [2,3] combined genetic algorithms with regex inference to design a tool for synthesizing regexes from positive and negative examples. Kim et al. [9] define a new normal form of regular expressions that significantly reduces the search space. Then Kim et al. [8] used neural example splitting to expedite the process. However, the quality of this approach depends on the quality of user-supplied examples, which is a challenge.

Multi-modal Regex Synthesis: A new approach to synthesizing regexes was proposed in recent years, namely multi-modal regex synthesis. Ye et al. [5,26] designed a regex synthesis framework that translates NL descriptions into sketches and synthesizes the results by examples. However, wrongly generated sketches cannot be corrected at a later stage. Based on the sketches, Ye et al. [25] proposed an optimized neural program synthesis method. Nevertheless, it has a relatively low accuracy rate on complex datasets. Li et al. [12] proposed TransRegex, which builds a seq2seq model to translate NL descriptions to regexes, then uses a neighborhood search to fix the results. However, the search space for repair can be enormous, which can be time-consuming and challenging to obtain results promptly. Rahmani et al. [19] proposed a new prompt method to convert NL descriptions into regexes using LLMs. Their algorithm enumerates components into a complete regex, which causes the combination explosion. It either does not support *intersection* and *complement* operations.

Compared to the existing methods introduced above, we propose a new framework that supports extended features, which is based on LLMs together with novel algorithms to repair regexes to address the problems faced by existing methods.

8 Conclusion

In this paper, we propose PowerSyn, a framework for multi-modal regex synthesis that supports extended features. It is based on LLMs together with novel algorithms to manipulate sub-expressions, which consider the matching relation, and are guided by positive and negative examples. The evaluation results demonstrate the significant efficacy of our approach. We explored our method in regex synthesis in this paper, one future work is to leverage the capabilities of LLMs to repair regexes.

Acknowledgements. We would like to thank reviewers for their helpful comments and suggestions. Work supported by the National Natural Science Foundation of China (Grant Nos. 62372439 and 61872339), the Natural Science Foundation of Beijing, China (Grant No. 4232038) and the Project of Construction and Support for high-level teaching Teams of Beijing Municipal Institutions.

References

1. Angluin, D.: Learning regular sets from queries and counterexamples. Inf. Comput. **75**(2), 87–106 (1987)
2. Bartoli, A., Davanzo, G., Lorenzo, A.D., Medvet, E., Sorio, E.: Automatic synthesis of regular expressions from examples. IEEE Comput. **47**(12), 72–80 (2014)
3. Bartoli, A., de Lorenzo, A., Medvet, E., Tarlao, F.: Inference of regular expressions for text extraction from examples. IEEE Trans. Knowl. Data Eng. **28**(5), 1217–1230 (2016)
4. Chapman, C., Wang, P., Stolee, K.T.: Exploring regular expression comprehension. In: Proceedings of the 32nd IEEE/ACM International Conference on Automated Software Engineering, ASE 2017, pp. 405–416 (2017)
5. Chen, Q., Wang, X., Ye, X., Durrett, G., Dillig, I.: Multi-modal synthesis of regular expressions. In: Proceedings of the 41st ACM SIGPLAN Conference on Programming Language Design and Implementation, PLDI 2019, pp. 487–502 (2019)
6. Davis, J.C., Coghlan, C.A., Servant, F., Lee, D.: The impact of regular expression denial of service (ReDoS) in practice: an empirical study at the ecosystem scale. In: Proceedings of the 2018 ACM Joint Meeting on European Software Engineering Conference and Symposium on the Foundations of Software Engineering, ESEC/FSE 2018, pp. 246–256 (2018)

7. Davis, J.C., Michael IV, L.G., Coghlan, C.A., Servant, F., Lee, D.: Why aren't regular expressions a lingua franca? An empirical study on the re-use and portability of regular expressions. In: Proceedings of the ACM Joint Meeting on European Software Engineering Conference and Symposium on the Foundations of Software Engineering, ESEC/FSE 2019, pp. 443–454 (2019)
8. Kim, S., Cheon, H., Han, Y., Ko, S.: Neuro-symbolic regex synthesis framework via neural example splitting (2022). arXiv:2205.11258
9. Kim, S., Im, H., Ko, S.: Efficient enumeration of regular expressions for faster regular expression synthesis. In: Proceedings of the 25th International Conference on Implementation and Application of Automata, CIAA 2021, pp. 65–76 (2021)
10. Kushman, N., Barzilay, R.: Using semantic unification to generate regular expressions from natural language. In: Proceedings of the 2013 Conference of the North American Chapter of the Association for Computational Linguistics: Human Language Technologies, NAACL 2013, pp. 826–836 (2013)
11. Lee, M., So, S., Oh, H.: Synthesizing regular expressions from examples for introductory automata assignments. In: Proceedings of the 2016 ACM SIGPLAN International Conference on Generative Programming: Concepts and Experiences, GPCE 2016, pp. 70–80 (2016)
12. Li, Y., et al.: Transregex: multi-modal regular expression synthesis by generate-and-repair. In: Proceedings of the 43rd IEEE/ACM International Conference on Software Engineering, ICSE 2021, pp. 1210–1222 (2021)
13. Liu, X., Jiang, Y., Wu, D.: A lightweight framework for regular expression verification. In: 19th IEEE International Symposium on High Assurance Systems Engineering, HASE 2019, pp. 1–8 (2019)
14. Locascio, N., Narasimhan, K., DeLeon, E., Kushman, N., Barzilay, R.: Neural generation of regular expressions from natural language with minimal domain knowledge. In: Proceedings of the 2016 Conference on Empirical Methods in Natural Language Processing, EMNLP 2016, pp. 1918–1923 (2016)
15. Loring, B., Mitchell, D., Kinder, J.: Sound regular expression semantics for dynamic symbolic execution of Javascript. In: Proceedings of the 41st ACM SIGPLAN Conference on Programming Language Design and Implementation, PLDI 2019, pp. 425–438 (2019)
16. Luo, B., Feng, Y., Wang, Z., Huang, S., Yan, R., Zhao, D.: Marrying up regular expressions with neural networks: a case study for spoken language understanding. In: Proceedings of the 56th Annual Meeting of the Association for Computational Linguistics, ACL 2018, pp. 2083–2093 (2018)
17. Michael IV, L.G., Donohue, J., Davis, J.C., Lee, D., Servant, F.: Regexes are hard: decision-making, difficulties, and risks in programming regular expressions. In: Proceedings of 34th IEEE/ACM International Conference on Automated Software Engineering, ASE 2019, pp. 415–426 (2019)
18. Park, J., Ko, S., Cognetta, M., Han, Y.: Softregex: generating regex from natural language descriptions using softened regex equivalence. In: Proceedings of the 2019 Conference on Empirical Methods in Natural Language Processing and the 9th International Joint Conference on Natural Language Processing, EMNLP-IJCNLP 2019, pp. 6425–6431 (2019)
19. Rahmani, K., et al.: Multi-modal program inference: a marriage of pre-trained language models and component-based synthesis. Proc. ACM Program. Lang. 5(OOPSLA), 1–29 (2021)
20. Shen, Y., Jiang, Y., Xu, C., Yu, P., Ma, X., Lu, J.: ReScue: crafting regular expression DoS attacks. In: Proceedings of the 33rd ACM/IEEE International Conference on Automated Software Engineering, ASE 2018, pp. 225–235 (2018)

21. Siddiq, M.L., Zhang, J., Roney, L., Santos, J.C.S.: Re(gex|dos)eval: evaluating generated regular expressions and their proneness to dos attacks. In: Proceedings of the 2024 ACM/IEEE 44th International Conference on Software Engineering: New Ideas and Emerging Results, NIER@ICSE 2024, pp. 52–56 (2024)
22. Spishak, E., Dietl, W., Ernst, M.D.: A type system for regular expressions. In: FTfJP 2012: 14th Workshop on Formal Techniques for Java-like Programs, pp. 20–26 (2012)
23. Turonová, L., Holík, L., Lengál, O., Saarikivi, O., Veanes, M., Vojnar, T.: Regex matching with counting-set automata. Proc. ACM Program. Lang. 4(OOPSLA), 1–30 (2020)
24. Ye, X., Chen, Q., Dillig, I., Durrett, G.: Benchmarking multimodal regex synthesis with complex structures. In: Proceedings of the 58th Annual Meeting of the Association for Computational Linguistics, ACL 2020, pp. 6081–6094 (2020)
25. Ye, X., Chen, Q., Dillig, I., Durrett, G.: Optimal neural program synthesis from multimodal specifications. In: Findings of the Association for Computational Linguistics: EMNLP 2021, pp. 1691–1704 (2021)
26. Ye, X., Chen, Q., Wang, X., Dillig, I., Durrett, G.: Sketch-driven regular expression generation from natural language and examples. Trans. Assoc. Computat. Linguist. **8**, 679–694 (2020)
27. Zhang, S., Gu, X., Chen, Y., Shen, B.: Infere: step-by-step regex generation via chain of inference. In: 38th IEEE/ACM International Conference on Automated Software Engineering, ASE 2023, pp. 1505–1515 (2023)
28. Zhong, Z., et al.: Semregex: a semantics-based approach for generating regular expressions from natural language specifications. In: Proceedings of the 2018 Conference on Empirical Methods in Natural Language Processing, EMNLP 2018, pp. 1608–1618 (2018)
29. Zhong, Z., et al.: Generating regular expressions from natural language specifications: Are we there yet? In: The Workshops of the Thirty-Second AAAI Conference on Artificial Intelligence, New Orleans, Louisiana, USA, February 2-7, 2018. AAAI Technical Report, vol. WS-18, pp. 791–794 (2018)

Formal Verification of RISC-V Processor Chisel Designs

Shidong Shen[1,2], Yicheng Liu[1,2], Lijun Zhang[1,2], Fu Song[1,2], and Zhilin Wu[1,2(✉)]

[1] Key Laboratory of System Software (Chinese Academy of Sciences) and State Key Laboratory of Computer Science, Institute of Software, Chinese Academy of Sciences, Beijing, China
{shensd,liuyc,zhanglj,songfu,wuzl}@ios.ac.cn
[2] University of Chinese Academy of Sciences, Beijing, China

Abstract. Chisel is an open-source high-level hardware construction language embedded in Scala to facilitate parameterizable, reusable circuit design generators. It is becoming increasingly popular and has been used to design many RISC-V processor variants. Formal verification has been adapted to check the (functional) correctness of RISC-V processor designs. However, the RISC-V instructions therein are specified in the low-level hardware languages Verilog/SystemVerilog, which are challenging to develop, maintain, and extend. This considerably lowers the advantage of RISC-V for designing highly customizable processors. In this work, we present the first end-to-end approach for formally verifying the correctness of RISC-V processor designs, fully at the Chisel high-level. Specifically, by utilizing the object-oriented and functional programming constructs offered by Chisel, we develop a high-level reference model of RISC-V instructions in Chisel. This reference model is a succinct, modular, and parameterized RISC-V processor design generator, thus can produce customized RISC-V processor variants. We then devise a novel queue-based synchronization mechanism between the RISC-V processor Chisel design and the reference model by which the correctness verification of the RISC-V processor design is reduced to the model-checking problem and off-the-shelf model-checkers can be harnessed. We implement our approach in an open-source tool and demonstrate its efficacy on two representative open-source RISC-V processor designs in Chisel (i.e., riscv-mini and NutShell). The experiment results confirm the efficacy of our approach, capable of discovering 7 real-world unknown non-conformance bugs and all the 10 manually injected bugs. It is also three-orders-of-magnitude more efficient than the state-of-the-art symbolic-execution based approach.

Keywords: Chisel · RISC-V · formal verification · reference model · synchronization · ISA conformance · model-checking

© The Author(s), under exclusive license to Springer Nature Singapore Pte Ltd. 2025
T. Bourke et al. (Eds.): SETTA 2024, LNCS 15469, pp. 142–160, 2025.
https://doi.org/10.1007/978-981-96-0602-3_8

1   Introduction

Background. RISC-V is a royalty-free and open standard Instruction Set Architecture (ISA) based on the well-established principles of Reduced Instruction
Set Computer (RISC). The RISC-V instruction set manual provides detailed
specifications of RISC-V ISA in two volumes. The first volume [30] specifies
the unprivileged ISA, including the base integer instructions (RV32I/64I) and
optional unprivileged extensions, such as Multiplication and Division extension
(M), and Compressed instructions (C). The second volume [31] specifies the privileged ISA and those beyond the unprivileged ISA, including privileged instructions and additional functionalities required for running operating systems and
attaching external devices. The scalable and extendable RISC-V ISA brings a
new level of flexibility in designing highly customizable processors.

Along with RISC-V, Chisel (Constructing Hardware in a Scala Embedded
Language) [2], an open-source hardware description language (HDL), was proposed. Chisel features hardware construction primitives and Scala's object-oriented and functional programming constructs, allowing designers to easily write
complex, modular circuit generators that can produce circuit designs in synthe-
sizable Verilog/SystemVerilog. This generation methodology enables the creation
of parameterizable, reusable components and libraries, such as the FIFO queue
and arbiters in the Chisel Standard Library. Compared to the classic HDLs
(e.g., Verilog, SystemVerilog, and VHDL), Chisel offers a higher level programming abstraction for hardware designs. Since its introduction, Chisel has been
widely used to design many RISC-V processor variants (e.g. RocketChip [26],
BOOM [4], riscv-mini [15], NutShell [23], and XiangShan [35]), and is playing an
indispensable role in the promotion of the agile hardware development methodology [17,37].

Motivation. Modern processors are becoming more and more complex, consequently, ensuring their correctness in the pre-silicon stage becomes a central
issue in the processor development. In this work, we focus on formal verification
for the (functional) correctness of RISC-V processor designs in Chisel, that is,
to check whether the implementations of RISC-V instructions in Chisel conform
to their specifications.

The state-of-the-art verification techniques for Chisel (namely, the open-
source tool riscv-formal [39] and the commercial tools FormalISA [1] and One-
Spin [24]) first compile Chisel designs into low-level implementations in Ver-
ilog/SystemVerilog, then check their conformance to the RISC-V ISA specifications in the form Verilog/SystemVerilog reference models or SystemVerilog
assertions (SVA) via model-checking. Though available, such low-level representation of RISC-V ISA specifications makes the development, maintenance,
diagnosis, and extension of the reference models or assertions challenging and
error-prone, hindering the flexibility of RISC-V ISA for designing highly customizable processors. Thus, a succinct, modular, and parameterized reference
model, as well as an accompanied formal verification tool, is highly-required.

Contribution. In this work, we propose the first *end-to-end* formal verification approach for the (functional) correctness of RISC-V processor designs, fully at the Chisel high-level[1]. Specifically, we make the following major contributions.

1. We develop a high-level, succinct, modular, and parameterized reference model for RISC-V ISA specifications in Chisel as a single-clock-cycle RISC-V processor generator, by utilizing the object-oriented and functional programming constructs offered by Chisel (cf. Sect. 3). The reference model implements all the common unprivileged instructions and various features of privileged instructions, including control and status registers (CSR), exception handling, and virtual memories. Our model not only strictly subsumes the functionalities of, but also is an-order-of-magnitude more succinct than the Verilog/SystemVerilog reference model in riscv-formal.
2. We propose an end-to-end formal verification approach for RISC-V processor designs in Chisel by devising a novel queue-based synchronization mechanism between the RISC-V processor DUT (design under test) and our reference model, to deal with the non-fixed delays resulted from the memory accesses as well as the additional challenges posed by the virtual memory in the DUT (cf. Sect. 4). With our synchronization mechanism, the correctness verification of DUT w.r.t. the RISC-V ISA specifications is reduced to the model-checking problem, that can be solved by off-the-shelf model-checkers.
3. We implement our approach in a tool using the open-source SMT-based model-checker Pono [20]. We validate the effectiveness and efficiency on riscv-mini [15] and NutShell [23], two representative open-source RISC-V processor designs in Chisel (cf. Sect. 5). The results confirm the effectiveness of our approach, discovered 7 real-world unknown ISA non-conformance bugs (2 in riscv-mini and 5 in NutShell) and all the 10 manually injected bugs (5 bugs per DUT). Compared with the state-of-the-art open-source tool riscv-formal [39][2], while our approach is comparable in terms of verification efficiency, riscv-formal *only* discovered 2 of 7 real-world bugs. We also compare with a recent symbolic-execution based tool [6,7], which is only able to discover 1 out of 7 bugs. Moreover, on this bug, our approach is significantly faster than the symbolic-execution based tool (0.52 s vs. 58 min).

Related Work. Formal verification has been widely studied and adopted for checking functional correctness of software and hardware designs [9]. Hereafter, we only discuss formal verification studies on RISC-V and Chisel.

As aforementioned, the open-source tool riscv-formal and the commercial tools FormalISA and OneSpin verify Chisel designs by first compiling them into low-level Verilog/SystemVerilog and then checking their correctness using Verilog/SystemVerilog reference models or SVA. Instead, we develop a high-level, modular, and parameterized reference model, that is a RISC-V processor design

---

[1] In other words, it is the first work for the formal verification of RISC-V processor designs in Chisel that do not go through low-level Verilog/SystemVerilog or SVA.
[2] We do not compare with the two aforementioned commercial tools FormalISA [1] and OneSpin [24]), as they are not publicly available.

generator in Chisel. It is more comprehensive yet more succinct than the Verilog/SystemVerilog reference model in riscv-formal, thus more convenient for maintenance, diagnosis, and extension of the reference model. We also propose the first end-to-end formal verification approach for RISC-V processor Chisel designs, which is more effective than riscv-formal with comparable verification efficiency (cf. Sect. 5).

Formal verification of CHERI-RISC-V processor designs was studied using SVA [12], where CHERI-RISC-V[3] is an extension of RISC-V ISA with an alternative model to offer memory safety. To reduce the manual effort of ISA modeling, a trace notation was proposed and used to model the RISC-V ISA [10], based on which a complete set of SVA properties are generated for detecting functional bugs in RISC-V processor designs.

KLEE, a dynamic symbolic-execution engine, has been utilized to analyze RISC-V processor designs in SpinalHDL [6,7]. They compile SpinalHDL designs into Verilog which in turn are compiled into C++. The RISC-V processor design in C++ is synchronized with a RISC-V Instruction Set Simulator in C++ as the reference model, on which dynamic symbolic-execution is applied to find non-conformance bugs. Dynamic symbolic-execution often suffers from the path-explosion problem when the DUT has many conditional branches, thus limited in efficiency for a high coverage analysis. The experimental results show that our approach is significantly more effective and efficient than this approach (cf. Sect. 5).

Recently, BDD-based formal verification was leveraged to verify the correctness of *non-pipelined* RISC-V processor designs with polynomial time and space complexity [32]. While efficient, their approach and closed-source tool cannot be applied to verify *pipelined* RISC-V processor designs such as riscv-mini and NutShell, due to the lack of support for clocks.

Informal verification (i.e., testing and simulation) for the functional correctness of RISC-V processor designs has been studies as well, e.g., [11,13,21]. There is also a trend of adapting effective software testing techniques (e.g. concolic testing and fuzzing) to the informal verification of hardware designs [8,14,19,36,38]. Nevertheless, they are orthogonal to this work.

Outline. Section 2 gives an overview of our end-to-end verification approach for RISC-V processor designs in Chisel. Section 3 describes the design of our reference model. Section 4 presents a queue-based synchronization mechanism between the RISC-V processor DUT and the reference model. Section 5 reports experimental results. We conclude this paper in Sect. 6.

The source code of our RISC-V ISA reference model and formal verification tool is available at: https://github.com/iscas-tis/riscv-spec-core.

2   Overview

In this section, we give an overview of our approach (see Fig. 1), comprising the following three key components.

---

[3] CHERI is an abbreviation of "Capability Hardware Enhanced RISC Instructions".

Reference Model. At first, following closely the official two volumes of the RISC-V ISA manual, we design a succinct and parameterized reference model for RISC-V processor design generator in Chisel with high confidence of correctness, where both the unprivileged and privileged instructions are covered.

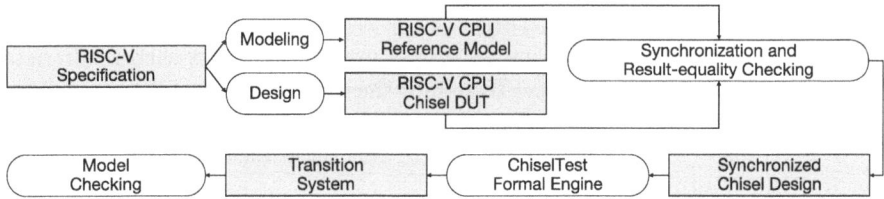

Fig. 1. Overview of our approach

Synchronization. To verify whether a RISC-V CPU Chisel design conforms to the RISC-V ISA specifications, the RISC-V CPU DUT is synchronized with the reference model and the results of the instruction executions in the DUT and the reference model are compared for equality checking. After synchronization, a synchronized Chisel design is obtained.

Model-Checking. The synchronized Chisel design is transformed by the formal engine in ChiselTest [16] to a transition system, which is then tackled by the model-checkers e.g. Pono [20], where various model-checking algorithms e.g. BMC [3], k-induction [28], and PDR [5], could be harnessed.

3   The RISC-V Reference Model in Chisel

In this section, we elaborate the design of our RISC-V reference model in Chisel. In particular, we illustrate how to model privileged instructions in a natural and succinct way by utilizing the object-oriented and functional programming constructs of Chisel.

The architecture of our RISC-V reference model is shown in Fig. 2. Intuitively, the RISC-V reference model can be seen as a modular, and parameterized RISC-V processor design generator in Chisel that can produce customized single-clock-cycle RISC-V processor variants.

As a result, it involves the common steps of decoding, executing, and register-status updating (a.k.a. write-back) in a typical RISC-V processor design. The step of register-status updating is responsible for updating the values of general registers and Control and Status Registers (CSR) after the execution of an instruction is finished. The reference model also involves several components for modeling privileged instructions, including exception handling and the address translation unit that translates the virtual addresses into physical addresses. Equipped with these components, the RISC-V reference model is capable of supporting the modeling of RISC-V 32/64 bit-widths Integer (I), Multiplication and

Division (M), Compressed (C), and Control and Status Register (Zicsr) instruction sets, as well as the three privilege levels, namely, Machine (M), Supervisor (S), and User (U), and finally the Sv39 virtual memory system.

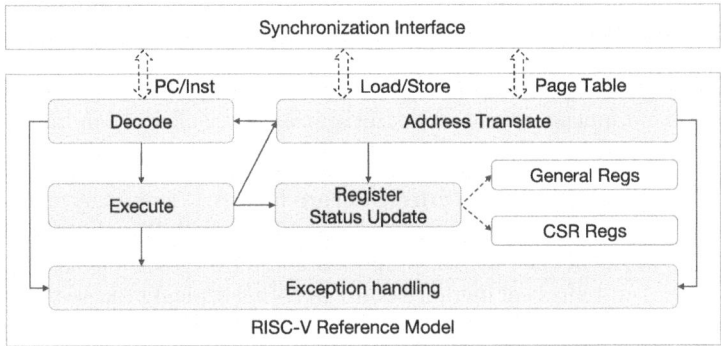

Fig. 2. The RISC-V reference model in Chisel

3.1   Succinct, Modular, and Parameterized Design

One of the notable features of our RISC-V reference model is its succinct, modular, and parameterized design generator in Chisel, that is,

- the reference model comprises only around 3,000 lines of Chisel code,
- the reference model resembles the modular structure of the RISC-V instruction set manual,
- the parameters therein can be instantiated to produce customized RISC-V processor designs with different bit-widths, and ISA extensions.

For a particular instantiation of the parameters, when the reference model is compiled into FIRRTL (a hardware intermediate representation language for Chisel) [18], only the ISA specifications that are related to this instantiation will be compiled in the generated FIRRTL code while the others are dropped. This design choice often reduces the sizes of the transition systems, thus alleviating the state-explosion problem of model-checking. On the other hand, if the low-level Verilog/SystemVerilog language is used to implement a RISC-V reference model, then the code size would be much larger and it is not very convenient to support different bit-widths or ISA extensions. For instance, in riscv-formal [39], around 30,000 lines of Verilog/SystemVerilog code are used to model the RISC-V ISA specifications, moreover, additional 2,551 lines of Python scripts are used to configure the bit-widths and ISA extensions of the reference models.

3.2 Modeling Privileged Instructions

The object-oriented and functional programming constructs of Chisel are utilized to model the two mechanisms related to privileged instructions, namely, exception handling and virtual-physical memory address translation.

Exception Handling. At first, thanks to Chisel's high-level language features, the enable bit in the exception vector can be turned on directly by calling the designated exception triggering functions, implemented in Chisel as well. Moreover, Scala's collection functions such as `foldRight` are very effective in implementing the priority arbitration for exceptions.

Virtual-Physical Memory Address Translation. The virtual memory system plays a vital role in modern operating systems, and Translation Lookaside Buffer (TLB) is one of the critical components in a processor for fast translation between virtual and physical memory addresses. In a typical processor design, the TLB component is usually implemented as a state machine to access the memory for multiple times. Nevertheless, our RISC-V reference model in Chisel only uses combinational logic, which should be finished in one clock cycle. As a result, it is necessary for the RISC-V reference model to have more copies of the memory read/write ports. In our reference model, we implement the virtual-physical memory address translation component for Sv39, which is a three-level page table virtual memory system. As a result, three additional page-read ports and one additional page-write port are included for the address translation, besides the conventional memory access interface for the load/store instructions. (See Fig. 3 for the architecture of the address translation component).

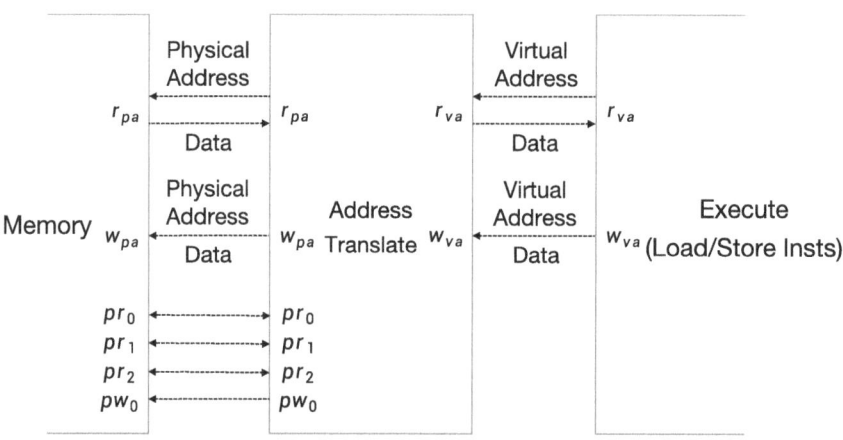

Fig. 3. Architecture of the address translation component

3.3   Validation of the Reference Model

Since the reference model is used as the specification in the formal verification of the ISA conformance of RISC-V CPU Chisel designs, the correctness of the reference model itself should also be guaranteed. Nevertheless, the formal verification of the correctness of the reference model is similar to the formal verification of the temporal logic specifications in model-checking, which is in some sense a dead-end. Therefore, we resort to the following two informal means to enhance our confidence on the correctness of the reference model.

– As a design choice, we utilize the high-level features of Chisel to make the reference model closely resembling the organization of the RISC-V ISA manual in a succinct and modular way. This definitely reduces the chances of introducing human-mistakes in the design of the reference model and eases the manual inspection of its correctness.
– Since the reference model can be seen as a parameterized single-clock-cycle RISC-V processor, we also use riscv-tests [25], the official RISC-V CPU test suite, to thoroughly validate the correctness of the reference model.

4   Synchronization

To facilitate the formal verification of the ISA conformance of the RISC-V CPU DUT with respect to the reference model, it is necessary to synchronize the DUT with the reference model. However, such a synchronization is non-trivial since there is a significant gap between the micro-architectures of the DUT and the reference model. For instance, while the reference model is a (parameterized) single-clock-cycle processor, the DUTs normally involve pipelines. To bridge this gap, in the synchronization, we take the signals in the last stage of the pipeline (usually the write-back stage) and check whether they are equal to those in the reference model.

  To this end, for many instructions (e.g. the integer computational instructions), the synchronization is not difficult since the number of clock cycles for their executions in DUTs have a *fixed* (constant) upper bound. However, the delays of load/store instructions can be *non-fixed*, since they involve memory accesses. In the sequel, we show how to deal with the non-fixed delays of the load/store instructions in DUTs during synchronization. Moreover, we also discuss how to tackle the additional challenges when virtual memory are used in DUTs so that the executions of the load/store instructions involve the translation of virtual addresses into physical addresses.

4.1   Synchronization of Instructions with Non-fixed Delays

When the execution of an instruction involves memory accesses, the delay can be non-fixed. For instance, some instructions may be implemented using state machines so that the delays in their executions may be greater than those of the other instructions.

Let us use the load instructions in NutShell to illustrate the non-fixed delays.

In RISC-V ISA, there are four load instructions, namely, LD, LW, LB, and LH. In contrast, NutShell [23], a 64-bit RISC-V processor, categorizes the load instructions into partial reads and full reads. The LW, LH, and LB instructions are *partial reads* that read 32, 16, and 8 bits respectively, while the LD instruction is a *full read*, that reads 64 bits. The delay for transmitting the signal to the write-back stage in the execution of a partial-read instruction is different from that of a full-read instruction.

To deal with the non-fixed delays of instructions in DUTs, we propose to utilize queues. When an instruction in the DUT is executed, some necessary memory access information (such as validity, address, data and width) is recorded in a queue. When the execution of an instruction is complete (usually the write-back stage in pipelines), the information can be retrieved from the queue and compared with the signals in the reference model. Since Chisel provides an implementation of queues in its library, it is relatively easy to implement the synchronization mechanism where queues are utilized to deal with non-fixed delays.

4.2 Synchronization of Instructions Involving Virtual Memory

The virtual memory poses additional challenges for the synchronization. As shown in Fig. 3, three page-read ports and one page-write port are used in the reference model to model the memory translations of load/store instructions. To deal with the delays resulted from the virtual memory, it is necessary to introduce five queues to store the memory access information of DUTs: one queue for each of the three page-read ports, and two queues for the read/write physical address involved in the load/store instructions (i.e., r_{pa} and w_{pa} respectively).

When a load/store instruction is executed in a DUT involving virtual memory, the corresponding memory access information is first extracted from the DUT and added into the three TLB read queues, then the reference model utilizes the information in the three TLB read queues to translate a virtual address into a physical address, which is finally compared with the value retrieved from the load/store queues that was added by the DUT to ensure that they are equal.

4.3 Equality Checking of the Execution Results

To verify that the implementation of an instruction in the DUT conforms to the RISC-V ISA specification of the instruction, it is necessary to check that the results after the execution of the instruction in the DUT and in the reference model are equal. Table 1 shows the set of signals of the DUT that are involved in the equality checking of the execution results in the formal verification. Usually, the signals in the DUT should be preprocessed before the equality checking.

Table 1. Set of signals to be checked for equality

Types of signals	Fields to be checked
Instruction	PC
General Regs	All general regs (x0 - x31)
CSR Regs	All implemented CSR regs
Exception	Valid, No, PC, Inst
Memory	Valid, Address, Data, Width
PageTable	Valid, Address, Data, Width

5   Evaluation

In this section, we evaluate the effectiveness and efficiency of our approach on two representative open-source RISC-V processor Chisel designs: riscv-mini and NutShell. Moreover, we compare the performance of our approach against the other two state-of-the-art approaches for formal verification of RISC-V processor designs, that is, riscv-formal and the symbolic-execution based approach in [6,7]. Both tools have been used in formally verifying several RISC-V processor designs and found real-world bugs [6,34].

5.1   Case Studies on Riscv-Mini and NutShell

We apply the approach proposed in this work to the formal verification of the ISA conformance of riscv-mini [15] and NutShell [23] w.r.t. the RISC-V ISA specifications.

- **riscv-mini** is a simple RISC-V processor with a 3-stage pipeline. It supports RV32I and the machine-level ISA. It also contains simple instruction caches (ICache) and data caches (DCache). It includes 3,499 lines of Chisel code in total. (See Fig. 4a for its architecture.)
- **NutShell** is a single-issue in-order RISC-V processor with a 9-stage pipeline. It supports the following instruction extensions: I, M, A, C, Zicsr, and Zifencei. Moreover, it includes three privilege levels, namely, M, S, and U. It also supports the Sv39 virtual memory system, and implements TLB to translate virtual addresses to physical addresses. As a result, it is capable of running Linux. It includes 8,859 lines of Chisel code in total. (See Fig. 4b for its architecture.) NutShell is configurable. For instance, it can be configured as a 32-bit processor (with a 5-stage pipeline).

RISC-V ISA Specification Conformance Checking. We use the assume statements of Chisel to restrict the op-codes of RISC-V instructions during the executions of the processors and the reference model. Then the formal verification of DUT's conformance to the RISC-V ISA specification is reduced to an

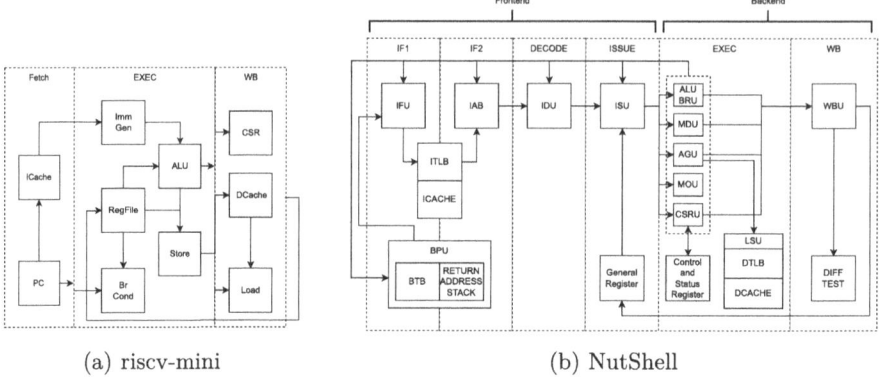

(a) riscv-mini   (b) NutShell

Fig. 4. Architecture of the two processors

instance of the model-checking problem, which is then solved by the Pono model-checker [20], a well-known efficient SMT-based open-source model-checker that can be easily integrated into the ChiselTest formal engine. The model-checking instances are in the BTOR2 format [22]. Each model-checking instance resulting from riscv-mini contains 3,395 total state bits and 378 total input bits, and each model-checking instance resulting from NutShell contains 71,581 total state bits and 7,312 total input bits. We utilize the bounded model-checking (BMC) engine of Pono to solve the model-checking problem[4], where the max step bound is set to 40. The model-checking experiments were run under Ubuntu 20.04LTS with 64 GiB RAM and 24 Intel(R) Core[TM] i9-13980HX CPU @ 5.60 GHz processors.

We find *2 RISC-V ISA non-conformance bugs* in riscv-mini and *5 RISC-V ISA non-conformance bugs* in NutShell. The 2 bugs found in riscv-mini have been reported to the designers as GitHub issues[5]. The 5 bugs found in NutShell have been confirmed by the designers.

Table 2 includes some statistics of the experiments related to the 7 bugs[6], where columns **Step** and **Time** show the number of steps and the execution time respectively when the bug was found, column **Assume** shows the instructions that are enforced by the assume statements, and column **Insts** reports the instruction represented by the counterexample when the bug was found, column **Hex** gives the hexadecimal encoding of the instruction, and column **VM** shows whether the virtual memory is enabled or not. The label R/N in the name of a bug represents that it is a bug of riscv-mini/NutShell.

---

[4] We also tried some other model-checking algorithms (e.g., PDR). It turns out that the transition systems generated from riscv-mini and NutShell are too large for them to finish in a reasonable amount of time (24 h).

[5] Please refer to the issues 71 and 72 at https://github.com/ucb-bar/riscv-mini/issues.

[6] The bugs N:E1 and N:E2 reveal that the values of some signals' bit-widths in NutShell do not conform to the RISC-V ISA specification, although they can be seen as the pragmatic choices made by designers.

We would like to remark that when the virtual memory is enabled in NutShell, we set the value of the first 20 bits of the `satp` register[7] to be `h80000` and the value of the `mstatus` register[8] to be `h000E0800`. Among the 5 bugs found in NutShell, the bugs N:E4 and N:E5 are correlated. When the bug N:E4 was found, the number of steps in the BMC algorithm is 29 and the execution time is 97 m31.34 s. Then we adapted the assume statement to enforce that `PPN[1:0]` is zero[9], thus bypassing the bug N:E4. Finally, we reran the model-checker Pono and discovered the bug N:E5 after 67 m11.29 s.

Table 2. Bugs found in riscv-mini and NutShell

Bug	Step	Time	Assume Insts	Insts	Hex	VM
R:E1	4	0.52 s	RV32I	BLTU x29, x1, -2	0xFE1EEFE3	✗
R:E2	5	2.58 s	RV32I	SW x1, 38(x1)	0x0210A323	✗
				SB x31, -1(x5)	0xFFF28FA3	
N:E1	10	2.56 s	RV32/64I	LD x4, -377(x1)	0xE870B203	✗
N:E2	29	47 m27.66 s	Load/Store	SD x1, 1976(x19)	0x7A19BC23	✓
N:E3	19	11 m25.44 s	Zicsr MRET, SRET ECALL, EBREAK	SRET SRET	0x10200073 0x10200073	✗
N:E4	29	97 m31.34 s	Load/Store	SD x0,48(x22)	0x020B3823	✓
N:E5	29	67 m11.29 s	Load/Store	LD x0,384(x2)	0x18013003	✓

In the sequel, we describe more details about the 2 bugs found in riscv-mini and 5 bugs found in NutShell.

R:E1. Instruction-address-misaligned exceptions are missed for branch instructions: riscv-mini enforces the instruction address alignment only for (unconditional) jump instructions (e.g., `JAL`), but not for (conditional) branch instructions (e.g., `BLTU`). As a result, when the addresses are misaligned in branch instructions, no exceptions will be triggered.

R:E2. Store address-misaligned exception does not flush the subsequent store instructions correctly: When the address in a store instruction is misaligned and an exception is triggered, riscv-mini does not flush the subsequent store instructions correctly. For instance, if the instruction `SW x1, 38(x1)` is followed by the instruction `SB x31, -1(x5)`, then although the execution of the first store instruction triggers an address-misaligned exception, the second store instruction, which should be flushed and not be executed, will still be executed partially in riscv-mini and a write request will be issued to the memory.

---

[7] The `satp` register is a read/write register that controls the supervisor-mode address translation and protection. It only exists when the supervisor mode is enabled.

[8] The `mstatus` register is a read/write register that keeps track of and controls the core's current operating state.

[9] PPN denotes the physical page number.

As we shall see in Sect. 5.2, riscv-formal fails to detect this bug, indicating that even on unprivileged instructions, riscv-formal can miss some bugs.

N:E1. Non-writable high bits of the mtval register: When an exception occurs, the high bits of the `mtval` register (more precisely, `mtval[63:39]`) in NutShell are not writable, which violates the RISC-V ISA specification.

N:E2. Invalid PPN[2] bits in Sv39 physical addresses: In RISC-V ISA specification, the physical addresses in the Sv39 virtual memory system should be 56 bits, while in NutShell, Sv39 physical addresses have only 32 bits.

N:E3. Missing privilege checking in the execution of xRET instructions: According to the RISC-V ISA specification, an xRET instruction (where x = M, S) can only be executed in a privilege mode that is the same as or higher than x. When the initial value of the `mstatus` register is set to be `h00001800`, and two consecutive `SRET` instructions are executed, after the execution of the first `SRET` instruction, the privilege mode is changed to U, as a result, the execution of the second `SRET` instruction should raise an exception. Nevertheless, NutShell fails to do so.

N:E4. Missing super-page checking in virtual address translation: According to Step 6 of the virtual address translation process in the RISC-V ISA specification (see Sect. 4.3.2 of [31]), some lower `PPN` bits of the Sv39 page table entries (PTE) should be zeros during the page-table translation. For instance, during the first translation (where level = 2), `PPN[level-1:0]` (i.e. `PPN[1]` and `PPN[0]`) should be kept as zeros. A violation of this restriction would raise a page-fault exception. Nevertheless, NutShell does not handle such unaligned super-page exceptions.

N:E5. Missing some corner cases on X, W, R, V bits of PTE: To determine whether a leaf PTE has been found, we should do some checks according to Steps 3 and 4 in the RISC-V ISA specification (Page 82, Volume 2).

Table 3. Truth table of X, W, R, V bits of Bug E5's PTE Flag.

X	W	R	V	Spec	NutShell
0/1	0/1	0/1	0	Page Fault	Page Fault
0	1	0	1	Page Fault	Page Fault
1	1	0	1	Page Fault	None
1	0	0	1	Found	Found
0/1	0/1	1	1	Found	Found
0	0	0	1	Not Found	Not Found

NutShell implements these checks by using nested conditional statements. After converting the counterexample reported by the Pono model-checker to the truth table (see Table 3), we can see that in the third case, according to the

RISC-V specification, a page-fault exception should be raised, while NutShell fails to do so.

A single corner case among 16 combinations of X, W, R, V bits is hard to be discovered by simulation or testing, which shows that formal verification is capable of discovering some deep bugs that might be elusive for informal verification methods (e.g. simulation or testing).

5.2   Performance Comparison with the Other Approaches

As reported in Sect. 5, our approach is able to discover real-world unknown bugs in the two open-source processor designs riscv-mini and NutShell. In the sequel, we compare the performance of our approach against the other two approaches of formal verification of RISC-V processor designs, that is, riscv-formal and the symbolic-execution based approach in [6,7].

5.2.1   Comparison with Riscv-Formal
We first compare the bug-detection capability of our approach and riscv-formal, then compare their scalability.

Comparison of the Bug-Detection Capability. We compare the detection capability of our approach and riscv-formal by checking whether riscv-formal can discover the 7 bugs found by our approach (see Table 2). It turns out that it can only discover 2 out of 7 bugs.

- Among the 2 bugs found in riscv-mini by our approach, i.e. R:E1–E2, riscv-formal fails to find R:E2, although it can find R:E1. It is because riscv-formal checks the ISA conformance *only* when an instruction is committed, but the flushed instruction in R:E2 is not committed, thus fails to detect. In contrast, our approach checks the conformance when memory read/write requests occur, thus does not miss the bug R:E2.
- Among the 5 bugs found in NutShell by our approach, i.e. N:E1–E5, riscv-formal cannot discover the four bugs related to virtual memories or privileged instructions, that is, N:E2–E5, namely, it can only find the bug N:E1.

Furthermore, the RVFI interface on which riscv-formal relies on is much heavier for the developers, compared to the interface in our approach, because it requires much more information from the DUT than ours.

Comparison of the Scalability. Besides the bug-detection capability, we would like to compare the scalability of our approach and riscv-formal on riscv-mini and NutShell. Since riscv-mini supports only the RV32I instructions and riscv-formal does not support the privileged instructions, we choose to ignore the privileged instructions and focus on the RV32I instructions. For technical convenience, we choose the 32-bit version of NutShell for the comparison. As a result of this choice, in the comparison, we can use the same configuration in our reference model for both riscv-mini and NutShell. Similarly, we can use the same configuration in riscv-formal for both riscv-mini and NutShell.

To facilitate the comparison, we manually inject into the two processor designs the following five bugs for RV32I instructions.

- #1. **Unsigned comparison for SLTI.** The SLTI (Set Less Than Immediate) instruction conducts a signed comparison between a register and an immediate value. We inject a fault in riscv-mini by neglecting the sign and apply an unsigned comparison.
- #2. **SUB with the highest bit set to 0.** We modify the implementation of the SUB (SUBtraction) instruction in riscv-mini by setting the highest bit of the result to 0.
- #3. **BNE to BEQ.** We modify the implementation of the BNE (Branch Not Equal) instruction in riscv-mini to the BEQ (Branch Equal) instruction.
- #4. **Incorrect signed comparison in BLTU.** The BLTU instruction compares two registers as unsigned integers. We manually introduced a bug by modifying it to use signed comparison, causing incorrect branching for large unsigned values.
- #5. **ADDI with the lowest bit set to 0.** We modify the implementation of the ADDI instruction in riscv-mini by setting the lowest bit of the result to 0.

Then we run our approach and riscv-formal to detect these bugs and compare their performance. When attempting to find a non-conformance bug for a DUT, we reduce the problem into the problem of checking multiple assertions against the DUT. Then we create multiple model-checking problem instances for these assertions, one instance for each assertion. Since the Pono model-checker is used as the backend in our approach, we run multiple Pono processes on the 24 Intel processors in parallel to solve these model-checking problem instances. On the other hand, in riscv-formal, we run multiple SymbiYosys [33] processes on the 24 processors in parallel, since SymbiYosys is used therein to solve the model-checking problem. Both our approach and riscv-formal will stop when any of their processes finds a bug.

Note that we record the time when the first bug is reported. The experiment results are reported in Table 4. From the results, we can see that the scalability of our approach is better than that of riscv-formal (except the bug #2).

Table 4. Scalability comparison of our approach and riscv-formal

Bug	riscv-mini				NutShell			
	Our approach		riscv-formal		Our approach		riscv-formal	
	Time[s]	Step	Time[s]	Step	Time[s]	Step	Time[s]	Step
# 1	2.28	4	3.43	4	10.32	6	29.14	6
# 2	6.72	4	1.81	4	14.84	6	14.73	6
# 3	0.66	4	3.41	4	5.47	6	32.44	6
# 4	0.50	4	3.50	4	6.54	6	32.77	6
# 5	1.62	4	3.36	4	10.28	6	32.75	6
Avg.	2.36	4	3.10	4	9.49	6	28.37	6

5.2.2   Comparison with Symbolic-Execution Based Approach

We compare the performance of our approach with the symbolic-execution based approach in [6,7]. For readability, we recall the workflow of the symbolic-execution based approach in the sequel.

- At first, the RISC-V processor design in the SpinalHDL (an open-source high-level hardware description language similar to Chisel) is translated into Verilog using SBT (a build tool for Scala projects).
- The Verilog code is translated into C++ using the tool Verilator.
- A Voter module is utilized to synchronise the C++ code corresponding to a RISC-V processor with a C++ RISC-V ISS (Instruction Set Simulator), where the RISC-V Formal Interface (RVFI) [27] is added to the RISC-V processor to facilitate its connection to the Voter module.
- The C++ code is compiled into LLVM bytecode by Clang.
- Finally, the symbolic-execution engine KLEE is harnessed for verification.

In [6], a non-pipelined RISC-V processor called MicroRV32 was verified. MicroRV32 supports RV32-IMC, but lacks Cache and TLB modules. It consists of 3,193 lines of Verilog code and 7,497 lines of C++ code (after translating Verilog to C++).

At first, we try to use the aforementioned symbolic-execution approach to detect the RISC-V specification non-conformance bugs in riscv-mini and Nut-Shell that were found by our approach (see Table 2).

We translate the NutShell and riscv-mini Chisel designs into SystemVerilog, add the RVFI, and establish the connections to the Voter module, so that KLEE can be utilized eventually to perform symbolic-execution. We set the time bound to 86,400 s (or 24 h) for detecting these bugs. It turns out that *the symbolic-execution based approach discovers only one bug in Table 2, namely R: E1, within the time 58 m39 s (Recall that R:E1 can be discovered by our approach in 0.52 s).* Note that the C++ RISC-V ISS does support privileged instructions and the poor performance of the symbolic-execution based approach is due to its poor scalability. Compared with MicroRV32, riscv-mini has 2,349 lines of Verilog code and 8,155 lines of C++ code, while NutShell has 18,039 lines of Verilog code and 19,513 lines of C++ code, after translating these Chisel designs into Verilog, then to C++ with Verilator [29]. Note that although the code sizes of riscv-mini and MicroRV32 are comparable, riscv-mini contains a *3-stage pipeline*, while MicroRV32 is a *non-pipelined* processor, therefore, these bugs are hard to detect in riscv-mini by the symbolic-execution based approach.

With the idea that the manually injected bugs might be easier to detect, we also manually inject into riscv-mini and NutShell the 5 bugs for RV32I instructions in Table 4. We also set the time bound to 86,400 s (or 24 h). It turns out that *the symbolic-execution based approach can discover only two bugs in riscv-mini, namely the bugs #3 and #4, within the time 85 m59 s and 1356 m10 s, respectively (Recall that the two bugs can be discovered by our approach in 0.66 s and 0.50 s, respectively).* It fails to discover the other 3 bugs in riscv-mini and all the

5 bugs in NutShell. These experimental results demonstrate that our approach is significantly more effective and efficient than the symbolic-execution based approach in the bug detection.

6   Conclusion and Future Work

In this work, we proposed the first end-to-end formal verification approach for the functional correctness of RISC-V processor Chisel designs, that is, whether a RISC-V processor Chisel design conforms to the RISC-V ISA specifications, where both unprivileged and privileged instructions are taken into account. In particular, we developed a succinct, modular, and parameterized RISC-V reference model in Chisel. We validated the effectiveness and efficiency of our approach on two representative open-source RISC-V processor designs. Our approach found 7 real-world unknown RISC-V specification non-conformance bugs in riscv-mini and NutShell. The experimental results show that our approach can discover more bugs than the state-of-the-art open-source formal verification approaches, i.e. riscv-formal and symbolic-execution based approach. Furthermore, our approach is also more efficient than them. We should emphasize that our reference model is of independent interest and might be used in some other verification approaches, e.g. simulation, emulation, and fuzzing.

For the future work, we would like to validate our approach on more open-source RISC-V Chisel designs. It is also interesting to combine the formal and informal approaches in order to achieve a nice balance between precision and efficiency in the verification.

Acknowledgments. This work is supported by the Strategic Priority Research Program of the Chinese Academy of Sciences, Grant No. XDA0320101.

References

1. Axiomise: FormalISA: RISC-V formal verification (2023). https://www.axiomise.com/riscv-formal-app/
2. Bachrach, J., et al.: Chisel: constructing hardware in a Scala embedded language. In: DAC, pp. 1216–1225 (2012)
3. Biere, A., Cimatti, A., Clarke, E., Zhu, Y.: Symbolic model checking without BDDs. In: TACAS, pp. 193–207 (1999)
4. RISC-V Boom: The Berkeley out-of-order RISC-V processor (2023). https://github.com/riscv-boom/riscv-boom
5. Bradley, A.R.: SAT-based model checking without unrolling. In: VMCAI, pp. 70–87 (2011)
6. Bruns, N., Herdt, V., Drechsler, R.: Processor verification using symbolic execution: a RISC-V case-study. In: DATE, pp. 1–6 (2023). https://doi.org/10.23919/DATE56975.2023.10137202
7. Bruns, N., Herdt, V., Drechsler, R.: Symbolic execution framework for RISC-V processor verification (2023). https://github.com/agra-uni-bremen/symex_processor_verification

8. Chen, C., et al.: HyPFuzz: formal-assisted processor fuzzing. In: USENIX Security, pp. 1361–1378 (2023)
9. Clarke, E.M., Henzinger, T.A., Veith, H., Bloem, R. (eds.): Handbook of Model Checking. Springer, Cham (2018). https://doi.org/10.1007/978-3-319-10575-8
10. Devarajegowda, K., Kaja, E., Prebeck, S., Ecker, W.: ISA modeling with trace notation for context free property generation. In: 2021 58th ACM/IEEE Design Automation Conference (DAC), pp. 619–624 (2021). https://doi.org/10.1109/DAC18074.2021.9586264
11. Fine, S., Ziv, A.: Coverage directed test generation for functional verification using Bayesian networks. In: DAC, pp. 286–291 (2003)
12. Gao, D., Melham, T.: End-to-end formal verification of a RISC-V processor extended with capability pointers. In: FMCAD, pp. 24–33 (2021)
13. Haedicke, F., Le, H.M., Große, D., Drechsler, R.: Crave: an advanced constrained random verification environment for systemc. In: SoC, pp. 1–7 (2012)
14. Kande, R., et al.: TheHuzz: instruction fuzzing of processors using Golden-Reference models for finding Software-Exploitable vulnerabilities. In: USENIX Security, pp. 3219–3236 (2022)
15. Kim, D.: RISCV-MINI, a simple RISC-V 3-stage pipeline written in chisel (2017). https://github.com/ucb-bar/riscv-mini
16. Laeufer, K., Bachrach, J., Sen, K.: Open-source formal verification for Chisel. In: WOSET (2021). https://woset-workshop.github.io/WOSET2021.html
17. Lee, Y., et al.: An agile approach to building RISC-V microprocessors. IEEE Micro **36**, 1 (2016). https://doi.org/10.1109/MM.2016.11
18. Li, P.S., Izraelevitz, A.M., Bachrach, J.: Specification for the FIRRTL language. Technical report. UCB/EECS-2016-9, EECS Department, University of California, Berkeley (2016). http://www2.eecs.berkeley.edu/Pubs/TechRpts/2016/EECS-2016-9.html
19. Lyu, Y., Mishra, P.: Scalable concolic testing of RTL models. IEEE Trans. Comput. **70**(7), 979–991 (2021). https://doi.org/10.1109/TC.2020.2997644
20. Mann, M., et al.: Pono: a flexible and extensible SMT-based model checker. In: CAV, pp. 461–474 (2021)
21. Naveh, Y., et al.: Constraint-based random stimuli generation for hardware verification. AI Mag. **28**(3), 13–13 (2007)
22. Niemetz, A., Preiner, M., Wolf, C., Biere, A.: Btor2, btormc and boolector 3.0. In: CAV, pp. 587–595 (2018)
23. Nutshell RISC-V CPU (2019). https://github.com/OSCPU/NutShell
24. Onespin formal verification solutions - siemens eda (2024). https://eda.sw.siemens.com/en-US/ic/questa/onespin-formal-verification/
25. RISCV-tests (2015). https://github.com/riscv-software-src/riscv-tests
26. Rocket chip RISC-V CPU generator (2023). https://github.com/chipsalliance/rocket-chip
27. RISC-V formal interface (RVFI) (2020). https://github.com/SymbioticEDA/riscv-formal/blob/master/docs/rvfi.md
28. Sheeran, M., Singh, S., Stålmarck, G.: Checking safety properties using induction and a SAT-solver. In: FMCAD, pp. 127–144 (2000)
29. Verilator: Open-Source SystemVerilog simulator and lint system (2024). https://github.com/verilator/
30. Waterman, A., Asanović, K.: The RISC-V Instruction Set Manual Volume I: Unprivileged ISA Version 20191213 (2019)
31. Waterman, A., Asanović, K., Hauser, J.: The RISC-V Instruction Set Manual Volume II: Privileged Architecture Version 20211203 (2021)

32. Weingarten, L., Datta, K., Kole, A., Drechsler, R.: Complete and efficient verification for a RISC-V processor using formal verification. In: 2024 Design, Automation & Test in Europe Conference & Exhibition (DATE), pp. 1–6 (2024). https://doi.org/10.23919/DATE58400.2024.10546693
33. Wolf, C., et al.: Symbiyosys (2022). https://symbiyosys.readthedocs.io/
34. Wolf, C.: Formal Verification of RISC-V Cores with RISCV-formal (2018). https://riscv.org/wp-content/uploads/2018/12/13.30-Humbenberger-Wolf-Formal-Verification-of-RISC-V-processor-implementations.pdf
35. Xiangshan: An open-source high-performance RISC-V processor (2023). https://github.com/OpenXiangShan/XiangShan
36. Xu, J., Liu, Y., He, S., Lin, H., Zhou, Y., Wang, C.: MorFuzz: fuzzing processor via runtime instruction morphing enhanced synchronizable co-simulation. In: USENIX Security, pp. 1307–1324 (2023)
37. Xu, Y., et al.: Towards developing high performance RISC-V processors using agile methodology. In: MICRO, pp. 1178–1199 (2022)
38. Xu, et al.: Functional verification for agile processor development: a case for workflow integration. J. Comput. Sci. Technol. (2023)
39. YosysHQ: RISC-V Formal Verification Framework (2016). https://github.com/YosysHQ/riscv-formal

The Principle of Staking: Formal Verification of Staking Smart Contract

Zhongyun Zhang[1] , Kundu Chen[2] , Weiqi Guo[3], and Wenbo Zhang[1(✉)]

[1] Shanghai Ocean University, Shanghai 201306, China
m220951666@st.shou.edu.cn, wbzhang@shou.edu.cn
[2] Beihang University, Beijing 100191, China
BY1606150@buaa.edu.cn
[3] Shanghai East Sea Marine Engineering Survey and Design Institute Co., Ltd.,
Shanghai 200137, China
guo_weiqi@ecs.mnr.gov.cn

Abstract. Recently, Proof-of-Stake (PoS) consensus mechanisms have been widely adopted by various blockchain platforms due to their superior performance and lower environmental impact. As a relatively new and somewhat unfamiliar consensus mechanism, PoS presents potential security risks. Staking is an extremely important concept in PoS, serving as the entry point to the PoS mechanism. It allows users to lock in their assets to obtain the right to participate in network consensus. As of today, research on it remains limited. Therefore, this paper aims to ensure the security of users' staked assets and the stability of the consensus network by analyzing the staking mechanism in PoS and modeling a general staking model. We enhance the security attributes of the model by adding a set of high-level properties. Finally, we verify its rationality and effectiveness in the Move language environment.

Keywords: Blockchain · Consensus mechanism · Smart contract · Formal verification

1 Introduction

Staking, initially a financial sector concept, refers to users pledging a certain amount of tokens to specific institutions in exchange for periodic returns. The advent of cryptocurrencies, especially the widespread application of the *Proof-of-Stake* (PoS) consensus mechanism [8], has elevated the importance of staking mechanism.

Staking is fundamentally integral to the Proof-of-Stake (PoS) consensus mechanism, which operates within a peer-to-peer network [16]. In this framework, stakers are selected based on the amount of cryptocurrency they commit to stake as a form of security deposit. This ensures that stakers have a vested interest in the network's integrity. Network nodes can send a certain amount

---

Z. Zhang and K. Chen—These authors contributed equally to this work.

T. Bourke et al. (Eds.): SETTA 2024, LNCS 15469, pp. 161–179, 2025.
https://doi.org/10.1007/978-981-96-0602-3_9

of tokens to a smart contract known as a *staking contract*, where these tokens are considered staked [7]. Simultaneously, the staking contract also distributes rewards back to stakers, which is the compensation promised by the network to stakers [18]. Therefore, the PoS consensus mechanism is a win-win mechanism for both the blockchain network and stakers.

As staking mechanisms have become increasingly intricate, they have led to the exposure of vulnerabilities in contracts and related attacks. Vulnerabilities come in many forms, ranging from simple and common ones like basic integer overflow attacks [30] and reentrancy attacks [27] to more specialized threats that target PoS consensus mechanisms, such as 51% attacks [35] and long-range attacks [28]. These vulnerabilities are not limited to staking contracts but also plague other types of smart contracts. Each one poses a significant challenge to the baseline of network security, constantly testing the resilience and security measures of blockchain networks. This constantly reminds researchers to be vigilant in safety.

Despite the efforts of security researchers in summarizing and proposing solutions for vulnerabilities in staking contracts [15], new attacks continue to emerge. On the one hand, this ongoing issue is due to the continuous evolution of development of staking concepts, inevitably leading to new vulnerabilities. On the other hand, it highlights the lack of a high-level model for the staking mechanism itself, leading staking contracts to lack thorough soundness checks. While many researchers have employed formal methods to model smart contracts, including theorem proving [29] and model checking [1], these studies often focus on general security properties. Typically, they start by defining a set of potentially risky features triggered by known vulnerabilities and then verify the presence of these features. These approaches typically operate at the language level rather than targeting specific functions or modules, limiting the comprehensiveness of ensuring the final security of contracts. Furthermore, compared to more complex staking mechanisms or staking contracts, the majority of researchers prefer to study simpler token mechanisms or token contracts, such as ERC20 [26], ERC712 [21], and so on. As a result, security research in the area of staking mechanisms is relatively scarce, and the security is somewhat lacking.

Therefore, the primary objective of this paper is to model staking mechanism, summarize its potential properties, and conduct formal verification. While this verification is not specific to any particular programming language, it remains an essential part of the verification process. The *Move* language [20] has been chosen as our target language for this paper, primarily due to its enhanced security features compared to other contract languages like Solidity [31]. The Move language enforces stricter resource and access control [11], reducing low-level errors in contracts and allowing us to focus more on the correctness of the model itself. In brief, the main contributions of this paper are as follows:

(1) We have analyzed the staking mechanism within PoS network. After analysis, we have established a general staking model and represented the model in a formalized manner.

(2) On the basis of the general model, we propose various constraints on the components of the model and the runtime conditions of the model and summarize them into a set of brief but important high-level properties to ensure the basic security of the model when interacting with the internal and external worlds.

(3) We convert the high-level properties of staking model to the specification language, and leverage the Move Prover [10], an SMT-solver interface for Move language to formally verify all of these properties. The results demonstrate that our staking model satisfies both the soundness and the feasibility.

The rest of this paper is arranged as follows. In Sect. 2, we introduce the relevant background knowledge, including staking mechanisms, the Move language and Move Prover. In Sect. 3, we analyze the commonalities of staking mechanisms to derive a general staking model. In Sect. 4, we discuss the high-level properties based on the model. The evaluation of the model will be carried out in Sect. 5. Finally, in Sects. 6 and 7, we address related work and provide a summary of our research.

2   Preliminary

2.1   Staking Mechanism

The staking mechanism required a user to deposit its tokens into a *staking pool* [12]. In order to gain a certain reward, the user must deposit tokens more than the required value to keep the staking pool activated. A staking pool is always conjured with a *delegation pool* [22]. Fundamentally, the delegation pool serves as an interface for the user, while the staking pool conducts the staking activities.

For most of the users who cannot meet the staking requirement of a staking pool, their initial interaction with the staking model typically involves accumulating their stake through a delegation pool. Once the delegation pool has accumulated enough stake to meet the staking requirement, it then transfers the stake to the staking pool for management. The outline of the staking mechanism is demonstrated in the Fig. 1.

Smart contracts can be used to deploy the staking pool, allowing any address to send tokens to the contract for staking [19]. An address that stakes tokens is referred to as a *staker*. A staking pool allows only one staker to exist. When the amount of staked tokens in the staking pool exceeds a predefined target value, known as *minimum amount*, the staking pool can be activated, and the staker is allowed to become a *validator* [4] and join the governance of the network.

In staking mechanism, the concept of an *epoch* is frequently employed to make necessary adjustments to the network after a fixed period of time [34]. Important adjustments include distributing rewards to stakers and adjusting the status of the pool. After each epoch ends, stakers can withdraw their tokens from the staking pool. After the withdrawal, if the existing staked token is less than the minimum amount, the validator reverts to a regular address.

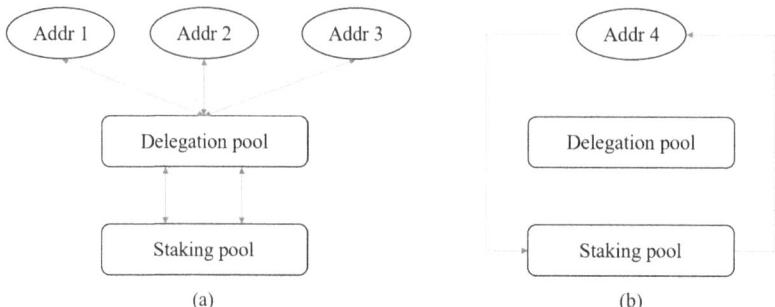

Fig. 1. The outline of the staking mechanism. (a) Common users engage with the dele-gation pool by contributing stakes and receiving tokens as rewards or upon withdrawal. (b) Users possessing the requisite token value can directly interact with the staking pool.

2.2   Move and Move Prover

As an emerging programming language, Move has its own innovations compared to other popular smart contract languages like Solidity. The essence of Move is the concept of *resources* [25]. In Move, a datatype is allowed to add or remove features, and shape its unique properties. A datatype that is non-duplicable and indestructible, and stored in the global storage, is referred to as a resource. This design ensures that the state of resources (like tokens) is easier to manage and track, thereby reducing the risk of errors in complex operations. In contrast, Solidity requires the manual specification for asset transfers, which heightens the potential for coding mistakes [24]. Move substantially reduces the attack surface of smart contracts by enhancing access control, authorization and type safety [3]. Meanwhile, its account model requires resources to be stored under unique *accounts*. Each Move account has a unique *address* used to identify and access the account and its resources. Therefore, users can maintain absolute and unique control over the account and the resources within.

The Move Prover is a formal verification tool specially made for smart contracts that are written in the Move language [36]. Move Prover features an expressive specification language called *Move Specification Language(MSL)*, designed to define contract behaviors. Leveraging automatic theorem-proving technology, it checks contract compliance with user-given specifications across all program variable assignments. The verification process involves compiling Move source code and MSL into Boogie, then using the Z3 SMT solver [9] to validate contract properties.

3   Staking Model

This section will introduce the basic framework of the *general staking model*. The objective of the general staking model is to illustrate the principle of the staking model, which enables the advancement of subsequent high-level properties and formal work.

3.1 Attributes

Based on the implementations of staking mechanisms in current mainstream blockchains such as Ethereum and Aptos, the attributes of the general staking model have been summarized into the following concepts:

– **Staking pool**: This term represents the repository where tokens are stored. The staking pool is the foundation and core of the staking mechanism.
– **Staker**: This role is attributed to the individual or entity tasked with the stewardship and operational management of the staking pool. They are usually in charge of the pool's maintenance, updates, and decision-making. Typically, blockchains also have validators responsible for verifying blocks. However, since the model does not involve a description of the work to achieve block verification, the duties of a validator are fewer and can be fully assumed by the owner, thus in this model, the staker also serves as the validator.
– **Staking pool state** (*Pending active, active, pending inactive, inactive*): These states delineate the lifecycle of a pool, ideally transitioning from inactive, to pending active, to active, to pending inactive, and subsequently reverting to inactive. Each blockchain's staking pool has a strictly designed status system. For example, Ethereum records four key time points to express the current state of the pool, such as reaching the conditions for activation, activation itself, exit, etc. In Aptos, the pool is directly marked with a state, where the pool only needs to record its current state, rather than many key time points. It is undeniable that both Ethereum and Aptos exhibit the presence of four statuses: pending active, active, pending inactive, and inactive. The design of these four states balances flexibility with security, facilitating the management of the states while avoiding issues that may arise from frequent state transitions. Specifically, a pool in the pending active state needs to meet the blockchain's requirements to become active, otherwise, it will directly revert to inactive.
– **Token state** (*Pending locked stake, locked stake, pending withdrawable stake, withdrawable stake*): These states categorize the tokens within the pool, streamlining pool management and mitigating the impact of fund additions or withdrawals on the staking pool's consensus network weight. The token states transition in parallel with the pool's status changes. To accommodate flexibility, transitions from pending withdrawable stake back to locked stake are permissible. Crucially, only tokens classified as withdrawable stake are eligible for withdrawal at any time.
– **Locked time**: This defines the lock period for tokens staked in the pool. It ensures that tokens are locked in the pool until the lock period expires. This double safeguard undoubtedly increases the cost of malicious behavior for network nodes. It also meets the needs of stakers who commit to long-term staking.

- **Epoch**: This represents a fixed period that divides the blockchain into continuous time segments. After each epoch passes, the blockchain undergoes some adjustments, including distributing rewards, updating statuses, and other very important operations. These adjustments act like a protocol, with some changes being made according to the content stipulated in this protocol at the end of each epoch and before the arrival of the next one.

These attributes collectively encapsulate the entire staking journey, from initiation to conclusion, providing a robust framework to underpin the entire staking model.

3.2   Events

In addition to attributes, the staking model also requires events that can interact with it. From the perspective of contracts, this is achieved through *view functions* and *transaction functions*. However, given that view functions do not involve state changes, this section will only discuss the key transaction functions that can change the state.

The transaction functions in Fig. 1 still appear complex, and the address of the delegation pool can be regarded as the whole of the Delegation pool and Addrs in (a) of Fig. 1. Therefore, the staking mechanism in Fig. 1 can be viewed as a communication between an address and a Staking pool.

Table 1. Staking Pool Key Functions Overview

Classifications	Functions
interface functions	Init
	addStake
	joinValidatorSet
	increaseLockUp
	unlockStake
	reactivateStake
	leaveValidatorSet
	withdraw
internal functions	onNewEpoch

Based on the simplified staking mechanism, transaction functions are divided into two types of events: *interface functions* and *internal functions*, as shown in Table 1. The interface functions for managing the staking pool are outlined as follows:

- **Init**: Initialization of the staking pool. This is the first event for stakers entering the staking model, as owning a staking pool is a prerequisite for staking.

- **addStake**: Adding tokens to the staking pool. Typically, for pools partici-
  pating in consensus work, added tokens are placed into pending locked stake
  to avoid affecting the pool's weight in the current epoch. For inactive pools,
  added tokens go directly into locked stake.
- **joinValidatorSet**: Staker applies to participate in consensus work. To join
  the consensus, the staking pool needs to be activated, hence the application
  changes the pool's status to pending active for review.
- **increaseLockUp**: Stakers wanting to stake long-term can increase the locked
  time of the staking pool.
- **unlockStake**: Stakers wishing to withdraw some tokens. This operation
  moves tokens from locked stake to pending withdrawable stake, awaiting the
  end of the locked time to transfer to withdrawable stake.
- **reactivateStake**: Stakers re-lock tokens that were prepared for unlocking.
  This operation is the opposite of unlockStake, moving tokens from pending
  withdrawable stake back to locked stake.
- **leaveValidatorSet**: Stakers apply to exit consensus work. There are two
  scenarios: one for stakers currently in action, changing the pool from active
  to pending inactive, and another for stakers who have applied but not yet
  started working, directly changing the pool from pending active to inactive.
- **withdraw**: Stakers redeem their tokens. Stakers withdraw tokens from withdrawable stake in the pool. For pools in inactive status, pending withdrawable
  stake ending its lock period is first transferred to withdrawable stake to avoid
  the embarrassment of tokens being stuck forever.

For internal functions, we use a single event to represent:

- **newEpoch**: Represents the adjustments made by the consensus network at
  the end of each epoch and the arrival of a new epoch. There are mainly two
  adjustments: distributing rewards and adjusting status. Adjusting status is
  relatively complex, as the status of some pools and the token status within
  those pools need to be adjusted. For example, for a staker who has triggered
  the leaveValidatorSet event, causing the pool's status to become pending
  inactive, the change to inactive status occurs at this time. A detailed definition
  of this function will be provided in Subsect. 3.3.

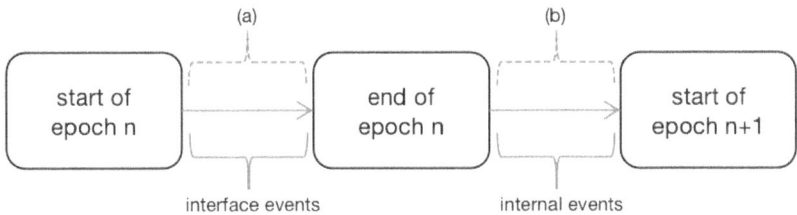

Fig. 2. Distribution of events in the n-th epoch.

Figure 2 illustrates the positions where interface events and internal events are triggered: (a) those within an epoch's time segment and (b) those occurring at epoch transitions. Transitions within segment (a) are triggered by interface events. The transitions in segment (b) are triggered by an internal event and are always automatically enforced by the blockchain network.

3.3 General Staking Model

We first provide the formal definitions of an account and a stake pool, followed by defining general staking model.

An account a can be represented by the binary tuple (ow, tk), where

- $ow \in Addr$ signifies the address of the owner, also known as the staker;
- $tk \in \mathbb{N}$ represents the quantity of tokens in the account.

The configuration of a stake pool is characterized by an septuple, denoted as $p = (ps, ow, lt, pl, ls, pw, ws)$, where

- $ps \in \{PA, A, PI, I\}$ is the staking pool state;
- $ow \in Addr$ is the address of the owner, also known as the staker;
- $lt \in \mathbb{N}$ is the locked time;
- $pl, ls, pw, ws \in \mathbb{N}$ represents the amount of tokens in pending locked stake, locked stake, pending withdrawable stake, withdrawable stake respectively.

The general staking model $\mathcal{P} = (S, s_0, E, \delta, m)$ is characterized by the following components:

- S represents a set of states;
- s_0 is the initial state;
- E represents a set of events;
- $\delta \subseteq (S \cup \{s_0\}) \times E \times S$ defines the partial transition function, mapping state-event pairs to subsequent states;
- $m \in \mathbb{N}$ represents the minimum staking threshold;

The model state is represented as a tuple (a, p, T) within the set S. Here, a represents an account, p denotes a staking pool, and $T \in \mathbb{N}$ represents the epoch number. Once initialization is complete, a and p consistently share a same owner. The automaton progresses from one model state to the next via function δ, activated upon the occurrence of event e, which is consistent with Table 1.

Starting from s_0, the only possible event is $Init(-, -)$. Assuming $Init(addr, T)$ is triggered by the account $a = (addr, tk)$ at epoch number T, the transition function is then defined as

$$\delta(s_0, (Init, addr, T)) = (a, (I, addr, 0, 0, 0, 0, 0), T)$$

For convenience, the notation $s[x = v]$ is used to denote the updated model state resulting from replacing the component x in state s with the new value v.

Starting from $s = ((ow, tk), (ps, ow, lt, pl, ls, pw, ws), T)$, if an event $e = addStake(addr, c)$ occurs where $addr = ow$ and $c \in \mathbb{N}$ represents the quantity of tokens for processing, the actual amount processed is $c' = \min(c, tk)$. The transition function is defined as

$$\delta(s, e) = \begin{cases} s[ls = ls + c'][tk = tk - c'] & \text{if } ps = PA \text{ or } I \\ s[pl = pl + c'][tk = tk - c'] & \text{if } ps = A \text{ or } PI \end{cases}$$

For an event $e = joinValidatorSet(addr)$ satisfying $addr = ow$ and $ps = I$, the transition function is defined as

$$\delta(s, e) = s[ps = PA]$$

For an event $e = increaseLockUp(addr)$ satisfying $addr = ow$, the transition function is defined as

$$\delta(s, e) = s[lt = lt + 1]$$

For an event $e = unlockStake(addr, c)$ satisfying $addr = ow$ and $c \in \mathbb{N}$, the transition function is defined as

$$\delta(s, e) = s[ls = \max(ls - c, 0), ws = ws + \min(ls, c)]$$

For an event $e = reactivateStake(addr, c)$ satisfying $addr = ow$ and $c \in \mathbb{N}$, the transition function is defined as

$$\delta(s, e) = s[ls = ls + \min(ws, c), ws = \max(ws - c, 0)]$$

For an event $e = leaveValidatorSet(addr)$ satisfying $addr = ow$ and $ps = PA$ or A, the transition function is defined as

$$\delta(s, e) = \begin{cases} s[ps = I] & \text{if } ps = PA \\ s[ps = PI] & \text{if } ps = A \end{cases}$$

For an event $e = withdraw(addr, c)$ satisfying $addr = ow$ and $c \in \mathbb{N}$, if the current state of the stake pool is I and the specified locked time has been reached, tokens in pending withdrawable stake are first transitioned to withdrawable stake:

$$s' = \begin{cases} s[ws = ws + pw][pw = 0] & \text{if } ps = I \text{ and } lt \leq T \\ s & \text{otherwise} \end{cases}$$

Then, adjustments are made for the value of tokens to be withdrawn, the transition function is defined as:

$$\delta(s, e) = s'[ws = \max(ws - c, 0)][tk = tk + \min(c, ws)]$$

For an event $e = (newEpoch)$, which signifies the arrival of the next epoch, a sequence of updates is triggered to modify the state of the model. The first step involves updating the epoch number:

$$s_1 = s[T = T + 1]$$

Then, rewards $r_{ls}, r_{ps} \in \mathbb{N}$ are distributed if the state of pool is in A or PI:

$$s_2 = \begin{cases} s_1[ls = ls + r_{ls}][pw = pw + r_{pw}] & \text{if } ps = A \text{ or } PI \\ s_1 & \text{otherwise} \end{cases}$$

The variables r_{ls}, r_{pw} represents the rewards allocated to pools. The calculation method for these rewards varies across different blockchains. Generally, rewards are distributed to pools in active and pending inactive states, as they are actively involved in the validation work. The amount of rewards is proportional to the staked principal. Pools in the other two non-working states will not receive any rewards.

The subsequent phase involves the adjustments to both token and pool states. If the state of pool is in A or PI, pending locked tokens are converted into locked stake:

$$s_3 = \begin{cases} s_2[ls = ls + pl][pl = 0] & \text{if } ps = A \text{ or } PI \\ s_2 & \text{otherwise} \end{cases}$$

Furthermore, pending withdrawable tokens are converted to withdrawable stake once the specified locked time has been reached.

$$s_4 = \begin{cases} s_3[ws = ws + pw][pw = 0] & \text{if } ps = A \text{ or } PI \text{ and } lt \leq T \\ s_3 & \text{otherwise} \end{cases}$$

The pool state is updated to be active if pool is in state PA or A and meets the minimum amount criteria:

$$s_5 = \begin{cases} s_4[ps = A] & \text{if } ps = PA \text{ or } A \text{ and } pl + ls + pw \geq m \\ s_4[ps = I] & \text{otherwise} \end{cases}$$

In summary, the transition for event $e = newEpoch$ can be encapsulated as:

$$\delta(s, e) = s_5$$

3.4   Lifecycle of a Staking Pool

To gain a good understanding of the general staking model, a simple example of one possible lifecycle of the model is presented here. Assuming a new, honest staker who has not yet participated in staking, his process from joining to exiting staking in three epochs should proceed as follows:

1. In the n-th epoch, a new staker creates a new and empty pool through the Init event, at which point the pool's status is "inactive";
2. The staker adds tokens to the pool through the addStake event;
3. When the number of tokens in the pool reaches the minimum amount, the staker applies to participate in the network consensus through the joinValidatorSet event. At this time, the node's status becomes "pending active";

4. At the end of the nth epoch, the newEpoch event is triggered, automatically qualifying the pool and changing its status to "active", while also automatically applying a locked time;

5. The n+1st epoch begins, during which the staker can initiate any event other than Init for their pool. Suppose the staker initiates an unlock event, requesting the unlock of all their staked tokens. The staker also initiates a leaveValidatorSet event, requesting to exit the network consensus. At this time, the pool's status becomes "pending inactive";

6. At the end of the n+1st epoch, the newEpoch event distributes rewards to the pool according to its contribution during the n+1st epoch and adjusts the status of the tokens in the pool. At this point, the pool's status should become "inactive", and all tokens are stored in "pending withdrawable";

7. The n+2nd epoch begins, the staker retrieves all the tokens from the pool to their account through the withdraw event, successfully exiting staking.

The workflow of a staking pool not only represents the process of a staker's participation and exit from staking but also is a microcosm of the staking model. Interface transitions and internal transitions work together to form a robust and versatile staking model.

4   High-Level Properties

Building on the foundation of the general staking model, we propose high-level requirements, or *high-level properties*, that the model should possess. High-level properties focus more on the logical layer of the model, which differs from low-level properties, such as integer overflow and array out-of-bounds. The design of the staking model itself thoroughly considers security while balancing flexibility. However, as a precaution, the high-level properties can serve as the last line of defense for the security of the general staking model. Furthermore, if there are staking contracts implemented on the basis of the general staking model, these high-level properties will also facilitate the contracts to verify their own security using formal techniques of theorem proving.

High-level properties are divided into *local properties* and *global properties*. Moreover, since our model's verification work is based on using the Move language on Aptos, our high-level properties are also formalized and defined by MSL[1]. Because it is difficult to clearly express properties in a concise manner using natural language, presenting MSL code helps readers better understand the properties themselves. Due to space limitations, we only introduce some of the high-level properties.

4.1   Local Properties

Local properties are specific to particular transitions.

---

[1] The full contract code is too long to be displayed here. Interested readers can find it in the GitHub repository referenced in Section Availability.

Property 1: Only the staker has permission to interact with staking pool.

This high-level property demonstrates the model's strict access control. Only the staker of the staking pool has the right to change the state parameters of the staking pool. It is usually necessary to check whether the staker's address in the staking pool matches the staker's address. In Aptos, the staker's address of the staking pool is extracted to create an "OwnerCapability" resource, which is stored under the staker's account. Therefore, as specified in Listing 1.1, the "*aborts_if*" clause states that the function should abort if there is no access right to the pool under the staker's account. For rigor, we also require that a staking pool indeed exists under the address in the "OwnerCapability" resource. This property is typically applied to interface functions. The specification is shown in Listing 1.1:

Listing 1.1. Code block: Property 1

```
1 // get staking pool address
  // from OwnerCapability resources
3 let pool_addr = global<OwnerCapability>
  (staker_address).pool_addr;
5 // staker has access
  aborts_if !exists<OwnerCapability>(staker_addr)
7 && !exists<StakePool>(pool_addr);
```

Property 2: When adding stakes, the change in the number of tokens in the account, the change in the number of tokens in the staking pool, and the number of tokens the staker intends to add must be consistent. The same applies to withdrawing money.

This property ensures that the amount of tokens staked by the user is correct, preventing any loss of assets. Therefore, the property can be further divided into two steps: a. The number of tokens decreased in the account is equal to the staked amount; b. The number of tokens increased in the staking pool is equal to the staked amount. The "*ensures*" clause specifies that there is a change of the amount in both the account and the staking pool respectively. This property typically occurs in the addStake event, and the description of the property in the withdraw event follows the same rationale. The specification is shown in Listing 1.2:

Listing 1.2. Code block: Property 2

```
1 // the token change in the account is correct
  ensures post_balance == balance - amount;
3 // the token change in the pool is correct
  ensures amount != 0 &&
5 if (is_current_epoch_validator(pool_addr)) {
      post_pl_value == pl_value + amount
7 } else {
      post_ls_value == ls_value + amount
9 };
```

Property 3: Internal transitions will not crash due to any reason.
The internal stability of the general staking model is widely regarded. A stable staking model will not experience unexpected termination during internal transitions. Thus, property 3 can be rephrased as the correct initial epoch state will always reach the corresponding termination state. In MSL, the partial description of this property is quite straightforward: the "aborts_if" clause specifies that the function should not abort in any case. This property should be applied to the new epoch event. In fact, this property also requires verifying that the correct initial state corresponds one-to-one with the termination state. However, the functions involved are quite complex which cause timeout, and the detailed verification process is explained in Sect. 5. The partial specification is shown in Listing 1.3:

Listing 1.3. Code block: Property 3

```
1 aborts_if false;
```

4.2 Global Properties

Global properties address security or the majority of transitions.

Property 4: The owner of a staking pool remains immutable.
The takeover of a staking pool could lead to the theft of all tokens within the pool. Therefore, the staker of the staking pool will be the pool's sole owner. Due to the unique design of Aptos, what we need to ensure is that the OwnerCapability in the model is always stored under the same account. The "ensures" clause specifies that for stakers who already own a staking pool, none of the transitions will change the identity of the pool's owner. The specification is shown in Listing 1.4:

Listing 1.4. Code block: Property 4

```
1 ensures forall addr: address
  where old(exists<OwnerCapability>(addr)):
3 old(global<OwnerCapability>(addr)).pool_address
  == global<OwnerCapability>(addr).pool_address;
```

Property 5: The total staked value in the staking pool should be constant (excluding addStake, withdraw, and newEpoch events).
This property requires that no unexpected circumstances can lead to the theft of tokens from the pool. It ensures that throughout the entire model, except for the addStake, withdraw events, and newEpoch, the sum of the four types of tokens in the staking pool remains constant under any transition. Therefore, by obtaining the sum of tokens in the pool for the rest of the transitions' pre-state and post-state, and specifying through the "ensures" clause that these two values should be equal. The specification is shown in Listing 1.5:

Listing 1.5. Code block: Property 5

```
  // get pre-state of the transition
2 let total_stake =
  pl_value + ls_value + pw_value + ws_value;
4 // get post-state of the transition
  let post_total_stake
6 = post_pl_value + post_ls_value + post_pw_value
      + post_ws_value;
8 // total stake should be constant
  ensures post_total_stake == total_stake;
```

5   Evaluation

In this section, we validate the specification of staking model and examine its performance. We employ Move Prover for verification, the procedure of solving is mentioned previously. Due to the staking model's complexity with non-quadratic operations and intricate references and queries, proof timeouts are likely. To prevent this, we split verification by function and property.

We categorize the properties of functions into pre-condition, post-condition, abort-condition, and other properties (including state update/modification, assumptions, references, etc.), and tally their occurrences in each function. For simplicity, we will only evaluate interface functions since internal functions are already encapsulated within the interface functions, and their properties are inherited by the interface functions as well. The result is shown in Table 2.

Table 2. The amount of conditions in each function.

Function	Abort	Pre	Post	Other	Sum
initialize_validator	8	0	3	0	11
add_stake	10	7	4	2	23
join_validator_set	14	0	2	1	17
increase_lockup	6	0	1	1	8
unlock	2	0	2	1	5
reactivate_stake	2	0	2	1	5
leave_validator_set	9	1	4	1	15
withdraw	9	0	2	2	13
on_new_epoch	1	13	0	0	14
global conditions	0	4	3	0	7

From the table, we find that the functions "add_stake", "join_validator_set", "leave_validator_set", "withdraw", and "on_new_epoch" are relatively complex. These functions have various pre-conditions and complex logic. In addition, we have separately categorized the common verification conditions shared by most functions, which are referred to as global conditions. Due to their wide applicability, the writing of verification conditions for global conditions will be more stringent.

The overall module verification process inevitably encounters timeout issues. To mitigate the impact of timeouts, we conducted verification for different properties separately. In such cases, we documented these functions causing timeouts, temporarily removed their related specifications, and re-verified them. Simultaneously, we also recorded the properties that couldn't be fully verified. The results are presented in Table 3.

Table 3. The time cost of verification.

Item	Passed	Verify Time	Timeout Func.
Property 1	Yes	3.20 s	-
Property 2	Yes	2.56 s	add_stake
Property 3	No	120 s[a]	on_new_epoch
Property 4	Yes	3.13 s	-
Property 5	Yes	2.96 s	-

[a] Given that the staking-related modules of Aptos are a foundational library, setting the timeout to 120 s is appropriate. A longer validation time would make contracts built on this foundational library more difficult to verify.

From Table 3, property 3 caused severe timeouts in the "on_new_epoch" function. Upon analysis, this function was found to be overly complex, containing numerous possible state transitions, which severely affected the efficiency of the verification, leading to timeouts. We have to use abstraction attempts in this case, that pre-defined the outcome of some operations to save time. In this case, we succeeded in passing this function within 120 s.

To fix it, we decompose the "on_new_epoch" step by step first. We individually verify each callee function and loop called within "on_new_epoch". For each function, we use "aborts_if" and "ensures" conditions to ensure the correctness of initial and terminal state, respectively. For functions with complex computations that lead to timeouts, we correctly limit the range of values, such as restricting the numerator of the fraction to between 0 and 100, instead of the default u64. An example is shown in Listing 1.6. For functions where we cannot limit the range of values, We have to use abstraction attempts, like behaviors in Listing 1.7. We set these functions as "opaque" to hide their computational processes during the verification of "on_new_epoch". They can be independently verified for correctness but do not need to participate in the verification process of the "on_new_epoch" function, thus avoiding an increase in computational load. For loops, we attempt to add spec at head of the loop to ensure the behavior of the loop. Second, we use "aborts_if false"; to ensure that no abnormal termination occurs during the execution of the function, as demonstrated in Sect. 4. By following the above two steps, property 3 can be proven. As a result, all of the properties can be verified after the adjustment.

Listing 1.6. Code block: Feasible limitation operations

```
1  // verification object in Move code
   // To prevent precision loss, fractions are usually presented
3  // in the form of a numerator, with the denominator being 100.
   let result = complex_calculations(commission_percentage);
5  // specification in MSL code with optimization
   // timeout disappear with the limitation below
7  requires commission_percentage >= 0
        && commission_percentage <= 100;
```

Listing 1.7. Code block: Abstraction operations

```
   // verification object in Move code
2  fun calculate_rewards_amount() { ... }
   // specification in MSL code with optimization
4  // timeout disappear with the operations below
   spec calculate_rewards_amount() {
6      pragma opaque;
       // verification is limited to the function itself
8      ensures [concrete] result == 0;
       // interact with caller functions using an uninterpreted spec
10     // function spec_get_result() to avoid complex calculations
       ensures [abstract] result == spec_get_result();
12 }
```

6   Related Work

PoS has emerged as a superior alternative to the Proof-of-Work (PoW) consensus protocol [22]. PoS encompasses two main aspects: the participation of stakers in the staking process and the subsequent consensus-reaching by validators. This paper focuses on the former, examining the staking model without delving into specific reward distribution algorithms and consensus algorithms. This section will highlight related work on consensus algorithms, their verification, and the study of reward mechanisms in staking pools.

Research on consensus algorithms is relatively extensive. There are primarily two types of PoS consensus protocols. The First, *Chain-based PoS* [23], relies on stake-based validator selection. Notable examples include Peercoin [16], followed by advancements in Ethereum 2.0 [6] and Tezos [14]. The second type, *BFT-based PoS* [33], combines PoS's energy efficiency with the fault tolerance and security benefits of BFT algorithms. This approach has been effectively implemented in next-generation blockchain projects such as Polkadot [32] and Algorand [13], etc. with Aptos [25] standing out for its exceptional efficiency and fault tolerance.

Significant efforts have also been dedicated to proving the security of consensus algorithms. For instance, Alturki [2] utilized Coq for algorithm security verification, while Losa [17] applied formal verification techniques to the Stellar consensus protocol. Such studies underscore the critical role of formal verification in ensuring the reliability of consensus mechanisms, a methodology also embraced in this paper.

Furthermore, the distribution of rewards to validators during the staking process has also garnered attention from researchers. Brünjes [5], as well as Gersbach [12] have investigated reward distribution schemes from the perspectives of both honest and malicious stakers. They conduct in-depth studies from the perspective of reward distribution in staking pools, aiming to prevent asset losses caused by unfair reward allocation schemes.

7   Conclusion and Future Work

This paper, motivated by the idea of exploring the essence of staking mechanisms in PoS, conducts an in-depth analysis of staking mechanisms. Based on the analysis of the implementation of staking mechanisms in mainstream blockchains, a general staking model has been summarized. To ensure the model's enhanced security, we propose a set of high-level properties as constraints on the model's behavior. Finally, we verify its performance using the Move Prover on the Move language.

This paper still has some shortcomings. For instance, due to our experimental process's dependency on the Move Prover, the work is challenging to verify in contexts of non-Move languages but relatively easier on Move-based blockchains like Aptos and Sui. Moreover, conducting experiments across multiple staking application scenarios will be our main goal and challenge in the future.

Acknowledgement. This research was funded by National Natural Science Foundation of China (62102243), Shanghai Sailing Program (21YF1417000). by X (grant number Y).

Data Availibility Statement. We have submitted our specification to the Aptos GitHub repository *aptos-core* main branch: https://github.com/aptos-labs/aptos-core/blob/main/aptos-move/framework/aptos-framework/sources. Our work is located in *stake, staking_contract, configs/staking_config* modules.

References

1. Abdellatif, T., Brousmiche, K.L.: Formal verification of smart contracts based on users and blockchain behaviors models. In: 2018 9th IFIP International Conference on New Technologies, Mobility and Security (NTMS), pp. 1–5 (2018). https://doi.org/10.1109/NTMS.2018.8328737

2. Alturki, M.A., et al.: Towards a verified model of the algorand consensus protocol in coq. In: Sekerinski, E., et al. (eds.) FM 2019. LNCS, vol. 12232, pp. 362–367. Springer, Cham (2020). https://doi.org/10.1007/978-3-030-54994-7_27

3. Benetollo, L., Bugliesi, M., Crafa, S., Rossi, S., Spano, A.: Algomove–a move embedding for algorand. In: 2023 IEEE International Conference on Blockchain (Blockchain), pp. 62–67. IEEE (2023)
4. Bhudia, A., Cartwright, A., Cartwright, E., Hernandez-Castro, J., Hurley-Smith, D.: Extortion of a staking pool in a proof-of-stake consensus mechanism. In: 2022 IEEE International Conference on Omni-layer Intelligent Systems (COINS), pp. 1–6. IEEE (2022)
5. Brünjes, L., Kiayias, A., Koutsoupias, E., Stouka, A.P.: Reward sharing schemes for stake pools. In: 2020 IEEE European Symposium on Security and Privacy (EuroS&P), pp. 256–275. IEEE (2020)
6. Buterin, V.: Proof of Stake: The Making of Ethereum and the Philosophy of Blockchains. Seven Stories Press (2022)
7. Chitra, T., Evans, A.: Why stake when you can borrow? arXiv preprint arXiv:2006.11156 (2020)
8. David, B., Gaži, P., Kiayias, A., Russell, A.: Ouroboros praos: an adaptively-secure, semi-synchronous proof-of-stake blockchain. In: Nielsen, J.B., Rijmen, V. (eds.) EUROCRYPT 2018. LNCS, vol. 10821, pp. 66–98. Springer, Cham (2018). https://doi.org/10.1007/978-3-319-78375-8_3
9. de Moura, L., Bjørner, N.: Z3: an efficient SMT solver. In: Ramakrishnan, C.R., Rehof, J. (eds.) TACAS 2008. LNCS, vol. 4963, pp. 337–340. Springer, Heidelberg (2008). https://doi.org/10.1007/978-3-540-78800-3_24
10. Dill, D., Grieskamp, W., Park, J., Qadeer, S., Xu, M., Zhong, E.: Fast and reliable formal verification of smart contracts with the move prover. In: TACAS 2022. LNCS, vol. 13243, pp. 183–200. Springer, Cham (2022). https://doi.org/10.1007/978-3-030-99524-9_10
11. Fynn, E., Bessani, A., Pedone, F.: Smart contracts on the move. In: 2020 50th Annual IEEE/IFIP International Conference on Dependable Systems and Networks (DSN), pp. 233–244. IEEE (2020)
12. Gersbach, H., Mamageishvili, A., Schneider, M.: Staking pools on blockchains. arXiv preprint arXiv:2203.05838 (2022)
13. Gilad, Y., Hemo, R., Micali, S., Vlachos, G., Zeldovich, N.: Algorand: scaling byzantine agreements for cryptocurrencies. In: Proceedings of the 26th Symposium on Operating Systems Principles, pp. 51–68 (2017)
14. Goodman, L.: Tezos—a self-amending crypto-ledger white paper. **4**, 1432–1465 (2014). https://www.tezos.com/static/papers/whitepaper.pdf
15. Hasanova, H., Baek, U., Shin, M., Cho, K., Kim, M.S.: A survey on blockchain cybersecurity vulnerabilities and possible countermeasures. Int. J. Netw. Manag. **29**(2), e2060 (2019)
16. King, S., Nadal, S.: Ppcoin: peer-to-peer crypto-currency with proof-of-stake. Self-Published Paper, August **19**(1) (2012)
17. Losa, G., Dodds, M.: On the formal verification of the stellar consensus protocol. In: 2nd Workshop on Formal Methods for Blockchains (FMBC 2020). Schloss Dagstuhl-Leibniz-Zentrum für Informatik (2020)
18. Matsunaga, T., Zhang, Y., Sasabe, M., Kasahara, S.: Reward and penalty mechanism in proof-of-stake consensus algorithm for blockchain. In: Proceedings of the 2020 International Conference on Emerging Technologies for Communications (ICETC2020), Virtual, E1-5 (2020)
19. Nadler, M., Schär, F.: Decentralized finance, centralized ownership? an iterative mapping process to measure protocol token distribution. arXiv preprint arXiv:2012.09306 (2020)

20. Nelaturu, K., Keilty, E., Veneris, A.: Natural language-based model-checking framework for move smart contracts. In: 2023 Tenth International Conference on Software Defined Systems (SDS), pp. 89–94. IEEE (2023)
21. Nelaturu, K., Mavridou, A., Stachtiari, E., Veneris, A., Laszka, A.: Correct-by-design interacting smart contracts and a systematic approach for verifying ERC20 and ERC721 contracts with verisolid. IEEE Trans. Dependable Secure Comput. (2022)
22. Nguyen, Q., Cronje, A., Kong, M., Kampa, A., Samman, G.: Stakedag: stake-based consensus for scalable trustless systems. arXiv preprint arXiv:1907.03655 (2019)
23. Pass, R., Shi, E.: Fruitchains: a fair blockchain. In: Proceedings of the ACM Symposium on Principles of Distributed Computing, pp. 315–324 (2017)
24. Patrignani, M., Blackshear, S.: Robust safety for move. In: 2023 IEEE 36th Computer Security Foundations Symposium (CSF), pp. 308–323. IEEE (2023)
25. Pierro, G.A., Ibba, G., Tonelli, R.: A study on diem and aptos distributed ledger technology. Int. J. Parallel Emergent Distrib. Syst. 1–17 (2023)
26. Rahimian, R., Clark, J.: Tokenhook: secure ERC-20 smart contract. arXiv preprint arXiv:2107.02997 (2021)
27. Samreen, N.F., Alalfi, M.H.: Reentrancy vulnerability identification in ethereum smart contracts. In: 2020 IEEE International Workshop on Blockchain Oriented Software Engineering (IWBOSE), pp. 22–29. IEEE (2020)
28. Sanda, O., Pavlidis, M., Seraj, S., Polatidis, N.: Long-range attack detection on permissionless blockchains using deep learning. Expert Syst. Appl. **218**, 119606 (2023)
29. Sun, T., Yu, W.: A formal verification framework for security issues of blockchain smart contracts. Electronics **9**(2), 255 (2020)
30. Torres, C.F., Schütte, J., State, R.: Osiris: hunting for integer bugs in ethereum smart contracts. In: Proceedings of the 34th Annual Computer Security Applications Conference, pp. 664–676 (2018)
31. Wang, Z., Chen, X., Zhou, X., Huang, Y., Zheng, Z., Wu, J.: An empirical study of solidity language features. In: 2021 IEEE 21st International Conference on Software Quality, Reliability and Security Companion (QRS-C), pp. 698–707. IEEE (2021)
32. Wood, G.: Polkadot: vision for a heterogeneous multi-chain framework. White Pap. **21**(2327), 4662 (2016)
33. Xiao, Y., Zhang, N., Li, J., Lou, W., Hou, Y.T.: Distributed consensus protocols and algorithms. Blockchain Distrib. Syst. Secur. **25**, 40 (2019)
34. Yaish, A., Tochner, S., Zohar, A.: Blockchain stretching & squeezing: manipulating time for your best interest. In: Proceedings of the 23rd ACM Conference on Economics and Computation, pp. 65–88 (2022)
35. Ye, C., Li, G., Cai, H., Gu, Y., Fukuda, A.: Analysis of security in blockchain: case study in 51%-attack detecting. In: 2018 5th International Conference on Dependable Systems and Their Applications (DSA), pp. 15–24. IEEE (2018)
36. Dill, D., Grieskamp, W., Park, J., Qadeer, S., Xu, M., Zhong, E.: Fast and reliable formal verification of smart contracts with the move prover. In: Fisman, D., Rosu, G. (eds.) TACAS 2022. LNCS, vol. 13243, pp. 183–200. Springer, Cham (2022). https://doi.org/10.1007/978-3-030-99524-9_10

A Contract-Based Framework for Formal Verification of Embedded Software

Xu Lu[1], Cong Tian[1(✉)], Bin Gu[2], Bin Yu[1], Chen Chen[1], and Zhenhua Duan[1]

[1] ISN and ICTT, Xidian University, Xi'an, China
ctian@mail.xidian.edu.cn
[2] Beijing Institute of Control Engineering, Beijing, China

Abstract. Contract-based design is a useful software engineering paradigm and has been exploited in many literatures for taming the complexity of embedded system development. A system is divided hierarchically into components in a top-down manner, where each component is associated with contracts structured in pairs of assumptions and guarantees. The strength of contract-based design enables stepwise refinement, compositional verification, and reuse of components etc. In this paper, we present a verification framework that builds upon contract-based design to ensure the correctness of embedded software. This framework can be integrated with many formal techniques, e.g., compositional verification, model checking, static analysis, runtime verification, that are shaped in a formal verification chain from the design perspective to the implementation perspective. First, a design level hierarchical model made up of components is abstracted for embedded software, and contracts relevant to components are specified and verified in temporal logic. Second, the behaviour models are constructed for the components located at the bottom of the hierarchical model, and verified using the same contracts at the first step. Third, the implementation of the bottom components are verified, still using the same contracts. Consequently, the consistency between design and implementation of embedded software is strictly proved. We provide a practical case study in the field of aerospace to illustrate the feasibility of our approach, where temporal logic LTL (Linear Temporal Logic) is employed for reasoning as contracts throughout the verification chain.

Keywords: Contract-based design · Temporal logic · Formal verification · Embedded software

1 Introduction

Nowadays, embedded systems have been applied in many safety-critical fields, e.g., aerospace, transportation, finance, medicine and so on. Embedded software plays an important role in embedded systems, that is the key part to realize system functions. In safety-critical scenario, failures or errors that occur in embedded software are hardly tolerable since they could result in loss of life or

© The Author(s), under exclusive license to Springer Nature Singapore Pte Ltd. 2025
T. Bourke et al. (Eds.): SETTA 2024, LNCS 15469, pp. 180–196, 2025.
https://doi.org/10.1007/978-981-96-0602-3_10

significant property damage. Therefore, the reliability of embedded software is particularly important and is still a difficult research problem [21]. Additionally, with the rapid development of advanced computer technologies and increase of market demands, embedded software is becoming more and more complex and its scale is growing larger and larger. As a consequence, how to ensure the safety-critical requirements of embedded software is confronted with serious challenge.

Relying on mathematically rigorous procedures, formal verification is able to help confirm that embedded software model or code behaves correctly, otherwise identify errors via searching through possible state space. Thus it is a research area of growing importance to meet the aforementioned challenge. Although formal verification is certainly be useful, it is yet too limited to cope with complete software verification, and suffers from a problem known as state explosion (poor scalability). This problem is further amplified by the rising complexity of embedded software and its usage for safety-critical tasks.

Contract-based design is a practical paradigm originated from software engineering for the design of complex systems, where each component is associated with contracts, i.e., runtime assertions that clearly describes the expected input-output behaviours. In fact, a contract is structured in a pair of assumption and guarantee that specify what a component must satisfy in response provided the environment obeys some given prerequisite. Unlike pre- and post-conditions of sequential programs, assumptions and guarantees are properties of the whole history/dynamics of a component. In this paper, aiming to reduce the burden of verification, we propose a formal framework to verify embedded software from design level to implementation level. The most significant strength of the framework is to ensure the correctness of system design and implementation, while further guarantee the correspondence between them, that is the major contribution of our work.

The framework consists of three verification phases. First, we exploits an existing contract-based proof system that allows for compositional reasoning. This enables us to formalize contracts of embedded software models in variety of temporal logics. The proof system reduces the correctness of contracts refinement to entailments of temporal logic formulas. Second, the inner behaviours of a bottom component are constructed by means of transition systems. The contracts associated with the component are checked whether they hold according to the behaviour model, where standard model checking techniques are adopted. Third, the implementation, actually the software code, of the bottom component is verified with respect to its contracts as in the second step. To this end, there are many off-the-shelf tools and methods available to be applied on code such as static analysis [28] or runtime verification [2].

The remainder of this paper is organized as follows: Sect. 2 gives a brief overview to the basic concepts of a contract-based proof system employed in this paper. Section 3 presents the framework of the three-step verification chain in detail. Section 4 instantiates the framework with a series of formal verification techniques. Section 5 shows the application of our approach on a practical case study in the field of aerospace. Section 6 discusses related work on contract-based theories. Section 7 summarizes our work and points out potential future research directions.

2   Preliminaries

The contract-based proof system in [14] is founded on traces. Let V be a set of variables which indicates the relevant information of the system, and T be the set of all traces over V which represent discrete or continuous evolutions of the values assigned to the variables in V. A system architecture is defined via components connected by their input/output ports. For the convenience of illustration, we assume a component owns one contract instead of a set of contracts. A contract C is a pair $\langle A, G \rangle$ of assertions, representing respectively an assumption and a guarantee for the component. A contract says that the behaviours of a component are guaranteed to be confined within expected scope, provided the component's environment obeys certain assumptions. An assertion is a property that is modeled here as a set of traces (subset of T) and is satisfied by a trace if the trace belongs to the assertion.

Definition 1. *Given a contract $C = \langle A, G \rangle$, and let I and E be two sets of traces. We say that I is an implementation satisfying C iff $I \cap A \subseteq G$, and E is an environment satisfying C iff $E \subseteq A$. If I (or E) satisfies C, I (or E) is also called an implementation (or environment) of C.*

An implementation is an instantiation of a component and is modeled as a set of traces. Since a component is paired with a contract, we say an implementation of the former is just an implementation of the latter. $\mathcal{I}(C)$ and $\mathcal{E}(C)$ are denoted, respectively, the implementations and the environments satisfying C. Two contracts C and C' are equivalent ($C \equiv C'$) if and only if $\mathcal{I}(C) = \mathcal{I}(C')$ and $\mathcal{E}(C) = \mathcal{E}(C')$. Intuitively, $C \equiv C'$ if they have the same implementations and environments.

Given a contract $C = \langle A, G \rangle$, C is in normal form iff $G = \bar{A} \cup G$, where $\bar{A}$ denotes the complement of A. We abbreviate the assertion $\bar{A} \cup G$ as $G^{nf(A)}$. It is easy to prove that contract normal form is equivalent to its original counterpart, i.e., $\langle A, G \rangle \equiv \langle A, G^{nf(A)} \rangle$.

Suppose a contract C is decomposed into sub-contracts $sub(C) = \{C_1, \ldots, C_n\}$. An implementation of C is typically obtained by composing implementations of the sub-contracts. Formally, an implementation I_C of C is given by $\bigcap_{i=1}^{n} I_{C_i}$, where I_{C_i} is an implementation of C_i. We say I_C is *induced* by $\{I_{C_i}\}_{1 \le i \le n}$. An environment of C_i is given by the intersection of implementations of other sub-contracts and an environment of C. Formally, an environment E_{C_i} of C_i for $1 \le i \le n$ is given by $E_C \cap \bigcap_{1 \le j \le n, j \ne i} I_{C_j}$, where E_C is an environment of C and I_{C_j} is an implementation of C_j. We say E_{C_i} is *induced* by E_C and $\{I_{C_j}\}_{1 \le j \le n, j \ne i}$.

Definition 2. *Let us consider a contract C which is decomposed into sub-contracts $sub(C) = \{C_1, \ldots, C_n\}$. We say $sub(C)$ is a **refinement** of C or C is **refined** by $sub(C)$ (written as $sub(C) \preceq C$) iff the following conditions hold:*

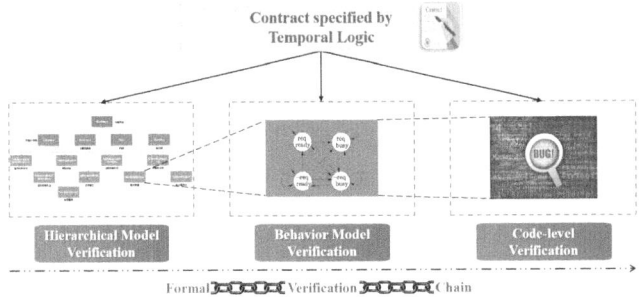

Fig. 1. Framework of the Verification Chain

1. *If I_C is induced by the implementations $\{I_{C_i}\}_{1 \leq i \leq n}$ where I_{C_i} is an implementation of C_i, then $I_C \in \mathcal{I}(C)$ (i.e., implementations of $sub(C)$ form an implementation of C).*
2. *If E_{C_i} is induced by E_C and $\{I_{C_j}\}_{1 \leq j \leq n, j \neq i}$ where E_C is an environment of C and I_{C_j} is an implementation of C_j, then $E_{C_i} \in \mathcal{E}(C_i)$ (i.e., an environment of C and implementations of other contracts form an environment of C_i).*

The following theorem declares a sufficient and necessary condition for the refinement relation.

Theorem 1 [14]. *Given a contract $C = \langle A, G \rangle$ and a set of contracts $sub(C) = \{\langle A_1, G_1 \rangle, \ldots, \langle A_n, G_n \rangle\}$. $sub(C) \preceq C$ iff the following conditions hold:*

$$\bigcap_{i=1}^{n} G_i^{nf(A_i)} \subseteq G^{nf(A)}$$

$$A \cap \bigcap_{1 \leq j \leq n, j \neq i} G_j^{nf(A_j)} \subseteq A_i, 1 \leq i \leq n$$

The conditions generated by Theorem 1 is also called proof obligations whose validation is sufficient to prove the correctness of the refinement relation among contracts.

3   A Framework of Formal Verification Chain

This section will illustrate in detail the verification framework. Existing methods usually verify software as a whole, no matter abstract models or source codes. Nevertheless, there exists a serious problem that cannot be avoided, known as state space explosion. Consequently, the verification process becomes infeasible in general. Our approach attempts to alleviate this problem with the help of contract-based mechanism.

As shown in Fig. 1, the framework mainly consists of three verification phases. To start with, certain kind of temporal logic is exploited as contracts to formalize important properties of embedded software. (1) In the first phase, a hierarchical model of system architecture is constructed by decomposing the system into related sub-components recursively. We associate each component with a contract which reflects its input-output behaviours. Here the purpose of the contract is to support the compositional verification of the system. (2) In the second phase, we explicitly build the inner behaviour model of the components at the bottom layer of the hierarchical model. Usually, this can be done by transition systems which can be verified via standard model checking technique. Here the contract is regarded as the property of the behaviour model. (3) In the third phase, we further verify the implementation, i.e., source code, of the components verified in the second phase concerning the contract. It should be noted that the contracts are shared among the three phases.

This framework aims to bridge the gap between the design and implementation of embedded software. Equally importantly, it is capable of reducing the complexity of verification task since we avoid the most difficult part, i.e., verifying the abstraction or implementation of a whole system directly. The behaviour model is also treated as a kind of implementation as well as code, although the former is in an intermediate abstract form.

3.1   Formal Guarantee of the Framework

Following the refinement relation of contracts, we can define a set of relevant contracts hierarchically until some contract cannot be refined.

Definition 3. *A Hierarchical Contract Model (HCM) is a tuple $\mathcal{H} = (C, \mathcal{H}^{sub} = \{\mathcal{H}_1, \mathcal{H}_2, \ldots, \mathcal{H}_n\})$, where C is a contract, and $\mathcal{H}^{sub}$ is a set of HCMs. Let $\mathcal{H}_i = \{C_i, \mathcal{H}_i^{sub}\}$ for $1 \leq i \leq n$, $\mathcal{H}$ is called a refined HCM if $\{C_1, C_2, \ldots, C_n\} \preceq C$ and every $\mathcal{H}_i$ is a refined HCM or an empty set.*

For an HCM $\mathcal{H} = (C, \mathcal{H}^{sub})$, an implementation of C is also called an implementation of $\mathcal{H}$. $\mathcal{H}^{sub}$ may be possibly empty if C is not decomposed, that is referred to as a *leaf contract*.

Example 1. *Assume there are four components with their contracts. The component $\mathcal{M}$ at the top layer is decomposed into $\mathcal{M}_1$ and $\mathcal{M}_2$, and $\mathcal{M}_1$ is further decomposed into two components at the bottom layer, i.e., $\mathcal{M}_{11}$ and $\mathcal{M}_{22}$. The HCM of $\mathcal{M}$ can be defined as $\mathcal{H} = (\langle A, G \rangle, \{\mathcal{H}_1, \mathcal{H}_2\})$, $\mathcal{H}_1 = (\langle A_1, G_1 \rangle, \{\mathcal{H}_{11}, \mathcal{H}_{12}\})$, $\mathcal{H}_2 = (\langle A_2, G_2 \rangle, \emptyset)$, $\mathcal{H}_{11} = (\langle A_{11}, G_{11} \rangle, \emptyset)$, $\mathcal{H}_{12} = (\langle A_{12}, G_{12} \rangle, \emptyset)$. If $\{\langle A_1, G_1 \rangle, \langle A_2, G_2 \rangle\} \preceq \langle A, G \rangle$ and $\{\langle A_{11}, G_{11} \rangle, \langle A_{12}, G_{12} \rangle\} \preceq \langle A_1, G_1 \rangle$, then $\mathcal{H}$ is a refined HCM.*

Theorem 2. *Consider a refined HCM $\mathcal{H}$. (1) There exists an implementation for $\mathcal{H}$ that is induced by the implementations of the leaf contracts of $\mathcal{H}$. (2) There exists an environment for each leaf contract $\mathcal{H}_{leaf}$ of $\mathcal{H}$ that is induced by the environment of $\mathcal{H}$ and the environments of other leaf contracts of $\mathcal{H}$ except $\mathcal{H}_{leaf}$.*

Proof. This can be proved via the structure of $\mathcal{H}$ in a bottom-up way. Without loss of generality, suppose $\mathcal{H}$ is shaped in the following structure where $\mathcal{H} = \mathcal{H}^0$.

$$\mathcal{H}^0 = \{C^0, \mathcal{H}^{sub_0}\}$$

$$\{\mathcal{H}_i^1 = \{C_i^1, \mathcal{H}_i^{sub_1}\}\}_{1 \leq i \leq n_1}, \{\mathcal{H}_i^1\}_{1 \leq i \leq n_1} = \mathcal{H}^{sub_0}$$

$$\{\mathcal{H}_i^2 = \{C_i^2, \mathcal{H}_i^{sub_2}\}\}_{1 \leq i \leq n_2}, \forall 1 \leq i \leq n_1, \exists j_1, \ldots, j_{m_i} : \{\mathcal{H}_{j_k}^2\}_{1 \leq k \leq m_i, j_k \in [1,n_2]} = \mathcal{H}_i^{sub_1}$$

$$\{\mathcal{H}_i^3 = \{C_i^3, \mathcal{H}_i^{sub_3}\}\}_{1 \leq i \leq n_3}, \forall 1 \leq i \leq n_2, \exists j_1, \ldots, j_{m_i} : \{\mathcal{H}_{j_k}^3\}_{1 \leq k \leq m_i, j_k \in [1,n_3]} = \mathcal{H}_i^{sub_2}$$

$$\ldots$$

$$\{\mathcal{H}_i^{N-1} = \{C_i^{N-1}, \mathcal{H}_i^{sub_{N-1}}\}\}_{1 \leq i \leq n_{N-1}}, \forall 1 \leq i \leq n_{N-2}, \exists j_1, \ldots, j_{m_i} :$$

$$\{\mathcal{H}_{j_k}^{N-1}\}_{1 \leq k \leq m_i, j_k \in [1,n_{N-1}]} = \mathcal{H}_i^{sub_{N-2}}$$

$$\{\mathcal{H}_i^N = \{C_i^N, \emptyset\}\}_{1 \leq i \leq n_N}, \forall 1 \leq i \leq n_{N-1}, \exists j_1, \ldots, j_{m_i} :$$

$$\{\mathcal{H}_{j_k}^N\}_{1 \leq k \leq m_i, j_k \in [1,n_N]} = \mathcal{H}_i^{sub_{N-1}}$$

(1) We simply assume any element in $\mathcal{H}^{sub_0} \cup \{\mathcal{H}_i^{sub_j}\}_{1 \leq i \leq n_j, 1 \leq j \leq N-1}$ is not empty[1]. Obviously, $\{\mathcal{H}_i^N = \{C_i^N, \emptyset\}\}_{1 \leq i \leq n_N}$ is the set of leaf contracts. Suppose there is an implementation I_i^N for $\mathcal{H}_i^N (1 \leq i \leq n_N)$. Since $\mathcal{H}^0$ is a refined HCM, $\forall 1 \leq i \leq n_{N-1}, \exists j_1, \ldots, j_{m_i} : \{C_{j_k}^N\}_{1 \leq k \leq m_i, j_k \in [1,n_N]} \preceq C_i^{N-1}$. Hence, $\forall 1 \leq i \leq n_{N-1}, \exists j_1, \ldots, j_{m_i} : \{I_{j_k}^N\}_{1 \leq k \leq m_i, j_k \in [1,n_N]}$ induces an implementation $\bigcap_{k=1, j_k \in [1,n_N]}^{m_i} I_{j_k}^N$ for $\mathcal{H}_i^{N-1}$.

Similarly, we continue to prove the implementations of the contracts at the $(N-1)$th layer can form implementations of the contracts at the $(N-2)$th layer. We know $\forall 1 \leq i \leq n_{N-2}, \exists j_1, \ldots, j_{m_i} : \{C_{j_k}^{N-1}\}_{1 \leq k \leq m_i, j_k \in [1,n_{N-1}]} \preceq C_i^{N-2}$. Hence, $\forall 1 \leq i \leq n_{N-2}, \exists j_1, \ldots, j_{m_i} : \{I_{j_k}^{N-1}\}_{1 \leq k \leq m_i, j_k \in [1,n_{N-1}]}$ induces an implementation $\bigcap_{k=1, j_k \in [1,n_{N-1}]}^{m_i} I_{j_k}^{N-1}$ for $\mathcal{H}_i^{N-2}$. Each $I_{j_k}^{N-1}$ can be replaced by the implementations of the contracts at the Nth layer, or in other words, the leaf contracts.

This can be done until we prove the implementations of the contracts at the bottom layer can form implementations of the contracts at the top layer. Therefore, conclusion (1) holds.

(2) Since $\mathcal{H}^0$ is a refined HCM, $\forall 1 \leq i \leq n_{N-1}, \exists j_1, \ldots, j_{m_i} : \{C_{j_k}^N\}_{1 \leq k \leq m_i, j_k \in [1,n_N]} \preceq C_i^{N-1}$. Hence, $\forall 1 \leq i \leq n_{N-1}, \exists j_1, \ldots, j_{m_i} : \{I_{j_k}^N\}_{1 \leq k \leq m_i, j_k \in [1,n_N] \setminus i}$ and the environment E_i^{N-1} for C_i^{N-1} induce an environment $E_i^{N-1} \cap \bigcap_{k=1, j_k \in [1,n_N] \setminus i}^{m_i} I_{j_k}^N$ for C_i^N.

Similarly, we continue to prove how to form the environments of the components at the $(N-1)$th layer. $\forall 1 \leq i \leq n_{N-2}, \exists j_1, \ldots, j_{m_i} : \{C_{j_k}^{N-1}\}_{1 \leq k \leq m_i, j_k \in [1,n_{N-1}]} \preceq C_i^{N-2}$. Hence, $\forall 1 \leq i \leq n_{N-2}, \exists j_1, \ldots, j_{m_i} : \{I_{j_k}^{N-1}\}_{1 \leq k \leq m_i, j_k \in [1,n_{N-1}] \setminus i}$ and the environment E_i^{N-2} for C_i^{N-2} induce an environment $E_i^{N-2} \cap \bigcap_{k=1, j_k \in [1,n_{N-1}] \setminus i}^{m_i} I_{j_k}^{N-1}$ for the C_i^{N-1}. Therefore, E_i^{N-1} can be replaced by environment $E_i^{N-2} \cap \bigcap_{k=1, j_k \in [1,n_{N-1}] \setminus i}^{m_i} I_{j_k}^{N-1}$ in the environment $E_i^{N-1} \cap \bigcap_{k=1, j_k \in [1,n_N] \setminus i}^{m_i} I_{j_k}^N$ for C_i^N, i.e., $E_i^{N-2} \cap$

---

[1] Note that the assumption is not rigorous. But this would not affect the correctness of the proof.

$$\bigcap_{k=1,j_k\in[1,n_{N-1}]\setminus i}^{m_i} I_{j_k}^{N-1} \cap \bigcap_{k=1,j_k\in[1,n_N]\setminus i}^{m_i} I_{j_k}^{N} = E_i^{N-2} \cap \bigcap_{k=1,j_k\in[1,n_N]\setminus i}^{m_i} I_{j_k}^{N}$$

is an environment of C_i^N. This can be done until to the top layer, i.e., $E^0 \cap \bigcap_{k=1,j_k\in[1,n_N]\setminus i}^{m_i} I_{j_k}^{N}$ is an environment of C_i^N. Therefore, conclusion (2) holds.   □

Theorem 2 provides us a principle to reduce the complexity of the verification process, since we do not need to prove the implementation of a system as a whole. Instead, a feasible way is to prove the correctness of the implementations and the environments of the bottom layer of an HCM, that is a much simpler task.

Example 2. *Continue with Example 1. We will show the implementation of $\langle A, G \rangle$ and the environments of $\langle A_2, G_2 \rangle$, $\langle A_{11}, G_{11} \rangle$, $\langle A_{12}, G_{12} \rangle$.*

Suppose the implementations of $\langle A_2, G_2 \rangle$, $\langle A_{11}, G_{11} \rangle$, $\langle A_{12}, G_{12} \rangle$ are respectively I_2, I_{11} and I_{12}, the environment of $\langle A, G \rangle$ is E. By Theorem 2, $I_2 \cap I_{11} \cap I_{12}$ is an implementation of $\langle A, G \rangle$, $E \cap I_{11} \cap I_{12}$ is an environment of $\langle A_2, G_2 \rangle$, $E \cap I_2 \cap I_{12}$ is an environment of $\langle A_{11}, G_{11} \rangle$, $E \cap I_2 \cap I_{11}$ is an environment of $\langle A_{12}, G_{12} \rangle$.

4   Instantiation of the Framework

Temporal logic allows the specification of system behaviour in terms of logical formulas. Many kinds of temporal logics exist today, roughly classified into discrete time, continuous time or hybrid semantics. Here we characterize sets of traces by means of a widely used temporal logic, LTL (Linear Temporal Logic), which is a logical formalism that is suited for specifying discrete, linear time properties on traces.

4.1   Linear Temporal Logic

LTL formulas over the set AP of atomic propositions are formed according to the following grammar:

$$\phi ::= p \mid \neg\phi \mid \phi_1 \vee \phi_2 \mid \bigcirc\phi \mid \phi_1 \mathbf{U}\phi_2$$

where $p \in AP$. Using the boolean connectives $\vee$ and $\neg$, the full power of propositional logic is obtained, i.e., other boolean connectives such as $\vee$, $\rightarrow$, $\leftrightarrow$ and boolean values $\top$, $\bot$ can be derived. The until operator $\mathbf{U}$ is able to derive the temporal modalities $\Diamond$ (eventually) and $\Box$ (always) as follows:

$$\Diamond\phi \overset{\text{def}}{=} \top\mathbf{U}\phi \qquad \Box\phi \overset{\text{def}}{=} \neg\Diamond\neg\phi$$

$\bigcirc\phi$ holds at the current moment, if ϕ holds in the next step. Formula $\phi_1\mathbf{U}\phi_2$ holds at the current moment, if there is some future moment for which ϕ_2 holds and ϕ_1 holds at all moments until that future moment. $\Diamond\phi$ ensures that ϕ will be true eventually in the future. $\Box\phi$ is satisfied if ϕ holds from now on forever.

A state s is a subset of AP that are true, while atomic propositions in $AP \backslash s$ are assumed to be false. LTL formulas are interpreted over infinite traces of states $\sigma = s_0, s_1, \ldots$. The notation $\sigma^i = s_i, s_{i+1}, \ldots$ is the suffix of σ starting at s_i. The satisfaction relation $\models$ of LTL is defined as follows.

$$\sigma \models p \quad \textit{iff} \quad p \in s_0. \qquad \sigma \models \neg\phi \quad \textit{iff} \quad \sigma \not\models \phi.$$

$$\sigma \models \phi_1 \vee \phi_2 \quad \textit{iff} \quad \sigma \models \phi_1 \text{ or } \sigma \models \phi_2. \qquad \sigma \models \bigcirc\phi \quad \textit{iff} \quad \sigma^1 \models \phi.$$

$$\sigma \models \phi_1 \mathbf{U} \phi_2 \quad \textit{iff} \quad \exists j \geq 0 : \sigma^j \models \phi_2 \text{ and } \sigma^i \models \phi_1 \text{ for all } 0 \leq i < j.$$

The semantics of LTL formula ϕ is defined as a language $Words(\phi)$ that contains all infinite words over the alphabet 2^{AP} that satisfy ϕ, i.e., $Words(\phi) = \{\sigma \in (2^{AP})^\omega \mid \sigma \models \phi\}$.

4.2 Instantiation of HCM Verification

When the contracts of components are specified by means of temporal logic formulas, the proof obligations defined in Theorem 1 can be specified in terms of temporal logic formulas as well. In the rest of this paper, contracts are expressed in LTL style. Provided that a contract $C = \langle \phi_A, \phi_G \rangle$ is refined by the contracts $sub(C) = \{\langle \phi_{A_1}, \phi_{G_1} \rangle, \ldots, \langle \phi_{A_n}, \phi_{G_n} \rangle\}$. The correctness of the refinement $sub(C) \preceq C$ can be verified by checking the validity of the following group of formulas:

– $((\neg\phi_{A_1} \vee \phi_{G_1}) \wedge \ldots \wedge (\neg\phi_{A_n} \vee \phi_{G_n})) \rightarrow (\neg\phi_A \vee \phi_G)$
– $(\phi_A \wedge \bigwedge_{1 \leq j \leq n, j \neq 1}(\neg\phi_{A_j} \vee \phi_{G_j})) \rightarrow \phi_{A_1}$
– $\ldots$
– $(\phi_A \wedge \bigwedge_{1 \leq j \leq n, j \neq n}(\neg\phi_{A_j} \vee \phi_{G_j})) \rightarrow \phi_{A_n}$

Now since the contracts are restricted to LTL, the validity is decidable and can be performed by standard model checking techniques for LTL. There are many tools available to do this [3,10,18].

4.3 Automata-Based LTL Model Checking

The behaviour model of a component can be built as a transition system.

Definition 4. *A transition system TS is a tuple $(S, Act, Tran, T_0, AP)$ where S is a finite set of states, Act is a finite set of actions, $Tran : S \times Act \times S$ is a transition relation, and $S_0 \subseteq S$ is a set of initial states. A TS starts in some initial state $s_0 \in S_0$ and evolves according to the transition relation $Tran$. A trace σ of a TS is an infinite sequence $s_0, s_1, \ldots$ such that $s_0 \in S_0$, and $a_i \in Act, (s_i, a_i, s_{i+1}) \in Tran$ for $i \geq 0$.*

Definition 5. *A Non-deterministic Büchi Automaton (NBA) $\mathcal{A}$ is a tuple $\langle Q, \Sigma, \delta, Q_0, F \rangle$ where Q is a finite set of states, $\Sigma = S$ is an alphabet, $\delta : Q \times \Sigma \longrightarrow 2^Q$ is a transition function, $Q_0 \subseteq Q$ is a set of initial states, and $F \subseteq Q$ is a set of accepting states, called acceptance set. A run for a* trace $\sigma = s_0, s_1, \ldots \in \Sigma^\omega$ denotes an infinite sequence $q_0, q_1, \ldots$ of states in $\mathcal{A}$ such that $q_0 \in Q_0$ and (q_i, s_i, q_{i+1}) for $i \geq 0$. $q_0, q_1, \ldots$ is accepting if $q_i \in F$ for infinitely many indices $i \in \mathbb{N}$. The accepted language of $\mathcal{A}$ is $\mathcal{L}_\omega(\mathcal{A}) = \{\sigma \in \Sigma^\omega \mid \text{ there exists an accepting run for } \sigma \text{ in } \mathcal{A}\}$.

The following theorem states that any LTL formula can be transformed into an NBA.

Theorem 3 [1]. *For any LTL formula ϕ there exists an NBA $\mathcal{A}_\phi$ with $Words(\phi) = \mathcal{L}_\omega(\mathcal{A}_\phi)$ which can be constructed in time and space $2^{\mathcal{O}(|\phi|)}$.*

The model checking problem for LTL is to check whether $TS \models \phi$. The basic idea is to try to disprove $TS \models \phi$ by "looking" for a trace σ in TS with $\sigma \models \neg\phi$. If such a trace is found, a prefix of σ is returned as a counter-example. Otherwise, it is concluded that $TS \models \phi$. One needs to first constructs an NBA $\mathcal{A}_\phi$ for the negation of the input formula ϕ (representing the "bad behaviours") and then applies the intersection techniques of TS and $\mathcal{A}_\phi$.

Let the behaviour model be an implementation I (transition system) with an environment E, and a contract $\langle A, G \rangle$. On the one hand, we have to prove I satisfies $\langle A, G \rangle$, i.e., $I \cap A \subseteq G$. According to the basic principle of model checking, the intersection $I \cap A \cap \bar{G}$ is checked to find counter-examples. On the other hand, we have to prove E satisfies A, i.e., $E \subseteq A$ which is usually much easier to be checked.

4.4 Runtime Verification Based on TRACE

TRACE[2] is a generic visualization and analysis tool for activities and their usage. It can help to understand complicated behaviours over time for all kinds of systems whose (concurrent) activities are declared in execution traces. We augment TRACE with LTL checking capability to achieve runtime verification of embedded software.

TRACE requires that abstract traces are expressed in a specific format which is centered around the concept of a "*claim*" sentence. A claim describes an activity on a single resource, including a start and end time stamp, a resource and a number of configurable attributes (e.g., the name of the activity). Wherein attributes are represented by a key-value mapping from attribute names to attribute values. What remains is how to encode execution traces of embedded software into TRACE format.

Formally, we define a claim as $\varsigma = \langle cid, t_{start}, t_{end}, attr^* \rangle$ that respectively indicate id, start time, end time and attributes of an activity. Given a set of program variables V, let the mapping $ps : V \longrightarrow \mathbb{R}$ be a program state at certain program point, and an execution trace of a program be $\rho = ps_0, \ldots, ps_n$. Suppose there is a finite set of atomic propositions $AP_{fin} \subseteq AP$ relevant to a program. The meaning of a proposition $p \in AP_{fin}$ at program state ps can be specified as a function $p : ps(V)^l \longrightarrow \mathbb{B}$, assigning to a set of program variables

---

[2] http://trace.esi.nl.

a boolean value at ps. Examples of propositions include relational expressions of the form $f(\boldsymbol{x}) > 0$ over variables $X \subseteq V$, where $\boldsymbol{x}$ is a string of variables and each of which is in X, $f : \mathbb{R}^l \longrightarrow \mathbb{R}, |\boldsymbol{x}| = l$. We assume that propositions are definable in first-order real arithmetic. To put it more plainly, for instance, given p representing the relational expression $x + y > 0$ and $ps = \{(x,0),(y,-1)\}$, we know p is false at ps. Therefore, for every $p \in AP_{fin}$, it is easy to check the truth value of p at any step of a trace. Practically, Z3 [25] is adopted to evaluate p in some cases (quantifiers or matrix occurs). We write the truth value of p at ps as $ps[p]$ which is either $\top$ or $\bot$.

Intuitively speaking, each program state in an execution trace is encoded into a claim sentence. Given an execution trace $\rho = ps_0, \ldots, ps_n$ and a finite set of atomic propositions $AP_{fin} = \{p_0, \ldots, p_m\}$, the encoding of ρ is formalized as $\varsigma_0, \ldots, \varsigma_n$, where

$$\varsigma_i = \langle cid_i, i, i+1, \{(p_j, ps_i[p_j]) \mid 0 \leq j \leq m\}\rangle \text{ for } 0 \leq i \leq n$$

cid_i is a unique label, ς_i lasts for a unit time step from i to $i+1$, and the attribute pair $(p_j, ps_i[p_j])$ represents p_j with its truth value.

Example 3 (program trace encoding). *Given an execution trace* $\rho = \{(x,0),(y,0)\}, \{(x,0),(y,1)\}$ *and a finite set of atomic propositions* $AP_{fin} = \{p_0 = (x + y > 0)\}$. *Thus* ρ *is encoded as claims* $\langle cid_0, 0, 1, \{(p_0, false)\}\rangle, \langle cid_1, 1, 2, \{(p_0, true)\}\rangle$.

Practically, we exploit two open source tools, KLEE [7] and GDB (GNU Debugger) [29], to assist to produce appropriate traces. As a dynamic symbolic execution engine built on top of the LLVM compiler infrastructure, KLEE provides a set of special functions which are useful in the context of symbolic execution. One of the functions interested in this paper is the ability to automatically generate test cases for high coverage of complex and environmentally intensive programs. GDB is a portable debugger that works for many programming languages, including Ada, C, C++, Fortran etc. It allows us to see what is going on inside a program (especially in certain key program points) while it executes.

During runtime verification, KLEE is employed to generate test cases that attempts to cover all possible branches of programs, while GDB is employed to extract critical trace segment by setting breakpoints in target programs. Let $var(\phi)$ be all variables related to the propositions appear in ϕ. Obviously, only variables in $var(\phi)$ have impact on the satisfaction of ϕ. Therefore, breakpoints are selected at the program points where the value of a certain variable $v \in var(\phi)$ is probably to change. Figure 2 shows the process of trace generation. At the beginning, KLEE is responsible for generating plentiful test cases for a program. Subsequently, GDB selects breakpoints with respect to the LTL specification expected to verify. Feeding each test case to GDB, a sequence of program states at all break points will be produced as the output. By doing so, an actual execution trace is generated ultimately. At this point, the generated execution traces are ready to be translated to TRACE format, and will be checked by TRACE with respect to LTL properties.

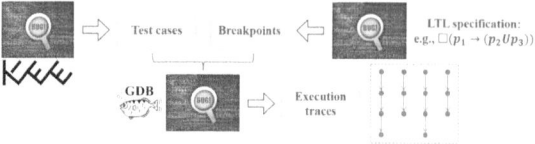

Fig. 2. Core idea of trace generation

Let the code be an implementation I which is in an environment E, and a contract $\langle A, G \rangle$. Analogous to the second phase, the intersection $I \cap A \cap \bar{G}$ is checked to verify the implementation, while $E \subseteq A$ is checked to verify the environment.

5 Case Study

This case study describes a Sun Search (SS) system, which aims to accomplish the function of solar capture. SS determines the current attitude of the satellite through collected data from gyro and sun sensor, then controls the satellite to rotate around pitch axis and/or roll axis in order to locate the sun. Once located, SS will keep the satellite's attitude towards the sun.

SS is composed of four subsystems (Sensor, Actuator, Controller and Data-Management) among which Controller is the central one that is responsible for collecting data from Sensor, communicating with DataManagement, and controlling Actuator to do appropriate actions.

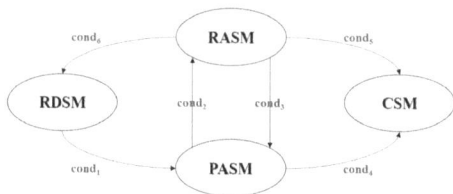

Fig. 3. Switch conditions of different modes

The complete sun search process is performed periodically. It is involved with four separate stages, namely modes: rate damping (RDSM), pitch adaption (PASM), roll adaption (RASM) and cruise (CSM). The detailed functions of the four modes are omitted here. Modes may be changed based on specific conditions in each cycle. The four modes do not alternate sequentially. Instead, they switch from each other based on specific conditions (Fig. 3). All modes should remain unchanged if none of the conditions hold.

In this section, experiments are conducted on a VMWare running Ubuntu 20.04.4, a AMD Ryzen 7 (4 cores) 2.90 GHz of CPU and 4 GB of RAM.

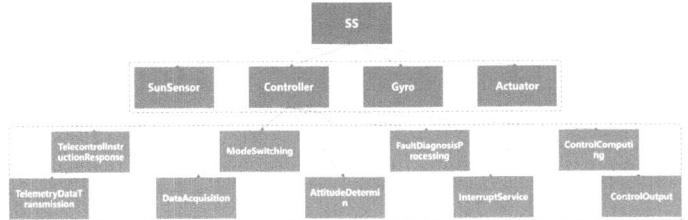

Fig. 4. Hierarchical model of Sun Search system

5.1 Verification of HCM

The hierarchical model consists of three layers as depicted in Fig. 4. The first layer is just the system SS, and the second layer are the four sub-systems including Controller. In the third layer, for the sake of simplicity, we only list the eight components consisted in Controller. The verification of mode related functions is what we concern, that is the core effect of ModeSwitching component.

We focus on the contracts specifying the state evolutions of components within a cycle. Let propositions $p_{rd}, p_{pa}, p_{ra}, p_c$ respectively denote the modes RDSM, PASM, RASM, CSM. Define $curMode \overset{\text{def}}{=} (p_{rd} \vee p_{pa} \vee p_{ra} \vee p_c)$. The contract of SS is $C_{SS} = \langle A_{SS}, G_{SS} \rangle$, where $A_{SS} = \top$ and $G_{SS} = \Box curMode$. C_{SS} restricts the scope of *mode* with the effects that the value of *mode* lies in one of the four modes.

The contract of Controller $C_{Cont} = \langle A_{Cont}, G_{Cont} \rangle$ formalizes the allowed mode switches without going into details. More precisely, the assumption A_{Cont} specifies the allowed modes along the trace, while the guarantee G_{Cont} points out the allowed alternation between two modes. For example, the next mode of RDSM can only be PASM except itself, and CSM cannot switch to other modes.

$$alter_1 \overset{\text{def}}{=} \Box(p_{rd} \to \Diamond(\Box p_{ps} \vee \Box p_{rd})) \qquad alter_2 \overset{\text{def}}{=} \Box(p_{pa} \to \Diamond(\Box p_{ra} \vee \Box p_c \vee \Box p_{pa}))$$

$$alter_3 \overset{\text{def}}{=} \Box(p_{ra} \to \Diamond(\Box p_{pa} \vee \Box p_{rd} \vee \Box p_c \vee \Box p_{ra})) \qquad alter_4 \overset{\text{def}}{=} \Box(p_c \to \Box p_c)$$

$$A_{Cont} : \Box curMode \qquad G_{Cont} : \bigwedge_{1 \le i \le 4} alter_i$$

We can check whether C_{Cont} is a correct refinement of C_{SS} (contracts of other components at the second layer are unrelated), i.e., $C_{Cont} \preceq C_{SS}$, by automated generating the following proof obligations $\phi_1 \wedge \phi_2$ whose validity can be checked by state-of-the-art LTL model checking tools.

$$\phi_1 = (\neg \Box curMode \vee \bigwedge_{1 \le i \le 4} alter_i) \to (\neg \top \vee \Box curMode) \qquad \phi_2 = \top \to \Box curMode$$

The contract of ModeSwitching $C_{MS} = \langle A_{MS}, G_{MS} \rangle$ is formalized as follows. More details about how to switch between modes are defined. $cond_i (1 \le i \le 6)$

is notated as a proposition to indicate the corresponding switch condition.

$$switch_1 \stackrel{\text{def}}{=} \Box(p_{rd} \wedge cond_1 \rightarrow \Diamond\Box p_{pa}) \quad switch_2 \stackrel{\text{def}}{=} \Box(p_{pa} \wedge cond_2 \rightarrow \Diamond\Box p_{ra})$$

$$switch_3 \stackrel{\text{def}}{=} \Box(p_{ra} \wedge cond_3 \rightarrow \Diamond\Box p_{pa}) \quad switch_4 \stackrel{\text{def}}{=} \Box(p_{pa} \wedge cond_4 \rightarrow \Diamond\Box p_c)$$

$$switch_5 \stackrel{\text{def}}{=} \Box(p_{ra} \wedge cond_5 \rightarrow \Diamond\Box p_c) \quad switch_6 \stackrel{\text{def}}{=} \Box(p_{ra} \wedge cond_6 \rightarrow \Diamond\Box p_{rd})$$

$$switch_7 \stackrel{\text{def}}{=} \Box(p_{rd} \wedge \Box\neg cond_1 \rightarrow \Box p_{rd}) \quad switch_8 \stackrel{\text{def}}{=} \Box(p_{pa} \wedge \Box(\neg cond_2 \wedge \neg cond_4) \rightarrow \Box p_{pa})$$

$$switch_9 \stackrel{\text{def}}{=} \Box(p_{ra} \wedge \Box(\neg cond_3 \wedge \neg cond_5 \wedge \neg cond_6) \rightarrow \Box p_{ra}) \quad switch_{10} \stackrel{\text{def}}{=} \Box(p_c \rightarrow \Box p_c)$$

$$A_{MS} : \Box curMode \qquad G_{MS} : \bigwedge_{1 \leq i \leq 10} switch_i$$

Other components does not change mode. We can check whether C_{MS} is a correct refinement of C_{Cont}, i.e., $C_{MS} \preceq C_{Cont}$, by automated generating the following proof obligations $\phi_3 \wedge \phi_4$ whose validity can be checked by state-of-the-art LTL model checking tools.

$$\phi_3 = (\neg\Box curMode \vee \bigwedge_{1 \leq i \leq 10} switch_i) \rightarrow (\neg\Box curMode \vee \bigwedge_{1 \leq i \leq 4} alter_i)$$

$$\phi_4 = \Box curMode \rightarrow \Box curMode$$

We use nuXmv to check the validity of $\phi_1 \wedge \phi_2$ and $\phi_3 \wedge \phi_4$. nuXmv is a symbolic model checker for finite- and infinite-state synchronous transition systems [8]. If the model part is left empty, nuXmv will give the validity result for the specification. In fact, the actual checking time is less than 0.01 s. Therefore, it can be inferred that $(C_{SS}, \{(C_{Cont}, \{(C_{MS}, \emptyset)\})\})$ is a refined HCM.

5.2   Verification of Behaviour Model

The behaviour model of component ModeSwitching is constructed (cf. Fig. 3), and the model is verified with respect to its contract. The verification process will still be handled by nuXmv.

   $mode$ is a variable of enumeration type that represents different modes. $cond_1$-$cond_6$ are boolean variables that indicates the switch conditions between different modes respectively. Suppose the switch conditions are independent from each other.

   The transition relation of the model consists of transitions between different modes and those occur in the same mode. $mode$ remains the same when all conditions do not hold in a cycle. For example, the condition of the transition from RDSM to PASM is $cond_1$. As another example, RDSM does not change to other modes if $\neg cond_1$ holds.

   The environment $E \subseteq A_{MS}$ is easy to be checked since E is just the whole system's environment. We only need to ensure the input mode is one of the four modes. Thus $E \subseteq A_{MS}$ holds trivially. The property $\neg A_{MS} \vee G_{MS}$ and behaviour model I are fed to nuXmv. nuXmv automatically negate the property to $A_{MS} \wedge \neg G_{MS}$, and prove whether there exists a counter-example in I. The results show that the model satisfies the property. The time consumption of the whole verification process is less than 0.01 s.

5.3   Verification of Code

We exploit the runtime verification approach based on TRACE to verify the code of ModeSwitching. Only the program variables of ModeSwitching associated with switch conditions are able to affect the contract. Hence, KLEE symbolizes those variables for the sake of generating test cases. The work mode is represented by a variable of unsigned int type, where four integer values corresponds to four modes. The ranges of other variables are not restricted.

The contract of code and that of behaviour model should be consistent. The former details the expressions of the switch conditions by means of program variables. The switch conditions $cond_1$-$cond_6$ are mapped into a group of boolean expressions. As an example, $cond_1$ is linked to the real switch condition $e = m\_countPublic > time\_D2P \vee m\_countMode > time\_D2P\_overtime$, which says that the stable operation time of three-axis angular velocity is greater than $time\_D2P$ cycles, or the execution time of current mode is greater than $time\_D2P\_overtime$ cycles. The truth value of $cond_1$ is consistent with that of e.

KLEE generates 40 groups of test cases in total, covering 22 branches of the code of ModeSwitching. In order to record the evolutions of the monitoring variables at runtime, we produce a script to automatically generate execution paths for each group of test cases. The implementation I is composed of all the execution paths. After that, the execution paths are translated to the format supported by TRACE, and verified together with the contract, i.e., $I \cap A_{MS} \cap \bar{G}_{MS}$ and $E \subseteq A_{MS}$. All test cases are passed in TRACE (no counter-example). The time of test case generation is 1.72 s, and the time of execution path production is 9.43 s, while the time of TRACE format translation is 0.04 s. The verification process are realized by our tool, including the functions of automatic script generation and automatic TRACE format translation. Obviously, execution path generation is the bottleneck of our tool from the efficiency point of view.

6   Related Work

Specifying contracts has been first advocated by Meyer with the design principle Design-by-Contract [24]. Using such methodology, development of software components occurs independently, without knowledge of any implementation details of other components. Instead, components rely on the contracts of each other. A refinement process similar to our compositional verification phase is espoused in [4,14]. Applications of hierarchical contracts have been recently discussed in [26,30], aiming at automatic synthesis and multi-agent mission.

ACSL (ANSI/ISO C Specification Language) is a behavioral specification language for C programs [6]. The paramount notion in ACSL is the function contract. ACSL uses Hoare style pre- and post-conditions and invariants, that follows the design by contract paradigm. In [27], a trace-based logic for reasoning about the behaviour of While programs is presented. The framework includes a proof system that is both sound and complete.

Lidström and Gurov propose a contract theory for sequential, procedural programs [22]. They latter apply the theory in real embedded software design [23]. Temporal TLA is used for reasoning at the system level, while properties of lower level components are specified in the form of ACSL. However, ACSL reasons in pre- and post-conditions style, the system level reasoning can only care about the temporal logic properties inter-procedurally (without going into details of procedures).

Cimatti et al. propose a fully formal contract framework [14,15] that relies on an expressive property specification language HRELTL [13] which extends LTL to be interpreted over hybrid traces. They have developed a verification engine called OCRA for checking the refinement of contracts [11]. This framework is used to check the validation of requirements for embedded systems [12] at the design level, ignoring implementations of components.

In [9], a compositional specification theory is presented for reasoning about components that interact by synchronisation of input and output (I/O) actions. The specification of a component constraints the temporal ordering of interactions of the environment. The theory includes a refinement preorder, enabling safe-substitutivity of components, but liveness properties are not considered.

Pacti is a recent tool which supports contract refinement verification [20]. However, the authors have only implemented support for polyhedral constraints, not for other popular constraint formalisms, such as LTL. SPIN [3] and NuSMV [10] support LTL property verification but only work with modeling languages Promela and SMV respectively. The tool provided in SPIN for extracting models from C programs failed to work on our subject programs. Model checking tools CBMC [16] and CPAChecker [5] cannot support LTL property verification. Ultimate LTL Automizer [17], a static analysis tool, works for LTL software model checking in the fashion of CEGAR (Counter Example Guided Abstraction Refinement). Our runtime verification approach complements static software model checking by independently analyzing each single execution trace of software implementations.

7   Conclusion

We address the problem of verifying embedded software to improve the scalability. Moreover, while design verification is important, it is also necessary to verify that an implementation preserves the design's correctness. For the above purpose, we propose a contract-based formal framework, with a three-step verification scheme. The correctness checking of a system proceeds from abstracted hierarchical model to the behaviour models of some components, until to the implementation of those components.

The main contributions of the paper are the following. First, the framework is generic that can be combined with many advanced verification techniques, especially enabling to verify complex temporal property. Second, we have proved the soundness of the framework. Third, we develop a prototype tool and demonstrate its feasibility with a real-world case study.

One of the directions for future research includes extending the framework with property mining methods in order to reduce experts' participation [19]. We believe a large part of the contracts can be obtained from requirements with the help of powerful AI techniques.

Acknowledgements. The authors really appreciate for the reviewing efforts of the reviewers. This research is supported by National Natural Science Foundation of China (62192734,62372347,62202361,62172322,61806158); China Postdoctoral Science Foundation (2019T120881,2018M643585).

References

1. Baier, C., Katoen, J.P.: Principles of Model Checking. MIT Press, Cambridge (2008)
2. Bartocci, E., Falcone, Y., Francalanza, A., Reger, G.: Introduction to runtime verification. In: Lectures on Runtime Verification: Introductory and Advanced Topics, pp. 1–33 (2018)
3. Ben-Ari, M.: Principles of the Spin Model Checker. Springer, Cham (2008)
4. Benveniste, A., et al.: Contracts for system design. Found. Trends® Electron. Des. Autom. **12**(2-3), 124–400 (2018)
5. Beyer, D., Keremoglu, M.E.: CPAchecker: a tool for configurable software verification. In: Gopalakrishnan, G., Qadeer, S. (eds.) CAV 2011. LNCS, vol. 6806, pp. 184–190. Springer, Heidelberg (2011). https://doi.org/10.1007/978-3-642-22110-1_16
6. Blanchard, A.: Introduction to C Program Proof with Frama-C and its WP Plugin (2020)
7. Cadar, C., Dunbar, D., Engler, D.R., et al.: Klee: unassisted and automatic generation of high-coverage tests for complex systems programs. In: OSDI, vol. 8, pp. 209–224 (2008)
8. Cavada, R., et al.: The nuXmv symbolic model checker. In: Biere, A., Bloem, R. (eds.) CAV 2014. LNCS, vol. 8559, pp. 334–342. Springer, Cham (2014). https://doi.org/10.1007/978-3-319-08867-9_22
9. Chen, T., Chilton, C., Jonsson, B., Kwiatkowska, M.: A compositional specification theory for component behaviours. In: Seidl, H. (ed.) ESOP 2012. LNCS, vol. 7211, pp. 148–168. Springer, Heidelberg (2012). https://doi.org/10.1007/978-3-642-28869-2_8
10. Cimatti, A., Clarke, E., Giunchiglia, F., Roveri, M.: NUSMV: a new symbolic model checker. Int. J. Softw. Tools Technol. Transfer **2**, 410–425 (2000)
11. Cimatti, A., Dorigatti, M., Tonetta, S.: OCRA: a tool for checking the refinement of temporal contracts. In: ASE 2013, pp. 702–705. IEEE (2013)
12. Cimatti, A., Roveri, M., Susi, A., Tonetta, S.: Validation of requirements for hybrid systems: a formal approach. ACM Trans. Softw. Eng. Methodol. **21**(4), 22:1–22:34 (2012)

13. Cimatti, A., Roveri, M., Tonetta, S.: Requirements validation for hybrid systems. In: Bouajjani, A., Maler, O. (eds.) CAV 2009. LNCS, vol. 5643, pp. 188–203. Springer, Heidelberg (2009). https://doi.org/10.1007/978-3-642-02658-4_17

14. Cimatti, A., Tonetta, S.: A property-based proof system for contract-based design. In: 2012 38th Euromicro Conference on Software Engineering and Advanced Applications, pp. 21–28. IEEE Computer Society (2012)

15. Cimatti, A., Tonetta, S.: Contracts-refinement proof system for component-based embedded systems. Sci. Comput. Program. **97**, 333–348 (2015)

16. Clarke, E., Kroening, D., Lerda, F.: A tool for checking ANSI-C programs. In: Jensen, K., Podelski, A. (eds.) TACAS 2004. LNCS, vol. 2988, pp. 168–176. Springer, Heidelberg (2004). https://doi.org/10.1007/978-3-540-24730-2_15

17. Dietsch, D., Heizmann, M., Langenfeld, V., Podelski, A.: Fairness modulo theory: a new approach to LTL software model checking. In: Kroening, D., Păsăreanu, C.S. (eds.) CAV 2015. LNCS, vol. 9206, pp. 49–66. Springer, Cham (2015). https://doi.org/10.1007/978-3-319-21690-4_4

18. Duret-Lutz, A., Lewkowicz, A., Fauchille, A., Michaud, T., Renault, É., Xu, L.: Spot 2.0—a framework for LTL and ω-automata manipulation. In: Artho, C., Legay, A., Peled, D. (eds.) ATVA 2016. LNCS, vol. 9938, pp. 122–129. Springer, Cham (2016). https://doi.org/10.1007/978-3-319-46520-3_8

19. Fuggitti, F., Chakraborti, T.: NL2LTL – a python package for converting natural language (NL) instructions to linear temporal logic (LTL) formulas. In: AAAI, System Demonstration (2023)

20. Incer, I., et al.: Pacti: scaling assume-guarantee reasoning for system analysis and design. arXiv preprint arXiv:2303.17751 (2023)

21. Knight, J.C.: Safety critical systems: challenges and directions. In: Proceedings of the 24th International Conference on Software Engineering, pp. 547–550 (2002)

22. Lidström, C., Gurov, D.: An abstract contract theory for programs with procedures. In: Guerra, E., Stoelinga, M. (eds.) FASE 2021. LNCS, vol. 12649, pp. 152–171. Springer, Cham (2021). https://doi.org/10.1007/978-3-030-71500-7_8

23. Lidström, C., Gurov, D.: Contract based embedded software design. In: David, C., Sun, M. (eds.) TASE 2023. LNCS, vol. 13931, pp. 77–94. Springer, Cham (2023). https://doi.org/10.1007/978-3-031-35257-7_5

24. Meyer, B.: Applying "design by contract". Computer **25**(10), 40–51 (1992)

25. de Moura, L., Bjørner, N.: Z3: an efficient SMT solver. In: Ramakrishnan, C.R., Rehof, J. (eds.) TACAS 2008. LNCS, vol. 4963, pp. 337–340. Springer, Heidelberg (2008). https://doi.org/10.1007/978-3-540-78800-3_24

26. Naik, N.V., Pinto, A., Nuzzo, P.: Contract-based hierarchical modeling and traceability of heterogeneous requirements. IEEE Trans. Comput.-Aided Des. Integrated Circuits Syst. (2024)

27. Nakata, K., Uustalu, T.: A Hoare logic for the coinductive trace-based big-step semantics of while. Log. Methods Comput. Sci. **11**(1) (2015)

28. Rival, X., Yi, K.: Introduction to Static Analysis: An Abstract Interpretation Perspective. MIT Press, Cambridge (2020)

29. Stallman, R.M., Pesch, R., Shebs, S.: Debugging with GDB: the gnu source-level debugger, v 7.3. 1. Free Software Foundation, Boston, MA, USA (2011)

30. Wang, T.E., Daw, Z., Nuzzo, P., Pinto, A.: Hierarchical contract-based synthesis for assurance cases. In: Deshmukh, J.V., Havelund, K., Perez, I. (eds.) NFM 2022. LNCS, vol. 13260, pp. 175–192. Springer, Cham (2022). https://doi.org/10.1007/978-3-031-06773-0_9

Formalizing x86-64 ISA in Isabelle/HOL: A Binary Semantics for eBPF JIT Correctness

Jiayi Lu[1] , Shenghao Yuan[2(✉)] , David Sanan[3] , and Yongwang Zhao[1,2]

[1] School of Cyber Science and Technology, and College of Computer Science and Technology, Zhejiang University, Hangzhou, China
[2] State Key Laboratory of Blockchain and Data Security, Zhejiang University, Hangzhou, China
shenghaoyuan0928@163.com
[3] InfoComm Technology Cluster, Singapore Institute of Technology, Singapore, Singapore

Abstract. Binary semantics forms a critical infrastructure for proving the correctness of Just-In-Time (JIT) compilation, an advanced technique to optimize runtime execution by translating the source bytecode of a program into target machine code. This paper presents a formal model of x86-64 binary semantics in Isabelle/HOL, as the foundation to verify the eBPF x86-64 JIT correctness for the Solana blockchain. First, we formalize a significant subset of x86-64 semantics, covering all the x86-64 instructions used in the Solana JIT. Second, we develop an encoder and decoder to establish a precise bidirectional mapping between assembly and binary code. Furthermore, we demonstrate the equivalence property of the x86-64 encoder-decoder pair, significantly simplifying the correctness proof of the Solana JIT compiler verification.

Keywords: x86-64 · ISA · Binary Semantics · eBPF Virtual Machine · Solana blockchain · Isabelle/HOL · Formal Verification

1 Introduction

As Paul Tyma stated in 1998, before the use of Just-In-Time (JIT) compilation, 'Java is slow. Java isn't just slow, it's really slow, surprisingly slow' [22]. JIT compilation has since emerged as an effective technique for speeding up program interpreters by dynamically translating source bytecode into target binary code, which is then executed as native machine code. This technique is now widely used in various interpreter-based implementations of programming languages, from Java to Linux eBPF [5] and its variants, specifically, the Solana blockchain eBPF virtual machine [21]. Given the widespread deployment of eBPF JITs in safety-critical environments, ensuring their correctness is essential for system security. Vulnerabilities within these JIT compilers could significantly compromise the security of Linux kernels or affect millions of transactions on the Solana platform.

T. Bourke et al. (Eds.): SETTA 2024, LNCS 15469, pp. 197–216, 2025.
https://doi.org/10.1007/978-981-96-0602-3_11

Formal verification, particularly through theorem provers like Coq [3] and Isabelle/HOL [17], offers a rigorous approach to mathematically ensuring the correctness of eBPF JITs. However, compared to standard compiler verification (*e.g.,* CompCert [12] that verifies the compilation from a subset of C to various target assembly languages), to verify a target-specific eBPF JIT is considerably more challenging due to the intricate nature of low-level binary semantics.

In the context of the Solana JIT, the main theorem for proving its correctness involves maintaining simulation preservation (see Subsect. 2.1 for details) between the source eBPF and the target x86-64 binary-level semantics. Essential to this proof is a formalized x86-64 binary semantics that incorporates the encoder-decoder equivalence property. This ensures the exact bijection between the binary and assembly representation, and the simulation to be conducted at the assembly level, thus profoundly simplifying the verification process.

However, existing research has yet to fully address this demand. Closely related work in Isabelle/HOL includes Sail [1] and X86_Semantics in AFP [23]. The Sail model translates an ACL2 [18] formal model of x86-64 ISA into its domain-specific language and produces corresponding Isabelle/HOL scripts. Nevertheless, the extensive use of bit-level semantics that Sail utilizes to formalize each x86-64 instruction noticeably complicates all subsequent proofs required for verifying the correctness of Solana JIT. Additionally, Sail lacks x86-64 encoding rules for proving encoder-decoder equivalence which is essential for streamlining the Solana JIT proofs. Meanwhile, the X86_Semantics in AFP only formalized a small subset of basic x86 instructions at the assembly level, insufficient for the comprehensive needs of the Solana JIT proof, and inadequate to fully bridge the gap between binary and assembly semantics.

Challenges. To establish a formal binary x86-64 model for the Solana eBPF JIT presents two major challenges:

- *Binary and Assembly Semantics Gap.* In contrast to the assembly level, binary semantics contains more complicated machine-level information. For example, a single assembly mnemonic can map to multiple, even exceeding ten, binary encodings (see Subsect. 4.3). Therefore, an effective formalization of binary semantics requires a bijective encoder-decoder pair for accurate machine execution. All the vital information(*e.g.,* operands, memory addresses, and instruction lengths) must be preserved throughout the bijection process. Furthermore, leveraging existing models like Sail poses challenges as it potentially increases the overall efforts to prove JIT correctness.
- *Encoding Complexity of the x86-64 ISA.* The x86-64 architecture is notoriously complicated [4,15,27]. The precise modeling of this architecture is critical, but the intricate CISC design demands a meticulous approach to handle properties such as variable instruction length, diverse bit-mode representations, and backward compatibility with legacy instructions. For the Solana JIT which targets a broad subset of the x86 ISA, this encoding complexity makes formalizing the decoder particularly demanding.

Contributions. Since existing models in Isabelle/HOL do not capture the semantics needed to necessarily support Solana eBPF x86-64 JIT verification, we have formalized a new binary x86-64 model capable of interpreting the x86-64 binary code generated by the Solana JIT. To establish confidence in our model, we base the formalization on the CompCert x86-64 semantic framework and enhance it by extending the capabilities to support more instructions. We choose Isabelle/HOL over other systems (*e.g.,* Coq or SMT solvers) to implement our model, due to its minimal trusted computing base (TCB) and the high degree of proof automation. In essence, this paper introduces the first binary formal semantics that encompasses Solana JIT implementation, along with an equivalence property demonstrated to simplify the JIT correctness proof. Our formalization lays the groundwork for a complete certification of the Solana eBPF JIT compiler. The contributions of this work are summarized as follows:

– *Formalization of x86-64 Binary Semantics.* We have formalized the semantics for all the necessary x86-64 instructions utilized by the Solana JIT (*i.e.,* 78 semantic definitions covering 190 assembly instructions, which correspond to 303 binary representations). Then we developed a formal model of the encoder-decoder pair, establishing an accurate bijection between the assembly and binary code. Our models are faithful to the behaviors of the instructions in the Intel 64 documentation, ensuring direct support for real-world scenarios.
– *Verification of Encoder-Decoder Equivalence.* We have provided the equivalence property of the x86-64 decoder-encoder pair, which distinguishes our work from existing research. This property guarantees that the binary semantics can be lifted up to the assembly level, thereby significantly streamlining the proof effort required for the main theorem of the Sonala JIT correctness.

All the formalization and proofs have been mechanized in Isabelle/HOL (see [14]), comprising approximately 8k lines of code total. This includes around 2.8k lines of specification for the x86-64 binary semantic model and 5.2k lines of proof for the encoder-decoder equivalence property.

The paper is organized as follows: Sect. 2 provides background materials. Section 3 proposes the semantic formalization of x86-64 ISA subset. Section 4 presents the encoder and decoder model and their equivalence proof is given in Sect. 5. Section 6 introduces related works and Sect. 7 concludes.

2   Preliminaries

This section first presents an overview of the Solana JIT correctness, addressing the foundational importance of binary semantics in this proof. Second, it introduces the x86-64 machine instruction format.

2.1   Solana JIT Correctness and x86-64 Binary Semantics Overview

eBPF (Extended Berkeley Packet Filter) originated for network packet filtering and has evolved to run sandboxed programs within the Linux kernel, enhancing its capabilities without modifying the kernel. Solana, an innovative blockchain platform, leverages Linux eBPF to implement its VM for executing Solana smart contracts. One key component of Solana eBPF VM is its JIT compiler that translates eBPF bytecode to x86-64 binaries to optimise performance.

The Solana eBPF JIT workflow is shown in Fig. 1. Consider the example of a user-provided eBPF binary instruction, $ins = 0x0CXY000000000000$, where X and Y are hexadecimal digits: 1) The instruction is decoded into the eBPF assembly $BPF\_ADD32\ R_X\ R_Y$ where $0x0C$ is the eBPF opcode of a 32-bit addition, and X/Y is the indices of the destination/source register; 2) Under the Solana per-instruction JIT rule (JIT_{rule}), two corresponding x86-64 assembly instructions are generated: one for a 32-bit addition and another for extending the result from 32-bit to 64-bit. The x86-64 $r_{X'}$ and $r_{Y'}$ are determined by a specific mapping function $fr : R_{BPF} \rightarrow r_{x64}$ that translates each eBPF register into a corresponding x86-64 register; 3) x86-64 instructions are encoded to L, a set of x86-64 binary instructions of dynamic sizes, using a Solana-specific encoding algorithm. This sequence, L, is referred to as the jited x86-64 code.

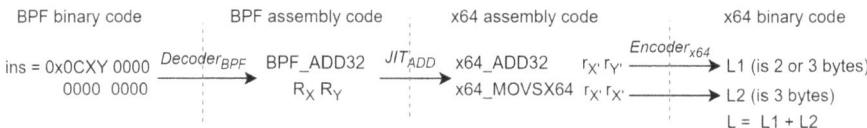

Fig. 1. Solana eBPF x86-64 JIT compiler workflow (for BPF_ADD_{32} instruction)

To prove the correctness of this JIT workflow, the main theorem posits a forward simulation, as shown in Fig. 2 (left). This theorem guarantees that each execution step ($step_{BPF}$) of the input eBPF binary code can be simulated by one or more execution steps ($step_{x64}^+$) of the output jited x86-64 code. The correctness of this simulation is established through value equality between each eBPF register R_i and its corresponding x86-64 register as determined by the mapping function fr, formally defined as $\approx \overset{\text{def}}{=} \forall i, [\![fr(R_i)]\!] = [\![R_i]\!]$. Given that the JIT

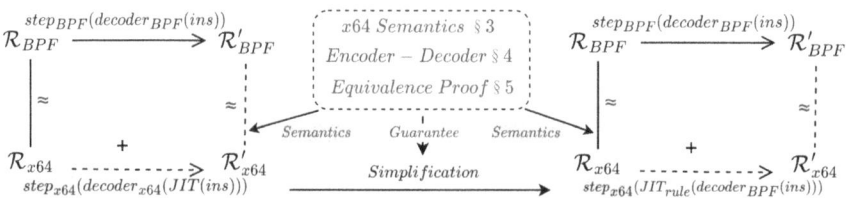

Fig. 2. Solana eBPF JIT simulation proof with the x86-64 binary target (left), our x86-64 binary semantics as an infrastructure for the Solana eBPF simulation proof (mid), and the simplified simulation proof with the x86-64 assembly target (right).

performs binary translation and takes *step* at the assembly level, two distinct decoder functions are utilized to handle the respective instruction sets.

Figure 2 also illustrates how this paper builds the infrastructure that forms the foundation for proving the correctness of the Solana JIT. Section 3 and Sect. 4 work together to provide binary semantics for the forward simulation to execute $step_{x64}$ and Sect. 5 guarantees a critical simplification process in this theorem by the encoder-decoder equivalence proof. This proof simplification is conducted as follows: The (per-*instruction*) JIT compiler is defined as a composition of functions: $JIT(ins) \overset{\text{def}}{=} encoder_{x64}(JIT_{rule}(decoder_{BPF}(ins)))$. The x86-64 binary model guarantees the equivalence property of the encoder and decoder, which simplifies $decoder_{x64}(JIT(ins))$ (Fig. 2 bottom left) into $JIT_{rule}(decoder_{BPF}(ins))$ (Fig. 2 bottom right). This simplification effectively elevates the JIT correctness proof from the x86-64 binary level to the assembly level.

2.2   x86-64 Machine Instruction Format

x86-64 ISA includes 16 general-purpose 64-bit registers, several special-purpose registers(*e.g.*, program counter), and a variety of instructions for arithmetic, control flow, system operations, etc. All formalized instructions conform to subsets of the general machine instruction format depicted in Fig. 3. Considering the complexity of the full x86-64 ISA and the redundancy of many components, we specifically focus on aspects of the x86-64 ISA employed by the Solana JIT.

Legacy Prefix (optional, 1-2 bytes)	REX Prefix (optional, 1 byte)	Opcode (mandatory, 1-3 bytes)	ModR/M (optional, 1 byte)	SIB (optional, 1 byte)	Displacement (optional, 1/2/4 bytes)	Immediate (optional, 1/2/4/8 bytes)

Fig. 3. x86-64 general machine instruction format

- *Legacy Prefix*: An optional 1-byte code divided into four groups, each with a set of allowable prefix codes. The Solana JIT only uses the operand-size override prefix (0x66) to specify a 16-bit operand size, ignoring others.
- *REX Prefix*: An optional 1-byte code '0100 WRXB' that enables 64-bit operands and accesses extended registers R8 to R15. W allows 64-bit operand size, R extends the ModR/M `reg` field, X extends the SIB `index` field, and B extends the ModR/M `r/m` field, SIB `base` field, or opcode `reg` field.
- *Opcode*: A mandatory code that defines instruction operations, consisting of an optional 1/2-byte escape prefix and a primary 1-byte opcode. The last bit of the primary opcode(w) indicates an 8-bit operand size when unset. The primary opcode can be extended by the ModR/M `reg` field.
- *ModR/M*: A 1-byte code following the opcode, specifying a register and/or memory operand. It includes a 2-bit `mod` field (for specifying the addressing mode), a 3-bit `reg` field (for the first operand or opcode extension), and a 3-bit `r/m` field (for the second operand).

- *SIB*: A 1-byte code required by certain ModR/M byte encodings to enhance memory addressing. It specifies a 2-bit `scale` factor, a 3-bit `index` register, and a 3-bit `base` register.
- *Address Displacement*: Included when the addressing mode requires a displacement, available in sizes of 1, 2, or 4 bytes.
- *Immediate data*: Included when the instruction calls for an immediate value, which can be 1, 2, 4, or 8 bytes, and is always the last field of the instruction.

Example. Figure 4 illustrates the encoding of the 16-bit **addw$_{ri}$** *R8 imm* instruction: adding the *imm*ediate value (assuming 0x1234) to the register *R8* (0b1000).

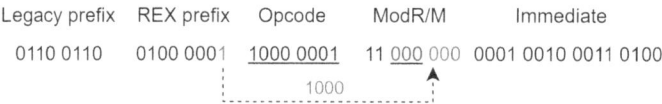

Fig. 4. Bianry representation of **addw$_{ri}$** *R8 imm*

This encoding begins with the legacy prefix (0x66). Since *R8* is an extended register, REX.B is activated and the `r/m` is set to 0b000 (colored in red). The opcode for this operation is 0x81, extended by the `reg` field 0b000 (colored in blue) to denote the addition of an immediate value to a register. The `mod` field is set to 0b11, indicating the `r/m` field represents a register operand, rather than a memory address. The binary instruction ends with a 16-bit immediate value.

In practice, the Solana eBPF JIT is more complex, as we have encountered a diverse array of instructions within different encoding patterns (see Subsect. 4.1). This diversity greatly complicates the decoding process as well.

3 Formalizing x86-64 ISA Subset

To formalize the binary semantics of x86-64, our methodology first lifts x86-64 instructions from the binary level to the assembly level by the faithful *decoder$_{x64}$* function (see Subsect. 4.3). Then, it interprets the corresponding assembly code under the defined x86-64 semantics. This section formalizes the detailed syntax, machine state and semantics of the x86-64 ISA subset required by the Solana JIT. Our formalization mainly focuses on the functional aspects of the ISA by defining mathematical formulas that depict the behavior of instructions on registers and memory. Given that the Solana JIT only generates instructions with sequential behaviors, the concurrency features of the x86-64 memory model are not covered in this paper.

3.1   Syntax

Figure 5 shows the syntax of our x86-64 formal model. The *processor registers* include the program counter *pc*, 16 general-purpose 64-bit registers *r*, the status flags *f* (*e.g.*, zero flag *ZF*, carry flag *CF*, etc.), and the time-stamp counter register *tsc*. The float registers are omitted as they are not needed by the Solana JIT. Memory access is facilitated through both the address *addr* and the size of the accessed memory block *mb*. *addr* defines three addressing modes in the Solana model:1) a single signed immediate value *d* as the address displacement;2) extends the first mode by adding a `base` register value;3) extends the second mode by adding an `index` register value with a 2-bit `scale` factor. The test conditions *η* encompass comparisons such as equal (=), below ($<_u$ for unsigned comparison), and less ($<_s$ for signed comparison), among others.

(IntReg)	*r*	::=	$RAX \mid RBX \mid RCX \mid RDX \mid RSI \mid RDI \mid RBP \mid RSP$
			$\mid R8 \mid R9 \mid R10 \mid R11 \mid R12 \mid R13 \mid R14 \mid R15$
(Rflags)	*f*	::=	$ZF \mid CF \mid PF \mid SF \mid OF$
(ProcReg)	*preg*	::=	$pc \mid r \mid f \mid tsc$
(Address)	*addr*	::=	$d \mid (r_{base}, d) \mid (r_{base}, r_{index}, scale, d)$
(MemBlock)	*mb*	::=	$M8 \mid M16 \mid M32 \mid M64$
(TestCond)	*η*	::=	$= \mid \neq \mid <_u \mid \leq_u \mid \geq_u \mid >_u \mid <_s \mid \leq_s \mid \geq_s \mid >_s \mid \cdots$
(x64Ins)	*ins*	::=	$\mathbf{addl_{rr}}\ r_d\ r_s \mid \mathbf{andq_{rr}}\ r_d\ r_s \mid \mathbf{rolw_{ri}}\ r_d\ ofs \mid \ldots \mid$
			$\mathbf{mov_{rm}}\ r\ addr\ mb \mid \mathbf{mov_{mr}}\ addr\ r\ mb \mid \ldots \mid$
			$\mathbf{jcc}\ \eta\ d \mid \mathbf{call_i}\ d \mid \mathbf{call_r}\ r \mid \ldots \mid$
			$\mathbf{rdtsc} \mid \mathbf{nop} \mid \ldots$

Fig. 5. The syntax of our x86-64 formal model

Our x86-64 model consists of four base sets of instructions.

– *Arithmetic and Logic Instructions:* We have formalized an extensive set of common arithmetic, logical, and bit manipulation instructions across various bit-width registers. For instance, $\mathbf{addl_{rr}}$ declares a 32-bit addition of the source register r_s to the destination register r, $\mathbf{andq_{rr}}$ defines a 64-bit logical AND between r_d and r_s, and $\mathbf{rolw_{ri}}$ formalizes a 16-bit left rotate on r_d using an 8-bit shift offset *ofs*;
– *Data Transfer Instructions:* We have defined necessary data transfer and conversion instructions executed by **mov** and its variants. For instance, $\mathbf{mov_{rm}}$ models data transfer from memory to registers (*i.e.*, memory load) and $\mathbf{mov_{mr}}$ models the opposition data transfer (*i.e.*, memory store), where *addr* points to the start location in the memory and *mb* dedicates the memory size to be manipulated;

- *Control Flow Instructions:* We have modeled the required semantics of instructions that govern the control flow. For instance, **jcc** formalizes a control transfer under the condition η, and **call** facilitates procedure calls using either a relative address displacement (**call$_i$**) or an absolute address stored in a register (**call$_r$**);
- *System Instructions:* We have formalized the specialized instructions for system-level functions. For instance, **rdtsc** models system API to read the time-stamp counter. **nop** is used for instruction alignment and timing adjustments without altering the program state.

3.2 Machine State

The program state is denoted as $\mathcal{S} ::= (\mathcal{R}, \mathcal{M})$, comprising pairs of the register state $\mathcal{R}$ and the memory state $\mathcal{M}$.

Register Map. The register state $\mathcal{R}$ is defined as an injective mapping from the processor registers to values,

$$(\text{Regmap}) \quad \mathcal{R} \in preg \rightarrow Val$$

where *Val* represents values of varying bit widths. For instance, when $\mathcal{R}(RAX)$ (or $[\![RAX]\!]$) conform to *Vint i*, it represents the value in *EAX*, which is the pseudo-register name of the lower 32-bit portion of *RAX*. The definition of *Val* also includes a special constructor *Vundef* denoting undefined value.

$$Val ::= Vundef \mid Vbyte\ int8 \mid Vshort\ int16 \mid Vint\ int32 \mid Vlong\ int64$$

Program Counter. Unlike assembly-level semantics where *pc* increments by 1 for non-control flow instructions, binary-level semantics increases *pc* by the byte size of each instruction, as determined by the *decoder$_{x64}$*. We define **nextinstr** function for updating *pc* to the address of the next instruction based on the input byte size *sz*. We use $\mathcal{R}(r)$ to denote the value of register r in register map $\mathcal{R}$, $\mathcal{R}\{r \leftarrow v\}$ for updating it to v, and $\mathcal{R}^{+sz}$ to signify **nextinstr**$(\mathcal{R}, sz)$.

$$\texttt{nextinstr}(\mathcal{R}, sz) \stackrel{\text{def}}{=} \mathcal{R}\{pc \leftarrow \mathcal{R}(pc) + Vlong\ sz\}$$

Memory. Our memory model is inspired by CompCert [13]. The memory state $\mathcal{M}$ is defined as a partial mapping from a 64-bit address to a byte.

$$(\text{Memory}) \quad \mathcal{M} \in int64 \rightharpoonup int8$$

The memory model provides several fundamental operations, including:

- $\texttt{load}(mb, \mathcal{M}, va) = \lfloor v \rfloor$: Read the value v in memory block mb at address va from $\mathcal{M}$.
- $\texttt{store}(mb, \mathcal{M}, va, v) = \lfloor \mathcal{M}' \rfloor$: Store value v into memory block mb at address va, returning the updated memory $\mathcal{M}'$.

$\texttt{load}$ and $\texttt{store}$ may fail in cases of invalid memory access. Therefore, those operations return option types, with $\lfloor v \rfloor$ (*i.e., Some v*) indicating success, and $\emptyset$ (*i.e., None*) indicating failure.

3.3   Semantics

We define the semantics of instructions that interact with registers and memory using the transition $(\mathcal{R}, \mathcal{M}) \xrightarrow{ins} (\mathcal{R}', \mathcal{M}')$. Typical instructions are selected from each of the four base sets to demonstrate the process of semantic formalization.

Arithmetic and Logic Instructions. The 32-bit $\mathbf{addl_{rr}}$ r_d r_s instruction first verifies that both the source register r_s and destination register r_d contain 32-bit integers, and uses function $\mathtt{bszie}$ to determine the instruction length n. The value in r_s is then added to r_d, followed by an update to pc.

$$\frac{Vint \; v_1 = \mathcal{R}(r_d) \quad Vint \; v_2 = \mathcal{R}(r_s) \quad \mathtt{bsize}(\mathbf{addl_{rr}} \; r_d \; r_s) = n}{(\mathcal{R}, \mathcal{M}) \xrightarrow{\mathbf{addl_{rr}} \; r_d \; r_s} (\mathcal{R}^{+n}\{r_d \leftarrow Vint(v_1 + v_2)\}, \mathcal{M})} \quad \text{(Add32)}$$

Data Transfer Instructions. x86-64 adopts the **mov** instructions to implement load and store operations. The function $\mathtt{eval\_addr}$ is to compute the 64-bit address $addr$ for memory access.

$$\frac{\mathtt{eval\_addr}(addr, \mathcal{R}) = Vlong \; va \quad \mathtt{bsize}(\mathbf{mov_{rm}} \; r_d \; addr \; mb) = n}{\lfloor v \rfloor = \mathtt{load}(mb, \mathcal{M}, va)}{(\mathcal{R}, \mathcal{M}) \xrightarrow{\mathbf{mov_{rm}} \; r_d \; addr \; mb} (\mathcal{R}^{+n}\{r_d \leftarrow v\}, \mathcal{M})} \quad \text{(Load)}$$

$$\frac{\mathtt{eval\_addr}(addr, \mathcal{R}) = Vlong \; va \quad \mathtt{bsize}(\mathbf{mov_{rm}} \; r_d \; addr \; mb) = n}{\lfloor \mathcal{M}' \rfloor = \mathtt{store}(mb, \mathcal{M}, va, \mathcal{R}(r_s))}{(\mathcal{R}, \mathcal{M}) \xrightarrow{\mathbf{mov_{mr}} \; addr \; r_s \; mb} (\mathcal{R}^{+n}, \mathcal{M}')} \quad \text{(Store)}$$

The $\mathbf{mov_{rm}}$ r_d $addr$ mb instruction first computes the exact address value va by $\mathtt{eval\_addr}$, then uses $\mathtt{load}$ to retrieve the value v in the memory block mb at the address va, loading it into register r_d. Conversely, $\mathbf{mov_{mr}}$ $addr$ r_s mb uses $\mathtt{store}$ to transfer the contents of register r_s into mb at va, and returns the new memory $\mathcal{M}'$. Both of the operations end with an update to pc.

Control Flow Instructions. Here we give the semantics of instructions that control execution flow. The **jcc** η d instruction takes an integer displacement d and conditionally performs a jump. Specifically, if the condition η, as assessed by the Rflags, is satisfied, the jump targets a specific address; otherwise, execution proceeds to the next sequential instruction. $\mathtt{eval\_cond}$ is used verify whether the status register value $\mathcal{R}(f)$ holds the condition η.

$$\frac{\mathtt{eval\_cond}(\eta, \mathcal{R}(f)) = True}{(\mathcal{R}, \mathcal{M}) \xrightarrow{\mathbf{jcc} \; \eta \; d} (\mathcal{R}^{+d}, \mathcal{M})} \quad \text{(Jcc-T)}$$

$$\frac{\mathtt{eval\_cond}(\eta, \mathcal{R}(f)) = False \quad \mathtt{bsize}(\mathbf{jcc} \; \eta \; d) = n}{(\mathcal{R}, \mathcal{M}) \xrightarrow{\mathbf{jcc} \; \eta \; d} (\mathcal{R}^{+n}, \mathcal{M})} \quad \text{(Jcc-F)}$$

The **call$_r$** r and **call$_i$** i instructions first push the current pc onto the stack. This is, decreasing the stack pointer register RSP by the byte size of pc (always 8 in our case) and storing pc at the location pointed by RSP. Then set pc to the 64-bit target address (va for absolute address or i for relative address).

$$\frac{\mathcal{R}(r) = Vlong\ va \quad \mathcal{R}' = \mathcal{R}\{RSP \leftarrow \mathcal{R}(RSP) - 8\} \quad \lfloor \mathcal{M}' \rfloor = \texttt{store}(M64, \mathcal{M}, \mathcal{R}(pc), \mathcal{R}(RSP))}{(\mathcal{R}, \mathcal{M}) \xrightarrow{\textbf{call}_r\ r} (\mathcal{R}'\{pc \leftarrow Vlong\ va\}, \mathcal{M}')} \text{(Call-R)}$$

$$\frac{\mathcal{R}' = \mathcal{R}\{RSP \leftarrow \mathcal{R}(RSP) - 8\}\ \lfloor \mathcal{M}' \rfloor = \texttt{store}(M64, \mathcal{M}, \mathcal{R}(pc), \mathcal{R}(RSP))}{(\mathcal{R}, \mathcal{M}) \xrightarrow{\textbf{call}_i\ i} (\mathcal{R}'^{+i}, \mathcal{M}')\ \text{(Call-I)}}$$

System Instructions. The Solana JIT employs a select set of system-level instructions, notably the **rdtsc**. This instruction reads the value from the 64-bit processor's timestamp counter tsc as v and distributes it across registers RDX and RAX. `lo_32` and `hi_32` are used to extract the lower and higher 32-bit values from v, respectively.

$$\frac{Vlong\ v = \mathcal{R}(tsc)}{(\mathcal{R}, \mathcal{M}) \xrightarrow{\textbf{rdtsc}} (\mathcal{R}'\{RAX \leftarrow Vint\ \texttt{lo\_32}(v), RDX \leftarrow Vint\ \texttt{hi\_32}(v), \mathcal{M})} \text{(rdtsc)}$$

4   Modeling x86-64 Encoder and Decoder

This section introduces a formal model of our x86-64 encoder-decoder pair tailored for the Solana JIT. We begin with the relevant x86-64 encoding specification. Then we present the encoder algorithm, which clarifies the process of translating assembly semantics into machine-readable binary codes. Finally, we illustrate the decoder algorithm, which elevates the x86-64 semantics from the binary level back to the assembly.

4.1   x86-64 Encoding Specification

To handle the complexity of CISC-styled instruction formats, we identify 24 fundamental x86-64 encoding patterns, *i.e.*, 4 primary patterns each comprising several subsidiary rules within the Solana JIT implementation. The first primary pattern, *R1*, addresses default operand configurations that commence directly with an opcode byte. Subsequent primary patterns, *R2* through *R4*, incorporate legacy, REX, and escape prefixes. For simplification, we list only the essential subsidiary rules but our formal model covers all the patterns used by Solana JIT.

- *R1*: *ins* that starts with an opcode byte, devoid of any prefix enhancements. Sub-patterns include:
  - *R1.1* [opcode]: *ins* exclusively comprising a singular opcode byte.

- *R1.2* [opcode + modrm]: *ins* that incorporates both an opcode byte and a ModR/M byte for registry access.
- *R1.3* [opcode + modrm + imm]: *ins* that integrates an opcode byte, a ModR/M byte, and a 1/2/4/8-byte immediate value.
- *R1.4* [opcode + displacement]: *ins* that features an opcode byte with a 1/2/4-byte displacement value, used for direct addressing (see Subsect. 3.1 memory addressing mode 1).
- *R1.5* [opcode + modrm + displacement]: *ins* that consists of an opcode byte, a ModR/M byte, and a displacement value, to enhance the addressing capabilities (mode 2).
- *R1.6* [opcode + modrm + sib + displacement]: *ins* that includes an opcode byte, a ModR/M byte, a SIB byte and a displacement value, applicable to enable complex addressing (mode 3).
- *R2*: *ins* with a REX prefix that enhances operand interactions by extending the default 32-bit operand size to 64 bits when REX.W is set, and by enabling access to the extended registers (R8-R15) through proper setting of REX.R, REX.X, and REX.B. Sub-patterns include:
  - *R2.1* [rex + opcode]
  - *R2.2* [rex + opcode + modrm]
  - *R2.3* [rex + opcode + modrm + imm]
  - *R2.4* [rex + opcode + modrm + displacement + imm]
  - *R2.5* [rex + opcode + modrm + sib + displacement + imm]
- *R3*: *ins* that operates on 16-bit operands requires the legacy prefix (0x66). Sub-patterns include:
  - *R3.1* [legacy + opcode + modrm + imm]
  - *R3.2* [legacy + opcode + modrm + displacement]
  - *R3.3* [legacy + rex + opcode + modrm + imm]
  - *R3.4* [legacy + rex + opcode + modrm + displacement]
- *R4*: Special *ins* that requires an opcode escape sequence prefix (0x0f) applied before the primary opcode. Sub-patterns include:
  - *R4.1* [escape + opcode]
  - *R4.2* [escape + opcode + modrm]
  - *R4.3* [rex + escape + opcode]
  - *R4.4* [rex + escape + opcode + modrm]

4.2   x86-64 Encoder

We define the x86-64 encoder Algorithm 1 following the previous specification. The algorithm processes each assembly instruction *ins* by first identifying and matching it to the corresponding instruction pattern (line 2). Upon successful pattern matching, the algorithm then converts *ins* into its binary representation, effectively encoding the assembly instruction into the target machine code.

The Algorithm 1 involves two important functions: The ConstructREX function (line 4, line 11) compiles the W, R, X, and B bits into a byte for the REX prefix. REX is included only if the lower 4-bit resultant value is non-zero; otherwise, it is omitted (line 6, line 14). Similarly, the ConstructModRM function

---

Algorithm 1: x86-64 encoder algorithm

Data: $(ins : instruction)$
Result: $(bin : x64\_binary)$
1 $encoder_{x64}$:
2 **switch** ins **do**
3   **case** $addl_{rr}\ r_d\ r_s$
4         $rex \leftarrow$ ConstructREX$(0,\ 8 \leq s,\ 0,\ 8 \leq d)$;
5         $modrm \leftarrow$ ConstructModRM$(0\mathrm{b}11, s, d)$;
6   **if** $rex = 0x40$ **then**
7   **return** $[\ 0x01, modrm\ ]$;   /* R1.2 */
8   **else**
9   **return** $[\ rex, 0x01, modrm\ ]$;   /* R2.2 */
10   **case** $addw_{ri}\ r_d\ imm$
11         $rex \leftarrow$ ConstructREX$(0, 0, 0, 8 \leq d)$;
12         $modrm \leftarrow$ ConstructModRM$(0\mathrm{b}11, 0\mathrm{b}000, d)$;
13         $l_{imm} \leftarrow$ u8_list_of_u16(imm)
14   **if** $rex = 0x40$ **then**
15   **return** $[\ 0x66, 0x81, modrm\ ] @ l_{imm}$;   /* R3.1 */
16   **else**
17   **return** $[\ 0x66, rex, 0x81, modrm\ ] @ l_{imm}$; /* R3.3 */
18   **case** nop
19   **return** $[\ 0x90\ ]$;   /* R1.1 */
20   **case** ...
21   ...;   /* handle other ins */

(line 5, line 12) combines the 2-bit mod, 3-bit reg, and 3-bit r/m fields into the ModR/M byte. For example, **addl**$_{rr}$ r_d r_s can match either *R1.2* (line 7) or *R2.2* (line 9), depending on the registers involved. The R and B bits in the REX byte are set to 1 if r_s and r_d access extended registers, respectively. The W bit is set to 0 for 32-bit operands, and the X bit remains 0, indicating that no SIB code is required for memory access. Finally, with the opcode 0x01 directly referenced in the manual, all the components are pipelined into a binary instruction.

The **addw**$_{ri}$ r_d imm instruction (line 10) matches either pattern *R3.1* (line 15) or *R3.3* (line 17), and is prefixed with 0x66 to signify a 16-bit operand size. We employ u8_list_of_u16 function to convert a 16-bit integer into a list of bytes (line 13) and use the '@' operator to concatenate these lists (line 15, line 17). The **nop** (line 18) instruction matches *R1.1*, for which the opcode 0x90 is directly returned (line 19). Other cases follow a similar pattern-matching process but are skipped for simplification.

Although a single assembly instruction may correspond to multiple binary encodings, our encoder is injective (see Lemma 1). This means that while the potential encodings vary based on the information specified in the assembly instruction, only one specific binary representation is generated for each instruction once the information is determined.

4.3 x86-64 Decoder

The decoder Algorithm 2 tackles a tougher challenge to map binary encodings back to the assembly forms. Similarly, our decoder is also injective. That is, for

---

Algorithm 2: x86-64 decoder algorithm

Data: $(pc : nat), (l_{bin} : x64\_binary)$
Result: $(asm : (nat \times instruction)\ option)$

1 $decoder_{x64}$:
2 $h0 \leftarrow l_{bin}[pc]$;
3 **if** $h0 = 0x90$ **then**

4   **return** $\lfloor (1, \textbf{nop}) \rfloor$;   /* R1.1 */
5 **else if** $h0 = 0x66$ **then**
6    $h1 \leftarrow l_{bin}[pc + 1]$;
7   **if** $h1$ *is not rex* **then**
8      $(mod,\ r_s,\ r_d) \leftarrow l_{bin}[pc + 2]$;
9   **if** $h1 = 0x81$ **then**
10       $imm \leftarrow \texttt{u16\_of\_u8\_list}(l_{bin}[pc + 3],\ l_{bin}[pc + 4])$;
11   **if** $mod = 0b11$ *and* $s = 0b000$ **then**

12   **return** $\lfloor (5, \textbf{addw}_{\textbf{ri}}\ r_d\ imm) \rfloor$;   /* R3.1 */
13   **else**
14   **return** $\emptyset$;

15   **else**
16       $\dots$;   /* R3.2 */

17   **else**
18     $(\_, w, r, x, b) \leftarrow h1$;
19     $\dots$;   /* R3.3, R3.4 */

20 **else if** $h0 = 0x0f$ **then**
21   $\dots$;   /* R4.1, R4.2 */
22 **else if** $h0$ *is not rex* **then**

23   $(mod,\ r_s,\ r_d) \leftarrow l_{bin}[pc + 1]$;
24   **if** $h0 = 0x01$ **then**
25   **if** $mod = 0b11$ **then**
26   **return** $\lfloor (2, \textbf{addl}_{\textbf{rr}}\ r_d\ r_s) \rfloor$;   /* R1.2 */
27   **else**
28   **return** $\emptyset$;

29   **else**
30     $\dots$;   /* R1.3, R1.4, R1.5, R1.6 */

31 **else**
32   $\dots$;   /* R2.1, R2.2, R2.3, R2.4, R2.5, R4.3, R4.4 */

each *ins* encoded into a sequence of bytes *bin*, our decoder will faithfully decode *bin* back to its original instruction. The decoder processes a list of x86-64 binary instructions l_{bin} and uses *pc* to mark the start of the current instruction. It outputs a corresponding assembly instruction and calculates the byte size of the instruction. This calculated size is essential for correctly branching to the subsequent instruction during the assembly execution.

The algorithm begins by examining the byte ($h0$) at position *pc* in l_{bin} (line 2). Based on the encoding rules (Subsect. 4.1), there are several possible outcomes:

– If $h0$ is a single opcode byte for a no-operand instruction, it matches pattern *R1.1*. For example, if $h0$ equals 0x90 (line 3), the decoder returns the **nop** assembly with a byte size of 1 (line 4).
– If $h0$ is the legacy prefix 0x66 (line 5), it matches patterns *R3.1* to *R3.4*. Analysis of the next byte $h1$ follows (line 6):
  • If $h1$ is not a REX prefix (line 7), it matches *R3.1* or *R3.2*. In this case, $h1$ serves as the opcode, and the following byte is the ModR/M byte. Using a mapping, the decoder extracts the mod, reg, and r/m (*i.e.*, r_d) fields (line 8), requiring further bytes to fully determine the instruction. For instance, if $h1$ is 0x81 (line 9) followed by a 16-bit immediate *imm*, and mod is 0b11 with reg at 0b000 (line 11), the instruction is confirmed as **addw$_{\text{ri}}$** r_d *imm* (line 12) with length of 5. u16_of_u8_list function is to convert two bytes into a 16-bit integer (line 10). In this case, reg field extends the opcode rather than serving as a direct operand.
  • If $h1$ is a REX prefix, the algorithm seeks to align with *R4.3* and *R4.4*. It extracts the REX.WRXB fields from $h1$ (line 18) and then proceeds with an analysis akin to the previously described, which will not be reiterated.
– If $h0$ is the opcode escape prefix 0x0f, it matches *R4.1* to *R4.4*, and the decoder should disassemble an instruction with an escape sequence (line 21).
– For other values of $h0$, the algorithm checks for a REX prefix (line 22):
  • If $h0$ is not a REX prefix, the decoder matches it with *R1.2* to *R1.6* to identify 32-bit instructions without extended registers, or certain 8-bit instructions. An example is provided with the parsing of the **addl$_{\text{rr}}$** r_d r_s instruction (line 24) with length of 2 (line 26).
  • If $h0$ is a REX prefix, the decoder matches it with *R2.1* to *R2.5*, *R4.3* or *R4.4* to identify either 8/32-bit instructions that access extended registers or 64-bit instructions (line 32).

In instances where none of the defined instruction patterns are met, the decoding is deemed invalid and the algorithm will return ∅ (line 14, line 28) because the Solana JIT does not generate this pattern.

5   Verifying Encoder-Decoder Equivalence

This section demonstrates that the formal model of our x86-64 encoder-decoder pair satisfies the equivalence property. The equivalence property confirms that the bidirectional mapping between assembly and binary instructions allows seamless conversion between the two without any information loss. This property is essential to verify the correctness of the entire Solana eBPF JIT compiler workflow, as shown in Fig. 1.

To prove equivalence, we first discuss two lemmas:

- *Encoder implies decoder*(Lemma 1): given that a list of x86-64 assembly instructions is encoded into binary form, prove that the encoded instructions can always be decoded back to the original assembly code.
- *Decoder implies encoder*(Lemma 2): given that a list of binary instructions is decoded into assembly form, prove that the decoded instructions can always be re-encoded to reproduce the original binary code.

We use $l \sqsubseteq_n L$ to represent a list l as a contiguous sublist within a larger list L starting at position n. Here, $l[i]$ refers to the i-th element of l.

$$l \sqsubseteq_n L \stackrel{\text{def}}{=} \forall\ i\ v.\ l[i] = \lfloor v \rfloor \Rightarrow L[n+i] = \lfloor v \rfloor$$

In the proof context, we declare $l_{bin} \sqsubseteq_n L_{bin}$ as an assumption to reflect that each jited x86-64 binary sequence l_{bin} of Solana JIT rule is a sublist within the complete jited x86-64 binary code L_{bin} of the entire Solana JIT compiler.

Lemma 1 (x86-64 Encoder_Implies_Decoder). *If $l_{bin} \sqsubseteq_{pc} L_{bin}$ and* $encoder_{x64}(ins) = l_{bin}$, *then* $decoder_{x64}(pc,\ L_{bin}) = \lfloor (length(l_{bin}),\ ins) \rfloor$

Proof. The proof begins by conducting a case analysis on the assembly instruction ins, where each instance generates a subgoal. We conduct further case analysis on each of its register-related operands and rely on the high degree of proof automation of Isabelle/HOL to solve all subgoals.

Lemma 2 (x86-64 Decoder_Implies_Encoder). *If $l_{bin} \sqsubseteq_{pc} L_{bin}$ and* $decoder_{x64}(pc,\ L_{bin}) = \lfloor (length(l_{bin}),\ ins) \rfloor$, *then* $encoder_{x64}(ins) = l_{bin}$

Proof. The proof also begins by case analysis on ins rather than on L_{bin} to maintain a more coherent and focused proof structure and reduce complexity. For each ins and its operands, relevant function definitions are unfolded to enable detailed examination at the bit level. We then conduct case analysis on l_{bin} to extract each byte and try to match it with ins. Simplification of the proof is achieved using the existing lemmas on bit operators provided by Isabelle/HOL.

Theorem 1 (Encoder-Decoder Equivalence). *If $l_{bin} \sqsubseteq_{pc} L_{bin}$, then* $decoder_{x64}(pc,\ L_{bin}) = \lfloor (length(l_{bin}),\ ins) \rfloor \iff encoder_{x64}(ins) = l_{bin}$

Proof. The proof is established directly by applying Lemma 1 and Lemma 2.

Status of the Proof. At the time of writing, the x86-64 binary model (including semantics, encoder, and decoder) and the proofs of Lemma 1 are done, sufficiently establishing the groundwork for proving the main theorem of Solana JIT correctness (Subsect. 2.1). While the mechanization of Lemma 2 continues due to the complex bit operations, completion of the full proof is anticipated soon.

6   Related Work

There have been many projects that formalize the semantics of various ISAs either as their main contribution or as part of their infrastructure. Pioneering work include research on ISAs such as x86 [4,8,15], ARM [6,29], RISC-V [19], SPARC [9,10,24], as well as verified Compilers *e.g.*, CompCert, CakeML [11]. We gain insights from these studies to inform our own research. This section mainly discusses related work on the formalization of x86 ISA and the verification of encoders and decoders. We compare our x86-64 formal model with existing studies and highlight our primary contributions to the verification of the Solana JIT.

Formalization of the x86 ISA. Various approaches have been taken to formalize the x86 ISA, but many do not align with our objectives. Our main goal is to provide the infrastructure that supports the verification of the Solana JIT correctness, which demands the x86-64 binary semantics and the equivalence proof of the encoder-decoder pair.

Sail is a language semantics framework tailored for describing ISA semantics. Sail x86-64 semantics is initially translated from an ACL2 formal model by Goel *et al.* [7] and then re-translated into Isabelle/HOL scripts. However, Sail significantly complicates the task of proving encoder-decoder equivalence due to its formalization of x86 semantics at the bit level. We shift to the byte level to avoid operations and transformations on individual bits.

Dasgupta *et al.* [4] employ $\mathbb{K}$ framework to define formal semantics for over 3000 user-level x86-64 instructions of Intel Haswell processor. This is so far the most comprehensive formalization of x86-64 ISA to our knowledge. However, it does not include specific mechanisms for instruction encoding and decoding.

Verbeek *et al.* [23] provide semantics for basic x86-64 assembly instructions in Isabelle/HOL, including arithmetic operations, jumps, and others. But this semantics is more limited than ours, covering only 120 instructions. It also maintains semantics at the assembly level and lacks mechanisms for binary analysis.

CakeML is a fully verified functional programming language compiler proven in HOL4 [20]. It supports verified end-to-end compilation into target concrete machine code for realistic x86-64 architecture, but the target proofs focus on the consistency between the assembly bytes in the memory and the binary sequences. Therefore, to our knowledge, there is no proof of encoder-decoder equivalence in the CakeML correctness theorem.

CompCert is a fully verified compiler for the C programming language in Coq. Its verification covers compilation passes beginning with the CompCert C AST, and extending to various target assembly languages (*e.g.*, x86-64, x84, ARM, RISC-V, etc.). The scope of verification still does not extend to the binary level. Nevertheless, subsequent projects based on CompCert have yielded significant insights (*e.g.*, FM-JIT [2], and CompCertELF [26,27]).

Verification of Encoders and Decoders. To delve into binary-level analysis of the x86 ISA, various projects incorporate encoders and decoders, ensuring their correctness through formal verification.

CompCertELF extends CompCert to support verified separate compilation from C programs to the Executable and Linkable Format (ELF). CompCertELF develops a verified encoder-decoder pair as a key component to link the CompCert assembly code with 32-bit x86 binary code in ELF format. Our model diverges distinctively from CompCertELF in several parts, serving different purposes. Firstly, it only supports the 32-bit x86 backend, whereas our binary model is built on the 64-bit x86 architecture and accommodates backward bit modes. Secondly, the encoder-decoder pair in CompCertELF doesn't satisfy the equivalence property, meaning that applying encoding and then decoding to instructions does not accurately reproduce the original assembly inputs.

Rocksalt [15] is another pioneering work that explores the x86 ISA at the binary level. It introduces a formally verified checker for Google's Native Client in Coq, targeting the 32-bit x86 processor. However, Rocksalt fails to develop a deterministic decoder since it lacks an encoder to prove consistency. Moreover, the subset of instructions it supports is relatively smaller compared to ours.

There are also some projects that focus on BPF JITs verification, which align more closely with our long-term goal of verifying the Solana JIT compiler. A common practice for them is also to employ encoders and decoders as part of the JIT correctness proof. However, these efforts are currently insufficient to fully support the Solana JIT proof. For example, Jitk [25] extends the CompCert to translate classic BPF to assembly for building verified in-kernel interpreters. Jitterbug [16] offers a framework for generating formal specifications to aid JIT correctness proofs, and has been applied to several real-world BPF JITs in Linux. Compared to our work, Jitterbug incurs a larger TCB by relying on external SMT solvers for symbolic execution. CertrBPF-JIT [28] provides a verified JIT compiler for RIOT-OS eBPF virtual machine in Coq, but it is currently limited to the ARM architecture and supports a small subset of arithmetic instructions which is too restricted for our application in the Solana JIT proof.

7   Conclusion and Future Work

In this paper, we present the infrastructure to verify Solana JIT correctness by formalizing a necessary subset of x86-64 binary semantics and demonstrating the equivalence proof of the x86-64 encoder-decoder pair. We first lift the target x86-64 binaries to the higher-level assembly representation, where we define the syntax, machine state, and semantics for all x86-64 instructions employed by the Solana JIT. We then tackle the complexities of low-level x86-64 ISA semantics by modeling the encoder and decoder specific to the Solana JIT. Our model adheres to the defined x86-64 encoding specifications for precise transition between the assembly and the binary level. Additionally, our proof of the encoder-decoder equivalence significantly simplifies the main theorem of the Solana JIT correctness, allowing further verification to be conducted at the assembly level.

Our future work will focus on a complete formal verification of the Solana x86-64 eBPF JIT compiler. While this study has established the foundational binary semantics for the x86-64 decoder correctness in Solana JIT, further research is going to explore additional facets, including the eBPF binary decoder and the JIT rules. Additionally, we are continuing to validate our binary semantics. We leverage the extraction mechanism Isabelle/HOL provides to automatically generate executable semantics in OCaml. The semantics will be validated against the official x86-64 test suite to establish confidence in our model.

Acknowledgements. This work has been supported by the Natural Science Foundation of China (Grant No. 62132014 and No. U2341212), and Hangzhou High-Tech Zone (Binjiang) Institute of Blockchain and Data Security.

References

1. Armstrong, A., et al.: ISA semantics for ARMv8-a, RISC-v, and CHERI-MIPS. Proc. ACM Program. Lang. **3**(POPL), 1–31 (2019)
2. Barrière, A., Blazy, S., Pichardie, D.: Formally verified native code generation in an effectful JIT: turning the CompCert backend into a formally verified JIT compiler. Proc. ACM Program. Lang. **7**(POPL), 249–277 (2023)
3. Bertot, Y., Castran, P.: Interactive Theorem Proving and Program Development: Coq'Art The Calculus of Inductive Constructions, 1st edn. Springer, Heidelberg (2010). https://doi.org/10.1007/978-3-662-07964-5
4. Dasgupta, S., Park, D., Kasampalis, T., Adve, V.S., Roşu, G.: A complete formal semantics of x86-64 user-level instruction set architecture. In: Proceedings of the 40th ACM SIGPLAN Conference on Programming Language Design and Implementation, pp. 1133–1148 (2019)
5. Fleming, M.: A thorough introduction to eBPF (2017)
6. Fromherz, A., Giannarakis, N., Hawblitzel, C., Parno, B., Rastogi, A., Swamy, N.: A verified, efficient embedding of a verifiable assembly language. In: Principles of Programming Languages (POPL 2019). ACM (2019). https://www.microsoft.com/en-us/research/publication/a-verified-efficient-embedding-of-a-verifiable-assembly-language/
7. Goel, S.: Formal verification of application and system programs based on a validated x86 ISA model. Ph.D. thesis, University of Texas at Austin (2016)
8. Goel, S., Slobodová, A., Sumners, R., Swords, S.: Verifying x86 instruction implementations. In: Proceedings of the 9th ACM SIGPLAN International Conference on Certified Programs and Proofs, pp. 47–60 (2020)
9. Hou, Z., Sanan, D., Tiu, A., Liu, Y.: A formal model for the SPARCv8 ISA and a proof of non-interference for the LEON3 processor. Archive of Formal Proofs (2016). https://isa-afp.org/entries/SPARCv8.html. Formal proof development
10. Hóu, Z., Sanan, D., Tiu, A., Liu, Y., Hoa, K.C., Dong, J.S.: An Isabelle/HOL formalisation of the SPARC instruction set architecture and the TSO memory model. J. Autom. Reason. **65**, 569–598 (2021)
11. Kumar, R., Myreen, M.O., Norrish, M., Owens, S.: CakeML: a verified implementation of ML. In: Proceedings of the 41st ACM SIGPLAN-SIGACT Symposium on Principles of Programming Languages, POPL 2014, pp. 179–191. Association for Computing Machinery, New York (2014). https://doi.org/10.1145/2535838.2535841
12. Leroy, X.: Formal verification of a realistic compiler. Commun. ACM **52**(7), 107–115 (2009). http://xavierleroy.org/publi/compcert-CACM.pdf

13. Leroy, X., Appel, A.W., Blazy, S., Stewart, G.: The CompCert memory model, version 2. Research report RR-7987, INRIA (2012). https://inria.hal.science/hal-00703441

14. Lu, J., Yuan, S., Sanan, D., Zhao, Y.: Solana x64 Semantics (2024). https://github.com/shenghaoyuan/Solana-x64-Semantics

15. Morrisett, G., Tan, G., Tassarotti, J., Tristan, J.B., Gan, E.: RockSalt: better, faster, stronger SFI for the x86. In: Proceedings of the 33rd ACM SIGPLAN Conference on Programming Language Design and Implementation, pp. 395–404 (2012)

16. Nelson, L., Geffen, J.V., Torlak, E., Wang, X.: Specification and verification in the field: applying formal methods to BPF just-in-time compilers in the Linux kernel. In: 14th USENIX Symposium on Operating Systems Design and Implementation (OSDI 2020), pp. 41–61. USENIX Association (2020). https://www.usenix.org/conference/osdi20/presentation/nelson

17. Nipkow, T., Wenzel, M., Paulson, L.C.: Isabelle/HOL: A Proof Assistant for Higher-Order Logic. Springer, Heidelberg (2002). https://doi.org/10.1007/3-540-45949-9

18. Ray, S.: Introduction to ACL2. In: Ray, S. (ed.) Scalable Techniques for Formal Verification, pp. 25–49. Springer, Boston (2010). https://doi.org/10.1007/978-1-4419-5998-0_3

19. RISCV-Coq Team: RISC-V Specification in Coq (2024). https://github.com/mit-plv/riscv-coq

20. Slind, K., Norrish, M.: A brief overview of HOL4. In: Mohamed, O.A., Muñoz, C., Tahar, S. (eds.) TPHOLs 2008. LNCS, vol. 5170, pp. 28–32. Springer, Heidelberg (2008). https://doi.org/10.1007/978-3-540-71067-7_6

21. Solana-Labs: Solana rBPF (2024). https://github.com/solana-labs/rbpf

22. Tyma, P.: Why are we using Java again? Commun. ACM **41**(6), 38–42 (1998). https://doi.org/10.1145/276609.276617

23. Verbeek, F., Bharadwaj, A., Bockenek, J., Roessle, I., Weerwag, T., Ravindran, B.: X86 instruction semantics and basic block symbolic execution. Archive of Formal Proofs (2021). https://isa-afp.org/entries/X86_Semantics.html. Formal proof development

24. Wang, J., Fu, M., Qiao, L., Feng, X.: Formalizing SPARCv8 instruction set architecture in Coq. Sci. Comput. Program. **187**, 102371 (2020). https://doi.org/10.1016/J.SCICO.2019.102371

25. Wang, X., Lazar, D., Zeldovich, N., Chlipala, A., Tatlock, Z.: Jitk: a trustworthy in-kernel interpreter infrastructure. In: 11th USENIX Symposium on Operating Systems Design and Implementation (OSDI 2014), pp. 33–47. USENIX Association, Broomfield (2014). https://www.usenix.org/conference/osdi14/technical-sessions/presentation/wang_xi

26. Wang, Y., Xu, X., Wilke, P., Shao, Z.: CompCertELF: verified separate compilation of C programs into elf object files. Proc. ACM Program. Lang. 4(OOPSLA), 1–28 (2020)

27. Xu, X., Wu, J., Wang, Y., Yin, Z., Li, P.: Automatic generation and validation of instruction encoders and decoders. In: Silva, A., Leino, K.R.M. (eds.) CAV 2021. LNCS, vol. 12760, pp. 728–751. Springer, Cham (2021). https://doi.org/10.1007/978-3-030-81688-9_34

28. Yuan, S., Besson, F., Talpin, J.P.: End-to-end mechanized proof of a JIT-accelerated eBPF virtual machine for IoT. In: Gurfinkel, A., Ganesh, V. (eds.) CAV 2024. LNCS, vol. 14681, pp. 325–347. Springer, Cham (2024). https://doi.org/10.1007/978-3-031-65627-9_16

29. Yuan, S., Talpin, J.P.: Verified functional programming of an IoT operating system's bootloader. In: Proceedings of the 19th ACM-IEEE International Conference on Formal Methods and Models for System Design, MEMOCODE 2021, pp. 89–97. Association for Computing Machinery, New York (2021). https://doi.org/10.1145/3487212.3487347

The Design of Intelligent Temperature Control System of Smart House with MARS

Yihao Yin[1,2,3], Hao Wu[2,3], Shuling Wang[3,4(✉)], Xiong Xu[3,4], Fanjiang Xu[3,4], and Naijun Zhan[4,5]

[1] Hangzhou Institute for Advanced Study (HIAS), UCAS, Beijing, China
[2] Key Laboratory of System Software, ISCAS, Beijing, China
[3] University of Chinese Academy of Sciences, Beijing, China
wangsl@ios.ac.cn
[4] National Key Laboratory of Space Integrated Information System, ISCAS, Beijing, China
[5] School of Computer Science, Peking University, Beijing, China

Abstract. MARS is a toolchain, supporting model-based design of cyber-physical systems (CPS), which integrates informal and formal design. With MARS, a system under development can be graphically modeled by the combination of AADL and Simulink/Stateflow, then the simulation of the graphical model can be conducted. Furthermore, the graphical model can be automatically transformed to Hybrid Communicating Sequential Processes (HCSP) for formal verification with HHL-Prover. Finally, ANSI-C code or SystemC code can be generated from the verified HCSP formal model with the guarantee of correctness. As a case study of CPS, in this paper, we apply MARS to design an intelligent temperature control system, including its modeling, simulation, verification and code generation. This case study demonstrates the advantages of the design of CPS with MARS, including the integration of modeling, simulation, verification and code generation; the integration of informal and formal design, thus providing balance between efficiency and rigidity.

Keywords: Simulink/Stateflow · Model-based design · HCSP · Code Generation · Verification

1 Introduction

The applications of embedded systems (nowadays called Cyber-Physical Systems (CPS)) are extremely broad encompassing nearly every aspect of modern life, especially in many safety-critical areas such as autonomous driving, medical devices, aerospace and so on. For such systems, any mistake of them may

T. Bourke et al. (Eds.): SETTA 2024, LNCS 15469, pp. 217–235, 2025.
https://doi.org/10.1007/978-981-96-0602-3_12

result in catastrophic consequences. However, complex CPS involve closely coupling of discrete control, continuous plants and communications, thus how to efficiently design reliable CPS is very challenging. Both industrial and academic communities have paid increasing attention to design safe CPS, which can be categorized into simulation-based, formal methods based, and their combination. Simulation-based approaches are advocated by industry, such as Simulink/Stateflow (S/S) [15] and AADL [5]. S/S has become a de facto model-based design tool in embedded industry, but it is insufficient for the design of safety-critical CPS because of the inherent incompleteness of simulation. AADL provides architecture modeling and analysis of CPS by simulation, and furthermore supports the automated code generation from AADL models to C code. However, it cannot support modeling continuous physical processes as well as their combination with software. Formal methods based approaches are advocated by academic community, which can be further classified into model-checking based and theorem proving based. In model-checking based approaches, a CPS is modeled as a hybrid automaton [1,8], and verification is done by computing reachable states [4,6,10]. In theorem proving based approaches, a CPS is modeled by a compositional modeling language, and verification is conducted through theorem proving, e.g. differential dynamic logic (dL) [18,31]. SCADE [2] tried to combine formal and informal, but failed to bridge the gap between informal graphical models and formal algorithm models.

In order to bridge the gap between informal and formal model-based design for CPS, in our previous work, we developed a toolchain called MARS [30], supporting modeling, analysis, verification, and code generation for CPS. MARS starts to design a graphical model for the system to be developed using the combination of AADL and S/S, by considering the functionality, physicality and architecture of the system in a unified framework [27]. Then, formal analysis and verification of the combined graphical model can be conducted via the translation of AADL and S/S into Hybrid CSP (HCSP), an extension of CSP for formally modeling hybrid systems [28]. The HCSP models can be simulated using the HCSP simulator. Additionally, to complement incomplete simulation, they can be verified using HHLProver (Hybrid Hoare Logic prover) implemented in Isabelle/HOL [23], as well as a more automated HHLPy prover [20]. Finally, implementations in SystemC or C can be automatically generated from verified HCSP models [24,29]. The transformation from the combined AADL and S/S to HCSP, and the one from HCSP to SystemC or ANSI-C, are both guaranteed to be correct [24,26]. MARS provides model-based design of safety-critical CPS by allowing switching between formal and informal seamlessly, depending on the efficiency, cost and rigidity.

In this paper, we apply MARS to the design of an intelligent temperature control system (ITCS), including its modeling, simulation, verification, and code generation. Specifically, the graphical model of the system is constructed using S/S, and then it is translated into an HCSP model, based on which simulation and verification are performed. From the verified HCSP model, we continue to generate ANSI-C code, which is guaranteed to be reliable given the correctness of the translation proved. The goal of this paper is to demonstrate the entire process of the model-based design approach, by applying MARS for the modeling, simulation, verification, and code generation of the case study, thereby validating the applicability of MARS for the design of complex embedded systems.

Paper Organization. The rest of the paper is organized as follows. Section 2 introduces some preliminary knowledge of this paper. Section 3 introduces the ITCS case study, and Sect. 4 presents the modeling, simulation, verification, and code generation of ITCS using MARS. Finally Sect. 6 concludes the paper.

2 Background

In this section, we introduce some preliminary knowledge for this paper, including Simulink, HCSP, and the MARS toolchain.

2.1 Simulink

Simulink [15] is a graphical environment for model-based design of dynamical systems, supporting description of both discrete-time and continuous-time behavior. A Simulink model contains a set of blocks, subsystems, and wires, where blocks and subsystems cooperate by exchanging data flows through connected wires. Wires can be considered as variables holding these data values. As basic units for building Simulink models, each block is defined with input and output ports, and methods that define how outputs and internal states are changed. Blocks can be grouped into subsystems to establish hierarchical diagrams. To ease modeling, Simulink provides an extensive library of pre-defined blocks and subsystems for building and managing diagrams, and also a rich set of fixed-step and variable-step solvers for analyzing dynamical systems through simulation.

2.2 HCSP

Hybrid CSP (HCSP) [7] is a formal language for describing HSs, which is an extension of CSP by introducing ODEs (ordinary differential equations) for modeling continuous evolution. HCSP includes common constructs such as assignment, internal choice, sequential composition and conditional statement. Besides, it includes more constructs explained as follows:

- Input $ch?x$ receives a value along the channel ch and assigns it to variable x. Output $ch!e$ sends the value of e along ch.
- Repetition c^* executes c for a nondeterministic finite number of times.
- Continuous evolution $\langle \dot{\boldsymbol{x}} = \boldsymbol{e}\&B \rangle$ evolves continuously according to the differential equation $\dot{\boldsymbol{x}} = \boldsymbol{e}$ as long as the *domain* B holds, and terminates whenever B becomes false. Communication interruption $\langle \dot{\boldsymbol{x}} = \boldsymbol{e}\&B \rangle \trianglerighteq []_{i \in I}(ch_i* \to c_i)$ behaves like $\langle \dot{\boldsymbol{x}} = \boldsymbol{e}\&B \rangle$, except it is preempted as soon as one of the communication events ch_i* takes place, and then is followed by the corresponding c_i.
- Parallel composition $pc_1 \|_{cs} pc_2$ behaves as pc_1 and pc_2 run independently except that all communications along the set of common channels cs between pc_1 and pc_2 are synchronized.

MARS enriches HCSP with constructs on modularity, including **module** for encapsulating a sequential process and **system** for parallel composition of modules.

2.3 MARS

The architecture of the toolchain MARS [30] is shown in Fig. 1, where AADL and S/S indicate graphical models that serve as input to the toolchain; HCSP indicates formal models, with their simulation and verification tools; and SystemC and ANSI C indicate generated code. To design a safety-critical system using MARS, users can choose to build graphical models from the top layer and do analysis through simulation by transforming the combined model to C, or build the formal HCSP models directly, which also have a simulator implemented. Formal verification of HCSP models is done by HHL Prover, which includes the interactive verifier implemented in Isabelle [31], the automatic verifier HHLPy for verifying HCSP sequential subset [20], and differential invariant generator for reasoning about ODEs [12]. Finally, implementations in SystemC [29] or ANSI-C [24] are automatically generated from the verified HCSP processes. Both the transformation from graphical models to HCSP models and the one from HCSP to SystemC or ANSI-C, can be done automatically and furthermore are guaranteed to be correct by proving the consistency between the models in different layers based on their formal semantics [24,28]. MARS supports the transformation of subsets of AADL and S/S, which include the main features of CPS including discrete-time control, continuous evolution, event-based control, *etc.*. Our approach allows model-based design of safety-critical CPS based on graphical and formal models and proven-correct translation procedures.

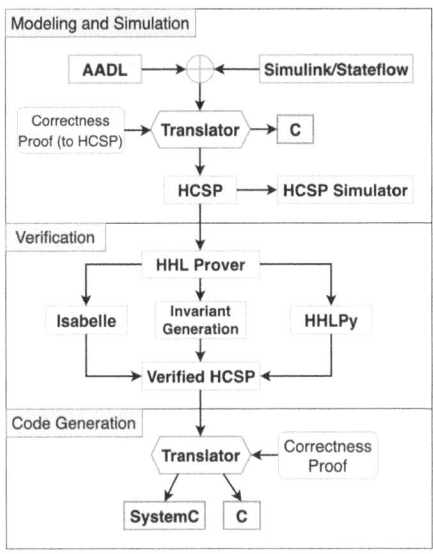

Fig. 1. The Architecture of MARS

3   An Intelligent Temperature Control System (ITCS)

The case study of ITCS is taken from the official website of S/S [15], as shown in Fig. 2. The system is modelled as an S/S diagram, assembled from a combination of continuous blocks, discrete blocks and subsystems, mimicking a real-world scenario wherein the indoor temperature is regulated by automatically toggling the heater on and off in response to changes in outdoor temperature. In this section, we introduce the S/S model of the case study from the overall top structure and the encapsulated subsystems respectively.

3.1   The Overall of ITCS

The system receives inputs from the left two constant blocks, which set the average outdoor temperature to 50 °F and the house temperature to 70 °F respectively. The control system is designed to maintain the indoor temperature at approximately 70 °F, with allowance of given up and down fluctuations. The system uses a sine function to represent the daily outdoor temperature variation and superimposes it over `OutTemp` (i.e. 50) to model the changing outdoor temperature. The F2C block converts the temperature from Fahrenheit to Celsius, then the converted `Tout` is sent to the House subsystem as one input. Concurrently, the constant house temperature 70 °F is also converted via F2C block and then the difference of it with the actual house temperature is calculated (i.e. `Terr`), to be input of the Thermostat subsystem, which determines whether the heater should be activated or not. The Thermostat block then transmits its judgment (i.e. `blowercmd`) as input to the Heater subsystem. The Heater subsystem receives the actual house temperature as another input and calculates the heat flow, i.e. HeaterOut. The heat flow is sent to the House subsystem as another input, and moreover, it is integrated via an integrator block and then multiplied with a constant via a gain block, to obtain the final cost, i.e. HeatCost. At the same time, the system calculates the real-time indoor temperature HouseTemp through the House subsystem. The final output graph is a line chart composed of the indoor and outdoor temperatures in the form of Fahrenheit degree, and the cost of the heater. The subsystems Thermostat, House and Heater will be explained subsequently.

3.2   The Subsystems

The model of ITCS consists of three subsystems: Thermostat, House and Heater, explained in the following parts.

Thermostat Subsystem. The Thermostat subsystem contains only one Relay block, as shown in Fig. 3a. It maintains an internal state that records the status of the switch. When the input signal exceeds a certain threshold (rise threshold, $215/9\,°C$ here), the switch closes and the output is 0, turning off the heater; when the input signal is below another threshold (fall threshold, $165/9\,°C$), the switch opens and the output is 1, turning on the heater; otherwise, when the input signal is between $165/9\,°C$ and $215/9\,°C$, the switch is not changed and the output keeps the value of the switch state. Due to the control of Thermostat subsystem, the indoor temperature can be maintained within a certain range.

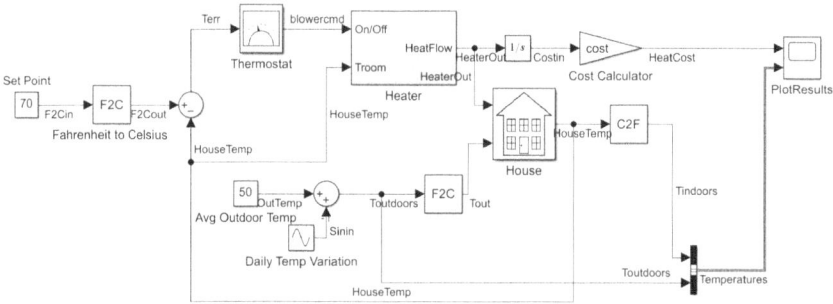

Fig. 2. The S/S Model of ITCS [15]

Heater Subsystem. The Heater subsystem implements the heater as shown in Fig. 3b. The input On/Off receives the output command of Thermostat subsystem (1 or 0), Troom is the actual house temperature from the House subsystem, and Theater is the temperature of the hot air from the heater, which is set to constant $50\,°C$ here. When the heater is on, the output `HeatFlow` is calculated by the following equation:

$$(\frac{dQ}{dt})_{heater} = (T_{heater} - T_{room}) * Mdot * C$$

where, $(\frac{dQ}{dt})_{heater}$ represents the heat flow from the heater into the room, $Mdot$ the air mass flow rate through the heater (kg/hr), C the heat capacity of air at constant pressure, and T_{heater}, T_{room} correspond to `Theater` and `Troom` respectively. The output `HeaterFlow` will serve as an input to both the integrator block and the House subsystem, as shown in Fig. 2.

House Subsystem. The House subsystem controls the indoor temperature of the house, as depicted in Fig. 3c. The input `In` receives the heat flow generated by the Heater, and `Tout` inputs the outdoor temperature. It calculates the final indoor temperature based on the inputs using the following equations:

$$(\frac{dQ}{dt})_{losses} = \frac{T_{room} - T_{outdoor}}{R_{eq}}$$

$$\dot{T}_{room} = \frac{1}{M * C} * ((\frac{dQ}{dt})_{heater} - (\frac{dQ}{dt})_{losses})$$

where, $T_{outdoor}$ represents the outdoor temperature `Tout`, T_{room} and C defined as above, R_{eq} the equivalent thermal resistance of the house, M the mass of air inside the house. As shown in the equations, $(\frac{dQ}{dt})_{losses}$ represents the loss rate of the heat in the environment, which is determined by the difference between the actual room temperature and the outdoor temperature, divided by the house thermal resistance. $\dot{T}_{room}$, the final gained heat rate of the room, also the derivative of the room temperature with respect to time, is the difference between the heat flow rate and the loss rate, divided by $M * C$. A loop is formed as the room temperature is also taken as an input of the Lossin block to calculate the loss rate of the heat. In S/S, the diagrams with algebraic loops are considered invalid, while the blocks which maintain internal states such as Integrator or Unit Delay blocks can break the loop. So with existence of the integrator block for `Troom` in House subsystem, the loop in this subsystem and also the main loop in the top diagram (due to the backward transition from House to previous parts) are both valid. Notice that different from $\dot{T}_{room}$, both $(\frac{dQ}{dt})_{losses}$ and $(\frac{dQ}{dt})_{heater}$ are named in the form of differential equations for ease of understanding their meanings and the relations between each other, without actual differential operations.

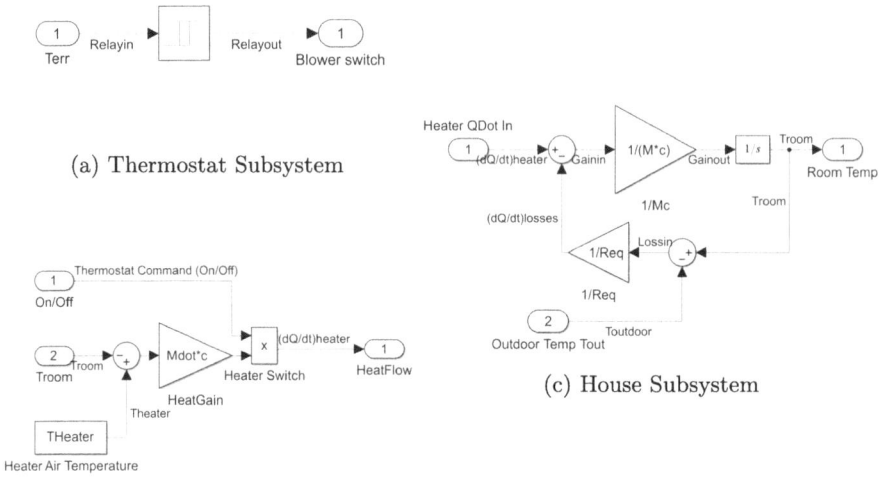

(a) Thermostat Subsystem

(b) Heater Subsystem

(c) House Subsystem

Fig. 3. The Subsystems

4   Formal Design of ITCS

In this section, we show how to conduct formal design of ITCS starting from the built graphical model, including constructing its formal model represented by HCSP, its simulation based on the HCSP model, verification of the HCSP model, and code generation from the verified HCSP model.

4.1   Translation to HCSP Model

We first apply the toolchain MARS to transform the S/S model of ITCS to HCSP formal model. Taking the S/S model presented in Fig. 2 in .xml format as input, the tool generates the HCSP model as shown in Fig. 4, which is to be served as the foundation for subsequent simulation and verification of ITCS. The generated HCSP model is a system from the overall structure, which contains one module transformed from the S/S model.

Before introducing the HCSP model, we briefly explain the strategy of MARS for transforming a S/S model. It first determines the sample times of all blocks, including the ones inside subsystems, based on which each block is classified as either discrete or continuous; then separates the whole diagram into discrete and continuous parts; finally, transforms the discrete and continuous parts individually first and then put them together in correct execution order to form the whole HCSP model of the S/S diagram. The complexity of the transformation is $O(n^2)$ where n denotes the number of blocks in source models due to the sorting procedure in correct execution order. The generated HCSP model for a given S/S diagram $\mathcal{D}$ has the following structure:

$$HCSP(\mathcal{D}) \,\hat{=}\, \text{Output; Init;}$$
$$\left(\text{Discrete;}\ \langle \dot{t} = 1, \dot{\mathbf{y}} = \Gamma(\mathbf{x}) \& t < period \rangle; \text{TimeUpdate;}\right)^{*} \quad (1)$$

It starts from Output, which is a sequence of assignments to the outputs of $\mathcal{D}$ by their respective values, followed by the initialisation of variables and then a repetition process. Init initializes some variables including internal state variables, the outputs of integrators and discrete constant blocks, and the auxiliary time variables introduced for managing the execution time of the whole model. Discrete represents the transformed process of discrete blocks of $\mathcal{D}$, and $\dot{\mathbf{y}} = \Gamma(\mathbf{x})$ is the combined vector of the ODEs for all integrator blocks after variable substitution corresponding to other non-integrator continuous blocks; TimeUpdate defines the update of the auxiliary time variables after each loop. The loop period $period$, constraining the domain of the ODEs, is the great common divisor of sample times of all discrete blocks of $\mathcal{D}$.

```
1  module P():
2  output HeatCost = Costin * cost,
       Temperatures = [9 / 5 *
       HouseTemp + 32, 50 + 15 *
       sin(0.262 * t)];
3  begin
4      t := 0;
5      _tick := 0;
6      F2Cin := 70;
7      Thermostat_sub_Relay1_state := 0;
8      tt := 0;
9      Costin := 0;
10     HouseTemp := 20;
11     {
12         F2Cout := 5 / 9 * (70 - 32);
13         Terr := F2Cout - HouseTemp;
14         blowercmd := (if Terr > 5*(5/9)
                 then 1 else (if Terr <
                 -5*(5/9) then 0 else
                 Thermostat_sub_Relay1_state))
15         Thermostat_sub_Relay1_state :=
                 blowercmd;
16         {tt_dot = 1, Costin_dot =
                 blowercmd * ((-HouseTemp +
                 50) * (Mdot * c)),
                 HouseTemp_dot = (blowercmd *
                 ((-HouseTemp + 50) * (Mdot *
                 c)) - (HouseTemp - 5 / 9 *
                 (50 + 15 * sin(0.262 * t) -
                 32)) * (1 / Req)) * (1 / (M
                 * c)) & tt < 0.001}
17         t := t + tt;
18         _tick := _tick + 1;
19         tt := 0;
20     }*
21 end endmodule
22 system P=P() endsystem
```

Fig. 4. The HCSP Model of ITCS

As presented in Fig. 4, the output list (Line 1) includes *HeatCost* representing the cost of heat, and the joint *Temperatures* for the indoor and outdoor temperatures, that correspond to the outputs of the S/S model. Each of the outputs is assigned to their respective values. The main body (Lines 4–20) implements the whole S/S diagram. It starts from the initialisation of a sequence of variables, among which *Costin* and *HouseTemp* are the outputs of two integrator blocks, *F2Cin* the output of a discrete constant block, *Thermostat_sub_Relay1_state* the internal state of Relay block, and *tt*, *t*, *_tick* the auxiliary time variables, then followed by a repetition process. At each round of the repetition, first the discrete blocks of the case study are executed in a correct order, then the two ODEs defining the derivatives of *Costin* and *HouseTemp*, plus the one with *tt* recording the execution time of each round, are put together to constitute the transformed process of the continuous part. Notice that variable substitution is performed on the right hand sides of each ODE, by replacing recursively the outputs of each non-integrator continuous block as functions of its inputs, till the equations only contain ODE variables and variables from the separate discrete part, e.g. *blowercmd* and *HouseTemp* occurring in the ODEs. Here 0.001 is the period of the whole diagram, and variables t and $\_tick$ represent the accumulated execution time and the number of execution loops respectively.

Notice that the equation of *HouseTemp* depends on the value of *blowercmd*, which is either 0 or 1, the output of Thermostat subsystem. We will consider the two different cases separately in the verification of ITCS.

4.2   Simulation

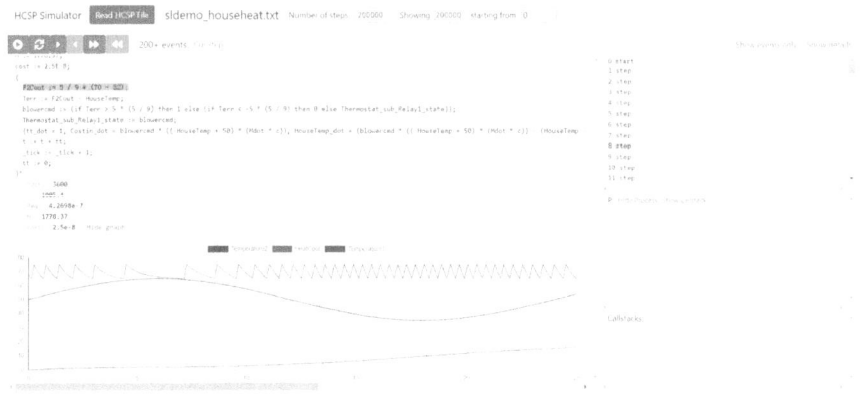

Fig. 5. Simulator interface after importing the HCSP model

MARS guarantees that the generated HCSP model and the corresponding source S/S diagram are consistent by formally defining their semantics and building the equivalence between them [28]. But for visualizing the behavior of the generated HCSP model, we also utilize HCSP simulator integrated in MARS to analyze the generated HCSP model, which reflects the behavior of the source S/S model as expected. HCSP simulator is designed to calculate the execution paths of HCSP processes and visualize them in the graphical interface. As shown in Fig. 5, the left "Read HCSP file" button is used to load the input HCSP models, and on the right, the number of simulation steps, starting position, and ending position can be set. On the left side of the interface, the loaded HCSP process is displayed, with the current executed statement highlighted, and below it, the values of process variables changing over time are displayed; On the right, the trace of all events produced during the execution is shown, including discrete steps, time progress or communication events.

Figure 5 shows the simulation result of the HCSP model of ITCS, by setting the step size to 0.001 s and number of steps to 200,000 respectively. Through the result, we can check whether its behavior aligns with expectation. On the left bottom of Fig. 5, the lines from top to bottom represent the indoor temperature change, the outdoor temperature change, and the cost incurred after the heater is turned on, respectively. The changes and fluctuations of the three curves conform to the design requirement, especially, the house temperature is always within a safe range, to be given in detail in the following verification part.

4.3   Verification

To remedy incomplete simulation, the verification of the HCSP model is needed to guarantee the design requirement strictly. In MARS, this is achieved by HHL Prover through a Hoare-logic style deductive verification method [11,31]. HHL Prover contains three parts: HHLPy [20] for deductive verification of sequential HCSP processes covering ODEs, achieving automation of verification through the annotation of differential and loop invariants and the integration with SMT solvers for solving logical formulas; the interactive Isabelle prover, that is implemented for the whole HCSP with concurrency and communication, conducting proof of HCSP specifications with pre-/post-conditions by manually choosing corresponding inference rules; and the invariant generation, which synthesizes differential invariants for reasoning about ODEs through template-based methods [12,19], to be employed for the former two provers if necessary.

This case study demonstrates the procedure for verifying a safety specification: "if the initial house temperature is within the range of $165/9\,°C$ to $215/9\,°C$, it will always remain between $145/9\,°C$ and $235/9\,°C$ (i.e. *the safe range*)". For simplicity, the initial system state is defined by the region $165/9 \leq T \leq 215/9$, while the unsafe region is $T \leq 145/9 \vee 235/9 \leq T$, where T stands for *House Temp*. Our objective is to verify that all system trajectories originating from the initial region will never enter the unsafe region.

For continuous-time systems, the most challenging part of Hoare-style reasoning is the synthesis of differential invariants. A differential invariant is a set of states Ω satisfying the following three conditions: (1) the initial region is contained in Ω (*Initial Condition*); (2) the unsafe region and Ω are disjoint (*Saturation Condition*); (3) Ω keeps continuous (differential) inductiveness, i.e., all trajectories starting from Ω remain within Ω (*Differential Inductive Condition*). In the following, we adopt a template-based approach for synthesizing a desired differential invariant. Please refer to [12,19,22,25] for more detailed introduction.

Step 1: Simplifying System. From the HCSP model, we see that the system consists of two modes, depending on whether *blowercmd* is 1 or 0, where the dynamics of the temperature are described by

$$\dot{T} = -3.334 \cdot T + 10.916 \cdot \sin(0.262t) + 114.315, \qquad \text{(mode 1)}$$

and

$$\dot{T} = -1.310 \cdot T + 10.916 \cdot \sin(0.262t) + 13.099, \qquad \text{(mode 2)}$$

respectively. The system will switch to mode 1 when $T < 165/9$, and switch to mode 2 when $T > 215/9$.

Note that the above expressions contain a trigonometric function, which will be difficult to reason about. To address this issue, inspired by [13], two fresh variables v and u are introduced to represent $\sin(0.262t)$ and $\cos(0.262t)$. Then, both mode 1 and mode 2 can be transformed to a 3-dimensional system in variables (T, v, u) with polynomial dynamics as follows:

$$\begin{pmatrix} \dot{T} \\ \dot{v} \\ \dot{u} \end{pmatrix} = \begin{pmatrix} -3.334 \cdot T + 10.916 \cdot v + 114.315 \\ 0.262 \cdot u \\ -0.262 \cdot v \end{pmatrix}, \qquad \text{(mode 1')}$$

and

$$\begin{pmatrix} \dot{T} \\ \dot{v} \\ \dot{u} \end{pmatrix} = \begin{pmatrix} -1.310 \cdot T + 10.916 \cdot v + 13.099 \\ 0.262 \cdot u \\ -0.262 \cdot v \end{pmatrix}. \qquad \text{(mode 2')}$$

Note that the derivative $\dot{v}$ is obtained by $\dot{v} = \frac{d\sin(0.262t)}{dt} = 0.262\cos(0.262t) = 0.262u$. The computation of $\dot{u}$ is similar. Moreover, we add a new constraint $u^2 + v^2 = 1$ as a state space constraint because $\sin^2(x) + \cos^2(x) = 1$.

Step 2: Setting Templates. Template-based synthesis leverages parameterization. A parameterized template for the target differential invariant is predefined, and constraints are formulated based on the definition of differential invariants. Satisfying these constraints yields the desired differential invariant.

For continuous-time systems, *barrier certificates* [19] are commonly employed for synthesizing differential invariants more efficiently. A barrier certificate is a continuously differentiable function Φ in system variables such that $\Phi \leq 0$ constitutes a differential invariant. For computability, barrier certificates are typically set to be polynomial functions.

Given our system's two polynomial subsystems, mode 1' and mode 2', we introduce two polynomial barrier certificates, Φ_1 and Φ_2, respectively. Each Φ_i is a parameterized polynomial of a user-specified degree d in variable T, v, u of the following form

$$\Phi_i = \sum_{\alpha_1+\alpha_2+\alpha_3 \leq d} c_{i,\alpha_1,\alpha_2,\alpha_3} T^{\alpha_1} v^{\alpha_2} u^{\alpha_3} \quad \text{for } i = 1, 2, \qquad (2)$$

where $\alpha_1, \alpha_2, \alpha_3 \in \mathbb{N}$ are exponents and $c_{i,\alpha_1,\alpha_2,\alpha_3}$ are unknown real coefficients.

Step 3: Solving Constraints. Similar to [9, Theorem 2], the constraints for Φ_1 and Φ_2 are given as follows, for $i = 1, 2$,

$$\forall(T, v, u).\ 165/9 \leq T \leq 215/9 \wedge u^2 + v^2 = 1 \implies \Phi_i(T, v, u) \leq 0, \tag{3}$$

$$\forall(T, v, u).\ (T < 145/9 \vee T > 235/9) \wedge u^2 + v^2 = 1 \implies \Phi_i(T, v, u) > 0, \tag{4}$$

$$\forall(T, v, u).\ u^2 + v^2 = 1 \implies \mathcal{L}_{f_i}\Phi_i(T, v, u) \leq \lambda_i\Phi_i(T, v, u), \tag{5}$$

$$\forall(T, v, u).\ u^2 + v^2 = 1 \implies \Phi_{3-i}(T, v, u) \leq \mu_i\Phi_i(T, v, u), \tag{6}$$

where λ_i is any real number, μ_i is any non-negative real number, and $\mathcal{L}_{f_i}(\Phi_i) = \langle \nabla\Phi_i, f_i \rangle$ is the Lie derivative of function Φ_i w.r.t. f_i (here, ∇ is the gradient notation and $\langle \cdot, \cdot \rangle$ is the dot product). Intuitively, constraint (3) ensures the initial region is contained within the region defined by $\Phi_i(T, v, u) \leq 0$, while (4) guarantees exclusion of the unsafe region from this region. Constraint (5) establishes that $\Phi_i(T, v, u) \leq 0$ is a differential invariant, ensuring mode i's safety. Finally, (6) maintains safety during mode switches. In our experiments, we set $\lambda_1 = \lambda_2 = -1$, $\mu_1 = \mu_2 = 10$, and the degree of barrier certificate templates to be 2.

To solve these constraints, we employ sum-of-squares optimization techniques to transform them into a hierarchy of semidefinite programming (SDP) relaxations, as detailed in [9,22,25]. In our experiments, we formulate the SDP constraints using JULIA package TSSOS [21] and solve them using the MOSEK solver [16]. We obtain the following solutions for Φ_1 and Φ_2:

$$\begin{aligned}
\Phi_1 = {}& 0.00553 \cdot T^2 - 0.00536 \cdot T \cdot v + 0.00014 \cdot T \cdot u + 0.69343 \cdot v^2 - 0.00037 \cdot v \cdot u \\
& + 0.68972 \cdot u^2 - 0.22240 \cdot T + 0.11975 \cdot v - 0.00345 \cdot u + 1.38315, \\
\Phi_2 = {}& -0.00278 \cdot T^2 - 0.00949 \cdot T \cdot v - 0.15400 \cdot v^2 - 0.00242 \cdot v \cdot u \\
& - 0.15705 \cdot u^2 + 0.07491 \cdot T + 0.15363 \cdot v - 0.00146 \cdot u - 0.31105.
\end{aligned}$$

The above synthesized invariants ensure the design requirement.

Currently, the differential invariant generation procedure for HCSP is not fully automated, as it often requires manual template refinement. Once a suitable differential invariant is found, it can be used in HHLPy or Isabelle provers of HCSP for further verification. But for this case study, the synthesized invariants ensure the design requirement directly, thus no further verification is needed.

4.4   Code Generation

The MARS toolchain supports the automatic code generation from HCSP model to C, with correctness guarantee, i.e. the generated C code and the source HCSP model are proved to satisfy the approximate bisimulation relation between their reachable states with given precision allowed in ODE discretization [24]. As a result, the safety properties (that can be considered as sets of system states) proved for the HCSP model are preserved for the generated code with tolerance of given precision. No more verification needs to be re-done at the code level.

For this case study, given any precision $\epsilon > 0$ allowed by the house temperature, our tool can generate the C code that is guaranteed to be approximate bisimilar with the HCSP model thus the original S/S model satisfies the given design requirement that the house temperature is always within the safe range with ϵ tolerance, i.e. $(145/9\,°C\text{-}\epsilon, 235/9\,°C\text{+}\epsilon)$.

By using MARS, the C code for ITCS is generated, part of which is presented in Fig. 6. The whole C implementation of ITCS consists of 97 lines, that is significantly less than the code automatically generated from S/S (to be shown later). Figure 6 presents the discretization code corresponding to the ODE part (Line 16 of Fig. 4), where h is the discretized step with respect to given precision. The ODEs of tt, $Costin$, $HouseTemp$ are discretized using Runge-Kutta method, implemented by a while loop: a sequence of discrete assignments on calculating the approximate values of continuous variables is performed in each loop, and when the boundary of the ODEs is reached, the loop breaks. The system's running results can be observed by executing the generated C code. Among the results in Fig. 8, we can see that the execution results of the generated C code from HCSP are almost identical to the ones of the HCSP model.

```
1  while (1) {                                11  ... ...
2      double tt_ori = tt;                     12  tt = tt_ori + (tt_dot1 + 2 *
3      double Costin_ori = Costin;                 tt_dot2 + 2 * tt_dot3 +
4      double HouseTemp_ori = HouseTemp;           tt_dot4) * h / 6;
5      double tt_dot1 = 1;                     13  Costin = Costin_ori +
6      double Costin_dot1 = blowercmd *            (Costin_dot1 + 2 *
           ((-HouseTemp + 50) * (Mdot *            Costin_dot2 + 2 *
           c));                                     Costin_dot3 + Costin_dot4) *
7      double HouseTemp_dot1 =                       h / 6;
           (blowercmd * ((-HouseTemp +    14  HouseTemp = HouseTemp_ori +
           50) * (Mdot * c)) -                     (HouseTemp_dot1 + 2 *
           (HouseTemp - 5 / 9 * (50 +             HouseTemp_dot2 + 2 *
           15 * sin(0.262 * t) - 32)) *           HouseTemp_dot3 +
           (1 / Req)) * (1 / (M * c));            HouseTemp_dot4) * h / 6;
8      tt = tt_ori + tt_dot1 * h / 2;          15  delay(threadNumber, h);
9      Costin = Costin_ori +                   16  if (!(tt < 0.001)) {
           Costin_dot1 * h / 2;               17      break;
10     HouseTemp = HouseTemp_ori +            18  }
           HouseTemp_dot1 * h / 2;            19  }
```

Fig. 6. Part of the C code generated from MARS

```
1  void ODEUpdateStates(SolverInfo *si)   11    house_initialize();
2  {/* the solver specified*/}            12    while ((rtmGetErrorStatus(house)
3  void house_step()                            == (NULL)) &&
4  { ...                              13        !rtmGetStopRequested(house))
5    if (IsMajorTimeStep(house)) {                {
6      ODEUpdateStates(&house->solver);  14      house_step();
7    ... ...                           15    }
8  }                                    16    house_terminate();
9  void main()                          17    ...
10 { ...                                18  }
```

Fig. 7. Part of the C code generated from Simulink

We also use S/S to generate the C code of ITCS, which amounts to 382 lines in total and is partly shown in Fig. 7. It includes the functions for updating continuous states with the specified solver for ODEs, the step function for executing the whole model, and the main function that initializes, steps in a while loop, and terminates the execution in sequence. The reason for the lengthy code from S/S includes: on one hand, the HCSP model transformed from the S/S diagram combines all the blocks of each connected part of the diagram with integrator blocks into one ODE vector, through variable substitution by hiding all outputs of intermediate non-integrator blocks, and as a result, the C code generated from the HCSP model will not include the local assignments corresponding to these blocks; On the other hand, S/S Coder needs to do settings related to ODE solver types, data logging, *etc.* for each S/S instance, while in our tool, all these settings are determined, which indeed lacks feasibility for some extreme cases, but promotes efficiency for normal cases that can be handled using the general ODE solver based on Runge-Kutta method. We will give a more comparison in next section. Figure 8 presents the comparison of execution results of the C code generated from HCSP model and S/S, the HCSP model and the original S/S model respectively. We can see that all of them are mostly consistent, except for some small fluctuations.

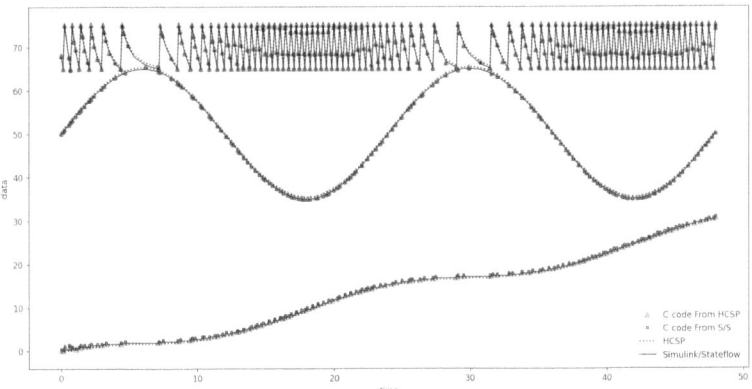

Fig. 8. Comparison of the execution results

5   Comparison with S/S

We compare our approach with S/S from three aspects throughout model-based development of systems: modeling and analysis, verification, code generation.

Modeling and Analysis. Based on a rich set of individually simple blocks and their hierarchical composition, S/S offers a powerful graphical modeling language for building embedded systems. Especially, it is capable of modeling dynamic systems involved with continuous physical plants and complex control logics. S/S does not have an official formal semantics, and instead, system analysis and design validation within S/S are based on numerical simulation, which provides a variety of ODE solvers especially the varying-step ones for solving ODEs with both efficiency and accuracy. MARS reuses S/S for the graphical modeling of software functionality and continuous plants of systems, and to remedy S/S, it further integrates AADL for the modeling of architectures [27]. MARS also provides HCSP language for the formal modeling of hybrid systems, with formal semantics defined, and supports the transformation from S/S diagrams to HCSP formal models. The transformation covers a subset of S/S graphical syntax related to the design of hybrid systems, which is also the focus of HCSP, and the correctness of the transformation is guaranteed by defining both the formal semantics of S/S and HCSP and proving their bisimulation between each other. MARS implements a HCSP simulator that invokes Python's Scipy package to have fixed-step solvers for solving ODEs.

Verification. Formal verification is necessary in the development process of safety-critical systems. S/S has a well integrated commercial verification toolset called Simulink Design Verifier (SLDV) [14], which offers static analysis and discrete-time verification of S/S models with a high degree of automation. However, same as Simulink, the verifier does not have a formal specification language with formal semantics, and instead, it represents the property to be proved also as a S/S model. As a result, the result of SLDV cannot guarantee soundness. In [17], the authors use SLDV to formally verify an automotive Simulink controller model and detect some bugs of SLDV. MARS reduces the verification of S/S models to the verification of the transformed HCSP formal model, due to the consistency guarantee of the transformation from S/S to HCSP. As shown in Fig. 1, MARS integrates HCSP verification tools based on a sound hybrid Hoare logic for reasoning about HCSP, implemented via interactive and automated theorem proving. Furthermore, it is able to reason about continuous time behavior of HCSP models involved with ODEs based on differential invariant generation. Due to the complexity of hybrid systems, the verification of HCSP related to invariant synthesis, communications and parallel composition, needs to be done manually, but its soundness and capability of handling these behaviors are very important for designing safety-critical control systems.

Code Generatation. In the previous section, we have already made some comparison between S/S and our approach for code generation of the case study. S/S has an integrated code generator, which is well developed and applied to many scalable practical embedded systems. However, the auto-generated C code may differ from the behavior of the original S/S model due to the lack of formal semantics, or potential bugs in the translation procedure from S/S to C. Thus, the code generated from S/S needs further verification for the safety. In [3], the authors perform formal verification of C code that is automatically generated from S/S controller models and find errors that are not inconsistent with the design requirement. Although these errors are found to exist as well for the original S/S model, it does not mean that the translation is correct, and in contrary, it shows the consequence of the original S/S lacking formal semantics and verification. In our tool, we implement a formally verified code generator from HCSP to C, which solves the above problem, but honestly, it is challenging for our tool to be applied for the development of large scale systems (mostly due to the verification intrinsic difficulty of complex systems).

6   Conclusion

In this paper, we show how to design an intelligent temperature control system with MARS. It consists of a S/S graphical model, a HCSP formal model transformed from the graphical model, the simulation and verification of the HCSP model, and the C code automatically generated from the verified HCSP formal model. Compared with the development of the system with S/S, the advantages of the design of CPS with MARS include: i) the correctness and reliability of the generated C code; ii) integration of modeling, simulation, verification and code generation, as well as integration of formal and informal design for CPS.

Acknowledgements. This work has been partially funded by the National Key R&D Program of China under grant No. 2022YFA1005100, 2022YFA1005101, and 2022YFA1005104, by the NSFC under grant No. 62192732 and 62032024, the CAS Project for Young Scientists in Basic Research under grant No. YSBR-040, and the Major Project of ISCAS (ISCAS-ZD-202302).

References

1. Alur, R., Courcoubetis, C., Henzinger, T.A., Ho, P.-H.: Hybrid automata: an algorithmic approach to the specification and verification of hybrid systems. In: Grossman, R.L., Nerode, A., Ravn, A.P., Rischel, H. (eds.) HS 1991-1992. LNCS, vol. 736, pp. 209–229. Springer, Heidelberg (1993). https://doi.org/10.1007/3-540-57318-6_30
2. Ansys Inc.: Esterel Technologies, SCADE Suite (2018). http://www.esterel-technologies.com/products/scade
3. Berger, P., Katoen, J.-P., Ábrahám, E., Waez, M.T.B., Rambow, T.: Verifying auto-generated C code from Simulink. In: Havelund, K., Peleska, J., Roscoe, B., de Vink, E. (eds.) FM 2018. LNCS, vol. 10951, pp. 312–328. Springer, Cham (2018). https://doi.org/10.1007/978-3-319-95582-7_18
4. Chen, X., Sankaranarayanan, S., Ábrahám, E.: Under-approximate flowpipes for non-linear continuous systems. In: FMCAD 2014, pp. 59–66 (2014)
5. Feiler, P., Gluch, D.: Model-Based Engineering with AADL: An Introduction to the SAE Architecture Analysis & Design Language. Addison-Wesley (2012)
6. Frehse, G., et al.: SpaceEx: scalable verification of hybrid systems. In: Gopalakrishnan, G., Qadeer, S. (eds.) CAV 2011. LNCS, vol. 6806, pp. 379–395. Springer, Heidelberg (2011). https://doi.org/10.1007/978-3-642-22110-1_30
7. He, J.: From CSP to hybrid systems. In: A Classical Mind, pp. 171–189. Prentice Hall International (UK) Ltd. (1994)

8. Henzinger, T.A.: The theory of hybrid automata. In: LICS 1996, pp. 278–292. IEEE Computer Society (1996)

9. Kong, H., He, F., Song, X., Hung, W.N.N., Gu, M.: Exponential-condition-based barrier certificate generation for safety verification of hybrid systems. In: Sharygina, N., Veith, H. (eds.) CAV 2013. LNCS, vol. 8044, pp. 242–257. Springer, Heidelberg (2013). https://doi.org/10.1007/978-3-642-39799-8_17

10. Kong, S., Gao, S., Chen, W., Clarke, E.: dReach: σ-reachability analysis for hybrid systems. In: Baier, C., Tinelli, C. (eds.) TACAS 2015. LNCS, vol. 9035, pp. 200–205. Springer, Heidelberg (2015). https://doi.org/10.1007/978-3-662-46681-0_15

11. Liu, J., et al.: A calculus for hybrid CSP. In: Ueda, K. (ed.) APLAS 2010. LNCS, vol. 6461, pp. 1–15. Springer, Heidelberg (2010). https://doi.org/10.1007/978-3-642-17164-2_1

12. Liu, J., Zhan, N., Zhao, H.: Computing semi-algebraic invariants for polynomial dynamical systems. In: EMSOFT 2011, pp. 97–106 (2011)

13. Liu, J., Zhan, N., Zhao, H., Zou, L.: Abstraction of elementary hybrid systems by variable transformation. In: Bjørner, N., de Boer, F. (eds.) FM 2015. LNCS, vol. 9109, pp. 360–377. Springer, Cham (2015). https://doi.org/10.1007/978-3-319-19249-9_23

14. MathWorks Inc.: Simulink Design Verifier – User's guide. https://de.mathworks.com/help/pdf_doc/sldv/sldv_ug.pdf

15. MathWorks Inc.: Simulink User's Guide (2013). http://www.mathworks.com/help/pdf_doc/simulink/sl_using.pdf

16. MOSEK ApS: MOSEK Optimizer API for Julia. Version 10.1.13 (2019). https://docs.mosek.com/latest/juliaapi/index.html

17. Nellen, J., Rambow, T., Waez, M.T.B., Ábrahám, E., Katoen, J.-P.: Formal verification of automotive Simulink controller models: empirical technical challenges, evaluation and recommendations. In: Havelund, K., Peleska, J., Roscoe, B., de Vink, E. (eds.) FM 2018. LNCS, vol. 10951, pp. 382–398. Springer, Cham (2018). https://doi.org/10.1007/978-3-319-95582-7_23

18. Platzer, A.: Differential dynamic logic for hybrid systems. J. Autom. Reason. **41**(2), 143–189 (2008)

19. Prajna, S., Jadbabaie, A.: Safety verification of hybrid systems using barrier certificates. In: Alur, R., Pappas, G.J. (eds.) HSCC 2004. LNCS, vol. 2993, pp. 477–492. Springer, Heidelberg (2004). https://doi.org/10.1007/978-3-540-24743-2_32

20. Sheng, H., Bentkamp, A., Zhan, B.: HHLPy: practical verification of hybrid systems using Hoare logic. In: Chechik, M., Katoen, J.P., Leucker, M. (eds.) FM 2023. LNCS, vol. 14000, pp. 160–178. Springer, Cham (2023). https://doi.org/10.1007/978-3-031-27481-7_11

21. Wang, J., Magron, V., Lasserre, J.: TSSOS: a moment-SOS hierarchy that exploits term sparsity. SIAM J. Optim. **31**(1), 30–58 (2021)

22. Wang, Q., Chen, M., Xue, B., Zhan, N., Katoen, J.: Encoding inductive invariants as barrier certificates: synthesis via difference-of-convex programming. Inf. Comput. **289**(Part), 104965 (2022)

23. Wang, S., Zhan, N., Zou, L.: An improved HHL prover: an interactive theorem prover for hybrid systems. In: Butler, M., Conchon, S., Zaïdi, F. (eds.) ICFEM 2015. LNCS, vol. 9407, pp. 382–399. Springer, Cham (2015). https://doi.org/10.1007/978-3-319-25423-4_25

24. Wang, S., Ji, Z., Xu, X., Zhan, B., Gao, Q., Zhan, N.: Formally verified C code generation from hybrid communicating sequential processes. In: ICCPS 2024, pp. 123–134. IEEE (2024)

25. Wu, H., Feng, S., Gan, T., Wang, J., Xia, B., Zhan, N.: On completeness of SDP-based barrier certificate synthesis over unbounded domains. In: Platzer, A., Rozier, K.Y., Pradella, M., Rossi, M. (eds.) FM 2024. LNCS, vol. 14934, pp. 248–266. Springer, Cham (2024). https://doi.org/10.1007/978-3-031-71177-0_16

26. Xu, X., Talpin, J., Wang, S., Zhan, B., Zhan, N.: Semantics foundation for cyber-physical systems using higher-order UTP. ACM Trans. Softw. Eng. Methodol. **32**(1), 9:1–9:48 (2023)

27. Xu, X., Wang, S., Zhan, B., Jin, X., Talpin, J., Zhan, N.: Unified graphical co-modeling, analysis and verification of cyber-physical systems by combining AADL and Simulink/Stateflow. Theor. Comput. Sci. **903**, 1–25 (2022)

28. Xu, X., Zhan, B., Wang, S., Talpin, J.P., Zhan, N.: A denotational semantics of Simulink with higher-order UTP. J. Log. Algebraic Methods Program. **130**, 100809 (2023)

29. Yan, G., Jiao, L., Wang, S., Wang, L., Zhan, N.: Automatically generating SystemC code from HCSP formal models. ACM TOSEM **29**(1), 4:1–4:39 (2020)

30. Zhan, B., et al.: Mars 2.0: a toolchain for modeling, analysis, verification and code generation of cyber-physical systems. arXiv abs/2403.03035 (2024)

31. Zhan, N., Zhan, B., Wang, S., Guelev, D.P., Jin, X.: A generalized hybrid Hoare logic. CoRR abs/2303.15020 (2023)

Universal Construction for Linearizable but Not Strongly Linearizable Concurrent Objects

Chao Wang[1]([⊠]), Peng Wu[2,5], Gustavo Petri[3], Qiaowen Jia[4], Youlin He[1], Yi Lv[2,5], and Zhiming Liu[1]

[1] Centre for Research and Innovation in Software Engineering, College of Computer and Information Science, Southwest University, Chongqing, China
`wangch1@swu.edu.cn`
[2] Key Laboratory of System Software (Chinese Academy of Sciences) and State Key Laboratory of Computer Science, Institute of Software, Chinese Academy of Sciences, Beijing, China
[3] Arm Research, Cambridge, UK
[4] China Great Wall Technology Group Co., Ltd., Shenzhen, China
[5] University of Chinese Academy of Sciences, Beijing, China

Abstract. Strong linearizability is a variant of linearizability and is more suitable for verification. In this paper we investigate the following two problems: (1) for which deterministic sequential specifications there exist linearizable but not strongly linearizable objects; (2) can we capture any violation scheme of strong linearizability for practical objects that are linearizable but not strongly linearizable.

To deal with the first problem, we propose two classes of deterministic sequential specifications called inclusively-permutative sequential specifications and exclusively-permutative sequential specifications. The first class of sequential specifications contains sequential specifications of counter, register, max-register, snapshot, set, queue, stack and priority queue. The second class of sequential specifications contains sequential specifications of blocking queue, blocking stack and blocking priority queue. To establish these results, we propose a uniform methodology to construct a wait-free, linearizable but not strongly linearizable object for these two classes of sequential specifications. Our universal construction is based on the classical universal construction, and it additionally permits each operation to change the "take-effect-order" of previous operations.

To deal with the second problem, we use bi-branch distinguishable executions to represent violations of strong linearizability. We investigate eight objects that are linearizable but not strongly linearizable, and we show that for each object, it has a pair of bi-branch distinguishable executions such that our universal construction can generate another pair of bi-branch distinguishable executions with the same set of histories.

T. Bourke et al. (Eds.): SETTA 2024, LNCS 15469, pp. 236–255, 2025.
https://doi.org/10.1007/978-981-96-0602-3_13

1   Introduction

Linearizability [1] is a *de facto* correctness criterion for concurrent objects. However, it is not suitable for randomized algorithms, because Golab et al. [2] have shown that their probability distributions may still vary when atomic objects are replaced with linearizable ones. This may incur potential vulnerabilities, and hence the notion of strong linearizability is presented in [2], as an extension of linearizability, to characterize such stronger criterion. Intuitively, strong linearizability requires that any execution can be interpreted incrementally, by associating each time point of the execution with a unique and fixed abstract state.

Filipovic et al. [3] proved that linearizability is equivalent to observational refinement. Verification of observational refinement in general requires to establish a forward simulation and a backward simulation [4]. Backward reasoning requires using prophecy variables and is in general complex. Compared to the verification of linearizability, the verification of strong linearizability is much more clear, since Rady et al. [5] proved that strong linearizability is equivalent to the existence of a forward simulation towards an atomic implementation.

Theoretically, according to the classical universal construction of Herlihy et al. in [6], it is well known that there is a wait-free and linearizable object for any deterministic sequential specification, and it is known that the objects generated by classical universal construction are strongly linearizable [7]. Practically, if the linearization points (the time point when an operation "takes effect") is fixed, such objects are strongly linearizable. However, many high performance objects are optimized to avoid contention and their linearization points are not fixed. Ad hoc objects such as MS queue [8] and Harris's linked list [9] have been proved to be not strongly linearizable [7]. A natural problem is, whether the existence of linearizable but not strongly linearizable objects is prevalent. In this paper, we present a systematic study to address this problem. Our investigation focus on searching for sequential specifications, for which there exist linearizable but not strongly linearizable objects, and we also intend to find typical schemes of how practical objects violate strong linearizability.

According to Rady et al. [5], each configuration of a strongly linearizable object can be related to a unique abstract state of its sequential specification via a forward simulation relation. To generate an object that is not strongly linearizable for a given sequential specification, one possible approach is to make some configurations of the object able to correspond to more than one abstract state with conflicts.Based on this idea we propose a universal construction $\mathcal{U}_{Spec}$ of a wait-free and linearizable object for sequential specification *Spec*, with intention of exposing behaviors that are not strongly linearizable. Our universal construction is inspired by the classical universal construction of a wait-free and linearizable object in [6]. As in [6], $\mathcal{U}_{Spec}$ maintains a linked list of nodes, and each operation will insert a node containing its method name and argument into the linked list. $\mathcal{U}_{Spec}$ uses the helping mechanism of [6] to ensure that each node be inserted into linked list in finite number of steps and is thus wait-free. In the classical universal construction, to obtain a return value, an operation requires to access the nodes of the inner linked list in a fixed order to ensure linearizability (essentially strong linearizability). To make a configuration of $\mathcal{U}_{Spec}$ able to correspond to more than one abstract state, we store the current history (at the time point when this operation is called) of each operation in its node, and permit each operation to select a linearization l for the longest history among the history of this node and the histories of the previous nodes in the linked list, as long as the return value of each operation in the previous nodes of the linked list and the return value of the same operation in l are the same. $\mathcal{U}_{Spec}$ is still linearizable since for each operation, l is a linearization for a history at some time point between its call and return actions.

A configuration of $\mathcal{U}_{Spec}$ can correspond to more than one abstract state, while each abstract state is obtained via a linearization, which can be considered a "permutation" of operations stored in the linked list. In this permutation, the operation of the current node (the last node of the linked list) can return a different value, while the return values of the operations in the previous nodes of the linked list are kept unchanged. To expose non-strongly linearizable behaviors due to different "permutations" of $\mathcal{U}_{Spec}$, we propose two classes of sequential specifications, and both classes are based on permutations of operations. The first class of specifications is called inclusively-permutative specifications. It requires that the last operation of the linked list should return a different value in certain permutation where this operation is not at the last place. The sequential specifications of counter, register, max-register, snapshot, set, queue, stack and priority queue belong to inclusively-permutative specifications. The second class of specifications is called exclusively-permutative specifications. It requires that the last operation of the linked list should return a different value in certain permutation where this operation is fixed at the last place. The sequential specifications of blocking queue, blocking stack and blocking priority queue belong to exclusively-permutative specifications.

To prove that an object is not strongly linearizable, we use the approach of [7,10], which chooses a pair $(e_1 \cdot e_2, e_1 \cdot e_3)$ of traces of the object, and proves that these two traces can not be interpreted incrementally. These are called bi-branch distinguishable executions in [10]. With this approach, we prove that for inclusively-permutative specifications and exclusively-permutative specifications, our universal construction is not strongly linearizable. To prove this result, we show that for each inclusively-permutative specification $Spec$, $\mathcal{U}_{Spec}$ can generate an execution e where a finite number of operations run concurrently, all operations but one already insert their nodes into the linked list and return, and the current operation generates a node and intends to insert it into the linked list. Then the current configuration can not correspond to one unique abstract state, since the current operation can choose a different linearization and return a different value in a future execution. Thus, the current configuration correspond to more than one abstract state with conflicts. Based on this observation we generate bi-branch distinguishable executions of $\mathcal{U}_{Spec}$ and prove that $\mathcal{U}_{Spec}$ is not strongly linearizable. The case for exclusively-permutative specifications can be similarly dealt with.

With [3–5], one can just know that there is no forward simulation relating a non-strongly linearizable object towards an atomic implementation of the target specification, but cannot tell in detail which executions make the object not strongly linearizable. Instead, our universal construction can establish the non-strongly linearizable object with explicit non-strongly linearizable executions. Moreover, surprisingly, we find that for objects that are known linearizable but not strongly linearizable, they share the same strong linearizability violation schemes under our universal construction, that is, for each of these objects, there is a pair of bi-branch distinguishable executions of the object and a pair of bi-branch distinguishable executions of $\mathcal{U}_{Spec}$, which share the same set of histories. We show this violation scheme with eight popular concurrent objects, some of which are optimized for high performance. Five of them are already known linearizable but not strongly linearizable: HW queue [1], a multi-valued single-reader/single-writer register object in [11], a snapshot object in [12], MS queue and Harris's linked list. The other three of them are known linearizable and we prove that they are not strongly linearizable via bi-branch distinguishable executions: Basket queue [13], time-stamped queue [14] and time-stamped stack [14]. These indicate that our universal construction is general enough for characterizing strong linearizability violation schemes for practical objects.

The main contributions of this paper are as follows:

– We propose a wait-free and linearizable universal construction $\mathcal{U}_{Spec}$ that permits each operation to change the order of taking effect and is potentially not strongly linearizable.
– We propose two classes of sequential specifications that cover widely-used sequential specifications: inclusively-permutative specifications and exclusively-permutative specifications. We prove that our universal construction is not strongly linearizable for inclusively-permutative and exclusively-permutative specifications.
– We prove that for each known linearizable but not strongly linearizable object, there is a pair of bi-branch distinguishable executions of the object that shares the same set of histories with a pair of bi-branch distinguishable executions of $\mathcal{U}_{Spec}$. To make this result more extensive we prove three new objects to be not strongly linearizable.

Related Work. Many efforts have been devoted on studying the theoretical aspects of strong linearizability. Helmi et al. [15] show that there is no strongly linearizable and non-blocking implementation of multi-writer registers, max-registers, snapshots, and counters from multi-reader/single-writer registers. Denysyuk et al. [16] show that there is no deterministic strongly linearizable wait-free implementation of snapshots, counters, or max-registers for three or more processes from multi-writer registers. Attiya et al. [17] show that there is no strongly-linearizable fault-tolerant message-passing implementation of multi-writer registers, max-registers, snapshots or counters. Attiya et al. [18] investigate the problem of whether there are wait-free and strongly linearizable implementations from realistic primitives with consensus number 2. Attiya et al. [19] propose strong observational refinement that preserves hyperproperties [20].

Golab et al. [2] indirectly prove that HW queue, a snapshot object in [12] and a multi-valued single-reader/single-writer register object in [11] are not strongly linearizable by showing that an adversary can change the resulting probability distributions when atomic objects are replaced by these objects. Hwang et al. [7] proved that MS queue and Harris's linked list are not strongly linearizable by generating executions that can not be interpreted incrementally. We show that our universal construction can generate a pair of bi-branch distinguishable executions that shares the same set of histories with the pair of bi-branch distinguishable executions of [7].

Herlihy et al. proposed the classical universal construction in [6] to generate wait-free and linearizable objects for any deterministic sequential specifications. Helmi et al. [15] proposed a universal construction to generate obstruction-free and strongly linearizable objects from multi-reader/single-writer registers for any deterministic sequential specification. To the best of our knowledge, we present in this paper the first universal construction for wait-free, linearizable but not strongly linearizable objects.

2   Background

In this section, we introduce the definitions of objects, two correctness conditions linearizability and strong linearizability, and a progress condition wait-freedom.

2.1   Notations

A finite sequence on an alphabet Σ is denoted $l = \alpha_1 \cdot \alpha_2 \cdot \ldots \cdot \alpha_k$, where $\cdot$ is the concatenation symbol and $\alpha_i \in \Sigma$ for each $1 \leq i \leq k$.

A *labelled transition system* (LTS) is a tuple $\mathcal{A} = (Q, \Sigma, \rightarrow, q_0)$, where Q is a set of states (a.k.a. configurations), Σ is an alphabet of transition labels, $\rightarrow \subseteq Q \times \Sigma \times Q$ is a transition relation, and q_0 is the initial state. A finite path of $\mathcal{A}$ is a finite transition sequence $q_0 \xrightarrow{\beta_1} q_1 \xrightarrow{\beta_2} \ldots \xrightarrow{\beta_k} q_k$ with $k \geq 0$, $q_i \in Q$ and $\beta_i \in \Sigma$ for each $1 \leq i \leq k$. A finite trace of $\mathcal{A}$ is a finite sequence $t = \beta_1 \cdot \beta_2 \cdot \ldots \cdot \beta_k$ with $k \geq 0$ and $\beta_i \in \Sigma$ for each $1 \leq i \leq k$, if there exists a finite path $q_0 \xrightarrow{\beta_1} q_1 \xrightarrow{\beta_2} \ldots \xrightarrow{\beta_k} q_k$ of $\mathcal{A}$ with $q_i \in Q$ for each $1 \leq i \leq k$.

2.2   Objects

Objects of high performance concurrent data structures have been widely used in concurrent programs to take advantage of multi-core architectures, such as *java.util.concurrent* for Java and *std::thread* for C++11. An object provides a number of methods, through which a client program interacts with the object. Objects and client programs may contain private memory locations for their own uses. For simplicity of notations, we assume that a method has just one argument and one return value, and the case for more arguments or more return values can be similarly dealt with.

An object or a client program may use the following primitive commands: τ, *read*, *write*, *cas*, *call* and *return*. The τ command is the internal command. A typical compare-and-swap ($cas(x, a, b)$) command compresses a *read* and a *write* command into a single one, which is meant to be executed atomically. It either changes the value of x from a to b successfully, or fails and does nothing if the value of x is not a.

An object or a client program can then be defined as a tuple of states, labels and a transition relation. Each state models a valuation of the control state and registers of one process. The transition of an object is the union of the transition of each method of the object. A client program can either use *read, write* or cas to change the memory, or use *call* to access an object and obtain the return value. A most general client is a special client program that is designed to exhibit all the possible behaviors of an object. Intuitively, it simply repeatedly calls an arbitrary method of the object with an arbitrary argument for arbitrarily many times. The detailed definitions of objects and client programs can be found in Appendix A.1 of our technical report [21].

As for the semantics of an object $\mathcal{O}$ for n processes, we consider all the n processes run concurrently a most general client, interacting with $\mathcal{O}$. The operational semantics of $\mathcal{O}$ for n processes is then defined as an LTS $[\![\mathcal{O}, n]\!]$, of which the details can be found in Appendix A.2 of our technical report [21].

2.3   Linearizability and Strong Linearizability

The behavior of an object is typically represented by histories of interactions between the object and the clients calling it through call and return actions. A history is a finite sequence of call and return actions. In a history, a return action $return(P_{i_1}, m_1, a_1)$ matches a call action $call(P_{i_2}, m_2, a_2)$, if both have the same process identities (i.e., $i_1 = i_2$) and for the same methods (i.e., $m_1 = m_2$). A history is sequential if it starts with a call action and each call (respectively, return) action is immediately followed by a matching return (respectively, a call) action unless it is the last action. A process subhistory $h|_i$ with $1 \le i \le n$ is a history consisting of all and only the actions of process P_i of h. Two histories h and h' are equivalent, if for each process P_i, $h|_i = h'|_i$. Given a history h, $complete(h)$ is the maximal subsequence of h consisting of all the matching call and return actions.

An operation o is a tuple $m(a) \Rightarrow b$, where m is a method, a is the argument and b is the return value. For operations without return value, we omitted return value and write them in the form $m(a)$ instead. In a history, operation o consists of a pair of a call action, denoted $inv(o) = call(P_i, m, a)$, and the follow-up matching return action, denoted $res(o) = return(P_i, m, b)$, for some process P_i, method m, argument a and return value b. A sequential specification is a prefix closed set of finite sequences of operations. Given a specification $Spec$, let $History(Spec)$ be the set of sequential histories corresponding to $Spec$, i.e., $History(Spec) = \{call(P_{i_1}, m_1, a_1) \cdot return(P_{i_1}, m_1, b_1) \cdot \ldots \cdot call(P_{i_k}, m_k, a_k) \cdot return(P_{i_k}, m_k, b_k) \mid (m_1(a_1) \Rightarrow b_1) \cdot \ldots \cdot (m_k(a_k) \Rightarrow b_k) \in Spec, i_1, \ldots, i_k \in \mathbb{N}^+\}$, where $\mathbb{N}^+$ is the set of positive integers. A history h induces a happen-before relation $<_h$ over operations, denoted $o_1 <_h o_2$, if $res(o_1)$ occurs before $inv(o_2)$ in h. Given a sequence e, let $history(e)$ be the projection of e into call and return actions.

Definition 1 (linearizability [1]). *A history h is linearizable with respect to a sequential specification Spec, if h can be extended (by appending zero or more return actions) to a history h', and there exists a sequential history $s \in History(Spec)$, such that*

- *complete(h') is equivalent to s.*
- *For operations o_1, o_2 of h, if $o_1 <_h o_2$, then $o_1 <_s o_2$.*

s is called a linearization of h. An object $\mathcal{O}$ is linearizable with respect to a sequential specification Spec for n processes, if for each trace e of $[\![\mathcal{O}, n]\!]$, history(e) is linearizable with respect to Spec.

A function f that maps sequences to sequence is prefix preserving, if whenever sequence l_1 is a prefix of sequence l_2 and they are both in domain of f, then $f(l_1)$ is a prefix of $f(l_2)$. Given a set E of sequences, let $close(E)$ be the prefix-closure of E.

Definition 2 (strong linearizability [2]). *A set E of traces is strongly linearizable w.r.t a sequential specification Spec, if there exists a function f that maps traces in close(E) into sequential histories, such that*

- *For each trace $e \in close(E)$, $f(e)$ is a linearization of history(e).*
- *f is prefix preserving.*

f is called a strong linearization function of E. An object $\mathcal{O}$ is strongly linearizable with respect to a sequential specification Spec for n processes, if the set of traces of $[\![\mathcal{O}, n]\!]$ is strongly linearizable w.r.t Spec.

For simplicity of notations, when no confusion occurs, a linearization is given as an operation sequence, instead of a sequential history; a strong linearization function is given as a function that maps traces to operation sequences, instead of into sequential histories.

Discussion About Sequential Specifications: In this paper each sequential specification *Spec* is defined as the set of traces of some LTS (called the LTS of *Spec*). A sequential specification is deterministic, if in the LTS of this specification, for each state q, each method m and each argument a, there is at most one edge with label of method m and argument a from q. In this paper, we concentrate on deterministic sequential specifications.

The definitions of sequential specifications of counter, register, max register, snapshot, set, queue, blocking queue, stack, blocking stack, priority queue and blocking priority queue can be found in Appendix A.3 of our technical report [21]. They are called *Ctr, Reg, MReg, Snap, Set, Queue, BQueue, Stack, BStack, PQueue* and *BPQueue*, respectively. Non-blocking queue permits deq() to return empty when there is no element, while blocking queue forbids deq() to return empty. The case is similar for stack and priority queue.

2.4   Wait-Freedom

Various liveness properties (progress conditons) have been proposed for concurrent objects to describe conditions under which method calls are guaranteed to successfully complete in an execution. Wait-freedom [22,23] is a typical liveness properties. Its definition can be found in Appendix A.4 of our technical report [21].

Intuitively wait-freedom requires each method call to return in finite number of steps. Our universal construction in later section will generate objects that are linearizable, not strongly linearizable and wait-free.

3   Universal Construction

In this section, we propose our universal construction and prove that it is wait-free and linearizable.

Rady et al. [5] proved that strong linearizability is equivalent to the existence of a forward simulation relation between an object and an atomic implementation of its specification. Thus, each configuration of a strongly linearizable object is related to a unique abstract state of its specification. In contrast, Herlihy-Wing queue (HW queue for short) [1] is known not strongly linearizable [2], and Herlihy et al. [1] stated that some configuration of HW queue should correspond to more than one abstract state. Based on these observations, the basic idea for our universal construction is to make some configuration able to correspond to more than one abstract state, while remaining wait-free and linearizable.

Inspired by the classical universal construction of Herlihy et al. in [6], we maintain a linked list of nodes. Each operation will generate a node with information of this operation, and insert it into the linked list via consensus. We use the help mechanism of [6] to permit other operations to help an operation to insert a node, and thus, inserting a node into the linked list can be done in a finite number of steps.

We now explain the meaning of "corresponding to more than one abstract state" with the following running example shown in Fig. 1. Assume that in execution e_1 of a non-strongly linearizable object, operation $enq(a_1)$ may do an action which "partly" modifies the abstract state, then operation $enq(a_2)$ runs until it returns. As the first future execution e_2, operation $enq(a_1)$ proceeds until it "completes" modification of the abstract state, and a follow-up operation $deq()$ returns a_1, which shows that $enq(a_1)$ takes effect earlier than $enq(a_2)$. As the second future execution e_3, the follow-up $deq()$ directly returns a_2, while ignoring $enq(a_1)$. This shows that $enq(a_2)$ takes effect earlier than $enq(a_1)$. The first case can be interpreted as $enq(a_1) \cdot enq(a_2) \cdot (deq() \Rightarrow a_1)$, while the second case can be interpreted as $enq(a_2) \cdot enq(a_1) \cdot (deq() \Rightarrow a_2)$. Herein, the time point of the end of e_1 thus corresponds to two abstract states: queue with content $a_1 \cdot a_2$ and queue with content $a_2 \cdot a_1$. It can be seen that the difference between these two operation sequences are due to the orders of operations. Executions of similar example occur in [1] for HW queue, where the return action of $enq(a_1)$ is before the call action of $deq() \Rightarrow a_1$ in $e_1 \cdot e_2$ in example of [1].

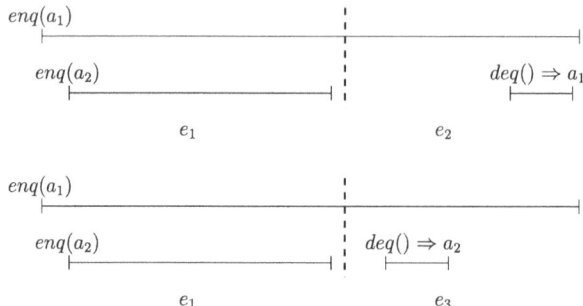

Fig. 1. Two executions of HW queue.

Based on the above discussion, our universal construction uses the following mechanism to synthesize different abstract states. Whenever an operation starts, we additionally record the current history in the node of the operation. Whenever the node of an operation is inserted into the linked list, it can select a linearization that contains the current operation and the operations in the previous nodes of the linked list, store the linearization into the node and compute the return value according to this linearization. There may be more than one candidate linearizations. Different linearizations are "permutations" of each other since they contain the same set of operations, except that the current operation may return different values in different linearizations. The return values of the operations in the previous nodes of the linked list should be kept unchanged in different linearizations. This extends the work of [6] since in their work an operation can only choose the unique linearization, which is generated via accessing the linked list sequentially.

Let us go into detail for our universal construction. To record history and generate id of operations, we use two atomic objects: history recorder and identity generators. As in the classical universal construction, to make consensus of adding which node into linked list, we use consensus objects to make decision.

A history recorder provides two methods $storeCall()$ and $storeReturn()$. It works as if maintaining a "queue" of call and return actions, and the "queue content" is considered a history. $storeCall(m, a, pid, oid) \Rightarrow h$ adds a call action of method m, argument a, process identity pid and operation identity oid into history recorder. It returns the history h which is obtained by adding such call action into queue content. Without loss of generality, assume that each action of history h additionally contains its operation identity. $storeReturn(m, b, pid, oid)$ adds a return action of method m, return value b, process identity pid and operation identity oid into history recorder. A identity generator provides only one method $genID()$, which is required to return a unique id. A consensus object [6] provides only one method *decide*(). Each process calls this method with its own input at most once. These calls return the same value, which is the input of one of the processes. In Appendix B.1 of our technical report [21] we prove that there are wait-free and strongly linearizable history recorder, identity generator and consensus objects. Thus it is safe to assume that the history recorder, identity generator and consensus objects of our universal construction are strongly linearizable and wait-free.

Given a deterministic sequential specification *Spec*, our universal construction for *Spec* is an object $\mathcal{U}_{Spec}$ with only one method *apply*(). It takes as the argument an invocation (m, a), which specifies the method m being called and its argument a, and returns a corresponding response.

Our universal construction maintains a linked list of nodes. Each node of the linked list is an instance of class Node, and we extend the definition of Node of [6] by adding operation id, history and linearization fields. Each node of our universal construction is a tuple $(oid, m, a, hist, lin, decideNext, seq, next)$ such that (1) *oid* stores the operation id, (2) m stores method name of the operation, (3) a stores the argument of the operation, (4) *hist* stores the history of the time point after call action of this operation, (5) *lin* is a linearization of *hist*, (6) *decideNext* is a consensus object used to decide which node is appended next in the list, (7) *seq* is the sequence number of the operation and is of type integer, and (8) *next* points to the next node in the linked list. The construction function of Node is of the form $Node(m, a, oid, his)$, it generates a new instance of Node; assigns value to method name, argument, operation id and history of this node, respectively; generates a new instance of consensus object and assigns it to the *decideNext* field of this node; sets *seq* field to 0; and leaves the *lin* and *next* fields uninitialized.

As in the classical universal construction of [6], our universal construction contains a specific Node instance called *tail*, which is the tail of the linked list. The head[] array of [6] is used to locate the head of the linked list, while head[i] is the latest node in the linked list that process P_i has observed. The announce[] array of [6] is used in the helping mechanism and is used to ensure wait-freedom. announce[i] is the node that process P_i currently intends to insert into the list.

In the construction function of our universal construction, we (1) generate a new instance of Node and assign it to *tail*, (2) set the *seq* field of *tail* to 1, and (3) set head[i] to be *tail* for each process P_i.

The pseudo code of method *apply* of $\mathcal{U}_{Spec}$ is shown in Method 1.

Method 1: *apply*

Input: Invoc (m, a)
1 Let pid be id of concurrent process and let oid $:= \mathcal{O}_{idGen}.genID()$;
2 h $:= \mathcal{O}_{his}.storeCall(m, a, pid, oid)$;
3 announce[pid] := new Node(m,a,oid,h);
4 head[pid] := Node.max(head);
5 **while** *announce[pid].seq == 0* **do**
6 | Node before := head[pid];
7 | Node help := announce[(before.seq+1)%n];
8 | **if** *help.seq == 0* **then**
9 | | prefer := help;
10 | **else**
11 | | prefer := announce[pid];
12 | Node after := before.decideNext.decide(prefer);
13 | l=genLin(tail,before,after);
14 | cas(after.lin,null,l);
15 | before.next := after;
16 | after.seq := before.seq+1;
17 | head[pid] := after;
18 head[pid] := announce[pid];
19 Calculate return value b of operation oid according to *lin* field of node of operation oid;
20 $\mathcal{O}_{his}.storeReturn(m, b, pid, oid)$;
21 return b;

Let us explain the pseudo code of method *apply* of $\mathcal{U}_{Spec}$ as follows. At Lines 1–2, we obtain the process id and operation id, add the call action to history recorder and obtain the newest version of history. Here $\mathcal{O}_{his}$ and $\mathcal{O}_{idGen}$ are wait-free and strong linearizable history recorder and identity generator objects, respectively. At Lines 3–4, current process announces its task into the announce[] array and updates *head[pid]*. Here $Node.max(head)$ returns a node with maximal sequence number in the linked list.

Lines 5–17 is a loop. In each round of the loop, as in the classical universal construction in [6], we insert the node into the linked list. Due to the help mechanism, such process can be done in finite number of steps and thus *apply()* method is wait-free. Please refer to [6] for the detailed explanation about the classical universal construction.

In each round, a node *after* is selected to be inserted into the linked list. Before the node *after* is inserted into linked list, we set the *lin* field of *after* with value $l = genLin(tail, before, after)$. We use cas command to ensure that the *lin* field of *after* is set only once. Let h_1 be the longest history among *hist* fields of *after* and the nodes in the linked list from *tail* to *before*. Then, the sequence $l = genLin(tail, before, after)$ should satisfy the following requirements: (1) l is a linearization of h_1, (2) the set of operations in l includes exactly the operation of *after* and the operations in the linked list from *tail* to *before*, (3) the return value of each operation (except the operation of $after$) in l is the same as that in the corresponding node of the linked list from $tail$ to $before$. Here to obtain the return value of an operation o_1 of node n_1 in the linked list, we execute according to lin field of n_1 and compute the return value of o_1 in this process. When there are more than one such candidate for l, $genLin(tail, before, after)$ returns one of them non-deterministically. This non-deterministic behavior does not exceed our definition of objects by, for example, assuming an additional process calling a method $repeat()$ that repeatedly sets a memory location x to 0 and 1. Thus, non-deterministically choosing an integer value a from $[1, k]$, where $2^j \leq k < 2^{j+1}$ for some $j \geq 0$, can be implemented by first reading x's value and setting it to the least important bit of a, then reading x's value again and setting it to the second least important bit of a, and so on. In this way, different values can be resulted for a under different schedules.

At Line 18 we update head[pid] as in [6]. Then we obtain the return value b of this operation in lin field of node of this operation at Line 19, add the return action in history recorder at Line 20, and returns b in Line 21.

The running example shown earlier in this section can now be reproduced with $[\![\mathcal{U}_{Queue}, n]\!]$. We can execute $enq(a_1)$ and $enq(a_2)$ concurrently, insert their nodes into the linked list of $\mathcal{U}_{Queue}$, and let $enq(a_2)$ return. Then we call $deq()$, generate its node, and we can choose its lin field to be either $enq(a_1) \cdot enq(a_2) \cdot (deq() \Rightarrow a_1)$ or $enq(a_2) \cdot enq(a_1) \cdot (deq() \Rightarrow a_2)$, which corresponds to the two conflict abstract states of $Qeueue$.

The following lemma states that $\mathcal{U}_{Spec}$ is wait-free and linearizable w.r.t. $Spec$. $\mathcal{U}_{Spec}$ is wait-free since each node can be inserted into the linked list in a finite number of steps, and recording a history, generating an operation id, calculating a linearization, setting a lin field and computing a return value can also be done in a finite number of steps. As for the linearizability of $\mathcal{U}_{Spec}$, given a trace e of $[\![\mathcal{U}_{Spec}, n]\!]$, let o be the last operation that inserts its node $node$ into the linked list, with $node.lin = l$. During the process when $node$ calculates l, it scans the $hist$ filed of all nodes in the linked list and the $hist$ filed of $node$, and selects the longest history h among them. Let S be the set of histories scanned during this process. For each node n_i in the linked list, $n_i.hist$ must contain the call action of the operation of n_i. Since the history recorder object $\mathcal{O}_{his}$ is strongly linearizable and $\mathcal{O}_{his}$ never removes any action, the content of $\mathcal{O}_{his}$ must increase monotonically. Thus, for any two histories in S, one must be a prefix of the other. Thus, h must contains all the call actions of the operations in the linked list and the call action of o, and obviously h is a prefix of $history(e)$. Since l is a linearization of h, and $history(e)$ can be obtained from h by adding possibly return actions of the operations of the nodes in the linked list and a return action of o, and possibly call actions of new operations whose nodes are not in the linked list, we can prove that l is still a linearization of $history(e)$. The detailed proof can be found in Appendix B.2 of our technical report [21].

Lemma 1. $\mathcal{U}_{Spec}$ *is wait-free and is linearizable w.r.t. Spec for each deterministic sequential specification Spec.*

4   Two Classes of Sequential Specifications

In this section, we propose two classes of sequential specifications: inclusively-permutative sequential specifications and exclusively-permutative sequential specifications. Then we prove that our universal construction is not strongly linearizable for these two classes of sequential specifications.

In our universal construction $\mathcal{U}_{Spec}$, more than one candidate linearization may be chosen in one operation. Each of these candidate linearizations is a "permutation" of another candidate linearization, except that the current operation may return different values. Based on this observation, we propose the notion of "permutation-based" sequential specifications, where permutations of other operations make the current operation return different values. Given a sequence s, let $perm(s)$ be the set of permutations of s, or in other words, each element of $perm(s)$ is a sequence obtained from s via changing the order of the elements in s.

The notion of inclusively-permutative sequential specification requires that the last operation $m(a)$ should return a different value when it is located after some permutation of a subset of previous operations of $m(a)$. "inclusively" indicates that the last operation $m(a)$ can "join the permutation" and be relocated at any position other than the last one.

Definition 3. *A deterministic sequential specification Spec is called a inclusively-per-mutative sequential specification, if there exists operation sequences l, l_1, l_2, method m, argument a and return value b, c, such that $b \neq c$, $l \cdot (m(a) \Rightarrow b) \in Spec$, $l_1 \cdot (m(a) \Rightarrow c) \cdot l_2 \in Spec$, and $l_1 \cdot l_2 \in perm(l)$.*

The notion of exclusively-permutative sequential specification requires that the last operation $m(a)$ returns a different value when being located after some permutation of previous operations of $m(a)$. "exclusively" indicates that the last operation $m(a)$ can not "join the permutation" and must located at the last position.

Definition 4. *A deterministic sequential specification Spec is called a exclusively-permutative sequential specification, if there exists operation sequences l, l', method m, argument a and return value b, c, such that $b \neq c$, $l \cdot (m(a) \Rightarrow b) \in Spec$, $l' \cdot (m(a) \Rightarrow c) \in Spec$, and $l' \in perm(l)$.*

Wang et al. [10] propose an approach called bi-branch distinguishable executions to prove that an object violates strong linearizability. It is based on the approach of proving object to violate strong linearizability in [7]. A pair e, e' of traces is called a pair of bi-branch distinguishable executions for object $\mathcal{O}$ and sequential specification $Spec$, if (1) they are both traces of $[\![\mathcal{O}, n]\!]$ for some n, (2) there exists e_1, e_2, e_3, such that $e = e_1 \cdot e_2$ and $e' = e_1 \cdot e_3$, and (3) for each function that maps prefix of e and e' to their linearization, such function can not be prefix preserving. In this section we use bi-branch distinguishable executions to prove our universal construction is not strongly lienarizable in some cases.

Let us use an example to demonstrate that $\mathcal{U}_{Spec}$ is not strongly linearizable when $Spec$ is inclusively-permutative. Given a inclusively-permutative specification $Spec$ and assume that $o_1 \cdot o_2 \cdot (m(a) \Rightarrow b) \in Spec$, $o_1 \cdot (m(a) \Rightarrow c) \cdot o_2 \in Spec$ and $b \neq c$. Then we show that the traces $e_1 \cdot e_2$ and $e_1 \cdot e_3$ in Fig. 2 are in $[\![\mathcal{U}_{Spec}, 3]\!]$ and they constitute a pair of bi-branch distinguishable executions. Herein the horizontal direction indicates time and the vertical direction indicates different processes.

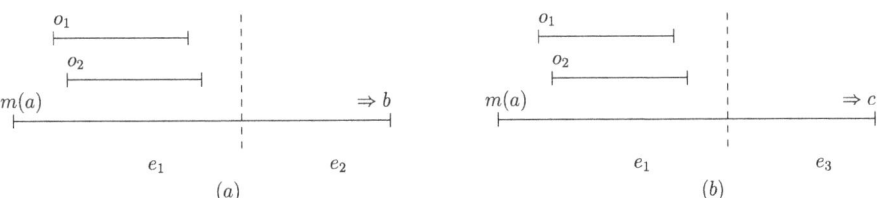

(a)   (b)

Fig. 2. Example for $\mathcal{U}_{Spec}$ not strongly linearizable when $Spec$ is inclusive-permutation

Let us first explain why $e_1 \cdot e_2$ is a trace of $[\![\mathcal{U}_{Spec}, 3]\!]$. We proceed as follows: (1) Call $m(a)$, o_1 and o_2, (2) put node of o_1 into linked list and let o_1 return, then put node of o_2 into linked list and let o_2 return. (3) Generate a node for $m(a)$ and set its lin field to be $o_1 \cdot o_2 \cdot (m(a) \Rightarrow b)$, put this node into linked list and return b. To explain why $e_1 \cdot e_3$ is a trace of $[\![\mathcal{U}_{Spec}, 3]\!]$, we do the first two steps of above discussion, and in the third step we set the lin field of node of $m(a)$ to be $o_1 \cdot (m(a) \Rightarrow c) \cdot o_2$ and return c.

To explain why $e_1 \cdot e_2$ and $e_1 \cdot e_3$ are a pair of bi-branch distinguishable executions, we prove by contradiction, and assume that there is a strong linearization function f for $\mathcal{U}_{Spec}$. Then $f(e_1)$ can be $(m(a) \Rightarrow d) \cdot o_1 \cdot o_2$, $o_1 \cdot o_2$, $o_1 \cdot (m(a) \Rightarrow c) \cdot o_2$, $o_1 \cdot o_2 \cdot (m(a) \Rightarrow b)$, $(m(a) \Rightarrow d) \cdot o_2 \cdot o_1$, $o_2 \cdot o_1$, $o_2 \cdot (m(a) \Rightarrow e) \cdot o_1$ or $o_2 \cdot o_1 \cdot (m(a) \Rightarrow g)$ for some d, e and g. If $f(e_1)$ contains $m(a)$ and the return value of $m(a)$ is b in $f(e_1)$, then since f is prefix preserving, the return value of $m(a)$ in $f(e_1 \cdot e_3)$ is b while the return value of $m(a)$ in $e_1 \cdot e_3$ is c, thus it is not the case that $f(e_1)$ contains $m(a)$ and the return value of $m(a)$ is b. If $f(e_1)$ contains $m(a)$ and the return value of $m(a)$ is not b in $f(e_1)$, then since f is prefix preserving, the return value of $m(a)$ in $f(e_1 \cdot e_2)$ is not b while the return value of $m(a)$ in $e_1 \cdot e_2$ is b, thus it is not the case that $f(e_1)$ contains $m(a)$ and the return value of $m(a)$ is not b. Thus, $f(e_1)$ does not contain $m(a)$. It is obvious that $f(e_1)$ contains o_1 and o_2, and $f(e_1 \cdot e_2) = f(e_1 \cdot e_3) = f(e_1) \cdot (m(a) \Rightarrow d)$ for some d. However, this is impossible since the return value of $m(a)$ in $e_1 \cdot e_2$ is different from that in $e_1 \cdot e_3$.

Based on intuition of above discussion, the following theorem states that $\mathcal{U}_{Spec}$ is not strongly linearizable when $Spec$ is inclusively-permutative. The detailed proof can be found in Appendix C.1 of our technical report [21].

Theorem 1. $\mathcal{U}_{Spec}$ *is not strongly linearizable when Spec is a deterministic inclusively-permutative sequential specification.*

Let us use an example to demonstrate that $\mathcal{U}_{Spec}$ is not strongly linearizable when *Spec* is exclusively-permutative. Given a exclusively-permutative specification *Spec* and assume that $o_1 \cdot o_2 \cdot (m(a) \Rightarrow b) \in Spec$, $o_2 \cdot o_1 \cdot (m(a) \Rightarrow c) \in Spec$ and $b \neq c$. Then we show that the traces $e_1 \cdot e_2$ and $e_1 \cdot e_3$ in Fig. 3 are in $[\![\mathcal{U}_{Spec}, 3]\!]$ and they are a pair of bi-branch distinguishable executions.

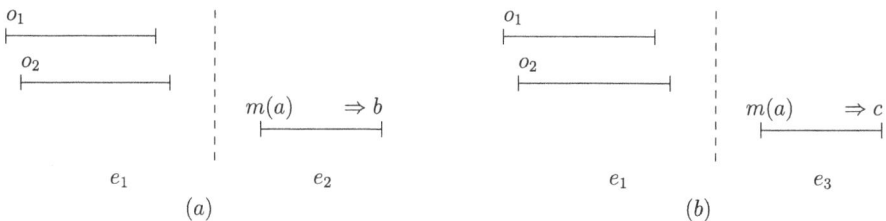

Fig. 3. Example for $\mathcal{U}_{Spec}$ not strongly linearizable when *Spec* is exclusive-permutation

Let us first explain why $e_1 \cdot e_2$ is a trace of $[\![\mathcal{U}_{Spec}, 3]\!]$. We proceeds as follows: (1) Call o_1 and o_2, put node of o_1 into linked list and let o_1 return, and then put node of o_2 into linked list and let o_2 return. (2) Call $m(a)$, generate a node for $m(a)$ and set its *lin* field to be $o_1 \cdot o_2 \cdot (m(a) \Rightarrow b)$, put this node into linked list and return b. To explain why $e_1 \cdot e_3$ is a trace of $[\![\mathcal{U}_{Spec}, 3]\!]$, we do the first step of above discussion, and in the second step we set the *lin* field of node of $m(a)$ to be $o_2 \cdot o_1 \cdot (m(a) \Rightarrow c)$ and return c.

To explain why $e_1 \cdot e_2$ and $e_1 \cdot e_3$ are a pair of bi-branch distinguishable executions, we prove by contradiction, and assume that there is a strong linearization function f for $\mathcal{U}_{Spec}$. Then $f(e_1)$ can be $o_1 \cdot o_2$ or $o_2 \cdot o_1$. If $f(e_1) = o_1 \cdot o_2$, then, since f is prefix preserving, $f(e_1 \cdot e_3)$ can only be $o_1 \cdot o_2 \cdot (m(a) \Rightarrow b)$, but $m(a)$ returns different values in $e_1 \cdot e_3$ and $f(e_1 \cdot e_3)$, thus $f(e_1)$ can not be $o_1 \cdot o_2$. If $f(e_1) = o_2 \cdot o_1$, then, for the same reason, $f(e_1 \cdot e_2)$ can only be $o_2 \cdot o_1 \cdot (m(a) \Rightarrow c)$, but $m(a)$ returns different values in $e_1 \cdot e_2$ and $f(e_1 \cdot e_2)$, thus $f(e_1)$ can not be $o_2 \cdot o_1$.

Based on intuition of above discussion, the following theorem states that $\mathcal{U}_{Spec}$ is not strongly linearizable when *Spec* is exlusively-permutative. The detailed proof can be found in Appendix C.2 of our technical report [21].

Theorem 2. $\mathcal{U}_{Spec}$ *is not strongly linearizable when Spec is a deterministic exclusively-permutative sequential specification.*

The following lemma states that many widely-used sequential specifications are either inclusively-permutative specifications or exclusively-permutative specifications. Thus our universal construction for them are all not strongly linearizable. The detailed proof can be found in Appendix C.3 of our technical report [21].

Lemma 2. *The sequential specifications of counter, register, max register, snap-shot, set, non-blocking queue, non-blocking stack and non-blocking priority queue are inclusively-permutative, and the sequential specifications of blocking queue, blocking stack and blocking priority queue are exclusively-permutative.*

5   Same Schemes of Strong Linearizability Violations for Practical Objects and Our Universal Construction

In this section we show that our universal construction is expressive enough to cover strong linearizability violation schemes (with bi-branch distinguishable executions) for practical objects, including:

- Five objects that are already known linearizable but not strongly linearizable: HW-queue, a multi-valued single-reader/single-writer register object in [11], a snapshot object in [12], MS queue [8] and Harris's linked list object [9].
- Three objects that are known linearizable: Basket queue [13], time-stamped queue [14] and time-stamped stack [14]. In this section we additionally prove that they are not stronly linearizazble.

We find that for each above practical object $\mathcal{O}$, there is a pair $(e_1 \cdot e_2, e_1 \cdot e_3)$ of bi-branch distinguishable executions of $\mathcal{O}$ and a pair $(e_1' \cdot e_2', e_1' \cdot e_3')$ of bi-branch distinguishable executions of $\mathcal{U}_{Spec}$ (with $Spec$ the corresponding specification of $\mathcal{O}$), such that $history(e_1) = history(e_1')$, $history(e_2) = history(e_2')$ and $history(e_3) = history(e_3')$.

Let us take the time-stamped queue object as an example, which is known linearizable. Let us briefly explain this object, and then state a pair of bi-branch distinguishable executions of time-stamped queue, and state how our universal construction generates a pair of bi-branch distinguishable executions with same histories.

In a time-stamped queue, each process is associated with a single-producer/multi-consumer pool (called SP pool), which is implemented as a linked list ended with a sentinel node. These pools are linked from an array $spPools[]$. Every element of the queue is stored in an SP pool. As shown in Fig. 4, a node of the linked list of time-stamped queue contains a data element, a timestamp, a pointer to the next node and a *taken* flag indicating whether this node has been removed. The workflow for a process to enqueue an element involves (1) adding a node to the SP pool of the process, (2) generating a new timestamp, and (3) attaching the timestamp to the node. The un-timestamped nodes are visible to other processes with the maximal timestamp value $\top$. To dequeue an element, we search all the SP pools for an element with the minimal timestamp, and then attempt to remove it from the SP pools. In Fig. 4, for simplicity we assume a timestamp is an integer. According to the timestamps in this figure, it can be seen that the next element to be dequeued is a. The flag *taken* is set to *true* for element c, which means that the queue does not contain c. It can also be seen that the node of element e has not been attached with a timestamp yet.

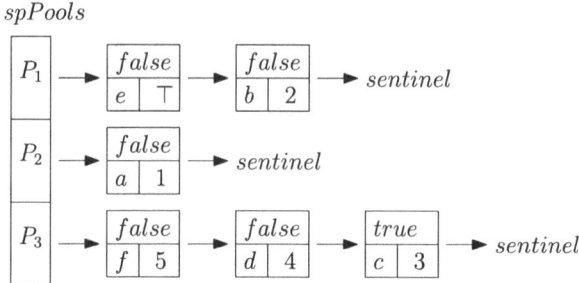

Fig. 4. A time-stamped queue.

The detailed code of time-stamped queue can be found in Appendix D.3 of our technical report [21].

The following lemma states that the traces in Fig. 1 constitutes a pair of bi-branch distinguishable executions of time-stamped queue. Its detailed proof can be found in Appendix D.3 of our technical report [21]. For simplicity, we use "The trace of Fig. 1 are a pair of bi-branch distinguishable executions of time-stamped queue" to indicate that there are a pair $e_1 \cdot e_2, e_1 \cdot e_3$ of traces as shown in Fig. 1, such that $e_1 \cdot e_2$ and $e_1 \cdot e_3$ are a pair of bi-branch distinguishable executions for $\mathcal{O}_{tsq}$, and the call and return actions of e_1, $e_1 \cdot e_2$ and $e_1 \cdot e_3$ are the same as that in Fig. 1. Here $\mathcal{O}_{tsq}$ is the object of time-stamped queue. In such e_1, $enq(a_1)$ (resp., $enq(a_2)$) generates a node and the time stamp ts_1 (resp., ts_2), and $enq(a_2)$ associate the node of a_2 with ts_2. Here we assume that $ts_1 < ts_2$. In execution e_2, $enq(a_1)$ associate the node of a_1 with ts_1. Since $ts_1 < ts_2$, $deq()$ returns a_1. In execution e_3, $deq()$ finds that the node of a_1 is still not timestamped. Thus, the node of a_1 has maximal time stamp, and $deq()$ returns a_2.

Lemma 3. *The traces of Fig. 1 are a pair of bi-branch distinguishable executions of time-stamped queue.*

The following lemma states that the traces in Fig. 1 constitutes a pair of bi-branch distinguishable executions of our universal construction $\mathcal{U}_{Queue}$. We already roughly explain how $\mathcal{U}_{Queue}$ generates these executions at the end of Sect. 3. Its detailed proof can be found in Appendix D.1 of our technical report [21].

Lemma 4. *The traces of Fig. 1 are a pair of bi-branch distinguishable executions of $\mathcal{U}_{Queue}$.*

In Appendix D of our technical report [21], for each of the eight objects mentioned in the beginning of this section, we introduce its code, generate a pair $(e_1 \cdot e_2, e_1 \cdot e_3)$ of bi-branch distinguishable executions of this object and a pair $(e_1' \cdot e_2', e_1' \cdot e_3')$ of bi-branch distinguishable executions of our universal construction, and then prove that they have the same set of histories. With this approach we prove that time-stamped queue, time-stamped stack and basket queue are not strongly linearizable.

6   Conclusion

In this paper, we propose a wait-free, linearizable universal construction to expose non-strongly linearizable behaviors of objects. We propose two classes of sequential specifications: inclusively-permutative specifications and exclusively-permutative specifications, which are rather pervasive to cover widely-used sequential specifications. Then we show that our universal construction is not strongly linearizable for these two general classes of specifications. Our work systematically reveals that many specifications have potential to be implemented in a manner that violates strong linearizability. This has rarely been studied from a theoretical perspective.

Our universal construction permits each operation to non-deterministically choose a linearization, while different linearizations are permutations of each other (except that some operation may return different values). This models the phenomenon that an operation may "partly" take effect in one step, but whether or not this operation indeed takes effect in this step depends on future executions. We find that for all known linearizable but not strongly linearizable objects, their strong linearizability violation schemes can be "reproduced" with our universal construction. Furthermore, with our universal construction for strong linearizability violation, we identify three more objects to be not strongly linearizable, which have not been investigated before.

Our universal construction is surely not strongly linearizable if the target sequential specification is inclusively-permutative or exclusively-permutative. An interesting open problem is whether there exists a linearizable but non-strongly linearizable universal construction for any sequential specification, if it admits a non-strongly linearizable implementation. Our universal construction is able to capture certain strong linearizability violation scheme for practical objects. It will be interesting to investigate how to generate a linearizable universal construction that can induce all strong linearizability violation schemes.

Acknowledgments. We sincerely thank the anonymous reviewers for their insightful comments. This work is supported in part by the National Natural Science Foundation of China (62002298, 62072443, 62372386 and 62032019), the National Key R&D Program of China (2022YFA1005100, 2022YFA1005101 and 2022YFA1005104), the Fundamental Research Funds for the Central Universities (SWU019036), and the Capacity Development Grant of Southwest University (SWU116007).

References

1. Herlihy, M., Wing, J.M.: Linearizability: a correctness condition for concurrent objects. ACM Trans. Program. Lang. Syst. **12**, 463–492 (1990)

2. Golab, W.M., Higham, L., Woelfel, P.: Linearizable implementations do not suffice for randomized distributed computation. In: Fortnow, L., Vadhan, S.P. (eds.) Proceedings of the 43rd ACM Symposium on Theory of Computing, STOC 2011, San Jose, CA, USA, 6–8 June 2011, pp. 373–382. ACM (2011)

3. Filipović, I., O'Hearn, P., Rinetzky, N., Yang, H.: Abstraction for concurrent objects. In: Castagna, G. (ed.) ESOP 2009. LNCS, vol. 5502, pp. 252–266. Springer, Heidelberg (2009). https://doi.org/10.1007/978-3-642-00590-9_19

4. Lynch, N., Vaandrager, F.: Forward and backward simulations. Inf. Comput. **121**, 214–233 (1995)

5. Rady, A.S.: Characterizing implementations that preserve properties of concurrent randomized algorithms (2017)

6. Herlihy, M., Shavit, N.: The Art of Multiprocessor Programming. Morgan Kaufmann (2008)

7. Hwang, S.M., Woelfel, P.: Strongly linearizable linked list and queue. In: Bramas, Q., Gramoli, V., Milani, A. (eds.) 25th International Conference on Principles of Distributed Systems, OPODIS 2021. LIPIcs, Strasbourg, France, 13–15 December 2021, vol. 217, pp. 28:1–28:20. Schloss Dagstuhl - Leibniz-Zentrum für Informatik (2021)

8. Michael, M.M., Scott, M.L.: Simple, fast, and practical non-blocking and blocking concurrent queue algorithms. In: Burns, J.E., Moses, Y. (eds.) Proceedings of the Fifteenth Annual ACM Symposium on Principles of Distributed Computing, Philadelphia, Pennsylvania, USA, 23–26 May 1996, pp. 267–275. ACM (1996)

9. Harris, T.L.: A pragmatic implementation of non-blocking linked-lists. In: Welch, J. (ed.) DISC 2001. LNCS, vol. 2180, pp. 300–314. Springer, Heidelberg (2001). https://doi.org/10.1007/3-540-45414-4_21

10. Wang, C., Jia, Q., Lu, Y., Wu, P.: Strong linearizability checking and determining for concurrent objects. J. Softw. **35** (2024)

11. Vidyasankar, K.: Converting Lamport's regular register to atomic register. Inf. Process. Lett. **28**, 287–290 (1988)

12. Afek, Y., Attiya, H., Dolev, D., Gafni, E., Merritt, M., Shavit, N.: Atomic snapshots of shared memory. J. ACM **40**, 873–890 (1993)

13. Hoffman, M., Shalev, O., Shavit, N.: The baskets queue. In: Tovar, E., Tsigas, P., Fouchal, H. (eds.) OPODIS 2007. LNCS, vol. 4878, pp. 401–414. Springer, Heidelberg (2007). https://doi.org/10.1007/978-3-540-77096-1_29

14. Dodds, M., Haas, A., Kirsch, C.M.: A scalable, correct time-stamped stack. In: Rajamani, S.K., Walker, D. (eds.) Proceedings of the 42nd Annual ACM SIGPLAN-SIGACT Symposium on Principles of Programming Languages, POPL 2015, Mumbai, India, 15–17 January 2015, pp. 233–246. ACM (2015)

15. Helmi, M., Higham, L., Woelfel, P.: Strongly linearizable implementations: possibilities and impossibilities. In: Kowalski, D., Panconesi, A. (eds.) ACM Symposium on Principles of Distributed Computing, PODC 2012, Funchal, Madeira, Portugal, 16–18 July 2012, pp. 385–394. ACM (2012)

16. Denysyuk, O., Woelfel, P.: Wait-freedom is harder than lock-freedom under strong linearizability. In: Moses, Y. (ed.) DISC 2015. LNCS, vol. 9363, pp. 60–74. Springer, Heidelberg (2015). https://doi.org/10.1007/978-3-662-48653-5_5

17. Attiya, H., Enea, C., Welch, J.L.: Impossibility of strongly-linearizable message-passing objects via simulation by single-writer registers. In: Gilbert, S. (ed.) 35th International Symposium on Distributed Computing, DISC 2021. LIPIcs, Freiburg, Germany, 4–8 October 2021 (Virtual Conference), vol. 209, pp. 7:1–7:18. Schloss Dagstuhl - Leibniz-Zentrum für Informatik (2021)

18. Attiya, H., Castañeda, A., Enea, C.: Strong linearizability using primitives with consensus number 2. In: Gelles, R., Olivetti, D., Kuznetsov, P. (eds.) Proceedings of the 43rd ACM Symposium on Principles of Distributed Computing, PODC 2024, Nantes, France, 17–21 June 2024, pp. 432–442. ACM (2024)

19. Attiya, H., Enea, C.: Putting strong linearizability in context: preserving hyper-properties in programsthat use concurrent objects. In: Suomela, J. (ed.) 33rd International Symposium on Distributed Computing, DISC 2019. LIPIcs, Budapest, Hungary, 14–18 October 2019, vol. 146, pp. 2:1–2:17. Schloss Dagstuhl - Leibniz-Zentrum für Informatik (2019)

20. Clarkson, M.R., Schneider, F.B.: Hyperproperties. J. Comput. Secur. **18**, 1157–1210 (2010)

21. Wang, C., et al.: Universal construction for linearizable but not strongly linearizable concurrent objects. Technical report ISCAS-SKLCS-24-01, State Key Laboratory of Computer Science, Institute of Software, Chinese Academy of Sciences (2024). https://lcs.ios.ac.cn/~lvyi/files/ISCAS-SKLCS-24-01.pdf

22. Herlihy, M.: Wait-free synchronization. ACM Trans. Program. Lang. Syst. **13**, 124–149 (1991)

23. Liang, H., Hoffmann, J., Feng, X., Shao, Z.: Characterizing progress properties of concurrent objects via contextual refinements. In: D'Argenio, P.R., Melgratti, H. (eds.) CONCUR 2013. LNCS, vol. 8052, pp. 227–241. Springer, Heidelberg (2013). https://doi.org/10.1007/978-3-642-40184-8_17

Cache Behavior Analysis with SP-Relative Addressing for WCET Estimation

Shangshang Xiao[1,2], Mengxia Sun[1], Wei Zhang[1,2(✉)], Naijun Zhan[3], and Lei Ju[2]

[1] School of Cyber Science and Technology, Shandong University, Qingdao, China
[2] Quan Cheng Laboratory, Jinan, China
sduzhangwei@sdu.edu.cn
[3] School of Computer Science, Peking University, Beijing, China

Abstract. Accurately bounding the worst-case execution time (WCET) is crucial for efficient real-time system design. Precisely analyzing whether a memory reference results in a cache miss or a cache hit significantly impacts the accuracy of the estimated WCET bound, as the latency of a cache miss is typically two orders of magnitude higher than that of a cache hit access. SP-relative addressing enables dynamic memory allocation on the stack, enhances thread safety, an therefore is widely adopted in embedded real-time systems. However, existing cache behavior analysis requires obtaining the exact address of each memory reference and pessimistically assumes that SP-relative addressing could access any memory address, resulting in an overestimated WCET bound. In this paper, we propose a new WCET analysis framework that first identifies the program segments in which the SP value remains constant for a accurate cache behavior analysis, and then comprehensively compute the WCET of the whole program based on the constraints between the SP value defined by the program's control flow. Experimental results show that, our method can tighten the estimated WCET bound by up to 36.31% and achieve an average improvement of 11.85%.

Keywords: WCET · Abstract interpretation · Cache analysis · SP-relative addressing

1 Introduction

Real-time systems [1,14] are extensively utilized in safety-critical fields such as autonomous driving, medical devices, and nuclear power plants, where tasks must operate within strict time constraints to guarantee reliability and safety. Therefore, bounding the worst-case execution time (WCET) during compile time is essential for the real-time verification. To ensure secure and precise timing

---

S. Xiao and M. Sun—The first two authors are Contributed equally to this work.

T. Bourke et al. (Eds.): SETTA 2024, LNCS 15469, pp. 256–274, 2025.
https://doi.org/10.1007/978-981-96-0602-3_14

verification, the estimated WCET bounds must be both tight (as close as possible to the actual worst-case execution time) and sound (no lower than any possible execution time).

Cache behavior analysis is crucial for accurate WCET estimation, given that the latency of a cache miss is typically two orders of magnitude greater than that of a cache hit. Current methods [3,10] often rely on abstract interpretation-based cache behavior analysis to predict the cache behavior of memory references, specifically assessing whether a memory block is evicted from the cache before its next access.

The memory address accessed by SP-relative addressing deepens on the SP register's value, which undergoes frequent changes during runtime, especially across function transitions. Moreover, the value of SP is path-dependent, which makes obtaining the exact value of it at compile time computationally challenging. Conventional methods struggle to precisely analyze the SP register values, and have to pessimistically assume that SP-relative addressing instructions might access any stack address, resulting in a substantial overestimation of cache interference.

Despite the unpredictability of the SP value at compile time, we observe that within specific program segments, such as loops without function calls, the SP value remains constant. In scenarios where the SP value in unchanged, even if its exact value is unknown, a more accurate cache interference analysis can be conducted based on the relative offsets among different SP-relative addressing instructions. To facilitate this, we introduce a novel analytical unit, called Hyper-Block, to identify program segments where the SP value remains consistent. By leveraging existing WCET analysis techniques, we can precisely calculate a tight WCET for each Hyper-Block and the corresponding SP value.

However, the change in the SP values between different Hyper-Blocks follows the control flow of the program, and the individually analyzed WCET bound for each Hyper-Block may result in an overestimated WCET bound. For example, the SP value in a caller Hyper-Block is never lower than that in the callee Hyper-Block. We formally model such constraints on SP values across distinct Hyper-Blocks and formulate the program's WCET as an Integer Linear Programming (ILP) problem to accurately compute the overall program's WCET. Experimental results conducted with the widely used MRTC benchmark program reveal that our method can tighten the estimated WCET bound by up to 36.31% and achieve an average improvement of 11.85%.

The subsequent sections of this paper are organized as follows: Sect. 2 delves into the related work, Sect. 3 provides an overview of cache analysis, Sect. 4 outlines the motivation behind this study, Sect. 5 introduces our proposed approach in detail, Sect. 6 evaluates the effectiveness of the proposed approach, and finally, Sect. 7 presents the concluding remarks for this paper.

2   Related Work

Research on cache analysis for WCET computation has been investigated for several decades. Ferdinand and Wilhelm proposed the abstract interpretation-based technique [5] to statically predict the cache behavior of programs. At present, abstract interpretation method has been successfully applied to instruction cache analysis [2, 23], data cache analysis [11] and multi-level caches analysis [8] of WCET estimation, and becomes a dominating approach for cache analysis with LRU replacement policy. Building on this cache analysis technique, Huynh et al. introduced a scope-aware persistence analysis [10] to capture the dynamic behavior of memory access, Zhang et al. further applied it to simulate dynamic cache behavior in preemptive multi-tasking systems [27], several works [17, 26, 28] considered the effect of interference from multi-core processors on cache analysis.

Existing cache behavior analysis methods generally require the exact address of each memory reference [15] to determine if it will result in a cache hit or miss. For instruction caches, executing an instruction leads to access to a concrete memory block. Since program access patterns to instructions are regular and predictable, current techniques can analyze instruction caches with high accuracy. However, data access patterns are significantly more complex [11]. To analyze data caches, it is crucial to determine all possible memory blocks that each instruction might access during execution [16]. This task is challenging because static data references often require extending invariant registers [18], which are generated by instructions that can be moved out of loops. For loop-affine array accesses, several methods are proposed [10, 19] to analyze array access patterns for data cache analysis.

Different from the loop-affine array accesses, the cache behavior analysis for SP-relative addressing is more complicated. R. T. White et al. [24] have noted that for stack data, the location of local variables for each function call can be determined accurately using address calculators and compiler analysis. By analyzing the program's control and data flow, the compiler and address calculator can predict stack data behavior even with multiple function calls and recursion. However, applying this approach to WCET calculations can lead to high computational loads and path explosion problems. Existing method [4] assumes that a SP-relative addressing may access any stack address and therefore leads to pessimistic cache interference analysis result, and WCET bound.

After obtaining cache behavior, integrating program constraints further enhances the accuracy of WCET predictions and helps address issues such as path explosion. Li, Malik, and Wolfe [13] proposed a method that combines cache models with Implicit Path Enumeration Technique (IPET) to simulate the impact of cache behavior on program execution time. This method considers dynamic changes in cache states, such as whether the cache contains the required data when accessing a specific memory address. Wilhelm et al. [25] focused on the precise modeling of loop constraints. Vivi et al. [21] proposed an infeasible path detection algorithm that finds pairwise conflicts between branches and assignments. Schoeberl, Brandner, and Puffitsch [20] discussed the necessity of considering specific program constraints in WCET analysis, such as function calls, task scheduling, and stack operations. Therefore, by designing functional constraints specific to a particular analysis method, combined with detailed information on the behaviour of the program, it is possible to exclude infeasible paths and avoid unreliable WCET estimates.

3   Background

This sections briefly presents the background knowledge of existing Abstract Interpretation-based WCET analysis method.

3.1   Control Flow Analysis

```
0000000000400604 <my_fabs>:
  400604:   d10043ff     sub sp, sp, #0x10
  400608:   bd000fe0     str s0, [sp, #12]
  ...// Some assembly code omitted here
  400614:   54000044     b.mi 40061c <my_fabs+0x18>
  400618:   14000004     b    400628 <my_fabs+0x24>
  40061c:   bd400fe0     ldr s0, [sp, #12]
  400620:   1e214000     fneg   s0, s0
  400624:   14000002     b    40062c <my_fabs+0x28>
  400628:   bd400fe0     ldr s0, [sp, #12]
  40062c:   910043ff     add sp, sp, #0x10
  400630:   d65f03c0     ret

0000000000400634 <main>:
  400634:   a9bd7bfd     stp x29, x30, [sp, #-48]!
  400638:   910003fd     mov x29, sp
  40063c:   90000000     adrp    x0, 400000 <__abi_tag-0x278>
  ...// Some assembly code omitted here
  400660:   1400000a     b    400688 <main+0x54>
  400664:   b9802fe0     ldrsw   x0, [sp, #44]
  400674:   97ffffe4     bl   400604 <my_fabs>
  ...// Some assembly code omitted here
  400688:   b9402fe0     ldr w0, [sp, #44]
  40068c:   7100101f     cmp w0, #0x4
  400690:   54fffead     b.le    400664 <main+0x30>
  400694:   52800000     mov w0, #0x0
  400698:   a8c37bfd     ldp x29, x30, [sp], #48
  40069c:   d65f03c0     ret
```

Listing 1. Assembly Code of the Program fabs

The worst-case execution Time (WCET) analysis is conducted utilizing the Control Flow Graph (CFG) of each program. The CFG is generally constructed based on the binary code of each program rather than the high-level languages to mitigate the effects of compiler optimizations. In specific, it is created through the decomposition of the program into a series of basic blocks, in which instructions must be executed sequentially without branch. The constructed basic blocks are subsequently linked based on their sequential execution order, forming the CFG. An illustrative example of a CFG is presented in Fig. 1. We first construct basic blocks by identifying the branch instructions in the disassembled code in Listing 1. Function my_fabs has three branch instructions: line4 points to line6, line5 points to line9, and line8 points to line10. Therefore the function are divided by these branch instructions into 4 basic blocks, and the CFG of my_fabs is constructed as the gray parts shown in Fig. 1. Similarly, by identifying all the branch instructions including function call and return instructions, the CFG of the program is constructed as shown in Fig. 1.

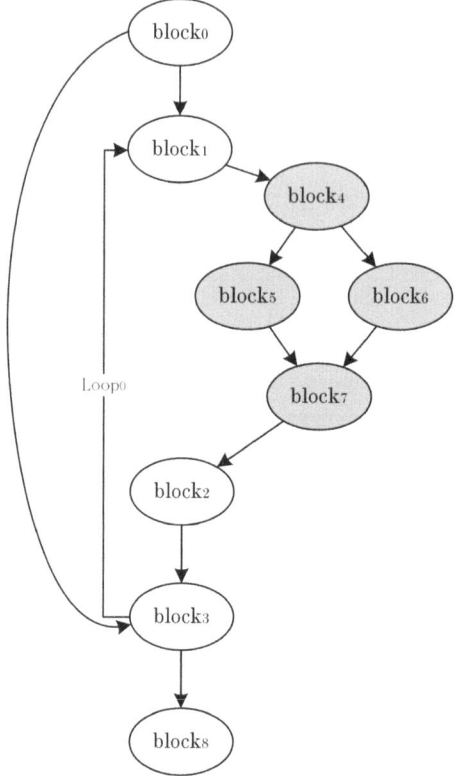

Fig. 1. CFG of the Program of Listing 1

3.2   Abstract Interpretation Based Cache Behavior Analysis

Based on the CFG, the analysis of cache behavior is conducted. Whether a memory reference results in a cache hit or miss significantly depends on the basic blocks (i.e., paths) the program traverses. To avoid exploring all possible program paths, existing methods typically employ abstract interpretation to statically analyze cache behavior. In essence, the abstract interpretation method merges concrete cache states from various paths into a singular abstract cache state, unveiling the worst-case scenario. The cache analysis rooted in abstract interpretation generally comprises three components: the Must analysis, which keeps only the memory blocks that are present in the cache on every path and maintains the maximum age of the accessed memory block, to predict whether a memory block is always in the cache; the May analysis, which retains all memory blocks across distinct paths and maintains the minimum age of the accessed memory block, to predict whether a memory block is likely to be in the cache; and the Persistence analysis, which maintains the maximum age of the accessed memory block and retains memory blocks that appear on at least one path, to predict whether a memory block is persistent. Then all the memory references are classified into four categories, as described in Table 1.

Table 1. Classification of Cache Access Behaviors

Classification	Cache Access Behaviors Described	Analysis
AH (Always Hit)	Every time the memory block is accessed, it is guaranteed to hit in the cache	Must
AM (Always Miss)	Every time the memory block is accessed, it is guaranteed to miss in the cache	May
PS (Persistent)	The first time the memory block is accessed, it misses; then all subsequent accesses hit in the cache	Persistent
NC (No classified)	The memory access cannot be classified into any of the above three categories	/

In the following we take the Must analysis as an example to illustrate the abstract interpretation based method. Firstly, three abstract cache states are defined for each basic block:

- **ACS_{in}**: It represents the abstract state (ACS) of the base block before execution begins. It is obtained by merging the post-execution abstract state (ACS_{out}) of all the predecessor nodes of the basic block. This merge operation requires the Join function of the Must analysis method. If no predecessor node exists, the ACS_{in} is set to none.
- **GEN**: It includes the memory blocks accessed by the basic block.
- **ACS_{out}**: It represents the abstract state of the base block after performing a series of memory access operations. First it needs to get access to the memory block through the Gen function, and update based on ACS_{in} status, which needs to apply the Update function of the Must analysis method.

Then, To describe the changes in cache state during program execution, two functions are defined over the abstract cache state to describe the changes in cache state during the program's execution.

- **Update**: The Update function for Must analysis is used to represent changes of the memory access over the ACS. Similar to actual cache replacement policies, each time a new memory access occurs, it is placed in the most "recent" position. The remaining memory blocks in the cache then follow the LRU (Least Recently Used) strategy.
- **Join**: The Join function is used to combined the abstract cache states of multiple basic blocks. It is similar to set intersection, and always has an upper bound of the position of the memory block. A memory block only stays in the abstract set state, if it is in both operand abstract set states. It gets the oldest age, if it has two different ages. For program in Listing 1, in the $block_6$, the memory block at address "sp+12" and "0x400028" is accessed, while in the $block_5$, only "0x400028" is accessed. Therefore in the $block_7$, the memory block at address "sp+12" will not left after the Join function while "0x400028" does.

Because programs contain loops or recursive structures, this process requires multiple iterations to explore all possible execution paths. Each iteration updates the abstract state based on the program's control flow and data flow until the abstract state stabilizes. The final ACS are obtained, the memory blocks that reside in each basic block ACS_{in} are treated as AH, which means that by the time execution reaches this basic block, the cache already contains these memory blocks and they will be hit without having to be reloaded. The analysis process of the other methods is similar to the Must method, but they differ in the Join function.

3.3   Implicit Path Enumeration

With the predicted cache behaviors of each memory reference and the pipeline architecture of the CPU, the WCET of each basic block can be computed. Then Implicit Path Enumeration Technique (IPET) is used for calculating the WCET of the program. Computing the WCET of the program is essentially equals to find the longest path within its CFG. IPET models the problem of finding the longest path as an Integer Linear Programming (ILP) problem.

We take the example in Fig. 1 to illustrate IPET. The objective function can be expressed as:

$$\text{WCET} = \text{MAX} \sum_{i=1}^{N} T_i \cdot X_i \tag{1}$$

where N is the count of basic blocks of the program, T_i is the WCET of the basic block i, and X_i is the execution count of the basic block i. The constraints is derived from the CFG of the program. For any basic block, its execution count is equal to the sum of the execution counts of all predecessor blocks, and also equal to the sum of the execution counts of all successor blocks:

$$X_i = \sum_{j \in \text{ all predecessors}} X_j = \sum_{k \in \text{ all successors}} X_k \tag{2}$$

For example, the execution count of block$_7$ (denoted as X_7) is the sum of X_5 and X_6, and it is also equal to X_2. The execution count of block$_1$ (represented as X_1) is the sum of X_0 and the loop bound of L_0, and equal to X_4, we denote the Loop bound of the loop i by L_i. Some of the constraints of the example program are expressed as followed:

$$X_7 - X_5 - X_6 = 0$$
$$X_7 - X_2 = 0$$
$$X_1 - X_0 - L_0 = 0$$
$$X_1 - X_4 = 0$$

4   Motivation

For data cache analysis, executing a single instruction can involve accessing multiple memory blocks. Therefore, before performing data cache analysis, it is essential to pre-process and determine the set of memory blocks that each instruction might access. A significant portion of these memory accesses are related to stack operations.

At runtime, global variables, static variables, and constants are stored in the global static area, allocated and freed by the system. The addresses of global variables are typically obtainable through static analysis, as they are determined at compile time and can be retrieved from the symbol table. In contrast, local variables and function parameters are stored in the stack area, with addresses dynamically allocated and released by the compiler based on the stack layout. This dynamic nature makes it challenging to precisely determine the addresses of local variables through static analysis.

Stack frame management is closely tied to the stack pointer, a register used to point to the current top of the stack, e.g., SP register in AArch64, %rsp and %rbp register in x86-64, and the B15 register in C66x DSPs. In this paper, we uniformly refer to it as the SP. SP-relative addressing is a method for accessing memory based on an offset from the SP register. This technique is commonly used to access local variables, function parameters, or return addresses on the stack. Since SP points to the top of the stack, SP-relative addressing allows for convenient reading or writing of data within the stack. For example, local variables can be accessed by adding an offset to SP, such as "mov r0, [sp, #-4]". Additionally, the value of SP can be manipulated to manage stack space. For instance, the instruction "sub sp, sp, #8" decrements SP by 8, allocating extra stack space for local variables. Conversely, "add sp, sp, #8" increments SP by 8, releasing the previously allocated stack space. These operations ensure proper positioning and management of local variables during function calls. SP-relative addressing simplifies and enhances the efficiency of managing function calls and returns, as adjusting SP is sufficient to handle new local variables and parameters.

Although providing advantages in memory management, SP-relative addressing poses challenges in WCET estimation, as **the value of the stack pointer (SP) register is typically not available at compile time.** The SP register dynamically changes as the program executes, its exact value is often dependent on the current state of the program stack during runtime, making it challenging to predict or determine beforehand at compile time. Especially in case of recursive or nested function calls, the stack pointer varies with each call, creating multiple layers of stack frames. Static analysis tools struggle to accurately predict SP positions across different function call frames without runtime information, making it difficult to determine the potential data blocks accessed by these instructions.

We show an example in Listing 1 to show the pessimism of the existing method. This example includes the *main* function and the *my_fabs* function, where the *main* function is responsible for initializing variables and call *my_fabs* to calculate the absolute value of a float.

Upon entering *main*, the stack pointer (SP) references the current stack top. The initial instruction in *main*, "stp x29, x30, [sp, #-48]!", stores x29 (the frame pointer) and x30 (the return address) onto the stack, moving the SP downwards by 48 bytes to reserve space for the new stack frame. Subsequently, the program transitions to *my_fabs*, causing the SP to descend once more to establish the stack frame for *my_fabs* (i.e., "sub sp, sp, #0x10"). In this example, the instructions "ldr s0, [sp, #12]" (line 7) and "ldr w0, [sp, #44]" (line 23) both reference memory addresses relative to the SP value. However, the SP values at the time of executing these instructions differ.

The stack pointer's value is path-dependent, making precise SP value determination typically needs to enumerate all possible execution paths, which is computational intractable. Existing methods [10,11] adopt a pessimistic approach by assuming that SP-relative addressing operations could potentially access any stack addresses, and therefore may consider that SP-relative addressing might contend with each other in the cache, resulting in a pessimistic analysis result.

5   Methodology

This section introduces a novel analysis framework that leverages a novel structure termed Hyper-Block to estimate the worst-case execution time. Conventional methods [10,11,28] struggle to accurately forecast SP-relative addressing, leading to a pessimistic estimation of the WCET bound. The proposed approach initially identifies the program segment where the SP address remains constant, termed Hyper-Block, aiming for a more precise WCET bound within each Hyper-Block, as detailed in Sect. 5.1. Subsequently, a novel technique is introduced to conduct a precise WCET analysis for the whole program by accurately determining the offset on SP values of different Hyper-Blocks, based on the call hierarchy among various procedures, as shown in Sect. 5.2.

5.1   Hyper-Block

Existing WCET analysis frameworks encounter challenges in accurately evaluating the stack pointer (SP) value, and have to assume a worst-case scenario where each SP-relative addressing operation could potentially access any stack address, leading to an estimated WCET bound, as discussed in Sect. 4. However, the SP value does not change randomly. Changes in the SP value generally occur during function calls or returns, remaining constant over prolonged duration. In cases where the SP value remains unchanged, despite its specific value being unknown, the offset concerning memory addresses accessed by SP-relative instructions can be statically determined. This capability facilitates a more precise cache behavior analysis.

Our analysis relies on the Global-Control Flow Graph (G-CFG) of the program, constructed from the Control Flow Graph (CFG) of each function and their inter-function call relationships as shown in Fig. 2. More specifically, we establish an G-CFG by analyzing the caller-callee relationships between functions using assembly code, which avoiding the impact of compiler optimizations. We establish connections between the basic block containing the function's call instruction and the entry basic block of the called function. Similarly, the exit basic block of the called function is linked to the return block in the calling function. This caller-callee relationship can typically be directly obtained through the jump instructions in the assembly code. However, for function pointers and indirect function calls where the target function cannot be determined explicitly, we adopt symbolic execution to identify all the potential functions they point to. In addition, we accept the user input to identify the caller-callee relationship for building a more accurate G-CFG. In order to perform a precise cache behavior analysis for SP-relative addressing memory references, we first identify program fragments where the SP value in constant, dented by Hyper-Block. A Hyper-Block is a sub-graph of the G-CFG, which contains multiple basic blocks that share the same function stack. In order to obtain a control flow between different Hyper-Blocks without violating the program structure, we construct Hyper-Block based on the G-CFG by the following steps:

1. from the inner-most loop to the outer loop of the G-CFG, group neighbouring basic blocks that reside in the same loop and same function as a Hyper-Block.
2. if all the basic blocks in a loop are grouped as a Hyper-Block, the Hyper-Block is considered as a basic block for the following Hyper-Block construction; otherwise, if the loop is divide into several Hyper-Blocks, the Hyper-Blocks are finally obtained.
3. iteratively perform the above steps until a fixed-point.

The algorithm for building Hyper-Blocks is detailed in Algorithm 1.

Algorithm 1: Hyper-Block construct

1: **for** each basic block i does not belong to any HyperBlock **do**
2:    Initialize $HyperBlock_i$ for i and Add $HyperBlock_i$ to HyperBlocks
3:    **for** each successor j of i **do**
4:       **if** j in same procudure AND no other path between i AND in same loop level **then**
5:          Add j to $HyperBlock_i.blocks$
6:       **end if**
7:    **end for**
8: **end for**
9: **for** each HyperBlock hb **do**
10:    **for** each head block b_h and tail block in b_t in hb **do**
11:       Initialize $dummy_{in}$ AND $dummy_{out}$
12:       $dummy_{in}.out = b.in$ AND $dummy_{in}.in = b.out$
13:    **end for**
14: **end for**

Figure 2 shows a typical example of how to construct the Hyper-Block. In the example, basic blocks with the same color belongs to the same function. Following the instructions, we firstly construct 6 Hyper-Blocks, {block$_1$, block$_2$, block$_3$}, {block$_6$, block$_7$, block$_8$, block$_9$}, {block$_{12}$, block$_{13}$, block$_{14}$}, {block$_{10}$},

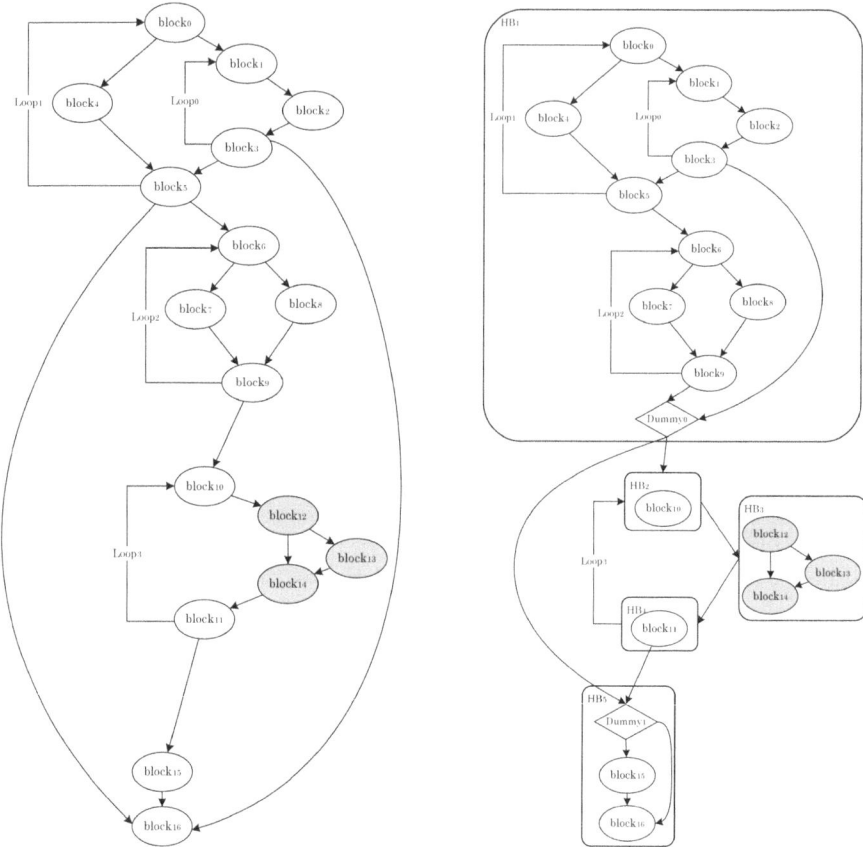

Fig. 2. G-CFG of the Program

Fig. 3. Control flow constructed by Hyper-Block

{block$_{11}$}, and {block$_{15}$, block$_{16}$}. Since all the basic blocks in loop0 and loop2 are all constructed as a Hyper-Block, respectively, {block$_1$, block$_2$, block$_3$} and {block$_6$, block$_7$, block$_8$, block$_9$} are considered a basic block and further to construct a new Hyper-Block, i.e., HB$_1$.

After dividing the G-CFG into several Hyper-Blocks, each Hyper-Block can be constructed as a smaller CFG to facilitate further analysis. If irregular branch structure occurs between Hyper-Blocks, special block called dummy node is required to add in the Hyper-Block. In the example of Fig. 3, block$_3$ and block$_4$ in the Hyper-Block1 both connect to block$_7$ in Hyper-Block5. To build a CFG with Hyper-Blocks, we introduce dummy node to create a dedicated entry and exit nodes of each Hyper-Block. If there are multiple exit blocks, a dummy node is created, and all outgoing edges from the exit nodes are connected to this node. This dummy node is then connected to the entry nodes of other Hyper-Block, with the edge types consistent with those of the original outgoing edges. Similarly, if there are multiple entry blocks, a dummy node will be created. This makes the dummy node the only entry node, and it connects to the exit nodes of other Hyper-Block, maintaining consistent edge types. Therefore, redundant edges of the same type between two Hyper-Block should be removed. For example, if there are two *nottaken* type edges between Hyper-Block 1 and Hyper-Block 3, only one should be retained.

5.2   WCET Computation

Once all the Hyper-Block are constructed, all the SP-relative addressing instructions inside a Hyper-Block share the same SP value. Then, we can simply and safely compute the WCET of each Hyper-Block with the existing WCET analysis method by enumerating the SP value from 0 to $set - 1$, where set denote the counts of cache set. Note that, whether two memory references cause cache contentions depends on the cache set they mapped rather than the exact memory address they accessed. Therefore, it is unnecessary to perform enumeration across the entire memory address space, while simply enumerating the SP value from 0 to $set - 1$ can significantly reduce analysis overhead. Moreover, to accurately determine whether two SP-relative addressing are mapped to the same cache set, we further enumerate such addresses by calculating the specific cache set of it in different SP value. Since step is carried out at the cache set granularity, its overhead is acceptable. Such enumeration yields a sound WCET estimation for each Hyper-Block. The proof is straightforward and is thus omitted.

Moreover, our method only leads to a linearly increased computational complexity, which is acceptable. Finally, we can generate a table that correlates various SP values with their respective estimated WCET bounds. We define function $WCET(HB_i, SP_j)$ to return the WCET of Hyper-Block HB_i, when the SP equals SP_j. Compared to Transformed-Control Flow Graph (T-CFG), which unfolds all the function calls and struggles to represent recursions, the G-CFG we use is essentially a function call graph, making it well-suited to represent recursive functions. We compute the WCET of each instance of a recursion by enumerating as mentioned above. Although different instances have different SP value, since we always seek the worst-case SP value across all instances, this approach remains safe in WCET estimation.

Although the WCET of each Hyper-Block can be computed by enumerating all the possible SP values, simply adding them together would yield a conservative estimation of the WCET, as the SP values that result the WCET of different Hyper-Block may not be simultaneously satisfied. For instance, for Hyper-Blocks that belongs to the same function, their SP value are same. So if the estimated WCET of these Hyper-Blocks corresponding to different SP values, the combination of the SP value are invalided, resulting in a overestimated WCET bound.

For the example shown in Fig. 3, we divide the G-CFG of the example into 5 Hyper-Blocks: HB_1, HB_2, HB_3, HB_4 and HB_5. We assume that the longest path of the program is:

$$HB_1 \mapsto HB_2 \mapsto HB_3 \mapsto HB_4 \mapsto HB_5$$

and the WCET of each Hyper-Block and the effected SP values are:

$$\mathrm{WCET}(\mathrm{HB}_1, 0), \mathrm{WCET}(\mathrm{HB}_2, 0), \mathrm{WCET}(\mathrm{HB}_3, \ 2)$$

$$\mathrm{WCET}(\mathrm{HB}_4, 1), \mathrm{WCET}(\mathrm{HB}_5, \ 0)$$

Since HB_1, HB_2, HB_4, HB_5 belong to the same function, their SP values should be same. However, the computed WCET of these corresponds to different SP values, i.e., 0, 0, 2, 0, respectively. So the combination of the SP values and the WCET are infeasible.

In order to safely compute the WCET of the program and avoid involving invalid combinations of SP values from different Hyper-Blocks, we formulate the constraints between SP values based on the control flow among Hyper-Blocks. Firstly, if Hyper-Block belong to the same function, they share the same stack and their stack pointers should be identical. Therefore, if HB_i and HB_j belong to the same function, we obtain the relationship:

$$\mathrm{SP}_{\mathrm{HB}_i} = \mathrm{SP}_{\mathrm{HB}_j} \tag{3}$$

Additionally, during task transitions, the SP value changes. In specific, the SP values increased when entering a new function for saving the state of the currently executing task (including the stack pointer), and decreases when returning to the caller function for restoring the state of the next task. Therefore, equations are established to relate the SP value between the caller Hyper-Block HB_i and the called Hyper-Block HB_j, as well as between the called Hyper-Block HB_m and the Hyper-BlockHB_n it returns to:

$$\mathrm{address}(\mathrm{SP}_{\mathrm{HB}_i}) + \mathrm{Size}_{\mathrm{HB}_j^i} = \mathrm{address}(\mathrm{SP}_{\mathrm{HB}_j}) \tag{4}$$

$$\mathrm{address}(\mathrm{SP}_{\mathrm{HB}_m}) - \mathrm{Size}_{\mathrm{HB}_n^m} = \mathrm{address}(\mathrm{SP}_{\mathrm{HB}_n}) \tag{5}$$

where $\mathrm{Size}_{\mathrm{HB}_j^i}$ denotes the change on SP value during Hyper-Block transition from HB_i to HB_j, $\mathrm{address}(\mathrm{SP}_{\mathrm{HB}_i})$ denotes the exact value of the SP in HB_i.

Since we only care the cache set that a SP-relative addressing mapped to, rather than the exact memory address. The above relationships can be transferred into the following SP constraint:

$$\mathrm{abs}(\mathrm{SP}_{\mathrm{HB}_i} - \mathrm{SP}_{\mathrm{HB}_j})\%set = \frac{\mathrm{Size}_{\mathrm{HB}_j^i}}{\mathrm{Size}_{\mathrm{line}}}\%set \tag{6}$$

$$\mathrm{abs}(\mathrm{SP}_{\mathrm{HB}_m} - \mathrm{SP}_{\mathrm{HB}_n})\%set = \frac{\mathrm{Size}_{\mathrm{HB}_n^m}}{\mathrm{Size}_{\mathrm{line}}}\%set \tag{7}$$

where $\mathrm{Size}_{\mathrm{line}}$ returns the cache line size.

With the above analysis on the SP values, we can derive the SP constraints and combine them with the program IPET constraints (i.e., as shown in Sect. 3.3). For the example in Fig. 3 the WCET can be formulated as:

$$\mathrm{Maximize} = \mathbf{X}(\mathrm{HB}_i) * \mathrm{WCET}(\mathrm{HB}_i, \mathrm{SP}_i) \tag{8}$$

Subject to:

ipet constraints :

$$X(\mathrm{HB}_1) - X(\mathrm{HB}_2) - X(\mathrm{HB}_5) = 0$$
$$X(\mathrm{HB}_2) - X(\mathrm{HB}_1) - X(\mathrm{Loop}_3) = 0$$
$$X(\mathrm{HB}_5) - X(\mathrm{HB}_4) - X(\mathrm{HB}_1) = 0$$
$$X(\mathrm{HB}_2) - X(\mathrm{HB}_3) = 0$$
$$X(\mathrm{HB}_3) - X(\mathrm{HB}_4) = 0$$

SP constraints :

$$\mathrm{SP}_{\mathrm{HB}_1} = \mathrm{SP}_{\mathrm{HB}_2} = \mathrm{SP}_{\mathrm{HB}_4} = \mathrm{SP}_{\mathrm{HB}_5}$$
$$\mathrm{abs}(\mathrm{SP}_{\mathrm{HB}_2} - \mathrm{SP}_{\mathrm{HB}_5})\% set = \frac{\mathrm{Size}_{\mathrm{HB}_5^2}}{\mathrm{Size}_{\mathrm{line}}}\% set$$
$$\mathrm{abs}(\mathrm{SP}_{\mathrm{HB}_5} - \mathrm{SP}_{\mathrm{HB}_4})\% set = \frac{\mathrm{Size}_{\mathrm{HB}_4^5}}{\mathrm{Size}_{\mathrm{line}}}\% set$$

where $\mathbf{X}(\mathrm{HB_i})$ returns the execution counts of $\mathrm{HB_i}$.

6 Evaluation

In this section, we evaluate the proposed method and compare it with the existing method [10]. In this method, which precisely model the access behavior of global variable. However, this method does not analyze SP-relative addressing accesses, pessimistically assuming that such accesses could target any memory address in the stack.

6.1 Evaluation Setup

We implement the proposed method based on the existing WCET analysis tool, Chronos [12]. For simplicity, we only focus on the single-core scenario without consider the shared cache contention. Note that, the proposed method focuses on a precise cache behavior analysis for SP-relative addressing and can be straightforwardly extended to deal with multi-core scenario by integrating it with the existing method [28]. In the experiment, we adopt the processor architecture of the TMS320C66x DSP CPU [22], a high-performance digital signal processor from Texas Instruments. The detailed cache configuration are summarized as follows (Table 2):

Table 2. Cache configurations in the experiment

Cache Level	Capacity	Block Size	Associativity	Hit Latency	Miss Latency
L1 Instruction	32 KB	32B	1	1 cycle	12.5 cycles
L1 Data	32 KB	64B	2	1 cycle	6 cycles

Similar to most relative works [7,9–11], we selected benchmark programs from the Mälardalen WCET Benchmark Suite [6]. All programs were compiled using the TI C6000-CGT compiler v7.4.4. The program uses the default stack start address (compilers usually assign a fixed base address to the stack), and resizes the stack size to 4 KB, which is the default stack size commonly used in embedded systems, which is also same as the GNU Compiler Collection for ARM.

6.2   Experimental Results

Table 3 shows the experimental results. we refer to the estimated WCET bounds derived from our proposed method and the traditional approach as WCET-Our and WCET-Con, respectively. We compare the WCET-Our and WCET-Con and use $\frac{\text{WCET-Con}}{\text{WCET-Our}} - 1$ as a metric to demonstrate the tightness of WCET bound produced by the proposed method. Experimental results in Table 3 reveals that, in comparison to the conventional method, our approach produces a tighter estimated WCET bound for all the benchmark programs. On average, our method achieves a 11.85% improvement in tightness.

Table 3. Estimated WCET bound in cycles from our method and the existing method

Benchmark	WCET-Con	Con-Timr	WCET-Our	Our-Time	$\frac{\text{WCET-Con}}{\text{WCET-Our}} - 1$
bsort100	658159	9.37 s	482852	401.50 s	36.31%
fdct	14624	84.76 s	11420	3511.47 s	28.06%
edn	3669718	48.38 s	2883263	2499.95 s	27.28%
insertsort	5676	7.74 s	4728	389.17 s	20.05%
matmult	550293	25.10 s	459668	794.64 s	19.72%
fir	161006	18.85 s	137000.5	317.20 s	17.52%
bs	642	6.78 s	546.5	76.16 s	17.47%
lms	3735553	52.86 s	3299397	3618.88 s	13.22%
cnt	1649631	11.71 s	1496112	5208.48 s	10.26%
djikstra	12186	276.96 s	11516	6513.51 s	5.82%
jfdctint	53509	75.21 s	50929.5	3158.24 s	5.06%
fibcall	1411	4.76 s	1363.5	72.34 s	3.48%
ud	23866	138.77 s	23080.5	16234.53 s	3.40%
crc	227066	69.84 s	220334.5	781.84 s	3.06%
floyd	10374	25.93 s	10158.5	1013.38 s	2.12%
ns	38355	25.60 s	38235	798.53 s	0.31%
expint	296891	40.81 s	296677	233.99 s	0.07%
prime	245877	8.16 s	245824	178.04 s	0.02%
Average					11.85%

Our method achieves a significant improvement for *bsort100* (36.3%), *fdct* (28.05%), *edn* (27.3%), *insertsort* (20.05%), and *matmult* (19.7%). This is due to the fact that these benchmarks contain a certain number of SP-relative addressing operations, which introduce significant cache interference between SP-relative addressing and global variables. For instance, in *insertsort*, which involves iterative array traversals and element insertions, out of its total of 32 data memory references, 12 are SP-relative addressing. Existing method can not determine the exact memory address of SP-relative addressing, and pessimistically classify all the data memory references as either AM or NC. Our approach identifies Hyper-Block and is capable to justify which SP-relative addressing instructions share the same SP value, enabling more accurate cache interference analysis.

The following List 2 is the source code for *insertsort*. All local variables (i.e., variable *i, j, temp*) and temporary data are stored in B15[1], B15[2] and B15[3]. With the execution of "i = 2" (line 8), the memory block associated with B15[1] to be loaded into the corresponding cache set, since B15[1], B15[2] and B15[3] belong to the same memory block, all the subsequent instructions related SP address are AH.

```
1   unsigned int a[11];
2   int main()
3   {
4     int  i,j, temp;
5     a[0] = 0;    /* assume all data is positive */
6     a[1] = 11; a[2]=10;a[3]=9; a[4]=8; a[5]=7; a[6]=6; a[7]=5;
7     a[8] =4; a[9]=3; a[10]=2;
8     i = 2;
9     while(i <= 10){
10        j = i;
11        while (a[j] < a[j-1])
12        {
13          temp = a[j];
14          a[j] = a[j-1];
15          a[j-1] = temp;
16          j--;
17        }
18        i++;
19     }
20     return 1;
21  }
22
```

Listing 2. Source Code of insertsort

Consequently, in *insertsort*, 11 data memory references are classified as AH. Similarly, in *bsort100*, with a total of 34 data memory references, 27 being SP-relative addressing, our method categorizes 21 data memory references as AH, a significant improvement over the existing method, which yields none.

However, for benchmarks like ns, expint, and prime, which have less inherently cache conflict for local variables, our method still performs better but the precision improvement is reduced. Our improvement in accuracy is 11.85%, while the analysis time increased by an average of 48.16 times. Considering that this analysis is conducted statically and performed only a limited number of times, the additional time overhead incurred for improved accuracy is worthwhile.

7   Conclusion

This paper introduces a novel cache behavior analysis approach for SP-relative addressing, leveraging the well-established abstract-interpretation method. By introducing a novel analysis unit called Hyper-Block, this method accurately identify the program segments where the SP value remains constant, enabling a more refined cache interference analysis for each Hyper-Block. Across various Hyper-Blocks, we systematically investigate the SP value transitions and encapsulate the program's Worst-Case Execution Time (WCET) calculation as an Integer Linear Programming (ILP) problem. Empirical results underscore the efficacy of the proposed technique in significantly refining the estimated WCET bounds.

Acknowledgments. This work is supported by National Natural Science Foundation of China (Grant No.62432005, 62302270), Shandong Provincial Natural Science Foundation (Grant No. ZR20220F003), Department of Science & Technology of Shandong Province (Grant No. SYS202201), Quan Cheng Laboratory (Grant No. QCLZD202302), Taishan Scholars Program (No. tsqn202211281).

References

1. Audsley, N.C., Burns, A., Davis, R.I., Tindell, K.W., Wellings, A.J.: Fixed priority pre-emptive scheduling: an historical perspective. Real-Time Syst. **8**(2–3), 173–198 (1995)
2. Ballabriga, C., Cassé, H.: Improving the first-miss computation in set-associative instruction caches. In: 2008 Euromicro Conference on Real-Time Systems, pp. 341–350. IEEE (2008)
3. Cullmann, C.: Cache persistence analysis: theory and practice. ACM Trans. Embed. Comput. Syst. **12**(1s) (2013). https://doi.org/10.1145/2435227.2435236
4. Ferdinand, C., Heckmann, R.: aiT: worst-case execution time prediction by static program analysis. In: Jacquart, R. (ed.) Building the Information Society. IIFIP, vol. 156, pp. 377–383. Springer, Boston, MA (2004). https://doi.org/10.1007/978-1-4020-8157-6_29
5. Ferdinand, C., Wilhelm, R.: Efficient and precise cache behavior prediction for real-time systems. Real-Time Syst. **17**, 131–181 (1999)
6. Gustafsson, J., Betts, A., Ermedahl, A., Lisper, B.: The mälardalen WCET benchmarks: past, present and future. In: 10th International Workshop on Worst-Case Execution Time Analysis (WCET 2010). Schloss Dagstuhl-Leibniz-Zentrum fuer Informatik (2010)
7. Gustafsson, J., Ermedahl, A., Sandberg, C., Lisper, B.: Automatic derivation of loop bounds and infeasible paths for WCET analysis using abstract execution. In: 2006 27th IEEE International Real-Time Systems Symposium (RTSS 2006), pp. 57–66 (2006). https://doi.org/10.1109/RTSS.2006.12

8. Hardy, D., Puaut, I.: WCET analysis of multi-level non-inclusive set-associative instruction caches. In: 2008 Real-Time Systems Symposium, pp. 456–466. IEEE (2008)

9. Hardy, D., Rouxel, B., Puaut, I.: The heptane static worst-case execution time estimation tool. In: Worst-Case Execution Time Analysis (2017). https://api.semanticscholar.org/CorpusID:20377524

10. Huynh, B.K., Ju, L., Roychoudhury, A.: Scope-aware data cache analysis for WCET estimation. In: 2011 17th IEEE Real-Time and Embedded Technology and Applications Symposium, pp. 203–212. IEEE (2011)

11. Lesage, B., Hardy, D., Puaut, I.: WCET analysis of multi-level set-associative data caches. In: 9th International Workshop on Worst-Case Execution Time Analysis (WCET 2009). Schloss-Dagstuhl-Leibniz Zentrum für Informatik (2009)

12. Li, X., Liang, Y., Mitra, T., Roychoudhury, A.: Chronos: a timing analyzer for embedded software. Sci. Comput. Program. **69**(1–3), 56–67 (2007)

13. Li, Y.T., Malik, S., Wolfe, A.: Efficient microarchitecture modeling and path analysis for real-time software. In: Proceedings 16th IEEE Real-Time Systems Symposium, pp. 298–307. IEEE (1995)

14. Liu, C.L., Layland, J.W.: Scheduling algorithms for multiprogramming in a hard real-time environment, pp. 174–189. IEEE Computer Society Press, Washington, DC (1989)

15. Lundqvist, T., Stenström, P.: An integrated path and timing analysis method based on cycle-level symbolic execution. Real-Time Syst. **17**, 183–207 (1999)

16. Lundqvist, T., Stenstrom, P.: A method to improve the estimated worst-case performance of data caching. In: Proceedings Sixth International Conference on Real-Time Computing Systems and Applications, RTCSA 1999 (Cat. No. PR00306), pp. 255–262. IEEE (1999)

17. Mancuso, R., Pellizzoni, R., Caccamo, M., Sha, L., Yun, H.: WCET (m) estimation in multi-core systems using single core equivalence. In: 2015 27th Euromicro Conference on Real-Time Systems, pp. 174–183. IEEE (2015)

18. Păsăreanu, C.S., Visser, W.: A survey of new trends in symbolic execution for software testing and analysis. Int. J. Softw. Tools Technol. Transfer **11**, 339–353 (2009)

19. Ramaprasad, H., Mueller, F.: Bounding worst-case data cache behavior by analytically deriving cache reference patterns. In: 11th IEEE Real Time and Embedded Technology and Applications Symposium, pp. 148–157. IEEE (2005)

20. Schoeberl, M., Schleuniger, P., Puffitsch, W., Brandner, F., Probst, C.W.: Towards a time-predictable dual-issue microprocessor: the patmos approach. In: Bringing Theory to Practice: Predictability and Performance in Embedded Systems. Schloss-Dagstuhl-Leibniz Zentrum für Informatik (2011)

21. Suhendra, V., Mitra, T., Roychoudhury, A., Chen, T.: Efficient detection and exploitation of infeasible paths for software timing analysis. In: Proceedings of the 43rd Annual Design Automation Conference, pp. 358–363 (2006)

22. Texas Instruments: C66x CPU and Instruction Set Reference Guide. Texas Instruments (2010). https://www.ti.com/lit/pdf/sprugh7. no. SPRUGH7

23. Theiling, H., Ferdinand, C., Wilhelm, R.: Fast and precise WCET prediction by separated cache and path analyses. Real-Time Syst. **18**, 157–179 (2000)

24. White, R.T., Mueller, F., Healy, C., Whalley, D., Harmon, M.: Timing analysis for data and wrap-around fill caches. Real-Time Syst. **17**, 209–233 (1999)

25. Wilhelm, R., et al.: The worst-case execution-time problem–overview of methods and survey of tools. ACM Trans. Embed. Comput. Syst. (TECS) **7**(3), 1–53 (2008)

26. Yan, J., Zhang, W.: WCET analysis for multi-core processors with shared L2 instruction caches. In: 2008 IEEE Real-Time and Embedded Technology and Applications Symposium, pp. 80–89. IEEE (2008)
27. Zhang, W., Gong, F., Ju, L., Guan, N., Jia, Z.: Scope-aware useful cache block analysis for data cache related preemption delay. In: 2017 IEEE Real-Time and Embedded Technology and Applications Symposium (RTAS), pp. 63–74 (2017). https://doi.org/10.1109/RTAS.2017.35
28. Zhang, W., Lv, M., Chang, W., Ju, L.: Precise and scalable shared cache contention analysis for WCET estimation. In: Proceedings of the 59th ACM/IEEE Design Automation Conference, pp. 1267–1272 (2022)

Timing Analysis of Cause-Effect Chains for External Events with Finite Validity Intervals

Xiantong Luo[1], Haochun Liang[1], Yue Tang[1(✉)], Xu Jiang[2], Nan Guan[3], and Wang Yi[1,4]

[1] Northeastern University, Shenyang, China
`tangyue@cse.neu.edu.cn`
[2] University of Electronic Science and Technology of China, Chengdu, China
[3] City University of Hong Kong, Hong Kong, China
[4] Uppsala University, Uppsala, Sweden

Abstract. In complex real-time systems, specific functionality is generally implemented by a cause-effect chain, which is a sequence of multi-rate real-time tasks with data dependency. One of the critical prerequisites for the correct operation of such systems is that the external event is timely captured by the first task of the corresponding chain, propagated to the last task and generates a response during a predefined time interval. Most of existing work assumes the external event keeps continuously valid and focuses on when the response will be generated. However, in actual scenarios, the external event may become invalid shortly after its occurrence and there will never be a response to it. This paper considers such external events with finite validity intervals and proposes techniques to analyze the minimum validity interval of an external event to guarantee the existence of a corresponding response. Experiments with both a randomly generated workload and a case study are conducted to evaluate and verify the proposed techniques.

Keywords: Cause-effect Chain · Validity Interval · Timing Analysis

1 Introduction

The complexity of real-time embedded applications and the number of functionalities within a system are rapidly increasing nowadays. A typical example is autonomous driving systems, where new advanced driver assistance systems and enhanced safety features necessitate the integration of a growing number of sensors and actuators and the execution of increasingly complex software functions. These complex functionalities are often implemented as sequences of tasks that may be activated independently [1], known as *cause-effect chains*. A typical example of such task chains can be observed in control systems, where modern controllers need to collect sensor inputs, filter data, extract features, and generate control commands for actuators, as shown in Fig. 1.

T. Bourke et al. (Eds.): SETTA 2024, LNCS 15469, pp. 275–292, 2025.
https://doi.org/10.1007/978-981-96-0602-3_15

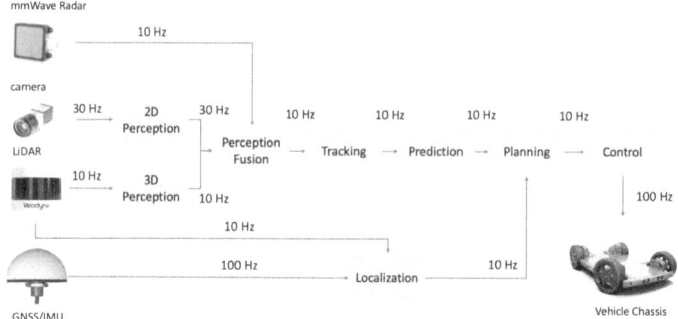

Fig. 1. Processing graph of an autonomous driving system in [2].

The end-to-end timing performance of a cause-effect chain, which describes the length of data propagation along the chain, is usually subject to some strict timing constraints, and failure to meet such requirements may lead to catastrophic consequences. For instance, when a pedestrian crosses the road, the Camera/Lidar task in an autonomous driving system captures the information about the pedestrian and makes appropriate decisions to avoid a collision. Formal methods are necessary to analyze the timing performance to ensure that end-to-end timing requirements are consistently honored. This has been a prominent topic of interest in both academia and industry [3–6].

Almost all existing work assumes that information from external events remains continuously valid, guaranteeing a corresponding response to any external events that occur. However, this assumption does not always hold true in real-world scenarios. For instance, if a pedestrian crosses the road and enters the car's blind spot before a response is generated, the car may make an incorrect decision. This is because the system might not detect the pedestrian's appearance, or the information may not successfully propagate to the task responsible for generating the control command.

Contributions. This paper addresses external events with finite validity intervals. It formally defines the validity interval of an external event and proposes a more general definition of reaction time for such external events. Based on this, this paper calculates the upper-bound of minimum length of validity interval to guarantee the existence of a reaction to any external event and analyzes the corresponding reaction time. Experiments with randomly generated workloads and a case study are conducted to evaluate the proposed techniques.

2   Preliminary

In this section, we first present a formal characterization of the system model, including the hardware platform, tasks, communication semantics, and cause-effect chains inspired by the event chain model in AUTOSAR-compliant automotive systems [7]. Secondly, we formally define the validity interval of an external

Table 1. Symbol table

Symbol	Description	Symbol	Description
τ_i	Task i in system	J_i^j	The j-th job released by τ_i
e_i	Worst-Case Execution Time of τ_i	$s(J_i^j)$	Start time of J_i^j
b_i	Best-Case Execution Time of τ_i	$f(J_i^j)$	Finish time of J_i^j
$T_i^{max}(T_i^{min})$	The maximum (minimum) inter-release time	$r(J_i^j)$	Release time of J_i^j
	between two consecutive jobs released by τ_i	$R(J_i^j)$	Response time of J_i^j
$\pi(\tau_i)$	Priority of τ_i	$\vec{c}$	Forward job chain
$\mathcal{R}(\tau_i)$	Response time of τ_i	$\overleftarrow{c}$	Data propagation chain
ρ	External events	$\vec{c}^*(\rho)$	Augmented forward job chain
$\mathcal{D}(\rho)$	Length of validity interval of ρ		with regards to an external event ρ

event, based on which we give a more generalized definition of reaction time, a widely adopted end-to-end latency metric. Table 1 summarizes the related symbols.

2.1 System Model

We consider a set of tasks deployed on a hardware platform consisting of several Electronic Control Units (ECUs). Each ECU is considered to be equivalent to the classical uni-processor system.

Tasks. A task is a piece of sequentially executable program and recurrently releases an infinite number of jobs, i.e., instances of the task. A task τ_i is characterized by a tuple: $(e_i, b_i, T_i^{max}, T_i^{min})$. e_i and b_i denote the Worst-Case Execution Time (WCET) and Best-Case Execution Time (BCET) of τ_i, respectively. T_i^{max} and T_i^{min} represent the maximum and minimum inter-release times between two consecutive jobs released by τ_i, respectively. The jth job released by τ_i is denoted by J_i^j. The *release time*, *start time* and *finish time* of J_i^j are denoted by $r(J_i^j)$, $s(J_i^j)$ and $f(J_i^j)$, respectively. The response time of J_i^j is denoted by $R(J_i^j) = f(J_i^j) - r(J_i^j)$, and the response time of task τ_i is denoted by $\mathcal{R}(\tau_i)$, which is the maximal response time among all its jobs.

Scheduling. Each task is statically mapped to an ECU, and the mapping is fixed in prior. A fixed-priority preemptive (FPP) scheduler is adopted to schedule all tasks (i.e., all jobs released by these tasks) mapped to the same ECU. Each task τ_i is assigned with a unique priority $\pi(\tau_i)$, and each job inherits the priority of the task releasing it. In particular, τ_i has higher priority than τ_j if $\pi(\tau_i) < \pi(\tau_j)$ holds. Tasks are assumed to have implicit deadlines, i.e., T_i^{min} is also the relative deadline of τ_i, and τ_i is *schedulable* if $\mathcal{R}(\tau_i) \leq T_i^{min}$. The problem of bounding $\mathcal{R}(\tau_i)$ has been extensively studied in literature [8]. In this paper, we do not focus on the schedulability of the system and simply assume that each task is schedulable under FPP.

Cause-Effect Chains. Tasks may communicate with each other to realize some specific functionality and thus form a set of independent cause-effect chains (called chains for short) with respect to their data dependency. A chain consists of an ordered sequence of tasks, denoted by $\mathcal{C} = \{\tau_1, \tau_2, ..., \tau_i, ..., \tau_{|\mathcal{C}|}\}$, where τ_i is the ith task in $\mathcal{C}$, and $|\mathcal{C}|$ is the number of tasks. We call τ_i the predecessor of τ_{i+1}, and τ_{i+1} the successor of τ_i for each pair of consecutive elements τ_i and τ_{i+1} in $\mathcal{C}$. In particular, the first and the last element in $\mathcal{C}$ are called the *source* and the *tail* task of $\mathcal{C}$, respectively.

Communications. There is a buffer of size 1 in between each pair of consecutive tasks τ_i and τ_{i+1} in $\mathcal{C}$, which is named the output buffer of τ_i and the input buffer of τ_{i+1}. A job J_i^j released by τ_i reads the data token from its input buffer at the beginning of its execution, i.e., $s(J_i^j)$, and produces an output data token into its output buffer at the end of its execution, i.e., $f(J_i^j)$. This communication policy complies with the implicit communication [1] implemented in automotive systems, e.g., AUTOSAR. When a new data token arrives, the old data token is overwritten. That is, only the latest available data token is read by each job. In particular, the data token read by the source task is derived by sampling. As in [5], we assume the sampling occurs at the start of each job of the source task.

For simplicity, we assume that the communication delay among jobs within the same ECU is zero. The communicating infrastructure between two jobs released by tasks mapped to different ECUs is modeled by an additional periodic task on the communication bus [7,9,10]. The job released by the communicating task is responsible for data transmission from one ECU to another.

We assume time is discrete. For any time $t > 0$, the notations t^- and t^+ are used to denote the time $t - \epsilon$ and $t + \epsilon$, respectively, where ϵ is an arbitrarily small positive number.

2.2   Validity Interval and Reaction Time

When an external event occurs, it triggers a status update within the system. The information about the external event is then captured by the source task of a cause-effect chain, processed and propagated to the tail task, and ideally yields a corresponding output response. An external event ρ is characterized by its length of *validity interval* $\mathcal{D}(\rho)$, which describes the length of time interval from the occurrence of ρ to the time instant when the status update triggered by ρ is covered by the occurrence of another external event. The length of time interval from the occurrence of the external event to the time instant when the response is generated is called the reaction time (also known as the first-to-first delay in [11]) of the cause-effect chain.

Previous work assumes the validity interval of an external event is infinite, and thus the information will always be captured and propagated along the chain and generate an output. However, as introduced in Sect. 1, this assumption may not always hold in actual scenarios. Consequently, a corresponding response to an external event may not always exist, and the reaction time becomes infinite. Existing work introduced alternative definitions of the maximum reaction time referring to augmented forward job chains [5]. In this paper, we generalize the definition by considering that the validity interval of an external event may be finite.

We first define 'dependent' from the perspective of data propagation.

Definition 1 (Dependent). *We say a job J_y^n is dependent on another job J_x^m, $y > x$, if there exists a sequence of jobs $\bar{c} = \{\bar{c}_x, \bar{c}_{x+1}, ..., \bar{c}_y\}$ satisfying that*

- $\bar{c}_y = J_y^n$.
- $\bar{c}_x = J_x^m$.
- *for $i \in [x+1, y]$, $\bar{c}_i$ reads the data produced by $\bar{c}_{i-1}$.*

We say a job $J_y^n, y \geq 1$ is *effective* if there exists a job J_1^m released by τ_1 satisfying that J_y^n is dependent on J_1^m. In the following, we assume it is effective when mentioning an arbitrary job $J_y^n, y \geq 1$. Next, we are ready to define the augmented forward job chain.

Definition 2 (Augmented Forward Job Chain). *An augmented forward job chain with regards to an external event ρ occurring at time instant t_0, denoted by $\vec{c}^*(\rho) = \{\rho, \vec{c}_1^*, \vec{c}_2^*, \ldots, \vec{c}_i^*, \ldots \vec{c}_{|\mathcal{C}|}^*\}$, satisfies*

- *C1. $\vec{c}_1^*$ is the first job released by τ_1 with $s(\vec{c}_1^*) \in [t_0, t_0 + \mathcal{D}(\rho)]$.*
- *$\forall i \in [1, |\mathcal{C}| - 1]$, $\vec{c}_{i+1}^*$ is the first job satisfying*
  - *C2. The start time of $\vec{c}_{i+1}^*$ is no earlier than the finish time of $\vec{c}_i^*$.*
  - *C3. $\vec{c}_{i+1}^*$ is dependent on J_1^x, where J_1^x is an arbitrary job with $s(J_1^x) \in [t_0, t_0 + \mathcal{D}(\rho)]$.*

The length of $\vec{c}^*(\rho)$ is denoted by $L(\vec{c}^*(\rho)) = f(\vec{c}_{|\mathcal{C}|}^*) - t_0$.

In Definition 2, an augmented forward job chain is constructed by always finding the first job (corresponding to **C1** and **C2**) released by each task reacting exactly to the considered external event (corresponding to **C1** and **C3**). When $\mathcal{D}(\rho)$ is not sufficiently long, it is possible that there does not exist a sequence of jobs satisfying both **C1** and **C3**, and thus an augmented job chain corresponding to ρ does not exist. In this case, we set $L(\vec{c}^*(\rho)) = \infty$. Reversely, when $\mathcal{D}(\rho)$ is sufficiently long, i.e., infinite, an augmented job chain always exists, and Definition 2 is the same as that in [5].

Now, we are ready to define the maximum reaction time of a chain $\mathcal{C}$.

Definition 3 (Maximum Reaction Time). *The maximum reaction time of a cause-effect chain $\mathcal{C}$ is upper-bounded by*

$$\mathcal{RT} = \max_{\forall \rho} L(\vec{c}^*(\rho)).$$

where ρ is an arbitrary external event, and $L(\vec{c}^*(\rho))$ is defined in Definition 2.

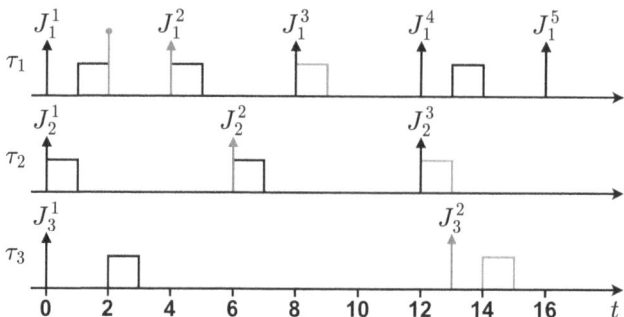

Fig. 2. Illustration of definitions.

An Example. Figure 2 shows the execution sequence of jobs released by tasks in a cause-effect chain $\mathcal{C} = \{\tau_1, \tau_2, \tau_3\}$. $T_1^{max} = T_1^{min} = 4$, $e_1 = b_1 = 1$, $T_2^{max} = T_2^{min} = 6$, $e_2 = b_2 = 1$, $T_3^{max} = T_3^{min} = 13$, $e_3 = b_3 = 1$. τ_2 has the highest priority and τ_3 has the lowest priority. The validity interval of external event ρ occurring at time instant 2 is 8. By Definition 2, the augmented forward job chain with regards to ρ, i.e., $\overrightarrow{c}^*(\rho) = \{\rho, J_1^2, J_2^2, J_3^2\}$, is constructed as follows: J_1^2 is the first job released by τ_1 satisfying $s(J_1^2) \in [2, 10]$ (corresponding to **C1**); J_2^2 is the first job released by τ_2 with start time no earlier than the finish time of J_1^2 (corresponding to **C2**) and J_2^2 is dependent on J_1^2 (corresponding to **C3**); J_3^2 is the first job released by τ_2 with start time no earlier than the finish time of J_2^2 (corresponding to **C2**) and J_3^2 is dependent on J_1^3 with $s(J_3^2) \in [2, 10]$ (corresponding to **C3**). When the validity interval of ρ decreases to 4, $\overrightarrow{c}^*(\rho) = \{\rho, J_1^2, J_2^2, J_3^2\}$ is no longer an augmented forward job chain of ρ since $s(J_1^3) \notin [2, 6]$.

2.3   Problem Definition

As illustrated in Fig. 2, the reaction time of an external event is not only affected by the execution sequence but also greatly dependent on the validity interval of the external event. In this paper, we seek to characterize the system's capability to perceive external transient events by addressing the following critical question: What is the minimum required validity interval for an external event to ensure that a response is generated corresponding to it?

3   Analysis

In this section, we first prove a sufficient condition for the existence of an augmented forward job chain regarding an arbitrary external event. We then derive the upper bound on the minimum length of the validity interval required to ensure a response to such an event, along with the corresponding maximum reaction time.

3.1   Sufficient Condition

To ensure that a response is generated for an external event ρ, the validity interval of the event must be of sufficient length to guarantee the existence of an augmented forward job chain with regard to ρ. We first present a sufficient condition for the existence of an augmented forward job chain concerning a fixed external event (Lemma 3) and then provide a sufficient condition for the existence of such a chain concerning an arbitrary external event (Lemma 5).

We first define a data propagation chain, which is a specialization of the 'dependent' relationship in Definition 1.

Definition 4 (Data Propagation Chain). *A data propagation chain, denoted by $\overleftarrow{c} = \{\overleftarrow{c}_1, \overleftarrow{c}_2, ..., \overleftarrow{c}_{|\mathcal{C}|}\}$, satisfies*

- *$\forall i \in [1, |\mathcal{C}|]$, $\overleftarrow{c}_i$ is released by τ_i.*
- *for $i \in [2, |\mathcal{C}|]$, $\overleftarrow{c}_i$ reads the data produced by $\overleftarrow{c}_{i-1}$.*

Next, we define a forward job chain, which is a reduced form of an augmented forward job chain that excludes the consideration of the external event.

Definition 5 (Forward Job Chain). *A forward job chain of $\mathcal{C}$, denoted by $\overrightarrow{c} = \{\overrightarrow{c}_1, \overrightarrow{c}_2, ..., \overrightarrow{c}_i, ... \overrightarrow{c}_{|\mathcal{C}|}\}$, satisfies*

- *$\forall i \in [1, |\mathcal{C}|]$, $\overrightarrow{c}_i$ is released by τ_i.*
- *$\forall i \in [1, |\mathcal{C}| - 1]$, $\overrightarrow{c}_{i+1}$ is the first job satisfying that the start time of $\overrightarrow{c}_{i+1}$ is no earlier than the finish time of $\overrightarrow{c}_i$.*

Next, we prove a property about a forward job chain in Lemma 2.

Lemma 1. *Let J_i^j and J_i^k be two arbitrary jobs with $j < k$. Let $\overline{c}$ and $\overline{c'}$ be the job sequences defined in Definition 1 and end with J_i^j, J_i^k, respectively. Then for $m \in [1, i]$, $r(\overline{c}_m) \le r(\overline{c'_m})$.*

Proof. We prove this by contradiction. Let $1 \le l \le i$ be the smallest value satisfying that $r(\overline{c}_l) > r(\overline{c'_l})$. Then for each $l + 1 \le l' \le i$, $s(c'_{l'}) \le f(c_{l'-1})$ holds, otherwise $c'_{l'}$ will read the data produced by $c_{l'-1}$ instead of $c'_{l'-1}$. Further, by Definition 2, $f(c_{l'-1}) \le s(c_{l'})$, then we have $s(c'_{l'}) \le f(c_{l'-1}) \le s(c_{l'})$. Then $s(c'_i) \le s(c_i)$, contradicting with the assumption that $s(c_i) = s(J_i^j) < s(J_i^k) = s(c'_i)$. Proved.

Lemma 2. *Let $\overrightarrow{c}_j$ and $\overrightarrow{c}_k$ be two jobs with $j < k$, and they are dependent on $J_1^{j'}$ and $J_1^{k'}$, respectively. Then $r(J_1^{j'}) \le r(J_1^{k'})$.*

Proof. We prove this by contradiction. Assume $r(J_1^{j'}) > r(J_1^{k'})$. Let $\overline{c}$ and $\overline{c'}$ be the job sequences defined in Definition 1, where $\overline{c}$ starts with $J_1^{j'}$ and ends with $\overrightarrow{c}_j$, and $\overline{c'}$ starts with $J_1^{k'}$ and ends with $\overrightarrow{c}_k$. Then by Definition 1, we have $r(\overrightarrow{c}_j) \le \overline{c'}_j$. By Lemma 1, $r(\overline{c}_1) = r(J_1^{j'}) \le \overline{c'}_1 = r(J_1^{k'})$, leading to contradiction.

Next, we derive the sufficient condition for the existence of an augmented job chain regarding an external event ρ occurring at t_0.

Lemma 3. *Let $\vec{c}$ be the forward job chain where $\vec{c}_1$ is the first job released by τ_1 with $s(\vec{c}_1) > t_0$. Let $\overleftarrow{c}$ be the data propagation chain with $\overleftarrow{c}_{|\mathcal{C}|} = \vec{c}_{|\mathcal{C}|}$. Then if $t_0 + \mathcal{D}(\rho) \geq s(\vec{c}_1)$, then $\vec{c}$ is an augmented forward job chain.*

Proof. By Definition 2, for each job $\vec{c}_j$ in $\vec{c}$, there must exist a job $J_1^{j'}$ released by τ_1 satisfying $\vec{c}_i$ is dependent on $J_1^{j'}$. Further, by Lemma 2, $s(J_1^{j'}) \leq s(\vec{c}_1)$. Then the lemma is proved.

Next, we provide sufficient conditions for the existence of an augmented forward job chain regarding an arbitrary external event.

Definition 6 (Successful Sampling). *A job J_1^x released by τ_1 completes a successful sampling if there exists at least one data propagation chain starting with J_1^x.*

Lemma 4. *Let $\vec{c}$ be a forward job chain and $\overleftarrow{c}$ be a data propagation chain with $r(\overleftarrow{c}_1) \geq r(\vec{c}_1)$. Then for $i \in [2, |\mathcal{C}|]$, $r(\overleftarrow{c}_i) \geq r(\vec{c}_i)$.*

Proof. Prove by contradiction. Let i' be the smallest index satisfying $r(\overleftarrow{c}_{i'}) < r(\vec{c}_{i'})$. Then $\vec{c}_{i'}$ executes after $\overleftarrow{c}_{i'}$ finishes, and $\overleftarrow{c}_{i'}$ is the first job whose start time is no earlier than the finish time of $\vec{c}_{i'-1}$, instead of $\vec{c}_{i'}$, leading to contradiction. Then the lemma is proved.

The sufficient condition to guarantee the existence of a response regarding an arbitrary external event is derived as below.

Lemma 5. *Let J_1^x and J_1^y denote two arbitrary consecutive jobs completing successful sampling. Let $B(J_1^x, J_1^y) = s(J_1^y) - s(J_1^x)$, and $\mathcal{B} = \max_{\forall x, y}\{B(J_1^x, J_1^y)\}$. For an arbitrary external event, if $\mathcal{D}(\rho) \geq \mathcal{B}$, there must be a response to it.*

Proof. Let ρ be an arbitrary event occurring at t_0. Since $\mathcal{D}(\rho) \geq \mathcal{B}$, let J_1^m be the first job with $t_0 + \mathcal{D}(\rho) \geq s(J_1^m)$ and completing a successful sampling. Let J_1^n be the first job with $s(J_1^n) > t_0$, and $\vec{c}$ be a forward job chain with $\vec{c}_1 = J_1^n$. Let $\overleftarrow{c}$ be the data propagation chain with $\overleftarrow{c}_{|\mathcal{C}|} = \vec{c}_{|\mathcal{C}|}$. Next we prove $J_1^m = \overleftarrow{c}_1$. We distinguish two cases.

- $J_1^m \neq J_1^n$. We prove by contradiction and assume $r(J_1^m) \neq r(\overleftarrow{c}_1)$. We distinguish two cases.
  - $r(J_1^m) > r(\overleftarrow{c}_1)$. Contradicting with the assumption that J_1^m is the first job completing successful sampling.
  - $r(J_1^m) < r(\overleftarrow{c}_1)$. Let $\overleftarrow{c}'$ be the data propagation chain starting with $r(J_1^m)$. By Lemma 1, $\overleftarrow{c}'_{|\mathcal{C}|} < r(\overleftarrow{c}_{|\mathcal{C}|})$. Then $\overleftarrow{c}'_{|\mathcal{C}|} < \vec{c}_{|\mathcal{C}|}$, contradicting with Lemma 4.

  Combining the two cases proves $J_1^m = \overleftarrow{c}_1$. Then, by Lemma 3, an augmented forward job chain must exist.
- $J_1^m = J_1^n$. Then by Definition 2, $\vec{c}$ is an augmented forward job chain.

Combining the above two cases, the lemma is proved.

By Lemma 5, the problem of deriving the minimum required validity interval to ensure a response to it has been reduced to bounding $\mathcal{B}$.

3.2   Upper-Bounding $\mathcal{B}$

Due to the complex runtime execution sequence and the extensive range of release and execution patterns for data propagation, determining a lower bound for $\mathcal{B}$ directly from data propagation's perspective presents a formidable challenge. It is difficult to ascertain the number of jobs released between two points, as well as the release pattern and offset for each pair of successive tasks in the chain. Additionally, the runtime execution sequence of each task must be considered, which could lead to an exponential increase in the number of possibilities.

To address this issue, we demonstrate that lower-bounding $\mathcal{B}$ can be equivalently transformed into bounding the maximum time disparity between the start times of two jobs, which are released by the source task and lead to two consecutive jobs released by the tail task in the chain. Consequently, our analysis will focus on two specific data propagation chains.

We begin with some preparatory lemmas. In the following, we use $\overleftarrow{c}^x$ to denote the data propagation chain ending with $J^x_{|\mathcal{C}|}$, and use $\overleftarrow{c}^x_j$ to denote the jth job in $\overleftarrow{c}^x$.

Lemma 6. *Let $J^x_{|\mathcal{C}|}$ and $J^{x+1}_{|\mathcal{C}|}$ be two arbitrary consecutive jobs released by $\tau_{|\mathcal{C}|}$. Let $\overleftarrow{c}^x$ and $\overleftarrow{c}^{x+1}$ be the data propagation chains ending at $J^x_{|\mathcal{C}|}$ and $J^{x+1}_{|\mathcal{C}|}$, respectively. Then*

$$\mathcal{B} \leq \max_{\forall x}\{s(\overleftarrow{c}^{x+1}_1) - s(\overleftarrow{c}^x_1)\} \tag{1}$$

Proof. To prove the lemma, it is sufficient to prove that two consecutive successful samplings must have two consecutive outputs corresponding to these two samples, respectively. Let J^x_1 and J^y_1 be two arbitrary consecutive jobs completing a successful sampling and $r(J^x_1) < r(J^y_1)$, then by Definition 6 there must exist two propagation chains $\overleftarrow{c}^{x'}$ and $\overleftarrow{c}^{y'}$ starting with J^x_1 and J^y_1, and ending with $J^{x'}_{|\mathcal{C}|}$ and $J^{y'}_{|\mathcal{C}|}$. We prove $y' = x' + 1$ by contradiction. Assume $y' \neq x' + 1$, and we distinguish three cases.

- $y' = x'$. Then by Definition 4, $J^{x'}_{|\mathcal{C}|}$ (*i.e.*, $\overleftarrow{c}^{x'}_{|\mathcal{C}|}$) reads the data from both $\overleftarrow{c}^{x'}_{|\mathcal{C}|-1}$ and $\overleftarrow{c}^{y'}_{|\mathcal{C}|-1}$, which will never hold.
- $y' < x'$. Then by Lemma 1, $J^{y'}_1 \leq J^{x'}_1$, contradicting with the assumption that $r(J^x_1) < r(J^y_1)$.
- $y' > x' + 1$. Let $Y = x' + 1$. By Definition 6, there must exist a propagation chain ending with $\overleftarrow{c}^Y_{|\mathcal{C}|}$, denoted by $\overleftarrow{c}^Y$. By Lemma 1, $r(J^y_1) \leq r(\overleftarrow{c}^Y_1) \leq r(J^y_1)$, contradicting with the assumption that J^x_1 and J^y_1 are consecutive jobs completing successful sampling.

Combining the three cases, the lemma is proved.

By Lemma 6, bounding $\mathcal{B}$ turns into the problem to bound $s(\overleftarrow{c}^{x+1}_1) - s(\overleftarrow{c}^x_1)$ for two consecutive jobs released by the last task in the chain. Next, we propose two methods for upper-bounding $\mathcal{B}$.

Lemma 7 (Bound 1). $\mathcal{B}$ *is upper-bounded by*

$$\mathcal{B} \leq \mathcal{R}(\tau_1) - e_1 + T_{|\mathcal{C}|}^{max} + \alpha + \beta \tag{2}$$

where $\alpha = \max_{\forall_x}\{r(\overleftarrow{c}_{|\mathcal{C}|}^x) - r(\overleftarrow{c}_1^x)\}$ *and* $\beta = \max_{\forall_x}\{r(\overleftarrow{c}_1^x) - r(\overleftarrow{c}_{|\mathcal{C}|}^x)\}$.

Proof. Let $J_{|\mathcal{C}|}^x$ and $J_{|\mathcal{C}|}^{x+1}$ be two arbitrary consecutive jobs released by $\tau_{|\mathcal{C}|}$. Let $\overleftarrow{c}^x$ and $\overleftarrow{c}^{x+1}$ be the data propagation chains ending at $J_{|\mathcal{C}|}^x$ and $J_{|\mathcal{C}|}^{x+1}$, respectively. Then we have

$$s(\overleftarrow{c}_1^{x+1}) - s(\overleftarrow{c}_1^x) \leq s(\overleftarrow{c}_1^{x+1}) - r(\overleftarrow{c}_1^x) \leq r(\overleftarrow{c}_1^{x+1}) - r(\overleftarrow{c}_1^x) + \mathcal{R}(\tau_1) - e_1$$

$$\leq r(\overleftarrow{c}_1^{x+1}) - r(\overleftarrow{c}_{|\mathcal{C}|}^{x+1}) + r(\overleftarrow{c}_{|\mathcal{C}|}^{x+1}) - r(\overleftarrow{c}_{|\mathcal{C}|}^x) + r(\overleftarrow{c}_{|\mathcal{C}|}^x) - r(\overleftarrow{c}_1^x) + \mathcal{R}(\tau_1) - e_1$$

$$\leq \mathcal{R}(\tau_1) - e_1 + \max_{\forall_x}\{r(\overleftarrow{c}_{|\mathcal{C}|}^x) - r(\overleftarrow{c}_1^x)\} + T_{|\mathcal{C}|}^{max} + \max_{\forall_x}\{r(\overleftarrow{c}_1^{x+1}) - r(\overleftarrow{c}_{|\mathcal{C}|}^{x+1})\}$$

$$\leq \mathcal{R}(\tau_1) - e_1 + T_{|\mathcal{C}|}^{max} + \alpha + \beta$$

Since $J_{|\mathcal{C}|}^x$ and $J_{|\mathcal{C}|}^{x+1}$ be two arbitrary consecutive jobs released by $\tau_{|\mathcal{C}|}$, by Lemma 6, the lemma is proved.

Lemma 8 (Bound 2). $\mathcal{B}$ *is upper-bounded by*

$$\mathcal{B} \leq \mathcal{R}(\tau_1) - e_1 + \gamma + T_1^{max} + \beta \tag{3}$$

where $\gamma = \max_{\forall_x}\{r(\overrightarrow{c}_{|\mathcal{C}|}^{x+1}) - r(\overrightarrow{c}_1^{x+1})\}$, β *is defined in Lemma 7.*

Proof. Let J_1^x and J_1^y be two consecutive jobs completing successful sampling. Let J_1^z be the first job with $s(J_1^z) \geq s(J_1^x)$. Let $\overleftarrow{c}$ be the data propagation chain starting with J_1^y, and $\overrightarrow{c}$ be the forward job chain starting with J_1^z. Then by Lemma 5, $\overrightarrow{c}_{|\mathcal{C}|} = \overleftarrow{c}_{|\mathcal{C}|}$. Then

$$s(\overleftarrow{c}_1^{x+1}) - s(\overleftarrow{c}_1^x) \leq s(\overleftarrow{c}_1^{x+1}) - r(\overleftarrow{c}_1^x) \leq r(\overleftarrow{c}_1^{x+1}) - r(\overleftarrow{c}_1^x) + \mathcal{R}(\tau_1) - e_1$$

$$\leq r(\overleftarrow{c}_1^{x+1}) - r(\overrightarrow{c}_{|\mathcal{C}|}^{x+1}) + r(\overrightarrow{c}_{|\mathcal{C}|}^{x+1}) - (J_1^z) + r(J_1^z) - r(\overleftarrow{c}_1^x) + \mathcal{R}(\tau_1) - e_1$$

$$\leq \mathcal{R}(\tau_1) - e_1 + \max_{\forall_x}\{r(\overrightarrow{c}_{|\mathcal{C}|}^{x+1}) - r(J_1^z)\} + T_1^{max} + \max_{\forall_x}\{r(\overleftarrow{c}_1^{x+1}) - r(\overleftarrow{c}_{|\mathcal{C}|}^{x+1})\}$$

$$\leq \mathcal{R}(\tau_1) - e_1 + \gamma + T_1^{max} + \beta$$

Theorem 1. $\mathcal{B}$ *is upper-bounded by*

$$\mathcal{B} \leq \min(\mathcal{R}(\tau_1) - e_1 + T_{|\mathcal{C}|}^{max} + \alpha + \beta, \mathcal{R}(\tau_1) - e_1 + \gamma + T_1^{max} + \beta) \tag{4}$$

Proof. Proved by combining Lemmas 7 and 8.

Next, we upper-bound the reaction time when the validity interval of an external event exceeds $\mathcal{B}$, i.e., when there must exist a response to an external event.

Theorem 2. *The maximum reaction time of a chain $\mathcal{C}$ is upper-bounded by*

$$\mathcal{RT} \leq min(\mathcal{RT}_1, \mathcal{RT}_2) \tag{5}$$

where $\mathcal{RT}_1 = \gamma + T_1^{max} + \mathcal{R}(\tau_{|\mathcal{C}|})$, $\mathcal{RT}_2 = \alpha + T_{|\mathcal{C}|}^{max} + \mathcal{R}(\tau_{|\mathcal{C}|})$, α, γ are defined in Lemmas 7 and 8, respectively.

Proof. Let ρ be an external event occurring at t_0, and $\overrightarrow{c}^*(\rho)$ be the augmented forward job chain regarding ρ. We first prove $\mathcal{RT}_1$. By Definition 2, Definition 5 and Lemma 8,

$$
\begin{aligned}
f(\overrightarrow{c}^*_{|\mathcal{C}|}) - t_0 &= f(\overrightarrow{c}^*_{|\mathcal{C}|}) - r(\overrightarrow{c}^*_{|\mathcal{C}|}) + r(\overrightarrow{c}^*_{|\mathcal{C}|}) - t_0 \\
&= r(\overrightarrow{c}^*_{|\mathcal{C}|}) + \mathcal{R}(\overrightarrow{c}^*_{|\mathcal{C}|}) - r(\overrightarrow{c}^*_{|\mathcal{C}|}) + r(\overrightarrow{c}^*_{|\mathcal{C}|}) - t_0 \\
&\leq \max_{\forall x}\{r(\overrightarrow{c}^{x+1}_{|\mathcal{C}|}) - r(\overrightarrow{c}^{x+1}_1)\} + T_1^{max} + \mathcal{R}(\tau_{|\mathcal{C}|}) \\
&= \gamma + T_1^{max} + \mathcal{R}(\tau_{|\mathcal{C}|})
\end{aligned}
$$

Next we prove $\mathcal{RT}_2$. Let J_1^x be the last job with $s(J_1^x) \leq t_0$ and completing a successful sampling, and $\overleftarrow{c}$ be the data propagation chain starting with J_1^x. Let $\overleftarrow{c}'$ be the data propagation chain ending with $\overrightarrow{c}^*_{|\mathcal{C}|}$. Then by Definition 4 and Lemma 4, J_1^x and $\overleftarrow{c}'_1$ complete consecutive successful sampling, and $\overleftarrow{c}_{|\mathcal{C}|}$ and $\overrightarrow{c}^*_{|\mathcal{C}|}$ are consecutive jobs released by $\tau_{|\mathcal{C}|}$. Then we have

$$
\begin{aligned}
f(\overrightarrow{c}^*_{|\mathcal{C}|}) - t_0 &\leq f(\overrightarrow{c}^*_{|\mathcal{C}|}) - r(J_1^x) \\
&\leq (f(\overrightarrow{c}^*_{|\mathcal{C}|}) - r(\overrightarrow{c}^*_{|\mathcal{C}|})) + r(\overrightarrow{c}^*_{|\mathcal{C}|}) - r(\overleftarrow{c}_{|\mathcal{C}|}) + r(\overleftarrow{c}_{|\mathcal{C}|}) - r(J_1^x) \\
&\leq \mathcal{R}(\tau_{|\mathcal{C}|}) + T_{|\mathcal{C}|}^{max} + \max_{\forall x}\{r(\overleftarrow{c}^x_{|\mathcal{C}|}) - r(\overleftarrow{c}^x_1)\} \\
&= \mathcal{R}(\tau_{|\mathcal{C}|}) + \alpha + T_{|\mathcal{C}|}^{max}
\end{aligned}
$$

Finally, we complete the analysis by upper-bounding α, β, and γ defined in Lemma 7 and 8, respectively.

Lemma 9. *α is upper-bounded by*

$$\alpha \leq \sum_{i=1}^{|\mathcal{C}|-1} T_i^{max} + (\mathcal{R}(\tau_i) - b_{i+1}) \cdot \delta \tag{6}$$

where $\delta = 0$ if $\tau_i \in hp(\tau_{i+1})$, and $\delta = 1$ otherwise.

Proof. Since $r(\overleftarrow{c}^x_{|\mathcal{C}|}) - r(\overleftarrow{c}^x_1) = \sum_{i=1}^{|\mathcal{C}|-1} r(\overleftarrow{c}^x_{i+1}) - r(\overleftarrow{c}^x_i)$, it is equivalent to upper-bound $r(\overleftarrow{c}^x_{i+1}) - r(\overleftarrow{c}^x_i)$. Recall that $\overleftarrow{c}^x_{i+1}$ reads the data token produced by $\overleftarrow{c}^x_i$. We distinguish two cases:

- $\tau_i \in hp(\tau_{i+1})$. Then $\overleftarrow{c}^x_{i+1}$ must be released before the successor of $\overleftarrow{c}^x_i$, otherwise it can not read $\overleftarrow{c}^x_i$. Then $r(\overleftarrow{c}^x_{i+1}) - r(\overleftarrow{c}^x_i) \leq T_i^{max}$.
- $\tau_i \notin hp(\tau_{i+1})$. Then $\overleftarrow{c}^x_{i+1}$ must be released before $T_i^{max} + \mathcal{R}(\tau_i) - b_{i+1}$, otherwise it can not read $\overleftarrow{c}^x_i$. Then $r(\overleftarrow{c}^x_{i+1}) - r(\overleftarrow{c}^x_i) \leq T_i^{max} + \mathcal{R}(\tau_i) - b_{i+1}$.

Combining the two cases, the lemma is proved.

Lemma 10. β *is upper-bounded by*

$$\beta \leq \begin{cases} \beta_1, & \tau_1 \in hp(\tau_{|\mathcal{C}|}) \\ min(\beta_1, \beta_2), & \tau_1 \notin hp(\tau_{|\mathcal{C}|}) \end{cases} \tag{7}$$

where $\beta_1 = \mathcal{R}(\tau_{|\mathcal{C}|}) - e_{|\mathcal{C}|} - \sum_{i=1}^{|\mathcal{C}|-1} b_i$, $\beta_2 = -\sum_{i=1}^{k} b_i$, k *is the task with largest index with* $\tau_k \notin hp(\tau_{|\mathcal{C}|})$.

Proof. We first prove the results without considering the relative priority of τ_1 and $\tau_{|\mathcal{C}|}$. By Definition 4, for an arbitrary x, for $1 \leq i \leq |\mathcal{C}|$, $\overleftarrow{c}_i^x$ finishes before $\overleftarrow{c}_{i+1}^x$ starts. Consequently, there must be at least one job of each task executed within the interval $[r(\overleftarrow{c}_1^x), r(\overleftarrow{c}_{|\mathcal{C}|}^x) + \mathcal{R}(\tau_{|\mathcal{C}|})]$, i.e., $r(\overleftarrow{c}_1^x) + \sum_{i=1}^{|\mathcal{C}|-1} b_i \leq s(\overleftarrow{c}_{|\mathcal{C}|}^x)$. Then

$$r(\overleftarrow{c}_1^x) \leq s(\overleftarrow{c}_{|\mathcal{C}|}^x) - \sum_{i=1}^{|\mathcal{C}|-1} b_i \leq r(\overleftarrow{c}_{|\mathcal{C}|}^x) + \mathcal{I} - \sum_{i=1}^{|\mathcal{C}|-1} b_i$$

where $\mathcal{I}$ is the maximum interference suffered by $\overleftarrow{c}_{|\mathcal{C}|}^x$, and can be derived by $\mathcal{R}(\tau_{|\mathcal{C}|}) - e_{|\mathcal{C}|}$. Then

$$r(\overleftarrow{c}_1^x) - r(\overleftarrow{c}_{|\mathcal{C}|}^x) \leq \mathcal{R}(\tau_{|\mathcal{C}|}) - e_{|\mathcal{C}|} - \sum_{i=1}^{|\mathcal{C}|-1} b_i$$

Next, we show the results can be further optimized when $\tau_1 \notin hp(\tau_{|\mathcal{C}|})$. Since $\tau_1 \notin hp(\tau_{|\mathcal{C}|})$, $r(\overleftarrow{c}_{|\mathcal{C}|}^x) > r(\overleftarrow{c}_1^x)$, otherwise $\overleftarrow{c}_{|\mathcal{C}|}^x$ must start before $\overleftarrow{c}_1^x$ and can not read the data sampled by τ_1 and propagated along $\overleftarrow{c}^x$. Let k be the task with largest index with $\tau_k \notin hp(\tau_{|\mathcal{C}|})$, there must be at least one job of $\overleftarrow{c}_i^x, i \leq k$ executed in $[r(\overleftarrow{c}_1^x), r(\overleftarrow{c}_{|\mathcal{C}|}^x)]$, then

$$r(\overleftarrow{c}_1^x) - r(\overleftarrow{c}_{|\mathcal{C}|}^x) \leq -\sum_{i=1}^{k} b_i$$

Lemma 11. γ *is upper-bounded by*

$$\gamma \leq \sum_{i=1}^{|\mathcal{C}|-1} T_{i+1}^{max} + (\mathcal{R}(\tau_i) - b_{i+1}) \cdot \delta \tag{8}$$

where $\delta = 0$ *if* $\tau_i \in hp(\tau_{i+1})$, *and* $\delta = 1$ *otherwise.*

Proof. Since $r(\overrightarrow{c}_{|\mathcal{C}|}^x) - r(\overrightarrow{c}_1^x) = \sum_{i=1}^{|\mathcal{C}|-1} r(\overrightarrow{c}_{i+1}^x) - r(\overrightarrow{c}_i^x)$, it is equivalent to upper-bound $r(\overrightarrow{c}_{i+1}^x) - r(\overrightarrow{c}_i^x)$. Recall that $\overrightarrow{c}_{i+1}^x$ is the first job whose start time is no earlier than the finish time of $\overrightarrow{c}_i^x$. We distinguish two cases:

– $\tau_i \in hp(\tau_{i+1})$. Then $\vec{c}_{i+1}^{\,x}$ must be released before $r(\vec{c}_i^{\,x}) + T_{i+1}^{max}$. Otherwise, there must be at least one another job released by τ_{i+1} whose release time is no earlier than $r(\vec{c}_i)$ and thus becomes the first job starting execution after $\vec{c}_i$ finishes, leading to a contradiction. Then $r(\vec{c}_{i+1}^{\,x}) - r(\vec{c}_i^{\,x}) \leq T_{i+1}^{max}$

– $\tau_i \notin hp(\tau_{i+1})$. Then $\vec{c}_{i+1}^{\,x}$ must be released before $T_{i+1}^{max} + \mathcal{R}(\tau_i) - b_{i+1}$, otherwise it can not be the first job whose start time is no earlier than the finish time of $\vec{c}_i^{\,x}$. Then $r(\vec{c}_{i+1}^{\,x}) - r(\vec{c}_i^{\,x}) \leq T_{i+1}^{max} + \mathcal{R}(\tau_i) - b_{i+1}$.

Combining the two cases, the lemma is proved.

4   Evaluation

In this section, we conduct experiments with randomly generated task sets and a case study to evaluate the proposed techniques.

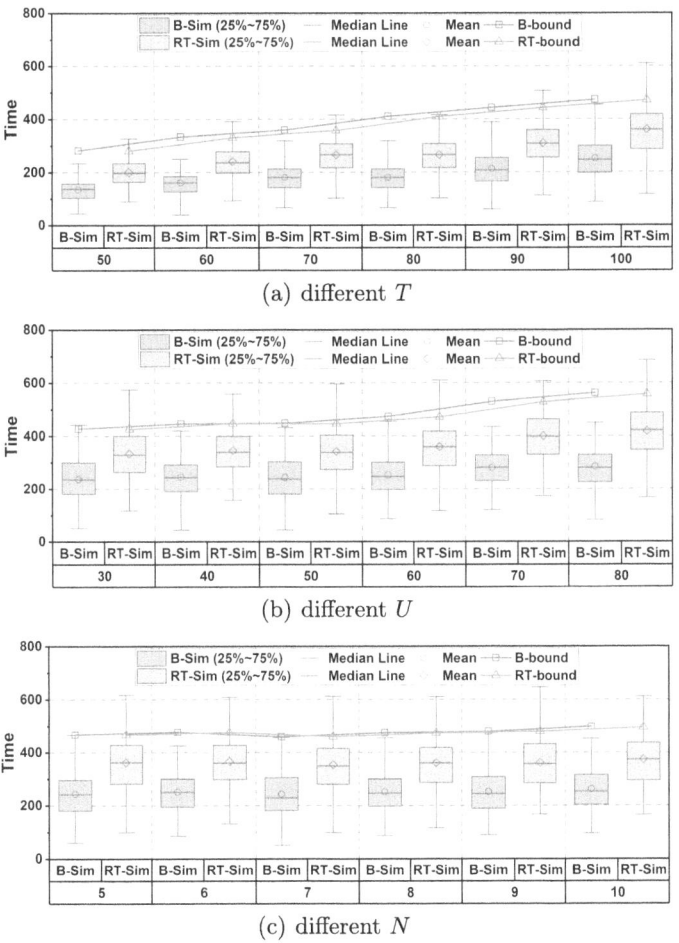

(a) different T

(b) different U

(c) different N

Fig. 3. Experimental results (randomly generated task sets).

4.1 Randomly Generated Task Sets

We compare the upper bound of the minimum validity interval to guarantee the existence of a response and the corresponding maximum reaction time, derived by simulating the actual execution sequence and the results calculated by Theorems 1 and 2.

Task Set Generation. We set a basic configuration: $U = 0.6$, $T = 100$ and $N = 8$, where U is the total utilization of the task set, the minimum inter-release time T_i^{min} of task τ_i is randomly generated in $[1, T]$, and N is the number of tasks in the analyzed chain. In each group of experiments, we vary one parameter while keeping others unchanged. We randomly generate 15 tasks in a task set and randomly pick some tasks to form a chain. The utilization of each task is generated based on UUnifast Algorithm [12]. The WCET of each task τ_i is calculated by multiplying its utilization with T_i^{min}, and the BCET is calculated by $\delta \cdot WCET$, where δ is randomly generated in $[0, 1]$. To determine T_i^{max}, we randomly choose value λ_i from $[1, 2]$ for each task and the maximum inter-release time T_i^{max} is decided by $\lambda_i \cdot T_i^{min}$. The inter-release time between consecutive jobs in simulation is randomly chosen in $[T_i^{min}, T_i^{max}]$. The actual execution time of each job is randomly chosen in $[BCET, WCET]$, and the simulation lasts until $2 \cdot LCM$, where LCM is the least common multiplier of the T_i^{max} of all tasks in the chain. The priority of tasks is assigned randomly, and the schedulability is checked before further analysis. For each value on the x-axis in Fig. 3, 200 task sets are generated. **B-sim** and **RT-sim** represent the maximum $\mathcal{B}$ and $\mathcal{RT}$ derived by simulating the actual execution sequence assuming the first jobs of all tasks start synchronously at time 0. **B-bound** and **RT-bound** represent the average theoretical upper bounds calculated according to Theorems 1 and 2 among all generated sets for each value on x-axis.

Results. Firstly, by Fig. 3 (a) and (b), both **B-sim** and **B-bound** increase with larger T and U. The reason is as follows: By the analysis in Sect. 3, for each pair of consecutive tasks, it takes a longer time for the information to be processed and propagated when downsampling occurs. With larger T and U, it becomes more possible that the disparity of inter-release time between a pair of consecutive tasks increases, and there is a higher possibility that downsampling occurs. Comparatively, both **B-sim** and **B-bound** keep relatively stable with increasing number of tasks in a chain. This is because the relationship between the number of tasks and the possibility of downsampling is less obvious. Secondly, both **B-sim** and **B-bound** increase with larger T, U, and N, which corresponds to the formula derived in Theorem 2. Finally, **B-bound** and **RT-bound** are always larger than **B-sim** and **RT-sim**, implying that our analysis generates safe upper-bounds.

4.2 Case Study

This case study is motivated by the autonomous driving system benchmark from [13][1]. There are four cause-effect chains $\{C_1, C_2, C_3, C_4\}$ in the system. The detailed information about the case study is shown in Table 2. Each task τ_i is represented by $(e_i, b_i, T_i^{min}, \pi(\tau_i))$, and has implicit deadline. Same as Sect. 4.1, we derive the upper bound of the minimum validity interval and corresponding maximum reaction time by simulation and theoretical analysis. The results are shown in Table 3. For each chain, it is shown that **B-bound** and **RT-bound** are always larger than **B-sim** and **RT-sim**, respectively, which implies the safety of the proposed analysis in Theorems 1 and 2.

Table 2. Description of the case study.

Task Parameter	Task Description	Task Parameter	Task Description
$\tau_0 = (7, 5, 500, 9)$	GPS	$\tau_5 = (25, 18.9, 500, 4)$	Camera
$\tau_1 = (12, 10, 500, 8)$	Lidar	$\tau_6 = (2, 1.8, 250, 3)$	EKF
$\tau_2 = (28, 22, 500, 7)$	Localization	$\tau_7 = (5, 3.2, 100, 2)$	Planner
$\tau_3 = (28, 25, 500, 6)$	Detection	$\tau_8 = (4.5, 1.8, 100, 1)$	Control
$\tau_4 = (28, 22, 500, 5)$	Fusion		

Cause-Effect Chains			
Chain 1	*Chain 2*	*Chain 3*	*Chain 4*
$C_1 = \{\tau_5, \tau_3, \tau_4\}$	$C_2 = \{\tau_0, \tau_2, \tau_6, \tau_7, \tau_8\}$	$C_3 = \{\tau_1, \tau_2, \tau_6, \tau_7, \tau_8\}$	$C_4 = \{\tau_5, \tau_3, \tau_4, \tau_7, \tau_8\}$

Table 3. Experimental results (case study).

	B-Sim(ms)			B-Bound	RT-Sim(ms)			RT-Bound
	Max.	Min.	Avg.	(ms)	Max.	Min.	Avg.	(ms)
C_1	506.4	499.5	502.1	1363.8	596.1	584.4	590.1	1349.0
C_2	525.4	493.2	507.8	1617.3	1304.5	1302.0	1303.6	1529.8
C_3	512.0	495.3	502.7	1678.7	1409.5	1405.5	1407.9	1605.7
C_4	505.0	498.0	501.4	1491.7	1204.5	1202.0	1203.7	1530.9

5 Related Work

Feiertag et al. [11] for the first time, identified four end-to-end timing semantics that characterize various timing latencies. Two of the most commonly considered semantics among them are reaction time and data age. Based on the activation

---

[1] [13] allocates the tasks to be executed on 4 ECUs. We increase the periods of tasks and choose appropriate priority assignments to make the task set schedulable with one ECU.

pattern, task chains can be distinguished into two types: time-triggered chain (also called cause-effect chain), where tasks are activated individually with their own periods, and event-triggered chain, where a task is activated by the data produced by its predecessor [14].

Time-triggered Chain. Becker et al. [15,16] analyzed the maximum data age by calculating data propagation paths based on reading- and data-intervals of jobs. Dürr et al. [9] calculated the upper bound of reaction time and data age for time-triggered chains composed of sporadic tasks by utilizing immediate forward and backward job chains. [4] upper-bounded the reaction time of cause-effect chains composed of periodic tasks. Klaus et al. [17] developed techniques to map task sets onto multi-core real-time systems efficiently. They also addressed the challenges of data-age bounds, synchronization overheads, and overall schedulability by automated system transformation and analysis. Abdullah et al. [18] computed the reaction time of synchronous periodic tasks under DBP. [19] also investigated the end-to-end delay of cause-effect chains for multi-rate LET tasks and examined the effects of release offset on system performance. [6] studied how to minimize synchronization overheads while guaranteeing the timing constraints with regard to data age.

Event-triggered Chain. The reaction time analysis problem for event-triggered chains with unbounded buffers reduces to the end-to-end delay analysis problem, for which established analysis techniques exist, such as the Compositional Performance Analysis framework [20] and the Real-Time Calculus framework [21]. [22] calculated the response time for a sequence of threads with synchronous and asynchronous communication. For event-triggered chains with limited-size buffers, [9] developed a delay analysis for non-skipped tasks under the RTC framework.

However, the above studies all assume that the external event is always valid and ignore how the length of the validity interval affects the reaction time.

6   Conclusion

Most existing analytical studies on cause-effect chain models assume that external events remain valid and focus primarily on when responses are generated. However, in real-world scenarios, external events may become invalid shortly after their occurrence, leading to a failure to respond. This paper extends traditional cause-effect chain model analysis by eliminating the assumption of perpetual validity, thereby enhancing the model's applicability to real-world situations. We provide a clear mathematical definition of the validity interval for external events and upper-bound the minimum length of the validity interval to guarantee a corresponding response to an arbitrary external event as well as the corresponding maximum reaction time. Finally, we validate the safety of our proposed validity interval and reaction time analysis via experiments.

Acknowledgments. This work is partially supported by Hong Kong GRF (grant numbers 15206221 and 11208522) and the National Natural Science Foundation of China (NSFC) (grant number 62402095).

Disclosure of Interests. The authors have no competing interests to declare that are relevant to the content of this article.

References

1. Hamann, A., Dasari, D., Kramer, S., Pressler, M., Wurst, F.: Communication centric design in complex automotive embedded systems. In: ECRTS (2017)
2. Guan, N., Dong, Z.: Industry challenge
3. Forget, J., Boniol, F., Pagetti, C.: Verifying end-to-end real-time constraints on multi-periodic models. In: ETFA (2017)
4. Kloda, T., Bertout, A., Sorel, Y.: Latency analysis for data chains of real-time periodic tasks. In: ETFA (2018)
5. Günzel, M., Chen, K.H., Ueter, N., von der Brüggen, G., Dürr, M., Chen, J.J.: Timing analysis of asynchronized distributed cause-effect chains. In: RTAS (2021)
6. Klaus, T., Becker, M., Schröder-Preikschat, W., Ulbrich, P.: Constrained data-age with job-level dependencies: how to reconcile tight bounds and overheads. In: RTAS (2021)
7. Lakshmanan, K., Bhatia, G., Rajkumar, R.: Integrated end-to-end timing analysis of networked autosar-compliant systems. In: 2010 Design, Automation & Test in Europe Conference & Exhibition (DATE 2010), pp. 331–334 (2010)
8. Lehoczky, J.P., Sha, L., Ding, Y.: The rate monotonic scheduling algorithm: exact characterization and average case behavior. In: RTSS (1989)
9. Dürr, M., Brüggen, G.V.D., Chen, K.H., Chen, J.J.: End-to-end timing analysis of sporadic cause-effect chains in distributed systems. ACM Trans. Embed. Comput. Syst. **18**(5s), 1–24 (2019)
10. Momete, D.C.: A unified framework for assessing the readiness of European union economies to migrate to a circular modelling. Sci. Total Environ. **718**, 137375 (2020)
11. Feiertag, N., Richter, K., Nordlander, J., Jonsson, J.: A compositional framework for end-to-end path delay calculation of automotive systems under different path semantics. In: Workshop on Compositional Theory and Technology for Real-Time Embedded Systems (2009)
12. Bini, E., Buttazzo, G.C.: Measuring the performance of schedulability tests. In: RTS (2005)
13. Verucchi, M., Theile, M., Caccamo, M., Bertogna, M.: Latency-aware generation of single-rate dags from multi-rate task sets. IEEE Real-Time Embedded Technol. Appl. Symp. (RTAS) **2020**, 226–238 (2020)
14. Vincentelli, A., Giusto, P., Pinello, C., Zheng, W., Natale, M.: Optimizing end-to-end latencies by adaptation of the activation events in distributed automotive systems. In: 13th IEEE Real Time and Embedded Technology and Applications Symposium (RTAS 2007), pp. 293–302 (2007)
15. Becker, M., Dasari, D., Mubeen, S., Behnam, M., Nolte, T.: End-to-end timing analysis of cause-effect chains in automotive embedded systems. J. Syst. Archit. **80**, 104–113 (2017)

16. Becker, M., Dasari, D., Mubeen, S., Behnam, M., Nolte, T.: Synthesizing job-level dependencies for automotive multi-rate effect chains. In: RTCSA (2016)
17. Klaus, T., Franzmann, F., Becker, M., Ulbrich, P.: Data propagation delay constraints in multi-rate systems – deadlines vs. job-level dependencies. In: RTNS (2018)
18. Abdullah, J., Dai, G., Yi, W.: Worst-case cause-effect reaction latency in systems with non-blocking communication. In: DATE (2019)
19. Martinez, J., Sañudo, I., Bertogna, M.: Analytical characterization of end-to-end communication delays with logical execution time. IEEE Trans. Comput. Aided Des. Integr. Circuits Syst. **37**(11), 2244–2254 (2018)
20. Henia, R., Hamann, A., Jersak, M., Racu, R., Richter, K., Ernst, R.: System level performance analysis-the symta/s approach. IEE Proc.-Comput. Digit. Tech. **152**(2), 148–166 (2005)
21. Thiele, L., Chakraborty, S., Gries, M., Kunzli, S.: A framework for evaluating design tradeoffs in packet processing architectures. In: Proceedings 2002 Design Automation Conference (IEEE Cat. No.02CH37324), pp. 880–885 (2002)
22. Schlatow, J., Ernst, R.: Response-time analysis for task chains in communicating threads. In: RTAS (2016)

Runtime Verification of Neural-Symbolic Systems

Shaojun Deng[1], Wanwei Liu[1(✉)], and Miaomiao Zhang[2]

[1] College of Computer Science and Technology, National University of Defense Technology, Changsha, China
{dengshaojun,wwliu}@nudt.edu.cn
[2] School of Software Engineering, Tongji Uniersity, Shanghai, China
miaomiao@tongji.edu.cn

Abstract. Neural-symbolic systems (NSSs), which are typically cyber-physical systems integrated with artificial intelligence modules, have received much attention in both academic and industrial fields. However, thorough verification (such as model checking) of such systems in general leads to prohibitively high costs due to the scale of the state space, and this makes it barely accomplishable within desired time-span. Consequently, light-weight verification techniques are introduced to deal with such cases, e.g., runtime verification (RV, for short).

In this paper, we investigate an RV framework for NSSs against signal temporal logic (STL) properties. To guarantee that the on-line monitoring could be accomplished in time, we utilize Euler-prediction to sample the system under scrutiny at discrete time-steps. Our framework supports both qualitative and quantitative on-line monitoring of STL specifications, and thus it terminates whenever a property is satisfied and/or violated by a finite prefix of the trajectory, and it can also provide the bounds of the quantitative satisfaction/violation w.r.t. the remaining execution. Notably, for the so-called piece-wise linear NSSs against affine STL formulas, our approach is exact. On top of it, a prototype tool is implemented, and is experimentally evaluated. The results demonstrate the feasibility of the presented runtime verification approach.

Keywords: Neural-symbolic system · Runtime verification · Signal temporal logic

1 Introduction

Neural-symbolic systems (NSSs, for short) can be seen as a specific application of neuro-symbolic AI, which are typically cyber-physical systems (CPSs) integrating artificial intelligence (AI). These ubiquitous systems are daily increasingly

This work is supported by the National Key R&D Program of China No. 2022YFA1005101, the National Natural Science Foundation of China under Grant No. 62032019 and No. 61872371.

used in autonomous vehicles, smart grids, medical devices, and industrial control systems [10]. Ensuring the safety, reliability, and performance of such systems has become increasingly urgent. Therefore, formal verification technique, such as model checking, is proposed to adopt for this purpose. However, such technique is mainly based on state-space exploration [7,8], and, the property under verification should also be taken into consideration — for the most cases, the specification is either applied to a semantic-transformation and is eventually transformed into a homogeneous structure with the model [3], or is applied to a syntactic-decomposition [2], so that an inductive checking can be performed. In general, these require that both the state-space and the transition-relation should be explicitly formulated. In contrast, such task is in general intricate for neural-symbolic systems, not only because of the extremely huge (or even infinite) state-space, more importantly, due to the opacity of the AI sub-system. Consequently, performing through and rigorous verification of NSSs in general leads to prohibitively high cost, and it can barely be accomplished in acceptable time. This makes such approach difficult to adopt in time-crucial verification tasks.

Runtime verification (RV) [4,11] is a lightweight technique used to monitor and check system behaviors, to ensure the system meets expected requirements. Compared to complete verification approaches (such as model checking), RV can detect potential issues in the actual operating environment of the system with lower overhead. Such verification framework generally comprises three subroutines: defining the properties the system must adhere to; collecting necessary data during system execution; and validating the correctness of the execution against these properties. The crux of RV is to effectively give a decision during the verification process with low time and space cost. Existing RV frameworks mainly deal with cyber-physical systems [15,16]. To make the task lightweight, they usually incorporate control theoretic approaches to dynamically adjust monitoring parameters, utilize temporal logic for specifying properties that converted into models such as timed automata, and ensure a sound verification process with minimal time overhead and high memory efficiency.

In this paper, we extend the runtime verification framework to that of a wide spectrum of NSSs — namely, the AI module can be either opaque or transparent, the CPS part can be either purely discrete or hybrid. In addition, our RV framework is suitable for specification language with powerful expressiveness, such as signal temporal logic (STL) [12,13], allowing for the verification of a wide range of properties within NSSs.

As previously mentioned, the issue lies in performing efficient computations during the system's runtime, particularly when dealing with the AI module. This module is often treated as a black box, lacking of explicit formulation, or is constituted with highly complex computational components and a vast number of parameters, which significantly increases the computational complexity in verification. To address this, we propose the way of sampling generation based on the *prediction-rectification* approach, which is enlightened by Euler's method for solving ordinary differential equations (ODEs).

Another challenge arises from the semantic structure of the specification language. Consider the STL formula $G_{[a,b]}\psi$, theoretically, to evaluate its truth value, we need to known that of ψ at every point $t \in [a,b]$, which makes such computation intricate due to the complexity of ψ's form. To this end, we focus on a kind of NSSs having special types: In which all parameters are rational numbers, and all control functions are essentially piece-wise linear. We call such an NSS to be a *piece-wise linear neural-symbolic system* (PLNSS). Indeed, such NSSs are commonly used in practice — data stored in a cyber system are represented by float numbers, and DNNs using piece-wise linear activation function are popular, which often act as the AI module. Further, if we require that all time-bounds occurring in an STL formula are rational numbers, and all its atoms are affine, namely, being of the form $\boldsymbol{c}^{\mathrm{T}}\boldsymbol{z} + d \gtrsim 0$, then we can circumvent this problem based on the following observation: Indeed, upon a trajectory of a PLNSS, truth value of any atom (and hence any subformula) of such a formula toggles only at some 'specific moments' — more accurately, there exists some rational number $\Delta t > 0$, such that any subformula's truth value toggles only at multiples of Δt. We call such specification language *affine* STL.

For PLNSSs and affine STL formulas, we can develop an exact runtime verification framework based on the rewriting approach, namely, no false positive/negative if the monitoring is successfully done. The basic observation is: in this setting, we may safely ensure the satisfaction of $G_{[0,\Delta t]}\psi$ once ψ is satisfied at both $t = 0$ and $t = \Delta t$. Therefore, in the case of $a > 0$, the truth value of $G_{[a,b]}\psi$ at $t = k \cdot \Delta t$ is just that of $G_{[a-\Delta t, b-\Delta t]}\psi$ at $t = (k+1) \cdot \Delta t$; likewise, $G_{[0,c]}\psi$ at $t = 0$ can be decomposed into ψ (at $t = 0$) and $G_{[0,c-\Delta t]}\psi$ (at $t = \Delta t$). Remember that due to the proviso of being affine, in the above a, b, c are all multiples of Δt. Using this technique, the RV task is boiled down to the situation of dealing with the discrete setting.

RV technique based on such syntactic-level transformation is complete for safety/co-safety properties, and it terminates once a bad-prefix/good-prefix is detected. Furthermore, the quantitative version of such light-weight rewriting can also deal with the non-terminated case — it provides a lower-bound and an upper-bound of the specification's quantitative semantics upon the remaining trajectory. Recall that the quantitative semantics of an STL formula embodies its degree of satisfaction (when the value is positive) and/or violation (when is negative) along a trajectory.

Contributions of our framework can be summarized as follows:

- First of all, we present a unified formalization of neural-symbolic systems, which generalizes that of CPS, pure physical systems, as well as pure cyber ones.
- Second, we propose an approach to performing an effective online trajectory sampling, which is specially tailored for dealing with the opacity of the neural-part.
- Last but not least, we have developed both the qualitative and quantitative RV techniques for NSSs against STL properties based on the rewriting app-

roach. Particularly, the newly presented approach is exact for PLNSSs w.r.t. affine STL formulas.

The remainder of this paper is organized as follows: In Sect. 2, we revisit some basic notions and notations related to neural-symbolic systems. In Sect. 3, we present the qualitative as well as the quantitative RV framework for neural-symbolic systems against STL properties. The proposed approach is implemented and evaluated in Sect. 4. In Sect. 5, we discuss some related work on NSS verification. Finally, we conclude this paper in Sect. 6.

2   Preliminaries

In this paper, we use $\mathbb{B}$, $\mathbb{N}$, $\mathbb{R}$, and $\mathbb{R}_{\geq 0}$ to denote the sets of boolean values (i.e., 0 and 1), natural numbers, real numbers, and non-negative real numbers, respectively.

An *interval* I is a subset of $\mathbb{R}$, being one of the forms $[a, b]$, $[a, b)$, $(a, b]$ or (a, b), where $a \leq b$, and we denote $a = \inf I$ and $b = \sup I$, respectively called the *left end* and the *right end* of I. For $t \in \mathbb{R}$, we denote by $I \pm t$ be the corresponding interval obtained from I by correspondingly shifting the both ends with t, without changing the form of I. Therefore, we have $\inf(I \pm t) = (\inf I) \pm t$ and $\sup(I \pm t) = (\sup I) \pm t$. For example, $[a, b] + 0.1 = [a + 0.1, b + 0.1]$, and $[a, b) - 0.2 = [a - 0.2, b - 0.2)$. Furthermore, let I be an interval having $\inf I \geq 0$ and $\sup I \geq 0$, then we use $I \dot{-} t$ for the interval having the same form as I, but $\inf(I \dot{-} t) = \max\{0, \inf I - t\}$, and $\sup(I \dot{-} t) = \max\{0, \sup I - t\}$. For example, $[2, 3) \dot{-} 0.5 = [1.5, 2.5)$, and $[2, 3] \dot{-} 2.5 = [0, 0.5]$.

Suppose that $D \subseteq \mathbb{R}_{\geq 0}$, then a continuous function $x : D \to \mathbb{R}$ is said to be a *signal* over D. Particularly, x is said to be a *discrete* (resp. *boolean*) signal whenever $\text{ran}(x) \subseteq \mathbb{N}$ (resp. $\text{ran}(x) \subseteq \mathbb{B}$). Suppose that $x_1, x_2, \ldots, x_m$ are m signals over D, then the vector $\boldsymbol{x} = (x_1, x_2, \ldots, x_m)^{\text{T}}$ is said to be an *m-ary signal vector* (or *signal group*) over D.

2.1   Neural-Symbolic Systems

A *neural-symbolic system* is constituted with a family of signals and several control functions. In detail, the signals can be categorized into the following groups:

- A set of *environmental-signals* $\boldsymbol{v} = \{v_1, v_2, \ldots, v_n\}$. In what follows, we interchangeably view $\boldsymbol{v}$ (and other signal sets) as a set or as a vector, provided there is no risk of ambiguity.
- A special subset $\boldsymbol{x}$ of $\boldsymbol{v}$, such signals are treated as inputs of the AI module.
- A set $\boldsymbol{y} = \{y_1, y_2, \ldots, y_k\}$ of discrete signals, which are outputs of the AI module.
- A set $\boldsymbol{c} = \{c_1, c_2, \ldots, c_m\}$ of *control-signals* and each of them is also discrete, and we require $\boldsymbol{y}$ and $\boldsymbol{c}$ to be disjoint.

An NSS also involves three control functions, listed as follows.

– The *physical control*, which is described by the differential equation

$$\dot{\boldsymbol{v}} = f(\boldsymbol{v}, \boldsymbol{y}, \boldsymbol{c}, t),$$

depicts the behaviors of the environmental signals.

– The *neural mapping*, can be figuratively established by some function

$$\boldsymbol{y} = \Psi(\boldsymbol{x}),$$

here Ψ is in general not explicitly given—in other words, Ψ sometimes acts as a "black-box" function, but it is *always callable* for any given input within its domain.

– The *cyber control*, which is formulated as

$$\boldsymbol{c}' = \delta(\boldsymbol{v}, \boldsymbol{y}, \boldsymbol{c}, \Delta t),$$

namely, δ gives the value of $\boldsymbol{c}$ at the "next discrete step", where Δt is the time-gap between the steps.

The *trajectory* of this NSS is just the signal tuple $(\boldsymbol{v}, \boldsymbol{y}, \boldsymbol{x})$ (sometimes, written as $\{\boldsymbol{v}(t), \boldsymbol{y}(t), \boldsymbol{x}(t)\}_{t \in D}$, where D is usually $\mathbb{R}_{\geq 0}$), which evolves under the guidance of the control functions.

Observe that an NSS becomes a CPS if $\boldsymbol{x} = \emptyset$ (and hence $\boldsymbol{y}$ is also $\emptyset$). Further, it becomes a pure cyber system in the case that $\boldsymbol{v}$ is empty. In our definition, an NSS generates a single trajectory once the initial values of all signals are set. Definitely, one can also extend this formalism via cooperating with nondeterminism in the cyber control, or with probabilistic mechanism in the physical control.

2.2 Signal Temporal Logic

Signal temporal logic extends LTL by adding time constraints and real-valued constraints. STL formulas can be defined with the following BNF

$$\varphi ::= \top \mid g(\boldsymbol{z}) \gtrsim 0 \mid \neg\varphi \mid \varphi \vee \varphi \mid \varphi \mathsf{U}_I \varphi,$$

where $\gtrsim \in \{>, \geq\}$, and I is an interval having $0 \leq \inf I$. In the above g is a continuous function, and $\boldsymbol{z}$ is a signal vector. Likewise, we also write $\tau, 0 \models \varphi$ as $\tau \models \varphi$. For convenience, we also introduce the following derived temporal connectives:

$$\mathsf{F}_I \varphi \overset{\text{def}}{=} \top \mathsf{U}_I \varphi;$$
$$\mathsf{G}_I \varphi \overset{\text{def}}{=} \neg \mathsf{F}_I \neg \varphi;$$
$$\varphi \mathsf{R}_I \psi \overset{\text{def}}{=} \neg(\neg\varphi \mathsf{U}_I \neg\psi).$$

We abbreviate $\mathsf{U}_{[a,a]}$ as U_a, we use $\mathsf{U}_{\geq a}$ for $\mathsf{U}_{[a,\infty)}$, and just use U for $\mathsf{U}_{\geq 0}$. Other syntactic sugar such as $\mathsf{F}_{\geq a}$, G can be accordingly defined in an analogous way.

Given a trajectory τ with signal tuple $(\boldsymbol{v}, \boldsymbol{y}, \boldsymbol{c})$ and $t \in \mathbb{R}_{\geq 0}$, then one can define the *qualitative satisfaction* as follows:

- $\tau, t \models \top$ trivially holds;
- $\tau, t \models g(\boldsymbol{z}) \gtrsim 0$ iff $g(z_1(t), z_2(t), \dots, z_m(t)) \gtrsim 0$, where $\boldsymbol{z} = (z_1, z_2, \dots, z_m) \subseteq \boldsymbol{v} \cup \boldsymbol{y} \cup \boldsymbol{c}$;
- $\tau, t \models \neg\varphi$ iff $\tau, t \not\models \varphi$;
- $\tau, t \models \varphi \vee \psi$ iff $\tau, t \models \varphi$ or $\tau, t \models \psi$;
- $\tau, t \models \varphi \mathsf{U}_I \psi$ iff $\exists t' \in I$ s.t. $\tau, t + t' \models \psi$ and $\tau, t'' \models \varphi$ for $\forall t'' \in [t, t + t')$.

Alternatively, we may define the *quantitative satisfaction* $[\![\bullet]\!]_{\tau,t}$ w.r.t. τ and t, which yields another type of semantics. Inductively:

- $[\![\top]\!]_{\tau,t} = \infty$;
- $[\![g(\boldsymbol{z}) \gtrsim 0]\!]_{\tau,t} = g(\boldsymbol{z})$;
- $[\![\neg\varphi]\!]_{\tau,t} = -[\![\varphi]\!]_{\tau,t}$;
- $[\![\varphi \vee \psi]\!]_{\tau,t} = \max\{[\![\varphi]\!]_{\tau,t}, [\![\psi]\!]_{\tau,t}\}$;
- $[\![\varphi \mathsf{U}_I \psi]\!]_{\tau,t} = \sup\limits_{t' \in I+t} \min\left\{[\![\psi]\!]_{\tau,t'}, \inf\limits_{t'' \in [t,t')} [\![\varphi]\!]_{\tau,t''}\right\}$.

We say that an STL formula φ is *strict* if all atomic subformulas of φ are of the form $g(\boldsymbol{z}) > 0$ when φ is equivalently written in negative normal form. Indeed, we have the following claim for the relation between qualitative and quantitative satisfaction.

Theorem 1. *For every strict STL formula φ, trajectory τ and $t \in \mathbb{R}_{\geq 0}$, we have: $\tau, t \models \varphi$ if and only if $[\![\varphi]\!]_{\tau,t} > 0$.*

We say that an STL formula φ describes a *safety property*, if each its violated trajectory has a 'bad-prefix'. Formally, if $\tau \not\models \varphi$, then there exists some $t \geq 0$, such that $\tau' \not\models \varphi$ provided that $\tau[0 : t] = \tau'[0 : t]$ — which means, $\boldsymbol{z}(t')$ yields a same value w.r.t. τ and τ' for every signal $\boldsymbol{z}$ and every moment $t' \leq t$. The formula φ is a *liveness property* if for every trajectory τ, there exists some $t \geq 0$ and some other trajectory τ' such that $\tau'[0 : t] = \tau[0 : t]$ and $\tau' \models \varphi$. i. o. w., each finite trajectory could be prolonged to satisfy a liveness property. Lastly, we say that φ is a *co-safety* (resp. *co-liveness*) *property* if $\neg\varphi$ is a safety (resp. liveness) one.

Theorem 2. *Every formula φ can be equivalently written as $\varphi_s \wedge \varphi_l$, where φ_s is a safety property and φ_l is a liveness property. Further, $\top$ is the only property which is both liveness and safety [1].*

2.3 Neural Networks

A deep neural network (DNN) consisting of L-layers can be described via a series of pairs $\{(\boldsymbol{W}_i, \boldsymbol{b}_i)\}_{i=1}^{L}$. Given an input vector $\boldsymbol{x}$, the corresponding output y can be inductively computed via the following process:

- first, let $\boldsymbol{z}_1 = \boldsymbol{x}$;
- for each $i < L$, we let $\boldsymbol{x}_{i+1} = \sigma(\boldsymbol{W}_i \boldsymbol{x}_i + \boldsymbol{b}_i)$, where σ is the activation function, to be defined later;

– finally, let y be the index of the maximum element of $\boldsymbol{W}_L\boldsymbol{x}_L + \boldsymbol{b}_L$.

Below lists some commonly used neural network activation functions:

– the ReLU function: $\sigma(\boldsymbol{x}) = \max\{0, \boldsymbol{x}\}$;
– the Sigmoidal function: $\sigma(\boldsymbol{x}) = \frac{\exp(x)}{1+\exp(x)}$;
– the Tanh function: $\sigma(\boldsymbol{x}) = \frac{\exp(x)-\exp(-x)}{\exp(x)+\exp(-x)}$.

Remember that in the above we take the convention of vectorized application of functions, namely, we use $g(\boldsymbol{x})$ for the vector $(g(x_1), g(x_2), \ldots, g(x_n))^{\mathrm{T}}$ in the case that $\boldsymbol{x} = (x_1, x_2, \ldots, x_n)^{\mathrm{T}}$. Observe that, a DNN using ReLU as the activation function actually admits a piece-wise linear mapping before the last step.

3 The Runtime Verification Framework

3.1 Sample Generation Based on Prediction-Rectification

The point of extending runtime verification from CPS to NSS is to deal with the opaque AI module, for it does not always provide an analytical description.

Provisos. In this section, let $\boldsymbol{v}$, $\boldsymbol{x}$, $\boldsymbol{y}$ and $\boldsymbol{c}$ be the environmental-, input-, output-, and control-signal sets of the NSS, respectively. And, the control functions/mappings of the NSS are given by

$$\begin{cases} \dot{\boldsymbol{v}} = f(\boldsymbol{v}, \boldsymbol{y}, \boldsymbol{c}, t) \\ \boldsymbol{y} = \Psi(\boldsymbol{x}) \\ \boldsymbol{c}' = \delta(\boldsymbol{v}, \boldsymbol{y}, \boldsymbol{c}, \Delta t) \end{cases}.$$

Meanwhile, let φ be the STL specification under scrutiny, we may safely assume that all constants (such as interval ends, coefficients) appearing in φ and related to the NSS are rational numbers, and suppose that we have some $\Delta t > 0$ which is a common divisor (or, common measure) of all the constants.

The Prediction-Rectification Signal Generation. Given a starting moment t_0 and a number N, suppose that the values of $\boldsymbol{v}(t_0)$, $\boldsymbol{y}(t_0)$ and $\boldsymbol{c}(t_0)$ are given, we can generate the series $\{\boldsymbol{v}[i], \boldsymbol{x}[i], \boldsymbol{y}[i], \boldsymbol{c}[i]\}_{i=1}^{N}$, where $\boldsymbol{v}[i]$ is the shorthand of $\boldsymbol{v}(t_0 + i \cdot \Delta t)$, and $\boldsymbol{x}[i]$, $\boldsymbol{y}[i]$, $\boldsymbol{c}[i]$ are defined analogously. Inductively, suppose that these values at step i are already calculated, then values at the 'next step' can be computed as follows.

(1) First of all, $\boldsymbol{v}[i + 1]$ can be approximately computed using $\boldsymbol{v}[i] + \Delta t \cdot f(\boldsymbol{v}[i], \boldsymbol{y}[i], \boldsymbol{c}[i], t_0 + i \cdot \Delta t)$.
(2) Recall that $\boldsymbol{x}$ is a subset (sub-vector) of $\boldsymbol{v}$, and hence $\boldsymbol{x}[i+1]$ is also obtained.
(3) Invoke the AI module with $\boldsymbol{x}[i + 1]$, and then we have $\boldsymbol{y}[i + 1]$.
(4) Finally, $\boldsymbol{c}[i + 1]$ is computed from $\delta(\boldsymbol{v}[i], \boldsymbol{y}[i], \boldsymbol{c}[i], \Delta t)$.

Note that the above computation is done at the moment $t = t_0$, and we regard such computation takes negligible time. In the first step of each raw, we use Euler's forward-prediction to conduct the approximation. This is called the *prediction phase*. Now, let $\boldsymbol{w}[i]$ be the juxtaposition of $\boldsymbol{v}[i]$, $\boldsymbol{y}[i]$ and $\boldsymbol{c}[i]$, i.e., the vector of predicted-values at moment $t_0 + i \cdot \Delta t$; and let $\widehat{\boldsymbol{w}}[i]$ be the corresponding actual-values. Once $\|\boldsymbol{w}[i] - \widehat{\boldsymbol{w}}[i]\|_\infty > \epsilon$ is detected at the moment $t_0 + i \cdot \Delta t$ (here ϵ is some preset tolerant), we immediately re-compute N newly-predicted values with the initial value $\widehat{\boldsymbol{w}}[i]$, i.o.w., the new computation takes the time $t_0' = t_0 + i \cdot \Delta t$ as the starting moment. This phase is called *rectification phase*.

PLNSS. In what follows let $\Gamma(t_0) = \{\boldsymbol{w}[i]\}_{i=0}^N$, thus this sequence depicts a prefix of the trajectory of the running system. There is no wonder that one can apply existing online RV technique against φ with such a sequence of samples. Nevertheless, we here interest in the situation that *we can perform an accurate monitoring with such samplings on discrete time-steps*. To this end, we in this paper particularly concern about NSS fulfilling the following properties:

(A) The environmental-control f is piece-wise constant, and either the number of linear-regions is finite, or f is periodic.
(B) The AI part is a neural network using ReLU as activation function, and all the parameters are rational numbers (maybe unknown though).
(C) The cyber-control function δ can be extended to a piece-wise constant function over $\mathbb{R}$, with rational turning points.

We call such a system *piece-wise linear neural-symbolic system* (PLNSS). Remember that Requirement (A) is the necessity guaranteeing f can be finitely (or unified) described; and Requirement (C) can almost be trivially achieved, because δ is defined upon a discrete domain.

In addition, we impose an additional constraint in the specification: each atomic proposition must be of the form $\boldsymbol{c}^{\mathrm{T}}\boldsymbol{z} + d \gtrless 0$. We call such STL formula an *affine* one.

With the proviso in the beginning of this section, we have the following claim about PLNSSs and affine STL formulas.

Theorem 3. *Let τ be the trajectory of a PLNSS, φ be an affine STL formula, then there exists some rational number $\Delta t > 0$, such that along τ, the truth value of φ toggles only at moments that are multiples of Δt.*

Proof. This proof can be done by induction on the formula's structure. But before that, we establish two preliminary observations:

(i) Let $q_1, q_2, ..., q_n$ be n distinct rational numbers. There exists a (largest) rational number q making $q_i = k_i \cdot q$ for $i = 1, 2, ..., n$, where each k_i is an integer. We denote this q as $\mathrm{cm}(q_1, q_2, ..., q_n)$.
(ii) For a PLNSS, each signal can be represented as a piece-wise linear function of t with rational coefficients. Over each period, it can be partitioned into a finite number of linear regions.

- This proposition trivially holds for the formula $\top$.
- For an atomic formula of the form $g(z) \geq 0$, where $g(z) = c^T z + d$ and $z = (z_1, \ldots, z_m)^T$, since each z_i is a piece-wise liner function of t, we can substitute them into $g(z) = 0$, and then obtain a set of linear equations for t with rational coefficients. The solution of these form a set of rational numbers $\{t_1, t_2, \ldots, t_n\}$. Let $\Delta t = \mathrm{cm}(T, t_1, t_2, \ldots, t_n)$, where T denotes the period of the system. Note that if the solution space of $g(z) = 0$ includes intervals, we just need to take the endpoints of these intervals, which must be rational numbers.
- If Δt is suitable for ψ, then it is also suitable for $\neg \psi$, straightforwardly.
- Suppose that Δt_i is suitable for ψ_i $(i = 1, 2)$, then we may choose $\mathrm{cm}(\Delta t_1, \Delta t_2)$ for $\psi_1 \vee \psi_2$.
- If Δt_i is suitable for ψ_i $(i = 1, 2)$, then $\mathrm{cm}(\Delta t_1, \Delta t_2, \inf I, \sup I)$ is competent for $\psi_1 U_I \psi_2$.

The above concludes the proof. $\qquad\qquad\qquad\qquad\qquad\qquad\qquad\qquad\qquad$ $\square$

According to Theorem 3, for a PLNSS and an affine STL formula, we need only concern a special sub-signal defined on discrete domain, rather than that on a continuous domain (namely, $\mathbb{R}_{\geq 0}$). Also note that this theorem just guarantees the existence of such Δt, yet its 'constructive way' of finding such a value does not practically work, due to the opacity of the AI module. Indeed, it is not necessary to detect the accurate value at the beginning of the prediction phase. In practice, we may first choose some Δt which is small enough (which is smaller than the half of the minimal gap of two crucial points in a period). Once we have detected $(c^T z(a) + d)(c^T z(a + \Delta t) + d) < 0$ at some moment $t = a$, according to the intermediate-value theorem, we may find some $\Delta t' < \Delta t$ having $c^T z(a + \Delta t') + d = 0$ using bisectional detection, and then Δt is refined to its common measure with $\Delta t'$. Alternatively, one can gather the derivatives of each 'piece', as done in [9], then one can also avoid missing the crucial points with the help of such information.

3.2 Qualitative Runtime Verification

We in this subsection provide a way of qualitative runtime verification for PLNSS against affine STL, which is also the basis of the quantitative version. The core part of our technique is *formula rewriting* [5, 14], and the intuition is: it simulates a running of automaton corresponding to φ on the (discrete) signal, each time, it takes the values of v, y, c at the next moment with time gap Δt, proceeds and transforms the formula under monitoring.

Let Γ be the sequence $\{w[i]\}_{i=0}^N$, then we define the *rewriting function* $\triangleright_{\Gamma, i}$ as follows:

(1) $\triangleright_{\Gamma, i}(\psi) = \psi$ if $i > N$; and otherwise

(2) $\triangleright_{\Gamma, i}(\top) = \top$;

(3) $\triangleright_{\Gamma, i}(c^T z + d \gtrsim 0) = \begin{cases} \top, & \text{if } c^T z[i] + d \gtrsim 0 \\ \bot, & \text{otherwise} \end{cases}$;

(4) $\triangleright_{\Gamma,i}(\neg\psi) = \neg\triangleright_{\Gamma,i}(\psi)$;

(5) $\triangleright_{\Gamma,i}(\psi \vee \eta) = \triangleright_{\Gamma,i}(\psi) \vee \triangleright_{\Gamma,i}(\eta)$;

(6) $\triangleright_{\Gamma,i}(\psi\mathsf{U}_I\eta)$

$$= \begin{cases} \triangleright_{\Gamma,i}(\psi) \wedge \triangleright_{\Gamma,i+1}(\psi\mathsf{U}_{I-\Delta t}\eta), & \inf I > 0 \\ \triangleright_{\Gamma,i}(\eta) \vee (\triangleright_{\Gamma,i}(\psi) \wedge \triangleright_{\Gamma,i+1}(\psi\mathsf{U}_{I\dot{-}\Delta t}\eta)), & \inf I = 0, \sup I > 0 \end{cases};$$

(7) $\triangleright_{\Gamma,i}(\psi\mathsf{U}_{[0,0]}\eta) = \triangleright_{\Gamma,i}(\eta)$, and $\triangleright_{\Gamma,i}(\psi\mathsf{U}_{I_\varepsilon}\eta) = \bot$, where I_ε is $[0,0)$, $(0,0]$ or $(0,0)$.

Remark 1. For Item (6), remind that both $\inf I$ and $\sup I$ are multiples of Δt, according to the construction — i.o.w., we have $\inf I = k \cdot \Delta t$ and $\sup I = \ell \cdot \Delta t$ for some $k, \ell \in \mathbb{N}$. Remember that $\bot$ is the abbreviation of $\neg\top$.

We denote by $\psi \xrightarrow{\Gamma} \eta$ if $\eta = \triangleright_{\Gamma,0}(\psi)$ in what follows. Then, we need to distinguish three cases:

1. $\eta = \top$, it indicates that $\tau, t_0 \models \psi$ holds — recall that t_0 is the starting moment to generate Γ;
2. $\eta = \bot$, it means that $\tau, t_0 \not\models \psi$, namely η is violated;
3. η is neither $\bot$ nor $\top$, we need to generate a next group of samples to proceed this uncertain case.

As the result, we may obtain a sequence

$$\psi_0 \xrightarrow{\Gamma_0} \psi_1 \xrightarrow{\Gamma_1} \psi_2 \xrightarrow{\Gamma_2} \cdots \xrightarrow{\Gamma_{i-1}} \psi_i \xrightarrow{\Gamma_i} \cdots$$

where $\psi_0 = \varphi$, and the start moment corresponding to Γ_i is $i \cdot N \cdot \Delta t$.

The following theorem guarantees the completeness of qualitative RV for safety/co-safety properties.

Theorem 4. *Let φ be a safety (resp. co-safety) affine STL property, and τ denotes the trajectory of a PLNSS. Then, $\tau \not\models \varphi$ (resp. $\tau \models \varphi$) iff φ can be rewritten into $\bot$ (resp. $\top$) within finite steps.*

3.3   Quantitative Runtime Verification

Given a sequence $\Gamma = \{w[i]\}_{i=0}^N$, and let Δt be the same as in the previous subsection, now consider the other rewriting operation $\bigcirc_{\Gamma,i}$ defined as follows:

(1) $\bigcirc_{\Gamma,i}(\psi) = \chi$ if $i > N$; and otherwise

(2) $\bigcirc_{\Gamma,i}(\top) = \infty$;

(3) $\bigcirc_{\Gamma,i}(c^\mathsf{T}z + d \gtreqless 0) = c^\mathsf{T}z[i] + d$;

(4) $\bigcirc_{\Gamma,i}(\neg\psi) = -\bigcirc_{\Gamma,i}(\psi)$;

(5) $\bigcirc_{\Gamma,i}(\psi \vee \eta) = \max(\bigcirc_{\Gamma,i}(\psi), \bigcirc_{\Gamma,i}(\eta))$;

(6) $\bigcirc_{\Gamma,i}(\psi\mathsf{U}_I\eta) = \begin{cases} \min(\bigcirc_{\Gamma,i}(\psi), \bigcirc_{\Gamma,i+1}(\psi\mathsf{U}_{I-\Delta t}\eta)), & \inf I > 0 \\ \max(\bigcirc_{\Gamma,i}(\eta), \min(\bigcirc_{\Gamma,i}(\psi), \bigcirc_{\Gamma,i+1}(\psi\mathsf{U}_{I\dot{-}\Delta t}\eta))), & \inf I = 0, \sup I > 0 \end{cases};$

(7) $\bigcirc_{\Gamma,i}(\psi\mathsf{U}_{[0,0]}\eta) = \bigcirc_{\Gamma,i}(\eta)$, and $\bigcirc_{\Gamma,i}(\psi\mathsf{U}_{I_\varepsilon}\eta) = -\infty$.

Remark 2. Note that in the above χ is a symbol acting as a place-holder. Thus, the output of this operation is an expression built up from χ, ∞, concrete numbers, together with the operators of $-$, max and min.

We say an occurrence of χ in $\bigcirc_{\Gamma,i}(\psi)$ is *positive* (resp. *negative*) if it is in an even (resp. odd) number of scopes of $-$.

The RV process in general consumes more than one sequence of signal samples, to this end, we define the following conception: Let $\Gamma = \{w[i]\}_{i=0}^{N}$ and $\Gamma' = \{w'[i]\}_{i=0}^{N'}$ with $w[N] = w'[0]$, then let $\Gamma \circ \Gamma'$ be the new sequence $\{w''[i]\}_{i=0}^{N+N'}$ where

$$w''[i] = \begin{cases} w[i], & i \leq N \\ w'[i-N], & i \geq N \end{cases},$$

called the *concatenation* of Γ and Γ'. In the following, we call N (resp. N') the *length* of Γ (resp. Γ'), denoted as $\mathrm{len}(\Gamma)$ (resp. $\mathrm{len}(\Gamma')$). Some properties of this operation are straightforward. For example, if $\psi_1 \xrightarrow{\Gamma_1} \psi_2$ and $\psi_2 \xrightarrow{\Gamma_2} \psi_3$, then we have $\psi_1 \xrightarrow{\Gamma_1 \circ \Gamma_2} \psi_3$. In addition, we have $\mathrm{len}(\Gamma_0 \circ \cdots \circ \Gamma_n) = \sum_{i=0}^{n} \mathrm{len}(\Gamma_i)$.

Let τ be the trajectory of the PLNSS, $\Gamma_0, \Gamma_1, \ldots, \Gamma_n$ are all the sequences sampled along τ so far, also let $\Gamma = \Gamma_0 \circ \cdots \circ \Gamma_n$ and let $t = \Delta t \cdot \mathrm{len}(\Gamma)$. We now let $[\![\varphi]\!]_{\tau,t}$ (resp. $\|\varphi\|_{\tau,t}$) be what obtained from $\bigcirc_{\Gamma,0}(\varphi)$ by replacing each positive (resp. negative) occurrence of χ with ∞, and each negative (resp. positive) one with $-\infty$. Then, we have the following theorem for quantitative runtime verification.

Theorem 5. $\|\varphi\|_{\tau,t} \leq [\![\varphi]\!]_{\tau,t} \leq [\![\varphi]\!]_{\tau,t}$.

Therefore, Theorem 5 provides the way to estimate the upper- and lower-bounds of the formula's quantitative satisfaction for the undetermined case.

4   Case Studies and Experimental Results

4.1   System Description

To demonstrate the applicability of our framework, we use the PLNSS provided by HYDAC in the context of the European project Quasimodo [6]. This case study involves a control system consisting of:

The Machine. The oil consumption pattern of the machine is periodic. A consumption cycle consists of 10 consumption periods, each lasting two seconds. For simplicity, just let the initial value of the amount of oil totally consumed be 0. Table 1 shows the consumption rate (r) of the machine in one cycle $(20s)$. We use the signal $v_{\mathrm{out}}(t)$ to record the amount of oil consumed by time t, then we have $v_{\mathrm{out}}(0) = 0$. Based on the machine's consumption pattern (i.e., $\dot{v}_{\mathrm{out}} = r$), within the time interval $[0, 20]$, we can establish the relationship for the oil consumption v_{out} about time t.

Table 1. Consumption rate of the machine in one cycle.

t (s)	[0,2]	[2,4]	[4,6]	[6,8]	[8,10]	[10,12]	[12,14]	[14,16]	[16,18]	[18,20]
r (L/s)	0	1.2	0	0	1.2	2.5	0	1.7	0.5	0

The Pump. The pump operates in two states: ON and OFF. It is assumed to be initially OFF at the start of each cycle. When the pump is switched to ON, it delivers oil into the accumulator at a rate of 2.2 L/s. The pump is also constrained by timing requirements, preventing it from switching between ON and OFF frequently. According to [6], the pump is assumed to activate no more than twice per-cycle. Followed by this assumption, there are at most four time points $(t_1 - - t_4)$ within a cycle to switch the pump ON or OFF. Thus, they have the following constraint:

$$0 \leq t_1 \leq t_2 \leq t_3 \leq t_4 \leq 20. \tag{$*$}$$

Additionally, there must be a minimum delay of 2 seconds between any two consecutive control actions (turning the pump ON or OFF). To fulfill this, the following artificial constraint is also imposed:

$$t_1 \geq 2, \ t_2 - t_1 \geq 2, \ t_3 - t_2 \geq 2, \ t_4 - t_3 \geq 2. \tag{$**$}$$

Let $v_{\text{in}}(t)$, with the initial value $v_{\text{in}}(0) = 0$, stand for the amount of oil pumped into the accumulator by time t.

The Accumulator. The accumulator stores oil under pressure from a fixed amount of gas. Let $v(t)$ denote the oil volume at time t, and v_0 represent the initial oil volume in the accumulator at the start of a cycle. Then, the oil volume in the accumulator is given by: $v(t) = v_0 + v_{\text{in}}(t) - v_{\text{out}}(t)$. The oil level v at time t (measured in liters) must always remain in the safety range (i.e. $[4.9, 25.1]$).

The Controller. In [21], a deep deterministic policy gradient (DDPG) method was employed to train a policy network as the controller for the oil pump system and ensured that the NSS's time-related constraints $(*)$ and $(**)$ are satisfied. This neural network uses ReLU as activation function, and we just treat it as a black-box, corresponding to some unknown mapping $\boldsymbol{y} = \Psi(v)$.

To convert $\boldsymbol{y}$ into a switching signal that satisfies constraints eq. $(*)$ and eq. $(**)$, the following transformation can be applied:

$$t_{k+1} = C \cdot y[i] + t_k + 2.$$

Here, C is a constant, and its value depends on the number of control switches in each cycle, $y[i]$ represents the value of the output from the $i - th$ neuron, t_k denotes the current control time point, and t_{k+1} denotes the next control time point. Here, $k \in \{1, 2, 3\}$, specifically, when calculating the first control time point, we have $t_1 = C \cdot y[1] + 2$. The four switching time points within a cycle, represented as (t_1, t_2, t_3, t_4), can be obtained through cyber control.

4.2 Experiments

In this section, we give the experimental results of the proposed approach upon the aforementioned PLNSS. All experiments were conducted on a machine equipped with an Intel Core i5-12400F CPU and 16 GB of RAM.

In this experiment, we focus on both qualitative and quantitative runtime verification of the safety of the aforementioned PLNSS. For qualitative RV, we concern about whether the signal (oil volume) within the safety range can consistently produce outputs within the safety range over a given time boundary. For the quantitative counterpart, we estimate the satisfaction degree of the specification in the current state of the system by incrementally evaluating the quantitative rewriting value w.r.t. the formula, providing estimates for the upper- and lower-bounds.

For *qualitative verification*, we monitor the property φ that for the initially safe input, if the oil amount remains in the safety range for 10 cycles (200 s). We can describe this using STL as follows:

$$\varphi = 4.9 \leq v \leq 25.1 \rightarrow \mathsf{G}_{[0,200]}(4.9 \leq v \leq 25.1),$$

being mind that $4.9 \leq v \leq 25.1$ is the shorthand of $(25.1 - v \geq 0) \wedge (v - 4.9 \geq 0)$. With the aim of verifying the property of this PLNSS, the objective of the qualitative verification is to answer the following research questions:

RQ1: Can the approximated trajectory obtained through prediction-rectification sampling accurately verify the system's safety during operation?

RQ2: How efficient is the online runtime verification framework based on prediction-rectification sampling for generating trajectories?

Besides these two research questions concerning accuracy and efficiency, we also check the following two issues to justify the exactness of the approach.

False positives: Where the system is actually safe but the approximated trajectory indicates it to be unsafe.

False negatives: Where the system enters an unsafe state, but the approximated trajectory indicates it to be safe.

Parameter Configuration. Based on the actual operating conditions of the oil pump system, we set the tolerant $\epsilon = 0.1$. We combine the results obtained from the previous bisection search with the actual runtime performance, let $\Delta t = 0.001$. Obviously, to ensure the safety of the oil pump system, the oil level at each moment must remain within a safe range. We sampled 200 times using different initial values $v_0 \in [4.9, 25.1]$, resulting in 200 different running trajectories. We focus on the following metrics: *False positive count, False negative count, Prediction error rate, Average Time and Memory consumption,* denoted by **FP**, **FN**, **PE**, **Time** and **Mem**. Our experimental results are shown in Table 2.

The experimental results indicate that our method did not produce any prediction errors and was able to exactly verify the safety of the PLNSS while maintaining low time and memory overhead.

Table 2. Qualitative runtime verification results.

FP	FN	PE	Time (s)	Mem (MB)
0	0	0.00	0.22	400.2

For *quantitative verification*, our goal is to quantitatively compute the satisfaction degree of future trajectories for the property based on the current signal value. With the aim of verifying the property of the PLNSS. The objective of the quantitative verification is to estimate the safety satisfaction in an infinite time domain and to decide whether we can stop monitoring whenever periodicity can be leveraged for this system. To ensure the system's safety, we set two different initial values $v_0 = 15$ and $v_0 = 20$ (both are within the safe range), and monitor their satisfaction degree over different time intervals $[0, T]$, namely, the property to be monitored is

$$\varphi = \mathsf{G}_{[0,T]}(4.9 \leq v \leq 25.1).$$

It is evident that the lower-bound of the satisfaction degree for such property is always $-\infty$. Therefore, we only need to focus on the upper-bound of that. We also recorded the switching time points for these two different initial values through cyber control at each time interval, specifically, we recorded the switching time points (t_1, t_2, t_3, t_4) for the last 20 s of each time interval. Our experimental results are shown in Table 3.

Table 3. Quantitative runtime verification results.

v_0	T (s)	(t_1, t_2, t_3, t_4)	$[\![\varphi]\!]_{\tau,T}$	Time (s)	Mem (MB)
15	20	(11.59, 13.70, 15.94, 17.95)	1.18	0.02	214.2
15	40	(7.92, 10.73, 13.83, 15.85)	1.14	0.06	232.7
15	60	(2.71, 7.06, 13.21, 15.29)	0.42	0.09	249.3
15	80	(2.68, 7.05, 13.25, 15.32)	0.30	0.12	268.4
15	100	(2.67, 7.05, 13.29, 15.33)	0.30	0.17	295.4
15	200	(2.67, 7.04, 13.26, 15.34)	0.30	0.28	398.4
20	20	(13.16, 15.17, 17.21, 19.21)	5.10	0.03	210.5
20	40	(11.39, 13.53, 15.79, 17.80)	1.07	0.07	230.7
20	60	(7.48, 10.40, 13.64, 15.67)	1.06	0.09	251.6
20	80	(2.67, 7.04, 13.26, 15.37)	0.31	0.16	275.4
20	100	(2.67, 7.04, 13.26, 15.37)	0.31	0.19	299.3
20	200	(2.67, 7.04, 13.26, 15.37)	0.31	0.32	392.3

We plot the two signals in Figs. 1 and 2. Combining them with Table 3, we can see that as the trajectory length increases, the safety satisfaction level of the sampled trajectory gradually decreases and eventually converges to the

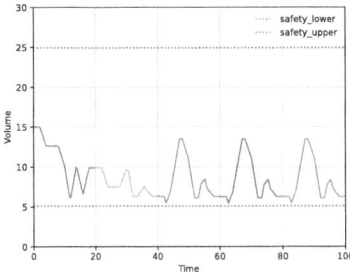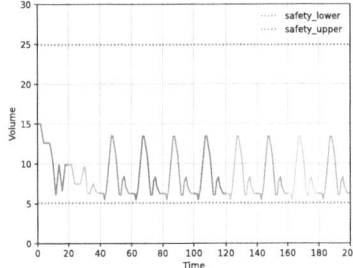

Fig. 1. Forward approximation sampling trajectory with an initial value of 15 over the interval $[0, 100]$ (left) and $[0, 200]$ (right)

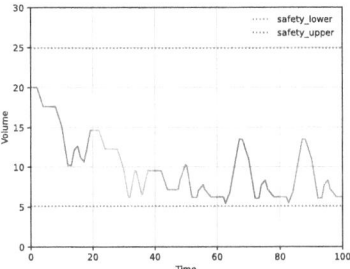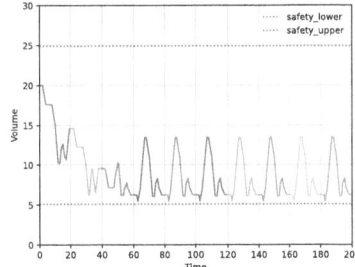

Fig. 2. Forward approximation sampling trajectory with an initial value of 20 over the interval $[0, 100]$ (left) and $[0, 200]$ (right)

same positive value. When the satisfaction level begins to converge to the same positive value, we can stop monitoring and consider the system to be safe.

5   Related Work

So far, there has been relatively few work done on the verification of NSSs. Previous work on NSS aimed to mitigate the limitations of neural networks (such as generalization issues) and symbolic systems (such as handling noisy data) by integrating them in hybrid models [10,18]. In our work, to ensure timely completion of online monitoring while minimizing data and computational resource usage, we employ Euler prediction to sample the monitoring system at discrete time steps. This method enables both qualitative and quantitative online monitoring of STL specifications through formula rewriting techniques. Many pieces of work involve verification using STL specifications. A tool called AMT 2.0 is presented in [17], designed for qualitative and quantitative analysis of hybrid continuous and Boolean signals that integrate numerical values and discrete events. In which signals are evaluated based on rich temporal specifications expressed in an extended signal temporal logic (xSTL), which integrates timed regular expressions within STL. The work most relevant to ours is [9], which is also based on formula rewriting techniques and the paper presents an efficient algorithm for robust monitoring of STL formulas against real-valued signals. The algorithm leverages state-of-the-art streaming algorithms from signal processing to compute the robustness degree linearly with respect to the size of the signal. This linear complexity ensures minimal overhead when integrated with simulation processes, facilitating the routine use of robustness-based monitoring in various applications. In comparison, the rewriting approach presented in this paper is more succinct. Another related work to ours is the predictive RV. [20] introduces a novel runtime verification technique with predictive semantics that allows for the prediction of property satisfaction or violation when the observed execution sequence is incomplete. In [19], a predictive RV framework is proposed for CPS aiming at enhancing system reliability by predicting potential runtime failures before they occur.

6   Conclusion

In this paper, we first present a unified formalization of neural-symbolic systems, extending the concepts of CPS, pure physical systems, and pure cyber systems. With this setting, we introduce an approach for effective trajectory sampling during runtime, specifically designed to address the opacity of the neural components. Subsequently, we develop both qualitative and quantitative runtime verification techniques for NSSs against STL specifications using a rewriting approach. Our approach is proven to be exact for PLNSSs with respect to affine STL formulas. Our method ensures that online monitoring could be accomplished in time. We implemented a prototype tool and demonstrated the effectiveness of our approach in terms of time and memory. Our verification framework theoretically resolves the technical intractability of NSS's validation. Nevertheless, further optimization on the scalability is still needed for its deployment and application in practical, such as more reasonable sampling strategy balancing precision and efficiency. Additionally, extending our RV framework to that having nondeterministic cyber control, or with probabilistic behaviors in the physical control is also a promising research direction in the future.

References

1. Alpern, B., Schneider, F.B.: Defining liveness. Inf. Process. Lett. **21**(4), 181–185 (1985)
2. Baier, C., Kwiatkowska, M.: Model checking for a probabilistic branching time logic with fairness. Distrib. Comput. **11**(3), 125–155 (1998)
3. Ball, T., Podelski, A., Rajamani, S.K.: Boolean and cartesian abstraction for model checking c programs. In: Margaria, T., Yi, W. (eds.) TACAS 2001. LNCS, vol. 2031, pp. 268–283. Springer, Heidelberg (2001). https://doi.org/10.1007/3-540-45319-9_19
4. Bauer, A., Leucker, M., Schallhart, C.: Runtime verification for LTL and TLTL. ACM Trans. Softw. Eng. Methodol. (TOSEM) **20**(4), 1–64 (2011)

5. Beffara, E., Bournez, O., Kacem, H., Kirchner, C.: Verification of timed automata using rewrite rules and strategies. In: The Seventh Biennal Bar-Ilan Symposium on the Foundations of Artificial Intelligence-BISFAI'01, pp. 15–p (2001)

6. Cassez, F., Jessen, J.J., Larsen, K.G., Raskin, J.-F., Reynier, P.-A.: Automatic synthesis of robust and optimal controllers – an industrial case study. In: Majumdar, R., Tabuada, P. (eds.) HSCC 2009. LNCS, vol. 5469, pp. 90–104. Springer, Heidelberg (2009). https://doi.org/10.1007/978-3-642-00602-9_7

7. Clarke, E.M.: Model checking. In: Ramesh, S., Sivakumar, G. (eds.) FSTTCS 1997. LNCS, vol. 1346, pp. 54–56. Springer, Heidelberg (1997). https://doi.org/10.1007/BFb0058022

8. Clarke, E.M., Emerson, E.A.: Design and synthesis of synchronization skeletons using branching time temporal logic. In: Kozen, D. (ed.) Logic of Programs 1981. LNCS, vol. 131, pp. 52–71. Springer, Heidelberg (1982). https://doi.org/10.1007/BFb0025774

9. Donzé, A., Ferrère, T., Maler, O.: Efficient robust monitoring for STL. In: Sharygina, N., Veith, H. (eds.) CAV 2013. LNCS, vol. 8044, pp. 264–279. Springer, Heidelberg (2013). https://doi.org/10.1007/978-3-642-39799-8_19

10. Ivanov, R., Weimer, J., Alur, R., Pappas, G.J., Lee, I.: Verisig: verifying safety properties of hybrid systems with neural network controllers. In: Proceedings of the 22nd ACM International Conference on Hybrid Systems: Computation and Control, pp. 169–178 (2019)

11. Leucker, M., Schallhart, C.: A brief account of runtime verification. J. Logic Algebraic Program. **78**(5), 293–303 (2009)

12. Maler, O., Nickovic, D.: Monitoring temporal properties of continuous signals. In: Lakhnech, Y., Yovine, S. (eds.) FORMATS/FTRTFT -2004. LNCS, vol. 3253, pp. 152–166. Springer, Heidelberg (2004). https://doi.org/10.1007/978-3-540-30206-3_12

13. Maler, O., Ničković, D.: Monitoring properties of analog and mixed-signal circuits. Int. J. Softw. Tools Technol. Transfer **15**, 247–268 (2013)

14. Martí-Oliet, N., Meseguer, J.: Rewriting logic as a logical and semantic framework. Electron. Notes Theor. Comput. Sci. **4**, 190–225 (1996)

15. Medhat, R., Bonakdarpour, B., Kumar, D., Fischmeister, S.: Runtime monitoring of cyber-physical systems under timing and memory constraints. ACM Trans. Embedded Comput. Syst. (TECS) **14**(4), 1–29 (2015)

16. Mitsch, S., Platzer, A.: Modelplex: verified runtime validation of verified cyber-physical system models. Formal Methods Syst. Des. **49**, 33–74 (2016)

17. Ničković, D., Lebeltel, O., Maler, O., Ferrère, T., Ulus, D.: Amt 2.0: qualitative and quantitative trace analysis with extended signal temporal logic. Int. J. Softw. Tools Technol. Transf. **22**, 741–758 (2020)

18. Yi, K., Wu, J., Gan, C., Torralba, A., Kohli, P., Tenenbaum, J.: Neural-symbolic VQA: disentangling reasoning from vision and language understanding. In: Advances in Neural Information Processing Systems, vol. 31 (2018)

19. Yu, K., Chen, Z., Dong, W.: A predictive runtime verification framework for cyber-physical systems. In: 2014 IEEE Eighth International Conference on Software Security and Reliability-Companion, pp. 223–227. IEEE (2014)

20. Zhang, X., Leucker, M., Dong, W.: Runtime verification with predictive semantics. In: Goodloe, A.E., Person, S. (eds.) NFM 2012. LNCS, vol. 7226, pp. 418–432. Springer, Heidelberg (2012). https://doi.org/10.1007/978-3-642-28891-3_37

21. Zhao, H, J., Li, Zeng: Safe reinforcement learning algorithm and its application in intelligent control for cps. J. Softw. **33**(7), 2538–2561 (2022)

Eidos: Efficient, Imperceptible Adversarial 3D Point Clouds

Hanwei Zhang[1,2], Luo Cheng[3,4], Qisong He[3,5], Wei Huang[6], Renjue Li[3,4],

Ronan Sicre[7], Xiaowei Huang[5], Holger Hermanns[2], and Lijun Zhang[3(✉)]

[1] Institute of Intelligent Software, Guangzhou, China
[2] Universität des Saarlandes, Saarbrücken, Germany
[3] Institute of Software, Chinese Academy of Sciences, Beijing, China
zhanglj@ios.ac.cn
[4] University of Chinese Academy of Sciences, Beijing, China
[5] University of Liverpool, Liverpool, England
[6] Purple Mountain Laboratories, Nanjing, China
[7] LIS, Centrale Méditerranée Marseille, Marseille, France

Abstract. Classification of 3D point clouds is a challenging machine learning (ML) task with important real-world applications in a spectrum from autonomous driving and robot-assisted surgery to earth observation from low orbit. As with other ML tasks, classification models are notoriously brittle in the presence of adversarial attacks. These are rooted in imperceptible changes to inputs with the effect that a seemingly well-trained model ends up misclassifying the input. This paper adds to the understanding of adversarial attacks by presenting **Eidos**, a framework providing **E**fficient **I**mperceptible a**D**versarial attacks on 3D p**O**int cloud**S**. **Eidos** supports a diverse set of imperceptibility metrics. It employs an iterative, two-step procedure to identify optimal adversarial examples, thereby enabling a runtime-imperceptibility trade-off. We provide empirical evidence relative to several popular 3D point cloud classification models and several established 3D attack methods, showing **Eidos**' superiority with respect to efficiency as well as imperceptibility. **Eidos** is an open-source project, and its code is available on GitHub at https://github.com/Uzukidd/eidos.

Keywords: Adversarial Attack · 3D Point Clouds · Robustness

1 Introduction

3D point clouds are a crucial format for representing shapes of 3D objects. Among others, they are the output produced by LiDAR sensors and thus of critical importannce in robotics and autonomous vehicle applications. They capture the surface geometry of the object by means of a discrete set of data points in 3D. The points within a point cloud are generally unordered, and this has been proven challenging when trying to apply (convolutional) Neural Network (NN) technology for 3D object recognition [15,22]. Recent advances, including PointNet [18], PointNet++ [19], and other works [3,14,34], address this challenge by capturing fine local structural information from the neighborhood of each point, leading to better performance on classification and segmentation

T. Bourke et al. (Eds.): SETTA 2024, LNCS 15469, pp. 310–326, 2025.
https://doi.org/10.1007/978-981-96-0602-3_17

tasks. With further advances in this direction, it can be expected that applications across "high-risk" sectors [4] are becoming in reach, including tasks like autonomous navigation and robot-assisted surgery, where any failure may have serious consequences.

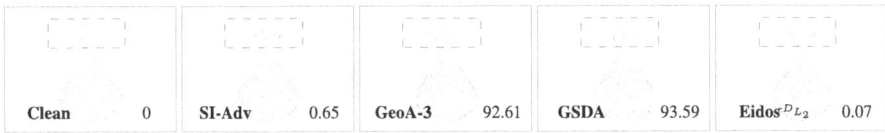

Fig. 1. Visualization of adversarial point clouds. It shows the original sample and adversarial distortions generated by different attack methods. **Eidos** here is used with D_{L_2} as imperceptibility regularization term. The number displayed in the bottom right denotes the mean L_2 norm of distortions, and it is clear that **Eidos** results in better imperceptibility than **SI-Adv**, **GeoA-3**, and **GSDA**.

A prominent shortcoming across many advanced ML techniques – especially those based on NN technology – is their susceptibility to input distortions, meaning that small distortions of the input may induce a misclassification by the NN. Techniques to identify such issues are often devised in an *adversarial* setting, where an adversary intentionally distorts the input slightly to induce a misclassification. For effective real-world applications, adversarial distortions need to be *imperceptible* and should be computable *efficiently*, i.e., the modifications should be subtle enough to avoid human detection and intervention, while also being computationally feasible. However, recent attempts [12,28,40] fail to efficiently achieve imperceptibility. The existing definitions of imperceptibility focus on different aspects, and when optimizations are based on just one definition, the results often do not align with what is imperceptible to the human eye. As depicted in Fig. 1, attacks computed by **SI-Adv** [9], **GeoA-3** [28], and also **GSDA** [8], all produce adversarial point clouds that fail to be imperceptibly different from the original (*cf*. the region inside the dash-dotted boxes). Incorporating multiple definitions therefore appears as a better approach to capture the true essence of imperceptibility, but this idea so far lacks computational efficiency [28]. To address these limitations, we present a novel adversarial attack framework that computes imperceptible adversarial distortion of 3D point clouds in an efficient manner. We name our method **Eidos** after Plato's term "eidos", which means the permanent reality that makes a thing what it is (as opposed to the particulars that are finite and subject to change). Translated to our practice, **Eidos** makes optimal adversarial 3D point cloud generation a reality.

Eidos is distinguished by its ability to work with a diverse set of imperceptibility regularization terms and to consider them altogether. For this, we formalize the adversarial attack as a constrained optimization problem, with the goal of minimizing the imperceptibility of adversarial distortion with the additional constraint of enforcing misclassification. With this formalization, we can study the relations between different regularization terms to guide the search for imperceptible adversarial distortions. Our work examines the power of the following imperceptibility regularizations: L2 norm, Chamfer Distance (CD), Hausdorff Distance (HD), and Consistency of Local Curvature (Curv), each of which echoing distinct imperceptibility traits of adversarial distortions.

As shown in Fig. 1, **Eidos** finds an adversarial example with extremely small distortion when only employing the L2 norm as an imperceptibility regularizer.

Two competing objectives make the optimization difficult. It has been observed that naively optimizing over the classification loss and imperceptibility together fails to generate adversarial distortions. Existing attacks, *e.g.* **GeoA-3** [28] use a hyper-parameter λ to control the balance between imperceptibility and misclassification. However, this may lead to failing attacks or oscillations on the boundary, and thus comes with a waste of computational resources. In contrast, **Eidos** tackles the efficiency problem by decomposing the optimization into two phases, inspired by boundary projection (BP) attacks [36] originally designed for 2D images. The IN phase aims at minimizing the classification loss quickly to identify adversarial examples. During the OUT phase, the search direction is determined by enforcing two conditions: minimizing imperceptibility and maintaining orthogonality to the gradient direction, thus preventing oscillations. Therefore, this two-phase optimization can find adversarial examples while minimizing the chosen imperceptibility in an efficient way. As we see in Fig. 1, **Eidos** can generate more imperceptible adversarial distortions than the state of the art.

We report on an extensive empirical evaluation of our approach, demonstrating its sensitivity and effectiveness. We assess effectiveness using success probability and imperceptibility metrics, while efficiency is measured as computation time. For sensitivity, we investigate different parameters of the algorithm, including step size, the number of iterations, and the number of imperceptibility regularization terms.

Contributions Our contributions are as follows.

- We propose an efficient framework, which facilitates the incorporation of a diverse set of imperceptibility metrics. We further explore the relationship between them in depicting the imperceptibility traits of point clouds while existing works do not discuss this in detail.
- Our approach *efficiently and effectively* handles adversarial optimization with several imperceptibility regularizations, avoids the competition between classification loss and imperceptibility, and provides a better trade-off than existing works.
- Our attack achieves decent performance against models with defense and easily adapts to black-box settings.
- We provide a comprehensive and fair evaluation of **Eidos** and the state-of-the-art.

Eidos is an open-source project, and its code is available on GitHub at https://github.com/Uzukidd/eidos.

2 Problem, Background, and Related Work

2.1 Problem Formulation

Preliminaries. Let $\mathcal{X} := \{\mathbf{x}_0, \cdots, \mathbf{x}_n\}$ denote a set of n 3D points represented by their 3D coordinates $\mathbf{x}_i := [x_{i,x}, x_{i,y}, x_{i,z}]^\mathsf{T} \in \mathbb{R}^3$. A classifier $f : \mathbb{R}^{n \times 3} \to \mathbb{R}^c$ maps a point cloud $\mathcal{X}$ to a vector $f(\mathcal{X})$ representing probabilities of c classes. The classifier prediction $\pi : \mathbb{R}^{n \times 3} \to [c] := \{1, \cdots, c\}$ maps $\mathcal{X}$ to the class label with maximum probability:

$$\pi(\mathcal{X}) := \arg \max_{k \in [c]} f(\mathcal{X})_k. \tag{1}$$

The prediction is correct if $\pi(\mathcal{X}) = t$ where $t \in [c]$ is the ground truth label.

Problem. Let $\mathcal{X} \in \mathbb{R}^{n \times 3}$ be a given 3D point cloud with known ground truth label t. An adversarial example $\mathcal{Y} := \mathcal{X} + \Delta \in \mathbb{R}^{n \times 3}$ is a 3D point cloud such that:

i) probability of the ground truth class is small enough to result in *misclassification*, i.e. $f(\mathcal{Y})_t < f(\mathcal{Y})_{k \in [c], k \neq t}$;
ii) the distortion Δ is *imperceptible*.

Imperceptibility. We list well-known metrics of distortion:

1. L_p *Norm*

$$D_{L_p}(\mathcal{X}, \mathcal{Y}) := \left(\sum_i (\mathbf{x}_i - \mathbf{y}_i)^p \right)^{\frac{1}{p}}, \tag{2}$$

   where $\mathbf{y}_i$ is the corresponding point of $\mathbf{x}_i$ in set $\mathcal{Y}$, assuming $|\mathcal{X}| = |\mathcal{Y}|$. Following the assumption made in [31] that the modification Δ is small enough, norm L_p, specifically L_2, is employed as an imperceptibility metric.
2. *Chamfer Distance*

$$D_{CD}(\mathcal{X}, \mathcal{Y}) := \frac{1}{n} \sum_j \min_i \|\mathbf{x}_i - \mathbf{y}_j\|_2^2 \tag{3}$$

   measures the distance between two point sets by averaging the distances of each point to its nearest neighbor from another set. This distance is popularly used in adversarial 3D points [9,28,31] but is less effective when a small portion of outlier points exist in the 3D point clouds.
3. *Hausdorff Distance*

$$D_{HD}(\mathcal{X}, \mathcal{Y}) := \max_j \min_i \|\mathbf{x}_i - \mathbf{y}_j\|_2^2 \tag{4}$$

   is a non-symmetric metric and attaches more importance to the outlier points in $\mathcal{Y}$.
4. *Consistency of Local Curvature* [28]

$$D_{Curv}(\mathcal{X}, \mathcal{Y}) := \frac{1}{n} \sum_j \|\kappa(\mathbf{y}_j; \mathcal{Y}) - \kappa(\mathbf{x}_i; \mathcal{X})\|_2^2 \tag{5}$$

$$\text{subject to } \mathbf{x}_i = \arg \min_i \|\mathbf{y}_j - \mathbf{x}_i\|_2, \tag{6}$$

   where $\kappa(\mathbf{x}_i; \mathcal{X})$ measures the local geometry of the local k point neighborhoods $\mathcal{N}_{\mathbf{x}_i} \subset \mathcal{X}$ of the point $\mathbf{x}_i$ and is defined as

$$\kappa(\mathbf{x}_i, \mathcal{X}) := \frac{1}{k} \sum_{\mathbf{x}_j \in \mathcal{N}_{\mathbf{x}_i}} | \langle \frac{\mathbf{x}_j - \mathbf{x}_i}{\|\mathbf{x}_j - \mathbf{x}_i\|_2}, \mathbf{n}_{\mathbf{x}_i} \rangle |, \tag{7}$$

   where $\langle \cdot, \cdot \rangle$ denotes inner product and $\mathbf{n}_{\mathbf{x}_i}$ denotes the unit normal vector to the surface at $\mathbf{x}_i$.

5. *KNN Smoothness* [25]

$$D_{Smooth}(\mathcal{X}) := \frac{1}{n}\sum_i d_i \cdot \mathbb{1}[d_i > \mu + \gamma\sigma] \tag{8}$$

$$w.r.t. \ d_i := \frac{1}{k}\left(\sum_{\mathbf{x}_j \in \mathcal{N}_{\mathbf{x}_i}} \|\mathbf{x}_i - \mathbf{x}_j\|_2^2\right), \tag{9}$$

where γ is a defined parameter while μ and σ are the mean and standard deviation of the distribution of distances among points, respectively. Unlike other metrics, KNN smoothness is not intended to assess the imperceptibility of modifications, but rather the naturalness of the modified 3D point cloud. This metric encourages every point to be close to its neighbors.

2.2   Attacks

In this part, we discuss related work in generating 3D adversarial point clouds and boundary projection attacks, sharing similar principles with our method in addressing the problem.

Boundary Projection (BP) Attack [36]. Let $\mathbf{x}$ denote an input image of true class t and $\mathbf{y}$ denote an adversarial example. The Boundary Projection (BP) attack generates adversarial examples by solving the optimization

$$\min_{\mathbf{y}} \ \|\mathbf{x} - \mathbf{y}\|_2^2 \tag{10}$$

$$\text{subject to } f(\mathbf{y})_t - \max_{k \in [c], k \neq t} f(\mathbf{y})_k < 0. \tag{11}$$

BP attack disentangles (10) and (11) into OUT case and IN case. In IN case, BP aims to find a solution satisfying (11), and searches along the gradient direction,

$$\mathbf{y}_{i+1} := \mathbf{y}_i - \alpha\mathsf{n}(\nabla_{\mathbf{x}}\ell(f(\mathbf{y}_i), t))), \tag{12}$$

where $\ell(f(\mathbf{x}, t))$ is the negative cross-entropy loss of classifier $f(\cdot)$, $\mathsf{n}(\cdot) := \frac{\cdot}{\|\cdot\|_2}$, and α is the step size. At initialization, $\mathbf{y}_0 := \mathbf{x}$ with fixed step size α to search adversarial examples as soon as possible. Once an adversarial solution is found, BP attack prioritizes reducing distortion with respect to (10).

Regarding (10), BP attack sets a target distortion $\epsilon = \gamma_i\|\mathbf{y}_i - \mathbf{x}\|$, where $\gamma_i < 1$ is a parameter that increases linearly with iteration i, and then searches in the tangent hyperplane of the level set of the loss at y_i, along the direction that is normal to the gradient

$$\mathbf{y}_{i+1} := (\mathbf{y}_i - \mathbf{v})\sqrt{[\epsilon^2 - r^2]_+} \tag{13}$$

$$\mathbf{v} := \mathbf{x} + r\mathsf{n}(\nabla_{\mathbf{x}}\ell(f(\mathbf{y}_i), t))) \tag{14}$$

$$r := \langle \mathbf{y}_i - \mathbf{x}, \mathsf{n}(\nabla_{\mathbf{x}}\ell(f(\mathbf{y}_i), t)))\rangle, \tag{15}$$

where $\mathbf{v}$ is an auxiliary vector to follow the tangent hyperplane and $[\cdot]_+$ takes the positive value. The above process can be iterative: if the current solution $\mathbf{y}_i$ crosses the boundary and thus triggers going back to the IN case, BP attack updates with (12) by setting $\alpha = r + \sqrt{\epsilon^2 - \|\mathbf{y}_i - \mathbf{x}\|^2 + r^2}$, which serves as an estimate of the step size required to cross the boundary along the given direction under a linear assumption.

Following the principle of BP [36], *i.e.* searching along the gradient of misclassification and minimizing the distortion along its orthogonal directions, we incorporate multiple metrics to assess the imperceptibility of unordered 3D point clouds and introduce Gram-Schmidt (GS) process to orthonormalize the gradient of different optimization terms. Such a framework allowed exploring various imperceptibility regularizations and identifying a trade-off between efficiency and imperceptibility. Our experiments reveal that some metrics conflict with each other.

Adversarial Attacks on 3D Point Clouds. Compared to 2D images, a 3D point cloud consists of a set of *unordered* points that represent the surface geometry of an object. Some measurements commonly used in 2D images, such as measuring the magnitude of distortion via L_2 norm or evaluating the photo-realistic of adversarial examples via PSNR and SSIM [27], are not faithful when evaluating the imperceptibility of distortion to 3D point clouds. Several attacks of 3D point clouds are gradient-based methods [7,10,12,21,25,28,33], inspired by the adversarial attacks against image classifiers. For instance, Su *et al.* [12] adapted FGSM [5], I-FGSM [11] and JSMA [17] by imposing constraints on the distortion for each point or the entire point cloud and enhanced clipping and gradient projection to preserve the distribution of points on the surface of an object. Building on this, MPG [33] introduces a Momentum-Enhanced Point-wise Gradient Method. In addition to perturbing point clouds, point addition and subtraction are proposed in the case of unordered point sets. To mislead the model, the attacker adds (removes) a limited number of synthesized points/clusters/objects to (from) a point cloud according to a saliency map [29,31,39] or gradient [33]. Within this category, attacks involving the imperceptible insertion or removal of a few points, like [12,13,29,31,38], are categorized as distribution attacks. Shape attacks [13], on the other hand, modify multiple points in specific areas of the point cloud. Moreover, adversarial attacks are also explored on mesh representations, for instance, mesh-attack [37] and ϵ-ISO [16].

Imperceptible Adversarial Distortions. We review several recent techniques for generating imperceptible perturbations in 3D point clouds that are resistant to adversarial attacks. Tsai *et al.* [25] proposed an attack based on K-Nearest Neighbor (KNN) loss, while **GeoA-3** [28] introduced consistency of local curvatures as part of geometry loss. Both of them utilize the C&W [2] to find adversarial examples, which is expensive. Normal Attack [24] incorporates both the gradient and tangent direction at each point as a form of smooth regularization. The normal-tangent attack (NTA) [23] employs a directional controlling loss to constrain the distortion along the normal or tangent direction of the gradient. Yeung *et al.* [10] consider minimal modification with respect to the L_0 norm as the definition of imperceptibility and formalize it into L_0-norm optimization problem. Other approaches focus on manipulating the point cloud representation itself. Graph Spectral Domain Attack (**GSDA**) [8] converts the point clouds coordinates into graph spectral domain and perturbs point clouds within that domain. Similarly, **SI-Adv** [9] regards shape-invariant as the definition of imperceptibility and performs a reversible coordinate transformation on the input point cloud to guarantee the preservation of shape. Adversarial attacks, *e.g.* **GeoA-3** and **GSDA**, producing imperceptible adversarial distortions often suffer from low time efficiency. **SI-Adv** is an efficient attack addressing imperceptibility. However, it only considers KNN smoothness and often generates outlier points. To overcome these limitations, we consider the imperceptibility regularization from [28] and provide insights into the trade-off between misclassification and imperceptibility regularization.

3   Method

Eidos tackles adversarial optimization efficiently by decomposing the optimization into two phases governed by different objectives, *i.e.* misclassification and imperceptibility. In the IN phase, we aim to find an adversarial point cloud, while in the OUT phase, we aim to optimize the imperceptibility metrics while keeping the current solution adversarial.

Algorithm 1 outlines our base principle of finding an adversarial example starting from the initial set $\mathcal{Y}_0 = \mathcal{X}$. Then, $\mathcal{Y}_i$ is updated iteratively in the direction of the gradient until an adversarial example is found, see *Line 4–5* in Algorithm 1. This is phase IN. The loss function is the misclassification loss $\ell(f(\mathcal{Y}_i), t) := f(\mathcal{Y})_t - \max_{k \in [c], k \neq t} f(\mathbf{y})_k$. The normalization function is defined as $\mathrm{n}(\cdot) := \frac{\cdot}{\|\cdot\|_2}$, and ϵ denotes the step size. In *line 6–9*, phase OUT treats the case of $\mathcal{Y}_i$ being adversarial and aims at improving imperceptibility, which can be based on a single metric like L_p norm, while keeping the solution adversarial. We obtain the normalized direction $\hat{\mathbf{d}}$ that decreases the imperceptibility regularization, which is then projected onto the tangent hyperplane of the level set of the loss at $\mathcal{Y}_i$, normal to $\hat{\mathbf{g}}$.

To account for multiple metrics used to measure imperceptibility, we enhance phase OUT by optimizing different imperceptibility regularization terms *alternatingly*. In Algorithm 2, *line 7–9* calculates the normalized direction $\hat{\mathbf{d}}_i$ for a set $\mathcal{D}$ of imperceptibility regularizations. In *line 10*, we use the Gram-Schmidt (GS) process to calculate an orthogonal set based on the gradients of misclassification and imperceptibility regularization terms, which allows us to optimize each of them independently. In *line 12–15*, our method searches along the direction that decreases imperceptibility regularization term D_j while saving the best solution with respect to the sum of all imperceptibility regularization terms. This is the core innovation of **Eidos**, together with the IN-OUT phase splitting.

4   Experiments

In this section, we first present our experimental setting, and then carry out an ablation study on coordinate transformation, imperceptibility regularization, and step size. More ablation studies on step size and the number of iterations, as well as the discussion of convergence are in the supplementary materials. We assess the performance of our method relative to **GSDA** and **SI-Adv** as the current state-of-the-art techniques regarding imperceptibility in this setting. Additionally, we compare with **GeoA-3** which

---

Algorithm 1. Eidos - Base

Input: $\mathcal{X}$: original point cloud to be attacked
Input: t: true label, K: maximum iterations
Input: ϵ: step size
Output: $\mathcal{Y}^*$

 1: $\mathcal{Y}^* \leftarrow \mathcal{X} \cdot \mathbf{0}$, $\mathcal{Y}_0 \leftarrow \mathcal{X}$
 2: **while** $i < K$ **do**
 3:    $\hat{\mathbf{g}} \leftarrow \mathsf{n}(\nabla_{\mathcal{X}} \ell(f(\mathcal{Y}_i), t)))$
 4:    **if** $f(\mathcal{Y}_i) == t$ **then** $\triangleright$ IN phase
 5:       $\mathcal{Y}_{i+1} \leftarrow \mathcal{Y}_i - \epsilon\hat{\mathbf{g}}$
 6:    **else** $\triangleright$ OUT phase
 7:       $\hat{\mathbf{d}} \leftarrow \mathsf{n}(\nabla_{\mathcal{X}} D(\mathcal{X}, \mathcal{Y}_i))$
 8:       $\mathbf{v} \leftarrow \hat{\mathbf{d}} - \frac{\hat{\mathbf{d}}\hat{\mathbf{g}}}{\|\hat{\mathbf{g}}\|_2^2}\hat{\mathbf{g}}$
 9:       $\mathcal{Y}_{i+1} \leftarrow \mathcal{Y}_i - \epsilon\mathbf{v}$
10:    **end if**
11:    **if** $D(\mathcal{X}, \mathcal{Y}_{i+1}) < D(\mathcal{X}, \mathcal{Y}^*)$ **then**
12:       $\mathcal{Y}^* = \mathcal{Y}_{i+1}$
13:    **end if**
14:    $i \leftarrow i + 1$
15: **end while**

---

incorporates the fusion of various imperceptibility metrics as a form of regularization. Last but not least, we evaluate our method against three common defense techniques and test our attack in a black-box setting.

4.1 Experiments Setting

Dataset. The ModelNet40 [30] dataset contains 12,311 CAD models from the 40 most common object categories in the world. There are 9,843 training objects and 2,468 testing objects. Following the previous setting [18,31], we uniformly sample 1,024 points from the surface of each object and re-scale them into a unit ball. For attacks, we randomly select 100 test examples from each of the 10 largest classes, *i.e.* airplane, bed, bookshelf, bottle, chair, monitor, sofa, table, toilet, and vase, as original point clouds to generate adversarial point clouds. Given our focus on untargeted attacks, we conduct experiments with 1,000 point clouds.

Networks. We take the pre-trained model of PointNet [18][1] trained with several data augmentations such as random point-dropping and rotation. We also use the pre-trained model of DGCNN [26][2] trained by Hu *et al.*. To verify our approach works on various architectures, we provide a comparison on Point-transformer[3] as well.

---

[1] https://github.com/shikiw/SI-Adv.
[2] https://github.com/WoodwindHu/GSDA.
[3] https://github.com/lulutang0608/Point-BERT.

Algorithm 2. Eidos

Input: $\mathcal{X}$: original point cloud to be attacked
Input: t: true label, K: maximum iterations
Input: ϵ: step size
Input: $\mathcal{D}$: a set of imperceptibility regularizations
Output: $\mathcal{Y}^*$

1: $\mathcal{Y}^* \leftarrow \mathcal{X} \cdot \mathbf{0}, \mathcal{Y}_0 \leftarrow \mathcal{X}$
2: **while** $i < K$ **do**
3:     $\hat{\mathbf{g}} \leftarrow \mathsf{n}(\nabla_{\mathcal{X}} \ell(f(\mathcal{Y}_i), t)))$
4:     **if** $f(\mathcal{Y}_i) == t$ **then**   ▷ IN phase
5:         $\mathcal{Y}_{i+1} \leftarrow \mathcal{Y}_i - \epsilon \hat{\mathbf{g}}$
6:     **else**   ▷ OUT phase
7:         **for** $D_j \in \mathcal{D}$ **do**
8:             $\hat{\mathbf{d}}_j \leftarrow \mathsf{n}(\nabla_{\mathcal{X}} D_j(\mathcal{X}, \mathcal{Y}_i))$
9:         **end for**
10:         $\{\hat{\mathbf{v}}_1, \cdots, \hat{\mathbf{v}}_m\} \leftarrow GS(\{\hat{\mathbf{g}}, \hat{\mathbf{d}}_1, \cdots, \hat{\mathbf{d}}_m\})$
11:         **for** $\hat{\mathbf{v}}_j \in \{\hat{\mathbf{v}}_1, \cdots, \hat{\mathbf{v}}_m\}$ **do**
12:             $\mathcal{Y}_{i+1} \leftarrow \mathcal{Y}_i - \epsilon \hat{\mathbf{v}}_j$
13:             **if** $\sum_j D_j(\mathcal{X}, \mathcal{Y}_{i+1}) < \sum_j D_j(\mathcal{X}, \mathcal{Y}^*)$ **then**
14:                 $\mathcal{Y}^* = \mathcal{Y}_{i+1}$
15:             **end if**
16:         **end for**
17:     **end if**
18:     $i \leftarrow i + 1$
19: **end while**

Attacks. Following the original setting of **GeoA-3** and **GSDA**, we use Adam optimizer [17] with a fixed learning schedule of 500 iterations. The learning rate and momentum are set as 0.01 and 0.9, respectively. For the weights of geometry-aware regularization of **GeoA-3**, we let $\lambda_1 = 0.1, \lambda_2 = 1.0, \lambda_3 = 1.0$. The penalty parameter is initialized as $\beta = 2,500$ and automatically adjusted by conducting 10 runs of binary search. We set $k = 16$ to define local point neighborhoods in **GeoA-3**. In **GSDA**, we let $k = 10$ for building the KNN graph, and let the penalty parameter $\beta = 10$ at the beginning and adjust it after 10 runs of binary search. The weights of Chamfer distance loss and Hausdorff distance loss in the regularization term are set to 5.0 and 0.5, respectively. We use the white-box version of **SI-Adv** with the step size 0.007 and maximum iterations 100. Adversarial examples are constrained by the L_∞ norm ball with 0.16 radius. For our method, we set maximum iterations as 100.

Evaluation Metrics. To quantitatively compare adversarial results across different methods, we use attack the success rate P_{suc} and the imperceptibility metrics outlined in Sect. 2.1. We use $k = 16$ to define local point neighborhoods for D_{Curv} and D_{Smooth} and $\gamma = 1.05$ for D_{Smooth}. As evaluation metrics, we denote L_2 norm as ¡, Chamfer distance as CD, Hausdorff distance as HD, consistency of local curvature as Curv, and KNN smoothness as Smooth. We report time in seconds, noted T, of each attack measured on a TITAN V 250W+Intel(R) Xeon(R) CPU E5-2630 v4 2.20GHz.

To compare the different attacks fairly, we follow the evaluation protocol [35] for operating characteristics: for $D \in [0, D_{max}]$,

$$\mathsf{P} := \frac{1}{N_{suc}} |\{\mathcal{Y} \in X_{suc} : D(\mathcal{Y}, \mathcal{X}) < D\}|, \quad (16)$$

where N_{suc} is the total number of the subset of adversarial point cloud X_{suc} that succeeded to deceive the network. This function varies from $\mathsf{P}(0) = 0$ to $\mathsf{P}(D_{max}) = P_{suc}$.

Table 1. **Eidos** success rate P_{suc} (%), average values of ¡$(1e - 1)$, CD $(1e - 4)$, HD $(1e - 2)$, Curv $(1e - 2)$, Smooth $(1e - 3)$ and time (s) of our attack constrained by D_{L_2} with different coordinate transformation against PointNet.

METHOD	P_{suc} ↑	¡↓	CD ↓	HD ↓	Curv ↓	Smooth ↓	Time ↓
T_{ori}	**100**	**0.71**	**0.61**	**1.41**	**0.12**	1.48	1.56
T_{rsi}	**100**	2.03	1.40	3.17	0.14	**1.25**	2.21
T_{gft}	**100**	0.49	0.47	1.05	0.12	1.55	10.28

4.2 Ablation

Before studying the impact of various imperceptibility factors, we start off by an ablation analysis on coordinate transformation and imperceptibility regularization. Specifically, coordinate transformation are central to the manner in which **SI-Adv** and **GSDA** incorporate their imperceptibility constraints. Further ablation studies then explore the impact of various parameters of our method, including coordinate transformation, imperceptibility regularization terms, step size, and the maximum number of iterations. Due to page limits, the experimental results on step size, and maximum number of iterations are in the supplement.

Influence of Coordinate Transformation. To improve imperceptibility, **SI-Adv** and **GSDA** transform coordinates. To evaluate how much these coordinate transformations contribute to the final results, we carry out the attack with fixed step size 0.06 for 100 iterations with L_2 norm constraint and:

T_{ori}: without any coordinate transformation;
T_{rsi}: with the reversible shape-invariant coordinate transformation of **SI-Adv**;
T_{gft}: with the Graph Fourier Transform (GFT) of **GSDA** before and after the optimization process.

Table 1 shows T_{rsi} and T_{gft} performing well only in the Smooth metric. In a nutshell, coordinate transformations are of little value for **Eidos** and thus not considered in the sequel.

Table 2. Eidos success rate P_{suc} (%), average values of ¡$(1e-1)$, CD $(1e-4)$, HD $(1e-2)$, Curv $(1e-2)$, Smooth $(1e-3)$ and time (s) of our attack constrained by different imperceptibility regularization with T_{ori} and T_{rsi} coordinate transformations against PointNet.

METHOD	P_{suc} ↑	¡↓	CD ↓	HD ↓	Curv ↓	Smooth ↓	Time↓
D_{L_2}	**100**	**0.71**	0.61	1.41	**0.12**	1.48	1.56
D_{CD}	**100**	5.07	**0.37**	0.93	0.16	1.56	1.84
D_{HD}	**100**	5.76	1.58	**0.26**	0.35	1.67	1.75
D_{Curv}	**100**	7.26	3.47	5.07	0.20	**1.20**	2.02

Influence of Different Imperceptibility Regularizations. Initially, we examine performance by separately optimizing imperceptibility regularization terms, such as D_{L_2}, D_{CD}, D_{HD}, or D_{Curv}, in Algorithm 1 with a fixed step size of 0.06. As shown in Table 2, we find that using the imperceptibility regularization induces optimality in the corresponding metric, except for D_{Curv} that gives the optimal results for Smooth. Figure 2 shows operating characteristics for Table 2. **Eidos** with D_{L_2} generates adversarial examples with extremely small ¡, with a few exceptions that have large ¡(around 2). Also, examples generated with D_{L_2} often have similar CD as if using D_{CD} instead. However, a few cases with a large value increase the average value in Table 2. With D_{HD} we obtain the worst results on Curv and vice versa. The correlation between these two imperceptibility regularization terms is relatively small, and thus it is difficult to optimize both of them together.

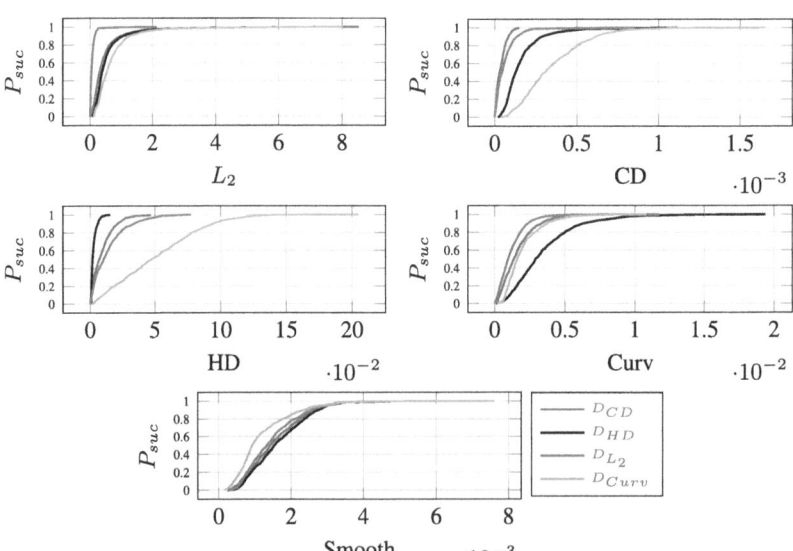

Fig. 2. Operating charateristics on PointNet for our attack constrained by different imperceptibility regularization.

In Table 3, we investigate the combination of different imperceptibility regularization terms with adaptive step size, following Algorithm 2. We observe that combining different imperceptibility regularization terms does not provide a dominant solution on all the metrics but provides a trade-off solution for the imperceptibility regularization we optimize for. We identify the significance of D_{L_2} in enhancing all imperceptibility metrics for adversarial distortions. Combining D_{HD} and D_{Curv} in **Eidos** yields the poorest results in ¡, CD, and Curv, aligning with the observation in Fig. 2.

Table 3. Eidos success rate P_{suc} (%), average values of ¡$(1e - 1)$, CD $(1e - 4)$, HD $(1e - 2)$, Curv $(1e-2)$, Smooth $(1e-3)$ and time (s) of our attack constrained by different imperceptibility regularization without coordinate transformation against PointNet.

METHOD	P_{suc} ↑	¡↓	CD ↓	HD ↓	Curv ↓	Smooth ↓	Time↓
D_{L_2+HD}	**100**	**2.23**	1.15	**0.52**	0.16	1.54	1.92
D_{L_2+Curv}	**100**	2.40	1.31	2.11	**0.09**	**1.33**	2.37
$D_{HD+Curv}$	**100**	5.83	2.22	0.99	0.17	1.45	2.58
$D_{L_2+HD+Curv}$	**100**	2.74	1.33	0.78	0.11	1.47	2.75
D_{all}	**100**	3.37	**0.88**	0.71	0.11	1.50	2.46

Step Size and Iterations. In the supplementary material, we report on the efficiency and sensitivity of our attack with respect to step size, testing six different fixed step sizes ($\epsilon \in [0.001, 0.01, 0.02, 0.03, 0.04, 0.05, 0.06, 0.1]$), as well as adaptive step size $\epsilon_{i+1} := \epsilon(1 - \gamma)$. In general, our approach turns out not to be sensitive to step size. A fixed step size works better with a single imperceptibility regularization term while adaptive step size performs better with multiple terms. We also conduct experiments with varying maximum iterations ($K \in [20, 40, \cdots, 200]$). The findings indicate a correlation between convergence and the imperceptibility regularization term. Details are available in the supplement.

Clean	**GeoA-3**	**GSDA**	**SI-Adv**	**Eidos**
(a) ✓monitor	✗flower-pot	✗mantel	✗mantel	✗mantel
(b) ✓sofa	✗flower-pot	✗bed	✗bed	✗bed

Fig. 3. Visualization of adversarial distortions produced by baseline methods and **Eidos**.

Table 4. Success rate P_{suc} (%), average values of ¡$(1e - 1)$, CD $(1e - 4)$, HD $(1e - 2)$, Curv $(1e - 2)$, Smooth $(1e - 3)$ and time (s) of our attack compared with baseline attacks against three networks.

METHOD	P_{suc} ↑	L_2 ↓	CD ↓	HD ↓	Curv ↓	Smooth ↓	Time ↓
			PointNet				
GeoA-3	97	44.86	4.81	0.73	0.36	1.73	125.48
SI-Adv	**100**	6.51	3.08	4.25	0.27	**1.20**	0.08
GSDA	97	54.47	4.70	2.65	0.51	1.54	138.73
Eidos	**100**	**3.37**	**0.88**	**0.71**	**0.11**	1.50	2.46
			DGCNN				
GeoA-3	100	195.45	6.95	0.46	0.23	2.04	307.05
SI-Adv	100	31.14	9.17	2.95	1.02	**1.72**	0.49
GSDA	100	145.36	6.06	0.54	0.27	1.94	329.83
Eidos	100	**23.65**	**4.48**	**0.45**	0.53	1.80	6.77
			Point-Transformer				
GeoA-3	61.4	47.50	5.81	0.43	0.69	1.91	267.79
SI-Adv	**100.0**	12.13	6.26	3.61	0.65	**1.47**	0.30
GSDA	61.8	57.03	5.83	2.13	0.84	1.76	291.32
Eidos	**100.0**	**6.86**	**1.78**	**0.37**	**0.24**	1.64	3.61

4.3   Comparison

We now compare our method directly to the mentioned state-of-the-art adversarial attacks. According to Table 4, our method outperforms the baseline methods, where **Eidos** refers to the version with all the imperceptibility regularizations incorporated. In PointNet and Point-Transformer, our method performs best on all the metrics except Smooth. In DGCNN, we outperform almost all combinations of baseline method and metric. **GeoA-3** and **GSDA** use a line search to balance misclassification and imperceptibility in adversarial optimization. However, they struggle to find an optimal parameter within reasonable computation budget for Point-Transformer (500 iterations for **GSDA** while 100 iterations for **SI-Adv** and **Eidos**).

Visualization   We visualize the adversarial point clouds generated by different attacks in Fig. 3. The adversarial distortions of **GeoA-3** and **GSDA** are perceivable due to unbalanced point distributions. **SI-Adv** seems closer to our attacks, but tends to introduce more outlier points.

Defenses.   We now study attack success rates under several state-of-the-art defense methods: Statistical Outlier Removal (SOR) [20] with $k = 2, \alpha = 1.1$; Simple Random Sampling (SRS) [33] with drop number 500; Denoiser and UPsampler Network

Table 5. Success rate P_{suc} (%), average values of L_2 norm ($1e-1$), Chamfer distance ($1e-4$), Hausdorff distance ($1e-2$), consistency of local curvature ($1e-2$), KNN smoothness ($1e-3$) and time (s) of our attack and the baseline attacks against PointNet with defense.

METHOD	P_{suc} ↑	L_2 ↓	CD ↓	HD ↓	Curv ↓	Smooth ↓	Time ↓
PointNet with SRS							
SI-Adv	77.3	8.39	4.36	3.87	0.36	**1.40**	8.78
Eidos	**82.0**	**4.68**	**1.65**	**0.84**	**0.18**	1.55	156.71
PointNet with SOR							
SI-Adv	100	17.06	7.08	3.71	0.65	1.88	0.19
Eidos	100	**9.63**	**1.80**	**0.39**	**0.22**	**1.76**	3.22
PointNet with DUP-Net							
SI-Adv	**90.8**	20.85	8.85	3.88	0.78	1.96	14.37
Eidos	76.6	**12.9**	**2.78**	**0.58**	**0.29**	**1.79**	98.77

Fig. 4. Operating characteristics of P_{suc} *vs.* HD and Curv on PointNet with DUP-Net w.r.t. Table 5.

(DUP-Net) [41] with $k = 2, \alpha = 1.1$, number of points as 1024 and up-sampling rate as 4. The results are shown in Table 5, where we only compare with **SI-Adv** as that is known to outperform **GeoA-3** and **GSDA** in defense [8,9]. **Eidos** clearly generates less perceptible adversarial distortions. To attack against randomness (SRS), we enhance the attacks by forwarding 100 times and averaging the gradients, which is commonly performed on attacks on images [1]. We see our method outperforming **SI-Adv** on SRS and SOR. With a limited distortion budget, *e.g.* left side of the red line in Fig. 4, our method achieves a higher success rate. Noteworthy, our method fails on hard examples, which require large distortions that are not alligned with the imperceptibility constraints.

Black-Box Attacks. Our framework aims to efficiently solve adversarial optimization with various imperceptibility regularizations. The method we compare with always uses the white-box scenario and only **SI-Adv** has a black-box version. Like **SI-Adv**, we adapt our method to the black-box scenario and compare it with **SI-Adv** and two famous query-based black-box attack algorithms, *i.e.*, **Simba** [6] and **Simba++** [32] in Table 6, where we perform better. In our experiments, we choose step size 0.32 because

Table 6. Success rate P_{suc} (%), average values of ¡(1e − 1), CD (1e − 4), HD (1e − 2), Curv (1e − 2), Smooth (1e − 3) and time (s) of our attack compared with baseline attacks under black-box setting against PACov with DGCNN as a surrogate model.

METHOD	$P_{suc} \uparrow$	$L_2 \downarrow$	CD $\downarrow$	HD $\downarrow$	Curv $\downarrow$	Smooth $\downarrow$	Time $\downarrow$
SI-Adv	100.0	37.30	7.63	8.76	0.46	1.45	96.34
Simba	100.0	39.26	11.11	10.40	0.60	1.64	100.07
Simba++	100.0	40.89	12.40	21.86	0.57	1.68	87.11
Eidos	100.0	**35.17**	**7.35**	**8.56**	**0.45**	**1.44**	108.77

according to **SI-Adv**, it is the best step size for **SI-Adv**. Our method outperforms **SI-Adv** in its best parameter.

5   Conclusion

This paper has presented **Eidos**, a method substantially improving the efficiency and imperceptibility of attacks on 3D point cloud classification tasks. It disentangles misclassification and imperceptibility, and supports generating adversarial point clouds across a range of imperceptibility metrics.

The empirical results show that **Eidos** clearly outperforms the state-of-the-art baseline methods that aim for imperceptibility. Interestingly, **Eidos** with the D_{L_2} metric often is efficient in improving across all the imperceptibility metrics. Further, our experiments on the defense model implicitly show that adversarial examples with small magnitudes are easy to defend against by using randomization.

Acknowledgements. This work has received financial support from CAS Project for Young Scientists in Basic Research (YSBR-040) and ISCAS New Cultivation Project (ISCAS-PYFX-202201). This work also has received financial support from VolkswagenStiftung as part of Grant AZ 98514 – EIS and by DFG under grant No. 389792660 as part of TRR 248 – CPEC. This work is part of the European Union's Horizon 2020 research and innovation programme under the Marie Skłodowska-Curie grant no. 101008233.

References

1. Athalye, A., Carlini, N., Wagner, D.: Obfuscated gradients give a false sense of security: circumventing defenses to adversarial examples. In: International Conference on Machine Learning, pp. 274–283. PMLR (2018)
2. Carlini, N., Wagner, D.: Towards evaluating the robustness of neural networks. In: 2017 IEEE Symposium on Security and Privacy (SP), pp. 39–57. IEEE (2017)
3. Duan, Y., Zheng, Y., Lu, J., Zhou, J., Tian, Q.: Structural relational reasoning of point clouds. In: 2019 IEEE/CVF Conference on Computer Vision and Pattern Recognition (CVPR), pp. 949–958 (2019). https://doi.org/10.1109/CVPR.2019.00104
4. EU: The artificial intelligence act (2023). https://artificialintelligenceact.eu

5. Goodfellow, I.J., Shlens, J., Szegedy, C.: Explaining and harnessing adversarial examples. arXiv:1412.6572 (2014)
6. Guo, C., Gardner, J., You, Y., Wilson, A.G., Weinberger, K.: Simple black-box adversarial attacks. In: International Conference on Machine Learning, pp. 2484–2493. PMLR (2019)
7. Hamdi, A., Rojas, S., Thabet, A., Ghanem, B.: AdvPC: transferable adversarial perturbations on 3d point clouds. In: Vedaldi, A., Bischof, H., Brox, T., Frahm, J.-M. (eds.) ECCV 2020, Part XII. LNCS, vol. 12357, pp. 241–257. Springer, Cham (2020). https://doi.org/10.1007/978-3-030-58610-2_15
8. Hu, Q., Liu, D., Hu, W.: Exploring the devil in graph spectral domain for 3d point cloud attacks. arXiv preprint arXiv:2202.07261 (2022)
9. Huang, Q., Dong, X., Chen, D., Zhou, H., Zhang, W., Yu, N.: Shape-invariant 3d adversarial point clouds. In: Proceedings of the IEEE/CVF Conference on Computer Vision and Pattern Recognition, pp. 15335–15344 (2022)
10. Kim, J., Hua, B.S., Nguyen, T., Yeung, S.K.: Minimal adversarial examples for deep learning on 3d point clouds. In: Proceedings of the IEEE/CVF International Conference on Computer Vision, pp. 7797–7806 (2021)
11. Kurakin, A., Goodfellow, I., Bengio, S.: Adversarial examples in the physical world. arXiv:1607.02533 (2016)
12. Liu, D., Yu, R., Su, H.: Extending adversarial attacks and defenses to deep 3d point cloud classifiers. In: 2019 IEEE International Conference on Image Processing (ICIP), pp. 2279–2283. IEEE (2019)
13. Liu, D., Yu, R., Su, H.: Adversarial shape perturbations on 3d point clouds. In: Bartoli, A., Fusiello, A. (eds.) ECCV 2020, Part I. LNCS, vol. 12535, pp. 88–104. Springer, Cham (2020). https://doi.org/10.1007/978-3-030-66415-2_6
14. Liu, Y., Fan, B., Meng, G., Lu, J., Xiang, S., Pan, C.: Densepoint: learning densely contextual representation for efficient point cloud processing. In: Proceedings of the IEEE/CVF International Conference on Computer Vision, pp. 5239–5248 (2019)
15. Maturana, D., Scherer, S.: Voxnet: a 3d convolutional neural network for real-time object recognition. In: 2015 IEEE/RSJ International Conference on Intelligent Robots and Systems (IROS), pp. 922–928. IEEE (2015)
16. Miao, Y., Dong, Y., Zhu, J., Gao, X.S.: Isometric 3d adversarial examples in the physical world. arXiv preprint arXiv:2210.15291 (2022)
17. Papernot, N., McDaniel, P., Jha, S., Fredrikson, M., Celik, Z.B., Swami, A.: The limitations of deep learning in adversarial settings. In: 2016 IEEE European Symposium on Security and Privacy (EuroS&P), pp. 372–387. IEEE (2016)
18. Qi, C.R., Su, H., Mo, K., Guibas, L.J.: Pointnet: deep learning on point sets for 3d classification and segmentation. In: Proceedings of the IEEE Conference on Computer Vision and Pattern Recognition, pp. 652–660 (2017)
19. Qi, C.R., Yi, L., Su, H., Guibas, L.J.: Pointnet++: Deep hierarchical feature learning on point sets in a metric space. In: Advances in Neural Information Processing Systems, vol. 30 (2017)
20. Rusu, R.B., Marton, Z.C., Blodow, N., Dolha, M., Beetz, M.: Towards 3d point cloud based object maps for household environments. Robot. Auton. Syst. **56**(11), 927–941 (2008)
21. Shi, Z., Chen, Z., Xu, Z., Yang, W., Yu, Z., Huang, L.: Shape prior guided attack: sparser perturbations on 3d point clouds. In: Proceedings of the AAAI Conference on Artificial Intelligence, vol. 36, pp. 8277–8285 (2022)
22. Singh, R.D., Mittal, A., Bhatia, R.K.: 3d convolutional neural network for object recognition: a review. Multimedia Tools Appl. **78**, 15951–15995 (2019)
23. Tang, K., et al.: Rethinking perturbation directions for imperceptible adversarial attacks on point clouds. IEEE Internet Things J. **10**(6), 5158–5169 (2022)

24. Tang, K., et al.: Normalattack: curvature-aware shape deformation along normals for imperceptible point cloud attack. Secur. Commun. Netw. **2022**(1), 1186633 (2022)
25. Tsai, T., Yang, K., Ho, T.Y., Jin, Y.: Robust adversarial objects against deep learning models. In: Proceedings of the AAAI Conference on Artificial Intelligence, vol. 34, pp. 954–962 (2020)
26. Wang, Y., Sun, Y., Liu, Z., Sarma, S.E., Bronstein, M.M., Solomon, J.M.: Dynamic graph CNN for learning on point clouds. ACM Trans. Graph. (tog) **38**(5), 1–12 (2019)
27. Wang, Z., Bovik, A.C., Sheikh, H.R., Simoncelli, E.P.: Image quality assessment: from error visibility to structural similarity. IEEE Trans. Image Process. **13**(4), 600–612 (2004)
28. Wen, Y., Lin, J., Chen, K., Chen, C., Jia, K.: Geometry-aware generation of adversarial point clouds. arXiv preprint arXiv:1912.11171 (2019)
29. Wicker, M., Kwiatkowska, M.: Robustness of 3d deep learning in an adversarial setting. In: Proceedings of the IEEE/CVF Conference on Computer Vision and Pattern Recognition, pp. 11767–11775 (2019)
30. Wu, Z., et al.: 3d shapenets: a deep representation for volumetric shapes. In: Proceedings of the IEEE Conference on Computer Vision and Pattern Recognition, pp. 1912–1920 (2015)
31. Xiang, C., Qi, C.R., Li, B.: Generating 3d adversarial point clouds. In: Proceedings of the IEEE/CVF Conference on Computer Vision and Pattern Recognition, pp. 9136–9144 (2019)
32. Yang, J., Jiang, Y., Huang, X., Ni, B., Zhao, C.: Learning black-box attackers with transferable priors and query feedback. Adv. Neural. Inf. Process. Syst. **33**, 12288–12299 (2020)
33. Yang, J., Zhang, Q., Fang, R., Ni, B., Liu, J., Tian, Q.: Adversarial attack and defense on point sets. arXiv preprint arXiv:1902.10899 (2019)
34. Yang, J., et al.: Modeling point clouds with self-attention and gumbel subset sampling. In: Proceedings of the IEEE/CVF Conference on Computer Vision and Pattern Recognition, pp. 3323–3332 (2019)
35. Zhang, H., Avrithis, Y., Furon, T., Amsaleg, L.: Smooth adversarial examples. EURASIP J. Inf. Secur. **2020**(1), 1–12 (2020)
36. Zhang, H., Avrithis, Y., Furon, T., Amsaleg, L.: Walking on the edge: fast, low-distortion adversarial examples. IEEE Trans. Inf. Forensics Secur. **16**, 701–713 (2020)
37. Zhang, J., et al.: 3d adversarial attacks beyond point cloud. arXiv preprint arXiv:2104.12146 (2021)
38. Zheng, T., Chen, C., Ren, K., et al.: Learning saliency maps for adversarial point-cloud generation. arXiv preprint arXiv:1812.01687 (2018)
39. Zheng, T., Chen, C., Yuan, J., Li, B., Ren, K.: Pointcloud saliency maps. In: Proceedings of the IEEE/CVF International Conference on Computer Vision, pp. 1598–1606 (2019)
40. Zhou, H., et al.: LG-GAN: label guided adversarial network for flexible targeted attack of point cloud based deep networks. In: Proceedings of the IEEE/CVF Conference on Computer Vision and Pattern Recognition, pp. 10356–10365 (2020)
41. Zhou, H., Chen, K., Zhang, W., Fang, H., Zhou, W., Yu, N.: Dup-net: denoiser and upsampler network for 3d adversarial point clouds defense. In: Proceedings of the IEEE/CVF International Conference on Computer Vision, pp. 1961–1970 (2019)

MILE: A Mutation Testing Framework of In-Context Learning Systems

Zeming Wei, Yihao Zhang, and Meng Sun$^{(\boxtimes)}$

Peking University, Beijing 100871, China
{weizeming,zhangyihao}@stu.pku.edu.cn, sunmeng@math.pku.edu.cn

Abstract. In-context Learning (ICL) has achieved notable success in large language models (LLMs) applications. By adding only a few input-output pairs demonstrating a new task, LLMs can efficiently learn the task during inference without modifying their parameters. Such mysterious ability of LLMs has attracted great research interests in understanding, formatting, and improving the in-context demonstrations, while still suffering from drawbacks like black-box mechanisms and sensitivity against the selection of examples. In this work, inspired by the foundations of adopting testing techniques in machine learning (ML) systems, we propose a mutation testing framework designed to characterize the quality and effectiveness of test data for ICL systems. First, we propose several mutation operators specialized for ICL demonstrations, as well as the corresponding mutation scores for ICL test sets. With comprehensive experiments, we showcase the effectiveness of our framework in evaluating the reliability and quality of ICL test suites. Our code is available at https://github.com/weizeming/MILE.

Keywords: In-context learning · Mutation testing · Large Language Models

1 Introduction

In the past few years, Large Language Models (LLMs) [2,30,46] have achieved milestone success across various tasks [15,38]. In particular, the In-Context Learning (ICL) [4,9] property of LLMs has been recognized as a key emerging ability of LLMs [21]. By prompting a few input-label demonstrations as the context, LLMs can be adapted efficiently to new tasks *without* modifying parameters. This enigmatic characteristic of LLMs has sparked significant research interest in comprehending [26,34,39] and utilizing [35–37] ICL in diverse scenarios.

However, ICL has been shown to have notable reliability issues, such as strong dependence on example selection [26], the order sensitivity of the demonstrations [22], and vulnerabilities against adversarial attacks [37]. To mitigate these issues, several works have been proposed to automatically organize demonstrations [22] or design intrinsically robust ICL mechanisms [10,43]. While these

© The Author(s), under exclusive license to Springer Nature Singapore Pte Ltd. 2025
T. Bourke et al. (Eds.): SETTA 2024, LNCS 15469, pp. 327–343, 2025.
https://doi.org/10.1007/978-981-96-0602-3_18

works mainly focus on improving the robustness of ICL, how to select high-quality test suites for evaluating ICL systems remains an open research problem. Moreover, since the computational cost of LLMs becomes significantly higher than classic deep neural networks, the need for high-quality datasets for efficient evaluations is further emphasized.

On the other hand, mutation testing [17] techniques have showcased impressive potential in studying the test suite reliability of machine learning (ML) systems [14,25,33,42]. By regarding the ML system as the software under test (SUT), several mutation testing methods have been designed for different ML paradigms including deep learning [13,25,28], reinforcement learning [31], and unsupervised learning [24]. Specifically, like mutation testing for software systems, these methods first apply mutators designed for the ML models or training data, then study the behavior differences between the original and mutant models. Since mutation testing is to assess the efficacy of test cases in characterizing faults in the ML model, test suites showcasing superior performance disparities between the original and mutant models are deemed of better quality.

In this paper, driven by the observation that ICL systems also encounter robustness issues and demand high-quality test cases, we propose **MILE**, a **M**utation testing framework for **I**n-context **LE**arning systems. First, we propose mutators specialized for ICL systems. Unlike mutation testing on conventional ML systems that consider both data and model mutators [13,25], we primarily focus on mutation operations on the ICL prompt since ICL systems typically use a static pre-trained LLM and mainly concentrate on designing demonstrations. Taking into account the characteristics of ICL, such as sensitivity to the orders and strong dependence on the labels, we propose a kit of mutators including demonstration-level ones and prompt-level ones. Meanwhile, we design corresponding mutation scores for MILE. Besides classic mutation scores, we propose a group-wise mutation score that helps identify how well test suites can characterize diverse defects, beyond just evaluating the test set as a whole.

We finally evaluate our MILE framework across benchmark datasets and popular LLMs. Following the common practice of existing mutation testing frameworks [13,25], we sample test data from uniform or non-uniform classes to simulate high- or low-quality datasets and calculate the mutation scores on them. The experiment results suggest that our mutation scores have a strong correlation to the quality of the test sets, showcasing the effectiveness of our framework in measuring the quality of test suites. In addition, we take an in-depth analysis of each mutator to better understand their sensitivity to the defects within the ICL prompts, which is helpful for mutation operation selection for testing ICL systems with different scenarios.

Overall, our contributions in this work can be summarized as follows:

1. We propose MILE, a mutation testing framework of in-context learning systems to comprehensively assess the effectiveness of their test cases.
2. We design demonstration- and prompt-level mutation operators specialized for ICL, as well as their standard- and group-wise mutation scores.
3. We evaluate and further analyze MILE across benchmark datasets and LLMs to showcase its effectiveness in assessing the quality of test cases.

2   Preliminaries

In this section, we provide background information and define formal notations for ICL and mutation testing.

In-Context Learning (ICL). ICL [4,9] is an intriguing property that emerges in LLMs in which they learn a specific task demonstrated by a few input-label pair examples. By keeping the model parameters static, prompting a system message that briefly describes the task and a set of input-label pairs demonstrating the task, the LLM can learn a mapping between the inputs and labels, and then predict the label of a new input query attached behind the demonstrations in the prompt. Specifically, the definition of an ICL system can be formulated as:

Definition 1 (In-context Learning System). *An ICL system consists of a pre-trained LLM $M(\cdot)$ that returns a response $M(p)$ for any prompt p, a system prompt p_s, and a set of in-context demonstrations $D = \{(x_1, y_1), (x_2, y_2), \cdots, (x_k, y_k)\}$. For any test prompt x_{test}, the model gathers all sources to form the ICL prompt $p^* = [p_s, x_1, y_1, x_2, y_2, \cdots, x_k, y_k, x_{test}]$ and return the final response by $M(p^*)$.*

An example of an ICL prompt for the RTE task [7] is illustrated in the following block. As instructed in the system message (lines 1–2), this task is to determine whether the hypotheses can be derived from the premises. Then, 2 demonstrations consisting of inputs (the premises and hypotheses) and labels (answer ↑ or ↓) are attached behind the system prompt. Generally, the shots (number) of demonstrations are much more than 2. Finally, the prompt ends with a querying input for inference. From the text, we can know that the hypothesis *"Qatar is located in Doha"* cannot be derived from the premise, which aligns with the *2nd* demonstration, so the correct output from the model should be ↓.

Example ICL prompt for RTE task

<s> Determine whether the hypotheses made based on the premises below are ↑ or ↓.
Premise: The Democrats' success in the 2006 elections means changes at the top in the House and Senate.
Hypothesis: Democrats won the 2006 elections.
Answer: ↑

Premise: IKEA offers fantastic and affordable solutions for your home furnishing needs.
Hypothesis: Ikea is a home.
Answer: ↓

Premise: VCU School of the Arts In Qatar is located in Doha, the capital city of Qatar.
Hypothesis: Qatar is located in Doha.
Answer:

Mutation Testing. Test cases play a crucial role in characterizing and evaluating the vulnerability and reliability of software systems. As a pioneering technique, mutation testing was first proposed in the 1970 s [17,18] to measure the quality of test suites for software systems. Generally, mutation testing aims to replicate potential faults and vulnerabilities in the system to determine which test cases can effectively detect them. To this end, the mutation testing first artificially mutates a normal system to introduce fault with a set of pre-defined mutation operators (mutators). Then, given a test suite, its quality judged by this testing framework is determined by the ratio of the mutants that are killed by this dataset, as formally stated in the following definition.

Definition 2 (Mutation Testing). *Consider a program P, a set of mutation operators $O = \{o_1, o_2, \cdots, o_m\}$, and a test set $T = \{(X_1, Y_1), (X_2, Y_2), \cdots, (X_n, Y_n)\}$ where each X_i is an input and each Y_i is a label. With each mutator o_i turns the program P into a mutant program $o_i(P) = P_i'$, a mutation testing process evaluates $o_i(P)$ on all (X_i, Y_i) and studies the difference between the performance of P and the mutants $\{o_1(P), o_2(P), \cdots, o_m(P)\}$.*

So far, mutation testing has been acknowledged as one of the most fundamental software testing techniques, which is widely adopted in scenarios like fault localization [27] and software repairment [12]. In particular, mutation testing has proven to be successful in evaluating the adequacy of test datasets by providing a metric to determine whether existing tests have good fault-revealing capabilities. In the context of ML systems, a representative application of mutation testing is to assess the quality of test sets by treating the model as a program, and when the mutated models (mutants) output false prediction, this mutant can be regarded as *killed*. We provide more related work on applying mutation testing for ML systems in Sect. 5.

3 Mutation Testing For In-Context Learning

In this section, we present MILE, our mutation testing framework for in-context learning systems. We begin with a brief overview of the testing pipeline and general design for mutation operator and score, then put forward our solutions to them respectively.

3.1 Overview

Similar to existing mutation testing techniques for ML systems, we devise a two-stage testing framework consisting of mutant generation and test set evaluation. However, in contrast to traditional machine learning approaches that train models from scratch (*i.e.* with random parameter initialization), ICL systems usually use a pre-trained static LLM and primarily focus on formatting in-context demonstrations [4,9]. Therefore, we only consider mutations in the demonstrations while keeping the LLM unchanged. Note that it is possible to

---

Algorithm 1: Pipeline of MLIE

Input : LLM M, System prompt p_s, In-context demonstrations
$D = \{(x_1, y_1), (x_2, y_2), \cdots, (x_k, y_k)\}$, Test set under evaluation
$T = \{(X_1, Y_1), (X_2, Y_2) \cdots, (X_n, Y_n)\}$, Mutation operators
$O = \{o_1, o_2, \cdots, o_m\}$

Output: Mutation scores and analysis

1 Obtain mutant prompts $D'_i \leftarrow o_i(D), \quad i = 1, 2, \cdots, m$;

2 Construct ICL model $\mathcal{M}(\cdot) = M([p_s, D, \cdot])$ and mutant models
$\mathcal{M}'_i(\cdot) = M([p_s, D'_i, \cdot]), \quad i = 1, 2, \cdots, m$;

3 Mutant_Outputs$\leftarrow$ [ ];

4 **for** $(X_i, Y_i) \in T$ **do**

5   **if** $\mathcal{M}(X_i) = Y_i$ **then**

6 | Mutant_Outputs.$append([\mathcal{M}'_1(X_1), \mathcal{M}'_2(X_i), \cdots, \mathcal{M}'_m(X_i)])$

7   **end**

8 **end**

9 **return** Mutation_Score(Mutant_Outputs, $[Y_1, Y_2, \cdots, Y_n]$);

---

use conventional model mutators for LLMs, but they face computational complexity bottlenecks. Additionally, due to the unique organization format of ICL prompts, it is challenging to apply other data mutators for general ML models to ICL.

The overall pipeline of our proposed MILE is elaborated in Algorithm 1. In line 1, we first obtain the mutated in-context demonstrations D'_i from D with all mutators. Then, by incorporating these demonstrations into the original LLM M, we obtain ICL models $\mathcal{M}$ and $\mathcal{M}'_i$ (line 2). The second stage is to evaluate the test set T with the mutants. In line 5, we first filter out the examples that are misclassified by the original model. Following existing work [25], we primarily illustrate our framework on classification tasks, but it can be easily adapted to other scenarios like regression tasks by adding a threshold function. Further, in line 6 for these passed test cases, we track all mutant predictions on them and finally calculate the mutation scores based on these outputs and true labels, as detailed in the following sections.

3.2   Mutation Operators for ICL

In this section, we propose several mutation operators specialized for ICL prompts. Considering the principle of the mutation operator, which is to characterize potential faults and the sensitivity of a program that may have suffered, we design mutators based on potential problems and the sensitivity of ICL prompts, and divide them into demonstration-level and prompt-level ones. The demonstration-level mutators change the input-label pair within a specific demonstration, while the prompt-level mutators modify the demonstrations in a more holistic manner.

Demonstration-Level Mutation Operators. First, we consider demonstration-level mutations for a single demonstration (x_i, y_i) that modify x_i or y_i to construct a mutant ICL prompt, including:

- **Noisy Labels (NL).** ICL is known to be sensitive to the noise of labels in the demonstrations [6,11]. However, recent research emphasizes the potential of scaling ICL to very large volumes [1] where ensuring label accuracy becomes challenging, leading to potential concerns about noisy labels within the prompt. Therefore, we first propose a Noisy Label (NL) mutator which randomly replaces a correct label in the demonstration: $y_i \leftarrow y', i \sim Uniform([1...k]), y' \in \mathcal{Y} - \{y_i\}$ where $\mathcal{Y}$ is all class labels.
- **Out-of-distribution Labels (OL).** Similar to the Noisy Labels mutator, we also consider another common reliability issue that the label assigned to data may be out-of-distribution (OOD), as the OOD detection is still a not fully addressed problem [20,40]. Unlike the NL mutator which injects a false label, this Out-of-distribution Labels mutator replaces the original label with one that does not belong to the task classes, $e.g.$ a special token: $y_i \leftarrow z, i \sim Uniform([1...k]), z \notin \mathcal{Y}$. Intuitively, the OOD label mutator may be more moderate than the noisy label mutator, as verified in our experiments.
- **Blurred Inputs (BI).** In addition to mutating the labels in the demonstrations, we further consider potential issues in the inputs x_i. As stated in prior research [26], high-quality inputs are essential for helping the language model better understand the task. Therefore, we suggest simulating questionable inputs in the demonstrations by blurring the input content: $x_i \leftarrow \tilde{x}_i, i \sim Uniform([1...k])$. In our implementation, we achieve this by simply truncating the input to its prefix.

Prompt-Level Mutation Operators. We also consider prompt-level mutation, where we maintain input-label pairs for each individual demonstration but explore mutating between different demonstrations, including:

- **Demonstration Shuffle (DS).** The order of the demonstrations can have a significant impact on the ICL prompts, as noted in previous studies [10,22]. Therefore, test cases for which the prediction changed after reordering the demonstrations would be considered as being near the decision boundary, indicating that they may be effective test cases [24,25]. This motivates us to propose the Demonstration Shuffle mutator that randomly re-orders all demonstrations in the prompt: $(x_i, y_i) \leftarrow (x_{\sigma(i)}, y_{\sigma(i)})$, where $\{\sigma(1), \sigma(2), \cdots, \sigma(k)\}$ is a random permutation of $[1...k]$.
- **Out-of-distribution Demonstrations (OD).** Similar to the proposed OOD Label mutator, we also consider another form of OOD mutator that introduces a self-consistent OOD demonstration (x', y') from a different dataset, which may also distract the model from the target task: $(x_i, y_i) \leftarrow (x', y'), i \sim Uniform([1...k]), (x', y') \sim \mathcal{D}$ which is another data distribution.
- **Demonstration Repetition (DR).** Finally, we consider the demonstration repetition mutator. The training data repetition mutator was suggested

for deep learning with the idea that the same data point might be gathered repeatedly from similar sources [25]. In the case of ICL prompts, repetition or very similar prompts might be seen as unnecessary [1]. As a result, we propose the Demonstration Repetition mutator that incorporates repeated demonstrations into the prompt: $(x_{i+j}, y_{i+j}) \leftarrow (x_i, y_i), i \sim Uniform([1...k]), j = 1, 2, ..., N$ where N is the times of repetition.

We present the implementation details of each mutator in experiments in Sect. 4. Based on these mutators, we further devise the mutation scores in the testing framework in the following.

3.3   Mutation Scores

We first consider the standard mutation score in the context of mutation testing, which is defined as the ratio of mutators killed by (*i.e.* misclassify any case in) the test set. Based on the notations presented in Sect. 2, this metric can be formulated as:

Definition 3 (Standard Mutation Score).   *The standard mutation score* MS_S *is defined by*

$$MS_S(M, O, T) = \frac{\#\{o_i | \exists j, \; M_i'(X_j) \neq Y_j\}}{\#O}, \tag{1}$$

where $\#S$ denotes the cardinality of set S. Please note that in this section we abuse the notation T to denote the test samples that are correctly classified by M. Apart from the standard metric, we are also interested in the test set's ability to identify different types of defaults. As outlined in the previous section, the ICL system may have various potential defects. Hence, a high-quality test set should be able to detect a variety of vulnerabilities, measured by the average number of mutator groups killed by the test cases. Motivated by this notion, we propose a **Group-wise mutation score** as follows:

Definition 4 (Group-wise Mutation Score).   *Suppose that the mutation operators can be divided into* K *groups* $O = \{O_1, O_2, \cdots, O_K\}$. *The group-wise mutation score* MS_G *is defined by*

$$MS_G(M, O, T) = \frac{\sum_{i=1}^{\#T} \sum_{j=1}^{K} \mathbb{I}(\exists o_l \in O_j, \; M_l'(X_i) \neq Y_i)}{\#T \times K}, \tag{2}$$

where $\mathbb{I}(\cdot)$ is the indicator function. Intuitively, MS_G measures how many groups of mutators can be killed on average, *i.e.* $\sum_{j=1}^{K} \mathbb{I}(\exists o_l \in O_j, \; M_l'(X_I) \neq Y_i)$. We divide this by K for normalization. This metric underscores the diversity among different mutator groups. This metric is useful for preventing inflation of mutation scores when a test case can only kill mutators from a few groups. In practice, we consider all mutators that are generated from the same operator in the previous section as one group, thus we generally have 6 mutator groups in this testing framework.

4   Experiments

In this section, we conduct evaluations across diverse datasets and LLMs to evaluate and comprehend our MILE framework. We start by elaborating the experiment set-ups, and then showcasing the effectiveness of MILE on measuring dataset quality. Finally, we analyze and compare the mutators for a better understanding of them.

4.1   Experiment Set-Up

Datasets. Following common practice in ICL research [43], we consider 5 popular datasets: **(1) SST-2** [29] (Stanford Sentiment Treebank) is a binary single-sentence classification dataset that is used for sentiment analysis. **(2) AGnews** [44] (AG's News Topic Classification Dataset) is a collection of news articles categorized into four different classes: World, Sports, Business, and Sci/Tech. **(3) RTE** [7] (Recognizing Textual Entailment) contains pairs of sentences where the goal is to determine if the second sentence logically follows from the first. **(4) MRPC** [8] (Microsoft Research Paraphrase Corpus) is a dataset for text pair classification on whether two sentences are semantically equivalent or not. **(5) QNLI** [32] (Question Answering Natural Language Inference) is a dataset for question answering through natural language inference with the task of determining if the answer is supported or contradicted.

The system prompts and input-label pair formats for these tasks are summarized in Table 1.

Table 1. System prompts and input-label pair formats for the tasks we used in the experiments.

Dataset	System Prompt	Content
SST2 [29]	The following are multiple film reviews with answers ($\leftarrow$ or $\rightarrow$).	Review, Answer
AGnews [44]	Classify the news articles into the categories of 1, 2, 3, or 4.	Title, Description, Answer
RTE [7]	Determine whether the hypotheses made based on the premises below are $\uparrow$ or $\downarrow$.	Premise, Hypothesis, Answer
MRPC [8]	Assess if each pair reflects a semantic equivalence relationship. Use $\leftarrow$ or $\rightarrow$ to indicate the answers.	Sentence 1, Sentence 2, Answer
QNLI [32]	Please determine whether the paragraph contains the answer to the corresponding question. Use $\uparrow$ or $\downarrow$ to indicate the answers.	Question, Paragraph, Answer

LLMs for Evaluation. In our experiment, we consider 3 popular open-sourced LLMs for our evaluation: **(1) Vicuna-7b** [46], **(2) Llama-2-chat-7b** [30] and **(3) Falcon-7b-instruct** [2], which all achieved notable performance across popular LLM benchmarks [19].

To ensure that these LLMs are capable of conducting ICL on these datasets, we evaluate the vanilla accuracy of the 3 models on the 5 benchmark datasets with **20 shots ICL**, which is commonly used in other popular evaluations and mostly achieves satisfactory performance. The accuracy under these evaluations is summarized in Table 2. In most cases, they achieve satisfactory accuracy on the tasks, verifying that their ICL inference is reasonable on these datasets. The 20 ICL examples are randomly sampled from the validation set for each task, with the numbers of demonstrations for all classes kept the same. To ensure a fair comparison, we fix the sampled demonstration sets in the ICL prompts in all the following experiments.

Table 2. Accuracy evaluation of the 3 LLMs across 5 datasets with vanilla 20 shots ICL.

Model	SST2	AGnews	RTE	MRPC	QNLI
Vicuna	92.8%	68.0%	71.2%	35.6%	56.4%
Llama-2	93.6%	61.2%	77.2%	68.4%	63.2%
Falcon	78.4%	27.6%	47.6%	68.4%	52.4%

Mutant Implementation Details. We provide the details of implementing each mutator. Note that for all mutators except Demonstration Shuffle (DS), we sample each input-label demonstration once to simulate $i \sim Uniform([1...k])$ in Sect. 3.2, so we obtain 20 mutant models from each mutator.

1. Noisy Labels (**NL**): For the sampled demonstration, we randomly flip the label to another possible class in this task.
2. OOD Labels (**OL**): For the sampled demonstration, we replace the label with a special token '&'.
3. Blurred Inputs (**BI**): For the sampled demonstration, we truncate the input with its first-half prefix.
4. Demonstration Shuffle (**DS**): To keep the number of mutants the same as other operators, we randomly generate 20 permutations of $[1...20]$ and apply these orders to the demonstration set.
5. OOD Demonstrations (**OD**): For the sampled demonstration, we replace it with 1 input-output pair randomly sampled from the WMT [3] dataset, which is a machine translation task from English to France.
6. Demonstration Repetition (**DR**): For the sampled demonstration, we insert two same demonstrations behind it.

Finally, with 20 mutants generated by each mutation operator, we collect 120 mutants in total for each vanilla ICL prompt.

Table 3. Standard Mutation Score MS_S comparison between the uniform sampled dataset (uni.) and non-uniformly sampled (non.) dataset.

Model	Vicuna		Llama-2		Falcon		Average	
Task	uni.	non.	uni.	non.	uni.	non.	uni.	non.
SST2	54.2%	20.4%	53.3%	20.4%	90.0%	44.6%	**65.8%**	28.5%
AGnews	78.3%	36.9%	94.2%	69.2%	60.8%	34.2%	**77.8%**	46.8%
RTE	47.5%	50.4%	94.2%	85.8%	4.2%	4.2%	**48.6%**	46.8%
MRPC	69.2%	50.8%	95.0%	73.3%	75.0%	45.8%	**79.7%**	56.6%
QNLI	98.3%	60.4%	95.8%	63.3%	3.3%	3.3%	**65.8%**	42.3%
Avg	**69.5%**	43.8%	**86.5%**	62.4%	**46.7%**	26.4%	**67.6%**	44.2%

4.2 Overall Assessment

Uniform and Non-Uniform Datasets. Our main evaluation aims to evaluate whether the mutation score can reflect the quality of the test set. Following existing evaluation frameworks [13,25], we simulate the quality of the test set through the aspect of the uniformity of the classes. Specifically, a good dataset consists of samples uniformly sampled from all classes, while a dataset consisting of samples from imbalanced classes is considered of poor quality.

As such, we first construct a dataset that is uniformly sampled from all classes (abbreviated as **uni.**), and also construct non-uniformly sampled datasets (abbreviated as **non.**). Specifically, 50% samples of the dataset are from one single class (called biased class), and another 50% samples are uniformly sampled from all classes. To make our evaluation results more robust, we create non-uniformly sampled datasets by enumerating all possible biased classes, and then report the average scores across these datasets. We first set the controlled number n as the half-size of the complete dataset, and control the size test set as $\frac{1}{2}n$ in our main evaluation. We also investigate the impact of dataset size on the mutation scores in the following.

Mutation Score Comparison. Based on the settings presented above, we evaluate the standard mutation score (MS_S) and group-wise mutation score (MS_G) on all datasets and models, and report them in Table 3 and Table 4 respectively.

As shown in Table 3, for all tasks the MS_S score of **uni.** dataset consistently outperforms **non.** dataset, with 67.6% *v.s.* 44.2% on average, indicating a strong correlation between the dataset quality and the mutation score from MILE. Such a significant gap applies to all 3 models, *e.g.* 69.5% *v.s.* 43.8% for the Vicuna model, verifying the university of this correlation among different LLMs. For most of the datasets, this property still holds, like the model-averaged score for SST2 exhibits a gap higher than 30%. There are also exceptional cases like QNLI and RTE tasks for Falcon, where the score is almost the same. However,

Table 4. Group-wise Mutation Score MS_G comparison between the uniform sampled dataset (uni.) and non-uniformly sampled (non.) dataset.

Model	Vicuna		Llama-2		Falcon		Average	
Task	uni.	non.	uni.	non.	uni.	non.	uni.	non.
SST2	13.7%	8.7%	18.0%	10.2%	51.0%	15.5%	**27.6%**	11.5%
AGnews	36.1%	10.2%	50.3%	12.7%	53.8%	3.8%	**46.7%**	8.9%
RTE	10.7%	7.3%	15.3%	12.0%	16.7%	18.0%	**14.2%**	12.4%
MRPC	24.1%	13.2%	47.7%	27.0%	70.3%	20.8%	**47.4%**	20.3%
QNLI	42.7%	27.2%	34.7%	18.3%	5.7%	9.7%	**27.7%**	18.4%
Avg	**25.5%**	13.3%	**33.2%**	16.0%	**39.5%**	13.6%	**32.7%**	14.3%

when reviewing Table 2 we can find that Falcon performs poorly on them (near random guess), thus these outliers do not affect our claims.

Further, from the group-wise mutation scores in Table 4, we can still observe a strong gap between the scores of **uni.** and **non.** datasets, with an averaged score of 32.7% for **uni.** to 14.3% for **non.** datasets. As a metric with considerations of mutant diversity, the MS_G score also aligns with the superiority of **uni.** over **non.** datasets in terms of the comprehensiveness of ICL evaluation. Moreover, the score itself also has an explicit semantic that indicates how many groups of mutants can be detected by each test case on average. For example, since Vicuna achieves 36% on uni. dataset in the AGnews task, we know that each sample in Vicuna can cover $36\% \times 6 \approx 2$ groups of mutants on average.

Varying Dataset Size. We also conduct an analysis of the scores by varying the size of the test set. To this end, we sampled multiple test sets with sizes $[20\%, 40\%, 60\%, 80\%, 100\%] \times n$. The results (averaged over 5 datasets) are summarized by the models in Fig. 1. For all models, the score superiority of the **uni.** datasets (blue lines) over **non.** datasets (red lines) are consistent among different set sizes, further confirming the strong correlation between the scores calculated by MILE. Moreover, an interesting observation is that MS_S gradually increases as the test set becomes larger, since intuitively a larger dataset can cover more mutants. However, the MS_G does not necessarily increase since it is averaged on instance-wise.

4.3 Mutator Analysis

In this experiment, we take a closer look at the sensitivity of the ICL model against each mutant group. This analysis aims to better understand the characteristics of each mutation operator, which is beneficial to selecting and allocating mutators for new LLMs or tasks when applying MILE.

Recall that in Sect. 3 we propose the group-wise mutation score as the average number of mutator groups killed by the test cases. Now, we use a refined metric

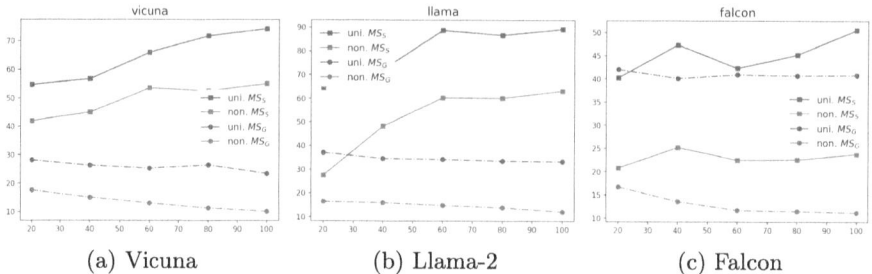

(a) Vicuna   (b) Llama-2   (c) Falcon

Fig. 1. Comparing mutation scores with different dataset sizes. Each figure represents the scores averaged over 5 datasets for a model. The X-axis denotes the ratio of the set size to n, and the Y-axis denotes the score (%). The blue lines represent the **uni.** dataset and red lines represent the **non.** datasets. The solid line and dotted line denote MS_S and MS_G, respectively. (Color figure online)

Table 5. Individual MS_G comparison for each mutant group. NL: noisy label; OD: OOD label; BI: blurred input; DS: demo shuffle; OD: OOD demo; DR: demo repetition.

Mutator	Demonstration-level			Prompt-level		
Model	NL	OL	BI	DS	OD	DR
Vicuna	45.5%	23.1%	11.6%	36.6%	23.2%	12.9%
Llama-2	50.2%	28.4%	15.6%	70.7%	31.0%	23.6%
Falcon	61.6%	55.8%	12.5%	69.2%	15.1%	39.5%
Avg.	52.4%	35.8%	13.2%	58.8%	23.1%	25.3%

to analyze the effectiveness of each mutation operator and the corresponding mutants. We first extend the definition of MS_G to the individual cases of a single mutant group O_j:

Definition 5 (Individual Group-wise Mutation Score). *For a single mutant group $O_j \subset O$, its individual group-wise mutation score is defined as*

$$MS_G(M, O_j, T) = \frac{1}{K} K \sum_{j=1}^{K} \mathbb{I}(\exists o_l \in O_j, M'_l(X_i) \neq Y_i). \tag{3}$$

Note that we can rewrite $MS_G(M, O, T) = \frac{1}{\#T} \sum_{j=1}^{\#T} MS_G(M, O_j, T)$. For mutant group O_j, the individual $MS_G(M, O_j, T)$ is the proportion of test cases that can kill anyone of the mutants, indicating the sensitivity of the ICL prompt against the mutation operator.

We summarize the individual MS_G scores in Table 5 with the scores averaged over 5 datasets. From all models, we can see that the NL (Noisy Label) and (DS) (Demonstration Shuffle) mutators exhibit significantly higher scores than other mutators, which aligns well with the fact that ICL prompts are quite

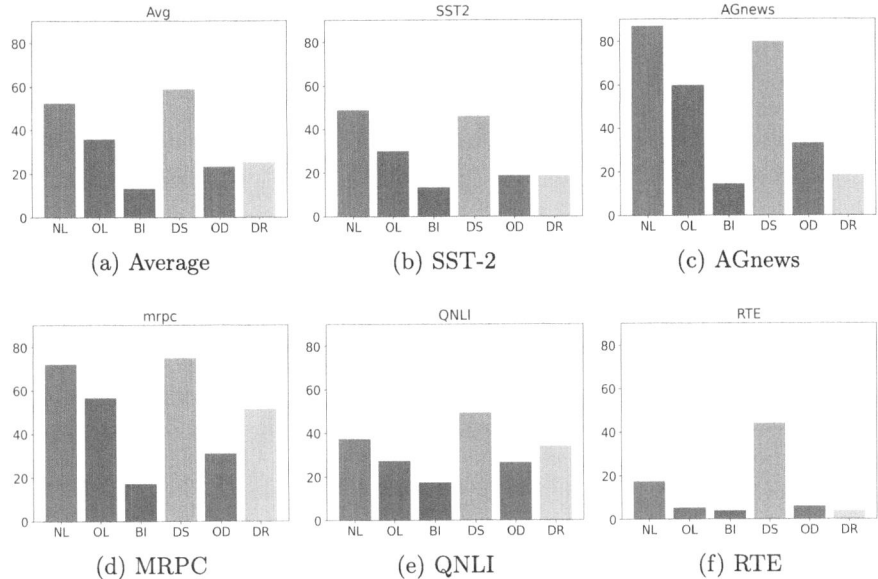

Fig. 2. Individual MS_G comparison for each mutant group on different datasets. The scores are averaged over 3 models.

sensitive to label noises [6,11] and demonstration orders [10,22]. Besides, the OL (OOD Label) mutator achieves a higher score than the other 3 mutators, including the OD (OOD Demonstration) mutator, confirming the sensitivity of the ICL prompts against label perturbation. When analyzing this property across different datasets, we can observe the strong transferability of the ranks among the mutators in Fig. 2, where the scores are averaged over 3 models. For example, the NL and DS mutators consistently have higher scores than other mutators, verifying the model sensitivity against them across different tasks.

In summary, as the mutator sensitivity can be transferred among different models and tasks, we can create a set of mutations for new models and tasks based on specific testing and test set selection needs. For instance, if there's a limited dataset size budget, using more sensitive mutators would help in selecting datasets that can effectively identify faults. On the other hand, using more moderate mutators may be beneficial in designing large-scale datasets to find more nuanced faults.

4.4 Threats to Validity and Limitations

In this paper, we acknowledge the following threats to validity and limitations. First, the selection of the LLMs and datasets can be a threat to validity. In our experiments, we have evaluated MILE across 3 LLMs and 5 datasets. Due to computational resource limitations, we only evaluate models limited to 7b size, thus selecting a larger model or closed-source model is a potential threat to validity. Additionally, we only used 20-shot ICL which is a common practice in other ICL evaluations, but any change in the number of ICL demonstrations could also pose a threat to validity. Besides, the random sampling of the uniform or non-uniform class datasets is also a threat to validity. To deal with this concern, we fixed random seeds in our experiments to ensure reproducibility. Also, we only consider uniformity as the simulation of dataset quality, thus cannot encompass all aspects of test set quality in practical scenarios, which we acknowledge as a limitation of evaluation. Moreover, it is also possible that the model is significantly sensitive or insensitive against some particular biased class during non-uniform sampling. In our experiment, we enumerated all possible biased classes and averaged all scores over these non-uniform datasets to address this issue. Finally, there are also exceptional cases that the score comparison between the two datasets does not align with our overall observation, but when revisiting the vanilla accuracy of the models in these datasets we can find that the model is not capable of conducting reasonable in-context inference on these tasks, and thus would not affect any of our claims.

5   Related Work

5.1   Robustness and Evaluation of In-Context Learning

Discovered from the GPT-3 model [4], the intriguing ICL ability of LLMs has attracted widespread interest in understanding [26,34,39], utilizing [35–37], improving [10,43] this learning paradigm. However, though having been studied by a series of works [10], the robustness issue of the in-context demonstrations is still an unaddressed problem. The ICL performance is very sensitive to the selection and order of demonstrations [22], as well as the noise in the labels [6,11], both posing safety concerns in their real-world applications. To select better demonstration sets, Wang et al. propose to select in-context demonstrations through the Bayesian lens that regard the LLMs as latent variable models [34]. Other works attempt to design intrinsically robust ICL against demonstration ordering like Zhang et al. propose BatchICL [43], an order-agnostic ICL inference algorithm, and Fang et al. propose InvICL [10], which identifies two crucial factors in the design of ICL including information non-leakage and context interdependence to achieve invariance in ICL.

Apart from focusing on the mechanism of ICL, few works have been dedicated to designing the evaluation specialized for ICL, and most of the existing works still solely conduct ICL evaluation with general LLM benchmarks like Alpaca Eval [19] or purely based on conventional natural language processing datasets like SST2. Recently, Chen et al. propose ICLEval [5], the first benchmark particularly designed for ICL evaluation with two key sub-abilities of LLMs, including exact copying and rule learning. Besides, the evaluation designed for the quality of test cases for ICL remains unexplored.

5.2   Mutation Testing for Machine Learning Systems

In recent years, leveraging mutation testing in machine learning (ML) testing has become a popular research topic [14,25,42]. The testing procedure typically consists of 2 stages, including mutating the ML system through different aspects to simulate potential faults within the system, and then evaluating the dataset on the original model and the mutant models to characterize the quality of the dataset or the system. As a pioneering study, Ma et al. propose the Deep-Mutation [25], which proposes various mutators for deep neural networks from source-level (training data and model architecture) to model-level (parameters and architecture after training). Then, under controlled experiments, they show that the mutation score is able to reflect the dataset quality for ML systems. Concurrently, Shen et al. propose Munn [28], including five mutation operators designed with the characteristics of neural networks and investigations on how mutation affects neural networks and how neural depth affects mutation analysis. Subsequently, Humbatova et al. propose DeepCrime [16], which defines 35 deep learning mutation operators and conducts empirical studies about real faults in deep learning systems.

Going beyond conventional deep learning systems, there are also other works dedicated to applying mutation testing techniques in other learning paradigms and scenarios. Hu et al. propose DeepMutation++ [13], extending the DeepMutation framework to both feed-forward and stateful recurrent neural networks. Lu et al. propose MTUL [23], a mutation testing framework for unsupervised learning systems. Besides, Wang et al. [33] propose to leverage mutation testing for adversarial example detection during inference, based on the intuition that adversarial samples are more sensitive against model mutations. Similarly, Zhang et al. propose to apply mutation testing to detect jailbreaking attacks against LLMs [45]. On the other position, Yu et al. propose GPUFuzzer [41], leveraging mutation techniques to craft jailbreaking prompts for LLMs. However, although preliminary work has been done on introducing mutation testing for LLMs, the use of mutation testing for ICL systems has not been explored.

6   Conclusion

In this paper, we propose MILE, a mutation testing framework of in-context learning (ICL) systems, aiming to evaluate the test suite quality for ICL models. For mutation operators, we consider demonstration-level and prompt-level ones, specialized for ICL prompts. Besides the standard mutation score, we also propose a group-wise mutation score to better understand the model sensitivity against inter-group mutants. With comprehensive experiments across popular LLMs and datasets, we demonstrate the strong correlation between the test set quality and mutation score calculated by MILE, showcasing the effectiveness of using MILE to evaluate the test suite quality. We further investigate the model sensitivity against different kinds of mutants and provide suggestions for designing mutators when applying MILE for different testing goals. Overall, our work provides a novel technique for evaluating and improving ICL systems.

Acknowlegement. This work was sponsored by the National Natural Science Foundation of China (Grant No. 62172019) and the Beijing Natural Science Foundation (Grant No. QY23041).

References

1. Agarwal, R., et al.: Many-shot in-context learning. arXiv preprint (2024)
2. Almazrouei, E., et al.: The falcon series of open language models. arXiv:2311.16867 (2023)
3. Bojar, O., et al.: Findings of the 2014 workshop on statistical machine translation. In: Proceedings of the Ninth Workshop on Statistical Machine Translation (2014)
4. Brown, T.B., et al.: Language models are few-shot learners. arXiv:2005.14165 (2020)
5. Chen, W., et al.: Icleval: evaluating in-context learning ability of large language models. arXiv:2406.14955 (2024)
6. Cheng, C., et al.: Exploring the robustness of in-context learning with noisy labels. In: ICLR 2024 R2-FM Workshop (2024)
7. Dagan, I., et al.: The pascal recognising textual entailment challenge. In: Machine Learning Challenges Workshop (2005)
8. Dolan, B., et al.: Automatically constructing a corpus of sentential paraphrases. In: IWP (2005)
9. Dong, Q., et al.: A survey on in-context learning (2023)
10. Fang, L., et al.: Rethinking invariance in in-context learning. In: ICML 2024 Workshop on Theoretical Foundations of Foundation Models (2024)
11. Gao, H., et al.: On the noise robustness of in-context learning for text generation. arXiv:2405.17264 (2024)
12. Ghanbari, A., et al.: Practical program repair via bytecode mutation. In: ISSTA (2019)
13. Hu, Q., et al.: Deepmutation++: a mutation testing framework for deep learning systems. In: ASE (2019)
14. Huang, X.O.: A survey of safety and trustworthiness of deep neural networks: verification, testing, adversarial attack and defence, and interpretability. Comput. Sci. Rev. **37**, 100270 (2020)
15. Huang, X., et al.: Understanding the planning of LLM agents: a survey. arXiv:2402.02716 (2024)
16. Humbatova, N., et al.: Deepcrime: mutation testing of deep learning systems based on real faults. In: ISSTA (2021)
17. Jia, Y., et al.: An analysis and survey of the development of mutation testing. IEEE Trans. Softw. Eng. **37**(5), 649–678 (2010)
18. Just, R., et al.: Defects4j: a database of existing faults to enable controlled testing studies for java programs. In: ISSTA (2014)
19. Li, X., et al.: Alpacaeval: an automatic evaluator of instruction-following models. https://github.com/tatsu-lab/alpaca_eval
20. Liu, W.O.: Energy-based out-of-distribution detection. In: NeurIPS (2020)
21. Lu, S., et al.: Are emergent abilities in large language models just in-context learning? arXiv:2309.01809 (2023)
22. Lu, Y., et al.: Fantastically ordered prompts and where to find them: overcoming few-shot prompt order sensitivity. arXiv:2104.08786 (2021)
23. Lu, Y., et al.: Towards mutation testing of reinforcement learning systems. J. Syst. Architect. **131**, 102701 (2022)

24. Lu, Y., et al.: Mutation testing of unsupervised learning systems. J. Syst. Archit. **146**, 103050 (2024)
25. Ma, L., et al.: Deepmutation: mutation testing of deep learning systems. In: ISSRE (2018)
26. Min, S., et al.: Rethinking the role of demonstrations: what makes in-context learning work? In: EMNLP (2022)
27. Papadakis, M., et al.: Metallaxis-FL: mutation-based fault localization. Softw. Test. Verif. Reliab. **25**, 605–628 (2015)
28. Shen, W., et al.: Munn: mutation analysis of neural networks. In: QRS-C (2018)
29. Socher, R., et al.: Recursive deep models for semantic compositionality over a sentiment treebank. In: EMNLP (2013)
30. Touvron, H., et al.: Llama 2: open foundation and fine-tuned chat models. arXiv:2307.09288 (2023)
31. Uesato, J., et al.: Rigorous agent evaluation: an adversarial approach to uncover catastrophic failures. arXiv:1812.01647 (2018)
32. Wang, A., et al.: Glue: a multi-task benchmark and analysis platform for natural language understanding. arXiv:1804.07461 (2018)
33. Wang, J.O.: Adversarial sample detection for deep neural network through model mutation testing. In: ICSE (2019)
34. Wang, X., et al.: Large language models are implicitly topic models: explaining and finding good demonstrations for in-context learning. arXiv:2301.11916 (2023)
35. Wang, Y., et al.: A theoretical understanding of self-correction through in-context alignment. In: NeurIPS (2024)
36. Wei, J., et al.: Chain-of-thought prompting elicits reasoning in large language models. In: NeurIPS (2022)
37. Wei, Z., et al.: Jailbreak and guard aligned language models with only few in-context demonstrations. arXiv preprint arXiv:2310.06387 (2023)
38. Wu, Q., et al.: Autogen: enabling next-gen llm applications via multi-agent conversation framework. arXiv:2308.08155 (2023)
39. Xie, S.M., et al.: An explanation of in-context learning as implicit bayesian inference. arXiv:2111.02080 (2021)
40. Yang, J., et al.: Generalized out-of-distribution detection: a survey. Int. J. Comput. Vis. (2024)
41. Yu, J., et al.: Gptfuzzer: red teaming large language models with auto-generated jailbreak prompts. arXiv:2309.10253 (2023)
42. Zhang, J.M., et al.: Machine learning testing: survey, landscapes and horizons. IEEE Trans. Softw. Eng. **48**(1), 1–36 (2020)
43. Zhang, K., et al.: Batch-icl: Effective, efficient, and order-agnostic in-context learning. In: ACL (2024)
44. Zhang, X., et al.: Character-level convolutional networks for text classification. In: NeurIPS (2015)
45. Zhang, X., et al.: A mutation-based method for multi-modal jailbreaking attack detection. arXiv:2312.10766 (2023)
46. Zheng, L., et al.: Judging LLM-as-a-judge with MT-bench and chatbot arena. In: NeurIPS (2024)

A Derivative-Based Membership Algorithm for Enhanced Regular Expressions

Mengxi Wang[1,2], Chunmei Dong[1,2], Weihao Su[1,2], Chengyao Peng[1,2], and Haiming Chen[1(✉)]

[1] Key Laboratory of System Software (Chinese Academy of Sciences) and State Key Laboratory of Computer Science, Institute of Software, Chinese Academy of Sciences, Beijing, China
{wangmx,dongcm,suwh,pengcy,chm}@ios.ac.cn
[2] University of Chinese Academy of Sciences, Beijing, China

Abstract. Enhanced regular expressions (EREs), which extend standard regular expressions with shuffle and counting operators, provide exponentially more succinct descriptions of regular languages. The membership problem, determining whether a given word w belongs to the language generated by an ERE E, is fundamental to numerous applications. However, efficient solutions for the membership problem of unconstrained EREs have remained elusive. This paper introduces a derivative for the counting operator and rigorously proves its correctness. We then leverage this derivative to design a membership algorithm for unconstrained EREs and analyze its time complexity based on a lemma establishing the relationship between the size of the derivative and the expression. We further propose algorithms based on the proposed derivatives to generate positive and negative words of specific lengths for EREs. The performance of the membership algorithm is then evaluated on real-world EREs. Finally, we validate the correctness of two existing inference algorithms that previously lacked formal correctness guarantees due to the absence of practical membership algorithms for unconstrained EREs.

Keywords: Membership · Enhanced regular expressions · Derivatives · Complexity · Positive and negative words

1 Introduction

Regular expressions (REs) have found widespread application in diverse fields, including reasoning concurrent systems, software engineering, deep packet inspection, and constraint solving [7–9,22,27,29] etc. Many of these applications utilize counting or shuffle (or interleaving) operators. The counting operator restricts the number of repetitions for specific subexpressions, while the shuffle

Chunmei Dong is currently employed at CMB Network Technology, Shenzhen.

operator enables the concatenation of patterns in any order. These operators significantly enhance the succinctness of REs. In fact, Gelade et al. [10] demonstrated that REs with shuffle are double exponentially more succinct than standard REs. However, incorporating counting and shuffle operators increases the complexity of their related decision problems: the equivalence problem for REs with counting and shuffle is already proven EXPSPACE-complete [12], while the problem for those without are only complete in PSPACE [23]. In this paper, we focus on the membership problem for REs with counting and shuffle operators, which we refer to as enhanced regular expressions (EREs).

The membership problem for a RE E and a string w involves determining whether w belongs to the regular language generated by E. Kilpeläinen and Tuhkanen demonstrated that membership testing for languages described by REs with counting operators is tractable [16]. Conversely, Mayer et al. proved that the membership problem for REs with shuffle operators is NP-complete [20]. Broda et al. present constructions of several succinct automata for REs with shuffle and intersection, though they do not address the complexity of this construction [2]. Notably, the membership problem for standard REs is complete in NL [15]. Gelade et al. further established a PSPACE upper bound for the membership problem of EREs via a specific NFA construction [12]. Hovland proposed a membership algorithm for a restricted subclass of REs (strongly 1-unambiguous regular expressions) with unordered concatenation (a confined form of shuffle) and numerical constraints, i.e. countings, [14]. Ghelli et al. presented algorithms based on constraint translation for a set of EREs [13] (later extended to handle unordered concatenation [6]). Wang presents a polynomial-time membership algorithm for single-occurrence ERE by constructing equivalent single-occurrence finite automata [28]. These approaches remain limited to EREs with specific restrictions, such as single-symbol occurrence and repetition. Consequently, a practical algorithm or the precise complexity of the membership problem for unrestricted EREs remains open problems.

Brzozowski introduced derivatives for standard regular expressions [4]. Sulzmann and Thiemann extended this concept to include REs with the shuffle operator [24]. This paper introduces a derivative for the counting operator in EREs and formally proves its correctness from a structural perspective. Based on these theoretical foundations, we propose a membership algorithm for unconstrained EREs. We then establish a lemma that elucidates the relationship between the size of the derivative and the size of the ERE, proving its correctness. This lemma enables us to analyze the time complexity of our membership algorithm. Based on the proposed derivatives, we further propose two algorithms for generating positive and negative words of fixed lengths for EREs. Experimental evaluation using both positive and negative examples derived from realistic EREs demonstrates the effectiveness and practicality of Algorithm 1. Furthermore, we leverage our algorithm to evaluate the correctness of previously untested inference algorithms for EREs due to the absence of reliable membership algorithms. Notably, the correctness of all algorithms operating on EREs and their subclasses can be similarly verified using our proposed methods. Moreover, XSD and Relax NG [5,21], two prominent schema languages, support counting (XSD) and unconstrained shuffle (Relax NG) respectively. Since the content models of these schemas are expressed as EREs, our membership algorithm proves valuable for XML validation [25], particularly for documents conforming to these schema standards.

This paper is organized as follows. Section 2 introduces the necessary concepts employed this work. Section 3 presents our membership algorithm for EREs, analyzes its time complexity, and provides algorithms for generating positive and negative words of specific lengths for experimental evaluation. Section 4 reports the experimental results, while Sect. 5 concludes with a discussion of future directions.

2   Preliminaries

Let Σ be a finite alphabet. A word $w = a_1 a_2 ... a_n$ is a finite sequence of symbols over Σ. Denote by Σ^* the set of all words over Σ. Standard regular expressions (REs) over Σ are defined recursively as follows: $\varnothing$ (the empty set), ε (the empty string), $a \in \Sigma$, the Kleene-star E^*, union $E_1 + E_2$, and concatenation $E_1 \cdot E_2$, where E, E_1, and E_2 are REs. For readability, we often use juxtaposition, $E_1 E_2$, to represent concatenation $E_1 \cdot E_2$. The language of an expression E, denoted by $L(E)$, is defined as follows: $L(\varnothing) = \varnothing$; $L(\varepsilon) = \{\varepsilon\}$; $L(a) = \{a\}$; $L(E^*) = L(E)^*$; $L(E_1 E_2) = L(E_1)L(E_2)$; $L(E_1 + E_2) = L(E_1) \cup L(E_2)$.

We extend standard REs to incorporate counting and interleaving as EREs, providing the corresponding definitions below.

Definition 1. *(See [11]) Let $\mathbb{N} = \{0, 1, 2, ...\}$ and $\mathbb{N}_0 = \mathbb{N} \backslash \{0\}$. Every RE is an ERE. For an ERE E, the counting expression $E^{[m,n]}$ is also an ERE, where $m \in \mathbb{N}$, $n \in \mathbb{N}_0 \cup \{\infty\}$ and $m \leq n$. The language of the counting expression is defined as: $L(E^{[m,n]}) = \bigcup_{i=m}^{n} L(E)^i$.*

Since E^* is simply an abbreviation for $E^{[0,\infty]}$, we omit the Kleene-star operator in the remainder of this paper. An ERE is in normal form if all its counting nullable subexpressions have a lower bound of zero (i.e., $m = 0$ for every subexpression $E_1^{[m,n]}$). Any ERE with counting can be normalized in linear time [11]. Consequently, we assume all expressions used in this paper are in normal form. An ERE E is nullable if $\varepsilon \in L(E)$. And a sub-expression $E_1^{[m,n]}$ is nullable if and only if its lower bound m equals zero.

For example, $L(a^{[2,4]}) = \{aa, aaa, aaaa\}$.

Definition 2. *[26] The shuffle operator (denoted by &) on two words is defined inductively as follows:*

1. *For $a \in \Sigma$, $a\&\varepsilon = \varepsilon\&a = \{a\}$.*
2. *For $a, b \in \Sigma$, and $x, y \in \Sigma^*$, $ax\&by = \{az | z \in x\&by\} \cup \{bz | z \in ax\&y\}$.*

For instance, $L(ab\&cd) = \{abcd, acbd, acdb, cadb, cabd, cdab\}$.

This definition extends to languages as follows. If L_1 and L_2 are two languages, then $L_1\&L_2 = \{w \mid w = x\&y, x \in L_1 \text{ and } y \in L_2\}$. We can further extend the shuffle operator to EREs. For EREs E_1 and E_2, $E_1\&E_2$ is an ERE, and $L(E_1\&E_2) = L(E_1)\&L(E_2)$.

EREs are simplified by the following axioms at linear time complexity:

$$
\begin{aligned}
E\varnothing &= \varnothing E = \varnothing, \\
E + \varnothing &= \varnothing + E = E, \qquad &\varnothing^{[m,n]} = \varnothing, \qquad &E\varepsilon = \varepsilon E = E, \\
E\&\varnothing &= \varnothing\&E = \varnothing, &E^{[0,0]} = \varepsilon, &E\&\varepsilon = \varepsilon\&E = E.
\end{aligned}
\tag{1}
$$

So we assume that all the EREs in this paper are simplified.

Definition 3. *For any ERE E, we define a function $Null\colon ERE \to \{\varnothing, \varepsilon\}$ to be*

$$
Null(E) = \begin{cases} \varepsilon, & \text{if } \varepsilon \in L(E), \\ \varnothing, & \text{otherwise.} \end{cases}
\tag{2}
$$

which can be calculated as follows:

$$
Null(\varnothing) = Null(a) = \varnothing,
\tag{3}
$$

$$
Null(\varepsilon) = \varepsilon,
\tag{4}
$$

$$
Null(E_1 + E_2) = Null(E_1) + Null(E_2),
\tag{5}
$$

$$
Null(E_1 E_2) = Null(E_1)Null(E_2),
\tag{6}
$$

$$
Null(E_1\&E_2) = Null(E_1)Null(E_2),
\tag{7}
$$

$$
Null(E_1^{[m,n]}) = \begin{cases} \varepsilon, & \text{if } m = 0, \\ \varnothing, & \text{otherwise.} \end{cases}
\tag{8}
$$

Definition 4. *[10, 11] The size of an ERE E over Σ, denoted by $|E|$, is the number of symbols and operators in E plus the sum of the sizes of the binary representations of all integers appearing within E.*

For a real number $i \geq 0$, $\lceil i \rceil$ denotes the smallest integer not less than i. Formally, the size of an ERE is defined as follows: $|\varnothing| = |\varepsilon| = |a| = 1$ for any $a \in \Sigma$; $|E_1 E_2| = |E_1 + E_2| = |E_1\&E_2| = |E_1| + |E_2| + 1$; and $|E^{[m,n]}| = |E| + \lceil \log m \rceil + \lceil \log n \rceil$. The size of a finite word w, denoted by $|w|$, is the number of symbols in w.

3   The Membership Algorithm and Applications

In this section, we first propose an extension of Brzozowski's derivatives to EREs in Sect. 3.1. Based on the extension, we propose a membership algorithm for unconstrained EREs in Sect. 3.2 and analyze its computational complexity in Sect. 3.3. As an application of the derivatives we present two novel algorithms to generate positive and negative words for EREs in Sect. 3.4.

3.1   The Theoretical Foundations

This section outlines the theoretical foundations of our derivative-based algorithm. We begin by introducing the concept and calculation rules for derivatives in the context of EREs.

For a language L and a finite word w, the derivative of L with respect to w is defined as $w^{-1}(L) = \{s \mid ws \in L\}$ [4]. The following theorem presents recursive rules for calculating the derivative of an ERE E with respect to a symbol a:

Theorem 1. *If E is an ERE, the derivative of E with respect to a symbol a can be calculated recursively as follows:*

$$a^{-1}(\varnothing) = a^{-1}(\varepsilon) = \varnothing, \tag{9}$$

$$a^{-1}(b) = \begin{cases} \varepsilon, & \text{if } b = a, \\ \varnothing, & \text{otherwise,} \end{cases} \tag{10}$$

$$a^{-1}(E_1 + E_2) = a^{-1}(E_1) + a^{-1}(E_2), \tag{11}$$

$$a^{-1}(E_1 E_2) = a^{-1}(E_1)E_2 + \text{Null}(E_1)a^{-1}(E_2), \tag{12}$$

$$a^{-1}(E_1 \& E_2) = a^{-1}(E_1)\& E_2 + a^{-1}(E_2)\& E_1, \tag{13}$$

$$a^{-1}(E_1^{[m,n]}) = a^{-1}(E_1)E_1^{[m\ \dot-\ 1,n\ \dot-\ 1]}, \tag{14}$$

where $\dot-$ is defined as $m \dot- 1 = \begin{cases} \infty, & \text{if } m = \infty, \\ 0, & \text{if } m = 0, \\ m-1, & \text{otherwise.} \end{cases}$

Proof. Derivatives for standard regular expressions have been established [4] as detailed in Eqs. (9) to (12). Sulzmann and Thiemann extended these derivations to encompass general synchronous shuffling [24] and exemplified in Eq. (13). This proof focuses on deriving the rule for counting EREs shown in Eq. (14). For a non-negative integer n and ERE E, let E^n denote the concatenation of E with itself n times, i.e., $E^n = \underbrace{E...E}_{n}$.

1. If $m = 0$, and if $n = \infty$, then

$$a^{-1}(E_1^{[0,\infty]}) = a^{-1}(E_1)E_1^{[0,\infty]},$$

which is consistent with the derivative of Kleene-star in [4]. Otherwise, $n \neq \infty$, and when $Null(E_1) = \varnothing$, we have:

$$a^{-1}(E_1^{[0,n]}) = a^{-1}(E_1^0 + E_1^1 + \ldots + E_1^n)$$

$$= a^{-1}(\varepsilon) + \sum_{i=1}^{n} a^{-1}(E_1 E_1^{i-1})$$

$$= \sum_{i=1}^{n} (a^{-1}(E_1) E_1^{i-1} + Null(E_1) a^{-1}(E_1^{i-1}))$$

$$= a^{-1}(E_1) \sum_{i=1}^{n} E_1^{i-1} = a^{-1}(E_1) E_1^{[0,n-1]}.$$

When $Null(E_1) = \varepsilon$, we have

$$\sum_{i=1}^{n} (a^{-1}(E_1) E_1^{i-1} + Null(E_1) a^{-1}(E_1^{i-1}))$$

$$= \sum_{i=1}^{n} (a^{-1}(E_1) E_1^{i-1} + a^{-1}(E_1) E_1^{i-2} + Null(E_1) a^{-1}(E_1^{i-2}))$$

$$= \sum_{i=1}^{n} (a^{-1}(E_1) E_1^{i-1} + a^{-1}(E_1) E_1^{i-2} + \ldots + + a^{-1}(E_1) E_1^0)$$

$$= a^{-1}(E_1) \sum_{i=1}^{n} \sum_{j=1}^{i} E_1^{j-1}$$

$$= a^{-1}(E_1) \sum_{i=1}^{n} E_1^{i-1}$$

$$= a^{-1}(E_1) E_1^{[0,n-1]}.$$

2. If $m \geq 1$, we have:

$$a^{-1}(E_1^{[m,n]}) = a^{-1}(E_1^m + E_1^{m+1} + \ldots + E_1^n)$$

$$= \sum_{i=m}^{n} a^{-1}(E_1 E_1^{i-1}) = \sum_{i=m}^{n} (a^{-1}(E_1) E_1^{i-1} + Null(E_1) a^{-1}(E_1^{i-1}))$$

$$= a^{-1}(E_1) \sum_{i=m}^{n} E_1^{i-1} = a^{-1}(E_1) E_1^{[m-1,n-1]}.$$

Similarly, when $n = \infty$, we get $a^{-1}(E_1^{[m,\infty]}) = a^{-1}(E_1) E_1^{[m-1,\infty]}$,

The definition is extended to words by: $\varepsilon^{-1}(E) = E$, $(wa)^{-1}(E) = a^{-1}(w^{-1}(E))$. The following theorem can be easily extended to EREs.

Theorem 2. [4] For a finite word w and an RE E, $w \in L(E)$ if and only if $\varepsilon \in L(w^{-1}(E))$.

3.2   The Membership Algorithm

Based on Theorems 1 and 2, we present a derivative-based membership algorithm for EREs in Algorithm 1. Algorithm 1 determines whether a given word w belongs to the language defined by an ERE E. It returns **T** (True) if $w \in L(E)$ and **F** (False) otherwise. The algorithm adopts the skeleton of Brzozowski's derivative-based membership algorithm for standard REs [4] and extends it to EREs, the correctness of which is guaranteed by Theorem 2.

Algorithm 1 initially assigns E to a variable named DE, representing the current derivative. Subsequently, it iterates through each symbol a in w from left to right. For every symbol, it calculates the derivative of the current DE with respect to a and updates DE with the result. If the computed derivative is empty ($\varnothing$), the algorithm terminates and returns **F**. Otherwise, it proceeds to scan the next symbol in w, recursively calculating derivatives until all symbols in w have been processed. Finally, if the last calculated derivative DE is nullable (i.e., $Null(DE) = \varepsilon$), the algorithm returns **T**; otherwise, it returns **F**.

Algorithm 1. MEMBERSHIP(E, w)

Require: An ERE E and a word $w = a_1 a_2 ... a_n$
Ensure: **T** if $w \in L(E)$ or **F** otherwise
1: $DE \leftarrow E$
2: **for** $i = 1, \ldots, n$ **do**
3:       $DE \leftarrow a_i^{-1}(DE)$;
4:       **if** $DE = \varnothing$ **then**
5:           **return F**
6: **if** $Null(DE) = \varepsilon$ **then**
7:       **return T**
8: **else**
9:       **return F**

For the expression $E = (a^{[0,3]} + b)(a + b^{[2,7]}\&c)$ and input word $w = aabbbc$, the membership testing process proceeds as follows:

1. Initialize the derivative DE with E: $DE \leftarrow E = (a^{[0,3]} + b)(a + b^{[2,7]}\&c)$.
2. Let w_i represent the i-th element of w. Reading $w_1 = a$, we calculate the derivative of DE with respect to a:

$$a^{-1}(DE) = a^{-1}((a^{[0,3]} + b)(a + b^{[2,7]}\&c)) = a^{[0,2]}(a + b^{[2,7]}\&c) + \varepsilon.$$

Since the derivative is not empty ($\neq \varnothing$), we update DE:

$$DE \leftarrow a^{[0,2]}(a + b^{[2,7]}\&c) + \varepsilon$$

as shown in Fig. 1.

3. Reading $w_2 = a$, we again calculate the derivative with respect to a:

$$a^{-1}(DE) = a^{-1}(a^{[0,2]}(a + b^{[2,7]}\&c) + \varepsilon) = a^{[0,1]}(a + b^{[2,7]}\&c) + \varepsilon.$$

We update DE:
$$DE \leftarrow a^{[0,1]}(a + b^{[2,7]}\&c) + \varepsilon$$

as shown in Fig. 2.

4. Reading $w_3 = b$, we compute the derivative with respect to b:

$$b^{-1}(DE) = b^{-1}(a^{[0,1]}(a + b^{[2,7]}\&c) + \varepsilon) = b^{[1,6]}\&c.$$

Updating DE:

$$DE \leftarrow b^{[1,6]}\&c$$

as shown in Fig. 3.

5. For $w_4 = b$, we calculate:

$$b^{-1}(DE) = b^{-1}(b^{[1,6]}\&c) = b^{[0,5]}\&c$$

and update DE:

$$DE \leftarrow b^{[0,5]}\&c$$

as shown in Fig. 4.

6. For $w_5 = b$, we calculate:

$$b^{-1}(DE) = b^{-1}(b^{[0,5]}\&c) = b^{[0,4]}\&c$$

and update DE:

$$DE \leftarrow b^{[0,4]}\&c$$

as shown in Fig. 5.

7. Finally, for $w_6 = c$, we have:

$$c^{-1}(DE) = c^{-1}(b^{[0,4]}\&c) = b^{[0,4]}.$$

Updating DE:
$$DE \leftarrow b^{[0,4]}$$

as shown in Fig. 6.

Since $\text{Null}(b^{[0,4]}) = \varepsilon$ according to Definition 3, we conclude that $w_1 \in L(E)$.

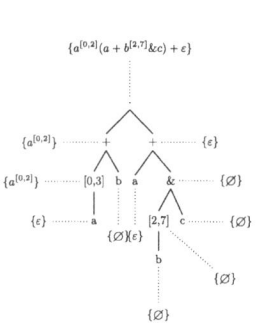

Fig. 1. Calculate the derivative of $(a^{[0,3]} + b)$ $(a + b^{[2,7]}\&c)$ w.r.t a.

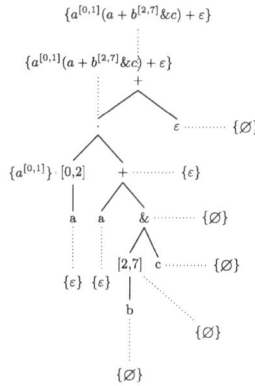

Fig. 2. Calculate the derivative of $a^{[0,2]}(a+b^{[2,7]}\&c) + \varepsilon$ w.r.t a.

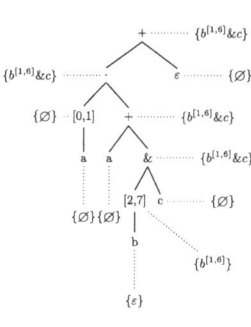

Fig. 3. Calculate the derivative of $a^{[0,1]}(a+b^{[2,7]}\&c) + \varepsilon$ w.r.t b.

Additionally, for word $w_2 = abcc$, as

$$w_2^{-1}(E) = w_2^{-1}((a^{[0,3]} + b)(a + b^{[2,7]}\&c)) = \varnothing,$$

$w_2 \notin L(E)$.

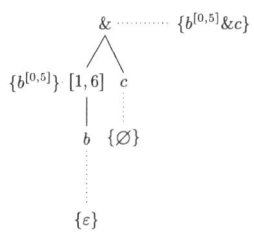

Fig. 4. Calculate the derivative of $b^{[1,6]}\&c$ w.r.t b.

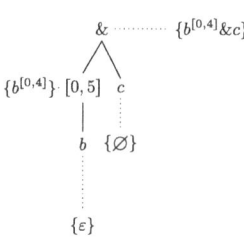

Fig. 5. Calculate the derivative of $b^{[0,5]}\&c$ w.r.t b.

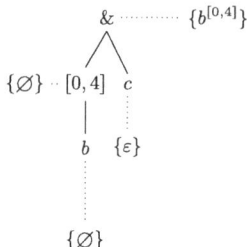

Fig. 6. Calculate the derivative of $b^{[0,4]}\&c$ w.r.t c.

3.3   Complexity Analysis

The time complexity of our algorithm is intrinsically tied to the size of derivatives. We establish an upper bound on derivative size through the following lemma.

Lemma 1. *For an ERE E and symbol a, we have $|a^{-1}(E)| \leq (r_E+1)|E|$, where r_E represents the sum of occurrences of counting, concatenation, and shuffle operators in E.*

Proof. When $a = \varepsilon$, $|a^{-1}(E)| = |E| \leqslant (r_E + 1)|E|$, the lemma is true. Now we consider the case $a \neq \varepsilon$ in the following. It is clear that when $E = \varnothing$ or $E = \varepsilon$, $|E| = 0$, $r_E = 0$, $|a^{-1}(\varnothing)| = |a^{-1}(\varepsilon)| = |\varnothing| = 0 \leqslant (r_E + 1)|E|$. If $E = b$ ($b \in \Sigma$), $|a^{-1}(b)| = |\varepsilon|$ or $|\varnothing| = 0 \leq (r_E + 1)|E| = |E|$. Suppose that the claim is true for regular expressions E_1, E_2, the proof proceeds by induction on the structure of E as follows.

1. For $E = E_1^{[m,n]}$, $r_E = r_{E_1} + 1$. If $m \geq 1$, $|E| = |E_1| + \lceil \log m \rceil + \lceil \log n \rceil$.

$$
\begin{aligned}
|a^{-1}(E_1^{[m,n]})| &= |a^{-1}(E_1)E_1^{[m-1,n-1]}| \\
&\leq |a^{-1}(E_1)| + 1 + |E_1| + \lceil \log m \rceil + \lceil \log n \rceil \\
&\leq (r_{E_1} + 2)|E_1| + \lceil \log m \rceil + \lceil \log n \rceil + 1 \\
&\leq (r_{E_1} + 2)(|E_1| + \lceil \log m \rceil + \lceil \log n \rceil) \\
&= (r_E + 1)|E|.
\end{aligned}
$$

In the same way, the theorem is still established when $m = 0$.

2. For $E = E_1 + E_2$, we get $r_E = r_{E_1} + r_{E_2}$, $|E| = |E_1| + |E_2| + 1$.

$$
\begin{aligned}
|a^{-1}(E_1 + E_2)| &= |a^{-1}(E_1) + a^{-1}(E_2)| \\
&= |a^{-1}(E_1)| + |a^{-1}(E_2)| + 1 \\
&\leq (r_{E_1} + 1)|E_1| + (r_{E_2} + 1)|E_2| + 1 \\
&\leq (r_{E_1} + r_{E_2} + 1)(|E_1| + |E_2| + 1) \\
&= (r_E + 1)|E|.
\end{aligned}
$$

3. For $E = E_1 E_2$, first we have $r_E = r_{E_1} + r_{E_2} + 1$, $|E| = |E_1| + |E_2| + 1$.

$$
\begin{aligned}
|a^{-1}(E_1 E_2)| &= |a^{-1}(E_1)E_2 + Null(E_1)a^{-1}(E_2)| \\
&\leq |a^{-1}(E_1)E_2 + a^{-1}(E_2)| \\
&\leq |a^{-1}(E_1)| + |E_2| + |a^{-1}(E_2)| + 2 \\
&\leq (r_{E_1} + 1)|E_1| + (r_{E_2} + 2)|E_2| + 2 \\
&\leq (r_{E_1} + r_{E_2} + 2)(|E_1| + |E_2| + 1) \\
&= (r_E + 1)|E|.
\end{aligned}
$$

4. For $E = E_1 \& E_2$, we have $r_E = r_{E_1} + r_{E_2} + 1$, $|E| = |E_1| + |E_2| + 1$.

$$
|a^{-1}(E_1 \& E_2)| = |a^{-1}(E_1)\& E_2 + a^{-1}(E_2)\& E_1|.
$$

For the case $r_{E_1} = r_{E_2} = 0$,

$$
\begin{aligned}
|a^{-1}(E_1)\& E_2 + a^{-1}(E_2)E_1| &\leq |\varepsilon \& E_2 + \varepsilon \& E_1| \\
&= |E_1 + E_2| = |E_1| + |E_2| + 1 \\
&\leq (r_E + 1)|E|
\end{aligned}
$$

Else for the case $r_{E_1} + r_{E_2} > 0$,

$$
\begin{aligned}
|a^{-1}(E_1)\&E_2 + a^{-1}(E_2)\&E_1| &= |a^{-1}(E_1)| + |E_2| + |a^{-1}(E_2)| + |E_1| + 3\\
&\leq (r_{E_1} + 1)|E_1| + |E_2|\\
&\quad + (r_{E_2} + 1)|E_2| + |E_1| + 3\\
&\leq (r_{E_1} + r_{E_2} + 2)(|E_1| + |E_2| + 1)\\
&= (r_E + 1)|E|.
\end{aligned}
$$

Now we analyze the calculation of derivatives. The derivative of a RE E w.r.t. a symbol a can be obtained in $O(|E|)$ time. First we convert E to a syntax tree in $O(|E|)$ time [3]. Then we calculate the derivative with Eqs. (9) to (14) in a bottom-up manner on the syntax tree, which also takes $O(|E|)$ time. For RE E and a word $w = a_1a_2a_3...a_n$, because our membership algorithm recursively calculates the ith derivative of E (denoted as DE_i, $i = 0, 1, ..., n-1$), so the time complexity of the algorithm is

$$
O(T) = O(|DE_0| + |DE_1| + |DE_2| + ... + |DE_{n-1}|),
$$

where

$$
DE_0 = E, DE_1 = a_1^{-1}(DE_0), DE_2 = a_2^{-1}(DE_1), ..., DE_{n-1} = a_{n-1}^{-1}(DE_{n-2}).
$$

Consider the worst case. From Lemma 1, for an ERE E, we have

$$
|DE_1| \leq (r_{DE_0} + 1)|DE_0| \leq |DE_0|^2.
$$

In the same way we can get

$$
|DE_2| \leq (r_{DE_1} + 1)|DE_1| \leq |DE_1|^2
$$

and

$$
\begin{aligned}
|DE_3| &\leq (r_{DE_2} + 1)|DE_2| \leq |DE_2|^2, ..., |DE_n|\\
&\leq (r_{DE_{n-1}} + 1)|DE_{n-1}| \leq |DE_{n-1}|^2.
\end{aligned}
$$

For $|DE_i| = |DE_{i-1}|^2$, we have

$$
\begin{aligned}
O(T) &= O(|DE_0| + |DE_0|^2 + |DE_0|^4 + ... + |DE_0|^{2^{n-1}})\\
&< O(|DE_0| + |DE_0|^2 + |DE_0|^3 + ... + |DE_0|^{2^{n-1}})\\
&= O\left(\frac{|DE_0|(1 - |DE_0|^{2^{n-1}})}{1 - |DE_0|}\right) = O(|DE_0|^{2^{n-1}}) = O(|E|^{2^{n-1}}).
\end{aligned}
$$

So the time complexity of the algorithm is less than $O(|E|^{2^{n-1}})$.

3.4   Generation of Positive and Negative Words of Specified Lengths

Positive and negative examples are essential in, e.g. example-based program synthesis algorithms [1]. String generation tasks frequently encounter length constraints, limiting the permissible length of generated results [19,31]. This section
leverages the derivatives introduced in Sect. 3.1 to present an application for
generating both positive and negative words of specified lengths.

We define $\mathsf{First}(E) = \{b \mid bw \in L(E), b \in \Sigma, w \in \Sigma^*\}$, which denotes the
set of first symbols in the language of E. To simplify derivatives, we employ
a rewrite system denoted as SIM (Fig. 7). Equations (15) to (17) are based on
the associativity, commutativity and idempotence of $+$; Equations (18) and (19)
are based on associativity and commutativity of $\&$; Equation (20) is based on
distributivity of $\&$ over $+$.

$$E_1 + (E_2 + E_3) = (E_1 + E_2) + E_3, \tag{15}$$
$$E_1 + E_2 = E_2 + E_1, \tag{16}$$
$$E_1 + E_1 = E_1, \tag{17}$$
$$E_1 \& (E_2 \& E_3) = (E_1 \& E_2) \& E_3, \tag{18}$$
$$E_1 \& E_2 = E_2 \& E_1, \tag{19}$$
$$(E_1 + E_2) \& E_3 = (E_1 \& E_3) + (E_2 \& E_3). \tag{20}$$

Fig. 7. The rewrite system SIM, where $E_i \in ERE$.

Utilizing Equations (15) to (17), the set of simplified derivatives of an ERE
E is finite [24]. Denoting the set of all derivatives of an ERE as $\mathcal{D}_E$, we define
$\equiv_{\mathsf{SIM}}$ as the least congruence relation generated by Fig. 7. The quotient set of
$\mathcal{D}_E$ with respect to $\equiv_{\mathsf{SIM}}$ is denoted as $\mathcal{D}_E / \equiv_{\mathsf{SIM}}$. Subsequently, we can construct
deterministic finite automata directly from EREs according to the following
definition.

Definition 5. *The derivative automaton $M_\mathcal{D}(E)$ of an ERE E is defined by a
5-tuple $(Q_\mathcal{D}, \Sigma, \delta_\mathcal{D}, E, F_\mathcal{D})$, where*
$Q_\mathcal{D} = \mathcal{D}_E / \equiv_{\mathsf{SIM}}$,
$\delta_d(q, a) = a^{-1}(q)$, *for $q \in Q_\mathcal{D}$ and $a \in \Sigma$,*
$F_\mathcal{D} = \{q \in Q_\mathcal{D} \mid Null(q) = \varepsilon\}$.

Evidently we have:

Theorem 3. $L(M_\mathcal{D}(E)) = L(E)$.

Building on this construction, we propose two algorithms as follows:

Algorithms 2 and 3 both take an ERE E and a positive integer k as input.
They initially set the witness word w to the empty string ε.

Algorithm 2 searches for positive words of length k accepted by E. Initially,
it sets a set of derivative $\mathcal{E}$ to $\varnothing$ (Line 1). It then selects a symbol a from

---

Algorithm 2. POSITIVE(E, k, w)

Require: An ERE E, a natural number k and a finite word w
Ensure: A positive word $w \in L(E)$ of length k or $\varnothing$ if w does not exist and a set
  1: $\mathcal{E} \leftarrow \varnothing$
  2: **for all** $a \in First(E)$ **do**
  3:      **if** $Null(a^{-1}(E)) = \varepsilon \land |w| = k - 1$ **then**
  4:          **return** wa
  5:      **else**
  6:          $E \leftarrow \mathsf{SIM}(a^{-1}(E))$
  7:          **if** $E \notin \mathcal{E}$ **then**
  8:              $\mathcal{E} \leftarrow \mathcal{E} \cup \{E\}$
  9:              **return** POSITIVE$(E, k - 1, wa)$
 10: **return** $\varnothing$

Algorithm 3. NEGATIVE(E, k, w)

Require: An ERE E, a natural number k and a finite word w
Ensure: A negative word $w \notin L(E)$ of length k or $\varnothing$ if w does not exist
  1: $\mathcal{E} \leftarrow \varnothing$
  2: **if** $|w| \leq k - 1$ **then**
  3:      **if** $First(E) \neq \Sigma$ **then**
  4:          Pick a from $\Sigma \setminus First(E)$
  5:          **return** $wa^{k-|w|}$
  6:      **else**
  7:          **for** $a \in First(E)$ **do**
  8:              $E \leftarrow \mathsf{SIM}(a^{-1}(E))$
  9:              **if** $E \notin \mathcal{E}$ **then**
 10:                  $\mathcal{E} \leftarrow \mathcal{E} \cup \{E\}$
 11:                  **return** NEGATIVE$(E, k - 1, wa)$
 12: **else**
 13:      **if** $Null(E) = \varepsilon$ **then**
 14:          **return** w
 15: **return** $\varnothing$

---

the *First* set of E (Line 2) and tests if $a^{-1}(E)$ is nullable, indicating that a is accepted by E. This test occurs when the length of the current witness word w is $k - 1$ (Line 3). If the condition holds, the algorithm returns the word wa (Line 4); otherwise, it rewrites E to its derivative with respect to a, simplifies the resulting ERE using the rewrite system SIM (Line 6). If E is not similar to any EREs in $\mathcal{E}$ (Line 7), the algorithm adds the simplified ERE to $\mathcal{E}$, decrements k, and updates w to wa (Lines 8 to 9). The search continues recursively until a positive word of length k is found or no such word exists in $L(E)$, in which case the algorithm returns $\varnothing$ (Line 10).

Similarly, Algorithm 3 begin with seting a set of derivative $\mathcal{E}$ to $\varnothing$ (Line 1). Then it checks if the length of w is less than $k-1$ (Line 2). If so, it attempts to find a symbol that leads the current derivative into the sink state of the completed DFA $M_{\mathcal{D}}(E)$ by testing if the *First* set of E is equal to the alphabet Σ (Line

3). If the *First* set is not universal (i.e., $\Sigma\backslash\mathsf{First}(E) \neq \varnothing$), then $wa^{-1}E = \varnothing$. By Theorem 1, $(wa\Sigma^*)^{-1}E = \varnothing$, and the algorithm returns a negative witness $wa^{k-|w|}$. If the *First* set of E is universal, the algorithm iterates through each symbol in the *First* set of E (Line 7) to rewrite E into its simplified derivatives (Line 8). If there is no such ERE similar to E modulo $\equiv_{\mathsf{SIM}}$ as recorded in $\mathcal{E}$, the search continues with the new ERE recorded, the word updated, and the parameter k subtracted by 1 as in Algorithm 2 in Lines 10 to 11. When the length of w reaches k, we check whether w is accepted by the initial ERE. Once the length of w reaches k, the procedure checks if the current w is accepted by the initial ERE (Line 13). If rejected (effectively a proper prefix of $L(E)$ at this point), the algorithm backtracks and continues searching; otherwise, it returns the k-length word. The search persists until a non-empty word is returned or no negative word of length k exists, in which case it returns $\varnothing$.

4   Experiments

We conducted two experiments using Java on a machine with a 2.4 GHz Intel Core i5 CPU and 8 GB of RAM. Section 4.1 evaluated the practical performance of our membership algorithm, while Sect. 4.2 demonstrated correctness checking for two previously unverified inference algorithms, made possible by the availability of a membership algorithm for unconstrained extended regular expressions.

4.1   Experiment on Performance

To evaluate the practical performance of our membership algorithm, we selected EREs from the corpus compiled in [17]. This corpus, comprising 1,107,596 EREs extracted from Relax NG, XSD, DTD, and RegExLib[1], represents a diverse and extensive collection of real-world expressions. We randomly sampled four sets of EREs based on expression size: $(1 \leq |E| < 50)$, $(50 \leq |E| < 100)$, $(100 \leq |E| < 150)$, and $(150 \leq |E| < 200)$, with 100 expressions in each set. For each set, we generated 10,000 positive words and 10,000 negative words using the methods described in Sect. 3.4. We then input these EREs and the generated words into our algorithm, recording the membership check running time for each instance. To enhance clarity, we divided the x-axis into disjoint sections of 200 symbols (e.g., 1–199 to 4,800–4,999) and plotted the average running time for each section based on word size.

Our experiments on positive words measured the membership checking runtime of four sets of EREs against their corresponding positive samples. For each set of 100 EREs, we calculated the average runtime across all positive words. The results are presented in Fig. 8. As shown in Fig. 8, the algorithm's runtime increases with both word size and expression size. Notably, the average runtime for EREs with $150 \leq |E| < 200$ is significantly longer than for the other three

---

[1] http://www.regexlib.com/?AspxAutoDetectCookieSupport=1.

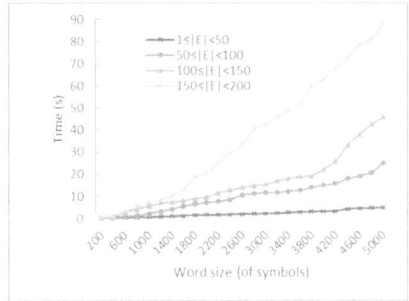

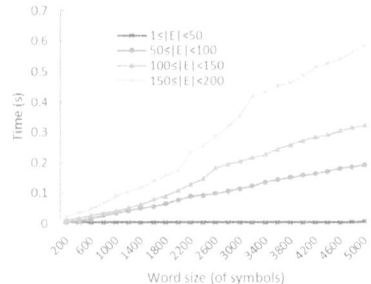

Fig. 8. Experiments on positive words   **Fig. 9.** Experiments on negative words

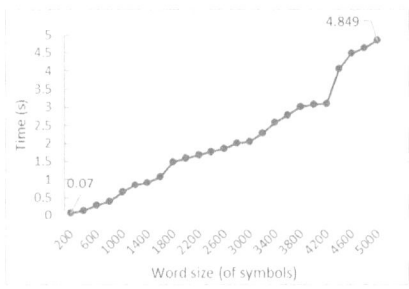

Fig. 10. Experiments on $(1 \leq |E| < 50)$

sets $(1 \leq |E| < 50$, $50 \leq |E| < 100$ and $100 \leq |E| < 150)$. While the runtime for long ERE is relatively higher, it is encouraging that the algorithm demonstrates efficiency on short expressions. Figure 10 provides detailed results for positive words with ERE sizes of $1 \leq |E| < 50$. We observe that average runtime across all word size segments remain below 5 s. Specifically, the average runtime for words smaller than 200 is only 0.07 s, while the algorithm takes an average of 4.849 s for words in the 4,800–4,999 size range.

Based on statistical analysis, 97.46% of the 1,107,596 EREs extracted from real-world data [17] have a size less than 50. This indicates that our algorithm not only provides a solution for the membership problem of unconstrained EREs but also proves effective and practical for the majority of real-world cases.

Experiments on negative words, as shown in Fig. 9, revealed remarkably efficient average runtime across all sets of EREs against their corresponding negative samples. This efficiency is consistent with our algorithm's design: it terminates as soon as the current derivative becomes empty ($\varnothing$) instead of processing the entire word.

4.2   Experiment on Correctness Checking

To evaluate the correctness of existing inference algorithms, we conducted experiments on two subclasses of EREs: ICHARE [30] and ICRE [18]. We selected these subclasses because they both support shuffle and lack constraints on repetition, unlike conflict-free REs, where repetition is limited to single symbols [6]. Our algorithm is the only known solution capable of handling this.

First, we utilized the GenICHARE algorithm [30] to learn ICHAREs from DBLP datasets: phdthesis, inproceedings, proceedings, www, and incollection. We then verified whether the learned ICHAREs encompassed all strings within the example sets. This involved checking if each string w in a sample set belonged to the language generated by the corresponding inferred ICHARE E, i.e., $w \in L(E)$. Experimental results confirmed that all words in the sample sets were contained within their respective inferred ICHAREs, demonstrating the correctness of the inference algorithm.

Similarly, we verified the correctness of the GenICRE algorithm [18] for inferring ICREs from DBLP datasets book and article. The results showed that GenICRE was also entirely accurate across all example sets. Table 1 summarizes the experimental results, encompassing dataset, dataset size, inferred EREs, membership checking time per dataset, and correctness rate. To conserve space, we employ abbreviated terms for words; a complete list of abbreviations is provided in Table 2. Notably, membership checking proved exceptionally efficient across all datasets. For instance, the expression $b^*n(l^?g^?cm^?k^?s^?s^?v^?o^?\&f^?\&q)(e^+|j|d)^?$ and 31,260 words in the incollection dataset were checked in only 6 s, implying an average checking time of less than 0.2 milliseconds per word. Even for the slowest dataset (article), containing 1,737,265 words, the average membership checking time remained below 2.5 milliseconds per word.

Table 1. Correctness Checking of Inference Algorithm on Different DBLP datasets

Methods	Dataset	Learning result	checking time	correctness
GenICHARE	phdthesis	$a^+c(u^*\&f^+i^?j^?\&k^?e^*l^?$		
	6953	$m^*\&p^?t^?q^*\&s^*)$	8.0 s	100%
GenICHARE	inproceedings	$a^*(l^?\&c\&g^*\&f^*i^?k^?\&$		
	1610138	$b^*j^?d^*\&no^?e^*\&q)$	3117.5 s	100%
GenICHARE	proceedings	$a^?(d^?\&cq^*e^?j^?r^?\&s^*\&b^*p^*\&l^*$		
	26502	$\&t^*h^?g^?\&m^*\&f^*\&i^*)o^*$	11.5 s	100%
GenICHARE	www 1557527	$(b^+|r)^?(a^*q^*d^?m^?\&c^+o^*f^?\&l^*)^?$	470.5 s	100%
GenICHARE	incollection	$b^*n(l^?g^?cm^?k^?s^?s^?v^?o^?$		
	31260	$\&f^?\&q)(e^+|j|d)^?$	6 s	100%
GenICRE	book	$(a^+|b^+)^?.((l^*|e^*|i^?)\&(c^?|u^*)\&g^*\&t^*$		
	14845	$\&p^?\&o^*\&n^+\&q^+\&s^*\&m^*)d^?j^?$	24 s	100%
GenICRE	article	$a^*((e^*|f^?|i^?)\&(c^?|h^?)\&(k^?|m^?)\&b^*$		
	1737265	$\&d^?\&g^*\&j^*\&l^?\&n^+\&o^?\&p^?\&q^?)$	4251 s	100%

Table 2. The list of abbreviations for words in DBLP

Word	editor	author	booktitle	cdrom	cite	crossref	ee	journal
Abbr	a	b	c	d	e	f	g	h
Word	month	note	number	pages	publisher	title	url	volume
Abbr	i	j	k	l	m	n	o	p
Word	year	address	isbn	series	school	chapter	publnr	
Abbr	q	r	s	t	u	v	w	

5   Conclusion

This paper introduces derivatives for regular expressions incorporating both counting and shuffle operators i.e., enhanced regular expressions (EREs), providing a structural proof of their correctness. We leverage these derivatives to develop a membership algorithm for unrestricted EREs. A key lemma establishes the relationship between the size of derivatives and the size of EREs, enabling us to analyze the time complexity of our algorithm. The experimental evaluation demonstrates both the effectiveness and practicality of our approach. Positive examples highlight its accuracy, while negative examples showcase its efficiency. Notably, our algorithm enables correctness verification for previously uncheckable inference algorithms due to the absence of suitable membership testing mechanisms.

Acknowledgements. The authors would like to thank the anonymous reviewers for their helpful comments and suggestions. Work supported by the National Natural Science Foundation of China (Grant Nos. 62372439 and 61872339) and the Natural Science Foundation of Beijing, China (Grant No. 4232038).

References

1. Angluin, D.: Learning regular sets from queries and counterexamples. Inf. Comput. **75**(2), 87–106 (1987)
2. Broda, S., Machiavelo, A., Moreira, N., Reis, R.: Location automata for regular expressions with shuffle and intersection. Inf. Comput. **295**(Part B), 104917 (2023)
3. Brüggemann-Klein, A.: Regular expressions into finite automata. Theoret. Comput. Sci. **120**(2), 197–213 (1993)
4. Brzozowski, J.A.: Derivatives of regular expressions. J. ACM **11**(4), 481–494 (1964)
5. Clark, J., Makoto, M.: Relax NG specification. oasis (2001). http://www.oasis-open.org/committees/relax-ng/spec-20011203.html (2004)
6. Colazzo, D., Ghelli, G., Sartiani, C.: Linear time membership in a class of regular expressions with counting, interleaving, and unordered concatenation. ACM Trans. Database Syst. **42**(4), 24 (2017)
7. David, C., Francis, N., Marsault, V.: Distinct shortest walk enumeration for RPQs. Proc. ACM Manage. Data **2**(2), 1–22 (2024)

8. Davis, J.C., IV, L.G.M., Coghlan, C.A., Servant, F., Lee, D.: Why aren't regular expressions a lingua franca? An empirical study on the re-use and portability of regular expressions. In: ESEC/FSE 2019, pp. 443–454 (2019)

9. Garg, V.K., Ragunath, M.: Concurrent regular expressions and their relationship to Petri nets. Theoret. Comput. Sci. **96**(2), 285–304 (1992)

10. Gelade, W.: Succinctness of regular expressions with interleaving, intersection and counting. Theoret. Comput. Sci. **411**(31–33), 2987–2998 (2010)

11. Gelade, W., Gyssens, M., Martens, W.: Regular expressions with counting: weak versus strong determinism. In: Královič, R., Niwiński, D. (eds.) MFCS 2009. LNCS, vol. 5734, pp. 369–381. Springer, Heidelberg (2009). https://doi.org/10.1007/978-3-642-03816-7_32

12. Gelade, W., Martens, W., Neven, F.: Optimizing schema languages for XML: Numerical constraints and interleaving. SIAM J. Comput. **38**(5), 2021–2043 (2009)

13. Ghelli, G., Colazzo, D., Sartiani, C.: Linear time membership in a class of regular expressions with interleaving and counting. In: CIKM 2008, pp. 389–398 (2008)

14. Hovland, D.: The membership problem for regular expressions with unordered concatenation and numerical constraints. In: Dediu, A.-H., Martín-Vide, C. (eds.) LATA 2012. LNCS, vol. 7183, pp. 313–324. Springer, Heidelberg (2012). https://doi.org/10.1007/978-3-642-28332-1_27

15. Jiang, T., Ravikumar, B.: A note on the space complexity of some decision problems for finite automata. Inf. Process. Lett. **40**(1), 25–31 (1991)

16. Kilpeläinen, P., Tuhkanen, R.: Regular expressions with numerical occurrence indicators-preliminary results. In: SPLST 2003, pp. 163–173 (2003)

17. Li, Y., Chu, X., Mou, X., Dong, C., Chen, H.: Practical study of deterministic regular expressions from large-scale XML and schema data. In: IDEAS 2018, pp. 45–53 (2018)

18. Li, Y., Mou, X., Chen, H.: Learning concise relax ng schemas supporting interleaving from XML documents. In: Gan, G., Li, B., Li, X., Wang, S. (eds.) ADMA 2018. LNCS (LNAI), vol. 11323, pp. 303–317. Springer, Cham (2018). https://doi.org/10.1007/978-3-030-05090-0_26

19. Liang, T., Tsiskaridze, N., Reynolds, A., Tinelli, C., Barrett, C.: A decision procedure for regular membership and length constraints over unbounded strings. In: Lutz, C., Ranise, S. (eds.) FroCoS 2015. LNCS (LNAI), vol. 9322, pp. 135–150. Springer, Cham (2015). https://doi.org/10.1007/978-3-319-24246-0_9

20. Mayer, A.J., Stockmeyer, L.J.: The complexity of word problems-this time with interleaving. Inf. Comput. **115**(2), 293–311 (1994)

21. Sperberg-McQueen, C., Thompson, H.: XML schema (2005). http://www.w3.org/xml/schema

22. Stanford, C., Veanes, M., Bjørner, N.S.: Symbolic Boolean derivatives for efficiently solving extended regular expression constraints. In: PLDI 2021, pp. 620–635 (2021)

23. Stockmeyer, L.J., Meyer, A.R.: Word problems requiring exponential time (Preliminary Report). In: STOC 1973, pp. 1–9 (1973)

24. Sulzmann, M., Thiemann, P.: Derivatives and partial derivatives for regular shuffle expressions. J. Comput. Syst. Sci. **104**, 323–341 (2019)

25. Tekli, J., Chbeir, R., Traina, A.J.M., Jr., C.T., Fileto, R.: Approximate XML structure validation based on document-grammar tree similarity. Inf. Sci. **295**, 258–302 (2015)

26. Ter Beek, M.H., Kleijn, J.: Infinite unfair shuffles and associativity. Theoret. Comput. Sci. **380**(3), 401–410 (2007)

27. Wang, X., Hong, Y., Chang, H., Langdale, G., Hu, J.: Hyperscan: a fast multi-pattern regex matcher for modern CPUs. In: NSDI 19, pp. 631–648 (2019)

28. Wang, X.: Membership algorithm for single-occurrence regular expressions with shuffle and counting. In: Bhattacharya, A., et al. (eds.) DASFAA 2022. LNCS, vol. 13245, pp. 526–542. Springer, Cham (2022). https://doi.org/10.1007/978-3-031-00123-9_41
29. Zhang, S., Gu, X., Chen, Y., Shen, B.: InfeRE: step-by-step regex generation via chain of inference. In: ASE 2023, pp. 1505–1515 (2023)
30. Zhang, X., Li, Y., Cui, F., Dong, C., Chen, H.: Inference of a concise regular expression considering interleaving from XML documents. In: Phung, D., Tseng, V.S., Webb, G.I., Ho, B., Ganji, M., Rashidi, L. (eds.) PAKDD 2018. LNCS (LNAI), vol. 10938, pp. 389–401. Springer, Cham (2018). https://doi.org/10.1007/978-3-319-93037-4_31
31. Zheng, Y., et al.: Z3str2: an efficient solver for strings, regular expressions, and length constraints. Formal Methods Syst. Des. **50**(2–3), 249–288 (2017)

NanoHook: An Efficient System Call Hooking Technique with One-Byte Invasive

Quan Hong[1,2] , Jiaqi Li[1,2] , Wen Zhang[3], and Lidong Zhai[2(✉)]

[1] School of Cyber Security, University of Chinese Academy of Sciences, Beijing, China
[2] Institute of Information Engineering, Chinese Academy of Sciences, Beijing, China
{hongquan,lijiaqi,zhailidong}@iie.ac.cn
[3] China Unicom Online Information Technology CO., Ltd., Beijing, China
zhangwen33@chinaunicom.cn

Abstract. System calls serve as the primary interface between the operating system kernel and user-space programs and can be hooked to trace, analyze, and modify program behavior. Minimizing the overhead introduced by system call hooking techniques is crucial to prevent performance degradation of the hooked program. Moreover, modifications to the process instructions by the hooking technique should be minimal to avoid unintended side effects. However, existing techniques struggle to balance these requirements. Techniques such as syscall user dispatch (SUD) and ptrace avoid modifying process instructions but introduce substantial overhead, whereas other low-overhead techniques often require modifying multiple bytes or instructions to redirect the system call to the hook function. This paper introduces NanoHook, an innovative system call hooking technique tailored for 32-bit programs. NanoHook leverages the specific jump behavior of 32-bit programs during system calls. This approach only requires binary rewriting of one byte of a particular instruction to hook system calls with minimal overhead. Experimental results demonstrate that NanoHook reduces the overhead, defined as the additional time required to execute a system call after introducing the hooking technique, by a factor of 6.7 to $13{,}335.6$ compared to existing techniques. When applied to Redis, NanoHook incurs only a 4% performance loss, significantly lower than the 8.3% to 94.85% performance degradation observed with other techniques.

Keywords: NanoHook · System call hooking · Instruction modification · Binary rewriting · Dynamic instrumentation · Software analysis

1 Introduction

Modern x86 CPUs offer four privilege levels, known as Ring0 to Ring3. Most operating systems typically use Ring0 for kernel mode and Ring3 for user mode.

T. Bourke et al. (Eds.): SETTA 2024, LNCS 15469, pp. 363–381, 2025.
https://doi.org/10.1007/978-981-96-0602-3_20

Ring0, with the highest privileges, enables direct interaction with physical hardware, whereas Ring3, the user mode, is restricted from directly accessing hardware resources like memory. System calls serve as the primary interface provided by Ring0, allowing user-mode programs in Ring3 to access necessary resources. Since all critical operations in user-space programs must be executed through system calls, system call hooking becomes a powerful tool for monitoring, modifying, and analyzing program behavior. System call hooking techniques are widely applied in various scenarios, including tracing tools [8,19], sandboxes [17,25], OS simulation layers [3,23], and providing binary compatibility support for new OS subsystems [21,29–31,34,35].

Motivation. Previous research has demonstrated that user-space OS subsystems [12,14,16,22,24,27], supported by kernel-bypass frameworks [15,32,37], are highly performant. For instance, lwIP [12] running on DPDK [15], a fast packet I/O framework, can sometimes achieve higher network performance than the kernel-space TCP/IP stack. However, to use such high-performance user-space OS subsystems, the source code of programs usually needs to be modified. Accessing and modifying the source code is not always feasible, particularly in closed-source or legacy software. In such cases, system call hooking techniques offer a solution, allowing user-space OS subsystems to be applied to the program without modifying its source code. In this scenario, the overhead introduced by the hooking technique is crucial, as lower overhead leads to more significant performance improvements. Additionally, the stability of the hooking technique is a crucial factor. Thus, it should minimize modifications to program instructions and implement system call hooking without being affected by the program's context.

Problem. There is still a lack of an ideal system call hooking technique to meet the needs of the above scenarios.

1. Existing kernel supports (e.g., ptrace and Syscall User Dispatch (SUD)) and *int3* signaling cause unacceptable performance degradation to hook-applied user-space programs.
2. Although LD_PRELOAD (Sect. 3.1) incurs relatively low overhead, it cannot hook functions not called via the Procedure Linkage Table (PLT).
3. In binary rewriting techniques, Detours [7] overwrites instructions that should not be modified; Instruction punning [9] and E9Patch [11] cannot exhaustively hook system calls (explained in Sect. 2.1). Thus, they cannot be used for systems requiring reliability. Although zpoline [38] (Sect. 3.1) can avoid these issues, it encounters conflicts between instruction rewriting and program execution when using multithreading. Moreover, zpoline can cause infinite loops and unpredictable behavior when applied to 32-bit programs (explained in Sect. 2.1).
4. Techniques based on specific kernel modifications or additional kernel modules such as Dune [4], which are not merged to the mainline, substantially diminish the portability of applications relying on them.

5. Although BSD Packet Filter (BPF) [28] and its extended version, eBPF, allow users to hook kernel-space functions, they have limitations in expressing complex operations like loops, constraining their ability to change and simulate system call behavior.
6. Modifying and recompiling user-space program source code is a common approach observed in Unikernel systems [6,20,26], but it is not always feasible as users typically lack access to the source code.
7. Linking the application binary with a specially modified standard library (e.g., libc) can replace system calls with specific OS subsystem function calls [21,29–31,35]. However, this method limits the choice of standard library implementations and cannot hook system calls invoked outside the standard library.

In summary, despite the significant advantages of user-space OS subsystems, their applicability has been limited by the lack of an ideal system call hooking technique.

Contributions. To address this issue, we propose NanoHook, an innovative system call hooking technique that offers several key advantages: 1) It minimizes hook overhead; 2) It only modifies one byte for a specific instruction; 3) It employs a simple approach to hook system calls; 4) It eliminates the need to modify user-space program files or add extra kernel modules; 5) It does not rely on specially modified standard libraries. To the best of our knowledge, no previous hooking techniques achieve these requirements simultaneously. We demonstrate the superiority of NanoHook in terms of hook overhead and performance through microbenchmarks (Sect. 3.2) and experiments applying NanoHook and other system call hooking techniques to real-world software (Sect. 3.3).

2   NanoHook

NanoHook leverages the feature of 32-bit programs when making system calls. When a 32-bit process initiates a system call, it executes the **call *%gs:0x10** instruction, leading to a jump to the __kernel_vsyscall function. This function then executes the *syscall/sysenter* instruction to request the kernel to complete the system calls initiated by the process. NanoHook locates the position of the **call *%gs:0x10** instruction in the process's virtual address space. Subsequently, leveraging the binary rewriting techniques, NanoHook replaces the lowest byte of the offset in this instruction. This ensures that during the execution of the instruction, the program will redirect to the hook function, thereby implementing system call hooking.

2.1   Challenge and Goal

The main challenge for binary rewriting-based system call hooking techniques is that the *syscall/sysenter* instructions occupy only two bytes. In contrast, other jmp/call instructions (except for short relative jumps) occupy more than two bytes. Overwriting *syscall/sysenter* instructions with jmp/call instructions that jump to arbitrary target addresses would overwrite adjacent instructions that should remain unchanged, resulting in unintended behavior [7]. Existing binary rewriting techniques, such as Instruction Punning and E9Patch, interpret the address offset bytes of jump instructions as instructions to avoid modifying adjacent instructions. However, the effectiveness of this strategy depends on the byte values of the subsequent adjacent instructions. Consequently, these techniques abandon replacement in some cases and fail to ensure exhaustive hooking [9, 11]. Although *int3* signaling, based on a single-byte instruction, can address this issue, it introduces significant hooking overhead.

zpoline addresses this issue by replacing the *syscall* instruction with a two-byte *callq *%rax* instruction. However, this approach requires rewriting the two-byte syscall instruction, which is not an atomic operation, potentially leading to unpredictable behavior in multi-threaded programs. In addition, zpoline encounters issues such as infinite loops and unpredictable behavior when applied to 32-bit programs. When a 32-bit program executes a system call, it jumps to the Virtual Dynamic Shared Object (vDSO) to execute the *syscall/sysenter* instructions, which are shared across the entire process. Replacing these instructions with *callq *%eax* causes any subsequent system calls in the hooking operation to also jump to the modified vDSO, creating an infinite loop. Moreover, in 32-bit programs, the *int 0x80* instruction follows the *syscall/sysenter* instructions in the vDSO. After zpoline replaces the *syscall/sysenter* instructions with *callq *%eax*, when the hook function returns, the *int 0x80* instruction executes, leading to unpredictable behavior due to altered register contents, as the system call has already been completed. NanoHook aims to overcome the shortcomings of existing binary rewriting techniques and provide a more reliable and efficient hooking technique for the system call hooking domain.

2.2   Methodology

System Call Process. NanoHook's design is inspired by the system call process in 32-bit programs. Before triggering a system call in a 32-bit user-space program, the system call number (e.g., 3 for read and 4 for write in Linux on x86 CPUs) is first set in the *eax* register. Subsequently, the parameters for the system call are stored in the *ebx, ecx, edx, esi, edi,* and *ebp* registers. Following the configuration of system call parameters, unlike 64-bit programs that directly execute the *syscall* instruction, 32-bit programs execute the *call *%gs:0x10* instruction. This instruction leads to a jump to the __kernel_vsyscall function in the vDSO. This function then executes the *syscall/sysenter* instruction, effecting the context switch to the kernel and subsequently invoking the appropriate system call handler based on the *eax* register. In the standard system call execution process, except for the special system calls mentioned in Sect. 2.4, all system calls are ultimately redirected to the __kernel_vsyscall function.

Binary Rewriting and Execution Flow. NanoHook's core concept leverages the mechanism by which the *call *%gs:0x10* instruction jumps to the

__kernel_vsyscall function. This instruction is an indirect absolute call that uses *gs* as the segment selector to locate the base address of the corresponding segment. It then retrieves the content at the offset 0x10 of the base address to obtain the address for the function call. This base address points to the Thread Control Block (TCB) header[1], a structure defined in the C library. The address of the __kernel_vsyscall function is stored at offset 0x10 in this structure. This value is initialized and assigned during process initiation.

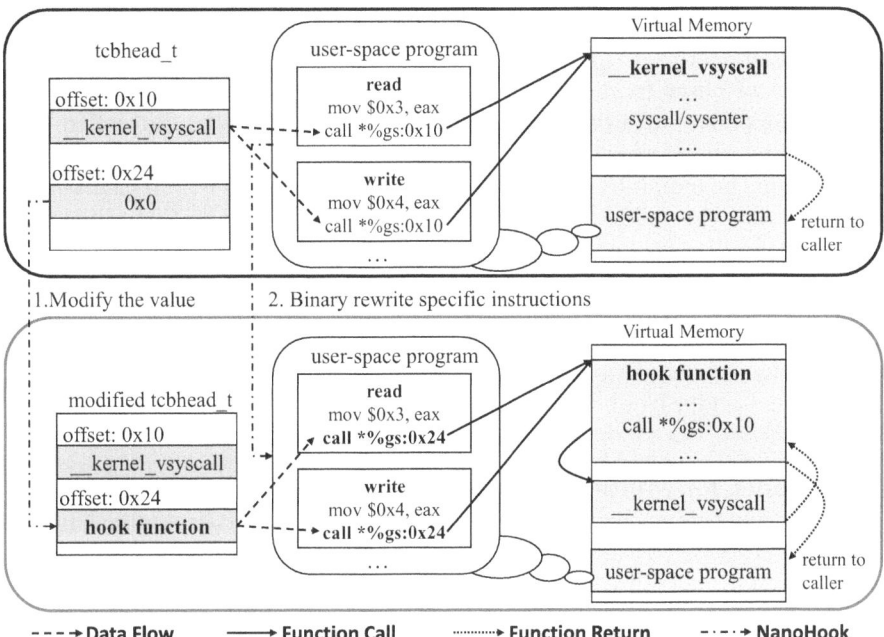

Fig. 1. NanoHook overview. The upper part shows the normal execution flow of the system call, while the lower part shows the execution flow of the system call after applying NanoHook.

To implement the system call hooking, we modify the process by which system calls jump to __kernel_vsyscall. The upper part of Fig. 1 depicts the standard execution process of a system call, while the lower part depicts the hooking process using NanoHook and the execution flow of system calls post-hooking. Specifically, NanoHook replaced the *call *%gs:0x10* instruction with *call *%gs:0x24* by modifying the lowest byte of the instruction offset. In essence, only one byte of the instruction undergoes modification, leaving neighboring instructions intact. The *call *%gs:0x24* instruction jumps to the address stored at offset 0x24 within the tcbhead_t structure. The memory region where the tcbhead_t structure is located is writable, so we directly store the hook function's address at offset

---

[1] https://elixir.bootlin.com/glibc/glibc-2.27/source/sysdeps/i386/nptl/tls.h.

0x24 within the tcbhead_t structure. After NanoHook is set up, the system call will execute the rewritten portion (*call *%gs:0x24*). This action jumps to the hook function and pushes the caller's address onto the stack. At this point, the hook function will have the same register state as the kernel-space system call handler. After the hook function executes, it jumps back to the caller's address to continue execution. In scenarios where executing the original system call is imperative, the hook function can specify a memory region that is not affected by the NanoHook binary rewrite to execute the *call *%gs:0x10* instruction. This instruction can ensure the normal execution of the system call.

NanoHook stores the hook function's address at offset 0x24 in the tcb_header structure and rewrites the lowest byte of the *call *%gs:0x10* instruction to 0x24. The choice of offset 0x24 is strategic, as it corresponds to a member of the __private_tm pointer array within the tcb_header structure. The __private_tm field is reserved by the system, with a default value of 0. Testing across various Linux distributions, including Ubuntu 22.04, Debian 11.7, RedHat 8, and CentOS 7.6, confirmed that this field is not utilized by programs, ensuring that altering its value does not disrupt normal operations of programs. The tcb_header structure, defined in the glibc source code, has included the __private_tm field since glibc version 2.20 (released on September 8, 2014) and continues to reserve it in the latest glibc-2.40 version. Even if this field is repurposed in the future, NanoHook can adapt by using other unused four-byte fields within the tcb_header structure, ensuring its usability.

TCB Header for Multithreaded Programs. The application object of the tcbhead_t structure is the thread. Therefore, the tcbhead_t structure shared in the entire process's virtual address space is only applicable to single-threaded programs. In a multi-threaded scenario, when the hooked program creates new threads, the program will generate and instantiate a new tcbhead_t structure for each thread. NanoHook relies on modifying the value at offset 0x24 in the tcb-head_t structure to the address of the hook function. However, this value remains at its default 0 in new threads. This results in NanoHook being unable to hook system calls initiated by new threads and may disrupt the program's operation. Specifically, when the new thread executes the *call *%gs:0x24* instruction, the process will redirect to address 0, causing the process to terminate.

To address this issue, we identify the system call made during thread creation. Subsequently, within the hooking function, we modify the tcbhead_t of the new thread (Sect. 2.2), ensuring that executions of the *call *%gs:0x24* instruction by the new thread correctly redirect to the hook function. To validate the effectiveness of this approach, we applied NanoHook to the Redis [33] program used in Sect. 3.3. This program creates multiple threads during its execution. The results demonstrate that this method effectively addresses the issues encountered by NanoHook when hooking system calls initiated by multiple threads.

2.3   Implementation

Our current prototype focuses on Linux. The core implementation of NanoHook includes binary rewriting and hook code instantiation, implemented in a shared library called libnanohook.so. The primary function for hooking is encapsulated in another shared library called libbasichook.so, which can modify system call parameters, execute the original system call logic, and alter return values. This design, also adopted by zpoline, helps to avoid infinite loops caused by invoking system calls within hook operations. We will delve into this in detail in Sect. 2.3. In our prototype, libnanohook.so is loaded via LD_PRELOAD, completing the system call hooking before the main function of the user-space program executes.

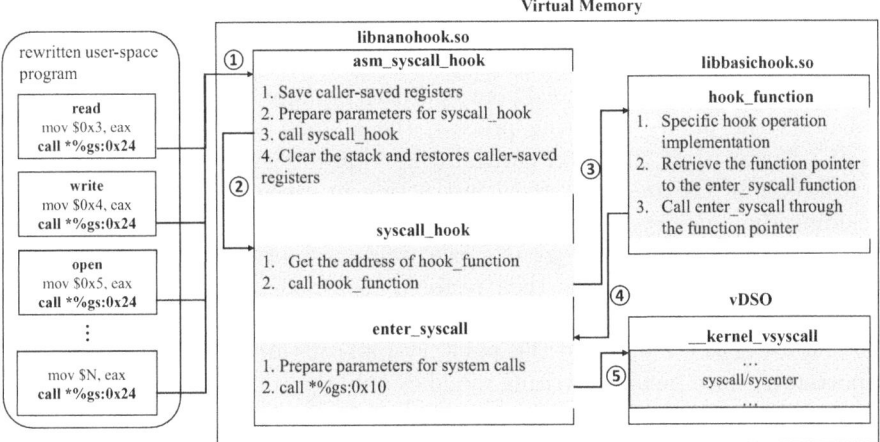

Fig. 2. Functions in libnanohook.so and libbasichook.so and their respective processes for handling system calls.

Setup Operations. NanoHook's setup operations consist of two critical steps: the instantiation of hook code and binary rewriting. These two steps are implemented in libnanohook.so, which is responsible for intercepting and handling hooked system calls. Figure 2 illustrates the roles of functions in the libraries libnanohook.so and libbasichook.so post-rewriting, along with the detailed execution process of system calls after hooking. In the hook code instantiation phase, the primary tasks include defining and declaring functions and embedding the corresponding assembly code. The entry point for all intercepted system calls is the *asm_syscall_hook* function, implemented in assembly language. This function begins by saving caller-saved registers according to the ABI standard. It then pushes the system call's register contents and other hook-related information onto the stack as parameters for the *syscall_hook* function. Finally, it invokes the *syscall_hook* function, which is written in C. After the *syscall_hook* function returns, the *asm_syscall_hook* function cleans up the parameters from the stack and restores the caller-saved registers. The *syscall_hook* function does not directly implement hook operations for different system calls. Instead, it calls the *hook_function* function from the separate library libbasichook.so, which implements the specific hook operations.

We also defined a function written in assembly language called *enter_syscall* in libnanohook.so, which is responsible for executing the original system call. The *enter_syscall* function primarily sets the system call registers according to the parameters on the stack and then executes the original system call via the *call *%gs:0x10* instruction. A function pointer to *enter_syscall* is also defined, providing a unified mechanism for executing the original system call during hook operations. This pointer can handle the various prototypes of system calls by accepting seven parameters corresponding to the *eax*, *ebx*, *ecx*, *edx*, *esi*, *edi*, and *ebp* registers. Unlike the LD_PRELOAD method, which requires defining a specific hook function and function pointer for each system call to store the address of the original system call, our approach is simpler and more convenient.

During the binary rewriting process, the address of the *asm_syscall_hook* function is stored at offset 0x24 within the tcbhead_t structure. Subsequently, all instances of the *call *%gs:0x10* instruction in executable memory regions, excluding the *enter_syscall* function, are replaced with *call *%gs:0x24*. During this stage, the user-space program's executable memory region is temporarily configured as writable and is then restored to a non-writable state after the binary rewriting completes. After this process, the user-space program's main function starts as usual, but at this point, system calls are hooked by NanoHook. Importantly, since binary rewriting modifies only the code loaded into memory, the original binary file of the user-space program remains unchanged.

Hook Function Development. As discussed in Sect. 2.3, specific hook operations are not implemented in libnanohook.so because executing system calls within the *syscall_hook* function could lead to an infinite loop. This loop occurs because the code executing the system call has been rewritten to *call *%gs:0x24*, causing the system call within *syscall_hook* to redirect back to *asm_syscall_hook*, creating a loop. Given the possibility of various system calls being executed within hook operations, avoiding this infinite loop issue is crucial. This problem is attributed to the default dynamic linker/loader, which automatically associates the library calls used in the hook operations with the rewritten library. To address this problem, we use *dlmopen*, an extension of *dlopen*. The *dlopen* function loads a library file into the memory of a user-space process. Building upon this basic feature, the *dlmopen* function accepts an additional argument, which allows the user to specify the namespace for loading the shared object, thereby associating its dependency libraries with the specified namespace. Therefore, *dlmopen* allows us to avoid automatic, unnecessary associations by loading the library that implements the hook operations into a separate namespace. To use dlmopen, we construct the core part of the hook operation as an independent shared library named libbasichook.so. During the setup phase, libnanohook.so uses dlmopen with the additional parameter value of LM_ID_NEWLM to load the library. Subsequently, we can use the *dlsym* to obtain a pointer to the *hook_function* in libbasichook.so. This function implements specific hooking operations for various system calls. The *syscall_hook* function in libnanohook.so can invoke *hook_function* through the obtained pointer, thereby performing the hooking operation.

2.4   Limitations

Here, we discuss the limitations of NanoHook.

Special System Calls. The context switch between user space and the kernel during system calls is time-consuming. For certain special system calls, the information they request from the kernel is not secret. Therefore, the kernel stores this type of information in memory accessible to the process. This allows these special system calls to be converted into regular function calls, thereby reducing the associated overhead. The kernel provides direct access to the execution code of these special system calls via the vDSO, enabling user-space programs to execute them without entering kernel mode. In the 32-bit vDSO of Ubuntu 22.04, there are only five such special system calls: time, gettimeofday, clock_gettime, clock_gettime64, and clock_getres. Similar to other system call hooking techniques, NanoHook cannot hook these special system calls by default, but this can be remedied by disabling vDSO.[2] Even if 32-bit vDSO is disabled in the Linux OS, the jump logic for system calls by 32-bit programs still exists. The difference is that it no longer jumps to the vDSO's __kernel_vsyscall function but instead jumps to the executable memory region of the dynamic loader/linker ld.so and then executes the system call using the *int 0x80* interrupt.

There is another category of special system calls that do not utilize the jump to vDSO to execute *syscall/sysenter* instructions; instead, they employ *int 0x80* for system calls. Such system calls include clone, clone3, rt_sigreturn, vfork, and sigreturn. Considering the limited number of these system calls, we can disassemble the executable region to locate the *int 0x80* instructions and then use existing hooking methods, such as zpoline, and *int3* signaling, to hook them. In conclusion, due to the limited number of these two types of special system calls[3] and the availability of alternative methods to hook them, their presence does not adversely impact the functionality and performance of NanoHook.

Other OSes and CPU Architectures. We have validated NanoHook's ability to hook 32-bit programs on various 64-bit Linux distributions, including Ubuntu 22.04, Debian 11.7, RedHat 8, CentOS 7.6, OpenSUSE 15.4, Fedora Linux 38, Rocky Linux 9.2, and AlmaLinux 9.2. Although not all distributions have been tested, 32-bit programs on Linux under the x86-64/i386 architectures theoretically exhibit the jump logic required for NanoHook during system call execution.

---

[2] Linux disables the vDSO in 32-bit programs when the kernel boot option specifies vdso32=0.

[3] In Ubuntu 22.04, 32-bit programs have 448 system calls, and these two special system calls only have 10.

NanoHook does not apply to operating systems such as Windows 10, FreeBSD 13.2, etc., as they do not exhibit the same jump logic during system calls as Linux. However, Windows provides a compatibility layer for Linux called the Windows Subsystem for Linux (WSL), and we confirm that NanoHook works on WSL2. NanoHook is also incompatible with CPU architectures other than x86 and x86-64 due to differences in instruction sets and system call conventions. Although NanoHook's applicability is limited to Linux systems on x86 and x86-64 architectures, considering the widespread use of such operating systems, we believe NanoHook can be applied to a large number of servers and desktop computers.

3   Evaluation

This section quantifies and evaluates the hook overhead introduced by various system call hooking techniques (Sect. 3.1) and assesses their impact on the performance of real-world software. We compared and analyzed different hooking techniques by deploying them separately within the same 32-bit program. The experiments were conducted on a virtual machine running Ubuntu 22.04. The machine has a kernel version of 6.2.0 and operates on the x86-64 architecture. For the host machine, the system was equipped with a 20-core 12th Gen Intel(R) Core(TM) i7-12700H CPU, clocked at 2300 MHz and 16 GB of DRAM.

3.1   Comparison With Existing System Call Hook Technique

We compare NanoHook with *int3* signaling (Sect. 3.1), SUD (Sect. 3.1), *ptrace* (Sect. 3.1), LD_PRELOAD (Sect. 3.1), and zpoline (Sect. 3.1). Here, we describe the mechanisms and properties of them.

int3 Signaling. The *int3*, a single-byte instruction (0xcc) that triggers a software interrupt, is commonly employed by dynamic debuggers to implement breakpoints. In Linux, executing *int3* causes an interrupt, leading to a context switch to kernel space, where the kernel handles the interrupt and sends a SIGTRAP signal to the executing process. The *int3* signaling technique leverages this behavior to implement system call hooks by using binary rewriting to replace all *syscall/sysenter* instructions with *int3*. A signal handler is then defined in the program to handle the SIGTRAP signal. This signal handler modifies the context saved when executing *int3* so that when execution is resumed, it redirects to the hook function. Both *int3* signaling and NanoHook achieve system call hooking by modifying just one byte of an instruction. However, the signal-handling process of *int3* signaling incurs significant overhead due to context manipulation by the kernel. In contrast, NanoHook can hook system calls with low overhead.

Syscall User Dispatch (SUD). SUD [5] is a kernel feature introduced in Linux 5.11, designed to provide a method for redirecting system calls to arbitrary user-space code. For the SUD feature, the kernel implements a hook point at the entry point of system calls. User-space processes can activate SUD and specify a memory region through the *prctl* interface. When SUD is activated, system calls can be directly executed in the specified memory region. However, when attempting to execute a system call outside the specified memory region, the kernel sends a SIGSYS signal to the user-space process. This mechanism allows user space programs to hook system calls by customizing the signal handler for the SIGSYS signal. As SUD is a kernel-supported feature, it does not require modification of user-space process instructions. However, similarly to *int3* signaling, the drawback of SUD lies in the overhead associated with signal handling, resulting in a significant performance impact on user-space programs.

ptrace. UNIX-like OSes provide the *ptrace* system call, enabling a tracer process to observe and control the execution of a traced process. When the tracer process invokes *ptrace* with the request value set to PTRACE_SYSCALL, the kernel arranges for the traced process to stop at the next entry or exit of a system call. At this point, the tracer process can modify the system call parameters at the entry point or alter the return value at the exit point, thereby achieving a hook on the system calls initiated by the traced process. Like SUD, *ptrace* is a kernel-provided feature, allowing system call hooks without modifying user-space instructions. However, the major drawback of ptrace is the significant overhead from context switches between the tracer and traced processes. Hooking system calls using *ptrace* introduces long delays for each system call, including the wake-up time for the tracer process, the execution time of the hook function, and the wake-up time for the traced process. This delay results in a substantial performance decrease for the traced process.

Function Call Replacement by LD_PRELOAD. The LD_PRELOAD feature, provided by the dynamic linker/loader (ld.so), allows a program to load the specified dynamic library before any others. This mechanism enables users to override functions in other libraries selectively. To hook system calls, one can declare and define functions with the same prototype as the system call wrapper functions in the dynamic library specified by LD_PRELOAD. Typically, the system call wrapper functions are implemented in standard libraries, such as libc. LD_PRELOAD introduces hooks via function pointer replacement, resulting in minimal overhead. However, the target of LD_PRELOAD hooking is functions rather than system calls. Replacing system call wrapper functions does not equate to hooking the underlying system calls. Since *syscall* and *sysenter* instructions are not directly associated with any function calls, LD_PRELOAD is limited in its ability to hook certain system calls. Firstly, glibc [13] is a typical example. In many cases, glibc does not use publicly exposed system call wrapper functions to invoke system calls; instead, it directly embeds *syscall/sysenter* within its internal functions, marked as invisible outside glibc, making LD_PRELOAD unable to apply hooks to system calls initiated by these internal functions. Secondly, LD_PRELOAD is unable to hook system calls initiated by system call wrapper functions that are not invoked through the Procedure Linkage Table (PLT). For instance, the *open_socket* function in libc calls the *socket* system call wrapper function using a relative call. Therefore, even if LD_PRELOAD replaces the *socket* system call wrapper function, it cannot hook the *socket* system call conducted by the *open_socket* function in libc.

zpoline. In 2023, Yasukata et al. introduced zpoline [38], a system call hook mechanism for x86-64 CPUs. The core idea is to replace the *syscall* instruction with a two-byte *callq *%rax* instruction and instantiate the trampoline code at virtual address 0. This mechanism can hook system calls with relatively low overhead while avoiding overwriting instructions supposed not to be modified. However, zpoline has two significant limitations. First, the kernel must permit mapping of virtual address 0, which must not be used for other purposes; otherwise, zpoline cannot be applied. This restriction somewhat narrows the technology's applicability. Second, enabling code execution at address 0 requires configuring the page as eXecute-Only Memory (XOM) to terminate read and write access. However, this requires a CPU that supports the Memory Protection Keys (MPK) feature. In comparison, NanoHook can overcome these limitations. NanoHook allows the specification of any address as the starting point of the trampoline code, eliminating the constraint of address 0. Additionally, unlike zpoline, which requires modifying 2 bytes of instruction, NanoHook only requires modifying 1 byte of instructions.

As described in Sect. 2.1, when applied to 32-bit programs, zpoline encounters issues such as infinite loops and unpredictable behavior. To better compare the overhead of NanoHook and zpoline, we improved zpoline to make it applicable to 32-bit programs. To address the infinite loop issue, we load the dynamic library implementing specific hooking operations into a new namespace and obtain its corresponding executable memory region. Subsequently, within the hooking function, the memory region during the execution of system calls is examined to determine whether to perform the hook operation. Additionally, we adjusted the return address saved on the stack after executing the *callq *%eax* instruction. This adjustment ensures that the *int 0x80* instruction is skipped when returning from the hook function, thus avoiding unpredictable behavior in the program.

3.2   System Call Hook Overhead

The "hook overhead" refers to the additional time incurred when executing a system call after applying a hooking technique. In this experiment, our primary focus is on the hook overhead itself. The differences in overhead between hooking techniques can be as small as a few dozen nanoseconds, which is much less than the overhead of cross-kernel system calls. To more accurately capture these subtle differences, we opted not to execute the original system call in the hook function but instead returned a dummy value. To avoid potential issues with this setup, we chose to hook the *getpid* system call, as it is one of the simplest system calls. With this setup, the hook overhead can be accurately measured by recording the time taken to execute *getpid* once after applying the hooking technique. To ensure the stability of our results, we hooked a specially designed program that iteratively calls *getpid* one hundred million times. We measured the total time taken to complete these iterations and divided it by the number of iterations to calculate the average time for executing one *getpid* system call.

Table 1. Average hook overhead and standard deviation, along with the percentage of standard deviation to overhead, for different hooking mechanisms.

Technique	Average Hook Overhead (ns)	Standard Deviation (ns)
ptrace	148024.76	11800.04 (7.97%)
int3 signaling	9956.72	105.85 (1.06%)
SUD	7708.47	133.08 (1.73%)
zpoline	74.71	0.46 (0.62%)
NanoHook	11.07	0.26 (2.35%)
LD_PRELOAD	3.28	0.45 (13.72%)

Table 1 presents the average and standard deviation of the hook overhead for different hooking techniques. LD_PRELOAD exhibits minimal overhead, nearly negligible, as it hooks through pointer replacement without executing additional instructions. The overhead of NanoHook is 3.4 times higher than LD_PRELOAD, primarily due to the necessity for the NanoHook to save and pass system call parameters. However, if the original system call were executed after the interception, LD_PRELOAD's overhead would exceed that of NanoHook, as LD_PRELOAD requires invoking *dlsym* to locate the address of the original system call's wrapper function. In contrast, NanoHook directly invokes the original system call through a function pointer, thereby incurring negligible additional overhead. The overhead of zpoline is 6.7 times higher than NanoHook, primarily due to the presence of a large number of *nop* instructions in the trampoline code. NanoHook is 694.5, 897.0, and 13335.6 times lighter than SUD, *int3* signaling, and *ptrace* respectively. The major overheads of *int3* signaling and SUD arise from signal handling for SIGTRAP and SIGSYS, while *ptrace* exhibits the most substantial overhead due to the cost of scheduling between the tracer and traced processes. Additionally, the overhead deviation of LD_PRELOAD is relatively large, accounting for about 13.6% of its average overhead. In contrast, zpoline shows the smallest deviation, representing 0.62% of its average overhead.

3.3   Application Performance

In this section, we quantify and evaluate the performance penalties introduced by NanoHook and other hooking techniques on real-world applications. We utilized

NanoHook and the existing hooking mechanisms described in Sect. 3.1 to hook
the system calls of Redis [33] and sysbench [18]. The version of Redis is 7.2.3
and the version of sysbench is 1.1.0. They are both installed as 32-bit programs.
We opted to compare NanoHook with the ptrace, zpoline, SUD, and *int3* signaling mechanisms. This experiment does not include LD_PRELOAD because its
limitation in being unable to hook many system calls within a program would
affect the evaluation results. Furthermore, employing LD_PRELOAD involves
the complex process of identifying all the wrapper functions for the system calls
used during the program's execution and defining a hook function for each,
whereas other hooking techniques can manage all intercepted system calls with
a single function. In Sect. 3.2, due to the simplicity of the target program's operations, involving only a few system calls, we can evaluate the hooking overhead
of LD_PRELOAD. Simultaneously, for reference, we also ran the same benchmark on the programs without applying any hooking techniques and reported
their performance in Fig. 3.

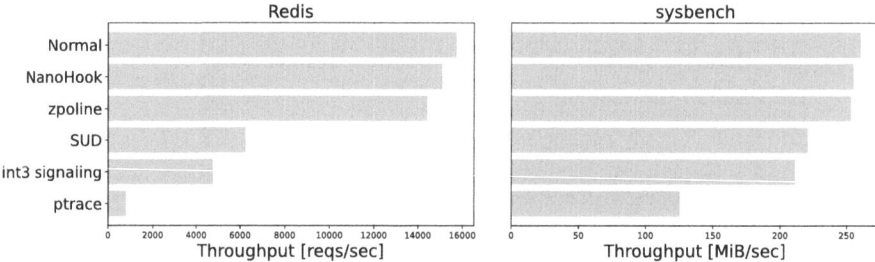

Fig. 3. Redis and sysbench throughput without and with various system call hook
techniques.

Redis. Initially, we launched the Redis server process on the machine. Subsequently, using the *redis-benchmark* as a benchmarking tool, we sent 100,000
GET requests to the Redis server process after applying various hooking techniques to the *redis-benchmark*. These requests were sent over 32 persistent concurrent connections. The results, presented in Fig. 3 (left), show the throughput
of redis-benchmark with and without different hooking techniques, allowing us
to evaluate their impact on program performance. It is evident that without any
hooking technique, the *redis-benchmark* achieves the highest throughput, sending 15,726.84 requests per second. The application of ptrace, *int3* signaling,
SUD, and zpoline reduced the throughput to 810.024 reqs/sec, 4764.05 reqs/sec,
6,242.25 reqs/sec, and 14,423.552 reqs/sec, respectively, corresponding to performance degradations of 94.85%, 69.71%, 60.30%, and 8.28%. NanoHook, however, only reduced the throughput to 15,097.458 requests per second, a 4.0% performance decrease. These results are consistent with the hook overhead shown
in Table 1, further demonstrating NanoHook's minimal impact on program performance.

Sysbench. We also evaluated NanoHook's impact on sysbench, a system performance benchmarking tool. Initially, we configured sysbench to execute the creation of a 1 GB file, which triggers a series of file-related system calls. Subsequently, we recorded the time required for sysbench to complete the file creation both with and without hooking, calculating and comparing sysbench's throughput in each condition. The results are depicted in Fig. 3 (right). Under normal conditions, sysbench achieved the highest throughput at 260.386 MiB/sec. When different hooking mechanisms were applied, performance experienced a decline. Specifically, the throughput of sysbench decreased by 51.86% with ptrace, by 18.85% with *int3* signaling, by 15.17% with SUD, and by 2.76% with zpoline. NanoHook, however, resulted in only a 2.08% reduction in sysbench's throughput.

The impact of hooking techniques on program performance can be quantified using the formula:

$$\frac{t_n + t_h}{t_n} = 1 + \frac{t_h}{t_n}$$

where t_n represents the time required for the program to execute normally, and t_h denotes the additional time incurred due to the hooking technique. When applying the same hooking technique to different programs, its impact on program performance is influenced by several key characteristics of the programs. Firstly, a critical factor is the number of system calls initiated during program execution. An increased number of system calls leads to a higher additional execution time t_h, thereby amplifying the impact of the hooking technique on program performance. For instance, in our experiments, Redis initiates significantly more system calls than sysbench. Consequently, the same hooking technique has a more pronounced impact on Redis's performance compared to sysbench. Secondly, the type of system calls performed by the program also plays an important role. Different types of system calls require varying amounts of time for execution. The longer the normal execution time of a system call (i.e., the larger t_n), the smaller the additional impact of the hooking technique on program performance. For example, sysbench primarily executes file-related system calls, which typically take longer than the network-related calls in Redis. Consequently, the same hooking technique has a more significant impact on Redis's performance compared to sysbench.

4   Discussion

NanoHook is an innovative and flexible system call hooking technique, with high efficiency. Although NanoHook is currently applicable to 32-bit programs on 32-bit and 64-bit systems, 32-bit programs are still widely used even in 2024. Firstly, modern 64-bit OSes generally offer multi-architecture support, allowing 32-bit applications to run seamlessly on 64-bit systems. Therefore, NanoHook can hook these 32-bit applications running on 64-bit systems. Secondly, as of 2024, approximately 15 Linux distributions, including Debian and Gentoo, still offer 32-bit versions [10]. In Debian's stable release alone, there are over 62,000

32-bit packages [1]. Thirdly, although 64-bit systems have become mainstream, many 32-bit programs remain in use due to legacy system requirements, specific business needs, or software vendor support. In particular, 32-bit processors are still prevalent in embedded systems and IoT. According to a report by Grand View Research, 32-bit controllers hold over half of the market share in embedded systems [2]. These devices often operate with limited resources, and the 32-bit architecture sufficiently meets their performance requirements. Similarly, numerous industrial control systems and medical devices, which prioritize stability and compatibility, are still based on 32-bit architectures. Migrating existing 32-bit applications to a 64-bit environment could introduce significant costs, complexity, and even new security vulnerabilities [36].

Lastly, for most applications, their memory usage typically does not exceed 3GB, making 32-bit the optimal size for these scenarios. The main advantage of transitioning to a 64-bit process lies in accessing larger memory and handling extensive data. For applications that do not demand these capabilities, converting to 64-bit yields no substantial benefits. To verify this, we compiled Redis 7.2.3 into 32-bit and 64-bit versions and launched the corresponding redis-server programs. We then used the redis-benchmark tool to send 100,000 GET requests to each over 32 persistent concurrent connections. The results showed that the 32-bit Redis achieved a throughput of 31,103.4 reqs/sec, slightly outperforming the 64-bit version, which achieved 30,154.825 reqs/sec. These results further reinforce our argument. These insights and data indicate that 32-bit systems and applications still have broad applicability and significance in many fields. Therefore, we believe that NanoHook still has wide applicability and significant application value.

NanoHook, with its flexibility and efficiency, can play an important role in various scenarios within the field of software engineering. Firstly, typical application scenarios for system call hooking, such as tracing tools and sandboxes, can use NanoHook to reduce the overhead introduced by hooking. Secondly, when users need to monitor, debug, analyze, or modify the program execution flow, they can employ NanoHook for hooking. It has a minimal impact on program performance and ease of use. Specifically, NanoHook's hooking operations are implemented in an independent library, allowing users to quickly tailor it to their needs. Additionally, NanoHook directs all hooked system calls to the same function, allowing users to perform different operations for various calls. Executing original system calls with different prototypes can be easily managed through a unified function pointer. It is relatively straightforward for users. Thirdly, in scenarios where applications aim to enhance performance by using more efficient user-space OS subsystems, NanoHook allows these programs to apply the userspace OS subsystem API without source code modifications. Its minimal hooking overhead allows NanoHook to maximize software performance. Fourthly, if a system call in the kernel has a defect but has not yet been patched, NanoHook can temporarily block the execution of certain system calls. It can also be used to fuzz the applications and the kernel by modifying system call parameters. Lastly, user-space eBPF [39] can implement syscall tracepoints via NanoHook, with minimal performance impact.

5   Conclusions

This paper presents NanoHook, a system call hook technique for 32-bit programs, capable of hooking system calls with low overhead by modifying only one byte of the specific instruction. The features of NanoHook give it a wide range of applications, including but not limited to sandboxes, tracing tools, and applying more efficient user-space OS subsystems to the software. With its unique combination of minimal overhead and flexibility, NanoHook offers an efficient and valuable solution in the realm of system call hooking. Future work will explore NanoHook's potential across diverse application scenarios, aiming to provide substantial support for research and practical applications in relevant domains.

References

1. Debian – packages (2024). https://www.debian.org/distrib/packages
2. U.S. Microcontroller Market Size & Trends — Industry Report, 2030 (2024). https://www.grandviewresearch.com/industry-analysis/us-microcontroller-market-report
3. Amstadt, B., Youngdale, E.: Wine (1993). https://www.winehq.org/
4. Belay, A., Bittau, A., Mashtizadeh, A., Terei, D., Mazières, D., Kozyrakis, C.: Dune: safe user-level access to privileged {CPU} features. In: 10th USENIX Symposium on Operating Systems Design and Implementation (OSDI 12), pp. 335–348 (2012)
5. Bertazi, G.K.: Syscall User Dispatch (2021). https://www.kernel.org/doc/html/latest/admin-guide/syscall-user-dispatch.html
6. Bratterud, A., Walla, A.A., Haugerud, H., Engelstad, P.E., Begnum, K.: IncludeOS: a minimal, resource efficient unikernel for cloud services. In: 2015 IEEE 7th International Conference on Cloud Computing Technology and Science (cloudcom), pp. 250–257. IEEE (2015)
7. Brubacher, D.: Detours: binary interception of Win32 functions. In: Windows NT 3rd symposium (windows NT 3rd symposium) (1999)
8. Cespedes, J.: ltrace (1997). https://ltrace.org/
9. Chamith, B., Svensson, B.J., Dalessandro, L., Newton, R.R.: Instruction punning: lightweight instrumentation for x86-64. In: Proceedings of the 38th ACM SIGPLAN Conference on Programming Language Design and Implementation, pp. 320–332 (2017)
10. Das, A.: 15 Linux Distributions You Can Rely on for Your Ancient 32-bit Computer (2023). https://itsfoss.com/32-bit-linux-distributions/
11. Duck, G.J., Gao, X., Roychoudhury, A.: Binary rewriting without control flow recovery. In: Proceedings of the 41st ACM SIGPLAN Conference on Programming Language Design and Implementation, pp. 151–163 (2020)
12. Dunkels, A.: Design and implementation of the lwIP TCP/IP stack. Swed. Inst. Comput. Sci. **2**(77) (2001)
13. Foundation, F.S.: The GNU C Library (glibc) (1988). https://www.gnu.org/software/libc/
14. Honda, M., Huici, F., Raiciu, C., Araujo, J., Rizzo, L.: Rekindling network protocol innovation with user-level stacks. ACM SIGCOMM Comput. Commun. Rev. **44**(2), 52–58 (2014)

15. Intel.: Data Plane Development Kit (2010). https://www.dpdk.org/
16. Jeong, E., et al.: {mTCP}: a highly scalable user-level {TCP} stack for multi-core systems. In: 11th USENIX Symposium on Networked Systems Design and Implementation (NSDI 14), pp. 489–502 (2014)
17. Kim, T., Zeldovich, N.: Practical and effective sandboxing for non-root users. In: 2013 USENIX Annual Technical Conference (USENIX ATC 13), pp. 139–144 (2013)
18. Kopytov, A.: sysbench (2005). https://github.com/akopytov/sysbench
19. Kranenburg, P.: strace (1991). https://github.com/strace/strace/tree/master
20. Kuenzer, S., et al.: Unikraft: fast, specialized unikernels the easy way. In: Proceedings of the Sixteenth European Conference on Computer Systems, pp. 376–394 (2021)
21. Kuo, H.C., Williams, D., Koller, R., Mohan, S.: A linux in unikernel clothing. In: Proceedings of the Fifteenth European Conference on Computer Systems, pp. 1–15 (2020)
22. Kwon, Y., Fingler, H., Hunt, T., Peter, S., Witchel, E., Anderson, T.: Strata: a cross media file system. In: Proceedings of the 26th Symposium on Operating Systems Principles, pp. 460–477 (2017)
23. Linux, U.M.: User Mode Linux (2005)
24. Liu, J., et al.: Scale and performance in a filesystem semi-microkernel. In: Proceedings of the ACM SIGOPS 28th Symposium on Operating Systems Principles, pp. 819–835 (2021)
25. LLC, G.: gVisor (2018). https://gvisor.dev/
26. Madhavapeddy, A., et al.: Unikernels: library operating systems for the cloud. ACM SIGARCH Comput. Archit. News **41**(1), 461–472 (2013)
27. Marinos, I., Watson, R.N., Handley, M.: Network stack specialization for performance. ACM SIGCOMM Comput. Commun. Rev. **44**(4), 175–186 (2014)
28. McCanne, S., Jacobson, V.: The BSD packet filter: a new architecture for user-level packet capture. In: USENIX winter, vol. 46, pp. 259–270 (1993)
29. Nikolaev, R., Back, G.: VirtuOS: an operating system with kernel virtualization. In: Proceedings of the Twenty-Fourth ACM Symposium on Operating Systems Principles, pp. 116–132 (2013)
30. Olivier, P., Chiba, D., Lankes, S., Min, C., Ravindran, B.: A binary-compatible unikernel. In: Proceedings of the 15th ACM SIGPLAN/SIGOPS International Conference on Virtual Execution Environments, pp. 59–73 (2019)
31. Raza, A., et al.: Unikernel Linux (UKL). In: Proceedings of the Eighteenth European Conference on Computer Systems, pp. 590–605 (2023)
32. Rizzo, L.: netmap: a novel framework for fast packet I/O. In: 21st USENIX Security Symposium (USENIX Security 12), pp. 101–112 (2012)
33. Sanfilippo, S.: Remote dictionary server (2009). https://redis.io/
34. Shen, Z., et al.: X-containers: breaking down barriers to improve performance and isolation of cloud-native containers. In: Proceedings of the Twenty-Fourth International Conference on Architectural Support for Programming Languages and Operating Systems, pp. 121–135 (2019)
35. Soares, L., Stumm, M.: {FlexSC}: flexible system call scheduling with {Exception-Less} system calls. In: 9th USENIX Symposium on Operating Systems Design and Implementation (OSDI 10) (2010)
36. Wressnegger, C., Yamaguchi, F., Maier, A., Rieck, K.: Twice the bits, twice the trouble: Vulnerabilities induced by migrating to 64-bit platforms. In: Proceedings of the 2016 ACM SIGSAC Conference on Computer and Communications Security, pp. 541–552 (2016)

37. Yang, Z., et al.: SPDK: a development kit to build high performance storage applications. In: 2017 IEEE International Conference on Cloud Computing Technology and Science (CloudCom), pp. 154–161. IEEE (2017)
38. Yasukata, K., Tazaki, H., Aublin, P.L., Ishiguro, K.: zpoline: a system call hook mechanism based on binary rewriting. In: 2023 USENIX Annual Technical Conference (USENIX ATC 23), pp. 293–300 (2023)
39. Zheng, Y., Yu, T., Yang, Y., Hu, Y., Lai, X., Quinn, A.: bpftime: userspace eBPF Runtime for Uprobe, Syscall and Kernel-User Interactions. arXiv preprint arXiv:2311.07923 (2023)

Faster Lifetime-Optimal Speculative Partial Redundancy Elimination for Goto-Free Programs

Xuran Cai[✉] and Amir Goharshady[✉]

Hong Kong University of Science and Technology,
Clear Water Bay, Hong Kong, China
xcaiay@connect.ust.hk, goharshady@cse.ust.hk

Abstract. Lifetime-optimal Speculative Partial Redundancy Elimination (LOSPRE) is one of the most classical, ubiquitous and effective techniques used by compilers for redundancy elimination, i.e. avoiding unnecessary recomputations of the same expression. State-of-the-art methods for LOSPRE over structured programs are based on treewidth, i.e. they first compute a tree decomposition of the control-flow graph of the program and then perform dynamic programming on this decomposition. In this work, we consider a different decomposition approach which is called series-parallel-loop (SPL) and was recently introduced in [8]. We present an efficient linear-time LOSPRE algorithm that builds upon SPL decompositions. We then provide extensive experimental results over the Small Device C Compiler (SDCC) benchmarks, demonstrating that our algorithm outperforms the highly-optimized treewidth-based approach of SDCC.

Keywords: LOSPRE · Structured Programs · Compiler Optimization · Control-flow Graphs · Graph Decompositions

1 Introduction

RE and its Extensions. Redundancy elimination (RE), i.e. avoiding repeated and unnecessary computations of the same expression, has been a goal of optimizing compilers since their early days. Put simply, if the same expression e is used in several different locations in a program, it might be beneficial to compute e once, store it in a temporary variable, and then use it whenever the program reaches any of the locations that need e. One of the first formalizations of this problem was provided in 1970 as Global Common Subexpression Elimination (GCSE) [17]. Later approaches considered removing redundancies that appear only in a subset of paths of the control-flow graph, leading to Partial Redundancy Elimination (PRE) [37]. An enhancement to PRE, introduced by Lazy Code-Motion (LCM) [33], focuses on achieving lifetime optimality by minimizing the lifetimes of the temporary variables it introduces. This is also

© The Author(s), under exclusive license to Springer Nature Singapore Pte Ltd. 2025
T. Bourke et al. (Eds.): SETTA 2024, LNCS 15469, pp. 382–398, 2025.
https://doi.org/10.1007/978-981-96-0602-3_21

helpful for reducing register pressure. Another classical improvement is that of Speculative PRE (SPRE) [7,28], which selects the path for adding computations based on profiling information with the goal of maximizing the benefits of PRE. Putting the ideas of LCM and SPRE together leads to Lifetime-Optimal SPRE (LOSPRE), which is currently the most expressive approach to redundancy elimination and subsumes all other methods mentioned above.

Example. Consider the C function in Fig. 1 (left). If the compiler directly compiles the code as written by the programmer without any optimization, it will lead to the intermediate representation shown in Fig. 1 (center). Note that the gray nodes in this IR all compute the same expression a+b. Applying LOSPRE to this expression will lead to the IR shown in Fig. 1 (right). In this case, a+b is computed only once and saved in a temporary variable temp. Then, all future uses of a+b are replaced by temp. Naturally, this optimization is sound only if there are no changes to the values of a and b between successive uses of temp. Moreover, it comes at a cost. Adding extra computations might change the code size and keeping temporary variables may increase register pressure, affecting performance. Such costs can be formalized and minimized by LOSPRE. See Sect. 2 for a more formal treatment.

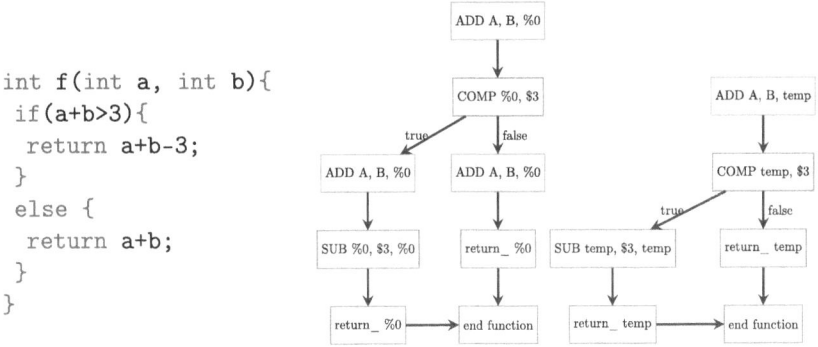

Fig. 1. A simple C function and its intermediate representation (IR) before and after optimization.

Sparsity of CFGs. A control-flow graph (CFG) is simply a graph that has one vertex corresponding to each statement of the program and a directed edge between two vertices whenever their corresponding statements may be executed successively. For example, in Fig. 1, we have shown the IRs as CFGs. Some applications use a coarser definition of CFG, in which every vertex corresponds to a basic block of program statements. In both cases, it is well-known that control-flow graphs of real-world programs are sparse, resemble trees and can be decomposed into sets of vertices of size at most 8 that are connected to each other in a tree-like manner. More formally, CFGs of goto-free structured programs have a treewidth of at most 7 [41]. This celebrated result has been used in a wide variety of program analysis, compiler optimization and model-checking problems [24], which rely on the small treewidth property to obtain faster algorithms for μ-calculus model-checking [38], data-flow analysis [12,27], MDPs [1,3,16], reachability analysis [10,40], algebraic program analysis [11,15,19], register allocation [5,35,41], optimizing cryptocurrency miners' revenues [4,36], cache management [2,13], reliability [26], chemical descriptors [18] and equality saturation [25]. The original bound in [41] applied to Pascal and C programs, but further works have extended it to other languages, such as Ada [6], Java [14,29] and Solidity [9], as well as to path decompositions [20]. There are also negative results, showing that bounded treewidth does not always help in verification [23]. Finally, the recent work [8] provides a new notion of decomposition, called series-parallel-loop (SPL), which exactly captures the set of control-flow graphs of structured goto-free programs and formalizes their sparsity.

Algorithms for LOSPRE. LOSPRE was initially solved by the min-cut-PRE (MC-PRE) algorithm of [42], which has a runtime of $O(n^3)$, where n is the number of nodes in the program's control-flow graph. The same work also shows that MC-PRE is equivalent to solving a weighted minimum cut problem on a directed graph. Thus, applying Karger's classical algorithm [32] leads to an improved runtime bound of $O(n^2 \log^3(n))$. An almost-quadratic runtime is considered too slow for many practical scenarios, especially just-in-time compilation [30,34,39]. This led to the development of suboptimal approximation approaches [30,39] or methods such as [31] that is empirically shown to work faster in practice while having the same asymptotic worst-case complexity. A breakthrough in LOSPRE was achieved by [34] in 2021, which provided a novel approach based on tree decompositions and treewidth. The algorithm of [34] considers the control-flow graph G of the program, computes a tree decomposition of G and then performs dynamic programming on this tree decomposition, leading to a LOSPRE solution that takes $O(\mathtt{tw}(G) \cdot 2^{\mathtt{tw}(G)} \cdot n)$ time, where n is the number of vertices in the CFG and $\mathtt{tw}(G)$ is its treewidth.

Our Contribution. In this work, we consider the problem of LOSPRE over structured goto-free programs. Our approach builds upon and extends the ideas of both [34] and [8] to obtain a faster linear-time algorithm for LOSPRE. More specifically, we exploit the sparsity of CFGs in order to design an algorithm with $O(n)$ runtime. However, unlike [34], we do not use tree decompositions. Instead, we use SPL decompositions, which were defined in [8]. This leads to a much simpler algorithm since SPL decompositions exactly capture the set of CFGs, i.e. we are not solving the problem on a larger set of graphs than necessary. Additionally, SPL decompositions do not ignore the directions of edges in the CFG. This simplicity pays off in practice. We provide extensive experimental results over the Small Device C Compiler (SDCC), which is a highly-optimized compiler using [34], and show that our approach obtains significant performance improvements over [34].

Organization. Section 2 provides a formal definition of the LOSPRE problem, following [34]. Section 3 is an overview of the SPL decomposition method of [8]. This is followed by our new LOSPRE algorithm in Sect. 4. Finally, Sect. 5 provides an experimental comparison of our approach and [34] over the SDCC benchmarks.

2 LOSPRE

In this section, we present LOSPRE. We use the terminology and notation of [34]. LOSPRE is an intraprocedural analysis that considers a single function of the program, modeled as a control-flow graph (CFG) $G = (V, E)$. For example, the two graphs of Fig. 1 are CFGs. A CFG always has a single entry node and a single exit node. The entry node corresponds to the beginning of the function and the exit node to its termination. The entry node has no incoming edge. Conversely, the exit node has no outgoing edge.

Use Sets. Consider an expression e. We define the *use set* U of e as the set of all nodes of the CFG in which the expression e is computed.

Life Sets. Our goal is to precompute the expression e at a few points, save the result in a temporary variable `temp`, and then use `temp` in place of e in every node of U. We denote the lifetime of the variable `temp` by L and call it our *life set*.

Invalidating Set. We say a node v of the CFG invalidates e if the statement at v changes the value of e. For example, if $e = $ `a+b`, then the statement `a = 0` invalidates e. We denote the set of all invalidating nodes by I. These nodes play a crucial role in LOSPRE since they force us to update the value saved in `temp` by recomputing e. We assume that the entry and exit nodes are invalidating since LOSPRE is an intraprocedural analysis that has no information about the program's execution before or after the current function.

Calculation Set. Given the sets U, L and I above, we have to make sure the value of our temporary variable `temp` is correct at every node in $U \cup L$. Thus, for every edge $(x, y) \in E$ of the CFG where $x \notin L$ and $y \in U \cup L$, we have to insert a computation `temp` $= e$ between x and y. Similarly, if $x \in I$, then the value stored at `temp` becomes invalid after the execution of x, requiring us to inject the same computation between x and y. Formally, the computation `temp` $= e$ has to be injected into the following set of edges of the CFG:

$$C(U, L, I) = \{(x, y) \in E \mid x \notin L \backslash I \ \wedge \ y \in U \cup L\}.$$

We call this the *calculation set*.

Example. Figure 2 shows an example of LOSPRE. The top part of the figure is a CFG in which the use set of an expression e is shown in gray, i.e. we need the value of e at vertices $U = \{2, 4, 5, 7\}$. The invalidating set is shown in orange, i.e. the vertices in $I = \{1, 6, 8\}$ invalidate e. The middle and bottom parts each show one possible optimization. We show the lifetime of our temporary variable in green.

In the middle part, the temporary variable is alive at $\{2,3\}$. Thus, the computation temp $= e$ has to be injected into the edge $(1,2)$. We can then use temp instead of e in locations $2, 4$ and 5. However, we need to recompute e in the edge $(6,7)$. In this case our computation set is $\{(1,2),(6,7)\}$. The edges in the computation set are shown in blue.

In the bottom part, the temporary variable is alive only at position 3. Thus, we first compute e when passing through $(1,2)$ so that we have its value at 2. We then recompute e when going through $(2,3)$ and save it at a temporary variable temp. This temporary variable is then used in place of e in 4 and 5. This example shows a tradeoff in which fewer repetitions of the computation lead to a longer lifetime for the temporary variable, which increases register pressure and is undesirable for register allocation.

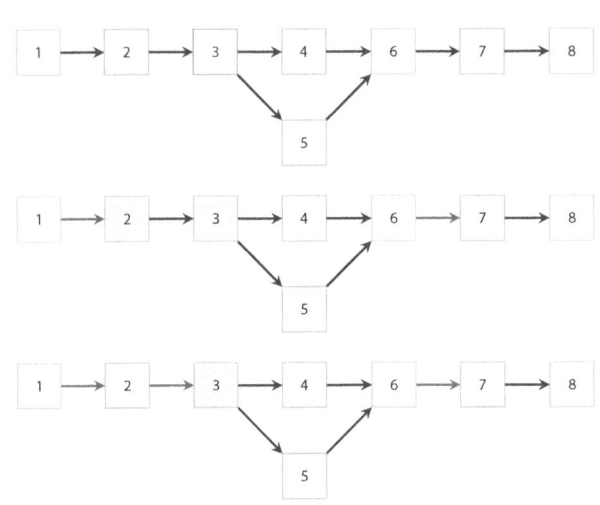

Fig. 2. An example of LOSPRE. The use set is shown in gray, the invalidating set in orange, and the life set in green. The edges of the calculation set are shown in blue. (Color figure online)

Costs. There are two types of costs associated with the process above: (i) injecting calculations into the edges in $C(U, L, I)$ and (ii) keeping an extra variable temp at every node in L. These costs are dependent on the goals pursued by the compiler. For example, a compiler aiming to minimize code size will focus on (i). On the other hand, if our goal is to ease register pressure, we would want to minimize (ii). LOSPRE is an expressive framework in which these costs are modeled by two functions

$$c : E \rightarrow K$$

and

$$l : V \rightarrow K.$$

where K is a totally-ordered set with an addition operator, c is a function that maps each edge to the cost of adding a computation of e in that edge and l is similarly a function that maps each vertex of the CFG to the cost of keeping the temporary variable `temp` alive at that vertex.

Based on the discussion above, we are now ready to define our main problem.

Definition 1 (LOSPRE). *Given a CFG $G = (V, E)$, a use set U, an invalidating set I and two cost functions $c : E \rightarrow K$ and $l : V \rightarrow K$, the LOSPRE problem is to find a life set L that minimizes the total cost*

$$\text{COST}(G, U, I, L, c, l) = \sum_{e \in C(U, L, I)} c(e) + \sum_{v \in L} l(v).$$

Examples of Cost Functions. Suppose our goal is to optimize for execution time. We use profiling to find frequencies of execution for each edge. We then set $K = \mathbb{R}$ and $c(x, y)$ to the frequency with which the edge (x, y) was executed. Finally, we set $l(x) = 0$ for all vertices x. As another example, suppose that we optimize for code size but also want to achieve lifetime-optimality, i.e. not keeping the temporary variable alive when it is not necessary. In this case, we let $K = \mathbb{R}^2$ (using lexicographic ordering) and assign $c(x, y) = (1, 0)$ to every edge (x, y) and $l(x) = (0, 1)$ to every vertex x.

3   SPL Decompositions

In this work, we build our algorithm on top of a decomposition method introduced in [8]. This decomposition method is called SPL (series-parallel-loop) and is an extension of series-parallel graphs with an extra loop operation. It is shown in [8] that a graph is a CFG of a structured program if and only if it has an SPL decomposition.

Structured Programs [41]. We say a program is structured if it can be generated using the following grammar:

$$\begin{aligned} P := &\ \epsilon \mid \texttt{break} \mid \texttt{continue} \mid P; P \\ &\mid \texttt{if } \varphi \texttt{ then } P \texttt{ else } P \texttt{ fi} \mid \texttt{while } \varphi \texttt{ do } P \texttt{ od.} \end{aligned} \tag{1}$$

Here, ϵ is any atomic operation that has no effect on control flow, such as an assignment to a variable. It is easy to define other structures such as `for` and `switch` as syntactic sugar. See [41] for details. We say a program generated by the grammar above is *closed* if every `break` and `continue` statement appears inside a `while` loop's body.

SPL Graphs [8]. An SPL graph $G = (V, E, S, T, B, C)$ is a directed graph (V, E) with four distinct special nodes $S, T, B, C \in V$, which are respectively called the *start*, *terminate*, *break* and *continue* nodes, generated by the grammar below:

$$G := A_\epsilon \mid A_{\texttt{break}} \mid A_{\texttt{continue}} \mid G \otimes G \mid G \oplus G \mid G^\circledast \tag{2}$$

We now explain the operations in this grammar.

Atomic SPL Graphs. There are three different atomic SPL graphs: A_ϵ, A_{break}, and A_{continue}. All of them contain only the four special nodes and only one edge as shown in Fig. 3.

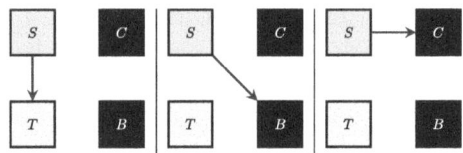

Fig. 3. Atomic SPL graphs: A_ϵ (left), A_{break} (middle), and A_{continue} (right) [8].

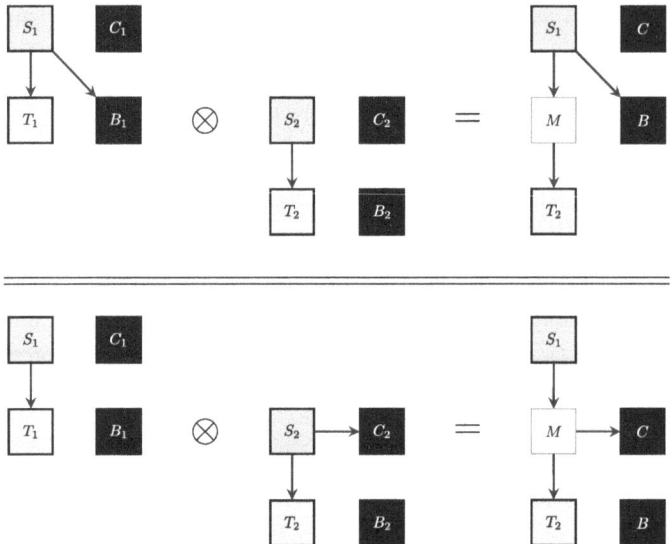

Fig. 4. Two examples of the series operation $\otimes$ [8].

SPL Operations. SPL defines three operations. Let $G_1 = (V_1, E_1, S_1, T_1, B_1, C_1)$ and $G_2 = (V_2, E_2, S_2, T_2, B_2, C_2)$ be two disjoint SPL graphs. Then, the graphs obtained by the following operations are also SPL graphs.

1. *Series Operation.* $G_1 \otimes G_2$ is generated by taking the union of G_1 and G_2 and merging the pairs of vertices $M = (T_1, S_2)$, $B = (B_1, B_2)$, and $C = (C_1, C_2)$. The distinguished vertices of $G_1 \otimes G_2$ are (S_1, T_2, B, C). It is easy to verify that the series operation is associative. Figure 4 shows two examples of the series operation.

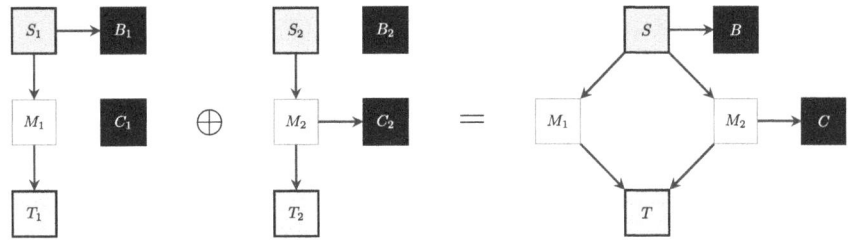

Fig. 5. An example of the parallel operation $\oplus$ [8].

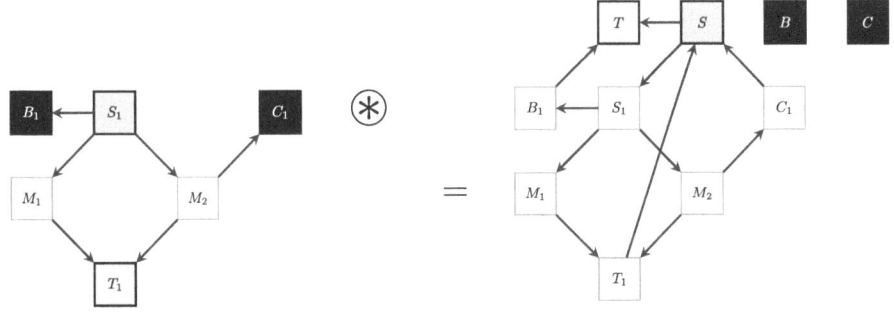

Fig. 6. An example of the loop operation [8].

2. *Parallel Operation.* $G_1 \oplus G_2$ is generated by taking the union of G_1 and G_2 and merging the pairs of vertices $S = (S_1, S_2)$, $T = (T_1, T_2)$, $B = (B_1, B_2)$, and $C = (C_1, C_2)$. The special vertex tuple of $G_1 \oplus G_2$ is (S, T, B, C). Fig. 5 shows an example of this operation.

3. *Loop Operation.* $G_1^{\circledast}$ is generated by adding four new vertices S, T, B, C to G_1 and then adding the following edges: $(S, S_1), (S, T), (T_1, S), (C_1, S)$, and (B_1, T). The special vertex tuple of $G_1^{\circledast}$ is (S, T, B, C). Fig. 6 shows an example of the loop operation.

We say an SPL graph $G = (V, E, S, T, B, C)$ is *closed* if there are no incoming edges to the vertices B and C.

SPLs as CFGs. Given the above definitions of structured programs and SPL graphs, we have the following homomorphism which maps every structured program to its control-flow graph. Moreover, this homomorphism preserves closedness, i.e. closed programs are mapped to closed graphs. A graph is an SPL graph if and only if it is the control-flow graph of a program [8].

$$\mathsf{cfg}(\epsilon) = A_\epsilon \quad \mathsf{cfg}(\texttt{break}) = A_{\texttt{break}} \quad \mathsf{cfg}(\texttt{continue}) = A_{\texttt{continue}}$$

$$\mathsf{cfg}(P_1; P_2) = \mathsf{cfg}(P_1) \otimes \mathsf{cfg}(P_2)$$

$$\text{cfg(if } \varphi \text{ then } P_1 \text{ else } P_2 \text{ fi)} = \text{cfg}(P_1) \oplus \text{cfg}(P_2)$$

$$\text{cfg(while } \varphi \text{ do } P_1 \text{ od)} = \text{cfg}(P_1)^\circledast$$

SPL Decomposition. Given a closed program P, we can first parse it based on the grammar in ((1)) to generate a parse tree. Subsequently, by applying our homomorphism above to this parse tree, we can derive a parse tree according to ((2)) for its control-flow graph. We use the term *SPL decomposition* to refer to the parse tree of the CFG according to ((2)). It is easy to verify that this process takes linear time. See Fig. 7 as an example.

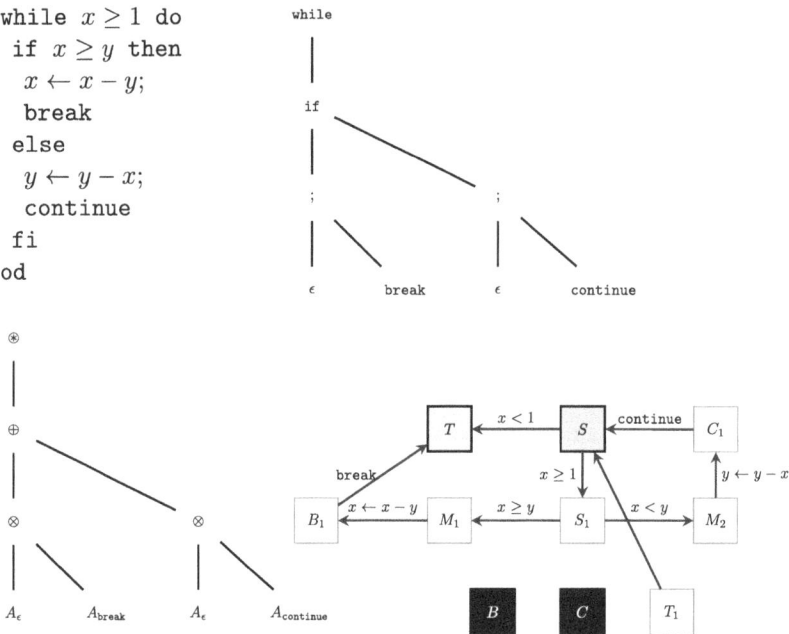

Fig. 7. A program P (top left), its parse tree (top right), the corresponding parse tree of $G = \text{cfg}(P)$ (bottom left) and the graph $G = \text{cfg}(P)$ (bottom right) [8]. The edges of the graph are labeled according to the statements in the program.

4 Our LOSPRE Algorithm

In this section, we present a linear-time algorithm for LOSPRE using SPL decompositions. As in Definition 1, the input to our algorithm consists of a closed program P, its control-flow graph $G = (V, E)$, a use set $U \subseteq V$, an invalidating set $I \subseteq V$ and two cost functions $c : E \to K$ and $l : V \to K$. Our goal is to find a life set $L \subseteq V$ that minimizes

$$\text{COST}(G, U, I, L, c, l) = \sum_{e \in C(U,L,I)} c(e) + \sum_{v \in L} l(v).$$

Step 1 (Initialization). Our algorithm computes an SPL decomposition of $G = \text{cfg}(P)$ by first parsing P and then applying the homomorphism of the previous section.

Step 2 (Dynamic Programming). Our algorithm proceeds with a bottom-up dynamic programming on the SPL decomposition. Note that each node u of the SPL decomposition corresponds to an SPL subgraph $G_u = (V_u, E_u, S_u, T_u, B_u, C_u)$ of G which is either an atomic SPL graph (when u is a leaf) or obtained by applying one of the SPL operations to the graphs corresponding to the children of u. See Fig. 7. Let $\Gamma_u = \{S_u, T_u, B_u, C_u\}$ be the set of special vertices of G_u. For every $X \subseteq \Gamma_u$, we define a dynamic programming variable $\text{dp}[u, X]$. Our goal is to compute this dynamic programming value such that

$$\text{dp}[u, X] = \min_{L \subseteq V_u \ \wedge \ L \cap \Gamma_u = X} \text{COST}(G_u, U, I, L, c, l).$$

Intuitively, we are considering a subproblem of the original LOSPRE in which the graph is limited to G_u. Moreover, we only consider those solutions (life sets) L for which $L \cap \Gamma_u = X$. The value in $\text{dp}[u, X]$ should then give us the minimum cost among all such solutions. Below, we present how our algorithm computes $\text{dp}[u, X]$ for every vertex u of the decomposition based on the $\text{dp}[\cdot, \cdot]$ values at its children:

(2.1) *Atomic Nodes:* If G_u is an atomic SPL graph, then the only vertices in G_u are the four special vertices. Therefore, we must have $L = X$. Our algorithm computes each $\text{dp}[u, X]$ as:

$$\text{dp}[u, X] = \text{COST}(G_u, U, I, X, c, l) = \sum_{e \in C(U,X,I) \cap G_u} c(e) + \sum_{v \in X} l(v).$$

(2.2) *Series Nodes:* Suppose $G_u = G_v \otimes G_w$ where v and w are the children of u in the SPL decomposition. Let $X \subseteq \Gamma_u$ and $X_v \subseteq \Gamma_v$ be subsets of special vertices of G_u and G_v, respectively. We say that X and X_v are *compatible* and write $X \leftrightharpoons X_v$ if the following conditions are satisfied:
 – $S_v \in X_v \Leftrightarrow S_u \in X$;
 – $B_v \in X_v \Leftrightarrow B_u \in X$;
 – $C_v \in X_v \Leftrightarrow C_u \in X$.
 Intuitively, compatibility means that the subsets X and X_v make the same decisions about including vertices in the life set L. Since $S_u = S_v$, they should either both include it or both exclude it. Similarly, B_u is obtained by merging B_v and B_w. Therefore, the decisions made for B_u and B_v must match. The same applies to C_u which is a merger of C_v and C_w.
 Now consider $X_w \subseteq \Gamma_w$. We say that X_w and X are compatible and write $X \leftrightharpoons X_w$ if the following conditions are satisfied:

- $T_w \in X_w \Leftrightarrow T_u \in X$;
- $B_w \in X_w \Leftrightarrow B_u \in X$;
- $C_w \in X_w \Leftrightarrow C_u \in X$.

The intuition is the same as the previous case, except that we now have $T_u = T_w$. Finally, we say that X_v and X_w are compatible and write $X_v \leftrightharpoons X_w$ if

- $T_v \in X_v \Leftrightarrow S_w \in X_w$.

This is because T_v and S_w are the same vertex of the CFG.

In this step, our algorithm sets

$$\mathtt{dp}[u, X] = \min_{\substack{X \leftrightharpoons X_v \\ X \leftrightharpoons X_w \\ X_v \leftrightharpoons X_w}} \mathtt{dp}[v, X_v] + \mathtt{dp}[w, X_w] - [T_v \in X_v] \cdot l(T_v) - [B_v \in X_v] \cdot l(B_v) - [C_v \in X_v] \cdot l(C_v).$$

This is because every edge in G_u appears in either G_v or G_w but not both. Thus, the cost of the edges would simply be the sum of their costs in the two subgraphs. However, when it comes to vertices, T_v and S_w are merged, as are B_v and B_w, and C_v and C_w. Hence, we have to make sure we do not double count the cost of liveness for these vertices. Since this cost is counted in both $\mathtt{dp}$ values at the children, we should subtract it.

(2.3) *Parallel Nodes:* We can handle parallel nodes in the same manner as series nodes, i.e. finding compatible masks at both children and ensuring that there is no double-counting of the costs of vertices. To be more precise, let $G_u = G_v \oplus G_w$. The compatibility conditions we have to check are as follows:

$$X \leftrightharpoons X_v \Leftrightarrow$$
$$(S_u \in X \Leftrightarrow S_v \in X_v \ \wedge \ T_u \in X \Leftrightarrow T_v \in X_v \ \wedge \ B_u \in X \Leftrightarrow B_v \in X_v \ \wedge \ C_u \in X \Leftrightarrow C_v \in X_v);$$
$$X \leftrightharpoons X_w \Leftrightarrow$$
$$(S_u \in X \Leftrightarrow S_w \in X_w \ \wedge \ T_u \in X \Leftrightarrow T_w \in X_w \ \wedge \ B_u \in X \Leftrightarrow B_w \in X_w \ \wedge \ C_u \in X \Leftrightarrow C_w \in X_w);$$
$$X_v \leftrightharpoons X_w \Leftrightarrow$$
$$(S_v \in X_v \Leftrightarrow S_w \in X_w \ \wedge \ T_v \in X_v \Leftrightarrow T_w \in X_w \ \wedge \ B_v \in X_v \Leftrightarrow B_w \in X_w \ \wedge \ C_v \in X_v \Leftrightarrow C_w \in X_w).$$

With the same argument as in the previous case, our algorithm sets

$$\mathtt{dp}[u, X] = \min_{\substack{X \leftrightharpoons X_v \\ X \leftrightharpoons X_w \\ X_v \leftrightharpoons X_w}} \mathtt{dp}[v, X_v] + \mathtt{dp}[w, X_w] - [S_v \in X_v] \cdot l(S_v) - [T_v \in X_v] \cdot l(T_v) - [B_v \in X_v] \cdot l(B_v)$$
$$- [C_v \in X_v] \cdot l(C_v).$$

(2.4) *Loop Nodes:* Finally, we should handle the case where $G_u = G_v^\circledast$. This case is quite simple. By construction, in comparison to G_v, the graph G_u has four new vertices

$$V_{\mathrm{new}} = \{S_u, T_u, B_u, C_u\}$$

and five new edges

$$E_{\mathrm{new}} = \{(S_u, S_v), (S_u, T_u), (T_v, S_u), (C_v, S_u), (B_v, T_u)\}.$$

The two graphs G_u and G_v do not share any special vertices, i.e. $\Gamma_u \cap \Gamma_v = \emptyset$. Moreover, for every edge $(x, y) \in E_{\mathrm{new}}$ we can decide whether (x, y) is in the calculation set solely based on X and X_v. This is because $x, y \in X \cup X_v$. More specifically, (x, y) is in the calculation set if and only if

$$\varphi(X, X_v, x, y) := [x \notin X \cup X_v \backslash I \ \wedge \ y \in U \cup X \cup X_v]$$

Thus, our algorithm sets:

$$\mathrm{dp}[u, X] = \sum_{x \in V_{\mathrm{new}} \cap X} l(x) + \min_{X_v \subseteq \Gamma_v} \mathrm{dp}[v, X_v] + \sum_{(x,y) \in E_{\mathrm{new}}} \varphi(X, X_v, x, y) \cdot c(x, y).$$

Step 3 (Computing the Final Answer). Let r be the root of the SPL decomposition. By definition, we have $G_r = G$. The algorithm outputs $\min_{X \subseteq \Gamma_r} \mathrm{dp}[r, X]$ as the minimum possible cost for the given LOSPRE input. This is because G_r is the entire CFG G and any solution L will conform to exactly one of the different possible values of X at r. As is standard in dynamic programming approaches, one can reconstruct the optimal life set L that leads to this minimal cost by retracing the steps of the algorithm and remembering which choices led to the optimal value at each step.

Theorem 1. *Given a LOSPRE instance consisting of a closed structured program P, its control-flow graph G with n vertices, a use set U, an invalidating set I and two cost functions $c : E \to K$ and $l : V \to K$, the algorithm above solves the LOSPRE problem of Definition 1 in $O(n)$ and outputs*

$$\min_L \mathrm{COST}(G, U, I, L, c, l) \qquad and \qquad \arg\min_L \mathrm{COST}(G, U, I, L, c, l).$$

Proof. Correctness is already argued above. Thus, we focus on the runtime analysis. The SPL decomposition has $O(n)$ vertices and can be computed in $O(n)$ as mentioned at the end of Sect. 3. At each vertex u of the decomposition, we have $2^4 = 16 = O(1)$ different possible values for X. The computations in Step (2.1) are over graphs with only four vertices and thus take $O(1)$ time. In Step (2.2) we have at most two compatible X_v's for each X. This is because inclusion or exclusion of the vertices S_v, B_v and C_v in X_v is uniquely determined by X and only T_v remains to be chosen. Similarly, for every fixed X, X_v, there is a unique X_w. Thus, computing each $\mathrm{dp}[u, X]$ in this step takes $O(1)$ time. In Step (2.3), every X induces a unique X_v and a unique X_w. Hence, this step takes $O(1)$ time to compute each $\mathrm{dp}[u, x]$ value. In Step (2.4), we try $2^4 = O(1)$ different X_v's for each X. Thus, the total runtime of Step 2 is $O(n)$. Finally, Step 3 takes the maximum of $2^4 = O(1)$ values. □

5   Experimental Results

Implementation. We implemented our LOSPRE algorithm in `C++` and integrated it with the Small Device C Compiler (SDCC) [21,22].

Baseline. We compared our algorithm's runtime with the treewidth-based approach of [34], which is the current state-of-the-art in LOSPRE. This approach has an asymptotic runtime of $O(\mathtt{tw}(G) \cdot 2^{\mathtt{tw}(G)} \cdot n)$ where $\mathtt{tw}(G)$ is the treewidth of G. We did not consider other previous methods since they are significantly slower with runtime bounds of $O(n^3)$ or $O(n^2 \cdot \log^3 n)$. Additionally, SDCC already includes a highly-optimized variant of algorithms for finding tree decompositions. Furthermore, [34] is also implemented as part of SDCC.

Machine. The results were obtained on an Ubuntu 24.04 machine, equipped with a 1.6 GHz dual-core Intel Core i5 processor and 4 GB of RAM.

Benchmarks. We exactly followed the setup of [34], utilizing the SDCC regression test suite as our benchmark set. This suite comprises a total of $20,244$ instances for LOSPRE. These benchmarks are embedded programs expected to operate in resource-constrained environments. Therefore, the focus is on code size optimization. More specifically, the goal is to minimize the total number of computations in the resulting 3-address code. Thus, we use $K = \mathbb{Z}^2$ with lexicographic ordering. The cost assigned to each edge (x, y) is $c(x, y) = (1, 0)$. We also enforce lifetime-optimality by assigning the cost $l(x) = (0, 1)$ to every vertex x. We only compare the runtimes. There is no output comparison since both our approach and [34] find an optimal solution for LOSPRE, creating 3-address codes of the same size. We enforced a time limit of 10 min and a memory limit of 4 GB for each benchmark.

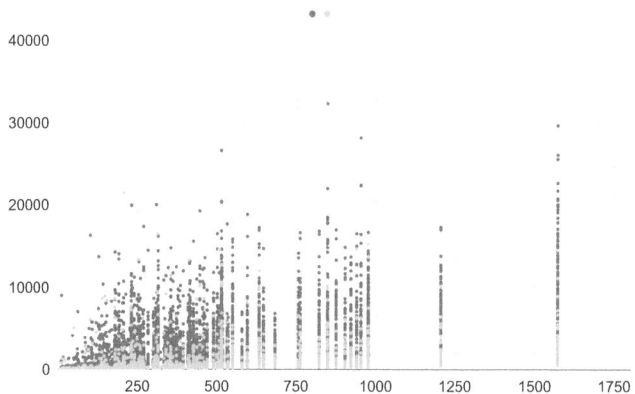

Fig. 8. Runtime comparison of the treewidth-based algorithm in [34] (red) and our approach (green). The x axis is the size of the CFG and the y axis is time in μs. (Color figure online)

Runtimes. Figures 8–9 provide runtime comparisons between [34] and our approach. On average, our algorithm takes $222.38\ \mu s$, while the treewidth-based approach of [34] has an average runtime of $1349.14\ \mu s$. The maximum runtime was $21,524\ \mu s$ for our algorithm compared to $32,284\ \mu s$ for [34]. Our algorithm

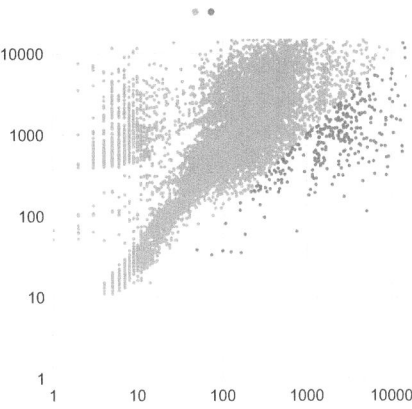

Fig. 9. Runtime comparison of the treewidth-based algorithm in [34] and our approach. The x axis is our runtime and the y axis is [34]'s runtime. Each dot represents one LOSPRE instance. Instances for which our approach was faster are shown in green and those for which [34] was faster are shown in red. The axes are in logarithmic scale. (Color figure online)

significantly outperforms [34] in the vast majority of benchmarks. We identified only 19 instances where our runtime exceeded 10,000 µs, whereas [34] takes more than 10,000 µs in 277 instances.

Discussion. In summary, our approach is approximately six times faster than the previous state-of-the-art for LOSPRE. This represents a significant improvement, particularly given that the treewidth-based approach of [34] is already highly optimized and included in the well-established SDCC compiler. We believe there are two main reasons for this speedup: (i) computing SPL decompositions is much faster than tree decompositions, and (ii) our algorithm's runtime does not depend on parameters such as treewidth and the constant factor hidden in our $O(n)$ asymptotic runtime analysis is small in practice.

6   Conclusion

We provided a novel algorithm for lifetime-optimal speculative partial redundancy elimination over structured goto-free programs. Our algorithm exploits the sparsity of the program's control-flow graph. However, unlike the previous state-of-the-art, we do not consider tree decompositions and treewidth. Instead, we build our algorithm based on the different notion of series-parallel-loop (SPL) decompositions. SPL decompositions can be computed much faster than tree decompositions and our algorithm's runtime is also independent of parameters such as treewidth. As a result, we observed a significant 6x runtime improvement in LOSPRE over benchmarks from the Small Device C Compiler. Our algorithm works directly on the CFG of a source program, whereas many compilers, such as LLVM, have an intermediate representation in the SSA form, which has been exploited for various compiler optimization tasks. An interesting direction of future research is to explore whether our speedups can be combined with those obtained from SSA representations. On the other hand, a significant limitation of our approach is that it can only be applied to goto-free programs. Extending the SPL decomposition and our algorithm to support goto statements is another interesting direction.

Acknowledgments. We are grateful to the anonymous reviewers for raising points that significantly improved this work. The research was partially supported by the Hong Kong Research Grants Council ECS Project Number 26208122.

References

1. Ahmadi, A., Chatterjee, K., Goharshady, A.K., Meggendorfer, T., Safavi, R., Zikelic, Đ.: Algorithms and hardness results for computing cores of Markov chains. In: FSTTCS, pp. 29:1–29:20 (2022)
2. Ahmadi, A., Daliri, M., Goharshady, A.K., Pavlogiannis, A.: Efficient approximations for cache-conscious data placement. In: PLDI, pp. 857–871 (2022)
3. Asadi, A., Chatterjee, K., Goharshady, A.K., Mohammadi, K., Pavlogiannis, A.: Faster algorithms for quantitative analysis of MCs and MDPs with small treewidth. In: ATVA, vol. 12302, pp. 253–270 (2020)
4. Barakbayeva, T., Farokhnia, S., Goharshady, A.K., Gufler, M., Novozhilov, S.: Pixiu: optimal block production revenues on Cardano. In: Blockchain (2024)
5. Bodlaender, H.L., Gustedt, J., Telle, J.A.: Linear-time register allocation for a fixed number of registers. In: SODA, pp. 574–583 (1998)
6. Burgstaller, B., Blieberger, J., Scholz, B.: On the tree width of ADA programs. In: Llamosí, A., Strohmeier, A. (eds.) Ada-Europe 2004. LNCS, vol. 3063, pp. 78–90. Springer, Heidelberg (2004). https://doi.org/10.1007/978-3-540-24841-5_6
7. Cai, Q., Xue, J.: Optimal and efficient speculation-based partial redundancy elimination, pp. 91–102. CGO (2003)
8. Cai, X., Goharshady, A.K., Hitarth, S., Lam, C.K.: Faster register allocation via grammatical decompositions of control-flow graphs (2024). https://hal.science/hal-04672403
9. Chatterjee, K., Goharshady, A.K., Goharshady, E.K.: The treewidth of smart contracts. In: SAC, pp. 400–408. ACM (2019)
10. Chatterjee, K., Goharshady, A.K., Goyal, P., Ibsen-Jensen, R., Pavlogiannis, A.: Faster algorithms for dynamic algebraic queries in basic RSMs with constant treewidth. ACM Trans. Program. Lang. Syst. **41**(4), 23:1–23:46 (2019)
11. Chatterjee, K., Goharshady, A.K., Ibsen-Jensen, R., Pavlogiannis, A.: Algorithms for algebraic path properties in concurrent systems of constant treewidth components. In: POPL, pp. 733–747 (2016)
12. Chatterjee, K., Goharshady, A.K., Ibsen-Jensen, R., Pavlogiannis, A.: Optimal and perfectly parallel algorithms for on-demand data-flow analysis. In: ESOP, pp. 112–140 (2020)
13. Chatterjee, K., Goharshady, A.K., Okati, N., Pavlogiannis, A.: Efficient parameterized algorithms for data packing. Proc. ACM Program. Lang. **3**(POPL), 53:1–53:28 (2019)

14. Chatterjee, K., Goharshady, A.K., Pavlogiannis, A.: JTDec: a tool for tree decompositions in soot. In: D'Souza, D., Narayan Kumar, K. (eds.) ATVA 2017. LNCS, vol. 10482, pp. 59–66. Springer, Cham (2017). https://doi.org/10.1007/978-3-319-68167-2_4

15. Chatterjee, K., Ibsen-Jensen, R., Goharshady, A.K., Pavlogiannis, A.: Algorithms for algebraic path properties in concurrent systems of constant treewidth components. ACM Trans. Program. Lang. Syst. **40**(3), 9:1–9:43 (2018)

16. Chatterjee, K., Lacki, J.: Faster algorithms for Markov decision processes with low treewidth. In: Sharygina, N., Veith, H. (eds.) CAV 2013. LNCS, vol. 8044, pp. 543–558. Springer, Heidelberg (2013). https://doi.org/10.1007/978-3-642-39799-8_36

17. Cocke, J.: Global common subexpression elimination, pp. 20–24 (1970). https://doi.org/10.1145/390013.808480

18. Conrado, G.K., Goharshady, A.K., Hudec, P., Li, P., Motwani, H.J.: Faster treewidth-based approximations for Wiener index. In: SEA, vol. 301, pp. 6:1–6:19 (2024)

19. Conrado, G.K., Goharshady, A.K., Kochekov, K., Tsai, Y.C., Zaher, A.K.: Exploiting the sparseness of control-flow and call graphs for efficient and on-demand algebraic program analysis. Proc. ACM Program. Lang. **7**(OOPSLA2), 1993–2022 (2023)

20. Conrado, G.K., Goharshady, A.K., Lam, C.K.: The bounded pathwidth of control-flow graphs. Proc. ACM Program. Lang. **7**(OOPSLA2), 292–317 (2023)

21. Dutta, S.: Anatomy of a compiler: a retargetable ANSI-C compiler. Circ. Cellar **121**(5) (2000)

22. Dutta, S., Drotos, D., Vigor, K., et al.: Small device C compiler (2003). http://sdcc.sourceforge.net/

23. Ferrara, A., Pan, G., Vardi, M.Y.: Treewidth in verification: local vs. global. In: LPAR, vol. 3835, pp. 489–503 (2005)

24. Goharshady, A.K.: Parameterized and Algebro-geometric Advances in Static Program Analysis. Ph.D. thesis, Institute of Science and Technology Austria, Klosterneuburg, Austria (2020)

25. Goharshady, A.K., Lam, C.K., Parreaux, L.: Fast and optimal extraction for sparse equality graphs. In: OOPSLA (2024)

26. Goharshady, A.K., Mohammadi, F.: An efficient algorithm for computing network reliability in small treewidth. Reliab. Eng. Syst. Saf. **193**, 106665 (2020)

27. Goharshady, A.K., Zaher, A.K.: Efficient interprocedural data-flow analysis using treedepth and treewidth. In: Dragoi, C., Emmi, M., Wang, J. (eds.) VMCAI 2023. LNCS, vol. 13881, pp. 177–202. Springer, Cham (2023). https://doi.org/10.1007/978-3-031-24950-1_9

28. Gupta, R., Berson, D., Fang, J.: Path profile guided partial redundancy elimination using speculation. In: Proceedings of the 1998 International Conference on Computer Languages (Cat. No.98CB36225), pp. 230–239 (1998)

29. Gustedt, J., Mæhle, O.A., Telle, J.A.: The treewidth of java programs. In: Mount, D.M., Stein, C. (eds.) ALENEX 2002. LNCS, vol. 2409, pp. 86–97. Springer, Heidelberg (2002). https://doi.org/10.1007/3-540-45643-0_7

30. Horspool, R.N., Pereira, D.J., Scholz, B.: Fast profile-based partial redundancy elimination. In: Lightfoot, D.E., Szyperski, C. (eds.) JMLC 2006. LNCS, vol. 4228, pp. 362–376. Springer, Heidelberg (2006). https://doi.org/10.1007/11860990_22

31. Jaiyen, B., Liu, J.: Implementing profile-guided speculative code motion in LLVM (2012)

32. Karger, D.R., Stein, C.: An Õ(n2) algorithm for minimum cuts. In: STOC, pp. 757–765 (1993)

33. Knoop, J., Rüthing, O., Steffen, B.: Lazy code motion. In: PLDI, pp. 224–234 (1992)

34. Krause, P.K.: lospre in linear time. In: SCOPES, pp. 35–41 (2021)

35. Krause, P.K.: Optimal register allocation in polynomial time. In: Jhala, R., De Bosschere, K. (eds.) CC 2013. LNCS, vol. 7791, pp. 1–20. Springer, Heidelberg (2013). https://doi.org/10.1007/978-3-642-37051-9_1

36. Meybodi, M.A., Goharshady, A.K., Hooshmandasl, M.R., Shakiba, A.: Optimal mining: maximizing Bitcoin miners' revenues from transaction fees. In: Blockchain, pp. 266–273 (2022)

37. Morel, E., Renvoise, C.: Global optimization by suppression of partial redundancies. Commun. ACM **22**, 96–103 (1979)

38. Obdržálek, J.: Fast mu-calculus model checking when tree-width is bounded. In: Hunt, W.A., Somenzi, F. (eds.) CAV 2003. LNCS, vol. 2725, pp. 80–92. Springer, Heidelberg (2003). https://doi.org/10.1007/978-3-540-45069-6_7

39. Pereira, D.J.: Isothermality: making speculative optimizations affordable (2007). https://api.semanticscholar.org/CorpusID:64227807

40. Sankaranarayanan, S.: Reachability analysis using message passing over tree decompositions. In: Lahiri, S.K., Wang, C. (eds.) CAV 2020. LNCS, vol. 12224, pp. 604–628. Springer, Cham (2020). https://doi.org/10.1007/978-3-030-53288-8_30

41. Thorup, M.: All structured programs have small tree width and good register allocation. Inf. Comput. **142**(2), 159–181 (1998)

42. Xue, J., Cai, Q.: A lifetime optimal algorithm for speculative PRE. ACM Trans. Archit. Code Optim, 115–155 (2006)

EDSLog: Efficient Log Anomaly Detection Method Based on Dataset Partitioning

Feng Liang and Jing Liu[(✉)] [ID]

College of Computer Science, Inner Mongolia University, Hohhot, China
`liujing@imu.edu.cn`

Abstract. With the growing demand for computility, the reliability of computility services has become increasingly crucial. Due to the escalating volume and complexity of tasks processed, computility services often need to operate under high load, which can easily lead to issues such as resource shortages and service interruptions. Logs in computility services meticulously record the operational information of each component; therefore, anomaly detection based on logs can effectively ensure the stable operation of computility services. This study aims to address two challenges in the field of log anomaly detection. First, this study addresses the previously overlooked issue of class-imbalanced log data. Second, given the massive volumes of log data, the time required for model training poses a significant challenge. To address these issues, we propose EDSLog, a novel efficient log anomaly detection framework based on dataset partitioning. Initially, EDSLog processes log sequences through the Weight-Based K-fold Sub Hold-out Method (WKHM), effectively alleviating the class-imbalance problem. Subsequently, EDSLog leverages Simple Recurrent Units (SRU) enhanced by a self-attention mechanism to extract features from log sequences. Finally, EDSLog determines whether the predicted log data are anomalous. Experiments show that EDSLog achieves the best evaluation metrics in class-imbalanced datasets while having the shortest total model runtime. Specifically, EDSLog achieved the highest F1 scores of 100 and 99.96 respectively on the BGL and HDFS datasets, where abnormal logs account for 0.1% of the data. Additionally, EDSLog's training speed was 35.62% faster than the model with the second shortest training duration among all models compared.

Keywords: Computility service · Log anomaly detection · Self attention · Dataset partitioning · SRU

1 Introduction

Computility services refer to the provision of diverse, ubiquitous, and inclusive computility resources, leveraging a variety of computational capabilities through cloud computing technology. In recent years, due to the rapid development of

T. Bourke et al. (Eds.): SETTA 2024, LNCS 15469, pp. 399–415, 2025.
https://doi.org/10.1007/978-981-96-0602-3_22

artificial intelligence, large models, and deep learning, the demand for computility has sharply increased, making secure and reliable computility services a subject of widespread attention. As computility services continue to expand in terms of functionality, customization, scale, and operate continuously around the clock, the complexity and pressure on computility service systems increase accordingly, potentially leading to faults such as resource shortages, data loss, and service interruptions [1–3]. Logs in computility services, which typically include timestamps, node locations, node types, operation commands, and login user information, are crucial data that reflect the operational status of each component, providing us with important clues to deeply understand abnormal behaviors [4,18]. Therefore, constructing an effective log anomaly detection framework to ensure the overall quality of computility services becomes particularly crucial.

Due to the success of deep learning in automatically learning complex patterns and relationships in large-scale data [5,10], many studies have turned to exploring the application of deep learning in log anomaly detection. DeepLog [4] is a deep learning-based log anomaly detection framework. It uses LSTM to capture complex patterns in log sequences for anomaly detection. PLELog [7] solves the problem of insufficient labels through probabilistic label estimation and designs an attention-based GRU [8] neural network to detect anomalies. CNN-text [9] starts from the semantic information contained in log messages, using CNN to extract the semantic content and conduct anomaly detection.

Although these research findings are significant, log anomaly detection still faces two challenges. **Firstly**, log data class-imbalanced. In mature computility service systems, anomaly log data usually represent a very small proportion of total log data, resulting in severe class imbalance. This presents a significant challenge to existing log anomaly detection methods. **Secondly**, the efficiency of models needs to be improved. Large computility service systems, such as Microsoft and Amazon, operate 24/7 and support hundreds of millions of users, thereby generating substantial log volumes. For instance, the distributed file system HDFS, commonly used in the computational service system discussed in this paper, generated 1.47 GB of log data in 38.7 h. Over time, the rate of log generation will significantly increase, leading to continuously growing volumes of log data. Consequently, there is a growing demand for models capable of efficiently handling these data volumes and swiftly detecting anomalies.

To address the aforementioned challenges, we propose EDSLog, a log anomaly detection framework. Firstly, to address class imbalance in log data, we introduce a dataset partitioning method called WKHM, which effectively mitigates model overfitting and inaccuracies in performance evaluation caused by class imbalance. Secondly, we then construct a log anomaly detection model using a Simple Recurrent Unit (SRU) [12] recurrent neural network combined with a self-attention mechanism [19]. The outputs of the multi-layer SRU are fed into the self-attention layer, which aids in learning the internal structure of log data and addressing long-term dependencies within the log sequences. The SRU based on the self-attention mechanism offers faster processing speed and improved performance compared to traditional recurrent neural networks.

To evaluate the performance of EDSLog, we utilized two of the most widely used public datasets, namely HDFS [13,14] and BGL [13,15]. Additionally, we processed these datasets by randomly deleting portions of normal or abnormal log data, achieving datasets with varying proportions of anomaly data. In our experiments, we also compared EDSLog with the WKHM and time-based training data selection methods. The results indicate that in datasets with anomaly log ratios from 0.1% to 10%, EDSLog significantly outperforms the comparison groups in terms of accuracy and F1 scores, and it also boasts the shortest processing time. These results fully demonstrate EDSLog's superior performance in anomaly log detection.

In summary, the paper provides the following contributions:

- This paper presents an innovative log anomaly detection framework, EDSLog, integrating the WKHM method for dataset partitioning and the SRU recurrent neural network for anomaly detection modeling. Compared to existing mainstream frameworks EDSLog demonstrated significant improvements across all comparative experiments, achieving the highest F1 scores of 98.97 on HDFS and 99.64 on BGL. Additionally, EDSLog also excelled in efficiency, taking only 26.64 min on HDFS and 10.15 min on BGL.

- To address the issue of class imbalance, this study proposes a novel dataset partitioning method, the WKHM. First, we evenly divide the entire dataset into k subsets, ensuring no overlap between them. Then, based on the time-series characteristics of the log data, each subset is further divided into training and test subsets according to a specified ratio. During model training, an incremental training strategy is employed, where each training subset undergoes T rounds of training in sequence. This ensures that the model gradually learns the characteristics of abnormal samples from different time periods, thereby enhancing its ability to identify abnormal samples. In the testing phase, weights are calculated based on the proportion of abnormal samples in each subset, and the final evaluation results are obtained by performing a weighted summation. Experimental results show that this method effectively addresses the issues of overfitting and inaccurate performance evaluation caused by class imbalance.

- We model complex log data using a combination of the self-attention mechanism and the SRU recurrent neural network. SRU exhibits faster speed and superior performance compared to traditional recurrent neural networks such as LSTM and GRU. Meanwhile, the self-attention mechanism is capable of capturing long-range dependencies in log data and offers the advantage of parallel computation. Experimental results demonstrate that the SRU-based log anomaly detection framework, which incorporates the self-attention mechanism, not only ensures efficiency in anomaly detection but also significantly enhances detection accuracy.

2   Related Work

2.1   Deep Learning Based Log Anomaly Detection

Deep learning has garnered increasing attention in log anomaly detection. In addition to methods utilizing LSTM [4], GRU [7], and CNN [9], as elaborated above, several novel approaches have emerged: Wang et al. introduced Light-Log [17], which performs log anomaly detection on edge devices utilizing a low-dimensional semantic vector space and a modified lightweight temporal convolutional network (TCN).

2.2   Methods of Data Set Partitioning

Hold-out. When using the hold-out method to process a dataset, the entire dataset D is divided into a training set S and a test set T, where S is used for model training, and T is used for model validation. Assuming D contains 200 samples, we divide the training and test sets in a 7:3 ratio. There are multiple ways to implement the holdout method for dataset division. Two commonly used methods are outlined below a) proportional split method: The first 140 samples are sequentially assigned to the training set, and the remaining 60 samples constitute the test set. This is the most common approach in the holdout method, and many studies on log anomaly detection adopt this method. In this paper, the holdout method mentioned subsequently refers to this approach. b) Stratified sampling method: In cases where the sample proportions are imbalanced, stratified sampling can be used to ensure that the proportions of various sample types in both the training set S and the test set T match those in the original dataset. This approach helps to ensure that the model is exposed to the same proportions of different sample types during both training and testing, thereby preventing model bias.

K-fold cross-validation. K-fold cross-validation is another common method for dataset division. This technique divides the dataset evenly into k parts, each referred to as a "fold". During model training, one fold is used as the test set, while the remaining $k-1$ folds are used as the training set. This process is repeated k times, ensuring that each part of the data is used for testing. Finally, the results of the k tests are averaged to obtain the final test result.

K-fold Sub Hold-out Method (KSHM). In the paper [22], the authors introduced KSHM, a dataset partitioning method designed for log anomaly detection. This method merges the advantages of the hold-out method and K-fold cross-validation, managing to preserve the time-series features within the dataset during partitioning. It further expands the sampling range without increasing the number of samples, thereby enhancing the model's ability to memorize effective features.

2.3   Methods Based on Log Data to Address Class-Imbalanced

In the field of log anomaly detection, common methods for handling data imbalance include oversampling and undersampling. In a study [21], the authors employed an oversampling technique, increasing the proportion of anomalous samples to 30% when it was initially below this threshold, thereby enhancing the model's ability to identify anomalous samples. In another study [20], the authors used the Tomek Link method for undersampling by identifying and removing majority class samples to achieve a more balanced dataset, thereby improving the model's ability to detect anomalous activities.

3   EDSLog Framework

3.1   Overview

This paper proposes an efficient log anomaly detection method based on dataset division, named EDSLog. This method effectively addresses the class imbalance in log data and significantly reduces the total processing time when handling large volumes of log data compared to other methods. The overall framework of EDSLog is illustrated in Fig. 1 and consists of two steps. First, to address the class imbalance in log data, we process the dataset composed of log using WKHM. Second, to fully and quickly learn the characteristics of the log data, each of the divided sub-datasets is fed into an SRU neural network model based on the self-attention mechanism for training. After training, the prepared test dataset is used to evaluate the trained model, yielding the final prediction results.

3.2   Dataset Partitioning Method WKHM

Dataset Partitioning and Class Imbalance Challenges. Prior to training a log anomaly detection model, dataset partitioning is a critical step in data preprocessing, typically guided by the dataset's characteristics. A prominent feature of log data is a class imbalance, where anomalous data constitutes only a small fraction of the overall log dataset. For instance, in the HDFS and BGL datasets, anomalous data accounts for less than 10% of the total. As system development and operational technologies evolve, this imbalance is expected to become more pronounced, potentially leading to model overfitting and inaccurate evaluation if not properly managed. Furthermore, log data is characterized by its vast volume and time-series nature. Common partitioning methods in log anomaly detection include the Hold-out method, K-fold cross-validation, and the KSHM method. Although K-fold cross-validation effectively utilizes limited data, it has several drawbacks: it disrupts time-series features, is time-intensive when handling large-scale data, and does not resolve the class imbalance. The Hold-out method preserves time-series features by proportionally splitting the dataset, but it struggles to adequately capture the characteristics of anomalous samples during training. While stratified sampling ensures class balance, it compromises time-series features. The KSHM method enhances the learning of

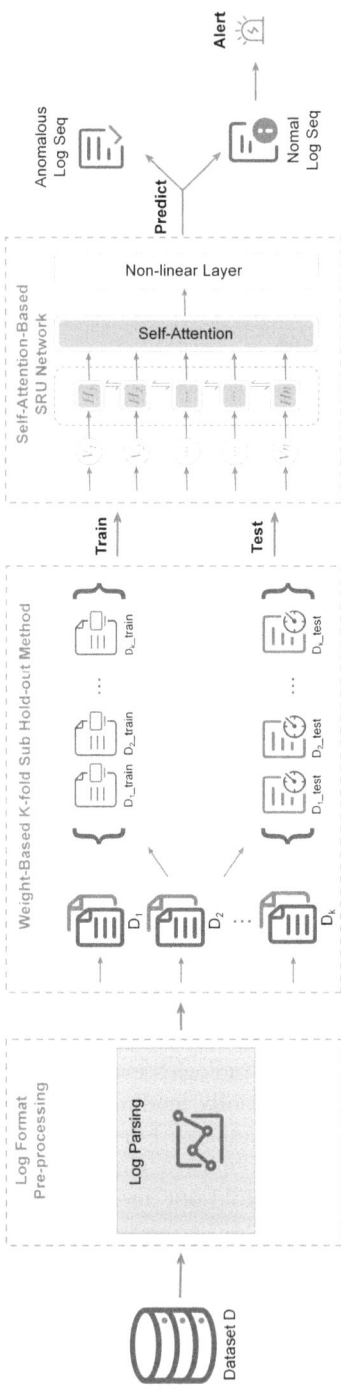

Fig. 1. Overview of EDSLog

anomalous samples while maintaining time-series features, yet it remains inadequate in learning from imbalanced sample characteristics and fails to ensure a fair representation of each class during model evaluation. Although over-sampling and under-sampling strategies based on class imbalance can mitigate the imbalance issue in certain scenarios, over-sampling might introduce noise, leading to model overfitting, and increase computational complexity and training time. Conversely, under-sampling may result in the loss of crucial information and disruption of time-series features, thereby impacting model performance.

Weight-Based K-fold Sub Hold-out Method (WKHM). In summary, it is evident that various dataset partitioning methods and data-based approaches to address class imbalance have their limitations. Consequently, to tackle these issues, we introduce WKHM, a weight-based k-fold hold-out method.

The primary workflow of WKHM is depicted in Fig. 2, comprising four key steps.

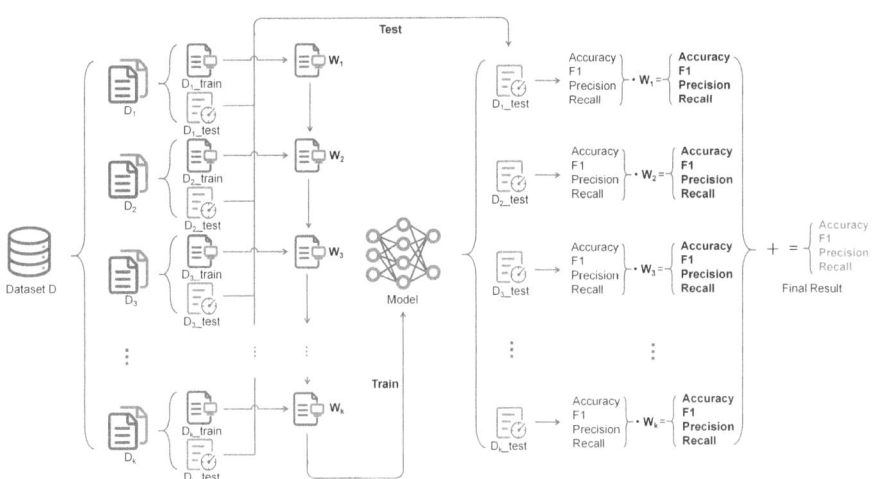

Fig. 2. Log Parsing

- K-fold partitioning of datasets: To address the issue of class imbalance in log data and ensure the robustness of evaluation results, we need to evenly divide the entire dataset into k subsets. The divided datasets are denoted as $\{D_1, D_2, D_3, \cdots, D_{k-1}, D_k\}$, and $D = D_1 + D_2 + D_3 + \cdots + D_{k-1} + D_k$, where $D_1 \cap D_2 \cap D_3 \cap \cdots \cap D_{k-1} \cap D_k = \varnothing$. At this point, the initial partitioning of the dataset is completed.
- training set and test set division: To preserve the potential time-series characteristics of the log data, we proceed with splitting the training and test sets

based on the foundation established in the previous step. Here, for each data subset, we apply the proportionate split method from hold-out validation to ensure the continuity of training data along the time dimension. In this study, a 7:3 split ratio is used. Each subset D_k is divided into D_{k_train} and D_{k_test}, with $D_{k\_train} \cap D_{k\_test} = \varnothing$, and the ratio of $|D_{k\_train}|$ to $|D_{k\_test}|$ is 7:3. To comprehensively evaluate the model's performance after training, we calculate weights $W_1, W_2, \ldots, W_{k-1}, W_k$ based on the proportion of abnormal log entries in each subset once the dataset has been split. Formula 1 is used to calculate these weights, which are based on the total number of abnormal entries T in the entire training set, where N_k represents the number of abnormal entries in the k-th training set.

$$W_k = \frac{N_k}{T} \tag{1}$$

- model training: To enhance the model's generalization ability and its capability to identify abnormal samples, we adopted an incremental training approach. Specifically, the model learns sequentially from datasets $D_1, D_2, D_3, \cdots, D_{k-1}, D_k$, each of which contains different distributions of abnormal data. In practice, these datasets are input into the model sequentially for T rounds of training.

- model validation: To comprehensively evaluate the effectiveness of the model training, we conduct tests after each round of training. The model's performance is assessed using the corresponding test sets $D_{1\_test}, D_{2\_test}, \cdots, D_{k\_test}$, and the evaluation results are weighted and summed according to the abnormal sample weights $W_1, W_2, \cdots, W_{k-1}, W_k$, ultimately producing the model's overall performance.

Through the aforementioned steps, the WKHM method enables the model to more comprehensively learn the characteristics of abnormal samples, ensuring that the model's performance across different classes is fairly reflected, avoiding overfitting, and ensuring that all classes are fairly and accurately represented during model performance evaluation. Additionally, this method preserves the time-series characteristics of the log data.

3.3   Self-attention Mechanism-Based SRU Neural Network

SRU Neural Network. Based on the reasonable partitioning of the dataset, to efficiently utilize the dataset obtained through WKHM, we can subsequently use the self-attention mechanism-based SRU recurrent neural network (as shown in Fig. 1) to effectively extract features from the training dataset and enhance the accuracy of anomaly detection results. Simple Recurrent Units (SRU) are a modification of the traditional Recurrent Neural Network (RNN), particularly the Long Short-Term Memory (LSTM) and Gated Recurrent Unit (GRU), as proposed by Lei et al. [12]. As variants of recurrent neural networks, LSTM and

GRU have been demonstrated to effectively process log data [4] [7]. They introduce a gating mechanism, ensuring that the computation at each step is based on
the result from the previous step. Consequently, recurrent computation is not
well-suited for parallelization [12]. Additionally, both LSTM and GRU utilize
a gating mechanism to control the flow of information, thereby mitigating the
issues of vanishing and exploding gradients. During this process, the computations in neural networks, particularly matrix multiplication, typically consume
substantial computational resources. However, the design of the SRU is notably
different. Its principal feature is that the gating computations depend solely on
the current recurrent input, implying that only the dot product operations are
dependent on previous steps. Consequently, matrix multiplication in the feed-
forward network can be parallelized more effectively.

SRU is primarily composed of two main components: the Light Recurrence
mechanism and the Highway Network structure. The detailed structure is shown
in Figs. 3 and 4.

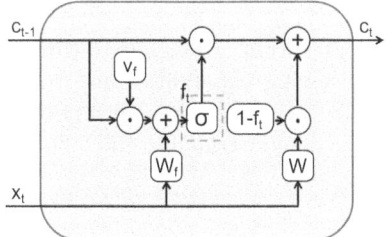 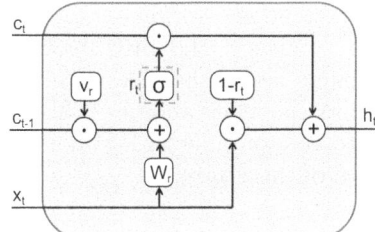

Fig. 3. Light Recurrence   **Fig. 4.** Highway Network

In summary, SRU, with its unique design, achieves highly efficient parallel processing and robust sequence modeling capabilities, establishing it as an
effective recurrent neural network architecture for log anomaly detection, as
demonstrated in the subsequent chapter of this study.

Self-attention Mechanism. The self-attention mechanism is introduced to
enhance the model's ability to capture long-range dependencies within log
sequences. The self-attention layer generates attention weights by calculating
similarity scores between each time step and then produces context vectors
based on these weights. In our model, the self-attention mechanism operates
on the output of the SRU to better capture important information within the
sequence. The specific calculations are as follows:

$$Q = W_q \cdot H, \tag{2a}$$
$$K = W_k \cdot H, \tag{2b}$$
$$V = W_v \cdot H \tag{2c}$$

where Q, K, V are the query, key, and value matrices, respectively, and W_q, W_k, W_v are trainable weight matrices. Next, the attention scores are computed as:

$$A = \text{softmax}\left(\frac{Q \cdot K^T}{\sqrt{d_k}}\right) \tag{3}$$

Finally, the context vectors are computed via weighted sum as follows:

$$C = A \cdot V \tag{4}$$

where C is the output of the self-attention layer, and the context vector represents the importance of each time step within the sequence.

The final layer of the model is a linear layer, which is used to map the output of the attention mechanism to a binary classification space. The computation of the linear layer is as follows:

$$\text{Output} = W_o \cdot H_{\text{Attn}} + b_o \tag{5}$$

where W_o represents the weights of the linear layer, H_{Attn} denotes the output of the attention layer, and b_o is the bias term.

In summary, the SRU based on the self-attention mechanism, through its unique design, achieves efficient parallel processing capabilities and robust sequence modeling abilities. This makes it an effective recurrent neural network architecture suitable for log anomaly detection, as demonstrated in the following section of this study.

4   Experimental Design

In this chapter, we introduce the datasets used in our experiments, describe the comparative models for log-based anomaly detection, detail the research settings and experimental environment, and outline the evaluation metrics.

4.1   Datasets Employed in the Experiments

In our study, we employed two widely recognized public datasets, HDFS and BGL, extensively used in prior research on log-based anomaly detection [4,7, 9,17,18], to assess the performance of EDSLog. **HDFS dataset:** This dataset contains 11,175,629 log entries generated by Hadoop MapReduce jobs running on over 2,000 Amazon EC2 nodes, with a total runtime of 38.7 h. The logs have been labeled by experts, resulting in 10,887,379 normal entries and 288,250 abnormal entries (approximately 2.9%), spanning 45 log templates. **BGL dataset:** This dataset originates from the BlueGene/L supercomputer at LLNL, California, which consists of 131,072 processors and spans a period of 7 months. It includes a total of 4,747,963 log entries. After expert labeling and parsing (with 34,470 non-conforming logs removed), 4,713,493 logs remain, comprising 4,365,033 normal and 348,460 abnormal entries (approximately 7.39% abnormal), spanning 378 log templates (Table 1).

4.2   Compared Approaches

In this study, we compared the EDSLog model with three representatively based on deep learning models in this field to assess EDSLog's performance enhancements. These three methods are DeepLog, PLELog and CNN-Text as mentioned in the introduction.

Table 1. BGL and HDFS datasets details

	log entries	templates	anomalies	anomaly log ratio	sizes
HDFS	11,175,629	11,175,629	288,250	2.9%	1.47G
BGL	4,747,963	4,713,493	348,460	7.39%	708 MB

4.3   Implementations and Environments

We implemented EDSLog using Python 3.8.12, Pytorch 1.10.0, and SRU 2.6.0. For the parameters in EDSLog, we set the size of the sliding window to 10, based on general experience, for the log data sequence S; To fully extract the temporal features of the sequence, we set the dimension of the hidden layer to $y = 256$ and k in WKHM to 5; To avoid overfitting, we set the number of SRU layers to 4; Finally, we chose to use the FocalLoss [6] based on category weights as the loss function and used an Adam optimizer with a learning rate of 0.001 for optimization. All experiments were conducted on a Linux server equipped with an Intel(R) Xeon(R) Gold 6129 2.30 GHz CPU, 192 GB of RAM, an NVIDIA V100 with 16 GB of GPU memory, and running CentOS 7.6.

4.4   Evaluation Metrics

Anomaly detection based on logs is fundamentally a binary classification problem; therefore, following existing works [4,7,9,11,17,18], we employ Accuracy, Precision, Recall, and F1-score to evaluate the performance of log-based anomaly detection methods. Furthermore, with the increasing volume of log data, the time consumed for training the model becomes significant. Therefore, we documented the duration of model training and the time required for model testing to comprehensively evaluate the efficiency of the log-based anomaly detection method.

5   Research Questions and Analysis of Results

5.1   RQ1: Can EDSLog Effectively Mitigate the Challenge of Class Imbalance Present in Log Data?

In this experiment, we aim to explore the performance of EDSLog in scenarios of class imbalance within log data. Simultaneously, considering the assessment challenges and biases in classification models introduced by class-imbalanced

Table 2. Results with different class distributions in BGL datasets

Model	Metric	0.1% (WKHM/Hold-out)	1% (WKHM/Hold-out)	5% (WKHM/Hold-out)	10% (WKHM/Hold-out)
CNN-Text	Accuracy	99.98/99.72	99.87/99.16	99.81/95.70	99.66/95.35
	Precision	99.98/99.93	99.87/99.16	99.86/97.19	99.65/96.54
	Recall	100/99.79	100/100	99.95/98.35	99.99/98.43
	F1_measure	99.99/99.86	99.94/99.58	99.91/97.77	99.82/97.47
DeepLog	Accuracy	99.98/99.92	99.93/99.29	99.52/84.37	99.16/71.85
	Precision	99.99/99.92	99.95/99.30	99.58/96.41	99.33/99.65
	Recall	100/100	99.98/100	99.94/86.89	99.80/69.34
	F1_measure	99.99/99.96	99.96/99.65	99.75/91.40	99.56/81.78
PLELog	Accuracy	40.82/9.79	43.35/8.50	77.63/20.28	79.78/27.65
	Precision	5.76/0.72	27.45/5.42	69.11/16.87	70.74/20.93
	Recall	84.25/100	89.45/99.77	99.02/99.37	99.95/99.82
	F1_measure	10.56/1.43	39.33/10.27	70.90/28.84	72.66/34.61
EDSLog	Accuracy	100/96.16	99.98/71.24	99.90/78.12	99.96/71.52
	Precision	100/99.96	99.98/99.53	99.90/96.43	99.97/91.78
	Recall	100/96.2	100/71.33	100/80.07	99.98/75.48
	F1_measure	100/98.04	99.99/83.10	99.95/87.49	99.98/82.84

Table 3. Results with different class distributions in HDFS datasets

Model	Metric	0.1% (WKHM/Hold-out)	1% (WKHM/Hold-out)	5% (WKHM/Hold-out)	10% (WKHM/Hold-out)
CNN-Text	Accuracy	99.84/97.82	98.87/89.94	96.35/80.40	92.00/84.42
	Precision	99.92/99.93	99.48/99.35	81.11/96.70	94.61/93.27
	Recall	99.92/97.89	99.38/90.44	98.65/82.31	96.76/89.42
	F1_measure	99.92/98.90	99.42/94.69	98.10/88.94	95.66/91.30
DeepLog	Accuracy	99.92/99.16	99.20/96.45	95.95/95.76	91.80/91.41
	Precision	99.92/99.16	99.20/96.45	95.95/95.76	91.80/91.41
	Recall	100/100	100/99.93	100/100	100/100
	F1_measure	99.96/99.58	99.60/98.16	97.93/97.84	95.70/95.51
PLELog	Accuracy	71.66/59.52	75.11/69.38	74.14/70.94	87.81/96.22
	Precision	27.27/2.14	40.04/5.58	27.10/5.58	44.88/33.75
	Recall	93.33/91.58	96.41/92.59	72.59/78.37	79.11/76.26
	F1_measure	34.73/4.19	47.17/10.53	26.74/10.42	47.14/46.79
EDSLog	Accuracy	99.92/99.87	99.23/99.10	96.68/95.78	92.24/91.52
	Precision	99.92/99.92	99.23/99.21	96.69/95.79	92.29/92.20
	Recall	100/99.95	100/99.89	99.98/99.98	99.89/99.12
	F1_measure	99.96/99.94	99.61/99.55	98.31/97.84	95.92/95.53

data, we will evaluate the effectiveness of the WKHM method in addressing these issues. Inspired by [16], and in order to test the model's performance in extremely unbalanced datasets, this experiment selected four abnormal ratios ranging from 0.1% to 10% to construct imbalanced datasets. Our primary strategy involved randomly removing normal data or anomaly logs from sequences to achieve specific anomaly ratios. According to [16], the selection strategy of training data significantly influences semi-supervised anomaly detection models based on logs. Although random selection of training data often yields better performance than chronological selection, it may lead to data leakage issues, compromising the model's accurate evaluation in practical applications. Consequently, in this experiment, we adopted a chronological training data selection strategy for PLELog, DeepLog, and CNN-Text (based on the proportional split hold-out method) and fine-tuned the model parameters, selecting the scenario with optimal performance for comparison. Additionally, to investigate the impact of WKHM on imbalanced log data classes, this study also modified the dataset partitioning methods for PLELog, DeepLog, and CNN-Text to WKHM for comparison with the hold-out method.

Tables 2 and 3 illustrate that in datasets with varying proportions of anomalous logs, all experiments showed a significant improvement in performance metrics after using WKHM compared to the traditional Hold-out method, with EDSLog demonstrating the best performance. This demonstrates that WKHM can effectively alleviate the issue of data imbalance. Specifically, CNN_Text, DeepLog, PLELog, and EDSLog achieved the highest F1 scores in the BGL dataset across four different anomalous log proportions, reaching 100, 99.99, 99.95, and 99.98, respectively. Similarly, in the HDFS dataset, the highest F1 scores achieved were 99.96, 99.61, 98.31, and 95.92 across the different anomalous log proportions.

Overall, the WKHM method effectively addresses the sample bias problem associated with the traditional holdout method when dealing with imbalanced datasets. It also accounts for the disparity between normal and anomalous samples in each sub-dataset during the final model performance evaluation. The method then performs a weighted summation of all evaluation results, ensuring a fair and accurate representation of each sample category within the dataset. Particularly in cases where anomalous data are scarce, traditional random sampling may result in an insufficient proportion of minority class samples (such as anomalous logs) in the training set, which is inadequate for training models with good generalization capability. By increasing the sampling weight of minority class samples, WKHM allows these samples to receive more attention during model training, thereby enhancing the model's ability to detect anomalies and increasing the overall classification accuracy. The EDSLog, in conjunction with the WKHM method, demonstrates the ability to maintain high accuracy across log datasets with varying proportions of anomalies, especially in highly imbalanced scenarios. The application of this method can significantly improve the accuracy and reliability of large-scale log analysis systems.

5.2   RQ2: How Does PLELog Perform in Terms of Efficiency?

In this experiment, our objective was to investigate the performance efficiency of EDSLog when handling massive volumes of log data. Inspired by [7], we systematically documented the duration of model training (Train), the time needed for model testing (Test), and the combined duration of training and testing (Total time).

Table 4 shows the training time and prediction time of EDSLog on HDFS and BGL. On the BGL dataset, EDSLog demonstrates a significantly shorter training time of 8.52 min compared to the other three methods. On the HDFS dataset, EDSLog also exhibits better training time efficiency (22.81 min), although the difference from DeepLog is not as pronounced as in the BGL dataset. However, it still achieves an improvement of approximately 42.57%. In terms of testing time, EDSLog incurs a higher time cost compared to PLELog in both the BGL and

HDFS datasets. For PLELog, its lower time cost is due to the aggregation of logs based on block_id during the data preprocessing stage, which reduces the amount of log data during prediction. For EDSLog, the higher time cost is attributed to the use of WSHM with a parameter k set to 5 for multiple predictions, leading to increased time expenditure.

The experimental results indicate that EDSLog significantly outperforms the second most time-efficient comparative method on both the HDFS and BGL datasets. This improvement is mainly due to the effective utilization of the SRU network based on the attention mechanism in EDSLog.

Table 4. Time cost of studied approaches

Model	Dataset	Train	Test	Total time
PLELog	HDFS	70.2 m	37.12 s	70.3 m
	BGL	19.41 m	7.46 s	19.53 m
DeepLog	HDFS	32.52 m	2.17 m	34.69 m
	BGL	19.84 m	1.90 m	21.74 m
CNN-text	HDFS	53.40 m	3.58 m	56.98 m
	BGL	20.49 m	1.43 m	21.92 m
EDSLog	HDFS	22.81 m	3.83 m	26.64 m
	BGL	8.52 m	1.63 m	10.15 m

5.3   RQ3: How Does the Effectiveness of EDSLog Compare with that of Other Methods?

In this experiment, we integrated all the comparison experiments mentioned above, aiming to more intuitively evaluate the performance advantages and efficiency improvements of EDSLog in log anomaly detection. In order to comprehensively assess EDSLog as well as three comparative models, we separately recorded the total time spent by the models as well as four commonly used performance indicators in the field of log anomaly detection: Accuracy, precision, recall, and F1 score. It is worth noting that the HDFS and BGL datasets used in this experiment are raw data, which differs from the specifically processed datasets used in RQ1.

As shown in Table 5, EDSLog performs exceptionally well on both the HDFS and BGL datasets when using WKHM. Specifically, it achieves the highest F1 scores of 98.97 and 99.79 on these two datasets, respectively. At the same time, the model also records the lowest total time, with only 26.64 min and 10.15 min, respectively.

The WKHM method in EDSLog effectively addresses the sample bias issue caused by class imbalance, while the SRU recurrent neural network based on the attention mechanism effectively and efficiently models the data processed by WKHM. Although some results show only slight improvements compared to the

Table 5. Comprehensive Performance Comparison

Method	Dataset	Partition	Total time	Accuracy	Precision	Recall	F1
DeepLog	HDFS	Hold-out	34.69 m	92.66	92.66	100	96.16
		WKHM	39.13 m	96.01	96.01	100	97.95
	BGL	Hold-out	21.75 m	92.88	99.28	93.06	96.07
		WKHM	21.93 m	99.25	99.31	99.93	99.62
PLELog	HDFS	Hold-out	66.30 m	59.08	4.16	81.57	7.92
		WKHM	65.40 m	76.58	31.16	73.52	36.24
	BGL	Hold-out	23.32 m	28.33	19.85	99.96	33.12
		WKHM	25.88 m	71.59	70.67	94.28	72.29
CNN-Text	HDFS	Hold-out	53.92 m	94.26	99.32	94.86	97.04
		WKHM	60.13 m	95.97	97.26	98.61	97.88
	BGL	Hold-out	21.97 m	95.85	97.10	98.50	97.80
		WKHM	23.15 m	99.27	99.79	99.47	99.63
EDSLog	HDFS	Hold-out	26.89 m	96.39	96.45	99.93	98.16
		WKHM	26.64 m	97.97	97.99	99.98	98.97
	BGL	Hold-out	11.01 m	91.07	94.73	95.77	95.25
		WKHM	10.15 m	99.59	99.77	99.82	99.79

baseline model, given the large volume of log data, even a 0.1% improvement represents tens of thousands of additional correctly predicted samples. In summary, the comprehensive experimental comparison results indicate that EDSLog is effective in the field of log anomaly detection.

6   Conclusion

In recent years, many log-based anomaly detection methods have been proposed, but they still face challenges, particularly with class-imbalanced log data and inefficiency in handling large datasets. In this paper, we propose a practical method, EDSLog, which first processes log sequences through WKHM. WKHM is a dataset partitioning method designed in this study, which enables models to fully learn the characteristics of anomalous data within log data. Additionally, it ensures that samples from various categories within the dataset are represented fairly and accurately during model performance evaluation. Then, EDSLog efficiently extracts features from log sequences using a Self-Attention-based SRU network, ultimately determining whether the predicted log is anomalous. Our experimental results on two of the most widely used public datasets demonstrate that the log anomaly detection method proposed in this paper, EDSLog, excels in addressing the class imbalance problem. Compared to comparative methods, it more effectively balances data across different categories, thereby enhancing the accuracy of anomaly detection. Furthermore, EDSLog exhibits exceptionally high efficiency when processing large-scale log data, with a significantly improved processing speed compared to other comparative methods. Overall, the aforementioned advantages of EDSLog indicate its great potential for practical applications.

Acknowledgments. This work was supported in part by the Natural Science Foundation of Inner Mongolia of China (No.2023ZD18), the Natural Science Foundation of China (No.62462047), the Engineering Research Center of Ecological Big Data, Ministry of Education, the fund of Supporting the Reform and Development of Local Universities (Disciplinary Construction) and the special research project of First-class Discipline of Inner Mongolia A. R. of China under Grant YLXKZX-ND-036.

References

1. Aydın, H., Orman, Z., Aydın, M.A.: A long short-term memory (LSTM)-based distributed denial of service (DDoS) detection and defense system design in public cloud network environment. Comput. Secur. **118**, 102725 (2022)
2. Chen, A., Fu, Y., Zheng, X., Lu, G.: An efficient network behavior anomaly detection using a hybrid DBN-LSTM network. Comput. Secur. **114**, 102600 (2022)
3. Roy, S., et al.: Why don't XAI techniques agree? Characterizing the disagreements between post-hoc explanations of defect predictions. In: Proceedings of IEEE International Conference on Software Maintenance and Evolution (ICSME), pp. 444–448 (2022)
4. Du, M., Li, F., Zheng, G., Srikumar, V.: DeepLog: anomaly detection and diagnosis from system logs through deep learning. In: Proceedings of ACM Asia Conference on Computer and Communications Security (AsiaCCS), pp. 1285–1298 (2017)
5. LeCun, Y., Bengio, Y., Hinton, G.: Deep learning. Nature **521**, 436–444 (2015)
6. Lin, T.-Y., Goyal, P., Girshick, R., He, K., Dollar, P.: Focal loss for dense object detection. IEEE Trans. Pattern Anal. Mach. Intell. (TPAMI) **42**(2), 318–327 (2020)
7. Yang, L., et al.: Semi-supervised log-based anomaly detection via probabilistic label estimation. In: Proceedings of IEEE/ACM 43rd International Conference on Software Engineering (ICSE), pp. 1448–1460 (2021)
8. Cho, K., van Merriënboer, B., Bahdanau, D., Bengio, Y.: On the properties of neural machine translation: encoder–decoder approaches. In: Proceedings of Eighth Workshop on Syntax, Semantics and Structure in Statistical Translation (SSST), pp. 103–111 (2014)
9. Mei, Y.D., Chen, X., Sun, Y.Z.: A software system anomaly detection method based on log information and CNN-text. Chin. J. Comput. **43**, 366–380 (2020)
10. Lu, S., Wei, X., Li, Y., Wang, L.: Detecting anomaly in big data system logs using convolutional neural network. In: Proceedings of Dependable Autonomic and Secure Computing (DASC), pp. 151–158 (2018)
11. Zhang, C., et al.: DeepTraLog: trace-log combined microservice anomaly detection through graph-based deep learning. In: Proceedings of the 44th International Conference on Software Engineering (ICSE), pp. 623–634 (2022)
12. Lei, T., Zhang, Y., Wang, S., Dai, H., Artzi, Y.: Simple recurrent units for highly parallelizable recurrence. In: Proceedings of Conference on Empirical Methods in Natural Language Processing (EMNLP), pp. 4470–4481 (2018)
13. Zhu, J., He, S., He, P., Liu, J., Lyu, M. R.: Loghub: a large collection of system log datasets for AI-driven log analytics. In: Proceedings of IEEE 34th International Symposium on Software Reliability Engineering (ISSRE), pp. 355–366 (2023)

14. Xu, W., Huang, L., Fox, A., Patterson, D., Jordan, M. I.: Detecting large-scale system problems by mining console logs. In: Proceedings of International Conference on Machine Learning (ICML), pp. 117–131 (2009)
15. Oliner, A. J., Stearley, J.: What supercomputers say: a study of five system logs. In: Proceedings of Edinburgh, pp. 575–584 (2007)
16. Le, V.-H., Zhang, H.: Log-based anomaly detection with deep learning: how far are we? In: Proceedings of the 44th International Conference on Software Engineering (ICSE), pp. 1356–1367 (2022)
17. Wang, Z., Tian, J., Fang, H., Chen, L., Qin, J.: LightLog: a lightweight temporal convolutional network for log anomaly detection on the edge. Comput. Netw. (CN) **203**, 108616 (2022)
18. Jia, T., Li, Y., Yang, Y., Huang, G., Wu, Z.: Augmenting log-based anomaly detection models to reduce false anomalies with human feedback. In: Proceedings of ACM SIGKDD Conference on Knowledge Discovery and Data Mining (SIGKDD), pp. 3081–3089 (2022)
19. Vaswani, A., et al.: Attention is all you need. In: Proceedings of Advances in Neural Information Processing Systems (NeurIPS), pp. 5998–6008 (2017)
20. Studiawan, H., Sohel, F., Payne, C.: Anomaly detection in operating system logs with deep learning-based sentiment analysis. IEEE Trans. Dependable Secure Comput. (TDSC) **18**(5), 2136–2148 (2021)
21. Xie, Y., Zhang, H., Babar, M. A.: LogGD: detecting anomalies from system logs with graph neural networks. In: Proceedings of IEEE 22nd International Conference on Software Quality, Reliability and Security (QRS), pp. 299–310 (2022)
22. Ou, X., Liu, J.: LogKT: hybrid log anomaly detection method for cloud data center. In: Proceedings of International Computer Software and Applications Conference (COMPSAC), pp. 164–173 (2023)

Author Index

GPSR Compliance

The European Union's (EU) General Product Safety Regulation (GPSR) is a set of rules that requires consumer products to be safe and our obligations to ensure this.

If you have any concerns about our products, you can contact us on ProductSafety@springernature.com

In case Publisher is established outside the EU, the EU authorized representative is:

Springer Nature Customer Service Center GmbH
Europaplatz 3
69115 Heidelberg, Germany

The manufacturer's authorised representative in the EU is Springer
Nature Customer Service Centre GmbH, Europaplatz 3, 69115 Heidelberg,
Germany. If you have any concerns regarding our products, please
contact ProductSafety@springernature.com

Printed and bound by CPI Group (UK) Ltd, Croydon, CR0 4YY

29/04/2026

02099541-0005